RECENT AMERICAN

LITERATURE

RECENT
AMERICAN
LITERATURE

DONALD HEINEY

Associate Professor of English,
University of Utah

BARRON'S EDUCATIONAL SERIES, INC.

Great Neck, New York

Preface

Recent American Literature is intended to serve as a concise but complete handbook of modern American literature to take its place alongside the already published volumes of the Barron's Educational Series. Such a book has not yet appeared; the standard histories of American literature customarily give scant attention to recent literary developments, and works of criticism which treat twentieth-century literature tend to be highly specialized, excessively recondite, and confined to a narrow aspect of the subject as a whole. The present volume, compiled in most cases from standard reference and critical sources and incorporating the judgments of established critical opinion, will provide a valuable and much-needed aid to the student, the teacher, the reviewer, and others whose daily business demands a convenient source of information on modern American writing.

The organization of the book has been planned to be as systematic as possible considering the nature of the subject matter. The general plan of the book is topical rather than chronological, since a half-century is too short a period in which to distinguish clear-cut chronological periods of literary development. "The Background of Modern American Literature" includes a discussion of the essential characteristics of American literature from the time of its origins, a brief survey of the foreign and native influences which went to make up its character, and a description of the changing social environment in American letters from 1900 to the present day. Parts 2-4 then treat various literary types in succession: fiction, the drama, poetry, and literary criticism. A bibliography provides a list of the more important works of each author treated in the text plus a short selection of secondary or critical materials for further study.

The sections treating individual authors have also been organized according to a consistent plan for the convenience of the reader. The discussion of each author begins with a critical summary of his position in the development of American literature, the specific qualities of his style, and the techniques, themes, devices, attitudes, and philosophical ideas most often noted in his work. The evaluations in these critical summaries are as objective as possible, arrived at through a consensus of criticism from standard sources rather than through the personal judgment of the writer. Next follows a biographical sketch, labeled "Life," in which the chief facts of the author's biography, especially as they bear upon the nature of his work, are presented. Again standard reference works have been used in compiling this material in order to assure a reasonable accuracy and soundness of judgment. Finally, in a section labeled "Chief Works," "Typical Works," "Important Poems," or "Typical Poems," the book presents summaries or analyses of the more important works of each author. This section is intended to serve as a convenient source of reference for the names of characters, details of plot, and general characteristics of a work rather than as a substitute for actual reading. Literature is intended to be read; a novel of Faulkner or a poem of Eliot can no more be understood by reading a secondary discussion of it than a symphony of Beethoven can be appreciated by listening to a music critic talk about it. After a work has been read, however, a concise synopsis which includes a well-judged critical evaluation is often helpful in recalling details and in making the pattern or theme of the whole work apparent. A summary of judgments which standard critics have made on the work is also helpful in enabling a reader to see it in its perspective or to fit it into the pattern of literary history. Such is the aim of the synopses in this volume. Thus it is hoped that *Recent American Literature* will add to the pleasure and understanding of the reader in his journey through the complex and fascinating American literature of our time.

Donald Heiney
January, 1958

Contents

1. The Background of Modern American Literature

A NEW LAND, A NEW LITERATURE

The history of American literature from colonial times to the present is the story of a search for a new literary idiom. American culture in its origins is an offspring of European culture; the peculiarly American "way of life," the American national personality, developed only gradually out of its European ingredients. But from the beginning of American history it is possible to discern new social elements—new attitudes and characteristics which developed out of the new social and environmental conditions of life on the American continent. Some of these American characteristics might be listed as follows:

Individualism: The American, under the influence of the frontier and the limitless space of the new continent, and faced with its hazards and dangers, is self-reliant and self-confident. Since he fixes his basic faith on himself, he is often eccentric; individual peculiarities are permitted in a land where the rigid social conventions of Europe have been left behind.

Democracy: The American is independent of the complicated and ossified social hierarchies of Europe, and tends to judge men on their merits rather than on their birth.

Provincialism: He feels at the same time a vague inferiority complex when he considers himself in relation to the older, wiser, more sophisticated culture of Europe. Sometimes, as in the case of T. S. Eliot, Ezra Pound, or Henry James, this results in a rejection of American "vulgarity" and a transfer of allegiance to European manners and European attitudes; at other times, as with Mark Twain, it takes a form of a satirical but somewhat self-conscious scorn for European artificiality and snobbism.

Optimism: America, the land of new hope, is a land where tragedy

1

seems out of place. The frontier, the new economic freedom, the apparently limitless possibilities of prosperity, combine to give the American a cheerful and positive attitude toward life. This attitude continues in American culture, as well as in American literature, until it is severely shaken by the social developments of the post World War I era and the Depression.

SOCIETY AND LITERATURE

As American society began to acquire the special characteristics that set it apart from the older societies of Europe, it demanded a correspondingly new literature—not merely a literature *about* the new things and new people of America, but a literature expressed in a new style, a new technique worthy of a new nation. Naturally, distinctive "American" characteristics can be found in American literature from its earliest beginnings. Irving, Cooper, Hawthorne, and Melville treated local folklore, frontier life, and religious institutions, and the generation of Poe and Whitman groped for a new poetry which would be distinctively American. But these attempts were sporadic and isolated. The mainstream of American literature to the time of Howells and James continued to be derivative from Europe; it was essentially a branch of European literature which treated American subject matter. It was only in the twentieth century, and particularly in the period of the nineteen-twenties, that American literature emerged for the first time as a distinctive and original idiom, a literature capable of taking its place with the other great literatures of western European civilization. Significantly, it was in this era that American literature first began to exert an important influence on European letters. Although poets like Poe and Whitman had previously enjoyed a considerable reputation on the continent, it was mainly in the period after the First World War that American literature came into its own in European eyes. The twentieth century is a climactic era in the history of American literature, the period in which the process which had been germinating for two hundred years at last reached its fruition. A study of American literature in the twentieth century, therefore, must first concern itself with identifying those national characteristics which set it apart from the other literatures out of which it developed.

THE EVOLUTION OF
MODERN AMERICAN LITERATURE

American literature in the twentieth century exhibits at least two qualities which make it distinctive: (1) it is ICONOCLASTIC and INDIVIDUALISTIC, that is, it is above all a literature of rebellion against conventions, whether social, moral, or literary; and (2) it is marked in technique and style by A SEARCH FOR A NATIONAL VERNACULAR, i.e., the modern American author consciously or unconsciously seeks to write in a way that is wholly American. It should be observed that this second tendency does not mean that American writers are necessarily nationalistic or patriotic; in fact those authors who are most "American" in style and mood (Steinbeck, Saroyan, Hemingway) are often severely critical of American culture on the social and political level. These tendencies of the twentieth century naturally have their foreshadowings in earlier American literature. It will be valuable, therefore, to examine briefly those elements in classic American literature which have had an obvious influence on authors in the twetieth century.

American culture from the beginning had characteristics which set it off sharply from the old cultures of Europe: democracy, the frontier, a new kind of freedom, a new concept of humanity. HENRY DAVID THOREAU (1817-62) expressed a typical American attitude when he rejected the sophisticated drawing-room civilization of Europe and set out in search of a life closer to the soil, a life in which a physical contact with nature would be combined with the individualism—even the eccentricity—of the frontiersman in a new land. In *Walden* (1854), his account of his hermit-life in the woods in a hut he built with his own hands, he expresses his desire "so to love wisdom as to live according to its dictates, a life of simplicity, independence, magnanimity, and trust." And in his "Essay on Civil Disobedience" (1849) he makes the provocative assertion that "that government is best which governs not at all," and vehemently declares his rejection of any regulative force other than his own conscience. His individualism was echoed by his friend RALPH WALDO EMERSON (1803-82), who applied it chiefly in the field of religious belief; he attacked all forms of organized religion, and proposed a faith based solely on intuitive spiritual experience. The tendency toward iconoclasm and individualism continued in American literature into the twentieth century; its influence is apparent in the irrepressible and satirical impudence of poets like Pound and Cummings and in the struggles of novelists like Dreiser against a narrow puritanical censorship.

Such tendencies in content were paralleled by others in literary technique. NATHANIEL HAWTHORNE (1804-64) and EDGAR ALLAN POE (1809-49) worked to convert the Europe *conte* or tale into what was to become the American short story, a genre which was to assume increasing importance in the twentieth century and which was to develop into something peculiarly and originally American. HERMAN MELVILLE (1819-91) developed a technique which in the long run was to be perhaps even more important: a realistic style which nevertheless contained overtones of philosophical significance. His *Moby Dick* (1851) and other novels, "rediscovered" in the period after the First World War, exerted an important influence on the American naturalistic movement; the example helped to give American naturalists a depth and a technical subtlety lacking in the earlier European naturalism of Zola and his school. A comparison of Zola with Faulkner, Wolfe, or Sherwood Anderson will make the difference clear. Whether or not a direct influence of Melville on such writers can be demonstrated, he is significant as a forerunner of the direction twentieth-century American literature is to take. WALT WHITMAN (1819-92) provided an equally important example for twentieth-century American poetry; the first American to experiment in "free verse" and rebel against the conventional forms of poetry, he also expressed the exuberance, the hedonism and antipuritanism, and the individualism expressed in the twentieth century by such poets as Sandburg, Pound, Cummings, and Hart Crane. His *Leaves of Grass* (1855) had been popular since its publication, but in the nineteen-twenties a new wave of enthusiasm for the book arose, and it was hailed by contemporary poets as a spiritual predecessor of their own poetry.

Finally, the attempts of the nineteenth-century authors to work out a genuinely American idiom, to achieve a vernacular style, especially in dialogue, should be mentioned. Perhaps the most important writer in this respect is MARK TWAIN (pseud. of Samuel Clemens, 1835-1910). His tales and stories, as well as his two best-known novels, *The Adventures of Tom Sawyer* (1876) and *The Adventures of*

Huckleberry Finn (1884) and his autobiographical *Life on the Mississippi* (1883) are vivid and simple, not only in their use of vernacular speech, but in their general style and mood; it might be said of these books that for the first time a great author had written as Americans actually talked. BRET HARTE (1836-1902) and humorists like JOSH BILLINGS (pseud. of H. W. Shaw, 1818-85) and ARTEMUS WARD (pseud. of C. F. Browne, 1834-67) also contributed, although their influence is less direct and obvious. The search for a realistic vernacular continued in the dialogue of writers from Stephen Crane to Eudora Welty. By 1930 a simple, vernacular, or "tough" dialogue was the stock-in-trade of American naturalists, and a tendency which was widely imitated in Europe.

PSYCHOLOGISTS, PHILOSOPHERS, AND PROPHETS

Several influences on twentieth-century literature from the realm of philosophy and the social sciences should also be mentioned. The socialist-radical movement, culminating in the work of KARL MARX (1818-83), began to find literary expression in America in the late nineteenth century and became even more prominent after 1900. Not only did authors like Clifford Odets and Granville Hicks frankly profess Marxism, but a large number of twentieth-century writers, for example, Steinbeck and Dos Passos, consciously or unconsciously presented Marxist concepts such as the conflict of social classes and the intransigence of the bourgeois-capitalistic ruling class. In the field of psychology, the Viennese psychoanalyst SIGMUND FREUD (1836-1939) publicized the importance of the subconscious life in forming human motivation and, even more important, through his revelation of the suppressed sexual element in human behavior paved the way for a franker and more revealing treatment of erotic themes in literature. There is scarcely an author in the twentieth century who can be said to have escaped some influence of Marx or Freud or both.

For American authors in particular, a second pair of late nineteenth-century thinkers should be cited. The American philosopher WILLIAM JAMES (1842-1910), brother of the novelist Henry James, formulated in his philosophy of Pragmatism a system of thought eminently suited to a new nation skeptical of traditional absolutism and preoccupied with solving the practical problems of material existence. In *Pragmatism* (1907) and *The Meaning of Truth* (1909) he defined a philosophy according to which an idea or "fact" has truth only according to its practical consequences; in other words, according to its usefulness. Pragmatism might be summed up in the expression, "Try it—if it works, it is right,"—an eminently American attitude. It is doubtful whether many twentieth-century authors were directly influenced by James' Pragmatism. He reflects rather than forms the intellectual temper of his time; such ideas were "in the air," and as such shared by novelists, playwrights, and poets.

Finally, HENRY ADAMS (1838-1918), scion of a distinguished Boston family, not only wrote novels of his own but presented in his autobiographical *Education of Henry Adams* (1907) and in his essays, of which *Mont-Saint-Michel and Chartres* (1904) is perhaps most important, a number of problems which were to occupy the attention of later American writers. These problems included (a) the place of the man of poetic or sensitive temperament in a practical society; (b) the relation between European and American culture, a subject which has fascinated American writers from Henry James to Henry Miller; and (c) the precarious balance between power and spirit, or materialism and idealism. This last concept, which Adams expresses in his autobiography in the famous phrase "the Virgin and the Dynamo," is the most important of the three to Adams himself and has perhaps been the most significant in the long run in twentieth-century literature; America, a materialistic nation with a literature which is dominantly realistic, has nevertheless sought constantly throughout the century for a synthesis of "the cult of the Virgin and the Worship of the Dynamo" which would raise the nation and its literature to a level above the realistic but provincial materialism of the frontier.

MAIN CURRENTS
OF THE TWENTIETH CENTURY

The year 1900 is more than an arbitrary chronological milestone in literary history: it marks the onset of a new era in literature as it does in the field of social relationships. On first examination the striking characteristic of twentieth-century literature is its extreme diversity. There is no one single school, no one tendency, which can be said to typify the age. Never before in literary history have there been so many cénacles, so many schools, circles, and movements existing simultaneously. This diversity is naturally only an aspect of a general diversity in social development: the twentieth century, having no one dominant social philosophy, cannot hope for a single and homogeneous kind of literature.

In addition, an important minority of twentieth-century authors show a tendency to retreat deliberately into obscurantism and esotericism. Literature has never, except in rare instances, been the preoccupation of the great masses of the population; but never before has literature been written for such a small and clannish group of *cognoscenti*. Comparatively speaking, the public which enjoys the poetry of T. S. Eliot or Wallace Stevens is an infinitely smaller percentage of the total population than the public which read the poems of Longfellow or Poe, or even that which patronized the plays of Shakespeare. Certain schools of poetry especially in the twentieth century tend to be difficult, heavy with allusion, and highly technical in construction.

At the same time the opposite tendency is discernible: many twentieth-century authors seek deliberately to create a literature for the masses, a literature which sacrifices none of its artistic quality in being presented in terms comprehensible to the man in the street. This experiment has, of course, been carried forth on a wide scale and in a highly organized manner in the Soviet Union, but the attitude is also apparent in the work of such American naturalists as Theodore Dreiser and John Steinbeck. Along with the tendency to broaden the basis of all the arts—music, the opera, drama, and painting—to make them assimilable by the masses of the population, there has been a comparable effort to democratize literature. Literature, however, is a verbal art requiring a certain background and vocabulary for proper appreciation; it is inherently a more difficult art to popularize than painting or music. Thus the democratization of literature has been accompanied by a simplifying, sometimes even a vulgarizing, of literary standards.

Amid the complexity of twentieth-century literary movements it is possible to distinguish two main tendencies. The first of these, the realistic-naturalistic movement, continues the tendency which began in Europe in the nineteenth century with Stendhal, Balzac, Tolstoy, and Ibsen. In the twentieth century this movement tends to become more militantly political, more liberal in outlook, and more consciously scientific in technique; but at the same time there is a tendency, especially in American naturalism, toward a symbolic or "mythic" quality which raises the style above a mere banal documentation, a recording of physical data. The tendency is apparent in such post-1945 novels as Hemingway's *The Old Man and the Sea* and Faulkner's *The Fable,* both of which are superficially realistic in style but mythic or symbolic in their underlying meaning.

The second great movement might be roughly termed "the reaction to realism;" it comprises the various forms of repudiation of external objectivity, including psychological fiction, neo-romanticism, impressionism, expressionism, and other forms of anti-realistic experimentation. It is less a literary school than a kind of residue, including all those authors who for one reason or another are not attracted to the realistic technique; it includes authors as different from each other as James Branch Cabell and Sherwood Anderson, as well as poets from Edgar Lee Masters to Conrad Aiken. It includes, however, a group which assumes increasing importance as the twentieth century proceeds: the school of psychological fiction. The term is a loose one; it may be used to describe the subtle internal analysis of Edith Wharton or Thornton Wilder, a technique which has almost no connection with the science of modern clinical psychology, or the psychopathological studies of Robinson Jeffers or Sherwood Anderson, which resemble case histories from abnormal psychology translated into literary form. These two tendencies—naturalism and psychological literature—are not mutually exclusive; they influence each other, and sometimes, as in the case of Katherine Anne Porter, they are combined in a single author. Since their origins are historically separate, however, it is useful to study them as entities, and to examine their separate influence on writers in the twentieth century.

THE PERIODS

A half century is too short a time to be broken up into neat chronological eras, each with its distinct "school of literature." Many authors who began writing before the First World War were still publishing in 1950; their "period" is simply the first half of the twentieth century. Nevertheless, from the point of view of social environment, distinct eras within the century may be distinguished. Since authors are not isolated from their culture but must necessarily write in a social environment, the changing temper of the times acts as an important influence on their work. An examination of these epochs, in most cases marked off by wars, economic changes, and other social phenomena, is essential to an undertanding of the literature that grew out of them.

The Fin-de-Siècle 1880-1914. This period might well be referred to as "the genteel age," although it is also the period when the beginnings of American realism can be discerned. It was in the main a period of prosperity; the national economy, at least in the North, had recovered from the effects of the Civil War, and industrialization was transforming the country at a dizzying rate. The far west, opened for settlement in the previous generation, was building, expanding, and prospering. The financial panic of 1893 scarcely slowed the nation in its triumphant progression toward its "Manifest Destiny" as a world power. The fervent nationalism of the times, which in its political form is perhaps best represented by the figure of Theodore Roosevelt, had its corresponding reaction in literature. It is not so much that the author of 1900 was patriotic as that he began consciously to think of himself as an American and to seek about for an American style and technique in which to express himself. Sometimes, as in the case of Henry James, he became preoccupied with the differences between the American and European cultures and with the psychological conflicts which took place when Americans encountered Europeans, whether at home or abroad.

But the age remained a genteel one, and its gentility was essentially that of Europe and New England, the miniature Europe-in-America that had dominated American letters since colonial times. Even a western-born author like William Dean Howells gravitated instinctively to Boston as the center of literary America. Under his editorship (1871-81) *The Atlantic Monthly* became, or remained, the severe and exacting arbiter of American literary taste. In spite of the encroachments of the machine age, and in spite of the innovations of such realists as Stephen Crane and Frank Norris, American literature remained essentially European, refined, and "old-fashioned" until the Victorian era and everything pertaining to it were swept away by the First World War.

The Roaring Twenties 1918-1929. At first it was not apparent that the war had ended an era; Warren G. Harding was elected to the Presidency in 1920 on a slogan of "back to normalcy." But a new youth had been created by the war, a youth emancipated, disillusioned, and cynical, a youth that Gertrude Stein in a famous phrase was to term "a lost generation." Instead of "saving the world for Democracy" the war had only created new hatreds, divisions, and menaces. But America emerged from the war prosperous: idealism had been betrayed, and in an era of easy money a new and cynical materialism took its place. It was the Jazz Age, the age of the Stutz Bearcat, the raccoon coat, the hip flask, and the Charleston; an age of youth, of short skirts, and of revolutionized morals. Prohibition, implemented by the Eighteenth Amendment in 1919 and put into effect in 1920, succeeded only in making cocktails smart, in enormously increasing the consumption of liquor, and of spreading the custom among women. "It don't prohibit worth a dime," proclaimed a popular jingle happily. Cynicism increased, and a new industry of crime and racketeering sprang out of the illegal liquor traffic. Stocks boomed, and new fortunes were made overnight. "America was going on the greatest, gaudiest spree in history and there was going to be plenty to tell about it," Scott Fitzgerald wrote.

To tell about it was the task of a new generation of writers. In spite of the general cynicism of the age, the Twenties were a tremendously creative period in literature and the arts. It was an age of technical experimentation and of daring innovations in content; it is safe to say that more new things were created in literature in that ten years than in the hundred years that preceded it. Sometimes, as in the case of Scott Fitzgerald, the new writers were frankly enthusiastic about the Jazz Age; but more often, as with Sherwood Anderson, Sinclair Lewis, and Ring Lardner, they caustically attacked the Babbitts and boosters of the new age and rejected the superficial hedonism of the tin lizzy and the cozy bungalow in the suburbs. But the attack on American middle-class mores was not political; the typical authors of the Twenties were sometimes vaguely left-wing in inclination, but their books were less political polemics than satires of private manners. In many cases the rejection of American culture took the form of expatriation: Gertrude Stein, Ezra Pound, Eliot, Hemingway, and others abandoned America for Europe, which attracted them through its lack of puritanism and its more sophisticated artistic attitudes. In poetry the era was frankly an age of experimentation. With the exception of a handful of "verse naturalists" like Robinson and Frost, few poets of the Twenties wrote anything that would have been recognized as poetry before 1900. It was the day of free verse, of radical experimentation in syntax, punctuation, and typography, and of the virtual abandonment of traditional verse forms. Eliot, Cummings, Pound, Stevens, and Marianne Moore created almost overnight a new concept of verse, virtually a new poetic language which lent new values to old words and revolutionized the traditional concept of what a poem could be. But this revolution in fiction and poetry, paralleled by similar revolutions in painting and the other arts, left the general public behind. While the bohemians and intellectuals were reading Eliot and Ezra Pound, the solid citizens in the suburbs were reading Eddie Guest, or more likely simply going to the movies. The split between the artist and the rest of society, which had always existed and which had widened toward the end of the nineteenth century, now became a gulf. In spite of the efforts of the Dos Passos and the Steinbecks to write about the struggles of the common man, and to write about them in his own language, the writer of the Twenties felt a sense of alienation from the general public stronger than American writers had ever felt before.

The Depression Era 1929-1941. On October 24, 1929, the bloated and spuriously prosperous stock market collapsed, and America's post-war prosperity was wiped out almost overnight. The national slogan changed from "Back to normalcy" to "Brother, can you spare a dime?" The gay cynicism of the Twenties became a resentful and bitter pessimism, and the national political temper began to swing to the left. A new social consciousness, a feeling of political responsibility, began to pervade the literature of the Thirties; where the writers of the Jazz Age had prided themselves on their political independence many authors of the Thirties turned to a "social protest" literature that was virtually a form of pamphleteering. The difference can be seen by comparing the apolitical individualism of the characters in Hemingway's *The Sun Also Rises* (1926) with the obvious political message in his later *The Fifth Column* (1938) and *For Whom the Bell Tolls* (1940), both conceived during the Spanish Civil War in 1937-38.

The era is also marked by a turn toward psychological literature, i.e., a rejection, on the part of some writers, of the materialism of the Twenties and a new interest in the inner life of the mind. Thomas Wolfe, with his verbose and poetic prose style and his preoccupation with subjective analysis, is perhaps the typical novelist of the Thirties as the terse and laconic Hemingway is the novelist of the Twenties. In poetry the interest in technical innovation which had flourished in the Twenties now gave way to a renewed concern with content, especially symbolic or mythic content. The poet of the Depression era retained the technical advances of the decade before, but he sought about for something new and significant to say with his new verbal tools, for a new poetic mythology. Sometimes this tendency took the form of a rejection of materialism and a new turn toward things of the spirit. T. S. Eliot's *Ash Wednesday* (1930) marks the beginning of a new school of metaphysical or quasi-religious poetry. Other poets turned to the political liberalism or radicalism that also preoccupied the novelists; MacLeish's *Frescoes for Mr. Rockefeller's City* (1933) epitomizes the new tendency toward criticism of capitalism and bourgeois hypocrisy. It was, in short, the poetry of the New Deal, and it is not surprising that MacLeish himself later became a high official in this administration.

Post-war 1945 and after. In spite of the general prosperity of the nation, the Second World War did not produce a Jazz Age corresponding to the one following the war of 1914-18. The American public did not enter the war in 1941 with the same naive idealism they had shown in 1917, and as a result they were less affected by a post-war disillusionment. There was, however, a political swing to the right, the symptoms of which extended from the victory of moderate Republicans at the polls in 1952 to the hysteria of McCarthyism and anti-intellectualism which swept over the nation immediately after the war and began to moderate only around 1953. Again, as in the Twenties, the nation was sharply divided; the temper of the general public was right-wing, nationalistic, and anti-intellectual, and consequently the intellectuals and artists were driven into a mood of alienation and criticism.

One characteristic of the age, however, a certain proportion of post-1945 authors shared with the general public: a turn away from skeptical materialism and a search for spiritual satisfaction. The beginnings of this tendency can be detected in the Thirties, as explained in the previous section, but it was intensified after 1945. In the case of the general public it took the form of a well-publicized and widely acclaimed "return to religion"—an increase in church-going, a heightened interest in theology, and much talk about "putting God back in education" and "a nation under God." Thinkers disagreed as to whether this phenomenon was a revival of genuine religious feeling or merely a neurotic escapism caused by the general insecurity of the age, but it is undeniable that it took place. In the field of literature the tendency is equally apparent, if somewhat less naive. Writers like Faulkner and Hemingway, who began in the Twenties as skeptical realists, seemed to develop social and spiritual consciousness in the Thirties and to end in something approaching mythological symbolism after the war (cf. The Fable, 1954, and The Old Man and the Sea, 1953). Another group of novelists, chiefly the younger generation, continued in the tradition of objective naturalism established by the writers of the Twenties; John O'Hara's Ten North Frederick (1955) is a highly documented naturalistic novel in the Dreiser tradition, influenced by Hemingway, Steinbeck, and Sinclair Lewis. The poets were likewise divided: some, chiefly the older generation, showed a spiritual or metaphysical tendency (e.g. Eliot's Four Quartets, published in 1943), while others, mostly younger poets, continued to imitate the adroit and technically complicated skepticism of the Twenties. In the case of both fiction and poetry the age of technical innovation was past; the Thirties, Forties, and Fifties were content to digest and perfect the new techniques invented by the writers of the Twenties. There was a certain imitative quality, a technical sterility, to the age; it seemed that all the new things had been invented, and the new generation of writers was forced to turn somewhat monotonously to rewriting the books, poems, and plays of the Twenties. Here and there a Tennessee Williams or a Eudora Welty seemed to show a flash of originality, but in general the post-1945 period was a time of assimilation and synthesis. American writers, having discovered their true national idiom during the Twenties, now set about perfecting and refining the literary techniques invented by the generation before them.

2. American Fiction
in the Twentieth Century

THE EUROPEAN INFLUENCES

The study of the evolution of literature is analogous to the study of evolutionary processes in living organisms; each literary generation derives from the preceding one just as generations succeed each other in the biological life-process. At the same time the process of evolution in literature is in one sense more complex: literary movements long dormant are frequently revived and renovated to fit the age, so that the influence of a literary movement may be felt across the gap of centuries. Medieval art, neglected since the Renaissance, was revived to inspire the British poets of the nineteenth-century Pre-Raphaelite movement, and the Trecento Italian poetry of Dante and Cavalcanti served as a model for the new poetic techniques of Pound and Eliot in the twentieth century. To comprehend the background of contemporary American literature we must therefore give a certain attention to the whole of literary history, and especially to the European literature of the century preceding.

Undoubtedly the dominant phenomenon in nineteenth-century European literature was the emergence of REALISM. From a literary point of view the triumph of realism was the triumph of the novel, in which it found its most apt expression. In its social aspect realism was a manifestation of the faith in science and liberalism which grew constantly during the century and only began to falter toward 1900. In content realistic literature is generally concerned with the affairs of the middle and lower classes; it treats economic, social, and technical matters (e.g., agriculture and industry) in addition to the traditional literary themes of love and gallantry, and it purports to utilize the vernacular of daily life instead of the artificial poetic diction of previous literatures.

The beginnings of realism can naturally be traced as far back as Homer; but in modern times a convenient arbitrary point of departure

14

is to be found in the work of STENDHAL (pseud. of Henry Beyle, 1783-1842). This brilliant French novelist, who wrote far ahead of his times, treated themes of the utmost romanticism, but he did so in a sparse, objective, and ironic manner which was greatly to influence subsequent realistic authors.

HONORÉ DE BALZAC (1799-1850) carried Stendhal's realism into the realm of subject matter as well as style. His *Comédie humaine,* a vast panorama of French society under the Empire and the Restoration, comprises twenty-four novels and a score of stories and tales. GUSTAVE FLAUBERT (1821-80) brought to the novel an even greater objectivity, a scientific penetration, and a painstaking exactitude in style. His *Madame Bovary* and his short tale *A Simple Heart* represent the high-water mark of French realism.

In England the realistic movement, latent in Defoe, Fielding, and Richardson, begins in earnest with CHARLES DICKENS (1812-70). Although Dickens had in mind no such pseudo-sociological plan as that of Balzac's *Human Comedy,* he nevertheless created a similar panorama of early nineteenth-century Britain. WILLIAM MAKEPEACE THACKERAY (1811-63) and ANTHONY TROLLOPE (1815-82) are the chief remaining figures of the British realistic movement.

Perhaps the most powerful of the European realistic novels were those of the great Russian triumvirate: FYODOR DOSTOYEVSKY (1821-81), IVAN TURGENEV (1818-83), and COUNT LEO TOLSTOY (1828-1910). Tolstoy's novels *Anna Karenina* and *War and Peace* are worthy of special mention as examples of Russian realism. In the Scandinavian countries the chief of several important realistic authors was the Norwegian dramatist HENRIK IBSEN (1828-1906), whose work is dominated by biting criticism of the middle class as well as antagonism toward bourgeois Philistinism and materialism. Ibsen's work was especially influential in Germany, where it served as one of the focal points of the naturalistic movement in the theatre, and in England, where it found a formidable champion and publicist in Bernard Shaw. In America the influence of Ibsenism was most apparent during the Twenties, although such post-1945 dramatists as Arthur Miller frankly borrowed Ibsen's techniques and attitudes.

Toward the end of the century the realistic movement on the Continent began to metamorphose into the school known as NATURAL-ISM. Compared with mid-century realism, naturalism tended to be more militantly scientific in its approach and even more concerned with degraded, often sordid levels of human existence. EMILE ZOLA (1840-1902) shares with the critic Hippolyte Taine the honor of founding the French naturalist school. Zola sought to make literature into a branch of the social sciences; the novel in his opinion ought to study social behavior as the chemist studies the behavior of compounds in a test tube. His formidable *Rougon-Macquart* series, an integrated novel sequence similar to Balzac's *Comédie humaine,* purported to present "a natural and social history of a family under the Second Empire." Zola was especially preoccupied with the operation of heredity, which he felt was the dominant motivating force in human destiny.

In Germany naturalism, as noted above, received a great impetus from the work of Ibsen. The chief German naturalists of the nineteenth century are the novelist THEODOR FONTANE (1818-98); the collaborators ARNO HOLZ (1863-1929) and JOHANNES SCHLAF (1862-1941), who wrote chiefly criticism, drama, and short stories; and GERHART HAUPTMANN (1862-1946), a versatile author who in the twentieth century turned to Symbolism and expressionism. Naturalism was less prominent in nineteenth-century English literature. Its leading exponent was THOMAS HARDY (1840-1924), whose novels are marked by a deep philosophical pessimism. Other important European naturalists are the Spaniard BENITO PEREZ GALDOS (1843-1920) and the Italian GIOVANNI VERGA (1840-1922).

There is an inevitable time lag in literary influences, especially when they are obliged to cross boundaries of language and nationality. America, separated from Europe geographically by an ocean and culturally by its tendency toward isolationism and provincialism, customarily lagged behind the literary tastes of Europe during the nineteenth century by at least a generation, and sometimes by more. The romantic period, for example, began in France shortly after the Revolution (*ca.* 1793) and in England only slightly later—the publication of *Lyrical Ballads* in 1798 is often cited as an arbitrary starting point. The European romantic movement may be said to have reached its height by 1815. In America, however, the same movement, impelled by the same causes and based on the same principles, reached its climax only in the era of Lowell, Whitman, and Lanier, roughly around 1850.

In the same manner American realism waited a cautious generation before it followed its European predecessors. The height of the movement in Europe—the age of Balzac, Flaubert, and Turgenev—may be placed approximately at the middle of the century. In America a true realistic novel can scarcely be detected before James' *The American* (1877) and the climax of American realism actually occurred around 1900. In fact, the inception of the American realistic movement was delayed until it underwent a second influence from European naturalists of the Zola school, thus confusing the characteristics of the two European schools in a single American movement. Stephen Crane and Frank Norris, who wrote around the turn of the century are as much naturalists as they are realists. Again, where the Zola school of naturalism may be said to begin in Europe with the publication of *Thérèse Raquin* (1867), the American naturalistic movement, which began with Norris and Dreiser, did not assume its final stature until after the First World War.

THE FIRST AMERICAN REALISTS: 1880-1914

Many names might be cited in a list of American authors who anticipated the realistic movement of the twentieth century: Harriet Beecher Stowe, Melville, Bret Harte, the Louisiana local-colorist G. W. Cable, the midwestern regionalists Edward Eggleston and Joseph Kirkland. The immediate founders of the realistic school, however, are four authors who dominated the period between 1880 and the First World War: W. D. HOWELLS, HENRY JAMES, FRANK NORRIS, and STEPHEN CRANE. Before Howells and James American realism was little more than a medley of folk tales, nature studies, and frontier romance; after Norris and Crane the way was paved for Dreiser and the naturalists of the Twenties. With the four in this important germinative period can be included four of lesser rank: HAMLIN GARLAND, the first to write realistically of farm life; JACK LONDON, whose tales of rugged men and violent adventure anticipated the Hemingway school; EDITH WHARTON, disciple of James, who in a sense bridges the gap between James' essentially nineteenth-century style and the more satirical and critical descriptions of the manners of the moneyed class by such twentieth-century realists as Scott Fitzgerald and John P. Marquand; and GERTRUDE ATHERTON, important as a realistic novelist of manners as well as a regionalist and ironist. To these may be added O. HENRY, founder of the twentieth-century magazine story and in addition an isolated literary phenomenon of great interest in his own right.

It can be convincingly argued that these writers are the first "modern" authors in American literature. If this is true, Howells and James are the least modern; their realism lies chiefly in their rejection of romantic sentimentalism and in their precise and observant depiction of manners. Norris and Crane are more daring in subject matter (slums, war, sex) as well as in style (terse, blunt, and vernacular); they are of the twentieth century in content as well as technique. It might be argued indeed that James is not a realist at all but a psychological novelist; and the fact that his work rose to a new popularity in the Thirties, when the public taste turned increasingly to psychological fiction, seems to support this view. Another way to view the difference between these authors is to argue that James, Howells, and Mrs. Wharton are the predecessors of the later "critics of middle-class manners"—(Sinclair Lewis, Marquand, Anderson, and Scott Fitzgerald); that O. Henry is the grandfather of the popular short story of the *Collier's* or *Saturday Evening Post* variety; that Norris and London are the founders of American sociological naturalism (Dos Passos, Farrell, et al.); and that Crane anticipates the sparse and economical naturalism of Hemingway and his imitators. Whatever the validity of such a generalization, it is clear that in this group of *circa* 1900 writers America had produced its first realists—and in James, perhaps, its first great novelistic stylist worthy of taking a place alongside Stendhal, Flaubert, and Turgenev.

All classifying of authors, whether by "school" or period, is of course arbitrary. Edith Wharton lived until 1937 and published one of her most important books in 1920. Yet she is clearly a pre-1914 writer in style and attitude; she admitted herself, in fact, that she felt almost a stranger in the new era of the Twenties. The same is true of Gertrude Atherton, who died as late as 1948. Hamlin Garland likewise lived and wrote into the post-1918 period, yet stylistically he precedes Crane; he was a successful author when Crane had not yet begun, and he gave Crane help and advice on the publication of *The Red Badge of Courage*. These nine authors are treated here as a group because they anticipate twentieth-century realism without totally achieving it; if they lived into the new era it was only as strangers, confused and sometimes resentful of the radical new school of fiction they had helped to found.

WILLIAM DEAN HOWELLS (1837-1920)

Howells, who ranked among the most popular American novelists at the turn of the century, is less read today; his chief importance is in the end perhaps a historical one. He was a prolific writer, an authoritative critic, and an energetic and perspicacious editor; his writing career extends over more than sixty years, and there is scarcely a realistic novelist of the next generation who was not influenced by him to some degree.

Howells evidently had ambitions to become something like an American Balzac. He deliberately wrote novels covering diverse aspects of American life (industry, farming, commerce, art, society, the family), and he sought, like Balzac, to create a "network" of characters who were to recur in his novels so that in a sense his books together would constitute one great work, an American *Human Comedy*. His real interests, however, were much narrower than those of Balzac. As a novelist he is mainly concerned with two aspects of American life: (1) the conflict between the new world of business and commerce and the genteel aristocracy of the eastern seaboard, especially the aristocracy of Boston; and (2) the moral and emotional problems involved in the institution of marriage.

Howells is rightfully considered important as one of the founders of American realism, but he is a realist only in a limited sense. He is a realist first of all in his subject-matter: the middle-class family, the economic aspects of middle-class life, industry, and commerce. Here he shows himself as the literary godfather of Sinclair Lewis and his school. He is a realist in plot in that he consciously avoids the "happy ending" or the dramatic climax dear to the romantic novelist. And he is a moral realist in his rejection of dramatic gestures, of heroic renunciation, of sentimental self-sacrifice. As an example, in *The Rise of Silas Lapham* the Lapham family imagines that Tom Corey is courting their younger daughter Irene. When it is found that he is

later held by Bernard De Voto, and as such assuming a position as an authoritative arbiter in American letters. Out of his *Harper's* articles came, in 1891, his chief statement of literary principle: *Criticism and Fiction.* In his later period he wrote a pair of utopian novels of a quasi-socialistic tendency, of which *A Traveler from Altruria* (1894) is best known. Although his literary output fell off toward the end of his life, he continued to write; his last novel, *The Leatherwood God,* appeared in 1916. He died in New York in 1920, on the eve of the triumph of realism for which he had helped to pave the way.

CHIEF NOVELS: *A Modern Instance* (1881) concerns the rise and decline of Bartley Hubbard, a journalist who also appears as a minor character in *Silas Lapham.* The story opens in Equity, a country town in Maine, where Hubbard, a Harvard graduate, is the frustrated and discontented editor of the local weekly. To amuse himself he enters into a flirtation with Marcia Gaylord, daughter of the old Squire Gaylord, an old-fashioned freethinker. In spite of himself he falls in love with Marcia, at least he imagines that he does; and she, her head turned by his sophistication and his dashing manners, comes to love him too. But when a minor scandal comes to light involving Bartley and a girl who works in his office, Marcia, idealistic and virtuous, regretfully renounces marriage. At this point in the novel an interlude introduces Bartley's friend Kinney, a local sage and amateur philosopher who is serving as cook in a nearby logging camp. From Kinney Bartley gets material for an article on the Maine logging industry. When he loses his job on the country paper, therefore, he elopes with Marcia, goes to Boston, and gets his start in the big-city newspaper world with the material he got from Kinney.

Bartley is an immediate success in Boston; the rest of the novel relates his gradual moral deterioration. He is brash, confident, ingenious, unprincipled—in short the kind of newspaperman that Howells, with his old-fashioned journalistic ideals, detested. As for Marcia, she is basically good, but her principles have been muddled by her godless upbringing at the hands of her skeptical father. Bartley becomes editor of *The Events,* a live-wire modern paper, and soon begins to cut ethical corners. Under the influence of big-city life he also turns to dissipation, and is brought home drunk one night by Ben Halleck, a shy and lame young man who has long loved Marcia in secret. When Bartley finds himself in financial trouble Halleck lends him money; in this and other ways he silently serves Marcia, although he knows his love is hopeless.

The climax comes when Bartley reencounters Kinney and steals some literary material from him which Kinney has intended to write up himself. Because of this he loses his job and finally abandons his wife and child to wander off west. For several years Marcia struggles along alone, aided by the banker Atherton and secretly protected by Halleck. Finally Bartley is located in Indiana, where he has filed divorce proceedings alleging desertion on Marcia's part. Marcia, her father, and Halleck go to Indiana and fight the case; Bartley flees again, and Marcia, now divorced, returns to Boston. Halleck is now free to marry her, but finds himself in one of Howells' puritanical moral dilemmas: as Atherton, the spokesman of the novel, explains, the fact that Halleck was in love with her when she was another man's wife is "an indelible stain." He renounces his happiness and hers too. Bartley is killed in a quarrel in Arizona, having through his lack of character ruined his own life and the lives of those around him.

There are two basic themes in this novel: (1) the condemnation of the aggressive and unprincipled ambition of Bartley, the personification of the new American business-man, and (2) the moral dilemma of Halleck, essentially a problem in the ethics of sexual relations. The first theme comprises the first important portrayal in literature of the American "booster," the type Lewis was to satirize in *Babbitt* and other novels. The second theme, the moral problem, is one recurring throughout Howells' work, and one which demonstrates his basic affinity to Henry James.

The Rise of Silas Lapham (1884) is Howells' best-known novel. The plot is similar to that of *A Modern Instance,* but the hero is treated more sympathetically, and in the end he manages to regenerate himself. Silas Lapham, son of a New England farmer, makes a fortune in the paint business out of a chemical his father had discovered on the farm. At one point in his career he had formed a partnership with one Rogers, but he later bought him out, and when the novel opens he is sole owner of his factory and business. In his new-found prosperity he moves his family to Boston; there his wife and his two daughters, Penelope and Irene, begin to move in social circles. Silas, feeling vaguely that his money has not brought him the satisfaction it ought to, decides to build an expensive and ostentatious house in the new Back Bay district; he hopes too that the house will aid his daughters in their attempt to rise in society. But his wife, the "conscience" of the family, feels somehow that their new wealth is morally tainted, since Rogers was bought out of the partnership for less than his share was later discovered to be worth. Silas agrees to reimburse Rogers, and both feel that the moral basis of the family has been restored.

Meanwhile Tom Corey, scion of a distinguished but no longer wealthy Boston family, becomes a frequent visitor at the house; it appears he is interested in Irene. His father Colonel Corey, content to live his life as a cultivated dilettante of independent means, has never been interested in making more money; but Tom, bored with his useless life, applies to Lapham to be taken into the paint company. Silas agrees, and Tom is a considerable success as a business-man. Now, however, Mrs. Lapham and the girls feel that their entire lives must be devoted toward impressing the Coreys and convincing these aristocrats that they are not vulgar provincials. They go to dinner at the Coreys'; the evening is a failure, since Silas, unaccustomed to wine, drinks too much and makes a fool of himself. At this point in the plot it is learned that his business affairs are not going well; he has taken Rogers, who is apparently a thorough-going rascal, back into the firm, and Rogers' schemes have brought the company to the brink of ruin.

The two plots—business and marriage—continue side by side. Tom proposes, but to Penelope instead of to Irene as expected. Penelope, out of a sense of sentimental and romantic loyalty to her sister, refuses, using as a second excuse her father's business failure. Disaster follows disaster; the partly-finished Back Bay house, uninsured, burns down, and the paint business collapses under new competition. Then Rogers comes to Silas with a way out: an English combine is ready to pay a high price for a mill which the firm owns. Both Silas and Rogers know the property is almost worthless, since the railroad which serves as its sole shipping outlet covets the mill and can force sale whenever it wants. Although Rogers claims such a deal is legitimate according to ordinary business ethics, Silas, after much soul-searching and consultation with his wife, rejects it. He is ruined, and starts over again to make another fortune by allying himself with the competitors who invaded his market. Penelope, listening finally to the arguments of common sense, marries Tom, and Irene is happy for their happiness.

This novel is basically a study of the American newly-rich, the conflict between the new race of industrial millionaires and the traditional aristocracy of New England. Lapham, representing "stalwart achievement," encounters the Coreys, "sterile elegance;" each has something to offer the other, but much misunderstanding and hostility must be cleared away first. Related, of course, is the question of business ethics: how high a price is Silas willing to pay for success? At the end, impelled by the strong ethical heritage of his New England ancestors, he accepts financial ruin rather than compromise his conscience. The Irene-Penelope-Tom plot studies another problem: the evils of romantic sentimentalism as it is derived from traditional novels. The minister Sewell, to whom the Laphams go for advice, is the spokesman for Howells' view on this subject—that human happiness is more important than the heroism of tragic renunciation.

A Hazard of New Fortunes (1889) is the most important work of Howells' later period, after he had moved to New York. It is also the most complicated of his novels; it contains many characters, several interwoven plots, and numerous sub-themes. Essentially it concerns two families: Basil March and his wife, who come from Boston to New York where Basil has been offered the editorship of a new magazine to be called *Every Other Week;* and the clan of old Dryfoos, a Pennsylvania farmer of German extraction who has sold his farm for a large amount to natural-gas interests and come to New York with his fortune. The manager of the magazine venture is the aggressive and unprincipled Fulkerson, who resembles the Bartley Hubbard of *A Modern Instance.* Another important character is Lindau, a German socialist and utopian who has lost an arm in the Union cause in the Civil War, a friend of March and later an employee of the magazine.

The first section of the novel is devoted largely to the apartment-hunting adventures of the Marches in New York City, a town which Howells for many years disliked for its hugeness, its callousness, and its sordid ugliness. The new magazine, backed by Dryfoos' money, goes well. But Dryfoos is not happy; his two daughters, Mela and

Christina, have turned into vulgar social climbers, and his son Conrad grows into a saintly idealist whose sympathies are with the laboring class and who detests his father's materialism. Dryfoos has, in fact, gone into the magazine venture chiefly to provide occupation for Conrad, but the son loathes the sordid sensationalism and commercialism which constitute Fulkerson's idea of how to run a magazine.

The climactic point of the plot is a dinner at which the socialist Lindau, hired by March as a translator, quarrels with Dryfoos, who is reactionary and bitterly anti-labor. The next day Dryfoos orders Lindau fired; March refuses, and the staff is split by the quarrel. Meanwhile a streetcar strike breaks out; Lindau, going into the streets to aid the strikers, is attacked by the police, and Conrad, coming to help him, is killed by a stray bullet. Dryfoos, stricken by his son's death, reexamines his conscience and begins to see the error and vulgarity of his life; he proposes to make it up to Lindau, but the old socialist has meanwhile died in the hospital. Old Dryfoos concludes sorrowfully that his son's death was a kind of atonement for the sins he has committed as a representative of the new capitalistic class.

This novel is by no means a socialist tract; March at the end sees that Lindau with his notions of class warfare has gone about a good cause in a wrong way, and that the non-violent way is better. "What's the use of our ever fighting about anything in America? . . . We can vote anything we want." Old Dryfoos is a study in newly-acquired wealth, something like Silas Lapham; on the farm he was successful and happy, respected by his neighbors, but when he becomes a capitalist he turns mean, selfish, and vindictive. The minor characters include Woodburn, a southern colonel and unreconstructed rebel "with his idiotic talk about patriarchal slavery" and Beaton, an artist who represents the bohemian attitude. Fulkerson, with his slick lingo and his brash sensational ideas, is another nineteenth-century "Babbitt," while March represents the ethical journalist in a moral dilemma. The novel includes a theory of human behavior that is essentially a modern and sociological one; "conditions make character, and people are greedy and foolish and wish to have and shine, because having and shining are held up to them by civilization as the chief good of life." This criticism of the American "success myth" reflects an attitude which Howells felt throughout his life and which was intensified by the experiences of his New York period.

HENRY JAMES (1843-1916)

James is not only the most important American realist of the period before the First World War; he is also the most expert stylist of his time, and perhaps of all American fiction. He is thus the first —and almost the only—American to achieve the synthesis of detailed observation and polished style which characterizes the great European realists: Stendhal, George Eliot, Flaubert, and Turgenev. It is significant that James was a personal friend of the last two authors; he is essentially a European in style, treatment, and literary attitude. If he is American at all, it is only in his subject matter, and in his slightly excessive respect for the superiority of European culture. Where the Mark Twains and W. D. Howells satirized European manners, James admired; yet in both cases the attitude was due to a partly repressed feeling of inferiority, a sense of provincial awkwardness before the finished perfection of European civilization. James overcame his native awkwardness, acquired polish, and moved in the highest social circles of Europe; but he never lost his innate American inferiority complex. "The soil of American perception is a poor little barren, artificial deposit," says the painter Theobald in *The Madonna of the Future*. "An American, to excel, has just ten times as much to learn as a European." This was James' own opinion, in spite of his lifelong admiration for native American wit, freshness, and naivete.

James' work falls clearly into three periods: (1) his early realistic stage, comprising the novels from *A Passionate Pilgrim* (1871) through *Washington Square* (1880), in which his style is straightforward, external and reasonably simple, not essentially different from the style of Howells; (2) his mature period of "psychological realism," beginning with *The Portrait of a Lady* (1881) and continuing through *The Tragic Muse* (1890); and (3) his final "difficult" or experimental period, opening with *The Spoils of Poynton* (1897) and including most of his later novels and tales, a period in which he becomes preoccupied with unusual point-of-view devices, with intricate syntactical experiments, and with subtleties of diction and dialogue. Philip Guedalla, feeling that the late James is deliberately and unnecessarily obscure, refers to the three styles as "James the First," "James the Second," and "The Old Pretender." Yet devoted Jamesians, a small but loyal fraternity, often prefer the complicated subtlety of the later work.

James as a stylist is sometimes difficult, but he is always highly refined, polished, perspicacious, and aesthetically accurate; he unerringly finds his way to the right word, and he is never clumsy or awkward as so many of his contemporaries are (Howells, Norris). His vocabulary is large, he is fond of Latinisms and of obscure or archaic words, and he has a weakness for sprinkling French expressions through his dialogues, especially in his later work. In the construction of his novels he is often intricate, and he is especially fascinated with point-of-view devices; the typical novel of his later period is related by a narrator who may take some small part in the action but who remains essentially on the sidelines as a spectator.

In subject matter James began as a realist and ended as a psychological novelist, yet his basic interest never changed. He is concerned chiefly with emotional relations among persons of breeding and gentility: tentative love, jealousy, misunderstandings of a complicated and subtle nature, degrees of social prestige, feelings of inferiority and superiority, and precise contrasts of national character. He balances these motivations with a precise, delicate, and unerring skill; no other American author is as adept as James at conveying subtle emotional distinctions. Thus his predilection for cultured, educated, or aristocratic characters is natural. He is not interested in presenting a complete and balanced view of life, including its vulgar life, as Zola was. He is concerned with psychological subtleties, and thus his technique requires superior minds—in his readers as well as in his characters. He is consequently open to a charge of snobbery. Even in works where he attempted to describe the life of the lower classes (e.g. *The Princess Casamassima*) his characters each have something exceptional about them; they are not average, neither are they "typical" of anything except the fiction of Henry James. He is not particularly interested in the economic side of life, i.e., in how goods are produced and how money is made. He is concerned instead with how money is spent; it seems to him a more interesting subject, and one not tainted with the sordid monotony of daily drudgery. To object to this is to object to James' very nature, and to his innate conviction about what literature should be. It should be remarked in his defense that he is intelligent enough to feel a genuine sympathy for the lower orders, and to hope for an amelioration of their condition. What he will not do is write about them realistically; he leaves this to writers like Crane and Norris. James is the founder, not of twentieth-century naturalism, but of the school of psychological realism presented by Edith Wharton, Thornton Wilder, and Katherine Anne Porter.

James' admiration for European culture led him to a lifelong interest in the conflict of the American and European personalities, i.e., in the problem of The American in Europe. He saw that Europeans were often regarded as overrefined, degenerate, and artificial by Americans, and that Americans were considered naive, vulgar, and ignorant by many Europeans. The misunderstanding caused personality conflicts, and even where the two races found each other agreeable (as in the many love-stories involving Europeans and Americans) the national differences provided opportunity for piquant contrasts of character. The typical American in a James novel is fresh, enthusiastic, not perhaps as cultured as he might be, but eager to learn, and basically "good" in spite of his disregard of the outworn conventions and social amenities of Europe. The European, on the other hand, is highly cultivated, urban, sometimes blasé and a little bored, but always correct. He is, however, sometimes unprincipled. In James the Americans often stand for morality, the Europeans for manners. This is true even in the case of characters like Daisy Miller, who seems a shameless flirt to the Europeans whose conventions she flagrantly violates. A third type of character occasionally found in such a novel is the objective spectator, half American and half European, or an American long expatriated like the Winterbourne of *Daisy Miller*. This character, of course, personifies the attitude of James himself—born an American, a European by choice, perceiving the unfortunate root of the misunderstanding but able only to view it as a more or less dispassionate observer. Thus James' view of America vs. Europe and his interpretation of character are intimately involved with his style and his theory of fiction, especially his interest in devices like the detached-narrator point-of-view.

James did not believe that art ought to have a moral; he despised the didactic, and even though he himself observed the utmost decorum he defended the right of the author to write about any subject, however offensive, that seemed to him significant. In many respects he was a model aesthete of the fin-de-siècle variety; he believed in art for art's sake, and he was interested chiefly in the enigma of the relation between life and art, between reality and fiction. Yet his work as a whole has a moral rather than an amoral tone. His characters are generally involved in some kind of a personal struggle; they do not always win, but it is nevertheless clear that James is on the side of virtue. A typical instance is that of *Daisy Miller,* where his tale takes the form of an investigation into whether Daisy was or was not an immoral creature. He finds that she was not; she died (that is, was punished) on account of her indiscretion, but she is still the most virtuous, and therefore the most admirable, character in the story. Although he was a believer, James had little interest in religious problems, and almost never treated them in his fiction. His ethics are those of conventional cultivated society, molded by good breeding but qualified by a strong individual sense of right and wrong: he admires love, fidelity, beauty, generosity, and tact. "To be completely great," he wrote, "a work of art must lift up the heart." If James is a realist, therefore, he is a realist of the spirit, a region of human conflict no less "real" than the battlefields of Crane or the slums of Dreiser and the naturalists.

LIFE: The life of Henry James was one of detachment and observation rather than action. He was born in New York in 1843, the son of the theological writer Henry James and the brother of the Pragmatist philosopher William James. The family had means enough so that neither son was obliged to work for a living. Thus James was detached by the nature of his upbringing from the American "success struggle" which preoccupied such novelists as his friend W. D. Howells.

As a boy Henry was privately educated by tutors. In 1855 the family went to Europe, where they stayed for three years. The visit was partly of an educational nature, since the father wished his sons to be citizens of the world, able to select for themselves the kind of lives they wanted to lead. Barred by a physical disability from serving in the Civil War, James entered the Harvard Law School in 1862. He liked Cambridge, and it remained his American home for the rest of his life. He visited Europe frequently, however, and ended as a more or less permanent expatriate. He began writing in the eighteen-sixties; his early work, critical articles and essays, soon gained the approval of W. D. Howells and C. E. Norton, editor of the *North American Review*. His first important fiction was *A Passionate Pilgrim* (1871), in which he took up for the first time the theme of The American in Europe. In 1875 he passed a year in France, associating freely with such famous authors as the Goncourts, Flaubert, Zola, Turgenev, and Maupassant. But he felt out of place in this group, comprised mainly of documentary realists with a slightly shocking penchant for the sordid. "They had no vision, no humanity, no taste for the intangible"; explains Van Wyck Brooks, "and, besides, he could not endure their Bohemian ways." He went to London, where he remained for a number of years, writing *The American* (1877), *The Europeans* (1878), *Daisy Miller* (1879), and most of the works of his middle period. In 1881 appeared *The Portrait of a Lady,* the first of his works in the new mature style and the novel which is generally considered his masterpiece. During the eighteen-nineties he turned to drama; his plays, excessively cerebral, had little success. He began writing novels again, producing another first-rate book, *The Spoils of Poynton,* in 1897. Other important novels of his later period include *What Maisie Knew* (1897), *The Awkward Age* (1899), *The Ambassadors* (1903), and *The Golden Bowl* (1904).

In 1915 James, chiefly out of sympathy for the Allied cause in the war, became a British citizen. He never married; he continued to write into the twentieth century, producing chiefly essays, stories, and drama in his last years. He died in London in 1916, shortly after receiving the Order of Merit for his services to the British nation.

CHIEF WORKS: *The American* (novel, 1877, dramatized by James in 1891) concerns the efforts of a young American millionaire, Christopher Newman, to make his way in French society and to win the hand of the aristocratic young Claire de Cintré, a widow. Newman, a capable and intelligent self-made man, is at first scorned by Claire's family, the Bellegardes, as a "commercial person." But he has a full sense of his own worth and is not rebuffed by their arrogance. The family reluctantly accepts him and the engagement is announced. Meanwhile Newman, democratic and interested in all kinds of people, meets Noémie Nioche, a young artist and coypist, and her father, from whom he takes French lessons. He introduces Noémie to Count Valentin, the younger brother of Claire, who is more friendly toward him than the other members of the family, and the young nobleman soon becomes infatuated with her. The Bellegardes presently break their promise to Newman and announce that the marriage is not to take place after all; Claire, whose main frailty is a weakness of will, has capitulated before her indomitable mother. Valentin, meanwhile, has fought a duel over Noémie and is fatally wounded. Going to his bedside, Newman learns from him of a family secret which he might use to force the Bellegardes into accepting the marriage. Without much difficulty Newman obtains the secret: that the old Marquise, Claire's mother, had callously allowed her ailing husband to die when he opposed the mercenary marriage of Claire to M. de Cintré, her first husband. After much soul-searching Newman decides not to resort to this blackmail even for revenge (Claire by this time has entered a convent); he is generous and decent, and he refuses to act according to principles which the decadent Bellegardes would find quite natural were they in his position. He is finally resigned to his loss.

The theme of this novel is one which is to recur throughout James' work: the psychological analysis of the conflict between decadent aristocracy (France) and virile commercialism (America). A second contrast is found in the attitudes of M. de Nioche (bourgeois materialism) and the Bellegardes (idealistic aristocracy) toward the problem of the sexual relations of their daughters. M. de Nioche never forgives Noémie for selling herself for money, but he accepts the money nevertheless and does not repudiate her. The Bellegardes, even though their fortunes are at a low ebb, refuse to allow Claire to marry an American millionaire for money; they prefer her to enter a convent, which has precedent in family tradition. The plot of this novel, with its family secrets, duels for love, and nunneries, is extremely romantic, but the style of psychological analysis rescues it from mere melodrama.

"Daisy Miller" (story, 1878) is, like many of James' short stories, actually a miniature novelette in structure and treatment of character. Winterbourne, a young American living more or less permanently abroad, encounters Daisy Miller in the watering-resort of Vevey in the Swiss Alps. The young American girl, a native of Schenectady, is traveling with her mother and brother, and is already the subject of gossip in Vevey because of her free and intimate manners with their courier, or household servant. Mrs. Costello, Winterbourne's aunt and patroness, advises him to have nothing to do with Daisy, averring that she is "not proper," but he is fascinated by her ingenuous and innocent manner and her youthful freshness. He takes her on an excursion to the Castle of Chillon, and shortly afterward the Millers depart for Rome, inviting Winterbourne to meet them there later in the winter.

When Winterbourne arrives in Rome he finds that the gossip about Daisy has turned to scandal: she goes openly about the street with young men, invites "foreigners" (Italians) to her hotel, and refuses to be escorted in public by her mother. As a climax she enters into a flirtatious romance with a young Italian adventurer named Giovanelli. She is finally ostracized and disowned by the American colony, headed by the somewhat stiff Mrs. Walker, who has tried to "rescue" her from her indiscretions and has been, as she thinks, rebuffed. The main drama of the story takes place in Winterbourne's mind as he tries to decide whether Daisy is a flirt and a person of no character or merely a high-spirited and somewhat naive girl who is prevented by her American provincialism from perceiving subtleties of social propriety. Finally Daisy, going imprudently to view the Colosseum by moonlight with Giovanelli, contracts a fever and shortly dies, but not before she sends a message to Winterbourne reassuring him that she was never engaged to Giovanelli. He concludes from this that she was innocent as he had thought and hoped, and that her apparent immorality was only the unfortunate result of her American freeness of spirit as misinterpreted by the Europeans and Europeanized Americans.

James wrote this story partly to defend the American girl from the unmerited censure she was receiving from Europeans, and from American expatriates in Europe, who confused natural exuberance with "fastness." Daisy is naive, somewhat sentimental, but well able to take care of herself; she is not immoral, and her tragic death is a kind of *deus ex machina* contrived merely to provide a dramatic finish for the story. Mrs. Costello and Mrs. Walker, rather proper middle-aged ladies, represent conventional opinion in this story; Giovanelli is intended as a personification of the European attitude, and Winterbourne is James himself, standing between Daisy and her detractors and viewing her with sympathetic eyes in an effort to understand her.

Daisy, of course, is American girlhood, or indeed the "American spirit" itself.

Washington Square (novel, 1881) is one of the few James novels laid in a totally American setting. The heroine, Catherine Sloper, is plain, honest, naive, but strong-willed, James' notion of the average American girl of the wealthy class. Her father, a successful New York doctor, has been greatly disappointed with the fruits of his success and hopes for much from his daughter in spite of her plainness. However the girl, encouraged by a romantic and sentimental aunt, Lavinia Penniman, makes the mistake of falling in love with the penniless fortune-hunter Morris Townsend, who is interested only in her prospects for inheritance after her father's death. With his greater knowledge of the world Dr. Sloper perceives Townsend's motives; and when Catherine dutifully reports to him that she has accepted Townsend's proposal, he forbids the marriage and threatens to cut off her inheritance.

To distract his daughter from her sorrow, the doctor takes her on a trip to Europe. Mrs. Penniman is left to entertain Townsend, whom she has come to regard virtually as a son, and whose interest she now places above her niece's. The stratagem of the voyage is futile; upon her return Catherine tells lover and father that she will no longer wait for paternal approval but will marry even if it means disinheritance. Her father is astounded and Townsend—interested in the money more than the girl—taken aback. He breaks off the engagement, presenting as an excuse to Catherine that he could not come between her and her father.

Gradually, as Catherine matures, she comes to understand Townsend's motives and realizes that her father has acted in her best interests. But when her father, shortly before his death, tries to elicit a final promise from her that she will never marry Townsend, she refuses out of pride, and as a result he virtually disinherits her. She does not regret the money, and grows gracefully into a maiden lady, kind to children and devoted to charitable acts. In Catherine's middle age Mrs. Penniman once again tries to arrange a marriage with Townsend, but Catherine, now older and wiser, refuses coldly; her pride is involved, and besides she feels little emotion toward the aging Townsend who now seems like a stranger to her. She prefers to live out her life in her comfortable position as a spinster and companion to the younger set in her social circle.

This novel, with its prosaic American setting and its straightforward style, is one of the least complicated of James' major works. It is interesting for its lucid exposition, for its depiction of New York society, but most of all for the skill with which James makes an interesting figure out of a girl who is virtuous, simple, and not intrinsically a fascinating person.

The Portrait of a Lady (novel, 1881) is representative of the best of James' mature work. The plot concerns the courtship, marriage, and development of character of Isabel Archer, a young American girl who has been left penniless by the death of her father. Taken to Europe by an eccentric aunt, Mrs. Touchett, the beautiful Isabel attracts the attention of a cousin, Ralph Touchett, scion of wealthy American relatives who live in Europe. Meanwhile she must decide what to do about two other suitors: the strong, reserved Caspar Goodwood (representing the American character) and Lord Warburton (a wealthy nobleman, symbol of European aristocracy). She refuses Warburton, but puts off Caspar with a promise of an answer in two years. Ralph Touchett, who is in love with her too, persuades his father to leave her half his fortune in order that she may be independent and make up her mind free of financial pressures.

After Mr. Touchett's death, therefore, Isabel goes to Italy with her new fortune. There, through the offices of the subtle expatriate Madame Merle, she meets Gilbert Osmond, who is actually a decadent fortune-hunter. He also proposes to her, and she, with too little experience of the world to perceive his true motives, is impressed with his suavity and accepts. The marriage is a failure; Isabel soon sees through Gilbert's superficiality and vanity, and Gilbert gradually realizes that his wife has more character than he thought—too much to be willing to serve as a mere reflection of his own personality. The rift is widened by a quarrel over Gilbert's daughter Pansy; Gilbert and Madame Merle plot to marry the girl to Warburton, Isabel's old suitor. Isabel is aware that Warburton still loves her and that Pansy is in love with a young man named Ned Rosier; she will have nothing to do with the match. Gilbert accuses her of interference in matters that are none of her business. Shortly after this, Isabel learns from the Countess Gemini, Gilbert's sister, that Pansy is actually the illegitimate child of Gilbert and Madam Merle. Disturbed by this discovery, she returns to England, where Ralph is dying; there she again meets her old American suitor Caspar, and finally realizes that he is the one she loves. But she has promised Pansy to return to Italy; she rejects this last chance for happiness and rejoins her husband and step-daughter, conscious of her marriage vows and of the child who has only her to look to for protection.

This intricate novel of psychological and moral interrelationships is in one sense another treatment of the Jamesian theme of the American in conflict with European culture (the virtuous Isabel vs. the cynical and devious expatriate Madame Merle) and in another sense the most personal of his novels, an intimate picture of a woman's soul presented with masterly psychological finesse. Isabel is virtuous, but here her resemblance to the Catherine Sloper of *Washington Square,* also the prey of a fortune-hunter, is at an end. Naive in the beginning, Isabel is nevertheless sensitive, perceptive, and intelligent; her virtue proceeds from a real strength of character and is not a mere negative modesty. She stands out sharply amid the collection of blasé Europeans, cynical expatriates, and international eccentrics who surround her. It takes Isabel a certain time to perceive the nature of the evil around her, but when she does perceive it she knows what to do. She is a typical example of the Woman of Character in James' work: generally American, often naive and credulous at the outset, an easy mark for fortune hunters and other conniving persons, but strong in her innocence and eventually triumphant over the webs of cynicism and evil in which she finds herself entangled. Isabel's sacrifice, like Daisy Miller's death, is an act of rebellion against the cynical conventions of a decadent culture.

In *The Princess Casamassima* (novel, 1886) James treats what seems for him an unusual subject: anarchist conspiracy in the slums of London. The central character, Hyacinth Robinson, is the illegitimate son of a Frenchwoman of low repute who dies in prison for the murder of an English nobleman, presumed father of the boy. He is raised by Miss Amanda Pynsent ("Pinnie"), a spinster dressmaker. In his youth his social consciousness is aroused by Anastasius Vecht, an anarchist violinist, and Eustache Poupin, a French refugee who fought in the Commune of '71. Hyacinth is clearly marked by his French and aristocratic heredity; he is sensitive and talented, and has the innate instincts of a gentleman. Apprenticed to a bookbinder, he soon begins to make his way in the world. But his friendship with Paul Muniment, a revolutionary, leads him into membership in a secret anarchist organization; in a moment of youthful enthusiasm he "pledges his life" to the movement.

Shortly afterward he meets the Princess Casamassima, a brilliant young woman of mixed Italian and American blood who is estranged from her aristocratic Italian husband. The two, separated by the entire social scale, nevertheless have much in common; they are sensitive, artistic, of finer clay than the ordinary, and both have a deep emotional sympathy for the unfortunate of the world. Under the tutelage of the Princess, Hyacinth begins to understand his true place in life. Although his sympathy for the masses is undiminished, he now sees that violence against the aristocratic classes would merely destroy beauty without ameliorating the misery of the poor. But he is still bound by his solemn pledge to the anarchist group, and when they order him to carry out a dangerous assassination he realizes he cannot refuse. Meanwhile the Princess, who has donated money to the cause, learns of his mission; she seeks to offer herself for the suicidal assassination in his place. But before she can carry out her sacrifice Hyacinth kills himself, unable to see any way out of his dilemma.

This novel, as might be expected, is not very successful in depicting the reality of life in the London slums. Its excellence lies first in the characters of Hyacinth and the Princess (whose girlhood and marriage are described in an earlier novel, *Roderick Hudson*) and second in the profusion of colorful and bizarre secondary characters: the Princess' companion Madame Gradoni, the dashing and unprincipled Captain Sholto, the dressmaker Pinnie, the aristocratic Prince Casamassima, the philanthropic Englishwoman Lady Aurora, the conceited and flirtatious shopgirl Millicent Henning, and a collection of minor anarchists and underworld characters. The plot is totally melodramatic, but it is related in a slightly ironic style that saves it from sentimentality. James' attitude toward the proletarian movement is ambiguous; he naturally deplores violence of the anarchist variety (none of which, incidentally, takes place in the novel) but the work nevertheless reveals a genuine sympathy for the poor of the world and a conviction that something must be done to alleviate their lot, even if this means the destruction of the aristocratic society in which James felt most at home.

The Aspern Papers (novelette, 1888) is narrated by an American editor who is an enthusiastic student of the works of the early nineteenth-century romantic poet Jeffrey Aspern, a figure modeled partly after Byron. He journeys to Venice in the hope of obtaining from one Juliana Bordereau, at one time a mistress of the long-dead poet, certain papers and mementoes of Aspern which are known to be in her possession. He finds the old lady living with an incredibly naive spinster niece, Miss Tina; Miss Bordereau herself proves inaccessible, but the niece quickly becomes his ally.

Driven impatient by his curiosity, the young American, taking advantage of Miss Bordereau's illness, opens her desk in the hope of getting a glimpse of the papers. She surprises him in the act and denounces him; he flees, and she suffers a relapse from excitement and shock. When he returns after a few days he finds she has died, after vainly attempting to destroy the letters. Miss Tina now offers them to him, but at a price: only if he were "in the family," she says, would it be right for her to let him have them. This thinly-veiled marriage proposal from the spinster horrifies the young man; he leaves, giving her no answer, and searches his conscience for the assurance that he has not actually made love to her. During his absence she comprehends his recoil; ennobled by her suffering, she burns the papers and dismisses him, preferring her dignity to the claim of her unworthy love.

The idea for this tale was suggested to James by the presence in Florence of Jane Clairmont, a relative of Shelley and the mother of Byron's daughter Allegra, and the alleged efforts of an American traveler to obtain some Shelley papers by entering her household as a lodger. The narrator, a literary critic once removed from the artist but nevertheless feeling an "artistic" justification for his deception of Miss Bordereau, argues for his right to lay bare the truth in the interests of scholarship regardless of the feelings of those he exposes. Miss Bordereau, on the other hand, denounces him as a "publishing scoundrel." In the end the central interest lies in the figure of Miss Tina, who acquires character as the story proceeds and who emerges at the end transformed by her heroic renunciation. The author's attitude toward the narrator is ambiguous, probably purposely so; we see the story only through his eyes, and yet his motives are decidedly questionable.

The Spoils of Poynton (novel, 1897) is a complicated and polished exercise in style, the first of James' novels in the new "difficult" manner of his later period. The heroine, Fleda Vetch, encounters the devoted aesthete Mrs. Gereth at a weekend spent with the Brigstocks, who are wealthy but vulgar and lacking in taste. The two are drawn together by their artistic sensitivity and become friends; Mrs. Gereth sees in Fleda a person capable of appreciating the exquisitely perfect synthesis of art and furniture she has achieved in Poynton, her home. Her whole life, in fact, centers around her home, and she lives in dread of the day her son Owen will install a bride in the house and banish her to a small "dowager's house."

Her fears are justified when Owen brings Mona Brigstock to Poynton and announces his intention of marrying her. The mother enlists the aid of Fleda in her flight against the intruder who seeks to rob her of "her" treasures, legally the property of her son. Fleda, who serves as an intermediary in the conflict between mother and son, soon finds herself in love with Owen; and he, bewildered by the bullying of the aggressive Mona, is ready to return her feelings. At this point Mrs. Gereth takes a decisive step: she moves into the small dowager house, taking with her as many of her fine things as she can cram into it. The lines of battle are drawn, and Mona refuses to marry Owen until his mother returns the "stolen" treasures.

Although Fleda sympathizes with Mrs. Gereth, she persuades her to return the possessions; but Mrs. Gereth agrees to do so only when Fleda promises that if she does Fleda will marry Owen herself. Owen presently proposes to Fleda, claiming that Mona's coldness has freed him of any moral obligation toward her, but Fleda insists that he discuss the matter with his "fiancée" first. Meanwhile Mrs. Gereth returns the furnishings; and Mona, her ultimatum satisfied, thereupon marries Owen.

Immediately after the marriage Mona, to demonstrate that it was not the material prize of the house she had fought for, embarks with her husband on a trip around the world, leaving Poynton in the hands of incompetent caretakers. Mrs. Gereth, deprived of the only possession she valued in the world, is broken in spirit, and it is almost an anticlimax when the house is burned through the negligence of the caretakers.

The point of this complicated study of psychological conflicts is that human relationships are more important than devotion to a mere cult of beauty. Mrs. Gereth, blindly devoted to her beautiful possessions, pays little heed to the nuances of moral character in those around her; for instance she mistakenly assumes that Fleda's promise has made her marriage with Owen an absolute certainty, and thus loses her "spoils" out of her very assurance that they are secured. Fleda, also a devotée of beauty but a more complicated character than Mrs. Gereth, is undone by her moral scruples; she attempts to be perfectly fair with Mona as well as loyal to Mrs. Gereth and Owen, and thus she spoils all through her excessive moral delicacy. Owen, handsome and pleasant although a little stupid, is a mere pawn for the forces around him, and in the end the vulgar Mona is the strongest person of the novel.

What Maisie Knew (novel, 1897) is an ingenious narrative told from the point of view of a little girl who finds herself caught in an intricate web of adult relationships. The story is laid in England. Maisie's parents, Beale and Ida Farange, are divorced, and she lives with each one for six months out of the year. The parents use the child as a weapon to take out their spite on each other, and gradually she comes to understand the battles going on over her head. Her mother engages an attractive governess, Miss Overmore, but discharges her when it is evident that Maisie is fond of her. The next nurse is Mrs. Wix, an incompetent and sentimental old woman who nevertheless wins Maisie's confidence and becomes her "emotional mother." Miss Overmore ingeniously manages to get taken on by Beale as a governess; but when Maisie comes to live in her father's household the young woman neglects her, since she has now become romantically involved with Beale, her employer. Meanwhile Ida's life has gone on; she becomes engaged to a suitor, Sir Claude. Miss Overmore marries Beale, but neither pair hits it off; Ida tires of Sir Claude, and he in turn falls in love with the new Mrs. Beale. Maisie, rejected by her mother, who dallies with a succession of lovers, turns to Sir Claude, journeying to France with him and becoming his confidante. The child now realizes that she has more character than the adults around her, and thus has a power over them; she asks Sir Claude to give up Mrs. Beale, and when he refuses she goes to live with Mrs. Wix, leaving the adults entangled in their hopeless confusion of passions.

The main interest in this novel apart from the ingenious point-of-view device is the character of Maisie herself, surely one of the most remarkable children in literature, and yet by no means precocious or unnatural. Mrs. Wix is also a fascinating character: sentimental, frowsy, and moralistic, she is nevertheless the wisest adult in the story, and the one good influence among the adults who surround Maisie.

The Turn of the Screw (novelette, 1898) is, for James, an excursion into an unusual genre: the ghost story. The heroine, who narrates the story in the first person, comes to a country-house in Essex to serve as governess for two orphaned children, Flora and Miles. She soon becomes aware of the presence in the neighborhood of two ghosts: Peter Quint, a former steward of the estate, and Miss Jessel, who had preceded the heroine as governess. Her horror is intensified when she realizes that Flora and Miles are aware of the presence of the apparitions, that they communicate secretly with them, in short that the children have come under the power of these evil beings. She takes Mrs. Grose, the housekeeper, into her confidence; the gossiping old woman believes the story, and helps to fill the governess in on the details of the history of the two, but never actually sees the ghosts herself. The governess is reluctant to inform the owner of the house—uncle of the two children—of her finding, since she is secretly in love with him, and imagines the derision with which he would greet such a ghost story. She decides instead to fight the ghosts through the soul of Flora. But she only succeeds in terrifying her so much that she loses her confidence entirely. When she tries the same tactics with Miles he becomes hysterical and dies (of terror?) in her arms, while the ghost of Quint regards the scene through the window.

For many years this tale was regarded as a simple ghost story. A recent school of criticism, however, has attempted to explain it in psychological or Freudian terms, arguing that the ghosts do not really exist but are merely delusions of the governess' sex-starved imagination. There is some interesting evidence for this theory; the governess herself (Chapter XIII) asks, "How can I retrace today the strange steps of my obsession?" If this theory is valid, then the governess, in her delusion, succeeds in convincing Mrs. Grose, Flora, and Miles of the reality of the ghost, the boy so effectively that she actually kills him from fright. But Wagenknecht remarks, "This view . . . has about as much critical standing as the aberrations of the Baconians," and the most that can be definitely said is that James' attitude toward the story is ambiguous.

The Turn of the Screw is also interesting as a Jamesian exercise in point of view. The first-person account of the governess is actually contained in a manuscript read forty years after the events by one Douglas, who had met the heroine years later when she was the governess of his sister. There is also an external narrator, identified only as "I," in this introductory frame story who stands between the reader and the original plot.

The Ambassadors (novel, 1903) climaxes James' lifelong interest in the contrast between European and American culture, and is perhaps his most important statement on that theme. The story opens as Lambert Strether, an intelligent and conscientious American editor, is sent by his wealthy and conventional fiancée Mrs. Newsome to rescue her son Chad from the distractions of Paris, including his supposed entanglement with a "wicked woman," and bring him back to take charge of the family business. Strether, upon his arrival, renews acquaintance with Waymarsh, an American who finds Europe baffling and unsympathetic, and meets Maria Gostrey, an American expatriate. These two figures serve as personifications of the two conflicting influences in the novel, Waymarsh representing the claim of American values and Maria pleading for European culture.

On meeting Chad and seeing what Paris, and more particularly his friend Mme. de Vionnet, have done for him, Strether begins to doubt the wisdom of taking him back to the more circumscribed life in Woollett, Massachusetts; he sees that Chad has in his grasp the opportunities that he himself had let escape in his youth and has always regretted. Finally, as his letters reveal to the formidable Mrs. Newsome that he actually approves of the influence of Paris and Mme. de Vionnet on Chad, this lady ceases to count on him; she sends as further ambassadors Chad's aggressively proper sister Mrs. Pocock, her husband Jim, and Jim's sister Mamie.

Mamie, who is considered Chad's presumptive fiancée by the family, is the only one who recognizes the significance of the change in him. She and Jeanne, daughter of Mme. de Vionnet, are drawn by

James in sharp contrast: the vital, ingenuous American spirit set off against the delicate, shy, and decorous European. Mrs. Pocock vetoes Mme. de Vionnet immediately, seeing not her charm but only her immoral relationship with Chad, and she convinces Strether that he has failed in his duty to Mrs. Newsome. Strether stands by Chad, even after he is brought to realize by an accidental encounter that the young man's relationship with the charming Frenchwoman would indeed be immoral in the eyes of Massachusetts. Making his decision, he convinces Chad that it would be unworthy of him to leave his mistress after all the richness of experience he has received from her. Thus Strether is left with the responsibility for Chad's remaining in Paris, even though he recognizes that the young man will probably eventually grow tired of the older woman. He does not, however, feel entirely at ease with his own conscience; and when an opportunity arises for him to remain in Paris with Maria he rejects it in order to remain perfectly sure in his own mind that his stay in France has been devoted entirely to the interests of Mrs. Newsome. Thus the novel ends inconclusively: Strether's attitude toward the situation is ambiguous, and Chad remains in Paris in his tenuous and obviously temporary relationship with Mme. de Vionnet.

The idea for this novel is taken from an admonition by William Dean Howells to Jonathan Sturges: "Live all you can: it's a mistake not to." Strether, regretting his own youthful prudence, sees in Chad the youth he might have been had he had the courage to abandon himself to intense experience in his early years. Thus Europe stands, as in many James novels, for experience, passion, and sophistication, and America for virtue and the dull life of the business world. In *The Ambassadors* Europe wins out, as it did for James himself. James, in fact, inserted himself into the novel in the person of Strethers; although the narrator of the story is not an autobiographical figure in the strict sense, he shares James' basic attitude toward the characters and their conflict. Jim Pocock is the type of the American business-man, out to enjoy himself in Paris and ready to leave intellectual and moral nuances to the women; his sharpness is directed entirely toward questions of business, and he has no interest in the subtleties of human relations. He serves as a horrible example of what would have awaited Chad had he returned to Woollett, and even of the fate that would fall on Strether if he married Mrs. Newsome.

The Ambassadors is perhaps the most severe of James' criticisms of the banality and materialism of American middle-class culture.

The Golden Bowl (novel, 1904) is the last complete novel of James and one of the most intricate products of his later "involved" period. The plot is a variation on the "love triangle" involving two couples whose affairs become entangled. The Italian Prince Amerigo, aristocratic but penniless, has an affair with the emancipated American girl Charlotte Stant, but they realize marriage is impossible since neither has any money. Later the Prince meets and marries Maggie Verver, daughter of the American millionaire Adam Verver. Maggie personifies the most admirable aspects of the American character: freshness, virtue, enthusiasm, and flexibility. The Prince, the type of the decadent aristocrat, is characterized through the symbol of the Golden Bowl which he at one time considers buying for Maggie: a gilded crystal bowl of exquisite proportions but marred by an internal and invisible flaw. Adam, also a model of the best American type, marries Charlotte, and the four, reunited in Italy, find a momentary happiness. But Maggie soon becomes aware of the previous relations of her husband and Charlotte, and perceives as well that their affair has now been renewed. She moves with tact and intelligence to fight her battle; and her delicacy of character so impresses both the Prince and Adam —who knows about the whole affair—that they agree to work with her to restore normal relationships among the four. Adam takes Charlotte back to America, and the Prince returns willingly to his wife, his love renewed by his new insight into her character and understanding.

In spite of its technical and stylistic intricacy, this novel deals with themes and characters common throughout the rest of James' work. Maggie is typical of his American girls, and perhaps the best of them; she is free of the silliness of Daisy Miller, the dullness of Catherine (*Washington Square*) and the naivete of Isabel (*The Portrait of a Lady*). The Prince is treated with more sympathy than most of the "decadent aristocrats" in James, and even Charlotte is likeable and convincing.

HAMLIN GARLAND (1860-1940)

In spite of the relatively slight importance of his work in a literary sense, Hamlin Garland occupies an important place in American letters: he is one of the first regionalists to treat local material realistically and without romanticizing. He represents a bridge between the sentimental local folklore of G. W. Cable and the stark rural realism of Caldwell or Steinbeck; he presents his material, which unlike many modern regionalists he knew from first-hand experience, realistically but with decorum. He is not remarkable as a literary technician; his style lacks the laconic modernism of Crane and the naturalistic toughness of Norris, and in some respects it is more conservative than the style of his literary godfather W. D. Howells. His main contribution to modern literature is in his subject matter. No American novelist before him had treated regional materials in the new "modern" way, showing farm life as it actually is instead of as it is seen through a veil of nostalgia by the sophisticated writer weary of the cities. "I have lived the life," he states in *A Son of the Middle Border,* "and I know that farming is not entirely made up of berrying, tossing the new-mown hay and singing *The Old Oaken Bucket* on the porch by moonlight." Although it seems surprising today, his straight accounts of rural life provoked an indignant reaction in a certain segment of the reading public when they were originally published; many readers wrote to him protesting against his vulgarity and cynicism. Today his work seems genteel, Victorian, almost prudish. The contrast indicates the degree to which literary freedom has progressed since the eighteen-nineties.

Yet it is not enough to say that Garland is a mere regionalist; his real theme is the contrast, or conflict, between town and country. His work treats two important processes: on the one hand the pioneer impulse which leads men to trend westward in search of open lands and new opportunities, and on the other hand the migration of the more sensitive and creative farm youth back toward the city. The first of these, the pioneer spirit, is typified by Garland's own father, dominated by a restless impulse to follow the continually advancing frontier to the west. The second, the rejection of the farm and the counter-migration to the city, is represented by Garland himself, who abandoned the Middle Border to seek a literary life first in the traditional Boston of his forefathers and then in Chicago, the new literary capital of the west.

In addition to Whitman, Howells, and Ibsen, two important influences on Garland's regionalism should be noted: Edward Eggleston's *The Hoosier Schoolmaster* (1871) and Joseph Kirkland's *Zury:*

the Meanest Man in Spring County (1887). These novels, both laid in middle-western settings, suggested to Garland the literary possibilities of such locales.

Garland referred to his own literary method as "veritism," by which he meant a combination of realism in subject matter and romanticism, or ethical idealism, in attitude. In other words he accepted, with reservations, the documentary techniques of the European realists, but rejected their callous "scientific" objectivity; Garland could never be indifferent toward the ethical implications of his material. There is a didactic element in all his work, especially in the period around *Jason Edwards: An Average Man* (1892). The chief social attitude in Garland is his sympathy for the western farmer, his poverty, his helplessness in the hands of the eastern financiers who set the prices for his crops, and the laboriousness and bleakness of his life. This attitude eventually led him to an interest in Henry George and the Single Taxers, the Farmer's Alliance, and Populist Party, and other groups which proposed revolutionary measures to alleviate the plight of the farmer. At one time he was virtually a propagandist for the Single Tax; *Jason Edwards* was written for this purpose, and *A Spoil of Office* (1892) was intended mainly to advance the cause of the Populist Party. Such writing declines with the disappearance of the problem that it treated; Garland today is remembered chiefly for his *Son of the Middle Border* and his simpler tales of life on the Dakota plains.

LIFE: Hamlin Garland was born in 1860 in a log cabin near West Salem, Wisconsin; his people were originally New Englanders. In 1869 his father, restlessly seeking a new land of opportunity, moved the family to a farm in Iowa, at that time virtually a frontier, where the Garlands made their home for twelve years. Here Garland received all the education he was to get: he attended the Cedar Valley Seminary in Osage, Iowa, where he got a groundwork in rhetoric and made a first acquaintance with Shakespeare, Hawthorne, and Whitman. In 1881 the family moved again, this time to the "Middle Border" region of Ordway, South Dakota, a bleak, arid, and inhospitable prairie where the utmost labor was necessary to wrest a living from the soil. Hamlin, although by this time aware that he was little fitted for the arduous life of the frontier, helped his father break land for the new farm, and in 1883 he staked out a homestead claim of his own in MacPherson County, South Dakota. This act, which seemed at first a false step, later provided the means for him to embark on his real career; in 1884 he sold his claim and with the proceeds came to Boston to prepare himself for a life as a professor of American literature.

In Boston, where he remained for nine years, he met William Dean Howells, at that time his literary ideal; and it was the great American realist who encouraged him in his own writing. By 1887 he had produced a number of poems as well as a volume of stories, published in 1891 as *Main-Travelled Roads*. Some of his stories were published in magazines, especially in *Arena,* whose young editor became his champion, and Garland was soon established as a talented young writer whose work was provoking national comment. The Boston period is also the era of his interest in the Single Tax and Henry George, whom he met personally and whose battle he assisted from the lecture platform. His first novels, *Jason Edwards: An Average Man* and *A Spoil of Office,* appeared in 1892. The following year Garland, now financially successful, moved his parents east to a house he had bought for them in the old home town of West Salem, Wisconsin. About the same time he transferred his own headquarters to Chicago, where the most important books of his middle period were written. In 1899 he married Zulime Taft, sister of the Chicago sculptor Lorado Taft; by this time the Middle Border farm boy had become an intimate of the vigorous and sophisticated Chicago literary circle. In 1915 he moved permanently to New York, where he had lived briefly after his Boston period. Two years later he published his autobiographical *Son of the Middle Border.* Its sequel, *A Daughter of the Middle Border,* although considered by critics inferior in quality to the earlier book, won him a Pulitzer Prize in 1922. In 1930 he moved with his wife to California, where he died in 1940. His late work (e.g. *The Mystery of the Buried Crosses,* 1939) is preoccupied with spiritualism and mysticism and is not considered important.

CHIEF WORKS: *Rose of Dutcher's Coolly* (novel, 1895) is the best of Garland's novels of the contrast between country and city, and the one of his fictional works that seems most likely to survive. The heroine, Rose Dutcher, is a Wisconsin farm girl who grows up as a tomboy on her widowed father's farm, vigorous, healthy, and self-possessed. Her sexual awakening and her tentative amorous experiments with her childhood sweetheart Carl are described with sensitivity but with discretion. Another important incident is a visit to a circus, where she is seized with a girlish crush for William de Lisle, a handsome and graceful acrobat whom she never forgets and who is to serve as a visionary ideal the rest of her life, a symbol of the beauty and sensual experience which she abandons the Wisconsin farm-land to seek. Grave and thoughtful by nature, she is an excellent scholar and soon attracts the attention of a visitor to her one-room schoolhouse, Dr. Thatcher, a Madison physician. He encourages her to come to the University of Wisconsin; she does so, at first boarding with Dr. Thatcher and his wife. But after the first year Dr. Thatcher recognizes in himself the beginnings of an illicit desire for the girl; he lays the matter before his wife, and they agree she must no longer stay in the house. Rose, in fact, charms everyone; in the cooperative house to which she moves she soon becomes a favorite. When she finishes the University her father, lonely, hopes for her to come back to the farm and even builds a new house for her, but she regretfully makes her choice: her life lies in the city, in the literary circles of Chicago, where she hopes to become a writer. She goes to Chicago and lives in a boarding house, where she learns much about the world, men, and life in general from her more sophisticated roommate Josie. She also forms an important friendship with Isabel Herrick, a woman doctor who serves as her adviser and introduces her into educated and cultivated society in Chicago. Garland, himself a farm-boy, describes life in these sophisticated circles with remarkable suavity; in fact the Chicago salon scenes are among the finest in the novel. In this group Rose meets Warren Mason, a talented writer but a drifter who cannot find his place in life and is making a living as a journalist. Rose has rejected several earlier chances for marriage; she has developed into a feminist, and refuses to accept a banal life as a mere housewife and mother. But Mason, with his advanced ideas, proposes to her a marriage in which they would live together as equals, as companions, and she accepts. When she breaks the news to her father he is heartbroken and desolate, and she too finds her heart wrung by the choice of abandoning her farm heritage. But she knows her destiny lies in the larger civilization of the city, with Mason, and she stands by her choice. The novel ends with the marriage.

This novel is typical of Garland's fiction in that it is often gauche, awkward, and sentimental in style, especially in the earlier chapters describing Rose's childhood. As it progresses, however, the awkwardness disappears, although traces of sentimentality persist; the Chicago scenes and the climax, the final parting with her father, are convincing and moving, more so than anything else in Garland's work. The novel is also remarkable in subject; it is one of the first American novels to take up the theme of the "awakening of adolescence" which is to become the stock-in-trade of novelists in the Twenties. The sexual aspects of Dr. Thatcher's attitude toward his young boarder are also described frankly, although with decorum. In its study of man-woman relationships and marriage the book lies under the influence of Ibsen, from whom Garland derived most of his feminist ideas. Rose is unwilling to marry Carl and drudge out her life as a farm-wife, but she is equally unwilling to accept what passes for marriage in cultivated circles in Chicago; she demands complete emotional and intellectual equality, which she finds in Mason.

Much of *Rose of Dutcher's Coolly* is obviously autobiographical, and it is a remarkable achievement on Garland's part that he has translated his own emotions and attitudes into a person of the opposite sex. The study of the inner life of a young girl is detailed and convincing; the influence on later novelistic studies of adolescence, especially on Willa Cather's *My Antonia,* is apparent. Garland's narrative skill, a part of his talent not often remarked, is visible in the dramatic scene of the storm on Lake Michigan (Chapter XXIII).

A Son of the Middle Border (autobiography, 1917) is considered Garland's most important work. Its merit lies mainly in its sincerity and in its documentary value, that is, in the accurate details it records of life on the Dakota "Middle Border" in the eighteen-eighties and of literary life in Boston and New York in the following decades. Its weaknesses are those of *Rose of Dutcher's Coolly* and the stories of *Main-Travelled Roads* and its sequels: sentimentality, gaucheness of style, and a certain naivete of literary and moral attitude. The sentimentality, in fact, is more prominent in this autobiography than it is in the earlier fiction, possibly because Garland is here viewing his boyhood through the nostalgic veil of years. And paradoxically the 1917 autobiography seems more prudish and Victorian than the novels of the nineties; there is none of the frank analysis of adolescent sexuality found in *Rose of Dutcher's Coolly* or in *A Little Norsk* (1892). Again the reason is probably that Garland is here writing about himself, in his own name. Among the most interesting scenes are the encounters with W. D. Howells, Edwin Booth, Walt Whitman, Henry George, Stephen Crane, and other intellectual and literary figures of the time; e.g. the passage in which Garland describes how he loaned Crane fifteen dollars so he could rescue part of the manuscript of *The Red Badge of Courage* from the clutches of a typist (Chapter XXXIV). The account, which covers Garland's life up to his move to Chicago around 1893, is continued in *A Daughter of the Middle Border* (1921). Other autobiographical works are *Boy Life on the Prairie* (1899), *Trail-Makers of the Middle Border* (1926), and *Back Trailers From the Middle Border* (1928).

Other Garland works should receive at least brief mention. *A Little Norsk* (1892) is the story of two Middle Border farmers who adopt a baby after its mother dies in a blizzard; it is similar to *Rose of Dutcher's Coolly* except that the heroine, a passive girl of Scandinavian extraction, lacks the intelligence and sensitivity of Rose and thus fails to escape from the bleak farm life. *Jason Edwards: An Average Man* (1892) and *A Spoil of Office* (1892) are two polemic novels presenting Single Tax doctrines and Populist agrarianism respectively; their obvious bias weakens their literary effect. *The Captain of the Gray-Horse Troop* (novel, 1902) deals with mistreatment of the western Indian by settlers and frontiersmen; and *Hesper* (novel, 1903) and *Cavanagh, Forest Ranger* (novel, 1910) treat similar western problems. Garland's stories are collected in *Main-Travelled Roads* (1891) and *Other Main-Travelled Roads* (1910), as well as other volumes which repeat some of the same stories. His chief statement of literary principle is contained in *Crumbling Idols* (1894), in which he sets forth the doctrine of "veritism" and calls for a new American literature based on native themes and centering around the life of the common man.

STEPHEN CRANE (1871-1900)

Crane is sometimes thought of as the founder of the terse, laconic school of Hemingway, Farrell, and the war writers of post-1945. It is true he is the first American to portray war realistically from the point of view of the individual soldier, and it is also true that he is the first to treat slums, prostitution, alcoholism, and other unpleasant subjects which are associated with the hard-boiled school of naturalism. This view of Crane, however, ignores another and perhaps even more important aspect of his work: his careful attention to style and imagery, the symbolic, almost mythic quality which he incorporated into his best work (*The Red Badge of Courage* and "The Open Boat"). Here he foreshadows Hemingway at his best, the Hemingway of *The Sun Also Rises* and the early stories like "The Snows of Kilimanjaro." Crane died young, at twenty-nine; in fact he published the two works mentioned above when he was only twenty-six. Superb as this work is, its promise was never fulfilled. But it is important as an influence, as an indication of the direction twentieth-century naturalism was to take; and three of his works—*Maggie, The Red Badge,* and "The Open Boat"—are important works of fiction in their own right.

In studying Crane's work it is difficult to speak of style and content separately; the two were welded together firmly in his mind, and they remain inseparably fused in his work. Crane had a certain way of looking at nature: he found the universe impersonal, imperturbable, and man a small, confused, and not very important automaton—but a thinking automaton, one who viewed his own mechanical behavior with a sort of bewildered curiosity. This is the situation of the boy Henry Fleming in *The Red Badge,* firing his rifle automatically, fleeing from battle scarcely realizing what he is doing, yet all the while observing his sensations with a curious detachment. Crane does not view experience objectively; in this sense he is not a realist. The reader sees experience only through the eyes of Crane's hero, and he sees it subjectively, transformed into symbols and moods that influence his emotions and even determine his actions. The colors of nature are always significant in Crane: red to indicate violence, danger, death, fear; blue for purity or repose; green and yellow for the ominous, the ghastly; and white for the mysterious, the ineffable, the "religious." Many critics have referred to him as an impressionist, and he was, it appears, actually influenced by the French impressionistic school of painting. He learned from them the significance of colors, the process of over-simplification, of reduction to essentials which takes place before Life becomes Art, and the necessity for an illusion of simplicity and casualness which is obtained only through the most careful attention to detail. Yet Crane was not a perspicacious stylist; he wrote quickly, almost intuitively, and when he did correct it was merely to remove superfluous adjectives and to delete details that seemed too specific—for example the names of characters and places. His fiction is based on careful research and therefore "authentic," but it is not highly documented with places, names, and statistics in the naturalistic manner. His style is sparse, bare, imagistic, and evocative, with all the nostalgic accuracy of a Japanese water-color.

This, however, is most true of his mature work: *The Red Badge* and the later tales. The Bowery tales, of which *Maggie* is the best known, represent Crane's style at a formative stage, influenced by his experience as a reporter and by the tradition of American folk humor (Mark Twain, Bret Harte). These works, the first in America to deal with the slums and the evil of big cities, are nevertheless neither naturalistic nor sociological; they are impressionistic mood-studies, pathetic with a slight suggestion of irony sometimes approaching genuine humor. His journalistic war-reporting in Cuba has the same slightly humorous quality, which is refined in *The Red Badge* to a subtle irony something like the pathetic automatism of a Charlie Chaplin comedy (*cf.* the scene in which the hero of *The Red Badge,* dazed by a blow on the head, wrestles desperately and grotesquely with the air in his efforts to stand up).

Anticipating Hemingway and the other naturalists of the Twenties, Crane has a keen ear for vernacular dialogue. He is one of the first American writers to transcribe common speech as it is actually spoken, not as it is portrayed by novelists who unconsciously correct its grammar and syntax. His dialogues are full of repetitions, inconsistencies, and non sequiturs; they might have been taken from actual recordings registered on the battlefield or in the Bowery slums. Here he succeeds in something that James and Howells disdained to attempt and which Norris only half achieved; and here also lies one of his important contributions to the novel of the twentieth century.

LIFE: Stephen Crane was born in 1871 in Newark, New Jersey, son of a Methodist minister. His education was sporadic; he spent a year at Lafayette College and another year at Syracuse University, but he was never a scholar, and he could scarcely even be described as well-read. In 1891 he became a newspaper reporter in New York City.

Meanwhile he dabbled in poetry and began writing sketches of the Bowery life he was encountering in his duties as a reporter. He wrote *Maggie, a Girl of the Streets* in 1893, but it proved too shocking in subject matter and too experimental in style to be acceptable to a publisher; he finally published it at his own expense. When the book appeared, however, it gained him two influential friendships: those of Hamlin Garland and W. D. Howells. In 1893 also he began to write *The Red Badge of Courage;* it appeared in serial form in 1894 and as a book in 1895. Its impact was instantaneous; it attracted the attention of Joseph Conrad, H. G. Wells, and other European men of letters, and made Crane a famous man overnight. It was, however, admired less in America than it was in Europe; many American critics attacked it on moral grounds, and others were unable to appreciate its unusual stylistic qualities. But the interest provoked by *The Red Badge* led to the reissue of *Maggie* and to the publication of several more Crane books: a book of poetry in 1895, *The Little Regiment* in 1896, and a pair of novels of modern American life in 1896 and 1897. The public, however, continued to view him as a war writer, and he spent most of the rest of his life as a war correspondent. In 1896, en route to Cuba to report the native insurrection, he suffered the shipwreck that gave him the material for "The Open Boat." He traveled to Greece to report the Turkish war, then visited England, where he found *The Red Badge* a best-seller, outselling even Tolstoy and Maupassant. Upon his return to America he was sent again to Cuba to write first-hand accounts of the Spanish-American War. Although he had written, in *The Red Badge,* the best combat narrative yet to appear in English, he had not at that time experienced an actual war; now, in Cuba, he saw war first-hand, and wrote accounts of it essentially no different from those in *The Red Badge.* His intuitive judgment in the earlier book had been infallible.

After his return from Europe Crane's marriage to a woman he had "rescued from the depths" caused him to be ostracized in more puritanical American society; in addition gossip arose that he was an alcoholic and even addicted to drugs. The truth was that his health was broken by his hardships and by his years in the slums. He returned to England ill, and was generously cared for by Joseph Conrad, who had become his fast friend. Finally he went to Germany to be treated for tuberculosis, where he died in a Black Forest health resort in 1900. "Sentimental critics have shed literary tears over Crane's early death," argues Barrett, "but his death at twenty-eight resulted in no loss to literature. He had exhausted his genius." Although many critics might challenge this assertion, it is true that Crane wrote nothing of great importance in the last four years of his life. Several minor works, including three volumes of short stories, were published only after his death. His work went into a kind of eclipse from his death to 1918, and it was actually only in the Twenties, when his importance in the development of the naturalistic movement became apparent, that his true stature was recognized by American criticism.

CHIEF WORKS: *Maggie, a Girl of the Streets* (novelette, 1893) is the best-known of Crane's "Bowery tales" and the work which first gained him a name in the literary world. Maggie Johnson, the heroine, is first seen as a ragged urchin in the slums of New York, with an alcoholic father and a brutal and vulgar mother. But she "blossoms in the mud-puddle;" she grows into a beautiful and virtuous girl, and finally attracts the attention of Pete, a young hoodlum friend of her brother Jimmie. Pete dazzles her with his flashy ways and his easy spending, and she soon imagines herself in love with him—the first love she has ever known in her life. The ignorant and bragging monologue of Pete as he tries to impress Maggie with his exploits (Section V) is one of the most strikingly original parts of the book. For a while Pete treats Maggie well, spending his money on her to take her to music-halls and restaurants. Meanwhile she works for a pittance in a collar-factory which is described in one of the first sweat-shop scenes in American literature, anticipating similar scenes in Dreiser's *Sister Carrie* (1900). But after he has "ruined" her (although details of the ruin are decorously omitted) he begins to tire of her. Maggie's mother, puritanical in spite of her harridan ways, throws her out of the flat when she learns the truth. Maggie hopes to throw herself onto the protection of Pete, but at this point he happens to meet an old girl-friend, the elegant prostitute Nell. Beside her Maggie looks dull and naive, and Pete soon abandons her. Maggie goes back to her mother, is rejected again with shrieks and blows, and is finally forced to roam the streets to support herself. It is only after the hardships of her life finally cause her death that her mother relents; the story ends as she cries in her grief. "I'll forgive her!"

It has been pointed out that, in spite of its reputation, this novelette is not really a study of prostitution; Maggie takes to the streets only out of dire need, and retains her inner virtue—her sense of guilt—to the end. In this sense the book is romantic rather than realistic; it is in the genre of the sentimental songs of the Nineties—e.g., "She's More To Be Pitied Than Censured"—a line which might well serve as the motto of the novel. The realistic aspects of the work are (a) the setting itself; it is virtually the first work of American literature to concern itself with big-city slums; and (b) the attempts at realistic slang and the vulgar speech of the streets, especially the inane repetitive quality of the dialect. The "immorality" of the work may have been shocking in the Nineties, but today it seems innocuously, almost romantically, sentimental.

The Red Badge of Courage (novel, 1895) concerns the adventures of a young Union soldier, Henry Fleming, in the Civil War battle of Chancellorsville, although the action is never identified by that name. As a boy back home on the farm Henry has wondered greatly about war, which he imagines as a spectacle of bravery, gallantry, and death. He is introspective although uneducated, and he worries a great deal over whether he will run from the battle when he finds himself in it. The battle is described in intimate detail, but always from the point of view of the common soldiers of Henry's regiment, who understand little of its broader pattern. Henry discusses the coming battle with Jim Conklin, a more experienced soldier who has befriended him, and is reassured when his friend admits that he would run from the battle if the going got too hot. Small narrative vignettes are included as the regiment moves into battle: a soldier who tries to steal a horse from a girl and is repulsed amid the jeers of his comrades, a dashing officer who is more concerned about a box of cigars than about the impending conflict. In spite of his uneasiness, Henry acquits himself well in his first engagement. He helps to repulse a Confederate attack, then another, and at length feels himself a hardened combat veteran. But finally the strain is too much; just as Jim Conklin had predicted, when the others begin to break and run Henry runs too, thoughtlessly and hysterically. As he withdraws from the scene of the battle his calm returns; then, in a famous scene (Chapter VII) he accidentally encounters the body of a Union soldier in a woody bower, and is filled with horror. He flees on, and soon encounters his friend Jim Conklin (identified by some critics through his "saintly" quality and by his initials with Jesus Christ), who has been wounded and ordered to the rear. Henry tries to take care of him, but his friend soon dies, in a grotesque and horrifying scene which nevertheless has its ironic aspects. Henry, wandering about bewildered, is struck on the head by a retreating soldier driven frantic by fear. His wound is serious, but he manages to find his way back to his broken regiment. There, instead of being denounced as a coward, he is treated as a hero; he has the "red badge" of a wound to certify his manliness. Still dazed, he decides to say nothing about the shameful manner of his injuring, and in a subsequent part of the battle he fights like a genuine wildcat, encouraging his comrades through his own fearlessness. In one sense Henry has been disillusioned about the myth of heroism, but in another way he has become a hero himself—not deliberately, in the way he thought heroes were made, but unconsciously, in the anger and confusion of battle.

Behind its straightforward narrative this novel is highly symbolic in detail and imagery. The dominant conflict of image is that between the red, violent, chaotic sensations of battle and the calm impersonal serenity of nature, unmoved by human strife. The first element is depicted in such images as the red stain of blood on the bandages and the famous line at the end of Chapter IX, after Henry stumbles upon the dead body in the woods: "The red sun was pasted in the sky like a wafer." The quality of tranquil nature is indicated by the idyllic descriptions of the woods, by the serene blue sky, and by such lines as the last one in the novel: "Over the river a golden ray of sun came through the hosts of leaden rain clouds." Henry, having passed through the "red sickness of battle," now regains his contact with the familiar and friendly things of the earth. Also important is the religious symbolism: the enigmatic figure of Jim Conklin, and such details as the chapel-like quality of the bower in the woods where Henry encounters the dead body.

The Red Badge was the first book to be written about the Civil War which did not treat the subject romantically, and as such it provoked much resentment; certain military and patriotic groups condemned it roundly as an insult to the reputation of the G.A.R. Others objected to it on stylistic grounds, complaining that it was too sparse, transparent, and inelegant. The novel remains, however, the first modern treatment of war in American literature; it would be extremely important for its influence on later war books even if it were not for its excellence in its own right.

"The Open Boat" (story, 1897) is the best known of Crane's later stories. The subject grew out of the sinking of the S.S. Commodore which Crane had experienced first-hand in 1896, and which he reported in straight journalistic style for the *Florida Times-Union* and the *New York Press*. In the fictional version the account is restricted to include only the thirty hours that Crane and his three companions spent in the boat. The three are the cook, the injured captain, and an oiler; Crane refers to his alter-ego only as "the correspondent." The technical problems of handling a small boat in a running sea are related in some detail. Meanwhile, underneath the account runs the story's dominant theme: the indifference of nature (the sea) toward man's struggle for existence. When they finally sight land they find it indifferent too: ". . . it was bitter and bitter to them that from it came no sign." When human beings finally appear on the shore, their efforts to rescue the castaways are described (Section IV) in masterful style solely through the dialogue of the men in the boat. Finally the four take the boat through the surf; it founders, and one of their number, the oiler, is drowned. Now humanity rushes to care for and cherish the three survivors. But the last sentence refers again to the sea; the three "felt that they could then be interpreters" for its enigma. This constitutes a statement of one of Crane's key aesthetic ideas: that life and nature can be understood only through intense participation in them; or to put it in literary terms, that you must live deeply before you can write effectively. The parallel to such modern writers as Hemingway is obvious.

FRANK NORRIS (1870-1902)

Norris is the first American author who can be accurately described as a naturalist. His best fiction (*McTeague, The Octopus*) might have been written by Emile Zola, had the great French naturalist chosen to visit California. It has been objected that there is a strong romantic strain in Norris, but so is there in Zola and his school; in both authors it takes the form of a kind of wordy mysticism, a weakness for turgid and rhapsodic generalizing. This tendency is most apparent in *The Octopus* and *The Pit;* in *McTeague* and most of the short stories it takes the form of a Victorian sentimentalism interspersed in the hard-boiled narrative (e.g., the love of Old Grannis and Miss Baker in *McTeague*). Norris had the same pretensions as Zola; he hoped to write a vast prose epic, a series of novels which would cover the growth of the American west as thoroughly as Zola's *Rougon-Macquart* series depicted the France of the Second Empire. His early death frustrated the plan, but the few novels he wrote show the pretentiousness of an author writing over his head, a man who has taken on a task too gigantic even for his considerable talent. The aspect of Zola which did not particularly impress Norris was the scientific part, the attempt to demonstrate such sociological influences as heredity and economic determinism. "Norris accepted determinism only in so far as it appealed to his dramatic sense," says his biographer Walker. He liked bigness—big characters, big struggles, and big forces—and the doctrine of economic determinism occasionally furnished him with such subjects. But essentially, as a story-writer, his interest was closer to the "romantic realism" of Kipling, London, and the other adventure-writers of his time. Sometimes his innate tendencies seem to betray his intentions; *McTeague* begins like Zola and ends like Zane Grey.

With his weakness for "bigness" Norris is not a subtle writer. He is not an expert stylist, neither is he skilled at keen characterization or delicate balancing of motivations or moral issues; here he is the farthest thing from Henry James that can be imagined. His main assets are (1) his careful personal observation and research, his attention to the details of daily life and to the economic or technical aspects of business and farming; in short his documentation; and (2) the epic quality, the sweep or scope, the grandeur he occasionally achieves through sheer power and building up of details. These two qualities, of course, could be attributed to Zola as well.

In *The Octopus* there is a kind of cult of elemental forces which ends in a tendency toward animism, i.e., the attributing of life to inanimate objects and forces. The railroad itself, the burgeoning of seed-life in the earth, the force of sexual love—even the west itself—seem imbued with mysterious significance. "It was one of those legendary passions that sometimes occur," he writes of the love of Vanamee and Angèle, "idyllic, untouched by civilization, spontaneous as the growth of trees, natural as dew-fall, strong as the firm-seated mountains." It is likely that much of this meretricious rhapsodizing is due to Norris' idea of writing an "American epic" in *The Octopus* and its sequels. With his tendency to oversimplification he tends frequently to lapse into clichés; e.g., Behrman, the railroad agent in *The Octopus,* is presented by Norris in all seriousness but is actually the stereotyped comic banker of the funny-papers, even to the watchchain which stretches across his fat paunch. Norris is not subtle in characterization; again he is the antithesis of James.

Norris' work may be clearly divided into three periods: (1) the artificial and unimportant medieval romances of his Paris days; (2) his tales of the San Francisco slums, comprising *McTeague, A Man's Woman, Vandover and the Brute,* and most of the stories published between 1894 and 1900; and (3) the "Epic of Wheat," the uncompleted trilogy which included *The Octopus* (1901), *The Pit* (1903), and *The Wolf* (never written). As in the case of Crane, it is doubtful whether his early death deprived the world of anything of importance; *The Pit* is inferior to *The Octopus,* and it seems unlikely that he could have come up to this level again.

Yet with all his faults Norris is an important author, historically if not intrinsically. He was the first to apply Zola-style naturalism to American subjects, and so provided a valuable precedent for Dreiser, Upton Sinclair, and many of the naturalists of the Twenties. He was the first to show the possibilities of the San Joaquin Valley as a locale, thus anticipating Steinbeck and Saroyan; his San Francisco slum stories advanced and improved the genre introduced by Crane, and his carefully documented studies of farming and the grain exchange anticipated not only Upton Sinclair but the sociological naturalists of the next generation (Dos Passos, Lewis, *et al.*). Yet in spite of Norris' epic ambitions, probably *McTeague,* with its colorful and dramatic characterizations of McTeague, Trina, and Marcus Schouler, will continue to be read when his more pretentious work—work important for its influence on other authors—will be forgotten.

LIFE: Norris was born in Chicago in 1870 of well-to-do parents. His family visited England in 1878 and moved to San Francisco in 1884; thenceforth Norris considered himself a native Californian. He spent the years 1887-89 in Paris, studying art and writing romantic poetry on medieval subjects; in 1892 one of these romances, *Yvernelle,* was published at his mother's expense. From 1890 to 1894 he attended the University of California, where he did not study very hard but began writing fiction, mostly short stories in the vein of Kipling. At Harvard (1894-95) he was a better student; under the guidance of Professor L. E. Gates he began writing *McTeague* and *Vandover*. After Harvard he served for a few years as a roving journalist, visiting Africa, fighting in the Boer War, and covering the Spanish-American War in Cuba. In 1899 *McTeague* appeared, causing the biggest literary sensation since *Maggie: a Girl of the Streets*. A victorian America was still too squeamish for "gutter realism." Norris married in 1900; meanwhile he was writing *The Octopus,* which was published in 1901. Its sequel, *The Pit,* appeared serially in 1902 and in book form the following year. *The Wolf,* which was to follow, was never written; Norris died in October, 1902 following an appendectomy, only three years older than Crane had been at his death.

CHIEF NOVELS: *McTeague* (1899) is based on Norris' early life in San Francisco but was actually conceived during the period when he was a graduate student at Harvard (1894-95). The literary influence of Zola's *L'Assommoir* (1877) and other treatments of the Paris slums is apparent. McTeague, born the son of a miner in the California gold country, learns dentistry from an itinerant tooth-puller and comes to San Francisco, where he practices as an unlicensed dentist in the working-class district of Polk Street. His friend, Marcus Schouler, is a bungling and incompetent veterinarian and a fervent though somewhat confused socialist. He introduces McTeague to his girl-friend Trina Sieppe; Trina comes to McTeague's office for some dental work, and the two fall in love and eventually marry. Marcus sulks for a while but steps aside, rather enjoying his rôle as a martyr.

The rest of the novel is concerned with the marriage of McTeague and Trina and with various lower-class citizens of Polk Street whose lives become involved with theirs. Although McTeague is not quite bright enough to understand Marcus' socialism, he is a fairly good dentist, and since Trina has won a lottery prize of five thousand dollars they are for a time financially secure. But Trina soon develops an abnormal, almost perverse avarice; she refuses to spend her money, and secretly hoards even the change which McTeague gives her to run the household. At this point Marcus begins to regret his sacrifice.

The two friends quarrel at a picnic, and in a wrestling match the stronger McTeague breaks Marcus' arm. In revenge Marcus informs the authorities of McTeague's illegal practice, and his income is cut off.

It is the beginning of the end. McTeague is too stupid to learn a profession, and too lacking in character to hold a job for wages very long. He turns to drink, becomes moody and surly, and finally disappears, abandoning his wife. She, by this time almost insanely avaricious, refuses to spend her capital; she tries to make a living manufacturing toys, but her hand is infected by the paint and finally has to be amputated. Reluctantly she draws her five thousand dollars out of the bank. Then McTeague returns, drunken and vicious, steals the money, and beats her unconscious. She dies the next morning.

A manhunt commences for McTeague, who flees first to the mining country of his youth and then south into the desert wastelands north of Death Valley. He forms a partnership with a prospector, finds a gold strike, then panics and flees on, leaving the gold to his companion. Finally he is cut off in the baking alkali desert by a member of a posse —by coincidence Marcus, who has followed him halfway across California in hope of revenge. The two struggle; McTeague kills Marcus, but not before Marcus has handcuffed himself to McTeague's arm. He presumably dies of thirst, shackled to the dead body of his former friend.

In this novel Norris, in addition to depicting slum life, which he does effectively and convincingly, is apparently trying to demonstrate a quasi-scientific theory of hereditary taint in the Zola manner. "Below the fine fabric of all that was good in him ran the foul stream of hereditary evil, like a sewer," he says of his hero in Chapter II. But the disasters that befall McTeague, Trina, and Marcus are caused as much by stupidity as by heredity. In any case the forces of destiny are not environmental, as they are in Howells; lower-class San Francisco is portrayed as sordid but basically decent, and the flaws of the three main characters lie within their own personalities.

There are a number of secondary plots, since Norris is attempting to draw a more or less complete picture of San Francisco slum life: the half-insane charwoman Maria Macapa, who marries the junk-dealer Zerkow and is murdered by him when he is finally convinced of the truth of her deluded story of hidden wealth; the idyll of Old Grannis and Miss Baker, two shy and lonely old people who join forces and find happiness; and the struggles and fortunes of the Sieppe family, Trina's relatives, a half comic and half pathetic set of German immigrants. The best parts of the book are the vignettes of Polk Street life and the characterizations of McTeague, Trina, and Marcus in their early happy days; after the murder of Trina the novel turns into something resembling a western dime novel, and the ending is hopelessly melodramatic. The story was made into a remarkable motion picture in 1923 by Erich von Stroheim.

The Octopus (novel, 1901) is a study of the struggle between the California wheat ranchers and the Southern Pacific railroad, the "octopus" which is strangling them economically. Norris changes the name of the railroad, and the town of Tulare, in the San Joaquin Valley, where the action takes place, is rechristened Bonneville, but the main lines of the story he relates are taken from actual incidents. Most of the characters, however, are fictional. The most important of these are Presley, a graduate of an eastern college, a youth with poetic aspirations somewhat resembling Norris himself in his early twenties; his friend Vanamee, a mystic and dreamer with a tragic love affair in his past, who makes his living as a sheepherder; the wealthy rancher Magnus Derrick; his son Harran; another son Lyman, who has become a lawyer in San Francisco; the German share-farmer Hooven; the small ranchers Osterman, Broderson, and Annixter; and the banker, railroad agent, and general villain S. Behrman, who secretly represents the interests of the master banker Shelgrim in San Francisco. All the ranchers involved are farming land deeded to the railroad by the government; the railroad has promised to sell it to them eventually for around $2.50 an acre, and on this basis they have settled on the land and improved it. Now the railroad begins its squeeze. It raises the rail charge for wheat; it promises a hop-farmer a low rate for shipping his crop, lends him money through Behrman on a mortgage, and then ruins him when his crop ripens by raising the freight rate to a prohibitive price. The railroad controls finance, politics, every aspect of life in the state; a single rancher, no matter how wealthy, is powerless against it. Finally the desperate ranchers band together in a League to fight for their rights. Magnus Derrick, in spite of the apprehensions of his conscience, agrees to try bribery in order to obtain political preference; finally he succeeds in getting his own son Lyman elected to the railroad commission. But the ranchers are betrayed; Lyman himself is a paid agent of the Trust, and the bribery is exposed. Now the railroad plays its final hand: it offers the ranches for sale to all comers at a high price, ignoring its earlier promise to sell the land for $2.50 an acre; and when the ranchers are unable to produce the money their ranches are sold to dummy buyers acting for the Trust. The ranchers are determined to protect their homes by force if necessary, and when the railroad posse comes to take possession a gun-battle breaks out. Norris copies the scene of battle from an actual incident, the Mussel Slough tragedy of 1880. Broderson, Osterman, Hooven, Harlan Derrick, and others are killed, but the railroad agent Behrman escapes unscathed. While this story unfolds, a sub-plot describes the railroad engineer Dykes, who is fired for no reason, driven out of the hop-growing business by the railroad, and eventually turns outlaw and holds up a train; he is pursued and captured after a wild-west train chase, and sentenced to life imprisonment.

An observer and occasional participant in the story is Presley, who plans to write a vast verse epic of the American west but finally realizes that this traditional form is unsuited to the subject. The aesthetic problem is one which also challenged Norris, and there is no doubt that *The Octopus* and its sequels are actually the epic which Presley is planning.

In the end the ranchers are broken, Magnus Derrick discredited through his dishonesty, the wives of the murdered men driven to beggary and prostitution. The railroad remains in triumphant possession of the wheat, which continues to spring forth from the ground indifferent to the struggles of men. Presley, melancholy and disillusioned, sets out for India in the very sailing ship which is to carry the ranchers' wheat to its market. By coincidence the nefarious Behrman comes to visit this very ship in port to inspect the wheat; he accidentally falls into the hold and is smothered by the grain. The ending, poetically apt though it may be, is scarcely believable; it seems as great an artistic flaw as the ending of *McTeague,* and for the same reasons.

Yet *The Octopus* is clearly Norris' masterpiece. In spite of its pretentious, awkward, and spuriously rhapsodic style, it manages to be convincing, even gripping; and the details of grain-farming and railroading have an unmistakable ring of authenticity. The general qualities of the novel have been earlier remarked. Interesting specific passages are the satire on women's clubs and genteel philanthropy in Section II, Chapter 1, anticipating Lewis and the other satirists of middle-class culture; the gripping account of Dyke's last flight and eventual capture; and the section toward the end of the novel (Section II, Chapter VIII) where, in alternating vignettes, the starvation of a rancher's widow is held up to ironic contrast with the callous gourmandising of the railroad executives and their wives. It should be noted, however, that the morality of the story is not clearly black-and-white; Norris takes some pains to make the position of Shelgrim, the railroad czar, seem logical if not moral, and the ranchers are shown resorting to violence, deceit, and fraud to gain their ends. In the final view the novel is an "epic of wheat," and the fate of the men who struggle for it seems almost incidental.

   The Pit (novel, 1903) continues the projected trilogy by following the wheat to the Chicago grain market. The central figure is Curtis Jadwin, an ambitious young grain speculator. He is married to the beautiful Laura Dearborn, but his young wife is bored and unhappy; Curtis' total energies are devoted to his business, and he pays almost no attention to her. She dabbles in an affair with a former suitor; but when Curtis, overspeculating, is wrecked financially, she turns to him again and their love is renewed. *The Pit* was a best-seller at the time of its original publication, but most of this success was due to the reputation Norris had earned with *The Octopus;* later critics have found the second novel of the trilogy inferior. One reason seems to be that the locale, urban and artificial, has less intrinsic interest than the primitive ranch-land of *The Octopus.* The projected third novel of the series, *The Wolf,* was still unwritten at the time of Norris' death.

JACK LONDON (1876-1916)

   Jack London is usually considered a naturalist by literary historians; he actually thought of himself as a sort of Nietzschean materialist. His "nature red in tooth and claw," however, is considerably idealized, and his conception of character is thoroughly romantic. His settings are exotic, at least to the American reader. London is a pulp-writer of genius; the quality of his work far transcends his technique and content.

   An omnivorous reader, London was influenced from many sources, including Nietzsche, Comte, Bergson, Kipling, and Marx. His chief borrowing from Nietzsche and Spencer was the idea of the superman, seen in its evil or negative aspect in the Wolf Larsen of *The Sea Wolf* and in a more positive treatment in the autobiographical Martin Eden. Yet London does not commit himself entirely to the superman concept. Van Weyden, the sensitive aesthete and impassioned lover, is as much the hero of *The Sea Wolf* as the sadistic Larsen; and the wild dog in *The Call of the Wild* is motivated mainly by his love and loyalty for his master Thornton rather than by his more primitive instincts.

As for Marx, he served to turn London's attention to the need for social reform and convert him to economic determinism; the tendency is seen especially in the socialistic treatises *The War of the Classes* (1905) and *The Human Drift* (1907) and in the "nightmare utopia" novel *The Iron Heel* (1907), one of the first modern novels to prophesy a fascist dictatorship. Nietzschism and Marxism, diametrically opposed and mutually incompatible, form the two poles about which London's work revolves.

London's prose style is forceful and colorful rather than precise. He tells his story through action (narration) rather than through words (exposition), and he seldom stops to preach or lecture to the reader. His early magazine experience taught him to make his prose command interest in every sentence. His subjectivity and enthusiasm lend a sincerity to his work which raises it far above the level of ordinary magazine fiction.

LIFE: London, the illegitimate son of the eccentric astrologer W. H. Chaney, was born in San Francisco in 1876; his mother was Flora Wellman, daughter of a respectable Ohio family. His youth was as romantic as any of his novels. He struck out as a vagabond at fifteen, was jailed for vagrancy, worked as an "oyster pirate" in San Francisco Bay, rode the freights over the Sierras, and sailed as a seaman on a sealing voyage. He read widely from his earliest youth. His reading was encouraged and guided by Ina Coolbrith, an Oakland poetess and librarian who was a major influence in shaping his literary character. In 1896 he joined the gold rush in the Klondike, where he acquired the material for *The Call of the Wild* and his other north-woods stories but found no gold whatsoever. He began to write shortly after this; his first story was accepted in 1899. In 1890 he had married

Bessie Maddern; three years later he abandoned his wife and two daughters to marry Charmian Kittredge, whose temperament better fitted his romantic character.

The Call of the Wild, which appeared in 1903, was widely publicized by the publisher and soon became a best-seller. From 1900 to 1916 London wrote fifty volumes and earned over a million dollars, all of which he spent as fast as he received it. He invested thousands in a ketch, the *Snark,* in which he and Charmian sailed to the South Seas, and even greater sums in a fantastic residence in California, Wolf House, which burned before it was completed.

A sporadic but impassioned socialist, London in 1905 ran for mayor of Oakland, but received only a few hundred votes. He was greatly influenced by the Communist Manifesto, but never sought to resolve his socialistic and humanitarian ideas with the blatant superman concept he had acquired from Nietzsche. He felt his socialistic ideas deeply enough, however, to go to jail for them and to devote to them large amounts of his time and money.

London fought a lifelong battle with the habit of drinking, part of which he described in *John Barleycorn* (1913). After 1913 his drinking caused his literary output to decline. His death in 1916 was probably by suicide, although uremic poisoning was alleged as the cause.

CHIEF NOVELS: *The Call of the Wild* (1903) is London's best-known work. The protagonist is a sled-dog who reverts to savagery. Buck, a sheepdog on a California ranch, is stolen and sent north for a sled-dog in the 1896-97 gold rush. He is sold to two French-Canadians who treat him fairly but harshly. His fellow dogs, however, are violently savage; they fight continually and frequently tear each other to pieces in their battles for supremacy. Buck, strong and courageous, excels in these battles and soon becomes leader of the pack. He passes into the custody of several owners and finally encounters John Thornton, who rescues him from a brutal beating at the hands of ignorant miners. Thornton nurses Buck's wounds, and the dog develops a strong affection for his new master. He saves Thornton's life twice and wins a thousand-dollar bet for him by pulling a heavy sled out of the ice. But on a gold-hunting expedition into the far north Thornton is killed by Indians. Buck, in a rage, slaughters several of the Indians, then joins the wolves of the forest as one of their own. He becomes to all purposes a wild animal, but once a year comes back to howl disconsolately over the river which holds Thornton's body.

The Sea Wolf (novel, 1904) is based on London's youthful sealing experiences. Humphrey van Weyden, a cultivated young man, is set adrift in the sea after a liner sinks and is rescued by the *Ghost,* a sealing vessel captained by the brooding and sadistic Wolf Larsen. Larsen brutalizes the entire crew and forces "Hump," as he is soon called, to work as a cabin boy. Conditions become steadily worse; the crew mutinies and the mate is drowned. Hump becomes mate; four more men are drowned in a storm, and the vessel is almost wrecked. Later a girl, Maud Brewster, and four men are picked up out of an open boat. Hump defends Maud when she is attacked by Wolf, and the pair become lovers. They escape from the ship in a small boat and take refuge on an island, where they reencounter Wolf in his wrecked ship and witness his death. The novel ends as the pair are rescued by a revenue cutter.

Several other works of London should receive at least brief mention. *The Game* (novel, 1905) is an elemental "Nietzschean" story of a prizefighter, Joe Fleming, who is finally killed in the ring while his young fiancée watches. *White Fang* (novel, 1906) was written as a complement of *The Call of the Wild;* it has, so to speak, the opposite plot. White Fang, one-fourth dog and the rest wolf, passes through the hands of a succession of owners. The conflict of the novel is that between the "call of the wild" of his wolf ancestry and his loyalty to his human masters. In the end, choosing humanity, he dies heroically while defending the home of his last owner, the engineer, Weedon Scott, from an escaped convict. *Martin Eden* (autobiographical novel, 1909) is a thinly-disguised account of London's own life including his sailor and worker days, his self-education, and his eventual success as an author. A love-plot concerns Eden's relations with Ruth Morse, a wealthy and educated girl who gives him his first impetus to improve himself. In the end the hero, feeling he has betrayed his own class and despising the moneyed class into which he has risen, takes his own life. *Smoke Bellew* (novel, 1912) is a picaresque account of the adventures of a journalist in the Yukon, and *John Barleycorn* (autobiographical novel, 1913) is an analysis of alcoholism and a plea for temperance based on London's own personal struggle with the drinking habit.

O. HENRY (pseud. of William Sidney Porter, 1862-1910)

Often considered the father of the American short story, O. Henry is more accurately described as the founder of a popular variety of story: the magazine story of the formula type, usually climaxed with a trick ending. Unlike the classic American short story (Hawthorne, Poe) the O. Henry story is based almost entirely on plot; mood and character are of incidental importance. Here it resembles the Italian novella of the Renaissance: salty, ingenious, very short, actually only an extended anecdote related with skill, irony, and humor. The genre in modern times is typically American, and it has played a large part in American magazine fiction since O. Henry's days.

The trick in a typical O. Henry story consists in withholding an important piece of information from the reader as long as possible, so that only as he finishes the story does he fully understand the significance of the previous action. The epitome of the device is found in "The Gift of the Magi," perhaps his best-known story, in which it is used in double form: the reader is kept ignorant of the nature of the Christmas gifts bought by both spouses until the last page, when the ironic coincidence of the truth is revealed. Another common trick is reversal, the *peripeteia* of Aristotle, in which a character does something for one reason but only succeeds in producing the opposite effect: e.g., "The Cop and the Anthem," in which the hobo's efforts to get into jail only succeed in keeping him out and vice versa. To O. Henry must be accorded the honor of discovering practically every formula which can be used to make a trick story; his work has served as an inexhaustible handbook for magazine writers and screen scenarists ever since.

LIFE: William Sidney Porter was born in Greensboro, North Carolina in 1862. His schooling was rudimentary, although he appears to have read widely as a boy. He worked briefly in a drug store and eventually made his way to Texas (1882), where after a variety of odd jobs including a spell as a ranch-hand he obtained a position as a teller in an Austin bank. He was married in 1887; his wife, the former Athol Anderson, was never in good health and was made virtually a permanent invalid by a difficult childbirth. Meanwhile Porter had worked for a Houston newspaper and founded a humorous weekly, which he called *The Rolling Stone.* In 1896 he was charged with embezzlement during his old job at the Austin bank and released under bail provided by friends. After some confusion over the legal aspects of the case Porter disappeared, passed through New Orleans, and eventually ended up in Honduras. He stayed there a number of months; not much is known about his activities in the Central American republic, although hints are provided in a book of short stories in Honduran settings, *Cabbages and Kings* (1904). He returned to America in 1897 to attend the bedside of his dying wife, and was obliged to surrender on the old charge; he was finally tried and convicted, and served three years in the penitentiary in Columbus, Ohio. This experience was the turning point in his career; he went into prison a journalist and emerged a mature and thoughtful author. In 1902 he went to New York and began turning out stories at a prolific rate; he remained there most of the rest of his life. Success came with *Cabbages and Kings* and was heightened by *The Four Million* (1906), stories laid among the humble classes of New York. He was married for a second time in 1907 to an old friend, Sallie Coleman of Greensboro, who served as a mother for his daughter by Athol, now grown. He died in New York in 1910, of cirrhosis of the liver aggravated by alcoholism.

TYPICAL STORIES: "The Gift of the Magi" (from *The Four Million,* 1906) is O. Henry's best-known story and one of his most ingenious. A poor young married couple in a New York tenement, Jim and Della Young, have only two treasures: Della's beautiful long hair and Jim's gold watch, an heirloom. Each sacrifices to buy the other a Christmas present: Jim sells his watch to buy Della a comb for her hair, and she sells her hair to buy a chain for his watch. Yet they are happy in their possession of "the gift of the Magi," the sacrifice of love which accompanied their otherwise useless presents.

"The Furnished Room," also from *The Four Million,* is grimmer. A young man, searching the city for his lost sweetheart who has come to New York to make her fortune as an actress, by coincidence rents the very room in which she has recently committed suicide. The young man suspects her presence from clues he finds and questions the landlady; but she, anxious to keep her tenant, denies any knowledge of such a young girl. In despair he seals the room and turns on the gas, with unconscious irony reenacting the drama of his sweetheart's death in the same room.

"Friends in San Rosario" (from *Roads of Destiny,* 1909) is based on Porter's practical experience as a banker. The two banks in a small Texas town are run by friendly rivals, "Major Tom" Kingman and Bob Buckley. A new and evidently severe bank examiner arrives, going first to Kingman's bank; the examiner is in a hurry, since he hopes to take the only train leaving town that afternoon. All goes well in the examination until Kingman suddenly confesses a shortage. The bank examiner demands an explanation, and Kingman provides a windy narrative which lasts so long that the examiner misses his train. Eventually the accounts are discovered to be correct, and at the end of the story the reader learns the reason for Kingman's curious behavior: he had received a secret note from Buckley explaining that his accounts were short and that cash to balance them was due to arrive on the very train the examiner hoped to take out of town. Kingman therefore detained the examiner with his long story to help his friend.

"The Ransom of Red Chief" (from *Whirligigs,* 1910) is a farcical kidnaping story in the genre of Tarkington's Penrod books, dominated by *enfant terrible* even more formidable than Penrod himself. Two crooks, passing through Alabama, kidnap a boy for ransom and hide him in a cave. But the boy, who has the time of his life playing Indian, raises so much trouble that the kidnapers are finally forced to take him back to his father. The father agrees to take the boy off their hands if they will pay him two hundred and fifty dollars; they pay gladly, and flee out of the state while the father struggles to hold the kicking and howling Red Chief at home.

"A Municipal Report" (from *Strictly Business,* 1910) purports to be a report on Nashville, Tennessee, where according to the author nothing ever happens. The story itself blasts the theory. The narrator, a journalist, comes to Nashville to visit a local author, Azalea Adair, on business. An ancient Negro, Caesar, who drives him there in a hack, turns out to be Miss Adair's protector, and the two dollars the narrator gives him for the ride find their way into her hands. Meanwhile the narrator has encountered a boring and raucous Civil War veteran and ne'er-do-well, Major Caswell, who he discovers is married to Miss Adair. The Major, it develops, is the curse of her life;

she is forced to write for magazines to support herself, but he habitually takes the money from her and spends it on drink. The next day the Major is murdered, and the narrator removes from the corpse's hand an incriminating clue: a button which he recognizes as having come from the overcoat of Caesar, the loyal retainer of Miss Adair. This story is one of O. Henry's most complicated in plot and construction, and one of his most successful. It is marred, however, by a certain conscious cuteness in style: when the doctor examines Caswell for the breath of life "his decision was that it was conspicuous by its absence." The portrait of old Caesar and the tongue-in-check description of Nashville are the high points of the story.

EDITH WHARTON (1862-1937)

Edith Wharton is sometimes mistakenly considered a "society novelist." It is true that she was intimately familiar with New York and Boston society and that her most typical novels are laid in these milieux. Her real interest, however, is in the psychological and spiritual motivations of her characters. Although her work influenced such American naturalists as Scott Fitzgerald and, surprisingly, John Dos Passos, she is the artist of the interior world rather than a recorder of external detail. Her characters are of course influenced by their social environment, but their real struggles are within themselves and their real victories are spiritual ones.

Mrs. Wharton's work differs widely in locale and treatment, and may be divided conveniently into three groups: (a) novels of the lives of humble people in rural settings, usually New England—e.g., *Ethan Frome;* (b) novels about the First World War, in which Mrs. Wharton, through sympathy for France, violently espoused the Allied cause—e.g., *A Son at the Front;* and (c) novels of society life in New York City and Europe, e.g., *The Age of Innocence, The House of Mirth,* and *The Custom of the Country.* Although *Ethan Frome* is her best-known novel among the ordinary reading public, it is in the last group that her finest work is to be found.

If it is necessary to find a classification for her, Mrs. Wharton might be termed a "psychological realist." She modeled her style on that of Henry James and is generally considered a member of the realistic school; but like James she is interested in the external data of life only insofar as they provide material for internal analysis. She believes the true drama of life takes place within the human soul; she is interested in fashionable society principally because of the moral crises it causes, especially in the minds of sensitive or artistic people. "Society" in the narrow sense guides itself almost entirely by a set of arbitrary and artificial conventions. It does not matter what vices or crimes an individual may commit as long as he does not openly attack these conventions. Most people capitulate to these conditions; they indulge in their private vices at pleasure but preserve a hypocritical respect for the conventions of polite behavior. It is all very well for a social leader to conduct a secret affair with her chauffeur, but to marry him is inexcusable. Mrs. Wharton's protagonists are often sensitive, artistic, highly moral persons who find this hypocrisy repugnant; they are willing to pay any price in order to be able to live honestly. This obsession eventually brings them to destruction; society imagines they are paying for their sins, but actually they are being made to suffer for their virtues.

In style Mrs. Wharton is conservative; she was little affected by the technical revolution in the novel that was going on all about her. She makes extensive use of reveries, of soliloquies, and of narrated soul-struggles on the pattern, "She might do this, but on the other hand perhaps she ought to do that." Here is apparent the influence of Henry James and Paul Bourget, both of whom she knew and admired personally. Her chief merits lie in her ability to make fictional characters seem real, to present moral conflicts with clarity, and to demonstrate the effects of social mores on mental life.

LIFE: Edith Newbold Jones was born in 1862 in New York City; her family was well-to-do and possessed ancestors going back to the Revolution. Her childhood was protected and monotonous, and as a result the little girl was forced to live mainly in the world of her imagination. In 1885 she married Edward Wharton, scion of an aristocratic Boston family, and traveled with her husband in Europe during the next few years. Although the marriage was generally successful, Mr. Wharton began to deteriorate mentally around 1900, and by 1906 his condition was hopeless. Mrs. Wharton, living alone in Paris, turned to writing seriously around the turn of the century; her first collection of stories appeared in 1899 and her first novel in 1902. Most of her American novels were written from memory in

France. She achieved her first wide success with *The House of Mirth* (1905). *Ethan Frome* (1911) and *The Age of Innocence* (1920) were even more successful; in the Twenties she was widely acclaimed as the leading American female novelist. Although her later works are considered inferior, Mrs. Wharton is still respected as the godmother of the modern psychological novel in America. She died in France in 1937.

CHIEF NOVELS: *The House of Mirth* (1905) is typical of Mrs. Wharton's work as a whole: it is laid in New York society and it contains all the problems inherent in her best novels. The title is derived from *Ecclesiastes* VII:4—"The heart of fools is in the house of mirth." Lily Bart, orphaned as a young woman, lives with her aunt Mrs. Peniston, who provides her with lodging and occasional gifts and accords her a remarkable freedom, paying scant attention to her comings and goings. Lily, who has been raised by her worldly mother to abhor the dingy and sordid in life, is determined to find a husband who can provide her with the luxury she craves, the luxury she believes is necessary to her temperament. But at twenty-nine she is still unmarried; her friends are growing bored with her status as an "extra woman" and she finds it increasingly difficult to find money to maintain her personal appearance. In short, she is dissatisfied, and feels herself to be in an ignominious and unworthy condition.

In hope of extricating herself from her situation she confides her financial embarrassment to Gus Trenor, a wealthy society host. He pays her gambling debts and offers to invest her savings for her, and it is not until she is forced to repulse his advances that she realizes she has compromised herself by accepting money from a man. The incident comes to the attention of Lawrence Selden, a charming young lawyer who loves her but does not have the money which Lily feels is essential in her future husband; and he begins to doubt whether the "real" Lily is, as he had thought, finer than her external behavior would indicate. Another suitor, the wealthy Simon Rosedale, wishes to marry her to consolidate his social position, but she finds him personally repugnant. To postpone a decision on her relations with him she accepts an invitation to go on a yachting cruise with her friends the Dorsets, failing to realize that this step, like her previous encounter with Trenor, will endanger her social reputation; Dorset's wife Bertha is engaged in an affair with a younger man, and she has invited Lily for no other purpose than to distract her husband. A quarrel breaks out, Lily is compromised socially, and finally finds herself rudely stranded in Europe. The Dorsets, who return to New York before she does, spread a misleading story about her behavior on the cruise, and when she returns to America she finds herself ostracized by polite society. Her wealthy suitor Rosedale rejects her, and her aunt virtually disinherits her.

At this point chance places in her hands certain compromising letters which Bertha Dorset had written to Lawrence Selden. She considers using these to blackmail her way back into polite society, and is actually advised to do so by Rosedale and Dorset. But she cannot bring herself to do it, especially since Selden would also be harmed by the disclosure. Without money and snubbed by her former friends, she sinks lower in society; she tries to work as a milliner's apprentice, but is a failure at this. In her last extremity of despair she visits Selden to thank him for his kindness to her, which has kept her from sinking completely under the weight of scandal. Then she returns to her boarding house, straightens out her affairs, using her aunt's legacy to repay Trenor, and half-intentionally takes an overdose of sedative. When Selden arrives the next morning to ask her to marry him he finds her dead, and learns only from her mementoes the truth of her innocence.

Lily Bart in some ways resembles the Daisy Miller of James; she is basically good, but is destroyed by a society whose conventions she has had the courage to violate. She is, however, a weaker character than Daisy; she is unduly attached to luxury, and somewhat naive about the consequences of her actions. Her dominating ambition in life is to maintain her freedom of spirit, a vision which has been inspired in her by Selden; but in her attempts to achieve this she breaks the conventions of society and is ruthlessly punished. The theme of the novel is that of the free and natural spirit punished by an artificial society. This novel, a best-seller in its time, was successfully dramatized by Clyde Fitch.

Ethan Frome (novel, 1911) is radically different in setting but similar in theme. Ethan, a taciturn New England farmer, out of sheer loneliness marries Zenobia, seven years older than he and a hopeless hypochondriac who spends on patent medicines the small profit he manages to wrest from the soil. He dreams of selling the farm, moving to the city, and becoming an engineer, but the plan comes to nothing; the domineering and egocentric Zenobia must live in a place she can "look down on," and refuses to leave the bleak New England farm. Ethan, unheroic by nature, accepts his lot stoically.

Then Zenobia's pretty young cousin Mattie Silver, left destitute by the death of her parents, comes to live with them and "do" for Zenobia. As a compensation for the lonely life on the farm, Mattie is permitted to attend an occasional church social in town, and it is necessary for Ethan to escort her to these affairs. Out of pity for the girl, who is continually nagged by the domineering "Zeena," Ethan comes to love her, and she returns his love.

When Zeena goes away to a neighboring town to see a new doctor Ethan and Mattie temporarily taste the joys of domestic life together. But on her return Zeena announces that she has hired a stronger girl to replace Mattie. Ethan, in despair, dreams of fleeing west with Mattie, but is constrained out of a sense of duty toward his wife as well as by his lack of means. Ethan and Mattie go to the station to meet the new hired girl; the same train is to take Mattie away. Impulsively they stop at a neighbor's farm and borrow a sled to coast down a dangerous slope; Mattie persuades Ethan to commit suicide with her, and he steers the sled into a tree. Ironically, they are only mutilated; Ethan is crippled and Mattie's spine is broken. Now it is Zeena who must care for Ethan and Mattie, who gradually turns into a querulous neurotic herself; the two have only thrown themselves into Zeena's power. Again social convention has triumphed over natural inclination.

The Custom of the Country (novel, 1913) is a somewhat satirical international novel of manners chronicling the social rise of the energetic Undine Spragg of Apex City. Raised in poverty in this small midwestern town, she comes to New York when her father suddenly makes a fortune. There her beauty almost instantly procures her admission to the best society. Contriving to conceal a history of broken engagements and a previous divorce, she marries Ralph Marvell, a young lawyer of good family but of limited means, who aspires to mold her tastes after his and help her through the maze of social custom. But Undine's extravagance soon forces him to abandon his practice for a more profitable business. Ralph derives little pleasure from the marriage, but consoles himself in his delight in his son Paul.

As for Undine, bored by her husband's literary interests and the cultivated conversation of his friends, she moves on to a flashier set, where she soon gets herself in more trouble; like Lily Bart, she borrows money from an admirer, Peter Van Degen. Soon, flinging aside all caution, she follows Van Degen to Paris and becomes his mistress. But when she divorces her husband under the impression Van Degen is to marry her, he fails to carry out his promise, and Undine finds herself adrift in Paris society.

But she is not long helpless; she soon makes the acquaintance of Count Raymond de Chelles, who aspires to marry her. First, however, her divorce must be transformed into an annulment and she must obtain custody of her child. Ralph, who has come to center his life around Paul, fights this latter scheme vigorously. When it appears likely that Undine will obtain custody of the child he tries to buy her off; meanwhile he learns certain unsavory facts about her life before she married him, particularly that she had been previously married to a vulgar and offensive business man named Elmer Moffatt. In a fit of despair he takes his own life.

Now a widow, Undine is able to marry Raymond, but once more she finds she has made a mistake; the excellent aristocratic circles into which she has risen turn out to be excessively refined and rather dull. Craving excitement, she is driven to fresh extravagances; she attempts to sell some tapestries out of the family mansion to a dealer, and discovers by coincidence that the dealer is actually an agent for her former husband Elmer Moffatt. An intrigue develops, her husband discovers the unsavory situation, and there is a scene; Undine is made to realize that she cannot bully the aristocratic Raymond into conceding to her wishes as she had her father and Ralph.

She goes to Moffatt and offers herself as his mistress, but he, inhibited by the puritanism of his Apex City background, insists that she first divorce Raymond so she can marry him. Although loath to give up her title, Undine does so. The closing scene shows her accepted into society as the beautiful wife of a billionaire, and her son a small, lost, and pitiful figure neglected by the mother who virtually destroyed his father to obtain custody of him.

Undine is in many ways similar to the Lily Bart of *The House of Mirth;* she feels luxury necessary to her temperament. But unlike Lily she has no sense of a finer life, no abiding moral standards. In short she is not a good girl, neither is she a strong character. She borrows her values from those around her; she desires the unattainable, and when she obtains it promptly throws it away to turn to cheap enjoyment. Her rootless past makes her little fit to appreciate the sense of tradition that dominates the lives of Ralph and Raymond; for her the present is all-sufficient. Lacking passion herself, she knows how to use her beauty to provoke the passions of others. Yet once she secures a man she loses interest in him, and thenceforth considers him only a provider. *The Custom of the Country* is a satirical attack on American marriage, an institution in which (in Mrs. Wharton's view) the wife is excluded from the real work of the husband and showered with luxury as a bribe for keeping out of his way. Undine is an extreme example of the evils which result from this system. Her superficial materialism and selfishness destroy the happiness of all about her except Moffatt, who accepts her as she is and fortunately possesses the wealth needed to provide the frivolous luxury she craves.

The Custom of the Country is the most "Jamesian" of Mrs. Wharton's novels, although Henry James himself, who treated the theme with more delicacy, found the novel excessively satirical. If the lines are bold, however, it has an energy lacking in James' more discreet treatments. A similar international plot is contained in *The Reef* (1912).

The Age of Innocence (novel, 1920), lacking the cutting satire of *The Custom of the Country,* is basically a more serious treatment of similar themes. Newland Archer, a young lawyer and member of New York and Newport society, is introduced on the eve of his engagement to Ellen Olenska, a cousin of his fiancée May Welland. Countess Olenska has separated from her Polish husband because of his low moral character, and the family is rallying around her to defend her from the social approbrium which will naturally result from her irregular situation. In order to bolster the social position of the family, Archer suggests that his engagement to May should be announced immediately, although he is inwardly distressed that his relationship with May should be used to serve such a purpose. As a lawyer and prospective member of the family, he advises Ellen against divorce, guessing that she was not entirely guiltless in her relations with her husband and fearing the scandal of an open suit. He finds himself, however, vaguely attracted to the sophisticated and Europeanized Ellen. Struggling against the impulse, he has the wedding date advanced, but it is no use; as the marriage approaches he realizes it is Ellen he loves, and that the shallow and conventional May will never satisfy his longing for a kindred spirit. It is finally Ellen who persuades him that he cannot sacrifice May's happiness to his own, and induces him to go through with the marriage.

Archer becomes increasingly restless after his marriage, as he sees a life of monotony with May stretching before him. Meanwhile Ellen's family applies pressure for her to return to her husband, and she, annoyed, leaves New York to live in Washington with her somewhat eccentric Aunt Medora, who has gotten to the point where she needs protection from her own vagaries. When Ellen is recalled to New York by illness of another relative, she and Archer renew their friendship; they find their love will give them no peace, and they despair of a future of shabby compromise and furtive meetings. The final decision, however, is made for them by May, who reveals secretly to Ellen that she is expecting a baby. Ellen, without disclosing her reason to Archer, decides to return to Europe, although not to her husband; at a farewell dinner for her it becomes clear to Archer that the assembled group all regard him as Ellen's lover. He plans to follow her, and is dissuaded only when May reveals to him the secret of her pregnancy. He renounces his love, and plans to live the rest of his life without excitement or joy.

For the remainder of his life he moves through a familiar routine, witnessing a gradual liberalizing of social mores that would have been considered impossible in his youth. He enters liberal politics, hitherto considered beneath the dignity of a gentleman, and is active in philanthropy. A good husband and a good father, he nevertheless feels he has missed the life of full experience as he had once envisioned it. Years later, after the death of May, he accompanies his grown son to Paris, where he has an opportunity to see Ellen. But after reflection he allows his son to go to her alone; although he and Ellen are still young enough to make a life together, he realizes he prefers his memory of her to a meeting with a woman who has possibly become a stranger to him with the passing of time.

This novel attempts a comprehensive study of the social mores of polite eastern society in the eighteen-seventies. It is an era of changing values and gradually relaxing mores; a married man may keep a mistress and provoke only light clubroom banter, a married woman may, with discretion, encourage a younger admirer, but appearances must be maintained. Such things must be kept from the ears of unmarried girls, and a wife is ostracized for openly abandoning a husband with whom life has become intolerable. The novel also includes an expert analysis of the part played by clan solidarity in public morals. The family stands behind a member whose personal misbehavior threatens a scandal, but casts out the offender as soon as the economic factor becomes involved; thus tribal loyalty is curiously confused with bourgeois materialism. Archer, the central character, grows from an ironic and slightly skeptical acceptance of these standards to a rebellious inward defiance. But he cannot overcome the conventions, and in the end he is forced to live in accord with them. The gradual social change permits his son to marry the illegitimate daughter of a man condemned by Archer's generation for business failure, but Archer himself is too old; he remains in the grip of nineteenth-century convention until the end of his days. It can be seen that *The Age of Innocence* treats the sort of problems found in Henry James and in Mrs. Wharton's own earlier work, but it does so in a franker and more objective way; it contains perhaps the most cogent criticism of upper middle-class American society to be published before Scott Fitzgerald and Sinclair Lewis. The novel, which won Mrs. Wharton a Pulitzer Prize in 1921, is generally considered her masterpiece.

GERTRUDE ATHERTON (1857-1948)

It is difficult to assess the quality of a best-seller of a previous age; some authors owe their popularity to the quality of their work, others become popular in spite of it. In the case of Gertrude Atherton the quality of her work was probably not equal to her popularity, yet the quality is higher than might be expected. Her work is comparable in many ways to that of Howells, and even more, in its faint feminine irony and its skill in depicting the emotions of the young, to Edith Wharton's. She is patently influenced by Henry James, whom she admired. In addition she is a regionalist of sorts; if for no other reason her work is valuable for its descriptions of a milieu depicted by no other major writer, the genteel San Francisco society of the end of the century. Frank Norris treats this society only incidentally, and not very successfully; other California writers of the era ignore it completely. Mrs. Atherton does so with modesty but with success. She is a romantic, perhaps, in her settings and in her elaborate love-intrigue plots, yet her romanticism is always tempered with a faint superior objectivity, a suggestion of irony that foreshadows the American novel of manners of the Twenties.

Mrs. Atherton's *The Conqueror,* a novelized biography of Alexander Hamilton, sold over a half-million copies, and her *Black Oxen* created a sensation in its time. Her work is diverse: she published essays, short stories, an autobiography (*Adventures of a Novelist,* 1932), and a history and description of California, *Golden Gate Country* (1945), published as part of the "American Folkways" series. Her most important works, however, are her novels of early California life, and the best of these is *The Californians,* for many years overshadowed by *The Conqueror* but now increasingly appreciated as her work is seen in the perspective of time.

LIFE: Gertrude Atherton was born Gertrude Franklin Horn in San Francisco in 1857. She was raised by her father, the California pioneer Thomas Lodowick Horn, who inculcated in her a taste for literature and sent her to be educated in various eastern schools. The last of these she left, as she later explained, because she had "absentmindedly got engaged to two young men at once and thought California was the safest place for me." The statement is typical of her ironic style. She married in 1876 and began publishing fiction soon after. Her first work of importance, however, was *The Doomswoman* in 1892. After *The Californians* (1898) her success was assured, and the rest of her life was uneventful. She travelled widely, living for several years in England and in Germany. Vigorous even in her old age, she remained active in San Francisco civic affairs and continued to write; her last book appeared in 1945 when she was eighty-three. She died in San Francisco in 1948.

CHIEF NOVELS: *The Californians* (1898, revised 1935) is a complex study of the interplay of the Spanish and American races in California and the social and amorous intrigues which develop out of this conflict. The story centers around the friendship of two girls: Magdalena ("Lena") Yorba, daughter of the proud California grandee

Don Roberto Yorba, and Helena Belmont, a dazzling American beauty. Don Roberto, who has accepted the coming of the Americans and has made many friends among them, has prospered while his indolent and extravagant countrymen have relapsed into dreams of the past. He is wealthy, and hopes through his wealth to obtain a fine husband for his somewhat plain daughter. But the girls quarrel over a suitor, John Trennahan; Lena at first unselfishly sacrifices him to her friend, then, when Helena rejects him because of his dubious past, rages at her for being afraid to undertake the job of moral regeneration which she, Lena, had been ready to do. Trennahan escapes to the South Seas, and Don Roberto, deprived of his hope for a son-in-law, grows morose and eccentric. Little by little the girls rebuild their friendship, and for a time Lena finds happiness in plans to become a writer. Then Trennahan returns; Magdalena, her native pride collapsing under the force of her love, agrees to marry him. Trennahan goes to demand her hand of Don Roberto, but it is too late: the old grandee has hanged himself out of disappointment over the failure of his daughter's marriage and his own life.

The dominant theme of this novel is the contrast between the aggressiveness and force of the American character and the carefree indolence of the Spanish grandees. Deprived of their lands and their status by the energetic Americans, the California Spaniards relapse into a nostalgic indolence, squandering their last wealth in gambling and careless hospitality. Don Roberto for a time appears to have conquered this racial weakness, but his daughter's "betrayal" by Helena and Trennahan breaks his heart. This romantic plot is related with verve and sensitivity but with a slight saving irony suggestive of Stendhal or Stephen Crane.

Julia France and Her Times (novel, 1912), a more popular, though not a better, work than *The Californians,* is Mrs. Atherton's most Jamesian work. It also contains her most romantic plot, a fantastic intrigue of pistols, noble suitors, and forced marriages. The heroine, Julia, grows up in the West Indies, is married against her will to an English officer who is the heir to a dukedom, and subsequently enjoys a number of interesting adventures in Europe and elsewhere. But if the novel begins romantically it takes a sociological turn; Julia, back in America, becomes a leader in the fight for female suffrage. The final conflict is one that would have intrigued James: Julia finds herself in love with a young American, Daniel Tay, and is forced to choose between marriage and her career in the suffrage movement. In the end she abandons her career and settles down serenely for a life with Tay, a resigned victim of the "splendid disease" of love, which demands that woman above all fulfill her natural duty of reproducing the race.

The Black Oxen (novel, 1923) owes most of its reputation to its unusual theme, although it is by no means a mere *succès de scandale*. Its heroine, the New York society belle Mary Ogden, marries a Hungarian nobleman and goes to live in Europe, returning only years later. When she does, at the age of fifty-eight, she is taken for her own daughter; she has been rejuvenated by a newly discovered glandular operation. The rest of the novel depicts the somewhat fantastic emotional problems of a middle-aged woman who has the body and passionate nature of a girl. The Countess Zattiany, as she is now called, at first romances with Lee Clavering, a young newspaperman, who continues to love her even when she reveals to him that she is old enough to be his mother. Eventually, however, she decides on a union more befitting her maturity; she marries an Austrian prince and returns to Europe to occupy herself with the diplomatic problems of her husband's career.

BETWEEN THE WARS:
REALISTS AND NATURALISTS

The dominant realistic movement which began with Howells, James, and Edith Wharton continued to hold sway over American letters after the First World War. Where the main body of European novelists had turned to realism in the nineteenth century and then reacted against it in the twentieth century, the Americans, following their example a generation behind them, arrived at the peak of their realistic movement around 1914. Meanwhile an even more important literary tendency began to develop out of the realistic movement: the school of naturalism, which dominated American letters during the important era of the Twenties.

Again the impetus came from Europe, although during the process of assimilation American naturalism acquired certain native qualities which set it apart from its continental models. In its original form the naturalistic movement arose out of an endeavor to apply to literature the method of the physical and social sciences. Although naturalism is foreshadowed in the work of Stendhal, Balzac, Ibsen, and others, the school properly speaking was established in Emile Zola (1840-1902), who not only laid down the theoretical basis for naturalistic literature but proceeded to follow his own precepts by creating some of the chief naturalistic works of the nineteenth century.

Zola, inspired by Claude Bernard's *Introduction to the Study of Experimental Medicine* (1865) and by Hippolyte Taine's deterministic and socio-eugenic theories, published in 1880 *The Experimental Novel,* a long essay or manifesto calling for the creation of a new scientific literature. The influence of heredity upon character was to be demonstrated with a scientific exactitude; literature was to observe and record life rather than interpret it. Vice and virtue were "products like sugar and vitriol"; they were to be utilized as a chemist uses reagents for the discovery of new scientific principles. In his *Rougon-Macquart* series Zola actually created a vast cycle of novels dissecting the rise, triumph, and degeneration of a single family and the operation of the principles of heredity on its members. Several units of the cycle, especially *L'Assommoir* (*The Dram-Shop,* 1877), *Nana* (1880), *Germinal* (1885), and *La Terre* (*Earth,* 1887) must be classed along with the greatest novels of the nineteenth century. The cycle, comprising twenty volumes in all, was widely imitated in the twentieth century; Dos Passos' trilogy *U.S.A.* (1930-38) is an example of the technique applied in modified form to the American scene.

Around Zola formed a school of young French writers determined to exterminate the literature of the past and create an idiom "worthy of the age of the locomotive." Edmond and Jules de Goncourt (1822-96 and 1830-70 respectively), Alphonse Daudet (1840-97), and Henry Becque (1837-99) produced work of first rank, and the circle also included many minor figures. The dramatic headquarters of the movement was the Théâtre Libre, an experimental theatre group managed by a former gas-company employee, André Antoine. During a seven-year period from 1887 to 1894 this group produced a hundred and twenty-four new plays, many of them destined to earn a permanent place in world literature.

Spreading from France, the naturalistic movement reached its height in Germany and Russia around the turn of the century; Arno Holz, Gerhart Hauptmann, and Maxim Gorky became the champions about whom the disciples rallied. In the Anglo-Saxon countries the movement caught on somewhat more slowly. Although Thomas Hardy and George Gissing are sometimes considered naturalists, English literature during the fin-de-siècle was actually dominated by the Pre-Raphaelite revival and by the "cult of decadence" of Swinburne and Wilde. The height of British naturalism was to occur in the twentieth century with John Galsworthy and his contemporaries. In America, as we have seen, the ground was broken by Stephen Crane and Frank Norris, with the assistance of Jack London and O. Henry, in the closing years of the century. Theodore Dreiser (1871-1945) might well be included among these late-nineteenth-century founders of American naturalism, since he published his first novel in 1900, but he is treated here instead among the twentieth-century naturalists because of his modernism in style and attitude and because his most important work, *An American Tragedy,* appeared only in 1925 in the middle of the naturalistic period of the Twenties.

European naturalism, as well as the American variety, differs from the realism of Flaubert, Turgenev, or Henry James in several respects, none of which is clear-cut and definitive. It tends to be more doctrinaire in its exposition of pseudo-scientific principles, it is less interested in character and more in the conflict of social forces, and it is concerned to a greater extent with the sordid, the shocking, and the depressing aspects of existence. By these criteria, however, there are naturalistic elements in many nineteenth-century authors, and Lewis and Scott Fitzgerald demonstrate many qualities of typical realists. Some further suggested qualities of naturalism as a literary movement are as follows:

(a) Naturalism is scientific or pseudo-scientific in its approach; it attempts to treat human beings as biological pawns rather than as agents of free will. The author does not attempt to judge his characters or to comment on their actions; he merely inserts them into a crucial situation and then pretends to stand back and watch them with the impassivity of the scientist. Although Dreiser and Sinclair claim to apply such principles to their novelistic technique, it has generally remained a synthetic theory and has only frequently been achieved in actual literary works.

(b) The naturalist attempts to make literature into a document of society. He writes "novel cycles" purporting to cover every aspect of modern life, or creates characters who are personifications of various social classes. Many naturalists (e.g., Dos Passos) gather copious data from actual life and include it in their literary works; they write novels around specific occupations such as railroading or textile manufacturing in which they utilize technical details of the trade for story interest. This aspect of naturalism represents an attempt to remove literature from the realm of the fine arts into the field of the social sciences.

(c) Because of the above-described documentary nature of naturalism, the technique often involves the conscious suppression of the poetic elements in literature. The prose style is flat, objective, and bare of imagery; it includes copious details and explanations, and is wary of highly literary metaphors. It endeavors to imitate scientific, technical, or sociological writing rather than the *belles-lettres* of the past, and in doing so ignores the great part of what is ordinarily considered literary beauty. Like the pseudo-scientific dogma described in (a) above, this quality is often more theoretical than practical. The best naturalists are those who do not totally abandon the literary traditions of the past. On the other hand some naturalists are merely writers lacking in the poetic instinct, writers who avoid a highly literary prose because they have little feeling for style and imagery; Dreiser might be cited as an example. For this reason many naturalistic novels seem gauche and awkwardly written to one familiar with the novels of Henry James, Flaubert, or Thackeray. To most of these rules Hemingway is a notable exception; not only is he devoid of scientific or sociological pretensions, but he is a highly personal writer with a careful and conscientious devotion to style, an author whose main concern is to communicate the essential quality of a personal experience rather than to portray a cross-section of a social milieu.

(d) Naturalistic literature tends to be concerned with the less elegant aspects of life; its typical settings are the slum, the sweatshop, the factory, or the farm. Where the romantic author selects the most pleasant and idealistic elements in his experience, the naturalistic author often seems positively drawn toward the brutal, the sordid, the cruel, and the degraded. This tendency is in part a reaction against earlier literature, especially the sentimentalism of the romantics. The real motivating forces in a naturalistic novel are not religion, hope, or human idealism; they are the basic urges of self-preservation, sex, and ambition.

It is apparent that there are important exceptions to this principle, at least among American naturalists. Dreiser, Tarkington, and Elliot Paul fastidiously avoid shocking detail, Lewis' scenes are laid chiefly in the middle class, and Scott Fitzgerald prefers to do his slumming at the Ritz. There is, in fact, some argument for classifying Hemingway, Lewis, and Fitzgerald as realists rather than as naturalists; such attempts to pigeonhole writers only demonstrates the unsatisfactory quality of all literary classifications.

(e) Naturalism is sometimes, but not always, socialistic or radical in politics. The sympathy of the typical naturalist (e.g., Dos Passos, Dreiser, Farrell) lies with the proletariat, and he sees social evolution mainly in terms of the conflict of classes. Industrial strife plays a large part in naturalistic literature, as does description of the exploitation of the worker, male and female, by the boss. Fitzgerald is practically devoid of politics, however, while Hemingway's liberal idealism is often submerged by his interest in war and bloodshed. Many critics have held that there is a strong romantic element in naturalism, and the liberalism of the naturalist, when it occurs, tends to be of an impassioned and quixotic variety. In spite of their purported objectivity, in fact, many naturalists seem less detached than angry. Naturalism is the literature of revolt, both political and literary.

THEODORE DREISER (1871-1945)

In addition to Dreiser's importance in his own right he is significant as a founding influence on the later American naturalist school. More than W. D. Howells or any other European such as Zola, he stimulated and made possible the work of the Lewises and Farrells of the postwar period. Not only did he help to establish the temper of the postwar novel, but his long struggles against puritan censorship in connection with *Sister Carrie, The "Genius,"* and *An American Tragedy* helped pave the way for public acceptance of the even more frank and hard-hitting novels of the Twenties.

Artistically Dreiser's work has severe flaws. His novels, amorphous and often awkwardly written, are none the less conceived on a gigantic scale; his very energy overcomes his stylistic deficiencies. Dreiser himself specifically discounted the influence of the European naturalists. He was deeply impressed, however, with the ideas of certain British skeptics and positivists of the nineteenth century: Spencer, Tyndall, and Huxley. He took his mechanistic skepticism from these sources in the same way that Zola borrowed from Bernard's *Experimental Medicine*. In the later years of his life he turned to an active study of physics and chemistry in an effort to widen his scientific background.

At the same time there was a certain mystical element in Dreiser's character which he apparently derived from his family background. His father was a devout German Catholic, and his mother was an amateur mystic who saw visions of Our Lady in the garden behind her home. Dreiser often shows, along with the mechanistic determinism of the positivists, an irrational preoccupation with life forces, with the mystic relations of various aspects of life, and with transcendental religious experience. There are other ambivalences in his temperament. An avowed determinist, he is none the less a socialist with a warm faith in the improvability of man and the possibility of social amelioration. A believer in the evolutionary "survival of the fittest" doctrines of Spencer, he is still compassionate toward the weak and helpless of the earth who are ruthlessly subdued by the strong. In the drama *The Hand of the Potter* (1916) Dreiser portrays a twisted, mentally deficient youth who commits a crime through perversion; yet it is obvious the author feels, and wishes us to feel, a sympathy for the youth who "after all didn't make himself." This is determinism mingled with Christian compassion. Actually Dreiser was unable to believe totally in either positivism or transcendentalism; he was a lifelong skeptic who found it difficult to believe in anything for very long.

It is this quality of pity in Dreiser's tragedies that raises them above mere mechanistic studies of degeneration; here he resembles Flaubert more than he does Zola. Yet he strives to remain totally objective; sinner and saint suffer alike in his novels, and indeed the amoral and carefree adventurers of the type of Drouet in *Sister Carrie* seem to be the only ones who always land on their feet. If there is any blame to be attached, it is society Dreiser would have bear the opprobrium; or perhaps it is the universe itself. Dreiser is half socialist and half cosmological pessimist in the manner of Thomas Hardy.

Dreiser's weakest quality is his style. Although he was trained as a newspaperman, he lacks concision; his sentences are sprawling and awkward, and he often gropes for the right word for paragraphs without finding it. He has very little aesthetic appreciation; for him language is a means of communication rather than an art form. His dialogue especially is often gauche and banal. At least, however, he does not have the stylistic delusions of grandeur of Thomas Wolfe; when Dreiser is obscure it is through awkwardness and not through spurious profundity.

His talent for characterization is also unimpressive; his heroes are given to sudden unmotivated acts, and success, as in the case of Carrie's stage triumph, sometimes arrives to them in a way that lacks verisimilitude. Dreiser's titanic energy and enthusiasm carry the story across these faults, however, and in the end the reader remembers only the magnificent sweep of the novel.

Dreiser, in many ways a sentimentalist, is not given to shocking or sordid detail. His scenes of misery in the slums and factories are convincing without being disgusting, and his treatment of love is almost romantic. The objection of puritanical readers to books like *The "Genius"* was based, not only on the characters' use of "God!" and similar ejaculations, but on the fact that virtue is punished and vice rewarded with no apparent moral foundation. This, however, is the way Dreiser conceived the universe to operate, and for him to present morality in any other way would have been a form of dishonesty. His novels are less immoral than pessimistic.

LIFE: Dreiser was born in Terre Haute, Indiana in 1871 of German-Catholic parentage. His brother, Paul Dresser, became a well-known song writer, the composer of *On the Banks of the Wabash*. The family was poor, and Dreiser's childhood was blighted by misery and humiliation. The father was intermittently unemployed during Theodore's first seven years; the children picked up coal along the railroad tracks and spent long hours delivering laundry the mother took in to earn a few dollars for food. Often their meals consisted of a single dish of mush or fried potatoes. Theodore and his brother underwent the experience of being sent home from school one winter because they had no shoes to protect them from the cold. In 1879 the family split up; eventually the mother opened a boarding house. The sensitive young Theodore was permanently marked by these early years; all his life he retained a sympathy for the underdog. It was undoubtedly the memory of his childhood which inclined him toward communism in his later years.

Dreiser attended a Catholic school in Terre Haute and later went on to the public schools of Warsaw, Indiana, where he began to show a precocious creativity. A high-school teacher, Mildred Fielding, encouraged him; later she made it possible for him to spend a year (1888-89) at Indiana University. He now began a period of unsettled wandering which lasted until he found his vocation with the writing of *Sister Carrie* in 1889-90. From 1892 he worked as a journalist and editor; he retained connections with the publishing business until 1911. During part of this time he held the responsible position of managing editor of Butterick Publications. Meanwhile he was writing articles and commercial magazine stories, and in 1899 he turned his hand to a novel. *Sister Carrie,* completed in 1900, was accepted by Doubleday, Page & Co. chiefly on the recommendation of Frank Norris, then serving as a reader for the firm. A contract was issued and the type set up. But when Mrs. Frank Doubleday, the publisher's wife, read the proofs, she was horrified that such a book should bear the imprint of the firm; her husband, after consideration, agreed. Dreiser attempted to hold the firm to the contract, but Doubleday made no effort to sell the small edition printed to avoid lawsuit, and the book passed almost unnoticed.

An even greater battle arose with *The "Genius"* in 1915. The novel was condemned by the Western Society for the Prevention of Vice, with headquarters in Cleveland, for "obscenity and blasphemy," and this organization enlisted the support of the New York Society for the Suppression of Vice. Intimidation was brought to bear on the publisher, who withdrew the book. Dreiser, encouraged by H. L. Mencken, joined battle and attempted to sue the publisher; a score of American men of letters lent their support. After long and fruitless litigation Dreiser gave up the battle in 1918; *The "Genius"* remained unpublished until 1923, when a new and sophisticated public was more receptive to literary frankness. But *An American Tragedy* was banned in Boston in 1927, and as late as 1937 the Hollywood "Hays

Office" refused to allow a film to be made of *Sister Carrie*. Dreiser's lifelong battle with censorship only confirmed his hatred of puritanism, Philistinism, and bourgeois hypocrisy.

His domestic life was likewise beset with difficulties. He married in 1898 upon insufficient consideration; his wife refused for forty years to agree to a divorce. Meanwhile he had formed an attachment with Helen Richardson, a distant relative who proved both congenial to his temperament and inspiring to his work. His inability to marry Miss Richardson until his wife died in 1942 inclined him to tolerance of irregular liaisons and of those unfortunate beings who are penalized for sexual mistakes in our society.

The contradictions of Dreiser's character are perhaps most apparent in his politics. During his early years he was a fervent humanitarian and enemy of capitalism; he wrote articles exposing slum and industrial conditions and spoke out warmly in defense of labor. A thorough-going individualist, he was wary of attachment to any party. But in 1927 he accepted an invitation to visit Russia under the auspices of the Soviet Bureau of Cultural Relations. His remarks upon his return pleased neither the Communists nor the capitalistic press, since he saw fit to criticize both America and the U.S.S.R. for their inadequacies. During the Thirties he appeared to drift closer to Communism. He followed the Party line toward the Second World War, refusing to endorse the war effort before 1914 and switching to a strong interventionist position after Russia was attacked. Yet even at the end of his life he condemned the standardization of thought and belief in the Soviet Union. Dreiser was attracted to Communism through his antagonism toward the evils of capitalism as he had known them and out of his Christian feeling of charity toward his fellow man. He died in Los Angeles in 1945; the speakers at his funeral included a Congregational minister and the left-wing writer John Howard Lawson.

CHIEF WORKS: *Sister Carrie* (novel, 1900) is a study of Carrie Meeber, an innocent Wisconsin girl who comes to Chicago to find work and falls into an intricate network of temptation. In writing the novel Dreiser borrowed on memories of his own sisters, two of whom abandoned the family to strike out on their own and found only misery. Carrie's temptations begin even before she arrives at the city;

on the train she encounters Charles Drouet, an energetic salesman and playboy whose attentions she hardly knows how to repulse. She rejects him, however, and takes up a respectable residence in Chicago with a relative. After some difficulty she finds a job in a shoe factory, but the work proves impossibly strenuous and sordid. Dreiser's description of the factory is drawn in the manner of the muckrakers of the eighteen-eighties; the bosses are conniving and lascivious, the factory degrading, ill-ventilated, and dangerous, and the hours heartbreakingly long.

Carrie soon wearies of all this, and presently a more attractive venture presents itself; she becomes Drouet's "sweetheart" and allows him to support her. After a while she aspires to greater triumphs. Drouet introduces her to George Hurstwood, a saloon manager who courts her for a time and even promises to marry her, although he has a wife and family he has not told her about. Hurstwood is a good dresser and a satisfactory employee, but at the bottom he is weak and indecisive. He loves good times and convivial companions, and he sees in Carrie a girlish charm which contrasts sharply with the coldness of his wife. The section describing Hurstwood's seduction of Carrie is titled, "The Lure of the Spirit: The Flesh in Pursuit." Hurstwood, seeking some means of eloping with Carrie, is tempted by an open safe in his employer's establishment; he steals a large sum of money and flees with Carrie on what he describes to her as their "honeymoon." But he lacks the decisiveness to carry his crime through to the end; he sends back most of the money to the employer, and the couple go to New York to start a new life. By this time Hurstwood has committed bigamy as well, and Carrie imagines herself his wife. When Hurstwood proves to have insufficient character to hold a steady job, Carrie leaves him; he degenerates rapidly and in the end commits suicide. Carrie goes on to become a successful actress, but her life is a spiritual vacuum and she fails to achieve happiness.

The chapter title "The Lure of the Spirit: The Flesh in Pursuit" expresses one of the themes of the novel: Carrie represents Spirit, the longing for a finer and higher form of life, artistic aspiration, and imagination, while Hurstwood, and to a lesser extent Drouet, stand for the material lusts which lie at the bottom of worldly ambition. An autobiographical element is indicated. Carrie represents the ideals, Dreiser's included, which can never be fully attained but without which life is meaningless. Hurstwood represents what Dreiser hoped he would never become: a characterless automaton with no higher goal than the satisfaction of his sensual inclinations. Yet Dreiser recognizes the Hurstwood in himself; the novel served to remind him to keep such inclinations well under control.

In contrast to previous stories of "fallen women," e.g., Crane's *Maggie, a Girl of the Streets, Sister Carrie* offers no moral judgment on the situation. There are no villains or heroes in the novel; Hurstwood, weak and characterless, is not guilty, and neither is Carrie. It is through sheer lack of character and through the influence of a corrupt capitalistic society that the lives of Carrie and her paramour are blighted.

The "Genius" (novel, 1915) is a classic story of a "misunderstood artist" adapted to the naturalistic style. Eugene Witla, a talented small-town boy, comes to Chicago and, by studying nights, wins an education as an artist. He holds a succession of menial jobs, then moves to New York and becomes a commercial artist and magazine illustrator. Gradually he becomes a figure of the Bohemian circle of Greenwich Village, and his reputation grows. After a time his original oils attract more attention than his commercial drawings. Dreiser portrays Witla as one of the "Ashcan Painters," an actual group of naturalistic artists including John Sloan and Everett Shinn.

Although Eugene's talent seems likely to win him artistic success, his career degenerates because he is unable to arrive at a satisfactory sex life. He is absolutely incapable, it seems, of understanding women, or of living on amiable terms with them. His preoccupation with love and romance becomes so obsessive that his artistic career often seems secondary. He romances unhappily with a long succession of women: Ruby Kenny, a sensual young Chicago model; Angela Blue, a "good girl," selfless and chaste, whom he eventually marries; Christina Channing, an actress and opera star; Carlotta Wilson, a bored and neurotic gambler's wife, and several others. Angela is the true sexual focus of his life; he is helplessly attracted to her beauty but feels himself unworthy of her because of his transitory adventures with other women. After his marriage Eugene, worried over these problems and exhausted by his tumultuous relations with Angela, gradually becomes artistically sterile. He turns to manual labor, to commercial art, to publishing, and to business in an effort to escape from his own nature. After Angela dies in childbirth he begins to arrive at a certain understanding of his own problems; he returns to painting and soon recaptures the success of his younger days. He also takes comfort in his daughter, who now provides him with the innocence and gaiety he has always sought in women.

There are two chief themes in The *"Genius."* The first is the traditional struggle of the artist against an uncomprehending and hostile public, a public whose ignorance of art is only equaled by its puritanical suspicion of the artist's way of life. Dreiser himself fought this struggle, and he was able to recount Eugene's torments at first hand. There is an almost religious fervor in the consecration Eugene brings to his painting, and an almost religious force in the energy which drives him to create in spite of the obstacles surrounding him. To Eugene, as to Dreiser, there is an element of the transcendental about the artist's vocation.

The second theme is that of the artist confronted by a choice of a normal family life and the sacrifices of an artistic career. Eugene cannot be both a good husband and a good painter; to the artist some things are denied. On one hand Eugene longs for the stability and serenity he hopes Angela's love will bring him; on the other hand he resents the restrictions and banality of conventional family life. The problem has a psychosexual aspect: Dreiser, postulating something like the Freudian libido, indicates that Eugene's creative energy can be directed to sexual satisfaction or to artistic creativity, but not to both at once. He wastes his creative energy in his marital relations with Angela, and can paint only when he denies himself this outlet.

Although The *"Genius"* is Dreiser's most autobiographical novel, he presents Eugene's career with great objectivity. With regard to the quotation marks in the title he explained, "I haven't committed myself at all. I merely put it up to the reader."

An American Tragedy (novel, 1925) is a study of social classes and of an individual's effort to rise from one into another; it involves also a moral analysis of guilt in the manner of Dostoyevsky's *Crime and Punishment.* Clyde Griffiths is a sensitive and unhappy youth whose parents are Kansas City street evangelists. Humiliated by his sordid family life and by the narrow bigoted morality his parents force upon him, he longs to escape into a finer and more rewarding environment. He feels, not without justice, that he is finer and more sensitive than the normal lot of individuals, and that life has unfairly condemned him to a banal and mean existence. But he lacks the force of character to fight his way to the top; his is a mere nostalgia for luxury rather than a true ambition. He works for a while as a bellhop in a Kansas City hotel, where he is vividly impressed with the contrast between his own poverty and the opulence and importance of the guests; he yearns to rise into this American plutocracy which seems to offer his only hope of self-realization.

Meanwhile a moral crisis presents itself. His sister Hester runs off with an actor who presently deserts her; she returns home pregnant, miserable, and without means. Clyde is moved by her plight, but instead of helping her he turns weakly to spend his money on Hortense Briggs, a vain and shrewdly calculating girl. One day Clyde, several other bellboys, and several girls set off on an escapade in a borrowed car. The driver runs down a little child and then wrecks the car trying to escape from the police; Clyde flees the scene, quits his job, and changes his name in an effort to avoid his part of the responsibility for the incident. Then an opportunity appears: a wealthy uncle, Samuel Griffiths, offers him a job in a collar factory in Lycurgus, New York. For a time Clyde's fortunes seem to rise. But after a while he finds himself in a curiously frustrating social situation. He is embarrassed in the company of his snobbish relatives, yet he is forbidden to approach the lower-class shop girls who work in his department. One of these girls, Roberta Alden, attracts him, and after a time he falls in love with her; their relations become intimate. Clyde, always indecisive, hesitates to break with Roberta even when his affections are transferred to another girl, the wealthy and socially prominent Sondra Finchley. Sondra is the key to all his ambitions; by the single stroke of marriage with her he imagines all his problems will be solved. At this critical moment Roberta discovers she is pregnant; she piteously demands that Clyde marry her. He is faced with a cruel moral dilemma: shall he stand by Roberta, thus abandoning what may be his last chance to rise in the world? At the critical moment he reads a news account of a boating accident in which a young girl is drowned while her companion's body is not found. Horrified at his own thoughts, he half-resolves to free himself by ending Roberta's life. He lures her to an upstate resort and rents a boat for a lake excursion. His preparations for the crime, however, are hopelessly incompetent.

He has registered under two different false names at hotels, and now he betrays by several signs the fact that he does not intend to return to the hotel. At the moment of decision he almost loses his nerve. Noticing his perturbation, Roberta reaches toward him; the boat capsizes accidentally and she is drowned. Clyde swims ashore and flees in guilty terror across the countryside. It is not certain whether he is guilty of Roberta's death, but he knows in his own mind that he did not exert himself to save her during the seconds she floated on the water. Arrested, he is tried for murder. The defense argues that he is a morally deficient person who is not responsible for his acts. But after he is found guilty and is awaiting his execution, Clyde begins to understand the moral implications of his act. Encouraged by his mother and by a sympathetic minister, he eventually resigns himself to his death as a necessary expiation for the moral cowardice he showed in refusing to accept the responsibilities life thrust upon him.

An American Tragedy is based on court records of an actual trial; Dreiser utilized large sections of the court transcript almost verbatim. But although the bare details are thus borrowed from reality, the implications and moral conclusions of the story are Dreiser's own. The title implies that the life of Clyde Griffiths is a tragedy; i.e., that he is a noble hero who is destroyed through the operation of inexorable forces, either within him or in his environment. One interpretation is that Clyde's "tragic flaw" is his ambition to rise in society regardless of the cost; in this sense the novel is a criticism of the "American Dream," the Horatio Alger tradition of unlimited opportunity and quick success in a new country where social barriers are flexible. Clyde, however, hardly seems to possess the strength of character that this interpretation demands; he is a weak person, and he commits his crime more out of a muddled desire to escape from his situation than out of ruthless ambition. In fact, as we have seen, there is a genuine doubt whether he consciously and deliberately willed the crime at all. He is perhaps "guilty" only in the legal sense. The other interpretation of the term "tragedy" as applied to this novel is that Clyde is destroyed by his environment, by the cruelty and callousness of a selfish capitalistic society. Although this interpretation is consistent with Dreiser's own political philosophy, there is not very much evidence in the novel to justify it. Clyde was not forced by capitalistic society to murder Roberta; he might have married her, or he might have abandoned both girls and gone off somewhere else to make a second start in life. "That young men can grow up in America with no higher ideals than those of Clyde Griffiths is a national disgrace, if not a national tragedy," remarks Wagenknecht, suggesting a third meaning of the word. And he adds, "Surely there can be no question that the book is deeply moving." Here lies its true importance: its human drama, the anguish of the decision that confronts Clyde, and the painstaking exactitude with which the human emotions of the drama are described. Like *Crime and Punishment,* the novel is a moving literary experience entirely apart from its perhaps questionable moral and philosophical conclusions.

The Financier (1912), *The Titan* (1914), and *The Stoic* (1917) together form a novel trilogy based on the career of Charles T. Yerkes, a Chicago transit mogul and "robber baron." The fictionalized Yerkes, Frank Cowperwood, bases his morality on something like the "law of the jungle" of Spencer's evolutionary ethic. He determines he is "going to be a lobster and not a squid"—i.e., that he is going to belong to the hunters among society and not to the hunted. These three novels are the most highly documented and detailed of Dreiser's works; they are also interesting as a panoramic picture of the industrial triumph at the end of the century.

BOOTH TARKINGTON (1869-1946)

Tarkington, a versatile writer, has unfortunately been viewed chiefly as a humorist until very recent times. It is true he has a sense of humor; if this is a fault in a serious novelist, he must stand convicted. A more serious accusation that may be brought against him is that he is a sentimentalist, but this is true of a good many other authors who are considered realists, from Daudet to Steinbeck. In spite of these liabilities, it is still true that he is a social satirist, an expert one, and one of the first American satirists of the twentieth century to treat the urban middle class, the social class which was only a few years later to occupy the attention of Sinclair Lewis. The significance of his contribution may be gauged by comparing the scenes of millionaire life in *An American Tragedy*—awkward, artificial, and unconvincing —with the accurate and penetrating pictures of the same classes in Tarkington's *Growth* trilogy. If Tarkington wrote too late to be the literary grandfather of Lewis and Fitzgerald, he is at least their "literary uncle."

Tarkington, however, is modern only in his subject-matter, and not always then. He is conservative in style and distinctly Victorian in the matter of decorum; there is little of the profanity, radicalism, and sexual frankness in his work found, for example, in the work of Crane, London, or Norris. He is not a thinker, and when he tries to be, he is often wrong; he suffered, for example, from a weakness for spiritualism which led him to include a real flaw in the plot of *The Magnificent Ambersons*. But he has the merits of a skilled professional writer: he is a careful observer, he has a knack for construction (suspense, ironic contrast, climax), and he has a marvelous talent for creating characters. He was inspired rather than influenced by James and Howells; his own style is earthier, less pretentious, and pervaded by an irony lacking in the other two novelists, who took themselves more seriously. His most important works are undoubtedly his studies of midwestern city life: the *Growth* trilogy, *Alice Adams, The Heritage of Hatcher Ide, Kate Fennigate,* and *The Image of Josephine*. These books resemble each other in style as they do in subject matter: they are basically serious, superficially ironic, detached and objective, documented with minute, well-chosen, and always significant details of life in the milieu he is describing. The other main category of his work is the *Penrod* series, which treats humorous adventures of boyhood more or less in the tradition of *Tom Sawyer,* but with greater irony and less nostalgia. A third category includes a single book: *Monsieur Beaucaire,* a satirical costume piece about an eighteenth-century French duke who masquerades as a barber to win the heart of a cold English lady.

Although he is not a thinker, Tarkington is capable of shrewd analysis of the growth and conflict of social classes, especially in his midwestern city stories. Several of his novels demonstrate the same social process: the birth and rise of a midwestern aristocracy, essentially Victorian and conservative, around 1890, and its gradual decline before a new rising class, the industrial and mechanical generation of the twentieth century. Often this social conflict is symbolized through the struggle of two families who represent the two classes; and it is a foregone conclusion that the struggle will end with the victory of the new class, the harbingers of the automobile, the factory, and the suburbs. On this framework Tarkington frequently builds a Romeo-and-Juliet story in which the lovers are separated by the basic hostility of their families and social classes: e.g., George and Lucy in *The Magnificent Ambersons* or Alice and Arthur in *Alice Adams*. Nevertheless Tarkington is not a sociological novelist; he is a student of American life, and he reflects sociological processes only insofar as these have changed the conditions in which the life of the American family takes place. In this, as in his flair for dialect and in his satirical treatment of stuffed shirts, small-town boosters, and society snobs, he resembles Sinclair Lewis, the one American author of the twentieth century with which he is most aptly compared.

LIFE: [Newton] Booth Tarkington was born in Indianapolis, Indiana in 1869; the city remained his home for most of his life and the setting for his best-known works. He was educated at Purdue and Princeton; although he never graduated through failure to make up a condition in Greek, he lived to see both Princeton and Columbia award him honorary doctorates. He began to write immediately after his college days; he published his first book, the semi-autobiographical *Gentleman From Indiana,* in 1899 and gained an enormous popular success with *Monsieur Beaucaire* in 1900. He traveled widely at various times in his life, and at one time served a term in the Indiana state legislature. He was married twice. During the latter part of his life he established what became virtually a permanent home at Kennebunkport, Maine.

Tarkington was not a prolific writer, but he was a steady writer; he continued to produce up to the year of his death. Most of his Penrod books appeared around the time of the First World War; his more serious midwestern novels extend from 1918 to 1945. He won a Pulitzer Prize in 1919 for *The Magnificent Ambersons* and another in 1922 for *Alice Adams;* during the early Twenties he held a position as one of America's most successful and popular novelists. His prestige among critics declined with the appearance of the more important naturalists in the late Twenties, but in recent years criticism had tended to regard him more seriously. In his sixties he was operated on for cataracts, and remained partly blind the rest of his life. He was, however, still productive at the time of his death in 1946.

CHIEF WORKS: *The Magnificent Ambersons* (novel, 1918), chron-

icles the rise and fall, through three generations, of the clan of Ambersons, the leading family in an unnamed town in the midwest (which
Tarkington refers to as the "Midland region"). The details, however,
are obviously drawn from the Indianapolis of Tarkington's youth. The
family's wealth and influence begin with old Major Amberson, who
acquires a fortune in the "Gilded Age" around 1875 and builds a fan-
tastically luxurious mansion in the growing Midland town. His daughter Isabel, torn between two suitors, rejects the dashing Eugene
Morgan and chooses instead the dull but steady Wilbur Minafer. This
proves to be the great mistake of her life. From her marriage, however, is born a son, George, the chief character of the novel.

As a boy George, over-indulged and spoiled, resembles a sort of
millionaire Penrod, and is heartily detested by most of the citizens of
the town. His character does not improve very much as he gets older.
He becomes, in fact, a conceited, fatuous, and weak-charactered
young man, although basically good-hearted. The first time in life he
is ever denied anything is when he meets Lucy Morgan, daughter of
his mother's old suitor, and falls in love with her. Lucy, who loves him
too, is nevertheless mildly derisive toward his egotism and rejects his
overtures. His vanity wounded, he breaks off the affair. Meanwhile
George's father dies and Eugene, Lucy's father, resumes his old courtship of Isabel. A talented inventor, Eugene has entered the new field
of automobile manufacturing and has become suddenly wealthy.
George, still piqued at Lucy, resents this courtship, and as "head of
the family" angrily turns Eugene out of the house, depriving his
mother of her last chance of happiness. At this point it becomes apparent that the fortunes of the Amberson-Minafer clan are in decline;
the theme of the struggle of social classes becomes apparent. The
Gilded Age aristocracy of the Ambersons inevitably gives way before
the vigorous new spirit of the automobile age; Isabel dies, George
finds himself virtually a pauper, and is forced to take a menial job to
support himself and his Aunt Fanny. Some years later George is injured on the street by an automobile, and far away in New York
Eugene, consulting a spiritualist medium, receives a suggestion (which
probably originates in his own mind) that the dead Isabel wishes him
to be reconciled with her son. The two families are united again, and
Eugene sees in George and Lucy a symbolic consummation of his
hopeless lifelong love for Isabel.

Such a synopsis, however, is unfair; the plot is the weakest part of this novel. The style, a charming mixture of sentimentality and irony, saves the work from mediocrity. The opening passage, a satirical essay on the social manners of the Gilded Age, is a masterpiece, as is the Penrod-like depiction of the boyhood escapades of George. Some of the dialogue is reminiscent of Scott Fitzgerald: "Don't you think," remarks young George naively, "that being things is rather better than doing things?" Another remarkable passage is the treatise on suburban "boosters" (Chapter XXVIII), which anticipates Lewis' *Babbitt* by a small margin of four years. *The Magnificent Ambersons* is the central novel of the trilogy *Growth* (published as a complete work in 1927), which also includes *The Turmoil* (1915) and *The Midlander* (1923).

Alice Adams (novel, 1921) is similar in style and setting to *The Magnificent Ambersons*. The heroine, seeking like the Clyde Griffiths of *An American Tragedy* to escape her sordid lower-middle-class background, tries to accomplish this through marriage with a wealthy young man. If she fails it is not through lack of effort. She surrounds her "intended," the aristocratic young Arthur Russell, with a web of tall tales and glamorized accounts of herself and her family, and for a time seems to make progress. The climax of the novel is a dinner-party which shatters all of Alice's hopes; Arthur clearly sees the vulgarity and instability of her family as well as the falsity of Alice's fictions about herself. Thenceforth the Adams family declines steadily; her brother becomes an embezzler, her father fails in business and then suffers a stroke, and the mother is forced to support the family by opening a boarding-house. The novel ends as Alice, resigned, enters a business college to begin her long and weary career as a wage-earner. The novel is more narrowly a study in character than *The Magnificent Ambersons;* Alice, superficial, naive, mercenary, yet engaging and basically good, is an unforgettable person. The climactic scene of the dinner party is a justly famous piece of narrative.

The "Penrod material" of Tarkington includes a number of books and short stories, although the character Penrod Schofield himself does not appear in all of them. The books about Penrod himself are *Penrod* (1914), *Penrod and Sam* (1916), and *Penrod Jashber* (1929). *Seventeen* (1916) is similar in style but treats different characters, and *The Flirt* (1913) and *Little Orvie* (1934) contain fiendish small boys of the same general type as minor characters.

GERTRUDE STEIN (1874-1946)

With the possible exception of James Joyce, Gertrude Stein has been heaped with more accusations of charlatanry than any other modern author; Sinclair Lewis openly accused her of "conducting a racket." The most conventional of her books must be considered eccentric, and certain things like the drama *Four Saints in Three Acts* seem downright incomprehensible to some. Nevertheless Miss Stein has had an incalculably important influence on younger authors, and her influence on Hemingway alone would mark her as an important literary personage. It appears that quite independently and originally she conceived certain devices of style and syntax which were taken up by a whole school of young American naturalists in the Twenties, and which have continued to filter their way into American literature until there is scarcely a modern writer who can be said to have totally escaped them. Her importance as time passes will probably lie in such influences rather than in her work itself, as fascinating as this may be to specialists and connoisseurs of the curious. It was Gertrude Stein above all who shattered the forms of conventional grammar and syntax, who demonstrated the possibilities of free association and the abandonment of conventional word-values in literary experimentation. Although she was the trail-breaker, she did not always do these things as well as her imitators, who could concentrate on refining the technique she had created out of nothing. As she herself said (of Picasso): "When you make a thing, it is so complicated making it that it is bound to be ugly, but those that do it after you don't have to worry about making it and they can make it pretty, and so everybody can like it when the others make it." It is relatively easy to be a good writer; it is hard to be a genuinely original one.

As an instance of her originality, Miss Stein was the first American author to try to transcribe banal daily speech, exactly as it occurs in life, into literature. As a student of psychology she learned that the human brain does not always operate on a sequential and logical level, that an ordinary conversation is full of repetitions and divergences. In *Three Lives* and in *The Autobiography of Alice B. Toklas* she attempted to utilize this natural conversation in prose narrative. But she went further; her psychological training had given her an interest in internal mental activity, especially in the process of associative thought. After her discovery of the French Symbolist poets she began to create something like automatic writing, a prose in which the imagination created word-pictures without the intervention of the intellectual or logical part of the brain. The mind, she felt, gives to words a special significance which is independent of their dictionary meaning; words provoke emotions and recollections through their sound and their associations as well as through their denotational content. In short, Miss Stein applied the findings of modern psychology on mental activity to the word theories of the Symbolists, and incorporated the resulting technique into narrative derived from her own literary materials. The most radical of her word-experiments are contained in *Tender Buttons* (1914) and *Four Saints in Three Acts* (1934); in both these words the literal or denotational content of the language is virtually nil. In her "sensible" works (*Three Lives* and the various autobiographical books) as well as in her more radical experiments she uses a language rich in adverbs and participles and rhythmic to the point of undulation. The phrases, devoid of metaphor and simile, are strung together with "and"; whole paragraphs are built around a single statement, phrased and rephrased until it becomes imbedded in the reader's consciousness. The lesson of this technique is clearly apparent in the styles of Hemingway and Dos Passos; Miss Stein was not entirely wrong when she proclaimed that she had taught Ernest Hemingway to write.

LIFE: Gertrude Stein was born in 1874 in Allegheny, Pennsylvania of German-American parents. Her childhood was spent in Vienna, in Paris, and in San Francisco; she attended schools both in Europe and in California. As an undergraduate at Radcliffe (1893-97) she came under the influence of two great teachers, Hugo Münsterberg and William James, and resolved to make psychology her life work. Her quick intelligence and excellent memory soon manifested themselves; James at one time remarked that she was the best woman student he had ever encountered. Her first published work was a paper, done in collaboration with Leon M. Solomons, entitled "Normal Motor Automatism," in the *Psychological Review* in 1896. It is likely that this paper, or the studies it reflected, determined the nature of her entire literary career; it was a study of automatic writing in normal subjects, and the examples quoted as well as the language itself foreshadow in an uncanny way the style of Miss Stein's later literary work.

Without finishing her degree at Radcliffe she went on to Johns Hopkins University with the idea of taking a medical degree. She studied medicine four years and again left without a degree; returning briefly to San Francisco, she abandoned America definitely for France in 1903. The date is an important one; it marks the founding of the Paris-expatriate cénacle of American authors which was later to include Hemingway, Pound, T.S. Eliot, Elliot Paul, and others. If Miss Stein was not the most important of these expatriates she was at least the first, and she consciously conceived of herself as the spiritual godmother of the group. Soon after (1907) she was joined by her friend Alice B. Toklas, who was to serve as her lifetime companion. The two young American spinsters took up residence on the Left Bank, eventually settling at 27, rue de Fleurus, an address that was to become the headquarters of avant-garde literary and artistic activity. Miss Stein entertained Matisse when he was still virtually unknown; she became the intimate of Picasso, Barque, and "Le Douanier" Rousseau, and acquired a fine collection of their paintings when they were still relatively inexpensive; a famous portrait of her by Picasso dates from this period. She also took under her wing a whole covey of young American expatriates of whom the most important were Pound, Sherwood Anderson, and Hemingway. She eventually broke with most of these people, usually because they became famous in their own right and escaped from her influence; she was inclined to run her salon with a firm and sometimes tyrannical hand. She had strong opinions about virtually everything, and had little patience with those who disagreed with her. Nevertheless her insight into literary talent and into social tendencies was remarkably sound; it was she who coined the term "a lost generation" which was so aptly applied to the intellectual youth of the Twenties.

In 1934 Miss Stein returned to America for the presentation of her play *Four Saints in Three Acts,* and was escorted on a lecture tour by Thornton Wilder. She soon returned to France; in her twenty years of foreign residence she had become a permanent expatriate. In spite of this she remained an American to the end of her days; her French was passable, but she continued to speak flowing, idiomatic, and colorful English in her daily life. During the Occupation of 1940-45 she and Miss Toklas retired to a villa in Culoz, in the Rhone Valley, where she was treated politely by the Germans although she was known to be an American. In 1945 she published an account of her Occupation experiences as *Wars I Have Seen,* and the following year appeared *Brewsie and Willie,* an amusing but perceptive sketch of the American GI's in Europe. She died in France the same year.

CHIEF WORKS: *Three Lives* (1909) contains a trio of matching novelettes, each an analysis of the life and character of a girl of the servant class in the city of Bridgeport. The book was undoubtedly suggested by Flaubert's *Three Tales;* indeed two of the novelettes are identical in structure and psychological treatment to the most famous of Flaubert's tales, *A Simple Heart.* "The Good Anna," the first novelette, describes a German housekeeper who watches jealously over her mistress, Miss Mathilda, and protects her from what she considers to be undesirable influences in her environment. Anna has no life of her own; she lives entirely for Miss Mathilda, her widow-friend Mrs. Lehntman, a German Doctor Shonjen who employs her during her youth, and her decrepit spaniel Baby. Her entire existence is vicarious; she is indignant at the persecution of her friends and scornful over their moral lapses. Their romances are the only passion in her life, and their afflictions her only tragedy. She dies at the end of the story, and her last thoughts are for her friends.

"Melanctha," the longest and most original of the three tales, concerns an impulsive, easy-going, and emotional young Negro girl whose life is blighted by her inability to understand men. In addition to a series of petty flirtations with various white and Negro men, she has two serious affairs: a long and bitter psychological struggle with the Negro Doctor Jefferson Campbell, who is too rational for her elemental emotions, and a fierce encounter with Jem Richards, a gambler who seeks to use her only as an instrument of his pleasure. Rose Johnson, a married friend, ostensibly tries to help, but actually patronizes her because she has not found a steady man as she, Rose, has. Melanctha is a moody creature entirely dominated by her emotions, which invariably lead her into the melancholy her name suggests.

The last tale, "The Gentle Lena," is very short; its heroine is a German immigrant girl who comes to Bridgeport and finds a place as a maid, is ill-treated by a succession of cooks and mistresses, and eventually drifts into a marriage with Herman Kreder, a young German tailor. Dully following the path destiny and her superiors have mapped out for her, she provides Herman with three children and dies bearing the fourth. Lena's main quality is her bovine complacency, which allows her to be dominated by the selfish and tyrannical people about her.

Three Lives is undoubtedly Miss Stein's most important work, her one book which seems most likely to assume a permanent place in American literature. This is due chiefly to its accurate and convincing characterizations; it is one of her few works of fiction to create believable and colorful people. More conventional in style than most of her work, it also contains some of her best dialogue: the natural, repetitive, flowing conversation which is her chief gift to other writers such as Hemingway and Anderson.

Tender Buttons (1914) was Miss Stein's first radically experimental work. It was originally printed in a small limited edition, and exerted little influence until it was reprinted in 1928. At the time she wrote this book Miss Stein was developing an interest in the problem of detaching words entirely from their dictionary meanings; she sought to use them merely as associative projectiles to strike the reader's brain. The book consists of three sections. "Objects" consists of aphoristic definitions of physical substances ranging from "a piece of coffee" to a piano; images of free association are used to provide a wandering, diffuse, but oddly pleasing surrealistic effect. "Food," the second section, contains similar associative definitions of meat and vegetables, stressing their visual and olfactory impact. "Rooms" presents longer and somewhat more abstract discussions of subjective experience, especially physical sensation. The technique of *Tender Buttons* has been compared to that of the cubist abstractions Miss Stein's friends Picasso, Braque, and Juan Gris were then painting. Since the work was read in its limited edition by several of Miss Stein's acquaintances who later became writers, its influence is probably greater than its publication figures would indicate.

The Autobiography of Alice B. Toklas (memoirs, 1933) is actually a journal of Miss Stein's own life, playfully written in the person of her companion Miss Toklas. This device makes it possible to comment impersonally on her own character, to praise (often with tongue in cheek) her own wit and genius, and in short to serve as her own

Boswell. The character of Miss Toklas is clearly defined through her "own" remarks: she is more naive, but less spiteful, than Miss Stein. The narrative begins with Miss Stein's childhood in Pennsylvania and continues through her youth to the period of the apartment in the Rue de Fleurus. There are fascinating accounts of Picasso, Matisse, Rousseau, and others, as well as shrewdly perceptive remarks on literary figures of the day.

Four Saints in Three Acts ("opera libretto," 1934) is one of Miss Stein's most controversial works. The opera was successfully performed on several occasions; the premiere took place with an all-Negro cast in Hartford, Connecticut in 1934. Music for the libretto was written by Virgil Thompson. Earlier versions of the work, without music, had appeared in 1929 and 1932.

Miss Stein's libretto for the opera is an exercise in surrealistic imagination, with little denotational meaning and no plot whatsoever. Actually there are fifteen saints, excluding those in the chorus, and five acts if the prologue is not included. If for nothing else, the libretto is remarkable for containing what is probably Miss Stein's most often quoted, if not her most meaningful, line: "Pigeons on the grass alas."

The relative success of this work as compared with *Tender Buttons* and other experiments is probably due to the fact that its audiences, diverted by the music and the spectacle, did not object to the lack of meaning of the text. Accompanied by music, the evocative but apparently senseless lines achieved a curiously pleasing effect. This is no criticism of Miss Stein's talent, since it was precisely her intent to divest literature of its logical content and to present it as a form of quasi-sensual pleasure.

Wars I Have Seen (autobiography, 1945) returns to the more comprehensible style of *The Autobiography of Alice B. Toklas;* the presentation is more straightforward, however, since Miss Stein in the earlier book was limited by her playful imitation of Miss Toklas' way of speaking. *Wars I Have Seen* contains some of her most conventional writing, and some of her best. The book is mainly concerned with the period 1940-45, the period of the German Occupation which Miss Stein and Miss Toklas spent in the Rhone Valley, although numerous observations on the First World War and other wars of history are included. Interesting pictures are presented of the life of the French countryside under the Occupation, the activities of the Resistance in the Rhone Valley as seen through the eyes of Miss Stein, and the change in the attitude of the German troops as their victory turned to defeat. The final section, "The Coming of the Americans," contains a vivid and moving account of the last days of the Occupation, one of the few passages in which Miss Stein stirs up any genuine excitement in her reader. The passage also reveals the extent of her warm and nostalgic love for America and Americans. As she explains in her account of the Liberation, she is fortunate in having two countries to be proud of, France and America; and this book reveals the extent of her love for both.

UPTON SINCLAIR (born 1878)

Upton Sinclair was for many years the most widely read American author in Europe, and even today he is better known on the continent than many a more talented American novelist. Part of the success of his fiction in translation is due to his directness and simplicity. His work is free from obscurantism or technical complexity, and his ideas are presented in concise, fresh, and obvious style. Sinclair is primarily a novelist of idea; his characterizations are weak and he wastes little time on plots. The ideas contained in his work are the old standbys of traditional socialism: the perfidy of the big business interests, the strangling influence of monopoly, and the general disregard of the common citizen in the great struggle to corner the world's resources and wealth.

As a stylist Sinclair may be roughly typed as a naturalist of the Zola school: he is scientific and perspicacious in his accumulation of data, objective in his treatment of character, and straightforward and unliterary, if occasionally excessively dramatic, in his language. He is, however, a versatile writer, one who can write in any style and whose works extend from books on personal hygiene to sociological essays and studies; he has written pot-boilers under a variety of pen-names, and in the Lanny Budd series he writes in a facile yet competent style suggestive of the better American magazine fiction. Like Zola, he seeks to write a literature which will find its place in the field of social sciences rather than in the arts; he is not "artistic" in the usual sense, and his main interests are in politics, finance, industry, and social questions. Since he is not very much interested in the art of the novel, his fiction is not remarkable from a technical point of view; it is precise and competent, and it is simple enough to be comprehended by the large reading public he desires to reach, and for his purposes this is enough.

Like many radical naturalists (e.g., Zola and Dreiser) Sinclair shows in his character a certain romanticism, even a shadowy tendency toward mysticism. He once declared that the three figures who shaped his thought were Jesus, Hamlet, and Shelley: the Prophet, the half-mad dreamer, and the romantic poet. From this attitude comes his idealism, from his idealism comes his burning interest in social questions, and from his social convictions come his hard-hitting and bitingly satirical naturalistic novels; the connection seems paradoxical, but is one found in many naturalistic novelists.

Sinclair was born only a decade after Crane and Norris, and his first successful book, *The Jungle,* appeared in 1906 only five years after Norris' *Octopus.* Yet Sinclair clearly belongs among the postwar authors, as Norris belongs with Crane, Howells, and the other predecessors of the realistic movement. The difference is immediately apparent if *The Octopus* and *The Jungle* are compared. Norris' novel is dramatic in plot, romantic in characterization (one of its central characters is a poet), and far from democratic in its basic argument; it is essentially a sympathetic defense of the wealthy ranchers in their struggle against the railroad. In *McTeague* Norris attempted a novel about the working class, but his characters are essentially freaks; far from hard-working proletarians, they are really nothing but grotesque social misfits. *The Jungle* is perhaps America's first proletarian novel; the degeneration of Jurgis is caused not by any basic flaw in his own character but by the viciousness and cruelty of the capitalistic society around him. Sinclair repeated the formula in *King Coal, The Brass Check, Oil!, Boston,* and other novels of his middle period; not only is this work consistently radical, but it takes a consistently realistic view of the American worker—or at least it attempts to study the working class sympathetically, from the inside, instead of satirically, from the outside, as Norris does. This of course has nothing to do with the quality of the two writers, and it may be argued that Norris is the greater talent; but it does show that Sinclair is more typical of post-1918 naturalism, and thus more "modern." He is, in fact, the most "typical" of the postwar naturalists in his conformity to the accepted rules and conventions of the school.

LIFE: Upton Beall Sinclair was born in Baltimore in 1878. His father, a habitual alcoholic, provided a memorable example for the boy's mind; Sinclair remained a teetotaler all his life. The family moved to New York when Upton was still a child. He went through the public school system at a phenomenal rate, emerging from grammar school at twelve, and worked his way through City College and four graduate years at Columbia. In 1900 he married Meta Fuller. Thenceforth Sinclair endeavored to make his living through free-lance writing, and for a half-dozen years the couple lived in the most discouraging poverty. In 1906 *The Jungle* made the best-seller lists; Sinclair invested the profits in Helicon Hall, a utopian living experiment in New Jersey. The building housed the then unknown Sinclair Lewis for a while, but soon burned to the ground. The incident is typical of the pattern of Sinclair's business and financial affairs.

During the Depression Sinclair, by this time an ardent socialist, became involved in politics on the West Coast. His EPIC Movement ("End Poverty in California") drew extensive support from independent voters; Sinclair ran for Governor of California in 1934 and might have won if it had not been for the vigorous and concerted opposition of business interests. Although his early muck-raking novels were widely read, Sinclair remained in relatively impecunious circumstances until the period of the Second World War, when his Lanny Budd series began to bring in money on a larger scale. To date his works have been translated into almost eight hundred separate foreign editions in fifty languages.

CHIEF NOVELS: *The Jungle* (1906) is a violent attack on the Chicago meat-packing industry. The hero, Jurgis Rudkus, is a Lithuanian immigrant who comes to Chicago and marries the young girl Ona, whom he has known in the old country. He quickly finds a job in a packing house, but the work is ill-paid and unhealthy. The newlyweds are cheated on a jerry-built house, then Jurgis is injured and loses his job. After this one misfortune follows another. He is jailed for striking a foreman, Ona dies in childbirth shortly after he returns from prison, and another child drowns in a flooded street. Thenceforth the degeneration of this strong and honest man is fast; he becomes a vagabond and petty criminal. He reaches the bottom of his despair when he finds Ona's cousin Marija working as a prostitute. Going numbly forth into the city, he wanders by chance into a socialist meeting, and there for the first time he perceives a way out of his misery.

King Coal (1917) follows a similar pattern. A fictional account of a strike in the Colorado coal mines, it is based on actual testimony recorded during an investigation of the Colorado strike of 1914-15. Its hero, Hal Warner, is a wealthy and educated playboy who becomes a miner in order to study the internal workings of the coal industry. He becomes a union organizer and works to correct the dangerous and unhealthy conditions under which the miners work; when the strike comes he abandons his social class to serve as one of its leaders. This novel evidently owes something in its structure and subject to Zola's *Germinal* (1885).

Oil! (1927) is a bitter and highly detailed exposé of the perfidy of the oil monopolies in California, based for the most part on the Teapot Dome scandals during the Harding administration (1923-24). Bunny Ross, the central character, is the son of an independent oil operator; when his father's business is threatened by the encroaching monopoly he becomes interested in the liberal movement. His friend Paul Watkins, who has fought in Siberia against the Reds as a member of the American Expeditionary Force, serves as a spokesman of Communist ideas. The novel also discusses national high finance in general, the causes of the First World War, and even crackpot religions in California; its discursiveness and its tendency to preach weaken its effectiveness as a work of fiction. Bunny ends up as a socialist, although he does not go so far as to accept totally the militant Marxism of his friend Paul.

Boston (1928) is a thinly fictionalized account of the Sacco and Vanzetti case, which provoked a fierce public controversy from the time of the alleged crime in 1920 until the execution of Sacco and Vanzetti in 1927. The story is seen through the experience of Cornelia Thornwall, a sixty-year-old widow who meets Vanzetti in a boarding-house and becomes a devoted partisan of the working class. When Sacco and Vanzetti are arrested for murder she works to defend them, along with her granddaughter Betty, but the two anarchists are doomed: they are betrayed not only by the judges and elected officials of Massachusetts, but by a traditional Boston society jealous of its prerogatives and resentful of the encroachment of the new foreign-born working class. The least objective of Sinclair's novels, *Boston* is nevertheless one of the most gripping, chiefly because of the interest inherent in the story.

Sinclair's Lanny Budd series should receive at least brief mention. Lanny, the hero of this set of interconnected novels, is born in Paris as the illegitimate son of a munitions manufacturer and rises in the world to become a daring American secret agent and diplomatist. The long series of novels begins with *World's End* (1940), in which Lanny's youth, including his European education, is described. In *Between Two Worlds* (1941) the story is continued from the end of the First World War to the time of the stock-market crash in 1929, roughly the "Roaring Twenties." *Dragon's Teeth* (1942) covers the period from 1930 to 1934, in which Lanny becomes involved with Nazism in Germany and is imprisoned as a result of his efforts to get a Jewish friend released from a concentration camp. *Wide Is The Gate* (1943) takes the story through the Spanish Civil War, and *Presidential Agent* (1944), *Dragon Harvest* (1945), *A World to Win* (1946), *Presidential Mission* (1947), *One Clear Call* (1948), and *O Shepherd, Speak!* (1949) narrate Lanny's experiences in the Second World War, including the Munich crisis and the events leading up to actual hostilities. By this time Lanny has become a secret agent, a confidant of Franklin Roosevelt, and an important figure in international diplomacy. As the war ends Lanny, provided with a million dollars by a philanthropic friend, plans to use the money to set up a radio station to propagandize for internationalism and world peace. While the Lanny Budd series is frankly popular writing, the novels are by no means badly written; their plots are sometimes melodramatic, but their style is straightforward, competent, and unpretentious. As a contribution to the genre of the historical novel they bear comparison with Jules Romains' *Men of Good Will* series and Roger Martin du Gard's *Les Thibaults,* as well as with Dos Passos' *U.S.A.*

SINCLAIR LEWIS (1885-1951)

Sinclair Lewis, the first American to win the Nobel Prize for Literature, is both a naturalistic chronicler of American life and a satirist whose barbs have been directed at practically every element of modern society. In the first sense his work comprises a pattern of American culture somewhat in the manner of Balzac's *Human Comedy* of Jules Romains' *Men of Good Will* series. He has analyzed suburban life, small-town society, the medical profession, organized religion, big business, and a host of other aspects of life in the twentieth century, and to each of these treatments he has brought the copious documentation, the careful selectivity, and the precise attention to detail of the naturalistic school. At the same time he aims the scorn and wit of a born satirist at everything he considers unworthy in America: hypocrisy, materialism, the monotony of small-town life, bigotry, vulgarity, and anti-intellectualism. His satire has earned him, not only the violent hatred of certain groups and individuals in America who found themselves only too recognizable in his novels, but, what is more unfair, a reputation as a misanthrope, an atheist, and an enemy of the "American way of life." Lewis is none of these things. He has a warm feeling of affection, even of kinship, for the characters whose weaknesses he describes. His sympathies are by no means entirely on the side of the sophisticated Carol Kennicott of *Main Street;* in the end Carol is wrong, and even Main Street finds some justification in the reader's mind. Lewis is far from pitiless toward George Babbitt, the materialistic booster whose name has become a dictionary synonym for suburban materialism; Lewis himself was born in a small middle-western town, and he retained many middle-class elements in his own character. At the bottom his satire is based on understanding; he hits the mark because he sees his characters from the inside out. His natural gift for caricature is so devastating, however, that he cannot help probing at weaknesses; his X-ray pictures of American life could not fail to elicit outraged protests from clergymen, capitalists, suburban patriots, and sentimentalists.

After *Main Street* (1920) Lewis seems to have had the idea of painting a complete cross-section of American life. He seldom repeated a theme; in this respect the originality and resources of his imagination are impressive. He satirized successfully suburban life (*Babbitt*), the medical profession (*Arrowsmith*), and organized religion (*Elmer Gantry*); he then went on to less satirical, but equally penetrating treatments of big business (*Dodsworth*), social welfare (*Ann Vickers*), the hotel business (*Work of Art*), American proto-fascism (*It Can't Happen Here*), the theatre (*Bethel Merriday*), organized philanthropy (*Gideon Planish*), marriage (*Cass Timberlane*), and the Negro problem (*Kingsblood Royal*). Each time he began his work with a careful and detailed study of the field to be covered. Where the technical details lay beyond his competence, as in *Arrowsmith*, he enlisted the aid of experts. These studies, however, are not objective documents on mere journalistic chronicles; they are works of art in which accuracy, in the last analysis, comes second to effect. Lewis in his artistic method is a caricaturist. His characters are not completely rounded humans but "types;" just as Balzac portrayed the miser, the ambitious youth, the neglected father, so does Lewis create the suburban booster, the small-town intellectual, the medical saint, and the hypocrite. He conveys these caricatures not through external description but through internal detail: nuances of speech, mannerisms, and characteristic actions.

Because of this method some of Lewis' characters suffer from a two-dimensional flatness. His clergymen are often so bumbling we cannot believe they would be entrusted with important parishes, and Dodsworth, as H. S. Canby has pointed out, is hardly the sort of man who would have risen to become head of a large corporation. Carol Kennicott, flighty, naive, and impractical, is an inadequate symbol of culture to oppose to the sterility of Main Street. Lewis is at his best as a satirist. His talent was negative; he had difficulty in drawing convincingly sympathetic heroes. Only the consecrated and idealistic scientist Arrowsmith impresses us as a truly admirable hero. Lewis could not totally scorn anything he found in America, but he found difficulty in totally admiring anything as well.

LIFE: Lewis was born in 1885 in Sauk Center, Minnesota, which, in spite of the denials of both Lewis and the citizenry of Sauk Center, seems to have served as model for the Gopher Prairie of *Main Street*. His father was a physician; Lewis had first-hand experience of life in the household of a country doctor which proved valuable to him in writing both *Main Street* and *Arrowsmith*. He graduated from Yale in 1908 and from that time to 1916 drifted about holding various jobs in journalism and magazine publication. He became an ardent socialist and was for a time associated with Upton Sinclair in the utopian colony of Helicon Hall. He began to produce fiction in 1912, and published numerous magazine stories, articles, and commercial novels in the period before 1920. In 1916 he abandoned journalism to turn to full-time writing, and in 1920 he published his first serious novel, *Main Street*. Other novels followed at the approximate rate of one every two years. He refused the Pulitzer Prize when it was offered to him in 1926, but accepted a Nobel Prize for Literature in 1930.

Lewis' first unsuccessful marriage lasted from 1914 to 1925. In 1928 he married the journalist Dorothy Thompson; this union of two temperamental artists produced a child, Michael, but ended in divorce in 1942. Lewis enjoyed an enormous success during the middle and latter part of his life; *Main Street* and *Babbitt* sold over a half-million copies each and were translated into all the major languages of the world, and his later novels were at least financial successes. He died in Rome in 1951.

CHIEF NOVELS: *Main Street* (novel, 1920) is a study of life in a rural midwestern town, and especially the efforts of the city-bred heroine to stimulate it into some semblance of intellectual activity. Carol Milford, a college graduate, plans to become a librarian and live an intellectual life among books and interesting personalities. But when she meets the young Dr. Will Kennicott she falls in love with him and agrees to go with him to Gopher Prairie, Minnesota as his bride. What follows is a succession of frustrations. Carol at first attempts to serve as a missionary of culture to the lethargic townsfolk. She organizes a little theatre, which falls flat; she investigates the local literary club, but flees from it in horror when the members dispose of the English poets in a single meeting and then go on to "English Fiction and Essays." The local minister is a bigoted nincompoop, and Erik Valborg, the town intellectual and promising material for an extra-marital romance, turns out to be vapid and cowardly. Carol gradually finds she is acquiring the enmity of the entire town; she is hated for her imagined air of superiority and resented for attacking the complacent and traditional pace of local society.

At length Carol abandons both town and husband to go to Washington; the war boom is on, and she secures a position as a clerk. But in Washington she is lonely; she begins to understand Gopher Prairie for the first time, and realizes there is a great deal of small town in her own personality. In the end she returns to Gopher Prairie, determined this time to approach small-town life in a more tolerant mood and to attempt to adjust herself to its peculiarities.

Main Street is in more than one sense an American *Madame Bovary;* in both novels the heroine is a frustrated young woman who is morally and intellectually superior to her physician husband, and in both cases the scene is laid in a small town whose stock types are paraded past the reader one by one. The more important sources of *Main Street,* however, lay in Lewis' own life. It has been remarked that Carol is in many ways a feminine transposition of Lewis himself, and that the story is a sort of allegory of his relation to American society.

Babbitt (novel, 1922) is a superficially satirical but perceptive study of the suburban middle class. The protagonist, George F. Babbitt, is a real-estate salesman in Zenith, a city resembling Minneapolis; he is aggressive, enthusiastic, optimistic, and devoid of any finer sentiments. His ideals are those of the "go-getter" and the "booster"—Zenith to him is the greatest little city in the world, selling real estate is the finest occupation known to society, and progress is constantly making Zenith and to a proportional extent America better and better in every way. Babbitt mistrusts liberals, artists, drifters, loafers, and clever people; he is rigidly moral in his domestic life, but is not averse to a fling with the "girlies" when he travels a few hundred miles to a convention. Babbitt, however, is not a total materialist; in fact he is not even a typical "Babbitt" as the term has later come to be understood. At the age of forty-six he begins to realize the superficiality of his life, and turns toward his friend Paul Riesling, an introverted and creative personality who is a sort of alter-ego to oppose to his own materialism. Paul, however, is basically an ineffectual person; he begins to degenerate, and finally is arrested for the murder of his wife. Babbitt, shaken, dabbles in radicalism and attempts a brief experiment in adultery with Mrs. Tanis Judique. The fear of social censure, however, proves too much for him; he prefers to be conventional and frustrated. At last he sinks back into the life of vulgarity and complacency he has tried in a perfunctory way to escape. In his son Ted, however, he sees promise of a vicarious escape. When Ted rebels against his school life and elopes against his parents' consent, Babbitt tries to tell him of the emptiness of his own life and encourages him to seek a finer existence on his own.

"Babbitt" has become an American byword; *Webster's Collegiate Dictionary* lists "Babbitt" and "Babbittry," the latter defined as "smug acceptance of the ethical and social standards of ordinary business and middle-class respectability; in allusion to the blatant hero of . . . Sinclair Lewis."

Arrowsmith (novel, 1925) presents a more positive idealism than any other work of Lewis. The author's father, a grandfather, an uncle, and a brother were all doctors. Encountering the profession in early life as he did, he retained a permanent respect for medicine and viewed it as one of the few fields in which true devotion and sincerity were possible. In *Arrowsmith* he portrays a hero who embodies his own personal ideal more than any of his other characters.

Martin Arrowsmith, the protagonist, is fascinated with medicine from boyhood. He struggles to educate himself and is eventually admitted to medical school. There he meets his first disillusionment; he finds that few of his fellow students and almost none of the doctors on the staff share his idealistic devotion to pure medicine. He begins to realize he will have to make a choice between a profitable, complacent career as a fashionable physician and a consecrated life as a research scientist. The rest of the novel follows the conflict between Arrowsmith's sincere idealism and the cynicism, selfishness, and muddled incompetency of most of the other doctors he meets. At first, influenced by Dr. Max Gottlieb, a brilliant European researcher, he determines to choose the path of pure science. He shows talent as a laboratory man, but meanwhile a personal problem intervenes. He has been courting a frivolous young graduate student; now he meets and falls in love with Leora Tozer, a nurse whose family live in a small town in North Dakota. When Leora goes home for the Christmas holidays Martin follows her, determined to make her his bride. In the small wheat town he tangles with Leora's relatives, who are narrow-minded and resent the intrusion of the outsider. A prolonged conflict takes place, but eventually he marries Leora.

Now that he is a family man, Martin decides he must choose some form of medicine more lucrative than pure research. He practices for a time in North Dakota, then becomes a public health inspector in Nautilus, Iowa. When his pompous and incompetent superior Pickerbaugh is elected to Congress, Martin finds himself Director of Public Health. But his idealism and sincerity spoil his chances of becoming a popular public servant; his efforts to clean up unhealthy conditions only make him enemies among the powerful. He resigns and works for a brief period as a member of the staff of the fashionable Rouncefield Clinic in Chicago, but the cynicism of his fellow physicians disgusts him. Disillusioned by the sordid commercialism of the clinic, he leaves for New York and becomes an assistant in Gottlieb's laboratory. There, under the guidance of the sincere old European scientist, he begins to find himself for the first time.

The climax of his career is a struggle against a bubonic plague epidemic in the West Indies; Leora and Martin's friend Sondelius succumb to the disease, and Martin is able to conquer the epidemic only by disobeying orders from the authorities. Deprived now of his family, he consecrates himself entirely to medicine; after a desultory and ill-fated second marriage he settles down to a life of pure research on a Vermont farm.

The chief theme of *Arrowsmith* is the contrast between the idealism of the true scientist and the sordid avarice of many members of the medical profession. The description of Martin's enthusiasm is related in a serious manner contrasting sharply with the satirical descriptions of other doctors, civic officials, small-town bigots, and nincompoops. Every aspect of the medical profession is criticized: medical schools, small-town practice, public health, fashionable clinics, and even research centers, which are shown to be continually harassed by the wealthy ignoramuses who pay for them. The sincerity of Martin, Gottlieb, and Sondelius relieves this otherwise sordid picture and shows the high idealism possible in the world of science. Much of the technical detail of this novel was supplied by the science writer Paul de Kruif.

Dodsworth (novel, 1929) is a study of the personal and domestic problems of a successful American business-man. Samuel Dodsworth, the protagonist, is a graduate of Yale and M.I.T. who knows machinery thoroughly; around 1903 he becomes interested in the then new field of automobile manufacturing. Soon he is an associate and stockholder in the Revelation Automobile Company, and through his ideas the company expands rapidly. Meanwhile he meets and marries Fran Voelker, a girl who has superficial interest but who is actually more interested in social climbing. Sam enjoys the excitement of his success in the business world, but Fran is bored with her existence; she convinces Sam that there must be more to life than making automobiles and enjoying the pleasures of one's home. Sam, who is in his forties, begins to wonder whether he isn't missing something, and he allows Fran to take him off to Europe to try to find it. The middle of the novel mainly concerns Fran's effort to make him into the type of cultured European snob she admires. Sam is at first amenable; he goes about politely meeting a succession of rude, egotistical, and superficial Europeans and does his best to assume a semblance of sophistication. When Fran decides that the finer life involves taking a lover, however, Sam balks. Divorce proceedings are begun, and Sam finds consolation in the company of Edith Cortwright, a sympathetic woman who accepts him for what he really is. Although Fran relents and seeks to recapture him, he rejects her and determines to build a new life on more sound moral principles.

Lewis criticizes several aspects of modern society in his novel. First, European "high society" is shown as superficial and snobbish, although European culture in the broader sense is by no means condemned. Second, the novel offers an interesting character study of a well-to-do wife with social aspirations. Fran, sexually cold, makes no effort to provide Sam with physical satisfaction. Neither does she accept him for what he is and offer him a genuine understanding; she is scornful toward the business which interests him so much and which provides both of them with their comfortable standard of living. Her aim is to make Sam resemble the fashionable social parasites she finds in Europe. She is highly cultured, but only on the surface; at heart she is interested only in social matters.

Sam, however, remains the central figure of the novel. Through him Lewis analyzes the problem of the American self-made man who wins wealth through his honest effort and talent and then finds he has no idea how to spend the money he has acquired. The swallowing up of the individual by big business is also portrayed; Sam's company is eventually bought out by the U.A.C., a large industrial combine, and Sam begins to feel like a nonentity amid the intricacies of higher finance. American business avails itself of individual talent and then, when it is done with the individual, casts him aside or swallows him in the web of bureaucratic organization.

Dodsworth, somewhat provincial and a little bull-headed, is nevertheless one of Lewis' more admirable characters. He talks intelligently instead of using the adolescent slang of Babbitt and Elmer Gantry; he is interested in literature and the arts, and is by no means unperceptive. Lewis admires the talented and hard-working industrial executive more than he does the narrow suburban booster of the type of Babbitt.

It Can't Happen Here (novel, 1935) is a satirical study of the triumph of a hypothetical American dictator, suggested by the success of fascism in Italy and Germany as well as by such American demagogues as Huey Long, who was assassinated the year the book was published. Its central character, Berzelius (Buzz) Windrip, begins in a small New England town and ends in the Presidency. The novel is concerned only secondarily with his rise to power, and concentrates chiefly on the fascist methods by which he rules the country after his election. He ruthlessly suppresses liberalism, wipes out labor unions, and extends his influence until he controls not only the executive wing of the government but also the judiciary and legislative. His antagonist in the novel is Doremus Jessup, a liberal newspaperman who has known him from the time of his beginnings in a small Vermont town. Jessup, persecuted by Windrip because he has worked against his election, joins a liberal underground movement led by Walt Trowbridge, a former senator and Windrip's opponent in the Presidential election. In addition to Jessup the liberal group includes Lorinda Pike, an intelligent woman of socialistic tendencies who becomes Jessup's companion; Jessup's daughter Sissy; and her fiancé Julian Falck. Windrip's American "Gestapo," the Minute Men, discover the plot, and Jessup and Julian are sent to a concentration camp. After several years Lorinda helps Jessup to escape to Canada, and when the Windrip government declares war against Mexico he takes an active part in the revolutionary uprising which results.

This "novel of the future" is an interesting exercise in extrapolation; its action begins in 1936 (i.e., one year after its publication) and continues through 1939, the year in which the fascist governments of the world actually succeeded in plunging Europe into war. It demonstrates a thesis which Americans often tend to forget: that if dictatorship should come to America it would come disguised in the nation's highest principles (e.g., "Minute Men"). The change of attitude which Jessup undergoes is significant; at the beginning of the novel he is vaguely liberal and dislikes violence. He and other liberals

permit, or tolerate, the accession to power of a totalitarian government. Then gradually Jessup realizes that passive liberalism is inadequate to cope with the situation; dictatorship must be fought through
an active revolutionary struggle. The novel thus reflects the militant
anti-fascism which developed in Lewis in the period immediately
before the Second World War.

ELLIOT PAUL (1891-1958)

Although he expected his reputation to be made on his novels,
Elliot Paul will be remembered chiefly for his two autobiographical
accounts of expatriate life in Europe and his part in founding the
important avant-garde review *transition*. *The Life and Death of a
Spanish Town* and *The Last Time I Saw Paris* are important documents in American literary history, whatever their intrinsic merit may
be: they sum up, perhaps better than any other two books, the nostalgia for Europe that led so many American intellectuals and writers
to abandon their country in the period between the two wars. They
bear comparison with similar books of Hemingway, for instance, *The
Sun Also Rises,* but there is an important difference: where Hemingway is concerned mainly with his own reactions to Europe and with
studies of other American expatriates, Paul tries to get at the essence
of European culture, especially the culture of the humble classes, the
working people among whom he chose to live. That Hemingway is
capable of this is shown by *For Whom the Bell Tolls.* Yet this is after
all an adventure story; it makes no serious attempt to give a comprehensive picture of the Spanish people. Paul is a better naturalist; his
goal is to portray an accurate cross-section of the life of a people.
But if his intention is sociological, his style is journalistic; in spite of
his personal connection with Jolas, Stein, Joyce, and other experimentalists he is relatively unconcerned with problems of literary technique. His intention is simply to get the idea across. "When you write
rapidly you write in your own style," he said in an interview with
Robert Van Gelder. "There is no good in trying for style by rewriting,
by torturing sentences. You knock the life out of it and probably out
of your ideas." Because of his journalistic background he often seems
to be writing for an audience which needs everything explained to it
and would be shocked by candid references to sex. When he mentions
France's chief Catholic novelist of the twentieth century he feels

obliged to explain, "Paul Claudel, a French writer, was sent to Washington as an ambassador." His accounts of the life of the flesh in the Rue de la Huchette are discreet, even prudish, when compared with *The Sun Also Rises* or Miller's *Tropic of Cancer*. It is for such reasons that *The Last Time I Saw Paris* became a best-seller, while *Tropic of Cancer* has not yet been admitted into the United States.

Paul began his literary career during his Paris period with three novels all more or less in the same style, impressionistic, consciously bohemian and anti-bourgeois in attitude, and rather immature in treatment: *Indelible* (1922), *Impromptu* (1923), and *Imperturbe* (1924). A group of novels in his middle period (*ca.* 1930) shows a more naturalistic technique, often attempting a cross-section of a community in the same way as *The Last Time I Saw Paris: Low Run Tide* (1929), the story of the decline of a New England fishing village, is typical of these. Since the Second World War he has devoted himself chiefly to an autobiography in several volumes under the general title of *Items on the Grand Account;* the volumes include, so far, *Linden on the Saugus Branch* (1947), *A Ghost Town on the Yellowstone* (1948), and *My Old Kentucky Home* (1949). He has also written a number of mystery stories of a satirical tendency.

LIFE: Elliot Harold Paul was born in 1891 in Malden, Massachusetts. After a few months at the University of Maine he went west to work at a number of odd jobs, then joined the Army Signal Corps to serve in France during the First World War. He stayed in France when the war was over, making his living writing for the Associated Press and for the Paris editions of the *Chicago Tribune* and the *New York Herald*. He soon became a familiar figure in the American expatriate circle: bearded, vigorous, a talented musician and a master of idiomatic French, popular with working-class Frenchmen and with the humble inhabitants of the Rue de la Huchette, just off the Boulevard Saint-Michel in the Latin Quarter. In 1927 he joined the French critic Eugène Jolas in founding the review *transition,* which became the most important center of expatriate writing in Paris during the Thirties and published authors of such stature as Gertrude Stein, Hemingway, Hart Crane, James Joyce, and W. C. Williams. In 1931 Paul went to live at Santa Eulalia, on the island of Ibiza in the Balearic Islands. In 1936 he managed to escape from Santa Eulalia just before the arrival of Fascist troops. In 1939 he returned to the United States, where he made his headquarters thereafter. He was married twice, the second time to Flora Thompson Brown, who appears along with Paul's son in *Life and Death of a Spanish Town*. Paul died in 1958.

CHIEF WORKS: *Life and Death of a Spanish Town* (autobiography, 1937) is two books in one: it is an account of Paul's life with his family in the Balearic town of Santa Eulalia del Rio on the island of Ibiza between 1931 and 1936, and it is a study of Spanish culture in general as exemplified in the life of this small town, especially in its reactions to the political events of 1931-36 and the outbreak of the Spanish Civil War. The term autobiography is not a very accurate one to apply to this book, since Paul is not writing about himself but about the town and its inhabitants; yet "journalism" does not adequately describe it either, since its approach is entirely subjective and literary. The first half of the book is a humorous but sympathetic study of folk-manners: the noble indolence of the Spanish temperament, the eternal conflict between Left (the fishermen, the town artisans, the intellectuals) and Right (the priests, the landowners, the Guardia Civil), and the contrast between the calm serenity of the Spanish town and the neurotic "go-getter" pace of life in America. The second half of the book, describing the events leading up to the Civil War and the outbreak of violence in Santa Eulalia, is markedly different in style; it is terse, dramatic, and militantly partisan in its bias for the Loyalist cause. The account of the shelling of the town by a Loyalist gunboat and the consequent evacuation of the town (Chapters 19-20) is a well-written and dramatic piece of narrative, as is the story of the final escape of Paul and his family from the island in a German destroyer. Although the style of this book is generally straightforward and conventional, there are occasional passages demonstrating the influence of Gertrude Stein and the *transition* writers, for instance this from Chapter 19, suggesting the Hemingway of *Big Two-Hearted River:* "When the pieces were well browned, I put a little bacon into the hot center, let the grease fry out, then added a cupful of *Marques de Argentera (tinto)* and let simmer slowly. Slowly bubbling, with especial care, for I wanted so badly to pay strict attention and watch slow bubbling, smelling tones of bacon and the sea and the wine from sunny slopes and thinking after all that it was a simple dish to make since worthy pig the sea had been working on the octopus for at least a dozen years and the sun had conjured vines from the earth and grapes that gave wine of an inimitable flavor." Passages such as these have the unmistakable quality of American expatriate writing of the Twenties.

The Last Time I Saw Paris (autobiography, 1942) covers the periods both before and after the events of *Life and Death of a Spanish Town,* roughly 1920-31 and 1937-39. During most of this period Paul lived in the Hôtel du Caveau in the Rue de la Huchette. *The Last Time I Saw Paris* is a detailed portrait of this short street, its shops and hotels, and its inhabitants. There are several dozen main characters, none of whom dominates the narrative; structurally the book is merely a documentary study of a typical Paris quarter. The treatment, however, is personal and informal. There are occasional lyric passages similar to the one quoted above from *Life and Death of a Spanish Town,* but in general the style is intended to appeal to the general American reading audience. The best parts of the book are the conversations with the young Hyacinthe Goujon, a sensitive, spirited, and dissatisfied girl whom Paul treats as a kind of symbol of the French temperament. Yet Paul is curiously reticent about personal confessions; his more intimate relations with the inhabitants of the street are only hinted, and the events described, although occasionally Rabelaisian, are nothing that an American student could not write home to his mother. Yet the book is a valuable document of the attitude of the typical American expatriate toward Paris in the Twenties and Thirties. It is interesting to compare it with the genteel admiration shown by Henry James for France (e.g., in *The Ambassadors*) or with the fervent francophilia of Edith Wharton (e.g. *A Son at the Front*). Paul is severely critical in some aspects of French culture: government corruption, technical inefficiency, the insolence and incompetence of public servants. "Never in the history of France has the ordinary citizen received good service of any kind." Yet in the end, knowing France better, he admires it more truly than did either James or Mrs. Wharton, who knew and admired its "civilization" rather than its daily life. *The Last Time I Saw Paris* is indispensable reading for an understanding of the American expatriate movement in the period between the two wars.

HENRY MILLER (born 1891)

It is difficult to assess the importance of an American writer whose two most important books have never been published in the United States, who is surrounded by a fervent and evidently maladjusted band of disciples, and who obviously owes much of the limited popularity he enjoys to the sensational aspect of his work. On the one hand it would be a mistake to take Miller on his own valuation, or that of his followers; on the other hand it is impossible to dismiss him as a mere pornographic exhibitionist. Probably his main importance in American literature is analogous to that of Scott Fitzgerald: he epitomizes and records a certain social phenomenon peculiar to his generation, in his case the revolt of the American expatriates in Paris against the puritanism, the sterility, and the "respectability" of their homeland. In a sense he is not really a novelist at all. Most of his so-called fiction is actually autobiography, although there is evidently a certain amount of exaggeration and hyperbolic drum-beating in it. It resembles the "fictionalized autobiography" of Elliot Paul except that where Paul remains an observer, chiefly interested in the lives of the people around him, Miller is interested primarily, perhaps exclusively, in himself. A certain amount of pose is involved; Miller obviously fancies himself as a rebellious and satanic hero who is as physically irresistible to women as he is obnoxious to the bourgeois. His fiction is unabashedly frank; if his two *Tropic* books are not pornography (and the American Customs authorities have decided that they are) they sometimes skirt it dangerously. Like D. H. Lawrence, he stands for the complete destruction of sexual and other taboos which stand in the way of the fulfillment of the individual; but unlike Lawrence he is often led by this credo into a preoccupation with the abnormal and degraded aspects of sexuality. But all these comments, while true, have nothing to do with his literary quality; they are remarks that might as easily be made about Cellini or Rousseau, both writers of autobiography with whom Miller shows an affinity of personality.

Upon actual inspection Miller's work is often energetic and talented, if not competent. Most of its faults are due to his own pose of genius: he is impulsive and careless in style, and often merely suggests through involved circumlocution what a better writer would have worked to express in concise and lucid form. His merits are those that go with his faults: energy, spontaneity, Rabelaisian humor, colorful if somewhat grotesque characterizations, a freshness of metaphor and dialogue. The best parts of his novels are the autobiographical passages, the pictures he draws of his own character in the process of formation. The sketches of male cronies, for example the confused and naive expatriate Fillmore in *Tropic of Cancer,* are also often superb. The characterizations of women are usually inferior; Miller is not interested in the more subtle or human aspects of female temperament.

An important aspect of Miller's work is the influence he has exerted on little-magazine and avant-garde writing in America. Numerous reviews (e.g., *The Tiger's Eye*) have been founded by his disciples or imitators, and whole bookstores have been devoted to his work, especially in the San Francisco-Berkeley area. His influence in Europe has also been important; in avant-garde literary circles in France, for example, he is often considered one of the most prominent American writers of the century. If *Tropic of Capricorn* and *Tropic of Cancer* are ever admitted to the United States, his reputation may at last be given a fair contest in his own country.

LIFE: Henry Miller was born in 1891 in New York of German-American parents; he spoke German himself until he began to go to school. During his boyhood he was a model juvenile delinquent; he quit City College in disgust, drifted from job to job, and by his own admission swindled his father out of a fund for his further education to spend the money on a female companion twice his age. Around the time of the First World War he dabbled with Communism; he met Emma Goldman in San Diego, but was unable to apply himself to the aims of the Party any more than he could concentrate on any other extended project. For five years beginning in 1920 he held one of the few steady jobs of his career: employment manager for a New York utilities company. This experience he incorporated almost verbatim into *Tropic of Capricorn.* His first book, *Clipped Wings,* was written in 1923; it was a study of twelve eccentric messengers, based on his telegraph company experience. He visited Europe briefly in 1928 and returned for a nine-year sojourn in 1930. In Paris he joined a group of avant-garde literary expatriates whose informal chief he soon became; he wrote his two most important novels during this period under conditions of extreme poverty and dissipation. He returned to American soil in 1939; a vitriolic essay on American culture, *The Air-Conditioned Nightmare,* appeared in 1945. Since the war he has lived chiefly at Big Sur, on the California coast near Monterey, where a considerable colony of writers, artists, and eccentrics has gathered around him.

CHIEF NOVELS: *Tropic of Cancer* (autobiographical novel, 1931) is based on the author's experience as an expatriate in Paris, where he lived in poverty in the St. Germain quarter in the midst of a frantic circus of eccentrics: his roommate Boris, the half-mad Van Norden, and many others, including a monotonous succession of women each irresistibly attracted to the hero. The better parts of the book are the chapters where Miller momentarily departs from the cataloguing of his amatory escapades and turns to the study of character: the description of the eccentric Hindu Nanantatee, or the disconnected episode in which the hero, desperate for money, travels to Dijon to take a job as lycée instructor and is bored to the brink of lunacy. Also justly famous is the passage near the end of the novel in which the hero encounters his friend Fillmore, who has married a French girl and settled down to respectable boredom. Fillmore, at the end of the encounter, has gone off in a drunken haze to return to America, and the hero has calmly pocketed the money Fillmore has given him to provide for his abandoned wife.

Tropic of Capricorn (autobiographical novel, 1939), although written subsequently, concerns an earlier period in Miller's life. It begins with a discussion of his family background and takes him through the interlude of his steady job, through his intellectual awakening and the discovery of his own personality, to the point in his life where he determined to abandon America and turn to a literary vocation in Europe. A more evenly written book, it lacks the blatant obscenity of *Tropic of Cancer* but lacks its shrewdly-drawn character sketches as well. The character of Miller's father is notable, however, and the description of the daily routine in a telegraph office is a little masterpiece of its kind. Most of *Tropic of Capricorn* is laid in New York City and Brooklyn.

Two non-fiction works of Miller deserve brief mention. *The Colossus of Maroussi; or The Spirit of Greece* (1941) is an unusual and highly subjective travel book, a favorite among Miller's inner circle of admirers; and *The Air-Conditioned Nightmare* (1945) is a caustic summary of American culture, based on Miller's reactions upon his return to America from his long exile in France. This second book, along with Philip Wylie's *Generation of Vipers* (1943), is one of the most violent rejections of American materialism and puritanism to appear in the twentieth century. It lacks Mencken's wit and Sinclair Lewis' social insight, however, and it is interesting chiefly for the light it sheds on Miller's personality and attitude.

In the post-1945 period two shorter works by Miller appeared in America in popular editions. *Nights of Love and Laughter* (1955) collects short pieces written between 1939 and 1947. The two most interesting of these are "The Alcoholic Veteran With the Washboard Cranium," a long monologue by a somewhat confused iconoclast whom Miller evidently met in a bar, and "Via Dieppe-Newhaven," an autobiographical account of an incident in which Miller, attempting to visit England during his stay in Europe, was barred from the country by the British authorities as a vagrant and an undesirable. A short excerpt from *The Colossus of Maroussi* is also included. *A Devil in Paradise* (1956) is an autobiographical novel laid in Big Sur; it is devoted chiefly to a character sketch of Conrad Moricand, an eccentric Swiss astrologer whom Miller brought to America out of charity and who proceeded to tyrannize over the household through his hypochondria, his egocentricity, and his elaborate and pathological fastidiousness. This short novel, which begins in the brash style of the *Tropic* books, succeeds in the end in drawing a vivid and poignant characterization; the reader is brought powerfully to share the mixture of aversion and pity which Miller feels for the grotesque figure of Moricand.

JOHN P. MARQUAND (born 1893)

Even more than Scott Fitzgerald, Marquand is the heir of the literary tradition of Henry James and Edith Wharton. He is conservative in his social attitude, yet he is satirical in his treatment of the very aristocrats he admires; he is a modernist in the sense that he recognizes the obsolescence of the tradition of New England gentility, yet in literary technique he is conventional, even old-fashioned. He has little sympathy with the more radical literary experiments of his age;

he rejects the characters of Steinbeck and Hemingway and Fitzgerald because to him they seem freakish, because "they were never like anyone I knew." Like Edith Wharton, he seems slightly shocked by the manners of the new age; he recognizes the existence of sexual license, profanity, and other vulgar realities of the post-1918 age, but he cannot bring himself to take them for granted as a Faulkner or a Hemingway does.

Like Howells and James, Marquand is basically a novelist of manners in the New England literary tradition. If he differs from these two, it is because he lived a half-century later under new conditions and among a new race of people. His typical hero is a New England gentleman of distinguished family who finds himself somewhat incongruously living in the twentieth century and tries to make the best of it. On the one hand his hero feels like a stranger amid the vulgar and crass materialism and the casual morality of the twentieth century, and on the other hand he rebels, as a twentieth-century man, against the rigid conventions of his traditional background, which he instinctively resents as obsolete. His continually recurring themes are the conflict between conformity and individualism and the waste of human power in creative individuals who are forced to live according to the standards set by earlier generations. Around this framework he builds novels of careful and profusely detailed precision. If he is a realist (and this is the most satisfactory way to classify him) it is in his thorough and studied mastery of his subject-matter, in the care with which he studies his upper-class milieu and transcribes its every detail faithfully into his fiction. In style Marquand is competent but unremarkable; his dialogue is slightly more terse and "modern" than that of Henry James, but is basically in the Jamesian tradition. He is fond of the flashback as a structural device and uses it extensively, especially in *Point of No Return,* where virtually the entire story is told in flashbacks. In *The Late George Apley* he uses an even more venerable form: the "papers" left behind by a great man, used by a biographer to construct an official picture of his life. It resembles both Howells' *The Rise of Silas Lapham* and Thomas Mann's *Doktor Faustus* (1947) in its construction and in its retrospective point of view. Marquand, who began as a popular magazine writer, learned conventional writing thoroughly, and he seldom departs from popular style, form, and construction even in his more pretentious works.

LIFE: John Phillips Marquand was born in Wilmington, Delaware in 1893; his mother's family was traditionally of New England, and his maternal grandfather was a brother of Margaret Fuller. During his boyhood he lived at Rye, N. Y. and at Newburyport, Massachusetts. In 1907 the financial slump greatly reduced the wealth of his family, and he was obliged to work his way through Harvard, which he did in three years. He worked as a journalist, served in the army in the Mexican campaign of 1916 and in the First World War, and tried advertising for a while, but presently quit and determined to make his living by writing. His first fiction, a romantic historical novel entitled *The Unspeakable Gentleman,* appeared in *The Ladies' Home Journal* in 1922. From that time until 1937 he wrote popular fiction, chiefly magazine stories of the formula variety; the period is also the era of the famous Mr. Moto stories, adventurous romances built around the figure of a Japanese secret agent (e.g., *Thank You, Mr. Moto,* 1936). His first novel of literary importance was *The Late George Apley* in 1937; it proved to be a popular as well as a critical success, and since then he has turned out similar novels steadily but slowly, at the rate of approximately one every two years. Meanwhile he continued to write formula fiction; the Mr. Moto books continued until the international events of 1941 made the theme unsuitable for light literature. In addition to *The Late George Apley,* his most important novels are *Wickford Point* (1939), *H. M. Pulham, Esq.* (1941), *So Little Time* (1943), *Repent in Haste* (1945), *B. F.'s Daughter* (1946), *Point of No Return* (1949), *Melville Goodwin, U.S.A.* (1951), and *Sincerely, Willis Wayde* (1955). Mr. Marquand has been married twice, the second time in 1937, and has five children.

CHIEF NOVELS: *The Late George Apley* (1937) is presented as the biography of an eminent Bostonian who is born in 1866 and dies in 1933, ostensibly written by the staid, conventional, respectful, and somewhat obtuse Horatio Willing. Thus the satire is double-edged; the reader sees the pedanticism and conventionality of Willing as well as the futility of the life of George Apley. Apley, born at the height of the era of Boston gentility, is thoroughly at home in the world of his youth. When he goes to Harvard, however, he falls in love with an "unsuitable" girl, Mary Monahan, and his family is forced to break up the affair and pack him off on a sea voyage. He conforms; he accepts the conventions of his family and society, works at an acceptable profession, and marries Catharine Bosworth, a fiancée selected by his family. As he lives into the twentieth century, however, Apley sees the traditions by which his family lived crumbling about him. His son marries a divorced woman and his daughter goes off with the kind of an "unsuitable" mate he was denied in college, he is confused by the "immoral" new novels and angered by prohibition, and he is finally struck down by the market crash of 1929, which leaves his personal fortune relatively untouched but destroys his faith in the established economic order. Before he dies in 1933 he begins to perceive the mistake of his life: that he tried to live it according to the standards of a previous generation. This novel, Marquand's most intricate technical accomplishment, was awarded a Pulitzer Prize in 1938.

  Wickford Point (novel, 1939) is the study of a slick popular writer named Jim Calder. In many respects his career parallels Marquand's: he is born about the same time of a respectable but not wealthy family, goes to Harvard, serves in the World War, and makes his living by writing formula fiction. The difference is that Jim Calder never writes a novel as good as *George Apley* or *Wickford Point;* as he himself eventually realizes, he lacks the true creativity needed to to be a great writer. The title refers to the estate of the Brills, Calder's conventional and snobbish relations; much of the novel concerns the life of the Brills, especially the marital crises and confusion of the attractive and popular Bella. *Wickford Point* is a triumph of technical competence. The story is told almost entirely through flashbacks; its approach to its material is discreetly satirical, and the portraits of Calder and Bella are especially perceptive and convincing.

  H. M. Pulham, Esq. (novel, 1941) is similar to *George Apley;* the main difference is that the action focuses more on the hero's personal love-life and less on his family and public affairs. Pulham, like Apley, abandons an earlier love under pressure from his family and instead marries a "suitable" girl. Twenty years later he meets his earlier sweetheart again, and decides to throw up everything and run away with her. At the last moment, however, his conventional character asserts itself, and he returns to his wife to live out a monotonous and respectable life. His conflict is paralleled by a similar one in the life of his wife Kay; she too considers running away with an old lover, but changes her mind and stays with Pulham.

Point of No Return (novel, 1949) established a well-known American metaphor. Charley Gray, a successful and rising banker, stops in the middle of his career and wonders whether it has been worth while. He decides, however, that it is too late for him to seek a more creative or spiritual way of life; he has passed the "point of no return" in his journey toward conventional success, and can only live out his life in the career he has chosen.

Sincerely, Willis Wayde (novel, 1955) is Marquand's most cutting and satirical portrait of an American business-man. The hero resembles Lewis' Babbitt more than he does anything else in Marquand's work; he has an infinite capacity for hypocritical rationalizing and sentimental self-deception. His life is devoted to a consecrated and solemn struggle for success; he does push-ups every morning, reads Dr. Eliot's Five-Foot Shelf of Harvard Classics as other people take medicine, and continues to make "business contacts" through his honeymoon. Yet in the end the reader is brought to sympathize with him, just as he is with Lewis' Babbitt; Wayde is after all "sincere," as the title implies, even in his materialism and his go-getter ideals, and in the end he is a victim of the standards around him more than of his own weakness. The final scene, in which his wife tucks him into bed with a kiss and a Nembutal, is masterful.

JOHN DOS PASSOS (born 1869)

Although Dos Passos is sometimes considered primarily a proletarian propagandist, his main contribution to literature has lain in the technical development of the novel. In the tradition of Zola, he treats humanity as a pattern of conflicting social masses rather than as an aggregation of individuals. This attitude owes something to the modern scientific tendency to study social groups with laboratory techniques (i.e., modern sociology) as well as to the Marxian idea of the class struggle; the Dos Passos "collective novel" is a sort of sociological experiment in fictional form. Unlike Zola, however, Dos Passos treats this sociological material with a new and radical technique; his style is far more original than his content. Dos Passos is one of the founders of the modern *roman fleuve* or pattern novel, a work lacking any plot in the usual sense and composed of an intricate patchwork of characters linked together by their common participation in a social situation. The apparent aimlessness of the *roman fleuve* is intentional; it is merely the purposelessness of nature seen at too close a vantage, a purposelessness which resolves itself to the detached observer as an ingenious machinery. Dos Passos worked experimentally with this technique in *Three Soldiers* (1921) and *Manhattan Transfer* (1925) and brought it to fruition in the trilogy *U.S.A.* (1930-36). His influence in this respect has been tremendous, especially in Europe; Jean-Paul Sartre has called him "the best novelist of our time" and imitated him frankly in his *Roads to Freedom* series. Along with Joyce, he has influenced a whole generation of young writers in the Thirties and later who sought new and radical forms for the novel.

Dos Passos' failings are those of most collective novelists: he seldom creates memorable characters, since he is little interested in individuals, and his work continually hovers on the brink of propaganda. But his books remain fixed in the reader's mind if his characters do not. Dos Passos is by inclination a creative artist; if he is momentarily carried by his passion to undermine a rotten capitalistic system, he never forgets that the duty of the artist is to create a striking and original world of the imagination.

LIFE: Dos Passos was born in Chicago in 1896 of middle-class parentage. He graduated from Harvard in 1916; he served in the First World War as an ambulance attendant and later as a private in the U.S. Medical Corps. He published *One Man's Initiation,* a somewhat immature novel, in 1920; his first important work was *Three Soldiers* (1921), a pacifistic novel based on his experience in the war; *Three Soldiers* was one of the first of the cynical novels of the Twenties denouncing war as a conspiracy of Wall Street and the munitions makers. Thus far his novel technique had been reasonably conventional; but in *Manhattan Transfer* (1925) he took a bold step forward. The complex pattern technique he attempted here in its raw form he strengthened in the *U.S.A.* trilogy, which began appearing in 1930 and which gained him acceptance as a major novelist.

During the early part of his career Dos Passos was a typical independent Marxist. He aided the fight of the Kentucky coal miners against their bosses and was jailed for his activity on behalf of Sacco and Vanzetti. *Three Soldiers* and *Manhattan Transfer* contain a great deal of proletarian propaganda; their political content is as one-sided as their fictional technique is objective. In the late Thirties, however, Dos Passos became an active anti-communist; he even condemned the New Deal as excessively collectivistic.

In 1939 Dos Passos began a second trilogy of American life, this time less technically radical, treating the period of the New Deal and the Spanish Civil War. The series, published under the general title of *District of Columbia,* began with *Adventures of a Young Man* (1939) and continued with *Number One* (1943), a study of an American demagogue modeled on Huey Long, and *The Grand Design* (1939), mainly concerned with the New Deal and the approach of the Second World War. His most recent novel, *Most Likely to Succeed* (1954), reflects a further turn to the right in his political and social attitude; it is satirical in style and sharply critical of radicals and bohemians in the period of the Thirties.

CHIEF NOVELS: *Three Soldiers* (1921) is a pacifistic study of a cross-section of the American army in the First World War, somewhat resembling Remarque's *All Quiet on the Western Front* in attitude and construction. The novel is interesting for its technical innovations; its form is totally "decentralized," without a central character and without a single plot to hold it together artistically. Although Dos Passos does not fully exploit the possibilities of the technique, we can see here the germ of the style which is improved in *Manhattan Transfer* and brought to perfection in *U.S.A.* The three soldiers of the title are Dan Fuselli, a shrewd Italian-American who fits easily into army life and remains cheerfully ignorant of the wider implications of the war; Chrisfield, an uneducated yokel from Indiana who is a misfit in the army and who eventually succeeds in murdering a personal enemy in the excitement of combat; and John Andrews, the most important of the three, a sensitive and creative college graduate who resents the stupid discipline of the army, deserts, acquires a French girl, studies music in Paris, and is arrested by M.P.'s at the end of the novel. Although the narrative seems confused, a pattern lies underneath: all the soldiers go into the army full of naive enthusiasm and chauvinism, and are rudely disillusioned by the experi-

ence of the reality of war. Another process takes place simultaneously: the awakening of the more perceptive American soldiers to
the sophistication and culture of Europe, the attraction of a world
they never suspected in their pre-1914 provincialism. Thus Dos
Passos demonstrates the formation of two important social attitudes,
the disillusionment and cynicism of the postwar generation and the
cult of everything European, and especially French, in America during the Twenties. Andrews, the only fully rounded and convincing
character in the novel, is well done; his attitudes toward the war and
toward French culture make him a symbol of the whole "lost generation" of intellectuals.

Manhattan Transfer (novel, 1925) is a cross-sectional panorama
of a city at work. The action begins in 1904 and continues through
the era after the First World War, the "Jazz Age." There is no consistent plot, neither are there protagonists in the ordinary sense; the
novel is a checkerboard composed of the careers of diverse and
disconnected characters each wandering his way through life in an
aimless and despairing fashion. None of these characters are ac-
quainted in the beginning, but their lives become linked through a
curious set of coincidences. In the end their destinies are intricately
interwoven; each is a part of society, and what each does has its due
impact on the others.

The most important of these characters are: Jimmy Herf, a frustrated reporter who suffers from the same sense of purposelessness
that many of Scott Fitzgerald's characters do; Stanwood Emery, a
young playboy who burns himself out pursuing a succession of women
and eventually dies in an apartment fire; George Baldwin, an excessively ambitious young lawyer; Oglethorpe, a degenerate capitalist;
and Congo Jake, a French seaman who becomes a successful res-
taurateur and, with the advent of Prohibition, a bootlegger. Knitting
the whole story together is Ellen Thatcher, a sensitive and unhappy
actress who marries two other characters of the novel in succession
and whose fortunes become linked with most of the others before the
novel ends. *Manhattan Transfer* is in many respects a careless and
immature work; the documentation is often inaccurate, and there are
an improbable and astonishing number of fatal fires, auto accidents,
crimes, suicides, and speakeasy brawls crammed into the action. The
attempts to reproduce New York dialects are also unimpressive,

especially in the case of the rich. Dos Passos attempts to evoke the tempo of the era by quoting snatches of popular songs, headlines, and public speeches, a device he was to develop more fully in *U.S.A.*

In *Manhattan Transfer* Dos Passos has not yet worked out the systematic political attitude he was to present later in *U.S.A.* Several characters are socialists or radicals, and the corruption of the capitalistic system is shown by implication, but the novel is by no means a revolutionary tract. The total effect is rather a pessimistic sense of futility, resulting from the inability of the characters to find any meaning in their lives. The postwar generation is portrayed as bitter and disillusioned; the collapse of their ideals after the war has left them in a spiritual vacuum in which nothing seems worth doing. The chief importance of the novel lies in the one-sided but convincing portrait it presents of the "lost generation" and in the stylistic innovations to be developed further in *U.S.A.*

U.S.A. (novel trilogy, 1930-36) is actually a single novel divided into three parts: *The 42nd Parallel* (1930), *Nineteen-Nineteen* (1932), and *The Big Money* (1936). The work was reissued in one volume in 1937. As in *Manhattan Transfer,* there is no comprehensive plot; the work is filled with a profusion of characters who grow up, mate, struggle, succeed or fail, and die without finding any particular meaning in their lives. The ostensible purpose of the work is to paint a complete panorama of American life in the era from 1900 through the Thirties. This is admittedly a staggering project. Dos Passos fails principally in that his picture of America is partisan rather than objective; the basic approach of the novel is that of classic Marxist criticism of capitalistic society. Capitalism, materialism, the factory system, and the "American way of life" are ruthlessly attacked. As a result of this basically negative approach there are few sympathetic characters; the reader finds it as difficult to admire Dos Passos' social workers and labor organizers as his swollen bosses and bankers.

U.S.A. is nevertheless an interesting and important novel if only from the point of view of technique. Only parts of it are narrative in the ordinary sense. Interwoven into the fictional plot are various forms of documentary materials. "Biographies" are short impressionistic accounts of the lives of eminent Americans ranging from Thorstein Veblen and Ford to Woodrow Wilson, written in a style resembling free verse with lines broken to indicate reading stress. These sketches include portraits of labor leaders and radicals, who are usually shown as martyrs of the capitalistic system, and biographies of business "moguls" and statesmen who have built the system and now control it. "Newsreels," the second type of documentary insertions, are paste-pot compositions made up of the speeches, headlines, and popular songs of the time; these sections are intended to evoke the mood of the age. Slanting is apparent here; the headlines are carefully chosen to demonstrate the viciousness of the capitalistic system and the irresponsibility of the idle rich. "The Camera Eye," the third type of inserted material, presents semi-autobiographical impressions written in stream-of-consciousness style. The unnamed protagonist of the Camera Eye sections grows gradually older as the novel proceeds; he represents the author's own consciousness as it moved through the era being described. The best of the documentary materials, however, are the Biographies; the sketches of Ford and Wilson are little masterpieces, and are frequently reprinted.

Each of the characters of *U.S.A.* has his own destiny and his own story; these destinies are interlinked, yet the threads are distinct and separate. The pattern is somewhat confused in the chronological presentation of the novel, and can best be analyzed if the careers of the chief characters are considered separately. These chief characters are as follows:

J. WARD MOREHOUSE is a self-made man, labor politician, and publicist who uses his winning manner to achieve great wealth and power. He marries twice; his first wife, Annabelle Strang, provides him with the money he needs to make a start in the world, and his second, Gertrude Staple, assists him in his career through her influence and advice. During the First World War he serves the government, and with this start he becomes a publicist and advertising executive in the postwar period. Symbolically he represents the ambition and opportunism which continually threaten to corrupt the labor movement.

ELEANOR STODDARD is an artistic and intelligent girl, refined in taste and sexually cold, who reacts violently against her sordid childhood by spending her life in a search for beauty. She becomes an interior decorator in New York, where she meets Morehouse and becomes his platonic companion. During the war she serves in the Red Cross. In the postwar period considerable success comes her way, but her monotonous and spiritually empty life leaves her dissatisfied.

RICHARD SAVAGE is a sensitive idealist who goes to Harvard, becomes an aesthete and something of a snob, but develops enough character to join a volunteer ambulance unit with the outbreak of the war in 1914. Later he serves as an officer in the American army. During the war his ideals are selfless and liberal, even radical; but in the postwar era he is driven by the cynicism he inherits from his generation to "sell out" and go to work for Morehouse's advertising agency. Savage represents the disillusionment of the intellectual class and its abandonment of the liberal ideal in the postwar period.

MARY FRENCH, daughter of a physician, spends her childhood in Trinidad. Like Savage, she is intensely idealistic in her youth; she retains this idealism longer than any other character in the novel. She becomes a social worker, then secretary to a union official. While working on the Sacco-Vanzetti aid committee she meets Don Stevens, a Communist Party member; the pair become engaged. But Don goes to Moscow and returns with a wife "assigned" him by the Party, and Mary's disillusionment with the radical movement comes at last. She continues to devote her life to the liberal cause, but her heart is no longer in it.

EVALINE HUTCHINS is an unhappy young woman who feels an inclination toward art but has little talent. Although at one time she is Eleanor Stoddard's partner in a decorating business, her life is a failure. She tries to forget this through experiments in sensualism, but becomes constantly more bored and neurotic. At last she takes her own life through an overdose of sleeping pills.

Secondary characters are Mac McCreary, an underprivileged boy from a shanty-Irish family who becomes successively a salesman of pornographic books, an itinerant printer, a reluctant husband and family man, and a revolutionary in Mexico; Janey Williams, a stenographer who cuts her family when she gets a "respectable" position as Morehouse's secretary; Charley Anderson, a talented inventor who becomes wealthy in the airplane business and turns into a typical capitalist; and Benny Compton, a Jewish labor agitator who is jailed several times, once for a long term in a Federal prison, and eventually becomes the paramour of Mary French.

Although *U.S.A.* presents a picture of the postwar generation similar to that found in *Manhattan Transfer,* its political message is stronger and more specific. In many respects it is a typical Marxist novel. The characters are divided sharply into "haves" and "have-nots"; the first are ruthless and corrupt, and the second bitter and frustrated. Most of the chief characters begin as idealists, and from there go on to one of two paths. The "haves" acquire success and gradually lose their idealism, "sell out," and turn to a ruthless self-aggrandizement; the backbone of the capitalistic class is made up of former idealists. The "have-nots" also begin as idealists, but find little success; the capitalistic world crushes them down, and even their own radical movement disillusions them through its cynicism and the opportunism of its leaders. It is individualism—i.e., opportunism and ambition—which continually threatens the radical movement. The renegades of labor are those, like Mac McCreary, who put their personal affairs ahead of their devotion to the movement. The capitalistic system is so firmly entrenched that democratic means are powerless to eradicate it; it is only through solidarity, mass action, and class warfare that the socialist state can be achieved. It is in virtue of the foregoing that *U.S.A.* is a Marxist novel. Its principal "heresies" with respect to Marxism are the unfavorable light in which it shows the proletariat, its exposure of the cynical tactics of labor leaders, and the implied criticism of the Soviet Union in cases such as that of Don Stevens.

The total impact of the novel is great; the reader is left with a powerful, if somewhat one-sided, picture of life in the Twenties and Thirties. The novel effectively presents the message that the capitalistic system is corrupt and anachronistic and that the hope of the future lies in some variety of radicalism. But Dos Passos is a better polemicist than he is a political planner; no real blueprint of the socialist state, no positive political ideology other than revolution is presented. Here Dos Passos reflects the attitude of the period he is describing; the intellectual temper of the pre-New-Deal era was critical rather than constructive. The novel is undeniably one of the most ambitious attempts thus far to present an encompassing panorama of American life in the twentieth century.

F. SCOTT FITZGERALD (1896-1940)

In addition to its intrinsic literary merit, which critics tend to regard more highly as time goes on, Scott Fitzgerald's work is important today as the record of an age: the Jazz Age period which began with the First World War and continued into the era of the Depression. At the same time it should be noted that Fitzgerald, like most creative artists, was not entirely a part of the society he portrayed. He installed himself well enough in this society to gain acceptance as the official literary spokesman of the Jazz Age; but at the same time, as Malcolm Cowley says, "he stood outside the ballroom, a little Midwestern boy with his nose to the glass, wondering how much the tickets cost and who paid for the music."

Fitzgerald is not a naturalist in the pseudo-scientific tradition; he never descends to shoddy or shocking realism, and there are obviously romantic elements in his work. His sympathies patently lie with the leisure classes. His love scenes are passionate in a spiritual way rather than in the physical sense; they seldom proceed beyond a kiss. Neither does he document his data methodically, although he attempted to keep notebooks for use in establishing his backgrounds. He is at his weakest in explaining the business and commercial operations of Wall Street, and at his best in transcribing the dialogue of the flappers, play boys, authors, and neurotic women among whom he passes his life. The most successful parts of his novels are those composed, like Chapter III of Book 2 of *The Beautiful and Damned,* entirely of dialogue. He has as little gift for exposition as he has for philosophical speculation, which he frequently attempts with no success whatsoever. Fitzgerald is further removed from the scientific naturalists in his lack of objectivity. He never achieves anything like a detached attitude toward his characters, and his best heroes and heroines are only thinly disguised portraits of himself. It is this characteristic that links him to Hemingway, as different as the two authors may be in other respects.

Fitzgerald's view of his age is perhaps more sound than Hemingway's. He is no social thinker, yet he intuitively grasped the significance of the stock market crash of 1929; it demonstrated to him immediately that the Twenties had been an artificial era, a never-never-land based on false illusions and false hopes, utterly lacking in reality. "The snow of twenty-nine wasn't real snow," he wrote in "Babylon Revisited." "If you didn't want it to be snow, you just paid some money." As great as his fascination was with the Jazz Age, he always observes it with a certain satirical detachment lacking in Hemingway, Dos Passos, and Paul; thus when the Depression embittered Dos Passos it merely impoverished Fitzgerald without greatly surprising him. The superficial reader often imagines Fitzgerald to be a snob. There is justice in the accusation, but if he was a snob he was at least an intelligent and conscious one. He was fascinated with wealth and success the way he was with the Jazz Age itself: as though they were delightful and fragile toys that should be enjoyed with the realization that they might break in one's hands at any moment. This was the story of his own life: his toys (marriage, success as a writer, wealth) did break in his hands, and he was left with the emptiness and futility which mark the later lives of his fictional heroes. The collection of journals, letters, and notes published in 1945 as *The Crack-Up* clearly reveal this personal tragedy. Yet if Fitzgerald could not escape the social collapse he himself predicted and understood, he greeted the disaster with courage; he himself seems in the end more admirable, a person of greater character, than any of the heroes of his novels. The difficulty is that Fitzgerald did not arrive at this mature understanding until he had written all his major novels; if he had written *This Side of Paradise* in 1940 its chief weakness, the unconvincing quality of Amory's regeneration at the end, might have been surmounted.

Fitzgerald's place in American literature is clearly defined: he records an age, and a particular social circle within that age, in the same way that Henry James does. Unfortunately he is not a stylist of James' caliber. Yet he is a more faithful realist, and this in a sense makes his work more valuable; his accurate dialogues, his careful observation of manners, styles, models, and attitudes, even of the prices of things, provide the reader with a vivid sense of reality which is lacking in James' more abstract style.

LIFE: Fitzgerald was born in St. Paul, Minnesota in a conventional middle-western suburban family. Although he dabbled in playwriting as an adolescent, his real life began when he came to Princeton in the fall of 1913. He left Princeton without a degree because of illness and poor grades, but the experience was the turning-point in his life. He wrote pieces for the *Tiger* and contributed to several campus variety shows before he left, and he remained a faithful Princeton alumnus to the end of his life. In the carefree, aristocratic, hard-drinking circle of the *Tiger* and the *Nassau Lit* he found a sense of belonging he had never known before and was never to achieve again. At Princeton he also formed several lasting friendships, of which the one with the critic Edmund Wilson was most important.

In 1917 he joined the army as a second lieutenant. He never served overseas, and spent most of his time in the service in training. On duty at Camp Sheridan, Alabama he met Zelda Sayre, whom he married in 1920. The marriage is described, with exaggerations and literary alterations, in *The Beautiful and Damned*. Zelda, in fact, served as model for a whole series of his heroines, and formed one of the most important influences on his life. She became intermittently insane after 1927 and during the later years of her life was confined in a sanatorium. From this marriage was born a daughter upon whom Fitzgerald centered his affections during the Thirties and to whom he wrote some important and revealing letters later published in *The Crack-Up*.

Fitzgerald's first important work, *This Side of Paradise,* appeared in 1920. It was an immediate success, and its author was forthwith hailed as the voice of the generation. Fitzgerald and his wife lived much abroad during the Twenties and early Thirties, especially in Paris and on the French Riviera. His major novels appeared from 1920 to 1934; a satirical novel about Hollywood, *The Last Tycoon,* was unfinished at his death but was published in 1941. Always a heavy drinker, Fitzgerald became a confirmed alcoholic during the Thirties. Although he maintained he could write only when stimulated by drink, the habit probably damaged both the quantity and the quality of his work. He had no business sense whatsoever and was continually in financial distress; this led him into hack-writing for popular magazines and into two abortive expeditions to Hollywood. He died in Los Angeles in 1940 of a heart attack aggravated by alcoholism. Although he had earned enormous sums at the height of his career, he was virtually penniless at his death.

CHIEF NOVELS: *This Side of Paradise* (1920) is Fitzgerald's most typical novel, although perhaps not his best. Ordinary as it may seem today, the book was a revelation when it was first published on the brink of the Twenties. It should be noted that this book was not written in the Jazz Age; on the contrary it helped to create the Jazz Age.

The plot is semi-autobiographical; it concerns the youth and young manhood of Amory Blaine, a spoiled and egotistical young Princeton student who turns to literature and the high life when his ambitions to become a football hero are balked. His life is principally molded by three women: Isabelle, a sort of inverted Fitzgerald who is more interested in romance than in love; Rosalind, whom he meets upon his return from the war where he serves as an officer, and who jilts him because she cannot give up the security of her wealthy background; and Eleanor Ramilly, a young madcap from an old Southern family who lures Amory into wild escapades. At the end of the novel Amory, made thoughtful by the funeral of Monsignor Darcy, an old beau of his mother's, decides to regenerate himself into "one on whom people can depend" as the churchman was. The action is evidently intended to show the development of an egotist into a "personage" or man of character and action; but since Fitzgerald at this time had not completed this transition himself, he has difficulty in demonstrating it in fiction. Autobiographical elements in this novel include the unhappiness of the brash young egotist in school and college because he is too small to play football, and the theme, recurring throughout Fitzgerald's work, of the "popular daughter," child of an old, usually Southern family who is surrounded by wealth and suitors but who comes to grief through an excess of success.

The Beautiful and Damned (novel, 1922) is a study of marriage in the Jazz Age modeled partly on Fitzgerald's own marriage with Zelda Sayres. Anthony Patch, a talented but indolent young playboy, finds no purpose in his life until he meets Gloria Gilbert, a popular debutante whose family originally came from the middle west. They marry and commence a wild orgy of spending, parties, trips, drinking, and gaiety which brings disaster on them both. Anthony becomes an alcoholic, and a wealthy, puritanical grandfather, Adam J. Patch, disinherits him when he discovers his immoral life. Rejected as an officer candidate in 1917, Anthony enlists as a private, and in a bleak Southern army camp seduces Dot, a naive small-town girl.

When Adam Patch dies, Anthony and Gloria spend their last cent fighting his will. Contrary to the expectations of the reader who is familiar with the clichés of naturalism, they do not lose this case; the will is broken, they come into thirty million dollars, and we know that Anthony's last chance to regenerate himself has been lost.

The theme of *The Beautiful and Damned* is well illustrated by a remark Anthony makes to the heartbroken Dot as he prepares to abandon her, a remark which sheds some light on Fitzgerald's own personal tragedy: "Dot . . . you'll forget. Things are sweeter when they're lost. I know—because once I wanted something and got it. It was the only thing I ever wanted badly . . . and when I got it it turned to dust in my hands."

The Great Gatsby (novel, 1925) is a character study of a wealthy Long Island parvenu, Jay Gatsby. Gatsby, who has acquired his fortune through bootlegging and other shady means, is the archetype of the American self-made man seen through the alcoholic and frenzied haze of the Jazz Age; he throws enormous and colossally expensive parties, he recalls his struggling youth with maudlin romanticism, and he seeks brutally and confidently to rearrange his friends' lives to suit himself. When he reencounters Daisy Fay, a youthful flame whose memory he has long cherished but who is now married to Tom Buchanan, he seeks to take up the affair where he left off; but Daisy lacks his decisiveness and the matter ends tragically. Daisy, driving Jay back from New York to Long Island in his car, runs over and kills a woman named Myrtle Wilson, who by an improbable coincidence is Tom Buchanan's mistress. Myrtle's husband, who has seen the car before in the possession of Buchanan, follows Jay, murders him, and kills himself. Gatsby's funeral is attended only by Nick, the bond-salesman narrator of the novel, and Jay's father. *The Great Gatsby* is a study of success and its poisoning influence on character, as well as a carefully drawn picture of the manners of the Long Island rich during the Twenties. The novel, usually considered Fitzgerald's most important, embodies a situation that recurs throughout his work: a poor boy is snubbed by a rich and beautiful girl, spends his life struggling to acquire wealth in order to become worthy of her or to "get even" with her, then finds, after he has achieved success, that his prize crumbles in his hands because the girl has fallen in society while he has risen, or because she was not what he had thought her to be. The "mystery" of Gatsby, uncovered by Nick Carraway as the novel proceeds, is that his extravagant and vulgar way of life represents an attempt, perhaps subconscious, to win the recognition of the beautiful Daisy who rejected him years before because he was poor and unknown.

Tender is the Night (novel, 1934) is laid in Europe, chiefly on the Riviera. Richard Diver, a young American psychiatrist, meets Nicole Warren, an attractive young American girl, in a sanatorium where she is being treated for schizophrenia. He marries her, cures her, but loses his strength as he pours it out to her. He returns to America and degenerates into a small-town practitioner who drowns his personal tragedy in drink. The story is told successively from the points of view of several characters, including Diver and Nicole. The theme of the novel is essentially the problem of the *homme épuisé,* the intelligent and capable hero who gradually degenerates through the draining away of his spiritual forces. Nicole's insanity is mainly drawn after the disease of Fitzgerald's wife, and the character of Diver is modeled partly on Fitzgerald himself. Another notable character is Abe North, an eccentric and alcoholic musician.

STORIES: Fitzgerald's stories are an essential part of any study of his work. Not only were they successful (his income for a time was derived chiefly from them, and he was paid some of the highest prices ever received by an American writer for short stories) but they often reveal his themes with greater simplicity and clarity than his novels, where the underlying motif sometimes tends to be buried in detail. The stories have been collected in four volumes: *Flappers and Philosophers* (1920), *Tales of the Jazz Age* (1922), *All the Sad Young Men* (1926), and *Taps at Reveille* (1925).

A few stories from these collections may be cited as typical. "The Diamond as Big as the Ritz" is a whimsical allegory (Fitzgerald calls it a fantasy) of the American monied classes. The hero, John Unger, comes from a small town called Hades to go to a fashionable prep school in the east. There he meets the effete Percy Washington, who confesses to him that his father is "by far the richest man in the world." On a summer vacation Percy takes John home to his western estate; it turns out to be a fantastic Montana castle, protected with anti-aircraft guns and built on a mountain which is one solid diamond.

John falls in love with Percy's sister Kismine, but their romance is interrupted by a furious aerial attack; Percy's father Braddock Washington tries futilely to bribe God by offering him the diamond, but the chateau is destroyed. As the story ends Kismine and John flee from "heaven" to Hades, concluding that "there are only diamonds in the whole world, diamonds and perhaps the shabby gift of disillusion." This early story contains one of Fitzgerald's infrequent comments on social injustice; the political content, however, is oblique and satirical, found mainly in remarks of the type which Kismine makes when fifty thousand dollars' worth of her father's slaves are killed in the air raid: "So few Americans," she complains, "have any respect for property."

"The Rich Boy," from *All the Sad Young Men,* is a study of the effect of large amounts of money on the character of a young man; it contains, on the first page, Fitzgerald's famous statement about the born rich: "They are different from you and me." The essential idea of the story is that hereditary wealth creates a complacency and self-satisfaction in the rich that ruins them for contact with the reality of life; their crack-up generally comes in the form of a love affair, since true human affection is one of the few things that cannot be bought. Anson, the hero, is effortlessly successful in his early life as a Yale student, as a Naval aviator, and as a broker and speculator on Wall Street. But he falls in love with "a conservative and rather proper girl," Paula Legendre, who after a long courtship rejects him because of his lack of character. Anson, turned cynical by the experience, dabbles in a purely physical affair with the social climber Dolly Karger, but finds that nothing satisfies him, not even his success in the financial world. At the end of the story he reencounters Paula, now happily married and a mother, and realizes for the first time the extent of the happiness he has missed. A counterplot relates his jealousy of the happiness of his Aunt Edna and her lover Cary Sloane; he eventually drives Sloane to suicide by threatening to expose them.

"Winter Dreams," also from *All the Sad Young Men,* is built on the theme developed more fully in *The Great Gatsby.* Dexter Green, a boy whose father owns "the second-best grocery store" in a Minnesota resort, serves as a golfing caddy for the spoiled young heiress Judy Jones and falls in love with her. He spends the rest of the story trying to climb the social scale to her level; he goes to a first-rate eastern university, makes a fortune in the laundry business, and arrives socially. Almost forgetting Judy, he becomes engaged to another girl; when he meets Judy again she momentarily surrenders to him physically, but now it is his turn to reject her; the magic moment has passed, and besides he realizes she is too selfish to be satisfied with any one man. "I'm more beautiful than anyone else," she complains. "Why can't I be happy?" In later years he hears about her from an acquaintance; she has married a Detroit business-man and become dull and commonplace. Dexter feels that he has lost something, but it is not Judy: it is the image of the fabulous Judy he fell in love with as a boy, a girl who never existed but who nevertheless dominated his life. It is interesting that the situation in this story is parallel to that in "The Rich Boy" except that the position of the sexes is reversed; Judy here plays the rôle of Anson, and Dexter corresponds to the "conservative and rather proper" Paula.

"Babylon Revisited" (from *Taps at Reveille*) is a longer and more important story; it includes a social perspective lacking even in Fitzgerald's novels, and is one of his most mature statements on the Jazz Age and its people. The theme is the passing of the Jazz Age and the contrast with the era after 1929. Charlie Wales, the hero, returns to Paris after the stock market crash and finds everything changed; his old friends have gone away, and the scenes of his Jazz Age debauches are curiously altered. The construction of the story involves a flashback: most of the story is devoted to Charlie's reminiscences of Paris in the Twenties. He and his wife Helen had lived a mad and fascinating life in those days; they quarreled frequently, and on one occasion he had even locked her out of the apartment in the snow, but these were things that were done in the Roaring Twenties. Now Helen is dead, and Charlie has come to Paris to visit his daughter Honoria, who is now in custody of Helen's sister Marion and her husband Lincoln. He hopes that Marion and Lincoln will give Honoria back to him, now that he is reformed in his personal life and lonely without Helen; but everything goes wrong. He loses his temper at Marion, a pair of high-living old friends arrive drunk at the wrong moment and make a bad impression, and at the end Charlie knows they will not let him have Honoria. Around this basic plot Fitzgerald builds an unobtrusive allegory of the contrast between the two ages. Marion and Lincoln, respectable, moral, and slightly stuffy, symbolize the new world of the Thirties; and Duncan Schaeffer and Lorraine Quarrles, whose tactless hilarity spoils Charlie's chance to regain his daughter, are ghosts out of the vanished Twenties. Honoria herself is perhaps associated through her name with Charlie's desire to regain his honor and self-respect. The antithesis between the two sets of symbolic characters is adroit; Marion and Lincoln are "right" in their way and the reader sees their position, just as he sees the superficiality of Duncan and Lorraine. There are no villains, and Charlie, caught between two worlds, wins our sympathy because he is the victim of a social change that is not his fault. The autobiographical elements of the story are obvious.

ERNEST HEMINGWAY (born 1898)

The publicity directed on Hemingway's colorful and adventurous life has often tended to obscure the fact that he is primarily a creative artist whose business it is to write. Although he is free from the pretensions of the aesthetic cultists, he approaches the craft of writing with a careful and conscientious devotion. He once remarked that his job as a writer was to "put down what I see and what I feel in the best and simplest way I can tell it." In spite of his occasional stylistic experiments and his rare excursions into politics, this has remained his ideal.

In the early Twenties Hemingway, a left-bank expatriate, contributed poetry to avant-garde reviews. He soon turned to the short story and the novel, but he retained an almost poetic interest in economy of language and in precision and brilliance of imagery. From the beginning he bore one of the marks of a great author: his style was original and unmistakable. A single paragraph of his prose is easily identifiable; he prints upon each sentence the mark of his temperament and style. Hemingway at his best establishes a characteristic mood, a literary ambience which is entirely personal and inimitable, as much as his disciples may try to imitate it.

An extremely subjective author, Hemingway is not interested in writing from sheer imagination or in making use of documentary materials in the traditional naturalistic manner. He writes only about those aspects of life he has encountered personally, although these are many: warfare, big-game hunting, sport fishing, bull-fighting, skiing, and life in the expatriate society of Paris. Conversely, there is very little he has done that he has not written about. In Africa in 1933-34 he was stricken with dysentery and had to be flown out to Nairobi for treatment. Many writers would consider this incident only an unfortunate interruption in a vacation, but out of the experience Hemingway wrote the superb story "The Snows of Kilimanjaro." Each of the locales of his life—Michigan, Wyoming, Paris, Italy, Spain, Switzerland, Africa, and Cuba—has had a novel or a cycle of stories written about it, and most of Hemingway's friends find themselves sooner or later converted to characters in his fiction. Like Joyce and Proust, Hemingway is a writer who uses the material of his own life to construct a transformed and artistically heightened fiction.

Because of the subjective nature of his approach to fiction, Hemingway's male characters are usually more believable than his women. His heroes themselves are lifelike in proportion as they are projections of his own personality. With a few exceptions, as with the Cohn of *The Sun Also Rises* and most of the bull-fighters of his fiction, his central characters are merely Hemingway as he pictures himself or as he would like to be. His work is autobiographical not only in the incidents related but in the attitudes and reactions of his characters to their situations. His female characters seem to be seen through masculine eyes; he is not a master of feminine psychology. The best of his women, e.g., the Pilar of *For Whom the Bell Tolls,* have a certain masculine quality about them. His love-heroines, e.g., Catherine in *A Farewell to Arms* and Maria in *For Whom the Bell Tolls,* are passive and erotic embodiments of male desire; they are devoid of intellectual individuality and seem to have little existence apart from their lovers.

The sensations which interest Hemingway, and therefore the experiences he relates in his fiction, are generally on the physical level. He is interested in sensation *per se:* the sensation of drinking wine chilled in a Spanish mountain stream, of passing one's fingers through the hair of a girl whose head has recently been sheared, or of being blown up by a trench-mortar shell in Italy. He dwells over these sensations and analyzes them with an intensity which would be Proustian if it were not so terse. Even the finer sensations in Hemingway—love or political loyalty—seem to be essentially physical reactions; the hero feels them with his body rather than his mind, and generally manages to make a response to them through some sort of bodily reaction. This is not to say that Hemingway views life from a bestial standpoint; on the contrary his sensations are extremely refined, and he is sometimes given to an immature and romantic sentimentality about them. His mind operates exclusively on the level of concrete image and is wary of dead abstraction. He is anxious to communicate to the reader "how it was," to recreate the exact physical sensations that he, or his heroes, felt under certain conditions. This is the most successful aspect of his technique. After reading Hemingway the reader is left with a strong impression of "how it was" to shoot lions in Kenya, to take part in the retreat from Caporetto, or to live in Paris in the early nineteen-twenties.

Hemingway derived his style from two chief sources: his early experience as a newspaperman and his encounter with Gertrude Stein and other avant-garde writers in Paris in the Twenties. As a journalist on the *Kansas City Star* he learned to write succinctly, to avoid superfluous adjectives and adverbs, and to pack the maximum content into the minimum space. In Paris he fell under the spell of Gertrude Stein's undulant prose, with its consecutive phrases connected by "ands" in an almost Biblical manner, its understatement, and its trick of repeating an image or an idea over until it has become imbedded in the reader's mind. During the Thirties he gradually weaned himself from this style, but his most characteristic works are written under the influence of Stein. In *For Whom the Bell Tolls* he returned to this style to create the best book of his later period. It has been rightly remarked that this style has ruined more budding authors than any other influence since Sterne, but it is still true that when Hemingway utilizes it he achieves a distinctive, powerful, and entirely personal idiom.

Actually the most typical Hemingway novels—*The Sun Also Rises, A Farewell to Arms,* and *For Whom the Bell Tolls*—are written in two styles in alternation. First there is the highly condensed description and narration, written in the flowing chain of images suggestive of free verse; the opening page of *A Farewell to Arms* and the fishing scenes in *The Sun Also Rises* are typical. The second style is the terse dialogue, almost bare of comment and full of conversational blind alleys and *non sequiturs,* which Hemingway's detractors find it so easy to parody. The dialogue style appears at its best in the conversations of the hero of *A Farewell to Arms* with his Italian comrades and in numerous short stories of the type of *The Short Happy Life of Francis Macomber*. It is through the alternation of these two styles that Hemingway avoids the monotony which has been the downfall of his imitators.

There are many scenes of violence, pain and tragedy in Hemingway, yet the total effect is seldom offensive. He relates the most violent of incidents in a totally matter-of-fact and objective manner. He never comments, and he never degenerates into pathos. His scenes of violence are effective through the facts related and not through appeals to sentimentality. His concept of character is "hard"—i.e., his heroes are laconic and cynical, and not given to gushing—yet we perceive that under their hardness they have the same impulses and emotions as the rest of mankind.

Although Hemingway is primarily interested in conveying experiences to the reader, his work is not devoid of ideas. The ideas, however, are latent and conveyed through physical sensation; Hemingway is anything but a philosophical novelist. Yet beneath the surface of his work is an integrated and consistent philosophy. The chief concepts in his work may be listed as follows:

(1) Like Dreiser, Hemingway is an advocate of NATURAL ACTION, although the two writers differ greatly in their concepts of nature. To Hemingway natural action consists chiefly in pursuing the impulses of the body, with the emphasis on the finer and more noble impulses. He is a hedonist in the classic sense, yet he is no mere seeker after sensation; perversions of bodily desires, including excesses, over-refinements, and artificially stimulated tastes, are opposed to natural action. Contrary to popular opinion, he is no believer in chest-pounding masculinity or in brute force. Cohn, who resorts to fisticuffs in *The Sun Also Rises,* is presented as wrong in doing so. A man who admires force for its own sake may well come to admire fascism, and Hemingway dislikes fascism precisely because it is dispensed by "legally constituted bullies." His attitude is often disparagingly called "adolescent," but it should be noted that the code of boyhood includes censure of bullies and an idealistic respect for fair play.

Natural action to Hemingway therefore implies, not mere bestial hedonism, but a healthy and intelligent exercise of one's sensual appetites. Prostitution, drunkenness, and brawling play a large part in his work; yet examination will show that the decent characters reject this way of life, or at least find little satisfaction in it. It would be too much to claim that Hemingway is a moralist, but at least he is no disciple of vice.

(2) Hemingway is a believer in RITUAL—naturally not the ritual of church or lodge, but the unspoken rituals which men have handed down, sometimes unconsciously, for generations. He views bull-fighting as a ritualistic form of art involving bloodshed and death rather than as a mere excuse for sadism. Hunting too has its ritual; there are rules which the hunter must observe, and even the hunted seem to accept the ritual as natural. Nick Adams is careful to throw back fish under the legal game size; not only the game laws but the ritual of fishing demand that no life be wasted unnecessarily. Francis Macomber, wounding a lion which then escapes into the bush, proposes to abandon it; but the hunter Wilson insists that the beast must not be left to suffer. The pair therefore risk their lives to put their erstwhile victim out of its pain. There is a similar ritual in warfare; Hemingway finds fascism particularly repugnant in that it does not observe this traditional code. It is by shooting civilians and bombing from the air that the fascists in *For Whom the Bell Tolls* reveal their ignorance of the code of warfare.

(3) Hemingway finds a sort of mystical experience, a quasi-metaphysical quality, in PAIN, VIOLENCE, and DEATH; in his work he utilizes this mystique as an element of tragic catharsis. He is ostensibly a pacifist and is constantly depicting the brutality and senselessness of war, but there is no doubt that he himself and his heroes live at the highest pitch in the midst of armed combat. War is a vast and intricate game, the most gripping of all games since it is the most dangerous; even one's opponents, provided they observe the rituals and play the game according to the rules, are to be respected. Hemingway is closer to the attitude of the professional officer than he is to the fervor of the civilian patriot.

A similar mystique is involved in hunting, one of the dominant interests in Hemingway's life. To him hunting is not so much a means of killing an animal as a contest between animal and man. Francis Macomber finds a deep spiritual satisfaction in hunting he has never found anywhere else in life; he is regenerated by the experience and develops character visibly. The animal in death, provided it has been fairly stalked and cleanly killed, Hemingway finds one of the most beautiful of sights. He distinguishes, however, between the natural and beautiful in the animal world—the lion, the kudu, and the buffalo —and the ugly and "monstrous," including the baboon and the hyena. It would be too much to argue that the animals derive an equal satisfaction from the hunt; yet the quarry often seems to be aware of the rules of the game and quite conscious that it is engaged in a gripping ritualistic contest with man.

Finally, sex and death each have their mystiques. In sexual experience Hemingway's characters often reach a height of understanding they cannot achieve on a purely intellectual basis; this is particularly true of the Frederick-Catherine affair in *A Farewell to Arms* and of the love of Robert and Maria in *For Whom the Bell Tolls*. In *The Sun Also Rises* Hemingway shows the dangers of obsessed sexuality in Cohn and Mike, and Jake is warped because this satisfaction has been denied him. Sexual activity is one of the normal functions; if it is denied, or if it is overemphasized, it becomes abnormal and unsavory. The mystique of death is connected with the sensation of the imminence of death. Those who have constant contact with death —soldiers, bull-fighters, and the seriously ill—see more clearly than other people; they are wiser and surer in their grip on reality. It is only the nearness of death which brings to Harry (*The Snows of Kilimanjaro*) a lucid insight into his own nature and his relations with others.

(4) Hemingway is by no means devoid of RELIGION, as the above discussion implies, although his concept of supernatural forces is not the conventional religious one. His position is practically that of a pantheist. Nature in its unspoiled state is hardly amiable or friendly, but there is a sublimity about it lacking in urban culture; at least it is clean and free from hypocrisy. Often, as in *The Sun Also Rises,* a clean and inspiring landscape is contrasted with the bitter, quarrelsome, and ugly people who inhabit it. Such "sublime" landscape Hemingway usually associates with mountain regions, with snow, and with clear, cold weather. The perverted "human" landscape is that of the plains, dripping with rain and soil with the mud of warfare or disaster. This might be considered a kind of private mythology in Hemingway's work. The symbolic contrast between

mountain and plain occurs in *The Sun Also Rises, A Farewell to Arms,* and *For Whom the Bell Tolls;* its most striking use is in *The Snows of Kilimanjaro,* where the hero's flight from the warm, damp plain to the snow-capped mountain symbolizes his escape from a sordid life into the purity of death. This demonstrates the religious element in Hemingway's cult of natural action and purity; Kilimanjaro is simultaneously a high snow-covered mountain, a token of purity, and a symbol of the death into which the hero passes at the end of the story. The contact with nature, whether in the Swiss Alps or in the lake country of northern Michigan, brings out the best in Hemingway's characters and exalts them spiritually in the way religious experience does for other people. In *A Farewell to Arms* the landscape of the Abruzzi is specifically associated with the priest who is the only truly religious character in the novel.

LIFE: Ernest Hemingway was born in 1898 in a prosperous Chicago suburb. His father, Dr. E. C. Hemingway, was a prominent Chicago physician and sportsman. Hemingway has written a number of tributes to his father in short stories, chiefly those laid in Michigan in which the hero is named Nick Adams. After finishing the public schools and traveling in France, Hemingway took a job on the *Kansas City Star.* Although he held this position only a few months, the journalistic training he acquired at this formative age marked his style for the rest of his career.

In 1917-18 he went to Italy to serve as an ambulance driver on the Austrian front, where he acquired some of the experiences he was to fictionalize in *A Farewell to Arms.* He was severely wounded in the summer of 1918; he was left with numerous scars, and his knee was patched with a platinum cap he was to retain the rest of his life. Returning to America, he married and went to work for the *Toronto Star.* In 1921 he returned to Europe and settled in Paris, where he joined the American expatriates who were forming a literary and artistic circle centering in the Saint-Germain quarter. Here he formed close attachments with Gertrude Stein, Sherwood Anderson, and Ezra Pound; this period had an important influence on his later style. *Three Stories and Ten Poems,* his first book-length publication, appeared in 1923. *The Torrents of Spring* (1926) marks his emancipation from Anderson and others who had previously influenced him;

it is a farcical parody of Anderson's style mixed with burlesque on Gertrude Stein, Henry James, Ford Madox Ford, and James Joyce. From 1924 on he traveled widely, seldom remaining in the same place for more than a few months. His literary output continued at a steady rate. His base during much of this time was Key West, Florida, which attracted him through a combination of solitude and sport fishing. In 1933-34 he traveled to Africa on a hunting expedition and emerged with the material for *Green Hills of Africa* (1935) and several of his best stories. *To Have and Have Not* (novel, 1937) was generally considered inferior to his earlier work; it was written in the lull following the African trip. In 1936-37 he made two trips to Spain to cover the Civil War, and out of the experience wrote the drama *The Fifth Column,* a number of stories, and the novel *For Whom the Bell Tolls.* In this period he engaged in considerable political activity on behalf of the Spanish Loyalists; the Civil War brought to the surface the anti-fascist sentiments he had been developing ever since his travels in Italy in the early Twenties. During the Second World War he served as a war correspondent in Europe; although technically a civilian, he actually took an active part in the campaign in France as an irregular raider. *Across the River and Into the Trees* (1950) made use of these war experiences.

Hemingway contracted, in all, four marriages, three of which ended in divorce. From his 1921 marriage with Hadley Richardson a son, John, was born, and his second marriage with Pauline Pfeiffer (1927) produced two more: Patrick and Gregory. His third wife (1940) was the journalist Martha Gellhorn, and the fourth, whom he met as a war correspondent in England in 1944, Mary Welsh. Since the war Hemingway has made his home on a farm, Finca Vigia, in Cuba, where he divides his time between fishing and writing. A novelette, *The Old Man and the Sea,* laid in Cuba and utilizing his fishing experience, appeared in 1952. In 1954 Hemingway was awarded the Nobel Prize for Literature; *The Old Man and the Sea* was specifically mentioned in the Nobel committee's citation.

CHIEF WORKS: *The Sun Also Rises* (novel, 1926) is a story of a set of expatriates in Paris who make a hectic trip over the Pyrenees to Pamplona for the bull-fights. The party includes Jake Barnes, an American who has fought in Italy and has been made impotent by a war wound; Bill Gorton, Jake's friend and fishing companion; Lady Brett Ashley, an English woman of breeding who is gradually degenerating into a nymphomaniac and adventuress; Michael (Mike) Campbell, who is waiting for Brett's divorce to become final so he can marry her; and Robert Cohn, a Jewish novelist who is obsessed with a racial inferiority complex and who is slighted and snubbed by the other characters. The early chapters are laid in Paris; Hemingway captures the mood of expatriate life so successfully that it seems unfortunate he did not treat such settings at greater length. After the trip to Spain there are jewel-perfect descriptions of tramping and fishing in the Spanish mountains; this section also contains classic accounts of the details of the bull-fight festival in a provincial Spanish town. While Jake and Bill are enjoying the countryside, however, Brett, Mike, and Cohn are involved in a sordid erotic triangle. Brett dallies with Michael and even goes off with Cohn for a few days, but does not fall in love until she meets Pedro Romero, a young matador. This affair brings the little group, and Romero along with them, almost to the brink of disaster. Finally Brett, in an act of generous renunciation, abandons Romero rather than wreck his career. Cohn, a skilled boxer, takes out his resentment on Jake, Mike, and Romero; Brett decides to marry Mike after all, and Jake, Bill, and Cohn are left in their original state of cynicism.

Although this novel seems negative and pessimistic upon superficial reading, its latent content offers a positive philosophy. Bill and Jake, the "natural" pair, are men of character; they contrast sharply with Mike and Cohn, who are continually bickering over Brett. Mike, Cohn, and Brett are the real representatives of the "lost generation" referred to in the novel's epigraph. Bill and Jake are at their finest when they are out in the sunshine fishing and drinking wine in the Pyrenees; Mike and Cohn are at their most typical in a hotel-room brawl or a tavern orgy. Bill and Jake are occasionally drawn into this environment temporarily, but they feel little kinship with it. They admire Romero because he is a man of tradition (or ritual) and therefore a man of character; he stands up to a beating by the larger Cohn without flinching. The idea that Bill and Jake, for all their superficial cynicism, are "religious" characters is pointed up by contrast with Brett, who feels an instinctive uneasiness in the presence of religion. She is symbolically denied entrance to a church at one point, and confesses her moral vacuum to Jake on another occasion. When she sacrifices her own happiness to Romero's career, an act of renunciation which the reader feels compensates for her previous sins, she remarks, "It's sort of what we have instead of God."

But Jake, the decent part of mankind in its struggle with the "lost generation," has been deprived of his virility by the war; he feels unable to take more than a passive rôle in the events of the plot. Idealism and sensitivity have been killed in the war, and now the "lost generation"—Mike and Cohn—comes to the surface. *The Sun Also Rises* is therefore more than a portrait of the postwar generation; it is a study of the forces which went to make up this generation and which drove its natural and latent idealism temporarily below the surface.

A Farewell to Arms (novel, 1929) is largely autobiographical in its external details. Its hero is Frederick Henry, an American lieutenant in the Italian ambulance corps during the First World War. Henry meets Catherine Barkley, an English nurse, and enters into an affair with her which at first he considers merely casual. When he is wounded by a mortar shell, however, he is thrown together with Catherine in a hospital, and the romance becomes more serious. Catherine is portrayed as a deeply feminine woman who has the ability to "make a home"—i.e., to create an atmosphere of stability and serenity—wherever she pauses, be it in a hospital room or in a sordid hotel. She is temperamentally monogamous; her intense love for Frederick has a deep maternal permanence about it. Under her care he begins to regain his health and to find a new meaning in life. During the period of his convalescence there are several interesting conversations with doctors, nurses, and fellow-patients; Henry's dialogues with the eccentric major of his outfit are particularly notable. Rinaldi, an Italian army doctor, is a minor classic among Hemingway's characters.

The turning-point of the novel is the retreat from Caporetto, a debacle in which the Italian army is completely disorganized and in which Henry narrowly escapes being shot as a deserter. At length he regains Catherine; they flee to the high mountains of Switzerland, where they find happiness for a time. But Catherine dies in childbirth and Henry is left disillusioned and cynical. The structure of *A Fare-*

well to Arms is that of the classic tragedy; the cathartic ending is
carefully prepared by foreshadowing and mood. Catherine dies not so
much because of the war as through the tragic fate which has determined that she and Frederick shall not succeed in their love; the
novel has been compared to *Romeo and Juliet* with its "star-crossed
lovers." The symbolic contrast between the plain (war, misery, corruption) and the mountain (happiness, purity, love) extends throughout the novel.

To Have and Have Not (novel, 1937) is generally considered an
inferior work, although as one of Hemingway's five full-length novels
it is nevertheless a book of importance. Its hero Harry Morgan,
cynical, defiant, and independent, is the owner of a Key West sport-
fishing boat. As the novel opens Morgan, trusting no one and living
shrewdly through his own wiles, is making his living by crossing to
Havana with the boat and chartering it to wealthy American sport-
fishermen. When one of these sportsmen cheats him out of his
charter-fee he is left destitute, and is forced to accept a job smuggling
Chinese to Florida. He accepts the money for this job and then
cynically puts his passengers ashore again in Cuba, although he is
forced to murder a man to accomplish this. In the second part of the
novel, several months later, he is shot while running liquor from
Cuba in his boat; the boat is confiscated and Harry loses his arm. In
the third section, having recovered from his wounds and his amputa-
tion, he is propositioned by a band of Cuban revolutionaries—
actually little more than gangsters—who want him to smuggle them
back into their country. This job is more complicated; it involves
stealing his boat back from the officials who have seized it. He
manages to steal the boat and get away with the Cubans, only to
realize when they murder his mate that they have no intention of
paying for their passage and will probably murder him when they
get within sight of Cuba. With great ingenuity and courage he manages to catch the Cubans off guard and kill them with their own
weapons, but he is mortally wounded in doing so. When he is found
by the Coast Guard he has just enough strength to speak the message
it has taken him all his life to learn: "No matter how a man alone
ain't got no . . . chance." Thus the ethical theme of this novel
anticipates that of *For Whom the Bell Tolls:* that man cannot stand
alone, that only in union with other men can he find the strength

to stand up to evil. Harry, cynical, confused, and lacking in moral conscience, is nevertheless no villain; he is simply not very wise, and learns his wisdom when it is too late. A sub-plot involves a satire on retired business-men, professors, would-be writers, and other members of the leisure class commonly found in resorts like Key West.

For Whom the Bell Tolls (novel, 1940) came out of Hemingway's experiences in the Spanish Civil War. The hero, Robert Jordan, is an American teacher who has come to Spain to fight for the Loyalists out of idealism. The early chapters describe his trip into the mountains north of Segovia and his contact with a secret guerrilla band he is to lead on an important mission: the destruction of a bridge on the highway leading out of the canyon into Segovia. The guerrilla band includes Pablo, its brooding and cowardly leader; Pilar, his courageous and colorful wife; and Maria, daughter of a government official, who has been mistreated by the Fascists before her rescue by the guerrillas. Jordan and Maria fall in love and become intimate; they hope to marry and go to America eventually, but they also realize that in their present situation they must seize every moment of pleasure while they can. For her part Pilar has no illusions; she has read Jordan's fate in his hand and knows he is soon to die.

As plans are laid to blow up the bridge a neighboring guerrilla squad is searched out and massacred by Fascist troops aided by plane, but there is nothing Pablo's band can do to help. In another scene Jordan makes his way through enemy lines to the Loyalist army; he is struck with the contrast between the devotion and bravery of the guerrilla bands and the confusion and corruption of the army in the plain. He now knows that the battle will be lost, but he returns to his mission. Finally, as a Fascist column comes down the canyon to finish off the battle around Segovia, the band attacks the bridge, drives off the guards, and drops the steel structure into the river with a few well-placed charges. The plans must be revised at the last minute, however, because of Pablo's treachery, and as a result Jordan is fatally wounded. The others offer to attempt to carry him off, but he insists on remaining with a machine-gun in a spot where he can ambush and mow down the pursuing Rebel column before he is killed.

On the factual level an adventure novel, *For Whom the Bell Tolls* is in a deeper sense a study of war and the reactions it provokes in men and women. Men are carried away by the partisan slogans of war, but women, wiser, see that life is more important than parties. Jordan the idealist is willing to give his life for his cause, but Maria's first loyalty is to her lover. Pablo is a third type: a moral coward, he becomes a defeatist and seeks to avoid personal danger. In doing so he endangers the whole group, imperils the project of blowing up the bridge, and even causes the death of Jordan. Pablo is wrong; but both Jordan and Maria are right in their way. Pilar stands somewhere between these extremes: a courageous and fervent patriot, she nevertheless understands the importance of individual human happiness.

Across the River and Into the Trees (novel, 1950) came out of Hemingway's Second World War experiences as *For Whom the Bell Tolls* came out of the Spanish Civil War. There, however, the similarity ends. The basic difference is that *Across the River* takes place after the war is over, and thus the combat incidents which interested Hemingway and would doubtless have interested his reader are merely mentioned in passing. In many respects the novel is autobiographical. The hero, the American colonel Richard Cantwell, is Hemingway's age, and he is credited with most of Hemingway's exploits in the Italian army in the First World War. In a sense Cantwell represents what Hemingway would have become had he chosen to become a professional soldier rather than a writer after the war, a choice he might well have made.

The scene is laid in Venice, where the fifty-year-old Cantwell loses himself in an affair with Renata, a "nearly nineteen" year old countess. Most of the novel is devoted to conversations with Renata and others; Hemingway uses the novel as an outlet for a motley set of personal ideas including his opinions of Second World War generals, theories of strategy, remarks on American politics, and innuendoes about his former wives. Young (in his *Ernest Hemingway,* N. Y., 1952) sums up the difficulty well when he remarks that Hemingway seems to be writing the novel under the impression he is being interviewed. "T/5 Jackson, Renata, and others act as straight men, setting up implausible questions so that Cantwell can pontificate." There are better passages: the hunting scenes, especially the opening chapter describing duck-shooting in Venice in winter, and the Colonel's description of America to Renata (Chapter XXXVII). In the end Cantwell dies of a heart attack in his car, shortly after he reminds his driver of the dying words of Stonewall Jackson: "Let us cross over the river and rest in the shade of the trees." In spite of such occasional fine passages, however, *Across the River* is the weakest of Hemingway's full-length works, and often reads like an unconsciously funny parody of his own style.

The Old Man and the Sea (novelette, 1952) is the most lyrical of Hemingway's longer works, apparently marking a turn away from the naturalistic style toward a more poetic form of expression. It retains, however, the terse and ironic understatement of his prewar work. The story is taken from an actual incident which Hemingway heard about during his fishing experiences in Cuba. The hero, Santiago, is an old Cuban fisherman who goes out alone in a small skiff to catch tarpon and marlin; his character is established through his conversations with a young boy, the only one in the world who appreciates him and admires his skill as a fisherman. After a long period of fruitless fishing the old man succeeds one day in hooking an enormous marlin, larger than his boat, the meat of which he can sell for a small fortune. For a day and a night he struggles with the fish and finally kills it. But as he attempts to tow it back to the cannery (it is too large to be taken into the boat) the marlin is torn apart by voracious sharks; when he reaches the harbor all he has left is a head and a bare skeleton. He knows he will never fish again: "Something in his chest was broken," but his spirit too was crushed, and the sea has defeated him. Yet there is a glory, almost a victory, in the stature of his defeat and in the unremitting courage with which he struggles against the sharks.

Most of the dialogue in this story is purportedly taking place in Spanish, which Hemingway "translates" literally to produce a curiously elegant and lyrical effect. The device is sometimes comic, as when Santiago and the boy discuss American big-league baseball in their poetic Spanish. But the more common result is a kind of Biblical dignity which is exactly suited to the subject of the book. The style is seen as well in the Spanish conversations in *For Whom the Bell Tolls* and in some of the bull-fighting stories (e.g., "The Capital of the World") as well as in some stories in which the dialogue takes place in Italian. In another sense *The Old Man and the Sea* belongs with Hemingway's hunting stories: it expresses the theme of the "kinship between hunter and hunted" in the sense of beauty and pity that the old man feels as he struggles with the fish. It has been pointed out that Santiago is established as a saintly, even Christlike figure through the scars on his hands as well as by his name and the austerity of his life; in a sense *The Old Man and the Sea* is a religious story. It is perhaps this aspect of the novelette which inspired the Swedish Academy to cite it specifically in awarding Hemingway the 1954 Nobel Prize. *The Old Man and the Sea* first appeared in *Life* magazine in the issue of September 1, 1952 and was later published in book form.

STORIES: Hemingway has published in all five volumes of stories, including a definitive volume, *The Fifth Column and the First Forty-Nine Stories* (1938), which includes all his shorter fiction published up to that time. This material may be roughly divided into three groups according to subject matter: (1) stories laid in America, including the Nick Adams fiction of the Michigan wilderness and the American stories of boxing and crime; (2) stories of Americans in Europe, including experiences of the First World War in the Italian army; and (3) African hunting stories.

Of the first group, "The Killers" (1927) is the best known. It is, in fact, Hemingway's most successful story in the popular sense; it was made into a successful motion picture and is often anthologized. The scene is laid in Michigan, the locale of Hemingway's own boyhood. The action is seen through the eyes of the boy Nick Adams, who remains a spectator instead of a central character, although in the end it is his emotional reaction to the situation which chiefly interests the author. Two Chicago hoodlums, Al and Max, come to an unnamed small town to murder Ole Andreson, a Scandinavian prizefighter who has gotten on the wrong side of the gangsters either by throwing a fight or failing to throw a fight, probably the latter. They order dinner in a lunch-room, where a dialogue takes place with George, the counter-man, Sam, the negro cook, and Nick himself, who works there. This dialogue is one of the best examples of the terse and hardboiled style which Hemingway has made famous. When the two gangsters depart, Nick, young and idealistic, feels that something must be done to save the doomed Ole. He goes to Ole's rooming-house to warn him, but Ole is tired of running away from his avengers and has decided to accept death: "After a while I'll make up my mind to go out." But Nick cannot share his resigned cynicism; he is too young and too optimistic. The story implies that this experience marks a turning point in his life, his first contact with evil and his resolution to struggle against it no matter what the cost. This story, short and superficially simple, is actually a minor masterpiece; its dialogue has been polished to perfection, and the ethical statement implied is typical of the best Hemingway.

"Big Two-Hearted River" (1925) is a long two-part story of Nick Adams' adventures tramping and fishing in upper Michigan; it contains the best statement of Hemingway's love for the outdoors as well as some masterfully detailed accounts of the technique of fishing and camping.

"In Another Country" (1927) is typical of the European stories. Outwardly simple, it contains some of Hemingway's most finished dialogue as well as his best examples of laconic irony. The material is drawn from Hemingway's own experience in a Milan hospital following his wounding on the Austrian front in 1918. The story consists almost entirely of conversations between the narrator, a wounded American officer, and an Italian major, before the war a great fencer, whose hand has been hopelessly crippled. The major takes a liking to the narrator and tries to teach him Italian, but grows angry when the American reveals that he "hopes to be" married. The reason is presently revealed: the major's wife has died, and he is unable to resign himself. This revelation breaks down the courageous reserve and self-control he has shown toward his war mutilation. He cries, but he still carries himself "straight and soldierly." The major personifies Hemingway's ideal of heroism, which here seems a fine and splendid one; the major has great physical courage and self-control, but is inwardly sensitive. The true hero is not a brute, nor is he a reckless fanatic; he is a man of emotional sensitivity who controls his instinctive weakness through sheer force of character.

"The Snows of Kilimanjaro" (1936) is one of several stories based on Hemingway's hunting expedition to Africa in 1933-34. Its experimental construction and style make it one of his most radical pieces of fiction from the technical point of view; it is essentially an exercise in stream-of-consciousness. The style alternates between the sparse dialogue and action of *The Sun Also Rises* and flashbacks, set in italics, recalling the hero's past career. These retrospective vignettes resemble Gertrude Stein more than anything else Hemingway has written; their thought is disconnected, their syntax undulating, and their imagery evocative. The story concerns Harry, a cynical and unhappy American writer who is wounded in a hunting accident in a remote district of Africa. In long dialogues with his wife, a former society girl he has married for her money and has grown to hate, he tortures her with reminders of his impending death. His resentment toward her comes from the fact that he has become forced to lead her way of life in order not to lose the money that goes with her; he has grown so used to this level of spending that he knows he can never get along without it. This is the problem of the "sell-out" of the writer, which greatly interested Hemingway at this time; *cf.* similar discussions in *Green Hills of Africa*.

At last Harry dies of gangrene; but at the moment of his death he has a dream in which a friend's airplane carries him off to the "great, high, and unbelievably white" peak of Kilimanjaro, whose supernatural quality has been established early in the story. To Harry in his hallucination the mountain symbolizes purity and escape: escape from the mean, bickering life he has led with his wife, escape from the commercialism into which his writing has degenerated, and, on a physical level, escape from the hot damp plain upon which he lies dying. Again, as in Hemingway's novels, snow, cold, and purity are equated with the finer nature in man and with all that is sublime in the physical world.

Julian, the friend mentioned in the story, is based on the character of Scott Fitzgerald. Several other actual persons are included under altered names.

"The Short Happy Life of Francis Macomber" (1936), also based on the 1933-34 African trip, is written in a more conventional style. An American couple, Francis and Margot Macomber, arrive in Nairobi and hire a professional hunter named Wilson to take them on a game expedition. Macomber is a rather spineless character; his wife despises him and makes no effort to conceal her affairs with other men. Macomber hopes the solitude of the safari will bring them together again. But on his first day of hunting he disgraces himself and loses his chance to win his wife's esteem; he wounds a lion, follows it into the bush, but bolts in terror when the lion charges. Margot now snubs him totally and begins to throw herself at Wilson. The latter is not particularly attracted to her, but as a professional hunter he has learned to accommodate himself to his clients' whims; he accepts her overtures. Macomber knows of the affair, but in his disgrace he is too weak to make any objection. At this point Margot hates Francis, Francis hates Wilson, and Wilson is beginning to despise them both. But the next day, hunting Buffalo, Macomber suddenly finds his courage in the excitement of the chase. In the course of a half hour (his "short happy life") he develops character and enthusiasm for life; both Wilson and Margot sense the transformation. Wilson congratulates him on his entry into manhood, but Margot, who realizes she can no longer control him as she has, is inwardly furious. Macomber presently goes with Wilson into the underbrush after a wounded buffalo, and as the two fire at the charging animal a bullet from Margot's gun kills Macomber from behind. When Wilson accuses her of murdering her husband she collapses in tears; but the implication is that she killed him rather than concede to his newly-won status as a man of character and courage.

THOMAS WOLFE (1900-1938)

An orderly and established civilization is always wary of Titans. Literary critics especially are inclined to condemn sheer, wild, and uncontrolled force and to admire control and technical perfection; for instance, Willa Cather, restrained, competent, a perfectionist in style, has generally been received more favorably by academic critics than Wolfe, who seems to defy standards of good writing. Wolfe as an author of incredible energy, power, creativity, and ego; he exhibits all the outward marks of genius. He has been criticized with justice for his naïveté, for his egocentricity, and especially for his blundering and inchoate style. It is true he shows certain technical and personal limitations, but he surmounts them well enough with the sheer force of his creativity to be assured of a place as one of the great authors of the twentieth century.

Everything Wolfe wrote was personal and subjective; he had little interest in environments other than his own. His novels are constructed entirely out of the persons and things he encountered during his own lifetime: his home town of Asheville, his family, the town characters of his boyhood, the University of North Carolina, Harvard, and New York City. But although Wolfe writes in great detail about all these things, he is really interested only in one thing: himself. If he was sure of any one fact it was that he himself was a genius. His two principal autobiographical heroes, Eugene Gant and George Webber, are marked men who are somehow different from the rest of humanity; they have monstrous bodies, they eat, drink, fight, weep, and make love on a gigantic scale, and they rage furiously at the banality and indifference which surround them. When Eugene Gant or George Webber receives a rejection slip (an accident which happens frequently to all authors) it is a tragedy of cosmic proportions; all other human calamity palls beside it. When George Webber deserts his mistress the world is shaken to its foundations, and the thunder and lightning continue for a hundred pages. Wolfe conceived his heroes on a gigantic scale which he thought only proper to the subject, but he lacked the insight to see his own emotions in their proper proportions.

The major theme of Wolfe's books is the "cult of genius," the genius, of course, being Wolfe himself. The genius as a type is marked from his birth as different from other children; he is moody, unpredictable, spasmodically violent, and unhappy. He is misunderstood by his fellow men, who persecute him because they unconsciously sense his superiority. He is forever doomed to loneliness; his stature isolates him like an elephant among monkeys. He loves mankind in the abstract, but shrinks from contact with it at close quarters; the bestiality, the materialism, and the shallowness of ordinary men fill him with horror. He creates his tremendous masterpieces, all the time wracked by torment, and then dies, murdered by a complacent and unfeeling society. The remarkable thing is that Wolfe actually lived this legend in many respects; if he errs it is chiefly in overestimating the enmity of ordinary mankind toward the genius.

If Wolfe's novels have any structure at all it is due to the efforts of his editors, Maxwell Perkins and later Edward C. Aswell. Wolfe himself was incapable of limiting the flow of words that streamed from his brain onto paper; it was a sort of compulsion. When the manuscript of *Look Homeward, Angel* was first presented to the publisher it was twice as long as *War and Peace*, or about twelve times as long as the ordinary novel. His editors were forced to attack this material with scissors and pencil and somehow cut it down to publishable length, inserting transitional links where necessary. Wolfe evidently wished to record everything that had hapened to him; he had to be persuaded to delete incidents which were intensely interesting to him but which had no organic connection to the novel.

In style Wolfe is inconsistent, awkward, and frequently inchoate. Some of his best passages are written in bare naturalistic narration. Other scenes are strongly influenced by Joyce; these are usually less successful, since Wolfe lacked Joyce's sensitivity for word values. The worst of his prose is to be found in the dithyrambic passages where he pulls out all the stops and loses himself in a tumult of adjectives; often these chapters degenerate into sheer nonsense. The same thing is true of his dialogue; it is best when it is simplest, and becomes mawkish as his characters grow passionate and lyrical. In his moments of greatest violence Wolfe's vocabulary fails him, and he retreats into such nebulosities as "inexpressible," "indescribable," "unspeakable," "inconceivable," "transcendent," "inexorable," and "ineffable." He himself was aware of some of his faults; in "The Story of a Novel" he cites his addiction to adjectives, his Whitmanesque "chants" which blunder on for pages in rhythmic but meaningless rhetoric, his long and tedious catalogues of things seen, of dimensions, textures, hues, architectural details, and countrysides, his fascination with the mere magnitude of experience, with "Amount and Number," his excessively explicit narrative, which could never leave anything to be inferred. He learned something from the critical reception of his first two novels, and became slightly more precise and objective in *The Web and the Rock* and *You Can't Go Home Again*. Yet the two later books lack the splendid energy of the Eugene Gant novels. In struggling for restraint Wolfe may have crippled the one irreplaceable gift he had: his titanic exuberance and creativity. His talent was essentially a romantic one. Of *Look Homeward, Angel* he says, "I really cannot say the book was written. It was something that took hold of me and possessed me, and before I was done with it . . . it seemed to me that it had done for me. It was exactly as if this great black storm cloud I have spoken of had opened up and, mid flashes of lightning, was pouring from its depth a torrential and ungovernable flood." This statement reflects a certain amount of pose, but it nevertheless summarizes Wolfe's own attitude toward the creative process. It is basically a romantic attitude, the theory of "possession" or divine inspiration which Coleridge claims inspired him to write "Kubla Khan."

Such a theory of art, naturally, is not conducive to economy and precision. When Wolfe began to write the sequel to *Look Homeward, Angel*, which he planned as a novel of two hundred thousand words, it grew into a Frankenstein monster which filled several wooden packing cases. The opening scene alone was longer than the average novel. Since no public could ever be induced to read such a novel, Wolfe and his editor were obliged to cut it drastically, although Wolfe complained, "My soul recoiled before the carnage of so many lovely things cut out upon which my heart was set." Finally, taking advantage of Wolfe's absence on a trip to Chicago, the editor sent it to the presses; the result was *Of Time and the River*, which many critics complained was unselective and unwieldy, although it contained only a tenth of what Wolfe had originally planned for it. Such was Wolfe's obsessive, almost pathological compulsion to write, to express everything he had thought and everything that had happened to him in order to assure it the immortality of the printed page.

After the sheer force of the language itself, the quality that remains in the mind of Wolfe's reader is the color and vividness of his characterizations. It is perhaps not accurate to say that Wolfe has a "skill in characterization;" his most convincing characters are drawn from life itself. Yet he is not without creative imagination in this respect; when the Eugene Gant books were criticized for their subjectivity he went out of his way, in *The Web and the Rock*, to create believable characters out of whole cloth. The best of these is the athlete Nebraska Crane, a completely fictitious invention, who is nevertheless a striking and convincing character. It seems, therefore, that Wolfe's skill in characterization is a genuine one; it is merely that the people who interested him, and therefore the ones about whom he wanted to write, were those who had stimulated his imagination through intimate personal contact in real life. Luckily Wolfe came from a colorful family and encountered many fascinating people during his life. Yet the success of his novels is not due only to this; a lesser author might have made dull novels even out of such material. It is interesting to compare the account of the affair between Monk

Webber and Esther Jack in *The Web and the Rock* with the novel *The Journey Down* by Aline Bernstein, the real-life model for Mrs. Jack, in which she depicts the same relationships from a different point of view and in a different literary technique. *The Journey Down* is not a bad novel, but the comparison will demonstrate the difference between talent and genius. Bernard DeVoto titled a famous essay on Wolfe "Genius Is Not Enough;" yet a novel can succeed on mere genius where it could not succeed on talent or skill alone.

Whatever his stature as a novelist, Wolfe is not a thinker. He has been hailed as a Whitmanesque champion of democracy, but he was equally influenced by the cranky and anti-democratic racism of Mencken, whom he greatly admired; there is anti-Semitism in his work, as well as hostility to negroes, half-breeds, Southern Europeans, and non-Anglo-Saxons generally. He is capable of referring to "the great Boob Public" in one paragraph and waxing eloquent over "all the poor blind fumbling Creatures that inhabit this earth" in the next. He has likewise been typified as a regionalist. This label is somewhat more valid, since all his novels begin with the same characters living in the same narrow and circumscribed rural region of North Carolina. But Wolfe does not share the Cult of the Land of the Southern agrarians; he despises everything that is mundane and mean, the agricultural life included. He is a regionalist only because he wrote entirely about himself, and because he passed the formative years of his life in Asheville, North Carolina. He was as little at home there as he was later in New York or Paris, but he nevertheless felt a genuine affection for the region of his youth. Like most Titans, he is inconsistent; he belongs with Rabelais and Whitman rather than with Flaubert or Henry James. Wolfe is perhaps not the greatest novelist America has produced, but he is certainly among the most gigantic of America's literary personalities.

LIFE: Wolfe was born in 1900 in Asheville, North Carolina, a mountain town near the Tennessee border. His father, William O. Wolfe, was a stonecutter and tombstone sculptor who had come to North Carolina from the East in his youth; his mother Julia kept a boarding house, and the family also included a brother Ben. The main events of his early life, concealed only by a few transparent name-changes, are to be found in *Look Homeward, Angel*. Thomas, precocious and well-read, was sent to the University of North Carolina at fifteen. He enjoyed a normal collegiate career, edited the student paper and magazine, and tentatively began writing plays; he graduated in 1920. Through the efforts of his mother he was enabled to continue his studies at Harvard, where he participated in George Pierce Baker's famous "47 Workshop" in playwriting and wrote a drama which was almost accepted by the Theatre Guild. Upon receiving his M.A. from Harvard he joined the English faculty of New York University, where he taught intermittently for six years. Legend has it that his scribbled comments on freshman themes were often longer than the themes themselves. During his N.Y.U. days he made two trips to Europe; on the second trip he began writing the material which was later to be organized into *Look Homeward, Angel.*

The main part of the book was written in America, chiefly in New York and Brooklyn. He made a third trip to Europe in 1928-29, and shortly after his return submitted the enormous manuscript to Scribner's. Maxwell Perkins, the Scribner's editor assigned to the book, began to cut the great mass down and organize it, and with the help of Wolfe produced a publishable manuscript. When *Look Homeward, Angel* was published later the same year it caused a tremendous stir. The respectable society of Asheville rose up in arms; one lady wrote Wolfe that although she disapproved of lynching she would not lift a hand to prevent his "big overgroan karkus" being dragged across the public square to the nearest tree. Numerous lawsuits were instigated, although most of them were later dropped. Critical reception to the book was mixed, although preponderately favorable. Wolfe deeply resented the comments of some critics that the style of the novel was awkward and formless; he castigated professional critics and academicians warmly in his later novels.

The second section of the Gant material was published in 1935 under the title *Of Time and the River.* By this time Wolfe had resigned his teaching position and was living on his royalties in Brooklyn. Shortly after the publication of this novel he left again for Europe, where he began the second, more objective cycle of autobiographical material in which the hero is named George Webber. He had finished an enormous mass of this material by 1938; but in July of that year he was stricken with a tenacious case of pneumonia while on a western trip. Complications ensued, and Wolfe died of a cerebral infection in September of 1938. His remains were brought back to Asheville on Pullman car K-19, the car on which the fictional Eugene Gant had first departed from Altamont. Soon after his death the publishers began working on the huge unfinished manuscript he had left; out of it they constructed *The Web and the Rock* (1939) and *You Can't Go Home Again* (1940). A set of "leftovers" formed *The Hills Beyond* (1941).

THE NOVELS: *Look Homeward, Angel* (1929) is Wolfe's most famous book and his most typical one; both his merits and his failings are here seen in their sharpest form. The novel is entirely autobiographical: Eugene Gant, the hero, is Wolfe himself, his parents are converted to W. O. and Eliza Gant, his brother Ben remains Ben, Asheville becomes Altamont, and the University of North Carolina (sometimes called Chapel Hill) becomes the State University at Pulpit Hill. Eugene is depicted, however, as a member of a large family: there are two sisters, Daisy and Helen, and three brothers, the dissolute Steve, Luke, and the quiet and bitter Ben. Eugene's early childhood is relatively happy, but his later years are marred by continual family strife. The moody and unstable father leaves the household intermittently and finally abandons his family for good; Eliza, driven by an obsession for property and security, opens a boarding-house. At the age of fifteen Eugene goes off to the University, where he is introduced to the world of ideas and begins to recognize his vocation for the first time. His brother Ben dies; the scene of his death from pneumonia, surrounded by the wrangling of the family and the self-pitying maundering of the father, is the height of the novel and a masterpiece of affective narration. After the death of Ben, Eugene, alienated from his saddened mother, realizes he must break with his family and plunge out into the world on his own.

Of Time and the River (1935) continues the story of Eugene Gant. He studies playwriting at Harvard under Professor Thatcher (George Pierce Baker), "tears the entrails" from two thousand books a year, and spends thousands of good hours brooding over a waitress with whom he has fallen in love. At Harvard he meets Francis Starwick, an affected and precious young littérateur; Eugene is impressed with Francis' sophistication and elegance, and they become friends. After his graduation Eugene goes to New York to teach English; later he and Francis go off on an escapade to Paris. Romantic complications occur, and then Eugene discovers that his idol Starwick is a homosexual. Disillusioned, he abandons him to wander over Europe alone until his money runs out. The novel also contains an account of the father's reconciliation with Eliza and his pathetic death.

The Web and the Rock (1939) is a fresh start; Wolfe begins attacking his autobiographical material all over again. The hero, George Webber, called "Monk" because of his extraordinary proportions, is a child of divorced parents; he goes to live with his Uncle Mark and Aunt Maw in the town of Libya Hill (still Asheville). There are many anecdotes of the Joyner clan, to which Mark and Aunt Maw belong. George's friend and protector is the half-Indian Nebraska Crane, athlete, adventurer, and later baseball star. Crane is one of the few entirely fictional characters in Wolfe's work. A notable incidental scene is the rampage and death of Dick Prosser, a pious Negro who goes berserk and is finally killed by a posse, who put his corpse on exhibition in a store window. The story continues with George's college days at Pine Rock College; his hero is the popular social leader Jim Randolph. After a brief interlude in New York with Jim and others, Monk goes to Europe; on the return trip he meets Mrs. Esther Jack (based on the character of Wolfe's friend Aline Bernstein), a Jewish costume designer, wealthy, attractive, understanding, yet maddening to Monk in her suave *savoir-faire* and her sophisticated society attachments, even in her self-assured Jewishness. Monk's affair with Esther occupies the rest of the novel. At last, emotionally exhausted and creatively empty, he blames the loss of his vitality on Esther and abandons her to go back to Europe.

In *You Can't Go Home Again* (1940) Monk comes back from Europe and renews his intimacy with Esther. His novel is accepted, and his relations with the editor Foxhall Edwards (Maxwell Perkins) are described. Aunt Maw dies; he returns to Libya Hill for the funeral but finds the town modernized and altered. He feels awkward and out of place, and realizes "you can't go home again"; the happiness of youth cannot be recaptured by returning to its geographical setting. Back in New York he goes to a lavish and abandoned party at Esther's, during which a fire breaks out and kills two elevator boys. This fact is kept secret from the revelers. It is this party which makes it clear to Monk that he is not of Esther's world; he breaks with her definitely. Monk's existence in Brooklyn during the Depression years is next described at great length. Later he goes to London, where he meets Lloyd McHarg (Sinclair Lewis), who praises and encourages him. The novel closes with an analysis of his break with Foxhall Edwards.

Although the tendency has been to view the Monk Webber novels merely as another version, or as a continuation, of the Eugene Gant sequence, there are essential differences. The background of the hero, in the first place, is not identical; for instance Monk is raised not by his mother but by an aunt, whose clan is described in some detail. More important, the literary approach of the second pair of novels is different; the Monk Webber material is more objective, and Wolfe makes a deliberate effort to stand farther off from his hero. In great measure he succeeds; Monk, although a less "titanic" character than Eugene, is better rounded and perhaps more believable. His faults and the instances of his "wrongness" are often frankly described; in his relations with Esther Jack, for example, he often seems wrong-headed and irrational and Mrs. Jack calm and reasonable. Yet this attempt at objectivity often weakens Wolfe's power; many passages in the Webber books are pedestrian, and the magnificent (although exasperating) ebullience of the Gant books is lacking. Muller convincingly argues in his volume on Wolfe that his death was perhaps not the great literary loss it seemed; he had written all he knew in *Look Homeward, Angel* and *Of Time and the River,* repeated himself less effectively in the second two novels, and would have found himself at a loss for something to express if he had gone on writing. Two novels of genius, however, are enough to demand of an author, and Wolfe's place of honor in American literature is assured.

JAMES T. FARRELL (born 1904)

Farrell is often treated as a disciple of Dreiser, and certainly there are many parallels between the two authors in attitude and style. There is an even closer resemblance, however, to Zola. Farrell is a model naturalist in the pseudo-sociological European tradition; his writing is more ruthless and callous than that of either Dreiser or Dos Passos, and he accepts the environmental doctrines of the European naturalist school. Nevertheless, Farrell is totally American in content; he has a sure touch for the slang of the Chicago slums, and he has never lost his contact with the lower-class Catholic Irish who make up the greater part of his characters. Though his technique may have been influenced by European examples, Farrell's experience and material are totally native.

According to his own statement, Farrell's writings are intended as an integrated panorama of American life in the form of a series of novels similar to Zola's *Rougon-Macquart* series, in which the influence of environment and heredity on a lower-class city population are demonstrated in detail. In practice his plan is a good deal more modest than Zola's; he is interested primarily in the lower class, where Zola sought to depict an entire nation, and his locales have been chiefly restricted to the Irish-populated slums of Chicago. He is less objective than Zola; his major works are essentially fictionalized autobiography, whether he calls himself Studs Lonigan or Danny O'Neill. Farrell also differs from Zola and many other naturalists in that he writes of the lower class from first-hand experience. He is not obliged to do research to document his novels; he has a wide fund of personal experience, involving many different occupations and activities, to draw upon. This experience gives to his naturalism a force and authenticity lacking in more academic authors.

Farrell's lower-class origins have contributed two other qualities to his work. In the first place he has little respect for decorum or gentility; his style is blunt, even vulgar, and the incidents he relates often approach the pornographic. In addition Farrell has developed into a bitter social partisan; he is critical of capitalism, respectability, even success in its ordinary forms, and his bitterness has in some instances brought him close to communism. He is too violently individualistic in personality to align himself with a program of any specific party; he has preferred to maintain a position as a vigorous foe of the inequality he encountered in the South-Side Chicago of his youth.

In addition to Zola, Farrell has cited as his favorite authors Dostoyevsky, Turgenev, Tolstoy, Gogol, Chekhov, Stendhal, Balzac, Flaubert, Proust, Joyce, and Dickens. The list is a significant one; with the exception of Chekhov and Proust all the authors are realists of one kind or another and not a single American is included. The omission of Dreiser is striking. But Farrell no doubt disliked the gauche dialogue, the emotional empathy with his characters, and the tendency toward sentimentalism which are Dreiser's weaknesses. As literary models Flaubert and Zola are more hard-minded and more objective; in addition they share the belief in environmental determinism which Farrell derived from his philosophical Marxism, and which Dreiser never grasped except in a muddled way. "If there is any hatred in my books," Farrell wrote, "it is not directed against people but against conditions which brutalize human beings and produce spiritual and material poverty." Such a credo cannot always be taken at face value; a good deal of Studs Lonigan's failure is due not to the environmental influence of the Chicago slums but to his own stupidity and innate lack of character.

In style as well Farrell shows, not so much the European influence, but the inspiration of European models. His style creates the illusion of a brutal and unpretentious spontaneity, although it is actually carefully worked; he is a slow writer and a careful one, and a stickler for detail. The chief defects in his work are those which come inevitably attached to his merits: his painstaking documentation often produces a tedious and repetitious prolixity, and his ruthless realism sometimes alienates more sensitive or idealistic readers. Yet *Young Lonigan,* which shocked readers in 1932, seems fairly innocuous in the age of James Jones and Norman Mailer, and a 1937 obscenity charge brought against *A World I Never Made* was thrown out of court. Like Bernard Shaw, Farrell has lived to outgrow his own radicalism; he is today a conservative writer. Yet the Studs Lonigan books, the major work of his career, remain as an invaluable document of the world and the time they describe, as well as one of the more interesting naturalistic experiments of the Depression era.

LIFE: Farrell was born in 1904 in the Chicago South Side, at that time one of America's most brutal slums. As a pupil in a Catholic high school he was an enthusiastic athlete; his dominating interest was in baseball, but he also won letters in football and basketball. Because of his education in parochial schools he has always retained an interest in priests, churches, and religious experience; his personal attitude, however, has remained independent and secular. Farrell attended the University of Chicago for about three years and for a time attended night classes at De Paul University, but his education remained incomplete; his personality was too active for him to sit quietly in a classroom for long. Meanwhile he had held a variety of odd jobs which later provided him with valuable literary material: gas-station attendant, express company clerk, clerk in a cigar store in New York City, and advertising salesman. He began to write around 1929; *Young Lonigan,* his first novel, appeared in 1932. It was only moderately successful, however, and real fame came to Farrell only with the obscenity charge brought against *A World I Never Made* in 1937. The same year he won the $2500 Book-of-the-Month-Club prize for the *Studs Lonigan* trilogy. From that time his writing has generally been popular both with the public and with critics, although criticism has tended to view his later work as not up to the quality of the Lonigan books. As his writing became successful Farrell moved to New York; he is married and the father of a son. He has made outspoken, even radical statements on politics from time to time, but he has never publicly espoused the cause of any particular party or group. In *The League of Frightened Philistines* (1945) he developed a rather unorthodox set of Marxian ideas on literary criticism, and roundly condemned the manner in which literary and publishing activities are presently carried on in capitalistic countries.

CHIEF NOVELS: The central work of Farrell's career is the trilogy *Studs Lonigan,* which consists of *Young Lonigan* (1932), *The Young Manhood of Studs Lonigan* (1934), and *Judgment Day* (1935). Studs Lonigan, the protagonist of the series, is far from a conventional hero; he is ignorant, brash, pugnacious, and at times brutal. He is intended, however, to serve as Farrell's personification of the Chicago South Side, and to a certain extent the entire American city proletariat. But Lonigan is less a worker than a loafer and ne'er-do-well; in this respect he resembles the "drifter" side of Farrell's own personality minus the detachment and creativity which have made him a major novelist.

In the first novel of the trilogy Lonigan, still a boy, is healthy, intelligent, and basically decent; the trilogy records his gradual corruption by his environment. The great struggle of his life is the incompatibility between the sense of sin instilled in him by his Catholic rearing and the brutal cynicism of the South Chicago streets. There are good influences in Lonigan's life: his mother encourages him to become a priest, and a girl, Lucy Scanlon, attempts to regenerate him. But inevitably he slips into the society of pool rooms, gambling, sexual degeneracy, and alcoholism of the young ruffians he encounters in the streets. Before *Young Lonigan* is finished it is apparent that his degeneration is inevitable. *The Young Manhood of Studs Lonigan* shows the completion of his transformation into an adolescent tough. He dabbles in petty crime, turns increasingly to alcohol, and narrowly escapes prison through an orgy in which members of his gang are incriminated in a rape. In *Judgment Day* his decline is complete. Another woman, Catherine Banahan, attempts to rescue him, but the process has gone too far. Lonigan, now approaching his thirties, has become a typical and unredeemable loafer and petty criminal of the South Side. Brooding over his weak heart, partly the result of his dissipations, he ruins himself through a series of bad judgments; he loses his small savings gambling on stocks, enters into an affair with Catherine and is unable to persuade her to have an abortion when she becomes pregnant, and finally finds himself unemployed and drifting in the early years of the Depression. At the end of *Judgment Day* he dies of heart disease at the age of twenty-nine, still ignorant of the forces—within him and in his environment—which have made him into a punk and a failure and finally destroyed him when his youth was scarcely over.

The best parts of the *Studs Lonigan* trilogy are those that are closest to Farrell's own experience. The characters of Studs and his father are well drawn; the women, including Studs' mother and the two girls who attempt to regenerate him, are stereotyped and less convincing. But although Studs is drawn largely from the experience of Farrell's own youth, the author and his character should not be confused; Studs is less Farrell than the sum of all the loafers, petty criminals, and ne'er-do-wells that Farrell observed in the Chicago of his youth. He has, however, put himself into the novel in another form; Danny O'Neill, the protagonist of Farrell's later novel cycle, appears in *The Young Manhood of Studs Lonigan* as a gas-station attendant and college student whose sensitive perceptions and more reasoned judgment raise him above the environment which has produced him. The main literary flaw in the trilogy is its profuse and repetitious detail, which often seems included merely to build up a feeling of authenticity; the three books might well have been compressed into a concise novel of one volume.

The second Farrell novel series centers around Danny O'Neill, a South-Side boy who succeeds in raising himself above the influence of the slums. Danny, more sensitive and thoughtful than Studs, eventually becomes a writer like Farrell himself. This series is generally considered inferior to the Lonigan material; Farrell's obvious sympathy for his character has blunted his powerful realism. The series includes *A World I Never Made* (1936), *No Star is Lost* (1938), *Father and Son* (1940), *My Days of Anger* (1943), and *The Face of Time* (1953). The volumes are not consecutive; for example *The Face of Time* finds Danny five years old, while *A World I Never Made* shows him as an adolescent.

Mention should also be made of several other novels which do not form a part of either series. *Tommy Gallagher's Crusade* (1939) is the story of a Catholic boy who is drawn by an anti-Semitic priest into a sordid right-wing political organization and finds himself on street corners passing out racist literature; the novel is the only literary treatment of any importance of the reactionary and racist movement within the Catholic Church in the Thirties, a movement which was eventually suppressed by the Church itself. *Ellen Rogers* (1941) is another story of adolescence on the Chicago South Side, but this time the protagonist is a girl; Ellen, from a good Catholic family, is ruined by her experiments in promiscuity with the boys of the South Side and finally commits suicide.

Bernard Clare (1946) begins a new series of novels, this time about a Chicago boy who comes to New York to become a writer. In *The Road Between* (1949) the character's adventures are continued, although his name is changed to Carr; and *Yet Other Waters* (1952) completes the series.

None of these post-1939 novels is considered up to the quality of *Studs Lonigan,* although *Ellen Rogers* is perhaps the best of them. A recurring difficulty is that Farrell, at the bottom an autobiographical writer, has difficulty conveying the emotions of the opposite sex. His women are never as convincing as his men, and in *Ellen Rogers* the character of Ed Lanson, the tough South Side boy who cheats Ellen and abandons her, is more believable than the heroine herself.

BETWEEN THE WARS:
REGIONALISM AND RURAL NATURALISM

The term "regionalism" has been applied to a diversity of literary techniques and schools. In American literature it has traditionally been used to describe folklore and "local color" writing in the tradition of G. W. Cable or Joel Chandler Harris. In twentieth-century American literature a new school of fiction in rural settings has appeared, a movement which has little connection with the nineteenth-century local colorists and which is connected instead to the dominant school of naturalism in modern fiction. Whatever label may be used to describe this movement, it is a significant and important one, and one which reflects a definite attitude of contemporary authors toward modern civilization.

The naturalistic movement, properly speaking, represented an attempt to create a literature for an age of science and industrialism. It thus tended to emphasize the more typically modern aspects of society: the factory, the city, the proletariat, suburban life, and the world of commerce. Its locales are generally urban or suburban, and its characters are persons who are in one way or another involved in the world of capitalism. In the twentieth century a wing of the naturalistic movement, however, has turned in the opposite direction: toward the land, the farm, and the peasant. This school represents in part a reaction to industrialism, and even to civilization itself. Such European authors as Knut Hamsun and Jean Giono, as well as Americans like Rölvaag and Steinbeck, are part of a back-to-nature movement which idealizes rural life and occasionally even suggests a sort of mystical primitivism.

The movement itself takes two principal forms. REGIONALISM (in the modern sense) may be defined as a form of pastoral literature laid in rural settings and making extensive use of local customs, language, and characteristics, but in which the chief interest lies in the personality and psychological motivation of the rural characters involved. Goethe's *Hermann und Dorothea* and George Eliot's *Adam Bede* foreshadowed this genre, and its chief modern American advocates are Hamlin Garland (see pp. 45-51), Ellen Glasgow, Willa Cather, and Faulkner. In some respects these authors, especially

Cather and Faulkner, are psychological and artistic rather than "agricultural" in their approach to the novel, but their settings are strongly influenced by regional characteristics.

RURAL NATURALISM, or AGRARIAN literature, on the other hand, is economic and technical in its approach; it is the rural equivalent of the city novel of industrialism. The practical problems of farming are related in great detail; the rural population is shown struggling against nature and the land rather than against each other. Naturally the two tendencies sometimes overlap; Steinbeck's *Of Mice and Men* treats of human conflict as well as of the struggle for life. The agrarian novel, however, does tend to show the peasant or farmer as a creature whose main problem lies in wresting a living from the land. The development of the genre can be traced to various nineteenth-century novels of the type of Zola's *La Terre;* its chief modern American advocates are Steinbeck and Ole Rölvaag.

Certain other authors treated in this section, notably Pearl Buck and Saroyan, are not ordinarily considered regionalists in the strict sense. Their affinity with this group lies in their preoccupation with a limited locale and people—China and the Chinese for Pearl Buck, and the San Joaquin Valley and the Armenian-Americans of the Fresno region for Saroyan. Both these authors have written books about other things and other people, yet their names are mainly associated with their "regionalistic" books, and their fame rests on this part of their work. Other authors who might have been included here, for instance Thomas Wolfe, have been classified elsewhere because it seemed that the psychological or personal element in their work outweighed the importance of the regional element.

The one section of America which has produced the greatest wealth of regional literature is the South. A number of reasons for this could be cited: the South, isolated from the rest of the nation socially and psychologically as a result of the Civil War, has retained a regional culture to a larger extent than any other section of the nation, and in addition its ante-bellum literary past (Poe, Lanier, *et al.*) has provided it with a kind of nostalgic tradition to maintain. Moreover, the antagonism which the South has nurtured for a hundred years against the North, Northern industrialism, Northern commerce, and Northern culture in general has provided it with an emotional focus, however negative, for literary adaptation; in other words the modern

Southern writer, in addition to having something to be "for," also has something to be "against," and his work gains a certain emotional sharpness thereby. Finally, the social problems caused by the legal emancipation of the Negro have provided a fertile ground for psychological and social conflict in fiction. It is difficult to imagine how an author like Faulkner would have written had he not lived amid the hatreds, the cruelties, the injustices, and the heroic acts of idealism caused by the Negro problem in the South.

The evident reason for the vigor and size of the regionalistic movement in recent American literature is a social one: a reaction against the slick and efficient modernism which has come to dominate American life in the first half of the century. A primitive people do not write pastoral literature; from Hesiod and Vergil to Knut Hamsun and Jean Giono pastoralism invariably reflects the nostalgia of the city-dweller for the country. America in the twentieth century is the most "civilized" (in the material sense) culture the world has ever known; it is therefore in some respects the most artificial, the most removed from the elemental realities of life, growth, and death. It is typical of the American writer of the twentieth century to reject this shining, mechanical, but monotonous world of the suburbs, the office, and the factory. Sinclair Lewis rejects it through satirizing it; Hemingway abandons it for Europe and adventure, and Cabell retreats from it into a world of fantasy. The regionalist escapes in another way: by returning to the country, the farm, the primitive, the inefficient, the elemental. Saroyan's whimsically indolent Armenians are as far from the Chamber of Commerce view of the "American way of life" as are the grotesque Georgia sharecroppers of Caldwell or the decadent Southern aristocrats of Faulkner. The retreat into the past is parallel: Willa Cather writes of the frontier, of American history, of seventeenth-century Quebec, and in doing so tacitly rejects twentieth-century America. Even her best-known novel in a contemporary setting, *The Professor's House,* has for its protagonist a man who rejects modern culture through his calm Epicureanism and his preoccupation with history and the past. Paradoxically, this rejection of urban American culture has produced some of America's best and best-known writers, the rural naturalists who are considered in Europe the "American school"—Faulkner, Caldwell, Steinbeck, and Saroyan.

ELLEN GLASGOW (1874-1945)

The term "regionalism" is often wrongly applied, yet the modern tendency among critics to limit its application to a small and highly specialized group of writers has tended to destroy its usefulness as a term. Certainly not all regionalists are slavish and uncritical admirers of the land they describe, nor need they be concerned solely with agrarian or social problems. A regionalist is essentially a writer who seeks to present to a wider audience a feeling for a people and a land he knows well. Ellen Glasgow satisfactorily fills this definition. Her major books are concerned with a well-defined and limited region, the Commonwealth of Virginia; and although her approach to fiction is basically a psychological or internal one she nevertheless shows her characters chiefly in relation to this region. She is not a "Southern patriot" like John Crowe Ransom, neither is she the reporter of sensational Southern horrors like Erskine Caldwell. Along with Faulkner, she is the most objective of the modern novelists who have treated Southern problems—although the objectivity of both authors sometimes seems dubious to Northern readers. "Taken together," says Wagenknecht, "her novels constitute a picture of Virginia from 1850 to our own time, but their emphasis is always upon the men and forces that are building the Virginia of the future and not upon the chauvinists who still bemoan the losses of the past."

Like Faulkner, Ellen Glasgow is interested in portraying the interrelationships of different social classes in the South. In Faulkner these classes are roughly (1) the decadent aristocrats, the former landowning class of the ante-bellum South; (2) the vulgar and materialistic commercial class; and (3) the Negroes. Miss Glasgow is not very much interested in the Negroes as a social class; in her novels colored people exist primarily as appendages to white families, and when they do exist independently they seem to show little race consciousness or solidarity. For her the social classes of Virginia consists of: (1) the "good families," the ante-bellum aristocrats of Faulkner, who are not treated at any great length in her later and more important fiction; (2) the "good people," the hardy back-country settlers, usually slaveless before the War, usually of Scotch-Irish ancestry and Presbyterian background, in other words the people from whom Miss Glasgow herself came; and (3) the educated, the intellectuals and professionals, of Southern ancestry but altered by a Northern education or by contact with big-city society. Since she lived in a decadent land in a decadent age, she is to a large extent a novelist of decadence, but she does not explore its unpleasant or abnormal side as thoroughly as Faulkner does; she retains throughout a genteel, almost Victorian sense of decorum, of what is fitting. Yet she is no prude; she portrayed free love and miscegenation in her fiction a generation before Faulkner. Her South is not so much corrupt as sterile. Yet she consistently shows the formation of new elements which are to transform and revivify Southern society. Her typical heroine is a young woman who perceives the indolence and flabbiness of character of the people around her and sets out vigorously to right matters, driven by an inflexible "vein of iron" (a favorite expression which Miss Glasgow uses in several novels) in her own character. Usually this heroine receives her first impulse through contact with an urban culture; Miss Glasgow seems to suggest that the impetus for the revival of the South must come from the outside, from the wider humanistic and educated tradition of western culture.

Although she is optimistic in this respect—about the future of the South—she is pessimistic in another respect—about the very nature of life itself. In Glasgow, as in Katherine Mansfield, the heroine invariably turns over a beautiful flower to find a repulsive snail underneath. Love especially is unsatisfactory; its attraction is irrational, disregarding considerations of compatibility and character, and its joys are ephemeral and costly. Many of her heroines are made unhappy through youthful love experiences, and more than one of them finds satisfaction later, in middle age, in a life of hard work devoid of masculine companionship. Because of this attitude, and because of her many strong portraits of women, she is sometimes regarded as a feminist writer. There is a certain justice in this view; her women are frequently stronger than her men, she is ironic about masculine fatuousness, and she is cynical about the satisfactions women can derive from love in a society in which men's pleasure is considered above all. Yet she is too objective to be a partisan, even for her own sex. There are many vigorous, admirable, and strong-principled men in her fiction; the intelligent and idealistic scholar John Fincastle in *Vein of Iron,* who sacrifices his career rather than compromise his principles, is typical. Likewise she portrays many women like the conniving and shallow Janet Rowan of the same novel, who does not want Ralph for herself but ruins his life rather than let her rival have him. Ellen Glasgow's apparent feminism is due mainly to the fact that she writes as a woman and that her strongest and most memorable characters are therefore usually of her own sex. She also treats the social problem of the place of woman, especially superior woman, in a man's world; but she is less partisan here than many a male writer, for example Ibsen or Shaw.

In spite of the objectivity of her attitude toward the South and the modernness of her portraits of women, one feels that Miss Glasgow is essentially a nineteenth-century author when compared with, say, Faulkner or Wolfe. Part of this is due to her decorum, to her lack of shocking or sensational detail, and to the artificial quality of her dialogue. If her whites speak like slightly stilted human beings, her Negroes speak like characters out of Joel Chandler Harris, an author for whom she confesses admiration. But in addition to these qualities there is a kind of naïveté about her work, a Victorian reluctance to come to grips with the physical realities of life. She is concerned hardly at all with the life of the senses. She describes what people eat, but not the sensation of hunger or the satisfaction of eating; she mentions love, but does not even attempt to communicate its physical aspect. Moreover there is a deep and old-fashioned sense of right and wrong in her work, a puritan conscience which she derives from her Calvinist background. When her heroines love out of wedlock, even out of the highest motives, they are invariably punished for it. The picture she shows of New York, even in her later novels, is that of a fascinating city of sin as a country schoolgirl might imagine it; when Dorinda (*Barren Ground*) goes to the metropolis she is first approached by a fascinating lady clad in black who wants her to enter into a disreputable house, and then rescued by a kindly doctor who gives her money to go back to Virginia and establish a dairy-farm. In *Vein of Iron* Ralph, in perfect seriousness, refers to the mink coat and orchids of an old flame who has gone off to live in Baltimore as "the uniform of ill fame." Miss Glasgow is on firmer ground when she sticks to her rural Virginia locales, the land she knew thoroughly and whose values and attitudes she appreciated.

In contrast to this aspect of naïveté in her work, mention should be made of her irony, a quality which some critics consider predominant in her style. She once stated that what Southern literature needed above all was "blood and irony," that is, a new vitality and passion plus the vantage-point of skeptical detachment which is "the safest antidote to sentimental decay"—a disease endemic in Southern literature from the time of the Civil War. The quality of irony is not often applied to her heroines, whom she views warmly and with sympathy; it is directed more often against rustics, bigots, small-town belles, politicians, and other minor types. A typical example is the Solomon Hatch of *The Miller of Old Church,* a dogged Fundamentalist who believes that "a man that's gone wrong on immersion can't be trusted to keep his hands off women." In this vein Miss Glasgow seems almost Mencken-like, as far as she is from that irascible critic in general attitude.

LIFE: Ellen Glasgow was born in Richmond, Virginia in 1874 of significantly contrasting parents: her mother came from the traditional Tidewater aristocracy of Virginia and her father from the hardy Scotch-Irish settlers of "the fertile wilderness between the Blue Ridge and the Alleghenies." Sickly as a child, she was unable to attend school, and was educated almost entirely out of her father's library; she read widely, mostly in the standard English poets and novelists. Later she encountered even more important influences: Balzac, Flaubert, Maupassant, the Russian novelists, finally Darwin and Huxley, whose philosophy contributed greatly to her thinking. She began to write when very young; she destroyed an early novel written when she was eighteen. Her first published novel, *The Descendant,* was a story of bohemian life in New York—although it came, as she herself admitted, out of a trip to the big city on which she never went out unchaperoned. The rest of her life was uneventful except for her writing; she passed it mainly in Richmond, although she traveled frequently and lived briefly in New York City. After *Virginia* (1913) her novels enjoyed a considerable popular success, although real critical acclaim came only with *Barren Ground* (1925), probably her most important book. Numerous prizes and awards came after 1940, and in 1942 she was awarded a Pulitzer Prize for *In This Our Life.* In all she wrote nineteen novels, a volume of short stories, a novelette, a volume of essays, and an autobiography; she was not prolific, but she wrote steadily, and her career was a long one. She died, still unmarried, in 1945.

CHIEF WORKS: *Virginia* (novel, 1913) is the first of Miss Glasgow's works in her mature style. Its heroine, Virginia Pendleton, is not only "the perfect flower of the Victorian ideal" but a personification of the Commonwealth itself in the post-bellum period around 1880. Far superior to those around her, she marries a weak and characterless young man, Oliver Treadwell. Oliver's ambition is to be a dramatist; and although Virginia's limited intellectuality excludes her from the area of her husband's aspirations, she clearly has more character and better judgment than he has. When Oliver finally achieves success as a dramatist he abandons her for another woman, since her lifetime of servitude has ruined her beauty. Virginia, however, struggles on courageously to devote herself to the future of her children, especially her talented son Harry. This novel, with its themes of the basic viciousness of the Victorian marriage relationship and the fatuousness of the Victorian male, is one of the most feminist of Miss Glasgow's works. Also included in the novel is a portrait of Cyrus Treadwell, tobacco grower, financier, and railroad man, a vulgar parvenu like the "Snopeses" found in Faulkner. This introduction of the theme of social change makes *Virginia* one of the first novels to treat the problem of the South with honesty and penetration.

Life and Gabriella: The Story of a Woman's Courage (novel, 1916) treats a similar theme but ends on a more positive note. Gabriella Carr is similar to Virginia except that she has a "vein of iron" in her character; when she finds herself in Virginia's position, married to a selfish and complacent husband (George Fowler) who eventually deserts her, she dismisses vain regret, turns her attention to a career, and soon wins success as a dressmaker and manager of a good-sized business. As the novel ends she marries Ben O'Hara, a westerner and therefore man of a new order, vigorous and democratic, who accepts her as a person as well as a woman; a marriage of happiness is achieved through a relationship of mutual respect.

Barren Ground (novel, 1925) is Miss Glasgow's finest achievement and her best-known work. Its basic plot is again that of *Virginia* and *Life and Gabriella:* a woman used and then cast aside by a worthless man. Like Gabriella, its heroine goes on to win success in life through

her energy and her inward "vein of iron," and in this case even wins
an ironic final victory over her seducer. Dorinda Oakley is born the
daughter of a hard-working but poor farmer in the village of Pedlar's
Mill in the barren Tidewater farm region of Virginia. She falls in love
with Jason Greylock, a handsome young doctor, and surrenders herself to him under the impression he is going to marry her. But Jason,
weak and indecisive, instead capitulates to his father's will and marries
the trivial Geneva Ellgood. Dorinda, fleeing the censure of the backwoods village, comes to New York. Searching for work, she is run over
by a taxi and rescued by the kindly Dr. Faraday, who takes her into his
house as a nurse when she recovers. Dorinda soon receives word
that her father is dying; she returns to Pedlar's Mill with her modest
savings, and Dr. Faraday lends her enough money to start a modern
dairy farm. With the knowledge of modern agricultural methods she
has gained by reading in the New York library she soon makes a
success of this; the farm prospers, and the timid country girl evolves
into a realistic, hard-minded, and competent spinster. Later she marries
Nathan Pedlar, a local storekeeper, easy-going and good-natured but
lacking Dorinda's drive; she remains the head of the family. When
Nathan dies heroically in a train wreck she lives the rest of her life
manless and independent, raising Nathan's son by a former marriage
and supervising the large staff of hands on the farm. Meanwhile Jason
has gone downhill; his neurotic wife commits suicide, and he is forced
to sell his farm to Dorinda, who takes a quiet but intense satisfaction
in the revenge. As the novel ends Jason, now alcoholic, sick, and
impoverished, is taken in by Dorinda and cared for until he dies; she
has conquered her old love for him, and she scarcely even pities him
in his humiliating end. Her triumph is complete. When a local farmer,
Bob Ellgood, proposes to her, she rejects him calmly, explaining, "I
am thankful to have finished with all that."

Although the theme of this work is one expressed in several other
novels by Miss Glasgow, it finds here its most vigorous and convincing statement. The New York scenes are weak, but the rest of the
novel is colorful and gripping without ever losing its basic ironic
objectivity. The portraits of Dorinda's family—her self-sacrificing,
bleakly religious mother, her conservative, dogged, and hard-working
father, her weak and ethically confused brother Rufus—are masterful. In spite of the impression given by a synopsis of the plot, it is

not primarily a feminist book; the social issue of the place of women is secondary to the personal study of Dorinda herself, one of Miss Glasgow's most real and living heroines. The history of the degeneration of Jason and the growing madness of his wife is also well done.

Vein of Iron (novel, 1935) is Miss Glasgow's best-known work from her later period. The setting is the town of Ironside in the Mountain Valley of Virginia. Ada Fincastle, the heroine, is born into a higher social class than Dorinda: the hardy and upright Scotch Presbyterians from which Miss Glasgow herself came. Her father, John Fincastle, is a cultivated and idealistic minister who loses his pulpit when he publishes an iconoclastic book of philosophy. The technique of the novel is, for Miss Glasgow, strikingly complex; the point of view switches constantly, and the first section is a novelistic exercise in which the action is seen from the vantage of several characters and related in styles suitable to their various personalities. The history of the novel extends into the Depression era, and the degeneracy of the post-1918 period is examined. With these changes in mind, it can be said that the theme of the novel is essentially that of the three novels examined above. Ada, born into the proud and upstanding Fincastle clan, is endowed with sensitivity by her delicate mother and with inner strength by her indomitable and puritanical old grandmother. While she is still a young girl she falls in love with Ralph McBride, a brilliant local youth who plans to become a law student, and he returns her love. But Janet Rowan, a perverse and discontented rival, resents Ada's success with Ralph; she easily traps the youth into a compromising situation and forces him to marry her, although she does not want him for herself. This tragic marriage, condoned by Ralph's mother and by Ada's rigidly moral grandmother and approved by the public opinion of the town, ruins Ralph's life. He becomes an automobile salesman; the marriage deteriorates steadily, and finally, on the brink of the First World War, Janet goes west to obtain a divorce. Ralph, who has joined the army, returns to Ironside for a brief visit, and he and Ada spend two idyllic days in a mountain cabin. From this encounter a child is born; Ralph has meanwhile gone off to France. Ada's grandmother at first refuses to have anything to do with the erring granddaughter, but when the time comes for the child to be born she relents and sustains Ada with her strength. After the war Ada and Ralph are married; they move with Ada's family to the Virginia metropolis of Queenborough (actually Richmond), and Ralph goes back to selling cars. The Depression hits the family hard; they lose their savings in a bank failure, and Ralph is fired from his job. Now Ada's "vein of iron" asserts itself; she supports the family by working in a department store, and sustains their courage through sheer force of character. When her father dies, leaving them some insurance money, they go back to Ironside to buy back the family house and live in it again. In the end the city, the world, the war, and the new America of the Jazz Age have brought only harm and misery to them, and they look forward to a new era of hope and prosperity in the rural village which gave them birth. Thus the concluding note of *Vein of Iron* is a rejection of the postwar world, with its alarming and confusing technical changes and the apparent degeneration of traditional mores. Ellen Glasgow obviously felt little at home in the America of the Twenties; she found it confusing and depressing, she does not write about it convincingly, and the last third of the novel therefore suffers structurally. The best part of the work is the narrative up to 1917, including the picture of the heroine's family and the story of the love-triangle involving Ada, Ralph, and Janet.

WILLA CATHER (1874-1947)

It is an oversimplification to treat Willa Cather solely as a regionalist, yet she fits this classification more closely than any other. Her dominant theme, the motif that winds its way through her work from one end to the other, is the one which preoccupies most modern American regionalists: the relation between town and country, or between the highly complex urban civilization of the twentieth century and the elemental simplicity of rural life. For Willa Cather, as for Garland, the rural life is the life of the frontier, and the urban world is the cultivated artistic and intellectual life of the Eastern seaboard. Her region is the vast area stretching from Nebraska southwest to New Mexico and Arizona, especially the great prairie area where she herself spent her girlhood. She is a psychologist rather than an agrarian; she is less interested in the way the harvest is wrested from the earth than in the effects of prairie life on various kinds of personalities. Her protagonists are for the most part foreign-born immigrants who come to the prairie region bringing with them the traditions and prejudices of the old world along with the wisdom of a more venerable civilization. Miss Cather admires the pioneer life not because it is elemental (*cf.* Steinbeck or Faulkner) but because it is stimulating and healthy; her ideal hero is a European provided with the traditions of his European heritage but rejuvenated by contact with the frontier. "I have never found any intellectual excitement more intense than I used to feel when I spent a morning with one of these pioneer women at her baking or butter-making," she wrote of her girlhood years.

Miss Cather is not a naturalist; her world is a poetized one where the brutal side of rural life is glossed over and where human passions are refined almost to the decorum of a Henry James. There are many romantic qualities in her work. She is interested primarily in the past: not only in the days of her own youth, but in the lost youths of her characters. Her pioneer women are constantly recollecting past times, past tragedies, past glories, and past joys; some of her novels seem composed almost entirely of reminiscences. One of her two most famous novels, *Death Comes for the Archbishop,* is practically an historical romance; it actually begins with that hoary device so dear to the nineteenth-century novelist, the solitary horseman riding across a plain. Miss Cather's essential interest, however, is in personality rather than in incident; she is romantic chiefly in her cult of the distant and misty past. She has little sympathy with the spirit of her own time; there is little of the liberal democratic fervor of Dreiser, and nothing whatsoever of industrialism, business, or modern politics. In such novels as *Alexander's Bridge* (1912) and *The Professor's House* (1925) she utilized contemporary settings and characters, but the characters in such novels are invariably intellectuals or artists who have little contact with the commercial and industrial main-current of twentieth-century life. Actually she admires most in American culture those elements drawn directly from foreign societies; her most sympathetic heroes are foreign-born. The "100% American" of the type of George Babbitt has little attraction for her.

The themes of Willa Cather's work are interlocking, or rather they are contained one inside the other, like a set of Chinese boxes. The main or "outer" theme, which contains the others, is that of the contrast between civilization and frontier. At the next level are the secondary themes, most of them involved with adjustment to frontier life. Examples are (1) the plight of the elderly and cultured immigrant who is unable to adjust to the crudity of life on the frontier (Mr. Shimerda in *My Antonia,* the pharmacist Euclide Auclair in *Shadows on the Rock*); (2) the revolt of the sensitive young person against the frontier and his search for tradition and stability in the intellectual centers of the east, or in Europe (Claude Wheeler in *One of Ours,* Jim Burden in *My Antonia*); (3) the conflict between native Americans and Europeans on the frontier (*O Pioneers!, My Antonia, One of Ours,* and several other novels and stories); and (4) the conflict between the generations, usually involving a hard and thrifty son and a romantic and dreamy father (Mr. Shimerda and his son Ambrosch). Within these basic conflicts can be found sub-themes, for example the friendship between the raw frontier boy and the professor who befriends him and introduces him to a wider culture, found in *The Professor's House, One of Ours,* and several other works.

As an analyst of the differences between European and American culture Willa Cather suggests comparison with Henry James, and indeed her first novel, *Alexander's Bridge,* lies strongly under James' influence. Her mature work, however, shows more originality; she reverses James' American-in-Europe theme and develops the problem of the European immigrant in American society, especially the frontier society of the west. In her girlhood in Nebraska she observed many types of immigrants: Czechs, Swedes, Norwegians, Germans, Russians. Many other American writers observed these people as well, but they described them from the outside (e.g., Garland's Middle Border tales). Willa Cather penetrates their psychology and shows them internally, in their innermost reactions to their environment. She sees in these people, even in illiterate peasants, the mark of an ancient civilization, a maturity, a contact with the past, lacking in the brash and successful American farmer or town merchant of the middle west. The archetype of these Europeans is the Bohemian settler Shimerda of *My Antonia,* a musician and a reader, cultured, melancholy, who eventually commits suicide because he is unable to adjust to the crude life of the Nebraska prairie. Yet in his failure he bequeaths to the growing American frontier a tradition, a cultural contact with the past, which enriches the new nation.

In style Miss Cather's work is restrained and artistic; she has a subtle feeling for words and avoids the awkwardness of the more "elemental" naturalists. Although she once declared that in writing *O Pioneers!*, the first of her mature novels, she decided "not to 'write' at all" and merely to concentrate on telling the story, her prose is actually carefully thought out and subtly arranged. She is a classic stylist, even in her theory of economy: "Art, it seems to me, should simplify," she wrote. When she revised *The Song of the Lark* in 1937, twenty-two years after its original publication, her main changes consisted of deletion of detail, superfluous documentation which she felt detracted from the central effect of the work. Sometimes, especially in her later novels, her style seems almost skeletal; Daiches refers to it as "the novel *démeublé.*" Here she is closer to Crane and Hemingway and to the Norwegian Knut Hamsun than she is to other American regionalists of the type of Faulkner and Steinbeck, or to her early model Henry James.

When Miss Cather's novels have a weakness it is generally in construction. Frequently they include disparate elements which she does not quite succeed in combining (e.g., in *One of Ours,* the early farm scenes and the later account of the European war); at other times she seems to have trouble with point-of-view problems, for instance the device of describing Antonia through the eyes of Jim Burden often causes the reader's attention to be distracted from the central drama of the story. Other novels (*Death Comes for the Archbishop, Shadows on the Rock*) are episodic and lack any single strong plot to tie them together; their unity is one of theme rather than of story. Her novels are often divided into "books" or sections which are unified works of art in themselves; this suggests that her talent was primarily that of a writer of novelettes and stories, which she combined to the best of her ability to make into novels.

LIFE: Willa Cather's exact birth date is uncertain, since her birth was never properly recorded. Standard reference sources give 1875 or 1876, but recent research has indicated 1874 as a more likely date. She was born near Winchester, Virginia, but the South had little influence on her; when she was eight years old she moved with her family to a ranch in Nebraska, where she spent the formative years of her girlhood. Here she wandered about the prairie on her pony, visiting remote farmhouses and making acquaintances with the immigrant farm women of the region. As a little girl she was given the rudiments of an education by her parents and grandmother; there were no public schools at hand. When she reached adolescence the family moved to Red Cloud, Nebraska, where she attended high school. As a student at the University of Nebraska (1892-95) she was a brilliant student and prominent in campus activities, serving as secretary of the literary society and editor of *The Hesperian,* a student magazine, which carried her first published fiction. From her graduation to 1901 she worked as a journalist; from 1901 to 1906 she served as a high-school English teacher in Pennsylvania. In 1906 she was offered a position on *McClure's Magazine* in New York; she accepted, and two years later was made managing editor. Meanwhile she had gained some success as a writer; her first volume of stories appeared in 1905. In 1911 she resigned her position on *McClure's,* and in 1912 her first novel, *Alexander's Bridge,* was published. Thenceforth she devoted herself entirely to writing. She remained unmarried, and subsequently traveled widely, especially in the Southwest; a series of novels based on Spanish-American and French-American history were inspired by her interest in this region. Her travels also led her to an interest in Canadian history; *Shadows on the Rock* (1931) is laid in the era of the French settlement of eastern Canada. Willa Cather died in 1947, secure in her position as America's foremost woman novelist.

CHIEF WORKS: *O Pioneers!* (novel, 1913) was Miss Cather's first full-length work in her mature style, following the Jamesian and derivative *Alexander's Bridge* (1912). In it she attacks for the first time in a novel the main theme of her work: the reaction of an immigrant family to the Nebraska frontier. The Swedish immigrant John Bergson, hard-working and devoted, has established his family on a farm near Hanover, Nebraska. As the novel opens he dies; the mother lacks character, and the responsibility for the family falls on the heroic and sensitive daughter Alexandra, the central figure of the novel. There are three brothers: Lou and Oscar, and the youngest, Emil, a favorite of Alexandra. Under her guidance the farm prospers; she forms a friendship with the restless young Carl Linstrum, but is unable to marry him because of her responsibilities. He goes away to the city to become an engraver, and Alexandra loses herself in the hard work of the farm. Meanwhile the scene has been set for another tragic love-drama: Marie Tovesky, a little Bohemian girl Alexandra has befriended, grows up and marries the farmer Frank Shabata. Emil, Alexandra's delicate young brother, falls in love with the young married woman; the two are discovered together and killed by Frank. Alexandra, long grief-stricken, recovers only when Carl Linstrum returns from the Klondike; the old friendship of the pair grows into a renewed love, and they decide to marry and devote their lives to the responsibilities and satisfactions of the farm. "Fortunate country, that is one day to receive hearts like Alexandra's into its bosom, to give them out again in the yellow wheat, in the rustling corn, in the shining eyes of youth." Even the violent tragedies that beset Alexandra cannot suppress her immigrant optimism and vitality. This novel is particularly interesting as an embryonic version or preliminary study for *My Antonia;* the main difference is that Alexandra is somewhat excessively depersonalized and symbolic, and thus does not seem as real a person as Antonia.

The Song of the Lark (novel, 1915) is the story of the daughter of a Swedish Methodist minister in the tiny town of moonstone, Colorado who becomes a famous opera singer. Thea Kronborg, the heroine, is encouraged in her precocious talent by her German music teacher, Professor Wunsch, and by Dr. Howard Archie, a local physician whose life has been ruined by an unhappy marriage. Luck follows Thea through her early career; she befriends a railroad worker, Ray Kennedy, and when he is killed in a train accident it is discovered that he has left her enough money in his will to go to Chicago to study. In Chicago she is taken in hand by the pianist Andor Harsanyi, who sends her to study with a great voice teacher, Madison Bowers. Her talent flowers, but she is discouraged and becomes ill. A friend, the wealthy young brewer Fred Ottenburg, invites her to recuperate on his Arizona ranch. They fall in love, but are unable to marry because of Ottenburg's estranged and mentally ill wife. Meanwhile Dr. Archie advances money for her to study in Europe; in ten years she becomes a great Wagnerian soprano, and returns in triumph to sing at the Metropolitan. As the novel ends she is about to marry Ottenburg, but she does so as a famous career woman and with the understanding that her main energies are to be devoted to her art.

This novel treats a theme which may be considered as second in importance in Miss Cather's work: the development of an artist from humble beginnings on the western frontier to success and fame in cultivated eastern and European society. In a sense it is the story of Willa Cather herself transferred to the realm of music. The main flaw of the novel is that the first half is more interesting than the second; after she wins success Thea becomes a little dull, and the author seems in doubt what to do with her. The best scenes are those of Thea's youth in the first pages of the novel.

My Antonia (novel, 1918) is the story of Antonia Shimerda, daughter of Bohemian immigrants in the Nebraska prairie land. The story is related by Jim Burden, a friend of Antonia who has much the same relation to the immigrant population of the prairie that Miss Cather herself had. The Shimerdas are sold bad land and have a hard struggle during the first years of their farming career. Mr. Shimerda is a dreamy and impractical musician who was goaded into leaving Europe by his wife, who hoped for greater opportunities for her son Androsch in the new world. Mr. Shimerda, crushed by the severity of pioneer life, commits suicide, and his daughter Antonia is forced to assume the burden of the farm work. Her splendid energy and optimism carry her through this ordeal; she is at her best when struggling against the challenge of the soil. Later the family moves to town and Antonia becomes a hired girl, but this change in her social status brings only ruin to her. She is deceived and abandoned by an unscrupulous railway employee; disillusioned, she returns to the country to bear her illegitimate child. Her life diverges from Jim's for a while, and when he encounters her next she is comfortably married to Anton Cuzak and is raising a large family; she has found her place in life. A sub-plot relates the careers of Pavel and Peter, two Russian immigrants who are continually dogged with ill luck.

This novel, usually considered Miss Cather's best by critics, nevertheless suffers from a structural flaw: the interest shifts from Jim to Antonia, and the reader has difficulty making up his mind which the story is about. The title is intended to suggest that it is about "Jim's Antonia," that is, about the character of the girl as seen through the young man's eyes. But in the third section we lose sight of Antonia almost completely as the author concerns herself with Jim's education at the University of Nebraska and his romance with the Swedish farm girl Lina Lingard. Yet in the end it is Antonia who dominates the book: vigorous, unselfish, possessing a certain sensitivity and yet realizing her basic limitations, she is content to devote her life to the hard labor of the farm and to her children, leaving the world of culture and education to the more fortunate Jim. The portrait of Mr. Shimerda is masterful; here Willa Cather most eloquently expresses her admiration for the European culture brought by the immigrants to the western prairie. On the other hand the bleakness and cruelty of life in the Old World is suggested by a story told by Pavel the Russian on his deathbed: years before, as a sledge-driver in Russia, he had thrown a bride and groom to the pursuing wolves to save his own life. This story, interesting in itself but having little organic connection with the main plot of the novel, well illustrates the difficulties in construction in which Miss Cather often finds herself.

One of Ours (novel, 1922) is Miss Cather's war novel; its title suggests that the hero is typical of the many midwestern boys who went to France in 1917 to "save the world for Democracy." The hero, Claude Wheeler, is first seen as a Nebraska farm boy. The chief characters of the early part of the book are his father, severe and insensitive; his understanding and sympathetic mother; the illiterate but cheerful and wise hired woman Mahailey; and Claude's freethinking, realistic, somewhat cynical Austrian friend Ernest Havel. Claude, seeking for a better life, goes off to Lincoln to his education, although his father obliges him to go to a shoddy denominational college instead of the University of Nebraska which Willa Cather herself attended. In Lincoln, however, he meets the Ehrlichs, a cultivated family of German background, and is introduced to the world of culture. His responsibilities to family and farm force him to give up his education, and he presently makes the mistake of marrying the colorless and excessively religious Enid Royce, who is more interested in prohibition work and entertaining preachers than she is in her husband. When a missionary relative in China falls ill Enid goes off to take care of her, and Claude goes back to live with his family. The second half of the novel concerns the First World War and its impact both on the farm community and on Claude himself; the changing attitudes of the region toward the impending war are described with skill and exactitude. Claude is commissioned in the army and goes to France, where he forms a friendship with the talented violinist David Gerhardt as well as with two separate French families who serve to introduce him to European culture. The war, France, David, and his French friends open Claude's eyes; in his mind he rejects his crude frontier background, and now knows what he wants to be. But his awakening is also his destruction; he is killed in a conventional heroic incident, leaving his mother and Mahailey to mourn him in Nebraska.

As previously remarked, the difficulty with this novel is that the two halves do not fit together. The first half is obviously the better, yet the section describing Claude's war experiences is a remarkable *tour de force;* it is hard-minded and masculine, although free from profanity, and is in every way comparable with such first-hand male accounts of the war as Dos Passos' *Three Soldiers.* Some of the best characters in the novel are the minor figures: Mahailey, Ernest Havel, the Ehrlich family, and Claude's thin-blooded, dyspeptic, puritanical, and materialistic brother Bayliss, a farm-machinery salesman who seems to Claude the personification of all that is sordid and dismal in the world. This novel was awarded a Pulitzer Prize in 1923.

A Lost Lady (novel, 1923) is one of the most "classic" and economical of the novels of Miss Cather's middle period. The setting is the railroad town of Sweet Water, Colorado, and the central character is Mrs. Forrester, a charming and vivacious young woman married to a railroad man and contractor many years her senior. The novel traces the decline of the heroine, which parallels the decline of the town after its future as a railroad center is blighted. The key incident in her life is her brief romance with the dashing bachelor Frank Ellinger. When Ellinger later marries, Mrs. Forrester turns her attention to the care of her now ailing husband; and when he dies she has an affair with the coarse and pushing business-man Ivy Peters. Again her lover marries, this time taking over the old Forrester mansion (symbol of the decline of the pioneer race and its replacement by the business-man). Years later she marries a wealthy Englishman in South America and manages to achieve a dignified and respectable old age, even though her known affair with Ellinger had made her a "lost lady" in her home town. This novel, like *My Antonia,* is related by a young man, Niel Herbert, who is slightly shocked at first by Mrs. Forrester's gay ways but eventually comes to admire her charm and vitality.

The Professor's House (novel, 1925) marks another temporary abandonment of the frontier setting. The middle-aged Godfrey St. Peter, historian at a midwestern university, is completely devoted to his studies in the Spanish period in American history; he is the epitome of the scholar and the introvert. When his wife Lillian demands a larger and more modern house, he insists on continuing to study in the attic of the old house, where he feels comfortable with his books and mementos. His daughters have married and gone away, and he finds little satisfaction in family life. As the story unfolds the reader learns the great event in his life: his encounter with Tom Outland, the one fine mind among all the students he has taught, who was killed in the First World War. A long flashback in Book Two relates Outland's life: as a cowhand in New Mexico he had encountered, with his companion Roddy Blake, an untouched cliff village inhabited by Indians in prehistoric times; the discovery fired his imagination and eventually led him to seek an education. Thus he came under the influence of St. Peter. Before he was killed Outland, by this time a brilliant physicist, had invented a gas device which had "revolutionized aviation." The patent for this invention came into the hands of his fiancée, St. Peter's daughter Rosamond; and when Rosamond marries the pushing and aggressive Louie Marsellus her husband becomes rich on the patent. All this depresses the Professor, and when a gas jet is accidentally opened in his room he can see no reason to shut it off; he narrowly escapes death and is rescued only through the loyalty of an old German seamstress, Augusta, who shares the room with him. This crisis, and his gratitude for the loyalty and affection of the old seamstress, reconcile him to continued existence, and he faces his old age with a kind of optimistic stoicism.

Like many Cather novels, *The Professor's House* actually contains two stories, that of St. Peter himself and that of Outland. In this case the two are more ingeniously welded than usual; the Professor remains the central figure, and Outland's life is tied to his own through their common interest in history as well as through the device of the invention. The chief impression the reader carries away from the book is the character of St. Peter, one of the most sympathetic and convincing persons in Miss Cather's work.

The Professor's House had hinted at Miss Cather's growing interest in the history of the Southwest, although it presented it only indirectly.

In *Death comes for the Archbishop* (novel, 1927) she treats the material at first-hand, and the result is a historical novel—one, however, in which the main interest is centered on a psychological study of the characters. The novel is set in the early nineteenth century in the region which is later to become New Mexico, and is based on actual historical documents. The key names are changed, however, the historical Bishop Lamy of Santa Fe becomes Jean Marie Latour, and his vicar-general Father Machebeuf is converted to Father Joseph Vaillant. The central figure is the French priest Latour, patrician, sophisticated, humanistic, and intelligent, who comes to the region to take over the office of Bishop of Santa Fe. Aided by his vicar Father Vaillant, Latour converts the Indians, builds missions, and brings civilization to a far-reaching desert and mountain empire. He is opposed, however, by the selfish and opportunistic Spanish priests of the region and by the ecclesiastical authorities in Mexico. His life is spent in struggle and loneliness; he finds little intellectual companionship in the rude missionary society. But he dies satisfied with his task and certain he stands on the threshold of a supernatural reward.

This novel is Miss Cather's most romantic work, and it is also her most popular. The sources of its popularity are obvious: it is straightforward in style and optimistic in tone, and it has the exotic charm of a historical setting. The title is misleading; the novel is not concerned primarily with death, and it is only at the end that Latour is made Archbishop. The story focuses on the character of Latour, on his inner struggle with his temptations of ambition and cultivated living, and on his saintly triumph in reorganizing and revitalizing the New Mexico Church. The heroism of the bluff and vigorous Father Vaillant is of a more physical sort; at the end of the novel, feeling that his task has been accomplished in New Mexico, he journeys northward to the infidel mining camps of Colorado to carry on the Church's work. Underlying the story of these two men is a wider pattern, the history of the European (specifically Spanish) influence on the Southwest and the gradual amalgamation of Spanish, Indian, and Anglo-Saxon elements to form the modern New Mexico.

Shadows on the Rock (novel, 1931) is another historical novel, this time laid in seventeenth-century Quebec under French rule. The construction is episodic; there is no single dominant plot. The central characters are the "philosophical apothecary" Euclide Auclair, who comes to the primitive settlement of "Kebec" to establish a pharmacy and serve as personal apothecary to his patron the Count Frontenac, Governor General of Canada, and Auclair's daughter Cécile, a "true Canadian" who prefers the new primitive country to the France she left as an infant. Connected to Cécile are the stories of Jacques Gaux, son of a sailor and a "fallen woman" of the town, whom she befriends and makes into her companion; Noël Pommier, the colorful and eccentric cobbler; and Pierre Charron, the romantic woodsman she eventually marries. The dominant theme of the novel is the formation of a new civilization in Canada, its character determined by its traditional French roots but markedly altered by the new soil into which it has been transplanted. Thus the basic concept of the book is not unlike that of the Nebraska frontier novels, which also study the effect of the transplantation of European culture into American soil. Much local color and folklore is included; in *Shadows on the Rock* Miss Cather undertakes a complete panorama of seventeenth-century Quebec history. The "shadows" of the title are the traditions and folk-tales, both of France and of the New World, which fall today over the "rock" on which Quebec is built.

STORIES: Willa Cather's first published book was a volume of stories which appeared in 1905 under the title *The Troll Garden*. All of the stories of this volume which Miss Cather wished to recognize, along with some later stories, were reprinted in *Youth and the Bright Medusa* (1920), which is therefore her most important and definitive story volume. The stories in this book are all concerned, in one way or another, with problems of art and artists, especially young artists in the early stages of their careers; the Medusa of the title is art itself, fascinatingly and often fatally attractive to the young. Of the stories included the best known are "Paul's Case," a study of a maladjusted boy in a Pittsburgh slum who revolts confusedly against his environment, embezzles money in order to pursue his dreams of an artistic life, and commits suicide when his money is gone; and "A Wagner Matinee," the story of a Boston girl who marries and goes west to live on the Nebraska frontier. After wasting her life in the dingy monotony of farm existence, she revisits Boston in her old age and through attending a single Wagner concert comprehends the value of what she has missed. The remaining stories in *Youth and* *the Bright Medusa* treat similar themes; several of them, e.g., "The Diamond Mine," "Coming, Aphrodite," and "Scandal," treat incidents in the lives of artistic women who more or less resemble the Thea of *The Song of the Lark*. A later volume, *Obscure Destinies* (1932), contains three long stories or novelettes dealing with life in Nebraska prairie communities.

OLE RÖLVAAG (1876-1931)

Like Willa Cather, the Norwegian-born Rölvaag is mainly concerned with problems of European settlers on the western prairie; he shares Miss Cather's admiration for the heritage of European culture, and he describes similar scenes observed in a similar era. In addition, his background and thematic content link him to a contemporary Norwegian novelist: Knut Hamsun, author of *Growth of the Soil* and a number of other novels depicting the advancement of the frontier in northern Norway. But Rölvaag lacks both Miss Cather's optimism and her stylistic perfection; and compared to Hamsun his prose technique is more conventional. His masterpiece, *Giants in the Earth* (1927), is the story of *Growth of the Soil* transferred bodily to the American prairies. There is another essential difference between the books of the two authors: Hamsun frankly champions the rural life and adulates the forces of natural reproduction, whereas Rölvaag confines himself to an objective description of the hardships of pioneering. Rölvaag hardly makes farming seem attractive; to his farmer heroes the prairie is merely a depressing waste which continually frustrates the efforts of humanity to wrest a living from it. In style Rölvaag is a traditionalist; his structure is direct and chronological and he approaches his characters through the conventional exterior narration of the realist. He wrote all his major works originally in Norwegian, and later collaborated with Lincoln Colcord in the English translations of the novels. His lifetime residence in America, however, as well as certain characteristics of his outlook, clearly justify the classification of his work as American literature.

LIFE: Ole Rölvaag was born on the island of Dönne in Norway in 1876; his family had been fishermen for generations. After a meager education he came to America at the age of twenty to work on a relative's farm in Dakota. He managed to work his way through a number of courses at Augustana College in South Dakota and then through St. Olaf College in Northfield, Minnesota; he received a B.A. from St. Olaf in 1905 and an M.A. in 1910. He became an American citizen in 1908. He returned to Europe intermittently throughout his career, and during the latter years of his life served on the faculty of St. Olaf. He died in 1931 of a heart attack.

CHIEF WORKS: *Giants in the Earth* (novel, published in Norwegian in 1924-25 and in English in 1927) is the first unit in a trilogy which in its entirety comprises a saga of pioneer life in South Dakota, dedicated by its author to "those of my people who took part in the great settling." Per Hansa, a Norwegian immigrant, struggles to wrest a living from his barren farm in the prairie country; he raises a sod hut and eats chiefly the products of his own labor for many years. Although Per himself is an ideal pioneer type, his wife Beret is moody, imaginative, and unhappy; she was destined by nature for a refined life in the city. Her complaints make both herself and Per unhappy, but he continues his dogged struggle against nature. When a son is born to them Per dubs it Peder Seier (Peter Victorious); he is proud of his child, although Beret is worried and unhappy because the baby has not been properly christened. Her religious conviction gradually turns into an obsession, a narcotic which makes the bleak prairie life endurable for her.

A significant episode is the scene in which Per Hansa discovers that earlier homestead stakes have been driven into the land now occupied by his friendly neighbors. He burns the stakes, so that when the earlier settlers return their claim is unsubstantiated. Beret learns his secret, and this act of her husband becomes a symbol of the loss of morality which she feels has accompanied their abandonment of their Norwegian homeland.

Beret's religious obsession and her sense of sin eventually cause Per Hansa's death. When a friend, Hans Olsa, dies in their house, she insists that Per Hansa go out in the blizzard to seek a minister. To her mind the extreme sacrament is more important than life itself. Per Hansa at last gives in to her nagging, goes for the minister, and is lost in the storm.

Peder Victorious (novel, in Norwegian 1926, in English 1929) continues the trilogy. The central figure is the son, Peder Victorious

Holm, who grows up as the favorite of his widowed mother. When Peder attends an American school the new perspective he gains there tends to alienate him from his mother, who stands rigidly in his mind as a symbol of an Old World way of life. A minister, Gabrielsen, encourages him to enter the ministry, but he finally decides to remain a farmer, thus casting his lot with the new way of life on the American soil. As the novel ends he decides to marry Susie Doheny, an Irish girl and sister of his fun-loving companion Charley, thus further uprooting himself from his orthodox Norwegian background.

Their Father's God (novel, 1931) was published almost simultaneously in Norwegian and English. This novel closes the trilogy; Peder, having married Susie Doheny, settles down to manage his mother's farm. When a child, Petie, is born the two young people differ over its religious education; the quarrel is essentially over the question of which culture (Irish or Norwegian) the child is to be raised in. Peder's mother Beret naturally takes his side, taking the child secretly to be baptized a Lutheran while Susie with equal secrecy has him baptized by a priest. Meanwhile Peder has entered politics, becoming quickly involved in the local rivalry between Irish and Scandinavian settlers. When Beret, on her deathbed, confesses the secret baptism Susie has a breakdown. Peder nurses her back to health, and the family peace is restored. Then, however, Peder's political opponents broadcast slanderous information about him which he believes could have come only from his wife, and he accuses her of putting loyalty to her race before love of her husband. The quarrel breaks out afresh, and finally Susie abandons him, taking her child back to her father's home. Thus the ending of the trilogy is a tragic one in harmony with Rölvaag's general pessimistic outlook; the diverse foreign elements on the Dakota frontier are unable to live together in peace, and eventually their religious differences and the cynical manipulations of politicians turn their mutual mistrust into outright hostility.

PEARL BUCK (born 1892)

It seems at first unsatisfactory to regard Pearl Buck as a regionalist, yet her main contribution to literature has been the presentation to American readers of a region which is virtually her homeland

Reared in China by missionary parents, she spoke Chinese before she spoke English. Her first published stories were laid in Chinese settings. Since then she has produced books, both fiction and non-fiction, on many different subjects from the problem of the American career woman to the raising of mentally retarded children; yet her main interest has remained China, and she is known to the general public as well as to academic criticism chiefly as the interpreter of Chinese culture to America. When she was awarded the Nobel Prize in 1938—only the third American to be accorded this high honor— the citation specifically referred to her "rich and truly epic descriptions of peasant life in China" as well as her "biographical master-pieces," presumably the fictionalized portraits of her missionary parents. It is worth noting that the two types of works mentioned, along with her own autobiography, comprise all her Chinese stories and tacitly exclude her works which treat only American characters in American settings.

The sense in which Mrs. Buck is not a regionalist is in her treatment, in her approach to the subject. She is not interested in local color; indeed her very choice of Chinese settings seems to have been little more than an accident of environment. Under other conditions she might easily have written books about Peruvians, Eskimos, or the sharecroppers of the American South. Her interest lies entirely in what is general, universal, and human in the Chinese people: the struggle of men to wrest a living from the soil, the intricate tensions of family relationships, the human reactions to violence and disaster, the effects of success and prosperity on the humble and hard-working, and the contrast between decadent aristocracy and crude but vigorous yeomanry. Yet she is not primarily interested in social processes or social relationships; her method is internal, analytical, and primarily concerned with the individual. The reader lives intimately with her fictional characters; they are not sentimentalized or glamorized, neither are they rendered brutal by an excessively naturalistic treatment.

The fact that Mrs. Buck's characters are foreigners, speaking an intricate foreign language which is almost impossible to translate adequately into English, involves her in certain stylistic difficulties. Under the conditions it is almost impossible, for example, to write natural dialogue; few American readers understand, or are interested in, the way Chinese really talk, and to make them talk like Americans (in slang, for instance) would be ludicrous. She approaches the problem by having them speak distinguished if somewhat stilted English, attempting through diction and syntax to recreate the peculiar dignity of the Chinese language as she knows it. The effect has often been described as "Biblical," and it is likely that she has consciously or unconsciously modeled the style on the English Bible. Many sentences begin with "Now" or "And," and occasional archaisms in construction and vocabulary heighten the effect. A flowing, dignified, almost epic quality results: "When the child was a month old Wang Lung's son, its father, gave the birth feasts, and to it he invited guests from the town and his wife's father and mother, and all the great of the town." In surmounting her problem Mrs. Buck has created a style with an unusual advantage. Since it is, so to speak, "translated from the Chinese," it is devoid of American idioms and slang, and thus is easily translatable into other languages. It is easy to see how the Swedish Academy committee, examining candidates for the Nobel Prize, might find a Swedish translation of *The Good Earth* more impressive than a Swedish version of Hemingway, Wolfe, or Faulkner, who would tend to lose their peculiar stylistic merit in translation.

LIFE: Pearl Buck, *née* Sydenstricker, was born in 1892 in Hillsboro, West Virginia, where her missionary parents had returned on a brief furlough. She traveled to China with them while still an infant, and for all practical purposes was reared solely in China. Growing up in Chinkiang, a city on the Yangtse River, she learned Chinese folklore and Buddhist and Taoist magic from a nurse. Even as a child she manifested a natural story-telling facility, and her juvenile stories were published in the *Shanghai Mercury* when she was still a girl. She received her formal education at a boarding school in Shanghai and at Randolph Macon Woman's College at Lynchburg, Virginia, where she was elected class president and wrote for a student paper. Returning to China, she found her mother seriously ill and spent two years nursing her; meanwhile she married Dr. John Lossing Buck, an "agricultural missionary." When her mother recovered, the family followed Dr. Buck to his work in a town in North China; they remained there for five years, then moved to Nanking, where Mrs. Buck taught English at the University of Nanking. In March 1927 the city was looted by Nationalist troops; the Bucks' house was burned and the family narrowly escaped death. The catastrophe also destroyed the manuscript of Mrs. Buck's first novel; by this time she was writing steadily, and had published in *The Atlantic Monthly* and other American magazines. Her first novel, *East Wind: West Wind,* appeared in 1930. In 1931 she wrote *The Good Earth* in three months; the novel was an immediate success, and she was awarded a Pulitzer Prize the following year. Although none of her subsequent books were considered to come up to the standard of this masterpiece, her work has generally been favorably regarded by critics. In 1933 she published a translation of one of China's most famous modern novels, *All Men Are Brothers;* her own *House of Earth* trilogy, the continuation of *The Good Earth,* was completed in 1935. The same year she was awarded the Howells Medal by the American Academy of Arts and Letters, and in 1938 she was awarded the Nobel Prize for Literature, a remarkable achievement when it is remembered that *The Good Earth* had appeared only seven years before. Beginning in 1938 she wrote several novels with American settings, of which *The Proud Heart* is best known. Around 1941 she began to return to her Chinese material. In recent years her work has been extremely versatile; she has published children's books, essays in defense or support of China and its people, an autobiography, and several collections of short stories. Mrs. Buck, who has lived more or less permanently in the United States since 1934, has two children, both daughters. Divorced in 1934, she married again in 1935 to Richard J. Walsh, president of a publishing firm and editor of the magazine *Asia*.

CHIEF WORKS: *The Good Earth* (novel, 1931) describes the lives of Wang Lung, a hard-working Chinese peasant, and his wife O-lan, passionately attached to the soil and struggling to raise themselves from the poverty of their class. The novel begins with the marriage of Wang Lung to O-lan, a slave girl from the formerly aristocratic but declining House of Hwang. The two work together through hardship, famine, flood, and sickness to wrest a living from their land and to increase their holdings, and eventually they achieve prosperity as the decadent Hwang clan declines. Three sons and two daughters are born to the marriage; Wang Lung, now wealthy, takes a concubine, the beautiful young Lotus, but O-lan serves him and her children patiently until her death. A sub-plot describes a family of shiftless relatives who come to live with Wang Lung; one year during the great flood Wang Lung's farm is miraculously spared by pillaging robbers, and he learns that his uncle is secretly allied to the robber band. Wang Lung cleverly succeeds in inducing the opium habit in this troublesome uncle and his wife, and they become too involved in their dreams to bother him further. After O-lan dies and his sons begin to marry, Wang Lung begins to enter into the decline of his life. He lives almost alone on his land, attended only by a single daughter and by his slave, the young Pear Blossom. As the novel ends he exhorts his sons never to relinquish the land he will bequeath them upon his death, but they are already secretly planning to sell the land and use the proceeds for various projects of their own. Lacking Wang Lung's dogged attachment to the soil, they belong to a new generation of "wreckers and builders;" one son is a revolutionary, and the other two are modern and practical in attitude. Thus the course of Wang Lung's career parallels the development of modern China and the emergence of progressive and revolutionary elements in her peasantry.

The Good Earth is the first volume of a trilogy titled in its entirety The House of Earth. The second volume, Sons (1932) follows the career of the three sons described in the earlier novel; they become respectively a merchant, a rich man, and a "good" war lord. The novel is said to be based on the traditional Chinese theme of the benevolent war lord, a kind of Robin Hood who robs the rich to aid the poor. A House Divided (1935) continues the story through the era of the Kuomintang and the agrarian reform. Yuan, a grandson of Wang Lung, is educated in America and returns to his country to aid his people in modernizing their agricultural system.

The Exile (novel, 1936) is a fictionalized biography of Mrs. Buck's mother, in which her father appears as a secondary character. The pendant to this novel is found in Fighting Angel (1936) another fictionalized biography in which the same marriage is seen from the point of view of the father. These two novels are probably Mrs. Buck's most important works after The Good Earth, and were specifically referred to by the Nobel committee in their award citation.

Dragon Seed (novel, 1941) marks Mrs. Buck's return to the

Chinese setting after several American novels. The scene is the Sino-Japanese war; the plot follows the fortunes of Ling Tan and his family through this national catastrophe. The remarkable scenes of the looting of Nanking are drawn from Mrs. Buck's personal experience. A sequel, *The Promise* (1943), depicts the Japanese conquest of Burma; the chief character, Lao San, is a son of Ling Tan who fights the Japanese in the army of Chiang Kai-shek. These later novels are particularly interesting as social and historical documents, and for the picture they present of Mrs. Buck's own experiences, but they are not considered the equal of *The Good Earth* in literary quality.

WILLIAM FAULKNER (born 1897)

The awarding of the Nobel Prize to Faulkner in 1950 has brought home to the American public the fact that in Europe he is considered the foremost living American author; today many American critics are inclined to agree in this judgment. The distinction is one to which he is well entitled. He is sometimes considered an agrarian naturalist in the manner of Erskine Caldwell; actually he is more meaningful and profound, as well as more artistically original, than any of the American naturalists with the possible exception of Hemingway. His novels are generally laid in rural settings, but the problems they treat are psychological and moral rather than physical. His great subject is the decline of the South: its economic sterility, its moral disintegration, and its struggle to resist the progressive and materialistic civilization of the North. The protagonists of his novels are the decayed aristocrats of the "Sartoris" type; whether their names are Sartoris, Compson, or Bundren, they are old Southern families past the peak of their prosperity and riddled with moral decay, yet still finer than their antagonists, the "Snopes" clan—the efficient, materialistic carpetbaggers, merchants, and entrepreneurs—who are gradually superseding them. In each of Faulkner's novels the Sartoris characters struggle futilely against the encroachment of the Snopeses. In *The Sound and the Fury* the Compson family struggles against a Snopes in their own midst: their brother Jason. In *Sartoris* the Sartoris and Compson clans are confronted by the Snopeses themselves; and these latter are seen at the height of their triumph in *The Hamlet*. Even in *Sanctuary*, the least profound and the most sensational of Faulkner's novels, the

"Sartoris" Temple Drake is defeated physically and symbolically by the perverted "Snopes" Popeye. Faulkner's mission is to preside over the spiritual death of the old South and to study the forces which are preparing its new awakening.

Faulkner is a highly individual author, and therefore difficult to classify. His earlier Yoknapatawpha County material (*Sartoris* and the early stories) is naturalistic regionalism, slightly influenced by the style of Sherwood Anderson and demonstrating as well a personal lyrical quality which was to become more prominent in his later work. Beginning with *The Sound and the Fury* (1929) his work may be more aptly described as "symbolic naturalism," and his style a radical form of stream-of-consciousness utilizing difficult and highly original experiments in chronology and point-of-view. An important section of *The Sound and the Fury* is quite literally "a tale told by an idiot." The trend away from realism continues throughout his career: *The Fable* is an allegory, virtually a fantasy, although parts of it are strongly realistic in a style resembling Dos Passos. Because of his interest in stream-of-consciousness techniques Faulkner may also be considered a kind of psychological novelist. In both *The Sound and the Fury* and *Light in August* the action centers around the events of a single day, but previous and subsequent incidents are filled in through recollections of the characters and through adroit and complex flashbacks, in either case seen internally, through the often semi-conscious reactions of the characters involved. The interest of the author is not so much in the incidents themselves as in the complicated mental reactions of the characters to the incidents—reactions so thoroughly non-verbal that new narrative techniques must be devised to communicate them. Here Faulkner resembles Proust and Joyce more than he does the American naturalists Farrell, Dreiser, or Hemingway.

From another point of view Faulkner is a regionalist, although his region is an imaginary one: "Yoknapatawpha County," including its county seat of Jefferson. Since Jefferson is described as seventy-five miles south of Memphis on the Illinois Central Railroad, it can easily be identified as Oxford, Mississippi, where Faulkner has passed most of his life; but at the same time Yoknapatawpha County is a fictional region only loosely related to the real Mississippi county. Unlike Wolfe, Faulkner has not faithfully and painstakingly recorded the

history of his own family. Certain incidents, like the murder of old
Colonel Sartoris, are drawn from family traditions, but in the main
Faulkner's characters are the product of his own imagination. For this
reason Faulkner is able to create characters of a greater diversity
than Wolfe: the gangster Popeye, the spinster Miss Burden, the
rebellious young Temple Drake, and the brooding Harvard student
Quentin Compson are equally forceful, real, and meaningful.

Faulkner, like Hemingway, is greatly concerned with erotic passions, with cruelty, and with the connection between the two. Where
Hemingway's cult of violence is uninhibited, almost innocent,
Faulkner's is twisted and melancholy; his mood resembles that of
Baudelaire or Poe. His characters are seldom moved by normal urges:
Quentin Compson (*The Sound and the Fury*) is in love with his
sister, Popeye (*Sanctuary*) is impotent, a character in *The Hamlet*
is romantic over a cow, and Joe Christmas (*Light in August*) becomes
the paramour of a spinster a generation older than he is. Except in
the case of *Sanctuary,* however, Faulkner does not relate these horrors
for mere shock effect; he is interested in aberration as a symbol of
Southern decline, and as such he treats it with the superb objectivity of
a true artist.

Faulkner's characters, although diverse, tend to fall into a set of
clearly defined groups. There are rebellious and nymphomaniacal
young girls of aristocratic families (Caddy Compson, Temple Drake);
there are half-witted country girls, easily exploited by town slickers
(Dewey Dell, Lena Grove); there are moody younger sons, reckless
and rebellious but proud of their family backgrounds (Quentin
Compson, Bayard Sartoris). But although Faulkner creates the same
characters over and over, he seldom repeats his stories; he finds a
new situation, plot, or structure for each novel.

There is little overt political content in Faulkner's work. It is
apparent, however, that he is by no means a liberal in the ordinary
sense. His sympathies are with the aristocratic and highly principled
Sartorises, as decadent as they may be, and against the parvenu
Snopeses. He shows little interest in humanitarianism or socialistic
planning, especially in his earlier works, and has been accused of
condescension toward Negroes. His later work, however, shows
evidence of a more liberal attitude: in *Intruder in the Dust* (1948)
he offers a positive solution to the Negro problem, although one

which may not be acceptable to Northern liberals, and since then he has frequently condemned racism, violence, and the activities of "White Supremacy" groups in the South. During the controversy over school desegregation in the South in 1954-56 Faulkner at first took a liberal stand endorsing the Supreme Court decision for desegregation and then, in a *Life* editorial, attacked the extremism of Northern pressure groups like the NAACP and warned the North to "go slow" now that it had won an important victory in principle. Actually Faulkner is no social thinker and is out of place in a political controversy. His approach to the Negro problem is purely aesthetic, psychological, and physiological; he describes both Sartorises and Negroes as they appear to him without idealizing them for didactic purposes. It should be pointed out as well that one of the most frequently recurring characters in his work is the strong-willed, courageous, and loyal Negro woman whose character is superior to that of the whites around her (Dilsey in *The Sound and the Fury,* Nancy in *Requiem For a Nun*). His strongest condemnation of slavery is perhaps that found in the long version of *The Bear,* where he develops at some length the idea that the fertile land of the South has been eternally cursed by this unnatural domination of man over man and by the sexual and psychological evils that have come out of it. It should not be imagined that because Faulkner uses the word "nigger" and sometimes shows Negroes as lazy and incompetent he is a fanatic white supremacist. He is an artist, and where this particular problem is concerned he faithfully records the events and attitudes of the culture he is describing.

LIFE: William Faulkner (the family's name is more correctly spelled Falkner) was born in New Albany, Mississippi in 1897. His family was a distinguished one; its founder, Col. William C. Falkner, was a Civil War hero and a novelist in his own right. To Faulkner his great-grandfather is a symbol, the epitome of the gallant aristocracy the war had destroyed. He recreates him in his fiction as Colonel Sartoris, a distinguished figure in the post-war gentry of Yoknapatawpha County. Faulkner's father, Murray C. Falkner, was for many years treasurer of the State University at Oxford (later the University of Mississippi); during the writer's lifetime the family, like the fictional Sartoris clan, was aristocratic and financially secure but no longer wealthy. Faulkner himself, exaggerating somewhat, describes its status as that of "genteel poverty." Anecdotes are told in Oxford of his eccentric habits and appearance in the days before his writing made him famous; his curious mixture of dignity and shabbiness earned him the nickname "Count-No-'Count." His education was incomplete; he quit school at the eleventh grade, but finished a year's work at the University after the war. His war experience played an important part in the formation of his character. Too short in stature for the Army Air Corps, he enlisted as a cadet in the Canadian branch of the Royal Flying Corps in 1918. He was trained as a pilot in Toronto but the war ended before he was commissioned. A legend that he was wounded in combat is unfounded; actually he was injured in a flying escapade while celebrating the Armistice in 1918. His disappointment at missing the experience of combat was a great one; the theme appears in several of his early stories and recurs years later in *The Fable*.

Faulkner began to write soon after the war; he thought at first he wanted to be a poet, and wrote fiction only to support himself while he wrote poetry. The poetry, although it showed talent, was not remarkable. He enrolled in the University, failed an English course, and restlessly went on writing. He was greatly aided during this period of his life by a friend, Phil Stone, an Oxford lawyer who gave him advice, encouragement, and financial assistance. On Stone's advice he went briefly to New York, where he worked in a bookstore and turned out a large number of stories. His first published work, a volume of poems entitled *The Marble Faun,* appeared in 1924. The following year he went to New Orleans, where he met Sherwood Anderson, by this time already an established author. Under Anderson's influence he wrote *Soldier's Pay,* his first novel; Anderson persuaded a publisher to print it, and Faulkner was launched as an author. From 1925 to 1929, however, he was forced to continue working part-time at odd jobs, including furnace-tending at the University of Mississippi. After a brief trip to Europe in 1925 he went on writing novels; *Soldier's Pay* (1926) and *Mosquitoes* (1927) and, to a certain extent, *Sartoris* (1929) were pot-boilers which he wrote in the hope of winning financial independence so he could write something more significant. The strategy was a mistake. Stone now persuaded him to try to write the best book he could, regardless of its marketability. The result was *The Sound and the Fury* (1929), a rewriting of a novel he had earlier abandoned. The novel was a critical success, although not a financial one. On the strength of it, however, he married Estelle Oldham (1929) and gave up his odd jobs to devote himself to full-time writing. *Sanctuary* (1931), which he allegedly wrote solely to make money, achieved its end; it created a sensation, became a popular success, and brought its author financial independence. From that time his reputation has constantly grown, although in 1946, immediately before interest in his work was revived by Malcolm Cowley's publication of *The Portable Faulkner,* there was a period when all of his nineteen volumes were out of print.

In 1933 Faulkner made the first of several expeditions to Hollywood to work as a screenwriter. For the most part, however, he has preferred to remain in Oxford, where he lives simply and takes little part in literary or intellectual activities. He has one child, a daughter. He was awarded the 1949 Nobel Prize for Literature in 1950 and delivered an impressive speech of acceptance before the Swedish Academy in which he upheld the dignity of man and presented an optimistic view of the future of civilization. Since 1950 criticism of his work has been extensive and generally sympathetic. His influence has been particularly important in Europe, but in America too he is commonly regarded as the greatest living American author.

CHIEF NOVELS: *The Sound and the Fury* (1929) marks Faulkner's first radical departure from the traditional form of the novel; it is also his most complicated book technically, and one of his most successful artistically. The title is from *Macbeth,* V:5: ". . . a tale told by an idiot, full of sound and fury, signifying nothing." The structure is extremely complex. The story is divided into four sections, each related through the mind of a different character, and there are countless flashbacks and switches in chronology. The "central time" of the action is 1928, but parts of all four sections take place in 1910. The main characters are Jason and Caroline Compson, heads of the aristocratic but declining Compson clan of Jefferson; Candace (Caddy), their daughter; Benjamin (Benjy), an idiot son; Quentin, the idealistic thinker of the family; Jason, a third son, materialistic and selfish; Dilsey, a self-effacing and intelligent old Negro servant;

and Luster, the fourteen-year-old Negro companion and bodyguard of Benjy. The kernel of the plot is as follows: Caddy is seduced by the worthless Dalton Ames and later married off to an opportunistic Northerner, who abandons her. Quentin, who only half-realizes he is in love with his sister, is filled with shame at her betrayal and finally drowns himself in Cambridge as a sort of expiation. Benjy is at first happy playing in his pasture, but the land is sold to pay Quentin's tuition at Harvard (symbol of the selling-out of the Southern land-holding class to the North). Later his brother Jason obtains legal guardianship over Benjy and has him sterilized (symbol of the extinction of Southern aristocracy at the hands of materialists); in the end Benjy is put into a state institution. Since the mother is self-centered and helpless, Dilsey presides over the disintegration of the family with loving patience and resignation. This novel makes extensive use of stream-of-consciousness narration, free association, and diffuse location in time.

As I Lay Dying (1930) relates the death of Addie Bundren, a farmer's wife in Yoknapatawpha County, and the efforts of her family to carry out her dying wish to be buried in the family plot in Jefferson. As in *The Sound and the Fury,* the story is seen through the eyes of various characters in succession, in this case Addie herself, Addie's husband Anse, her daughter Dewey Dell, and her sons Cash, Darl, Jewel, and Vardaman. As Addie dies she supervises Cash in the construction of her coffin; the doggedly precise Cash explains carefully in his section just why he built the coffin as he did. The family are burdened with a staggering set of obstacles in their efforts to carry Addie's body to Jefferson. A flood wipes out a bridge, the mules are almost drowned in the river, Cash's leg is broken in a wagon accident, Darl, losing his wits, sets fire to a barn and is packed off to the insane asylum, and Dewey Dell, seeking a "remedy" for her illegitimate pregnancy, is seduced by a cynical town druggist. As the journey proceeds it assumes the proportions of a saga. When the mother is finally buried, Anse buys himself a set of store teeth and suddenly marries "a duck-shaped woman with pop eyes" he encounters in the town. His obligation to his dead wife is fulfilled, and he now looks only to the future.

Light in August (1932) opens as a country girl, Lena Grove, comes to Jefferson on foot seeking Lucas Burch, the father of the child she is about to bear. When she reaches the town, however, her destiny becomes involved with that of Joe Christmas, a young saw-mill worker with a touch of Negro blood. Christmas, an orphan, has been raised to manhood by a dour Scotch farmer; a bitter experience with a small-town harlot has made him antisocial and brooding. His wanderings throughout the South have at last led him to Jefferson, where he becomes the protege of a mysterious spinster named Burden, daughter of carpetbaggers who settled in the town after the Civil War. He lives in a cabin on Miss Burden's land and eventually becomes her lover. When Lucas Burch, fleeing Lena, arrives in town Christmas utilizes him as a partner in his secret bootlegging enter-prises, which involve highjacking liquor from trucks and selling it to the town loafers by the bottle.

All this is background; the key action of the novel takes place on the day Lena arrives in town. On the morning of this day Miss Burden, brooding over her imminent old age, attempts to kill Christmas and herself with an obsolete Confederate pistol; the weapon misfires, and Christmas, emotionally overwrought, kills her with a razor. Burch, drunk, sets fire to the house, is caught, and arrested for the murder; he escapes by putting the blame on Christ-mas. When Lena gives birth to her child the sheriff forces Burch into a reconciliation with her, but he flees on first opportunity. Lena, too dim-witted to waste much time in regret, goes blithely on to Memphis to take up a new life. In the meantime Christmas has been captured in a nearby town and brought back to the Jefferson jail. When he escapes he is tracked to the house of the Rev. Hightower, a dis-graced minister, and brutally slain by Percy Grimm, a conceited young national guardsman. *Light in August* is structurally similar to Joyce's *Ulysses:* it focuses on the events of a single day and describes the reactions of various characters to these events.

Sanctuary (1931) is the most lurid of Faulkner's novels in con-tent, although relatively conventional in technique. This unbeatable combination made it an enormous popular success; it was later made into a motion picture upon which Faulkner collaborated. The heroine is an intelligent but rebellious and neurotic young college girl, Temple Drake. She flees on an escapade with Gowan Stevens, the character-less young nephew of the lawyer Gavin Stevens, who later reappears in *Intruder in the Dust*. Through Gowan's drunkenness the car is wrecked, and he leads Temple to a lonely farmhouse where she falls into the hands of a gang of moonshiners. The leader of this band is the strange and perverted social misfit Popeye, himself impotent, who derives a vicarious satisfaction from Temple's violation at the hands of Alabama Red, another member of the gang. Gowan, beaten, disappears, and Temple subsequently undergoes various exotic and painful adventures including a confinement in a Memphis brothel whose madam is at first proud to gain the patronage of the important Popeye but later shocked by his depravity. Alabama Red is killed by Popeye in the act of making an unscheduled visit to Temple, who eventually escapes. Meanwhile Goodwin, another of the bootleggers, has been arrested for a murder actually committed by Popeye. He is defended by Horace Benbow, a lawyer who wishes to expiate his selfish and conventional life by fighting for this unpopular cause. Benbow attempts to use Temple's evidence to save his client, but she has been so unbalanced by her experience that she only prejudices the jury against Goodwin. Goodwin is lynched by a mob, Benbow barely escapes, and Temple goes off to Paris to forget her three months' nightmare. Popeye, the evil focus of the whole drama, escapes to Florida and is later hanged for a murder he did not commit. Faulkner at one time declared that he wrote *Sanctuary* solely to create a sensation and make money. It did both these things; it is not, however, as bad a novel as Faulkner's statement, or a summary of its plot, would suggest. Temple's character is vividly established, and the plot achieves more suspense and general interest than it does in most of Faulkner's work. There is also an underlying symbolism— the rape of the South at the hands of an impotent North (Popeye)— but the theme is not of any importance in the basic structure of the book and means little to the ordinary reader. An important sequel to *Sanctuary* is found in *Requiem for a Nun* (see p. 221).

Absalom, Absalom! (1936) is one of Faulkner's most intricate and difficult novels. Its plot centers around the career of the Mississippi planter Thomas Sutpen, who dies in 1869; but the story is seen through the eyes of young Quentin Compson in 1910. The mysterious and demonic Sutpen comes to Jefferson when it is still a frontier community. He buys a hundred-square-mile section of land ("Sutpen's Hundred"), imports a French architect to build a mansion, and brings in a wagon-load of slaves. After he has finished furnishing the house in expensive taste, he consolidates his position in the community by marrying Ellen Coldfield, daughter of a leading citizen of Jefferson. Although he is considered strange and unfriendly, he grows immensely rich; he invites his neighbors to lavish dinners and entertains them with wrestling matches between his slaves. His wife bears him a son, Henry, and a daughter, Judith. Both of these children have strange qualities; Judith takes an unnatural pleasure in the ferocious combats of her father's slaves. Henry goes off to the University and there meets Charles Bon; by coincidence Charles is Henry's half-brother. Thomas Sutpen has been married before to a West Indian woman, but has abandoned her after discovery of her Negro blood. Now this ghost of his first marriage returns to haunt him; Charles meets his half-sister Judith and falls in love with her. At this point the source of Sutpen's wealth is revealed; it came from the dowry of the first wife he has abandoned.

The war intervenes. Then, as Charles is about to marry Judith, he is mysteriously killed by Henry Sutpen. Henry flees and drops out of sight for many years. Meanwhile Thomas Sutpen returns from the war to find his wife dead, and develops an obsessive desire to perpetuate his line. Since Charles is dead, Henry a fugitive, and Judith vowed to spinsterhood, he plans a second marriage with Rosa Coldfield, one of the narrators of the novel. Rosa flees from him in indignation, and in 1867 Sutpen, still seeking an heir, enters into a liaison with Milly Jones, granddaughter of the loafer and sometimes tenant farmer Wash Jones. In 1869 Milly bears a child, and Wash kills Sutpen in a rage. Henry returns to Jefferson and is killed in the burning of the mansion. Gradually the Sutpen clan dies out; the last survivor of the line is an idiot illegitimate son of Charles Bon. Miss Rosa, the last person to know the inside history of the family, dies in the winter of 1910.

The structure and style of this novel are complex; the story is related from diverse points of view, always in retrospect, and the language of presentation is purposely chaotic. The major part of the narrative is related by Quentin Compson to his indifferent Harvard roommate Shreve McCannon. Quentin himself acquires the story only obliquely; he hears part of it from his father, part from Rosa Coldfield, and part of it from family documents and letters. The rise, triumph, and decline of the Sutpen clan is symbolic; it represents the history of the Southern landowning class from 1830 to 1910. Thomas Sutpen, at first creative, vigorous, and ruthless, eventually becomes old, degenerate, and obsessive. His clan attenuates into idiocy as the Snopeses of the South begin their rise to supremacy. The character of Quentin, who also appears in *The Sound and the Fury,* is skillfully drawn through his relations with the Northerner Shreve McCannon.

The Hamlet (1940) is less a novel than an integrated set of sketches, some of them first published as magazine stories, centering around the crossroads village of Frenchman's Bend in Yoknapatawpha County. The dominant theme is the emergence and rise to power of the Snopes clan in the eighteen-nineties, and the central character in Flem Snopes, the most efficient and ruthless of his clan.

The novel is divided into four sections. In the first, titled "Flem," the hamlet of Frenchman's Bend with its ruined ante-bellum mansion is dominated by the Varner family, who own the local store and control the region's economy. The Snopes clan soon arrive and begin to work their way into the community. Flem, one of several sons of old Ab Snopes, goes to work for the Varners as clerk in their store, and through his uncanny and intelligent perspicacity soon makes himself an essential part of the business. He saves his money and presently buys the local blacksmith shop as an investment; he has begun the first of his "capitalistic" enterprises. The section also introduces V. K. Ratliff, a shrewd but friendly itinerant peddler who serves as an observer and commentator in the novel. A comic interlude relates how Ab Snopes sells the farmer Pat Stamper a horse which has been "fattened" by blowing it up with a bicycle pump.

The second section, "Eula," relates the history of Will Varner's daughter Eula, whose phenomenal sexual charms attract half the men in the region before she is twelve. When one of her swains gets her with child, Flem quietly makes a deal with Varner to marry her, thus acquiring the most desirable woman in the county and simultaneously assuring his penetration into the Varner family.

"The Long Summer," the third section, contains two main incidents. In an ironically related idyll, Ike, an idiot offspring of the Snopes clan, becomes romantic over a cow and finally "elopes" with it. Meanwhile Mink Snopes and the farmer Jack Houston quarrel over a bull which wanders into Houston's pasture, and Mink murders

Houston from ambush. He hides the body in a hollow tree, and he and his brother turn to squabbling over the money Houston was carrying when he died. At the end of the section the Snopes clan agrees to cure Ike of his infatuation by killing his cow and feeding him a steak from it.

In "The Peasants," the final section, Flem Snopes achieves two crowning triumphs. Returning from Texas with his bride, he brings along a herd of wild horses in charge of a Texan hostler. The Texan sells the beasts to the local farmers and then vanishes, whereupon the horses break out of their corral and disappear into the country-side. When the farmers remonstrate with Flem he claims he has nothing to do with the horses. Later he carefully drops hints that treasure is buried on the grounds of the old mansion, which he now owns. By "salting" the ground with coins he manages to trick the astute Ratliff and two other men into buying the place for an ex-orbitant price. The money from these and other successful ventures in his pocket, he then moves on to Jefferson and greater triumphs, leaving the village ruined and demoralized.

The Hamlet is the most satirical of Faulkner's novels; parts of it are virtually parody. Ike's romance with the cow and the various horse-dealing incidents are related in the tradition of American folk humor; they suggest Mark Twain or Bret Harte. Behind this satire, however, lies a serious pattern: the rise of the brash Snopes clan and its victory over the traditional Varners, who are squeezed dry and cast aside like a lemon before the novel is over. Thus The Hamlet shows the beginning of the process of the commercialization of the South, the climax of which is shown in The Sound and The Fury, Light in August, Absalom, Absalom!, and other novels. In a broader sense the theme is the struggle between the Snopeses, whatever name they assume, and the Sartoris tradition of aristocracy. The dominant quality of the Snopeses, the shrewd and ruthless aggressiveness which earns them their success, is clearly shown in this novel. The charac-ters of Ratliff and Houston are also superbly drawn.

Intruder in the Dust (1948) presents a more optimistic analysis of the problem of the South than any of Faulkner's earlier works. The plot, centering around a lynching story, is banal and has often been treated by lesser authors; the interest of the novel lies in its mem-orable characterizations and in its implied socio-political ideas.

The action opens as Lucas Beauchamp, an eccentric old Jefferson Negro, is accused of the murder of a white man, Vinson Gowrie. Feeling among the "white trash" runs high, not only because Lucas is seized near the body with a pistol in his hand, but because he has a long reputation as a "high-nosed nigger" who has refused to accept the inferiority of his race. A lynching seems certain. The affair causes a vague feeling of guilt in the boy Charley Mallison; years before he fell in a creek and was taken to Lucas' place to dry out, and the Negro's intelligent friendliness on that occasion has remained in his mind ever since. Charley's uncle, the lawyer Gavin Stevens, agrees to take Lucas' case, but Lucas will tell the attorney nothing. It is to the boy that he confides his innocence; he asserts to Charley that if Vinson's corpse is dug up it will be found not to have been shot with Lucas' pistol. In the middle of the night Charley, his friend Aleck Sander, and the courageous spinster Miss Eunice Habersham go to the cemetery and exhume the body; to their surprise it is not Vinson, but the loafer and petty criminal Jake Montgomery. Meanwhile, as the mob from Vinson's home district, Ward Four, clusters around the jail, Miss Habersham guards the prisoner with the weapon of her feminine dignity, and the sheriff and Stevens go back to dig the corpse up again. This time the grave is empty. Both corpses are found buried in the river-bed, and Vinson's relatives are persuaded that Lucas could not have committed the crime. The solution to the mystery gradually comes out. Crawford Gowrie, partner of his brother Vinson in a lumber business, has been stealing lumber from the shed at night. Detected by Lucas, he has killed his brother and thrown the evidence toward Lucas in order to silence the Negro. Later he has been forced to kill Montgomery to cover his tracks. Lucas, freed, is used as a decoy to capture Crawford, who commits suicide in jail.

It is the lawyer Gavin Stevens in this novel who serves as the spokesman of Faulkner's own ideas. Stevens' conversations with the sheriff and with his nephew Charley constitute a comprehensive statement on the Negro problem in the South as it stands today. It is the men of good will—Stevens, the sheriff, Charley, the Negro Lucas, and their kind—who must set about fighting lynching and discrimination with courage. But the job must be done by the South itself. Intervention of the North, through "Yankee" legislation, will turn both the men of good will and the ignorant Snopeses and crackers against the North; they will unite in a fanatic defense of Southern independence, and the Negro's lot will be worse than before. If the South is allowed to handle the problem itself progress will be slow, as all true progress is; the Civil War adequately demonstrated that no mere Constitutional Amendment has the power to free the Negro. The South, led by its young and educated, must progress in its own way; and Faulkner in this novel shows a constructive and optimistic picture of how this may be done.

Requiem for a Nun (1950) is a sequel to *Sanctuary;* it follows the life of Temple Drake eight years after the action of the earlier novel. Ostensibly a novel, *Requiem for a Nun* is cast in dramatic form and is in fact virtually a play; it has been produced on the stage with little adaptation. The incidents of the story become apparent only through gradual revealment. Temple, it develops, has married Gowan Stevens, the college boy whose drunken accident eight years before threw her into the hands of the perverted Popeye. Two children have been born from the marriage. Shortly before the novel opens, one of them, a girl six months old, has been murdered by Nancy Mannigoe, a Negro servant. Nancy has been condemned to hang for the crime, but for some undisclosed reason Temple feels an obsession to save her. She is aided by Gavin Stevens, the cultured and intelligent lawyer who had earlier appeared in *Intruder in the Dust* and a number of Faulkner's stories. Gavin, who is Gowan's uncle, had nevertheless defended Nancy at her trial for murdering his own nephew's child. In a scene in the office of the Governor of Mississippi and in a flashback to the time of the crime, the true facts are revealed. During her ordeal in the Memphis brothel Temple had become infatuated with Alabama Red, a member of Popeye's gang, who was killed by Popeye when he was surprised trying to climb into her room. Certain shameless letters she had written to him had come into the possession of his brother Pete. When Pete comes to her to attempt to blackmail her with the letters, she sees in him the sexual image of the dead Red, and is ready to allow herself to be "kidnaped" by him. Nancy, a prostitute and dope addict who is nevertheless a religious and inwardly decent person and who is determined to prevent Temple's surrender to evil, finally smothers the baby to prevent her mistress from going off with Pete; she hopes through her execution for this crime to obtain expiation for her life of vice. Gowan, the young husband, learns the full details of the sordid history when he hides in the Governor's office as Temple tells the story. The Governor refuses to grant a reprieve, and Nancy dies forgiven by Temple and secure in her inward religious faith. But there is no such solace for Temple, who has to face a life in which both she and her husband know every detail of her own vicious past.

Temple, who is not basically an evil person in *Sanctuary,* is here seen corrupted and destroyed by the evil that was done to her by Popeye and his confederates. Evil begets more evil, and the chain is broken only by the unselfish sacrifice of Nancy. Gowan is also involved in the moral tangle; he began the whole chain of evil through his drunken escapade, and now he finds himself punished through the death of his child and the corruption of his wife. Although Gavin Stevens is the spokesman of Faulkner's ideas in *Intruder in the Dust,* here he seems less important; it is the strong, courageous, and selfless Nancy, a sinner yet a true Christian martyr, who provides the positive message of the novel. Even Temple is impressed by her unshakeable religious faith at the end, although she realizes it is something that she herself could never attain. This novel demonstrates the idealistic and religious tendency in Faulkner's later work, a tendency which is to emerge as the dominant quality in *The Fable.*

Requiem for a Nun is also interesting from a structural point of view. The middle section of the novel is written as a drama with lines of dialogue alternated with stage directions. This section includes the flashback scene in which Temple is prevented from fleeing with Pete by Nancy's murder of her child. Preceding this is a long expository chapter written in the style of *Absalom, Absalom!* and the other prewar novels in which the history of the Jefferson courthouse is described in detail from the time of its construction around 1830. Following the central dramatic section is another chapter relating the history of the jail in which Nancy is confined, and the novel then ends with a short scene in drama form depicting the final interview between Temple and Nancy shortly before the Negro woman is executed. Thus *Requiem for a Nun* is a more pretentious book technically than *Sanctuary,* as well as a more sincere work of art. Yet its unusual form, lacking in action and devoted mainly to remembered incident, cripples its interest; in the end it is a less gripping narrative than *Sanctuary.* The two "historical essays" included are valuable sources of information about the history of the fictional Yoknapatawpha County.

The Fable (1954) is radically different from anything else Faulkner has written, and was long awaited as the climactic achievement of his career. Upon its publication in 1954 it was revealed to be a long and technically difficult parable of humanity and war, the most idealistic of Faulkner's novels but in some way the most unsatisfactory. The plot is so complicated as to defy synopsis. The setting is the First World War, and the story is built around the actual incident of the "false armistice" of May, 1918, and the folk-legend of the appearance of a Christ-like figure in the trenches who came to bring peace to the battle-weary armies. In Faulkner's novel the Christ-figure is an anonymous French corporal whose career clearly parallels that of the Passion: he has twelve disciples, one of whom, his friend Polchek, betrays him and later commits suicide; two women who follow him are named Marthe and Marya (Mary); he is executed between two criminals, his body is taken by his women to a farm where it is blown up (i.e., the Ascension) by a chance shell, and he is later chosen by a series of coincidences as the Unknown Soldier whose remains are interred at the foot of the Arch of Triumph. Behind his story lies the mysterious organization known as *Les Amis Myriades et Anonymes à la France de Tout le Monde* with its saint-like leader, the American Negro Reverend Tobe Sutterfield. A long digression, adapted from Southern folklore, tells the story of an English horse-trainer and two Negroes who travel around the South winning horse-races with a stolen thoroughbred. Another important sub-plot concerns the French division commander General Gragnon, whose career is ruined when an entire regiment, under the influence of the Christ-like corporal, mutinies when it is ordered to attack and thus precipitates the false armistice. The most interesting narrative passages of the novel, however, are those dealing with a young British aviator (called only "David"), eager to get into combat, who arrives in France just in time for the mutiny and the false armistice. His sole combat sortie is a weird mission to escort a German general behind the Allied lines to confer with the Allied high command over the crisis caused by the mutiny (i.e., the militarists, the generals, band together regardless of nationality against the "men of good will" when a dangerous pacifistic movement arises). David, who does not understand the significance of the mission, gradually becomes aware of a vast and mysterious plan contrived to effect the meeting: the guns in his own plane have been loaded with blank ammunition, and both the German and Allied anti-aircraft guns have secretly been provided with dud shells so that the planes may cross the lines unscathed. Later in the novel David, fearing he has joined the war too late to take part in combat, falls into despair and presumably commits suicide.

In many ways *The Fable* is the weakest of Faulkner's major works; its various plots are poorly coordinated, much space is given to incidents which are not relevant to the central theme, and the whole novel suffers from a kind of vague and maundering spuriousness. Much of the difficulty is due to the fact that Faulkner has abandoned his Mississippi material, where he is thoroughly at home, to deal with Europe, which he visited only once, and the First World War, which he saw only from America and Canada. In support of this view it might be argued that the best parts of the book are those closest to Faulkner's own experience: the story of the stolen horse, a tale something like those related in *The Hamlet,* and the parts dealing with flying, drawn from Faulkner's own service as a Canadian air cadet. The main ideas of the novel are expressed in a long dialogue between the corporal and the Allied commander-in-chief (pp. 342ff). The passage is evidently modeled on the famous "Grand Inquisitor" chapter from Dostoyevsky's *The Brothers Karamazov;* the general, like the Grand Inquisitor, argues that mankind must be cynically manipulated for its own good, and the corporal, like Dostoyevsky's Christ, holds fast to his faith in man's essential goodness and wisdom.

STORIES: "A Rose for Emily" (1931) is an allegory of decadence built around the life of a simple Jefferson spinster, Miss Emily Grierson. The events, however, are related by indirection and seen only from the point of view of public rumor; thus the structure and chronology are more complicated than the story would seem to demand. The basic plot, disclosed by gradual revelation, is as follows: after the death of her father the unmarried Miss Emily lives alone in an old house with a single Negro servant. Stricken by her father's death, she seldom goes out. Then a construction company comes to lay sidewalks in Jefferson, and Miss Emily falls in love with Homer

Barron, a strong and vigorous Yankee foreman. The affair continues for some time; then, presumably, Homer loses interest in what for him has been merely a passing diversion. But for Miss Emily her passion for Homer is the center of her life; she poisons him, preferring to retain him dead rather than allow him to escape alive. For thirty years she keeps the corpse in a tightly sealed upstairs bedroom, never going out, refusing to pay her taxes, considered a little crazy but still respected by the town. Then she dies; the Negro man steals unobtrusively away, and her secret is revealed. On the pillow next to Homer's decayed body the townspeople find "a long strand of iron-gray hair."

The most obvious interpretation of this story is that it depicts the "seduction" of the aristocratic South (Miss Emily) by a vigorous and enterprising North (Homer). The North for all its vigor is corrupted by its selfish and materialistic exploitation of the South; then the South, having destroyed its seducer, lives on to the end proudly cherishing the shreds of its traditional aristocratic dignity.

"Barn Burning" (publ. 1939) is a popular Faulkner story frequently anthologized. The hero, the boy Colonel Sartoris Snopes, is the son of a ne'er-do-well sharecropper, Abner Snopes, who nevertheless admired his old Civil War commander Colonel Sartoris enough to name his son after him. Thus the boy's character is symbolically a battleground in which the qualities of Snopes and Sartoris struggle for supremacy. As the story opens the Snopeses are driven out of a town where the father has burned a barn out of revenge. They move to another part of the county, and the father hires out to work a farm on shares from Major de Spain, the wealthy and aristocratic landowner who appears in several other Faulkner stories. But the father, sullen and arrogant, starts off on the wrong foot by soiling an elegant imported rug in de Spain's house, is forced ignominiously by the Major to clean the rug, and resolves again on the only kind of revenge he knows: barn-burning. The boy, seeing now that his father's irrational criminality is destroying the family, is torn with an inner conflict: is his first loyalty to his father or to the abstract concept of justice? He decides for justice, goes to Major de Spain and warns him, and the Major kills his father in the act of burning the barn. The boy is left in "grief and despair," but Faulkner holds out hope for tomorrow; a Snopes has made a choice for human dignity, and thus it is seen that decency and idealism appear spontaneously even in the most degraded of human clans. The last paragraph is significant: the season is spring and the boy "did not look back"— there is promise for the Snopeses, and for the South, in the future.

"The Bear" (1942) has been published in at least two forms: the shorter and simpler version was published originally as a short story in *The Saturday Post* (May 9, 1942), and a longer and more complicated version appeared in *Go Down, Moses* (1942) as well as in Malcolm Cowley's *The Portable Faulkner* (1946). The short version, a straightforward narrative, describes the growing to manhood of the young boy Isaac McCaslin through his experience of hunting Old Ben, a semi-legendary crippled bear who roamed the forests near Jefferson. From the time his memory begins Isaac has heard tales of the giant bear to whom bullets are "so many peas blown through a tube by a boy," and at last, when he is ten, he is allowed to join the annual hunting party including his father, Major de Spain, General Compson, the Negro Tennie's Jim, the half-Indian half-Negro hunter Sam Fathers, and the white woodsman Boon Hoggenback. Under Sam's tutelage he becomes, year by year, a skilled hunter and tracker; the year he is eleven he sets out alone to find the bear. At first he has no luck; then, guided by a suggestion from Sam, he leaves behind him the paraphernalia of civilization (the gun, his watch, compass, and stick) and goes into the forest alone. Thus meeting the wilderness on equal terms, he finds Old Ben; the two confront each other silently in the depths of the forest, and then Old Ben goes his way. During the succeeding years the boy kills his first deer and prepares himself for a second meeting with the bear. When he is fourteen he meets Old Ben again, and this time he is armed. But at the crucial moment he does not fire; he throws down his gun instead and runs to save his small dog, which is dashing itself suicidally on the bear. Later he understands why he did not shoot. His father reads to him a passage from Keats' "Ode on a Grecian Urn" in which the poet consoles the figured lovers on the urn by telling that, although their love must remain unconsummated, it will remain eternally virginal and unspoiled. The boy comprehends that the experience with the bear was a "moment of truth" which would have been shattered had he destroyed Old Ben, his partner and co-equal in the experience. Old Ben in this story is a symbol of primeval nature, "apotheosis of the old wild life at which the puny humans swarmed and hacked in a fury of abhorrence and fear." It is only through contact with this primitive reality that the boy Isaac becomes a man. Thus behind the story lies a cult of primitivism, a quasi-religious respect for savage and primeval life, which can be detected in some degree throughout Faulkner's work.

The *Go Down, Moses* version of "The Bear" is much more complex, and suffers artistically from its deliberate obscurity and its long passages of rambling discourse. It is, however, a key work if one is to understand Faulkner's basic ethical and metaphysical values. The narrative has been changed in several respects; the longer version centers on the story of a savage and valiant dog, Lion, who corners Old Ben and is mortally wounded as the giant bear is killed by Boon Hoggenback's knife. This long version is divided into five sections or chapters, four of which expand the story of the *Post* version and continue the narrative through the killing of the bear. Section IV is a long dialogue in which Faulkner, speaking through McCaslin, makes one of his most important statements on the problem of the South, arguing that the land has been eternally cursed by the evil institution of slavery, and that only through relinquishing the land can the curse be effaced. An even broader implication lies at the next level: that men were meant to hold God's earth in common, and that all land everywhere, since the beginning of history, has been cursed by the evil of private ownership.

JOHN STEINBECK (born 1902)

Steinbeck is a model example of the modern American nostalgia for the primitive, the counter-reaction to the triumphant urbanization of American culture which took place in the first half of the twentieth century. He stands at the opposite extreme from the Horatio Alger myth, for he admires everything that is not a material success: the have-nots, the misfits, the racial minorities unjustly deprived of their civil and economic rights, the simple, the poor, and the oppressed. His rural heroes, illiterate and sometimes weak-minded, are nevertheless essentially noble; far from realistically described, they are actually poetized rustics in the traditional romantic manner. It is true that Steinbeck is a naturalist, and that his novels are based on first-hand research, carefully documented, and essentially faithful to the facts. But everything is transformed: the creative process simplifies character, idealizes qualities, and casts over the whole a web of significance so that what might have been mere documentary reporting becomes a form of art comparable to the Greek tragedy or the Homeric epic.

Steinbeck is a regionalist as well as a naturalist; his region is the Salinas Valley in central California and the nearby Monterey coast, a rather exotic enclave in American civilization populated with Mexican farmworkers, Italian fishermen, and assorted artists, bohemians, and eccentrics. In addition to Steinbeck both Henry Miller and Robinson Jeffers have made literary use of this region. But neither Jeffers nor Miller has found in the Monterey country the wealth of native material that Steinbeck extracts from it. Whether he describes the country faithfully is, in the end, a question of secondary importance; his Monterey and Salinas counties are as much imaginary realms as the Yoknapatawpha County of Faulkner. Here live his poetic Mexicans, his sentimental cannery workers, his eccentric and colorful fishermen; here his rural tragedies unfold in the atmosphere of the naturalistic novel mingled with that of the Greek pastoral. Like Willa Cather, Steinbeck is fascinated with the foreign elements in the American population; and like most regionalists he believes the elemental life of the country infinitely superior to that of the city. When his characters are established securely on the land they are hard-working and good-hearted, if somewhat inclined to drink and argumentation. When their agricultural activities are dislocated—when the Joads are driven from Oklahoma, or when a seductive woman intrudes her way into the agrarian dream of Lennie and George in *Of Mice and Men*— tragedy and bitterness result.

Steinbeck, like many naturalists, presents scenes of great cruelty and passion in his novels. *The Grapes of Wrath,* upon its appearance in 1939, excited a torrent of puritanical indignation almost equal to that which greeted Dreiser's *Sister Carrie.* Steinbeck is not interested in mere frankness for shock effect, however. His characters use profanity because they know no other way of speaking; it is a sort of tic or mannerism with them. This is the reason profanity is so frequent in the speech of illiterate people; foul language is as conventional in some groups as polite formulae are in cultured society. Actually Steinbeck's characters are seldom deliberately cruel, and are more likely to be gentle. When they commit crimes it is usually through accident (*The Grapes of Wrath*) or out of sheer stupidity (*Of Mice and Men*), and they generally regret such acts as soon as they realize their full implications.

In politics Steinbeck during the Thirties was a consistent independent liberal. Some of his novels are mere allegory or folklore, devoid of any social content (*The Wayward Bus, The Pearl, Of Mice and Men*). *The Grapes of Wrath* is compassionate toward the plight of migrant Oakies, but offers little as a solution but the organized philanthropy of the New Deal. *In Dubious Battle* is a strike story which ostensibly glorifies the left-wing labor movement, but violence is tacitly condemned, and official Communism found the "line" of the novel unacceptable. During the Second World War Steinbeck wrote outright war propaganda in *Bombs Away* (1942) and something very close to it in *The Moon Is Down* (1942). Steinbeck is generally sympathetic to the proletariat and to the rural laborer. He has not, however, adhered consistently to the platform of any one party or movement.

Steinbeck is more conscious of style than most naturalists; there is a certain poetic quality to his prose. Several of his novels represent attempts to create a synthetic folklore, utilizing the traditional stylistic devices of the folk-tale. He makes strong use of rhythm and repetition: Lennie's theme of "George . . . are we gonna have rabbits, George?" is woven into *Of Mice and Men* like the recurring motif of a sonata. His descriptions of nature are terse but highly charged with imagery. Sometimes he feels the same tenderness toward the sea or the hills that he does toward his rural folk-heroes. Occasionally, especially in *Of Mice and Men,* he consciously creates the classic tragedy; the catastrophe of George and Lennie proceeds inevitably out of their tragic flaws in the same manner as the catastrophe of Agamemnon. The figures are drawn on a smaller scale, it is true, but it is precisely Steinbeck's point that humble and illiterate people may have their tragedies too.

Steinbeck's fiction technique is "dramatic" in another sense: it is based largely on dialogue, connected together with brief descriptive passages, and is almost barren of formal exposition. The situation of the characters and their previous history are explained through conversation rather than through explicit exposition by the author, just as they must be on the stage. For this reason Steinbeck's novels and stories are easily dramatized; several of them have been converted into successful plays and films. At least two of them, *The Moon Is Down* and *Burning Bright,* were deliberately written as "dramatic stories" which can be converted into dramas with a minimum of adaptation; they consist entirely of dialogue interspersed with brief passages of action which are really nothing but stage directions. The others among his novels which are most dramatic in style are *Of Mice and Men, In Dubious Battle, The Grapes of Wrath,* and *The Pearl.* The group of his works which are not easily convertible into dramas includes especially the semi-humorous Monterey stories: *Tortilla Flat, Cannery Row,* and *Sweet Thursday.* Here there is much exposition, usually ironic or whimsical, written from the abstract point of view of public opinion or rumor in the Monterey community.

Steinbeck's work is diverse not only in style but in quality. His styles may be roughly classified under four headings: (1) naturalistic tragedies (*Of Mice and Men, The Grapes of Wrath, In Dubious Battle,* etc.), (2) the whimsical Monterey idylls (*Tortilla Flat,* etc.), (3) pastorals (*The Red Pony* and similar lyrical-sentimental works) and (4) miscellaneous adventure stories laid outside the Salinas-Monterey region (*The Moon Is Down, Bombs Away,* etc.). Of these, groups (1) and (3) are superior in quality, although *In Dubious Battle* is not usually considered the literary equal of the others. The stories in group (2) are considered well done but of lesser importance; Steinbeck is here writing for a popular audience and seeking frankly to amuse. Group (4) is consistently inferior; the two works cited are little more than propaganda, and Steinbeck's lack of intimate personal contact with his material produces a quality of abstraction that destroys their effectiveness. A fifth group of minor works might be cited: the symbolic parables, including *Burning Bright* (1950) and *The Pearl* (1948). Steinbeck, the artist of primitives, is no primitive himself; he is a competent professional writer who is always conscious of formal literary technique and of literary history, and who can write in a diversity of styles to suit his material.

LIFE: Steinbeck was born at Salinas, California, in 1902 of educated middle-class parents. He was educated in the Salinas high school and at Stanford University, although he did not finish his degree. His principal interest in college was biology, a preoccupation he has retained throughout his life. As a young man Steinbeck worked on newspapers and held a variety of odd jobs; he began writing during a winter as a caretaker in a snowbound Lake Tahoe resort. His first three books were unsuccessful, but *Tortilla Flat* (1935) won him considerable recognition. *Of Mice and Men* (1937) was even more successful; and *The Grapes of Wrath* (1939) created a storm of controversy which made him a famous figure overnight. Except for a period of war reporting and for numerous fishing and scientific expeditions, he has remained since in Monterey or in nearby Los Gatos, where he continues to turn out stories drawn from the life of the region. His most recent works are *The Wayward Bus* (1947), *The Pearl* (1948), and *East of Eden* (1953).

CHIEF WORKS: *Tortilla Flat* (novel, 1935) is actually a set of connected incidents rather than a single integrated narrative; it has the structure of *Pickwick Papers* or of Daudet's *Tartarin* stories. The setting is the uphill Mexican district of Monterey, California, called Tortilla Flat, populated by the colorful Mexican-Americans Steinbeck calls *paisanos*. The chief characters of the narrative are Danny, prodigious drinker of wine and free-hand battler; his friends Pilon, Pablo, Big Joe Portagee, and Jesus Maria Corcoran; the beggar Pirate; the wine-merchant Torrelli; and a number of sentimentally promiscuous ladies. Danny comes back from the First World War to find himself an heir and a property-owner; an uncle has died leaving him two houses in Tortilla Flat. Danny moves into one of the houses and rents the other to Pilon, who moves into it with all his friends and presently burns it down. Thenceforth all of them live with Danny in his house, and when they discover that Pirate possesses a hoard of hidden coins they invite him to move in with them too, along with his five dogs. A fantastic and slipshod household is established. The six men and five dogs live by occasional odd jobs, by begging handouts from restaurants and by adroit thefts from their neighbors. In spite of their basic amorality, however, and their many and colorful sins, they win the reader's sympathy through their naive and innocent charm. The chief incidents are a farcical hunt for buried treasure (VIII), Danny's gift of a motorless vacuum cleaner to a lady-friend whose house is not wired for electricity (IX), the poignant incident of the Mexican soldier whose baby dies in spite of the ministrations of the Tortilla Flat inhabitants (X), Pirate's gift of a golden candlestick to the Church (XII), Danny's madness, caused by brooding over the responsibility of his possessions (XV), and the gloriously destructive party at which Danny is cured of his melancholy (XVI). In the last chapter (XVII) Danny destroys himself heroically and magnificently by leaping into a ravine, and the novel closes with a description of his funeral and the dispersal of his friends, who solemnly burn the house before they go as a tribute to Danny.

This novel, the book which made Steinbeck famous, is the most successful of the three works of its type. In style it is a kind of mock epic; Steinbeck pokes fun at the epic tradition on the first page, and there is a thread of ludicrous heroism running through the narrative. The dialogues are sentimental; the style of lyrical "translation" from the Spanish in which the familiar second person (thee-thou) is rendered literally lends a kind of spurious poetic quality to the conversations. The characterizations are romantic, although ironic, and little distinction is drawn between the characters of Danny and his friends. *Tortilla Flat* is far from realism; its characters are exotic to begin with, they are seen entirely from the outside, they are romanticized and poetized, and the novel in the end is almost a fantasy. Yet this is the source of its charm: it lacks the sordid realism of Steinbeck's more serious work, but it creates its own mythical world of great interest and fascination.

In Dubious Battle (novel, 1936) is a strike story, Steinbeck's bitterest and most partisan narrative, and at the same time one of his most powerful novels. Jim Nolan, a young employee of a San Francisco store, is beaten by the police while innocently watching a radical demonstration and as a result is fired from his job; bitter, he joins the Communist Party. He is introduced to Mac, an organizer, who is to be his mentor in Party work. Mac, hard-bitten, cynical, and realistic, is militant Marxism personified; he welcomes trouble and bloodshed because they will provoke the class hatred he can manipulate for Party purposes, and he cynically finds ways to use the deaths of Party comrades for propaganda purposes. The central action of the novel is a strike among itinerant apple-pickers ("fruit tramps") in the fictional Torgas Valley. Before the Party cell comes from San Francisco to organize them, the pickers have little class consciousness and passively accept their cut in wages. Mac and his comrades succeed in persuading them to strike, but brutal violence and destruction are involved: a man is killed during a riot over the arrival of strikebreakers, the lunch-wagon of a Party sympathizer is burned and he is beaten, several men including Jim are shot in a battle with the strikebreakers, and Anderson, a farmer who has agreed to let the striking pickers camp on his land, is ruined financially when vigilantes burn his barn containing his entire apple crop. Mac secretly encourages this violence, since he knows it will build up the hatred needed to solidify the working class in the Valley as well as in the rest of the country. The strike is a failure; the pickers are reduced to starvation, some of them are shot, and as the novel ends Jim Dolan is killed by vigilantes who ambush him through a ruse. But Mac's purposes have been served; his main interest has not been in the plight of the Torgas Valley pickers but in the Party's long-term plans for revolution, which are best served when workers are martyred and a strong class feeling is stirred up. A doctor, Burton, serves as a philosophical commentator and spokesman for the intellectual class in the novel, and thus perhaps serves as Steinbeck's mouthpiece. The attitude of the author, however, is ambiguous; *In Dubious Battle* is at first glance a piece of Party propaganda, yet the Party tactics are often seen to be foolish, irrational, and gratuitously destructive. Communist criticism did not approve of the novel, probably because it shows so many human weaknesses and passions in consecrated Party workers; and it is likely that this cool reception helped to turn Steinbeck away from Communism toward other and more moderate forms of liberalism. The style of *In Dubious Battle* is violent, coarse, and forceful; the climactic ending, in which Mac, carried away by anger, harangues the crowd in an effort to use Jim's murder for propaganda purposes, is especially well done.

Of Mice and Men (novel, later drama, 1937) is a folk tragedy laid in the setting of a California ranch. To the ranch come George Milton, an impractical but intelligent and hard-working laborer, and Lennie Small, his strong, half-witted, and gentle companion. The pair have formed a sort of tacit partnership: George protects Lennie from the pitfalls of a clever and unscrupulous society, and Lennie puts his enormous strength at George's disposal. The pair meet Candy, a decrepit old man who has managed to save a few dollars through the years, and the three enter into a sentimental partnership to retire and buy a little ranch of their own. Candy is to furnish the money, George the brains, and Lennie the brute strength. Their dream occupies their entire attention; they can talk of nothing else. Soon it becomes a kind of drug which makes their hard life bearable. Lennie, however, comes to disaster in a moment when George is not there to protect him. Curley, the conceited young ranch owner's son, has married a flirtatious young woman who is a continual source of trouble on the ranch. The wife, bored, dabbles with Lennie; she is fascinated by his strength and tries her seductive tricks on him. Lennie, bewildered, crushes her like an egg without knowing what he is doing. He is aware he has done something wrong, and, afraid George will punish him, he stumbles away in flight. George, however, tracks him down and finds him before the posse reaches him, and kills him with a revolver as he lulls him with tales of their dream ranch.

The Red Pony (novelette, 1938) has been published in several forms: a short version as a story in 1937, the complete novelette, comprising four sections which are virtually individual stories, as part of *The Long Valley* in 1938, and a revised version with added material published as a separate volume in 1945. The four connected stories relate the youth and coming to maturity of Jody Tiflin, a boy on a California ranch. In "The Gift" Jody's father gives him a red pony, and under the tutelage of the wise and experienced ranch hand Billy Buck he learns how to ride it, feed it, and take care of it. But the pony takes cold and dies; in the magnificent closing scene of the story Jody, hysterical with sorrow and anger, beats off the buzzards which are attacking the corpse with his bare hands. In "The Great Mountains" an old *paisano* named Gitano (i.e., Gypsy) comes to the ranch to ask for work, claiming he was born on the land and that it once belonged to his family. Jody associates the old Mexican with the mountains to the west of the valley, an unknown wilderness which represents for him the primeval and the mysterious. But time has passed Gitano by; he is old and good for nothing, and Jody's father will not hire him. At the end of the story Gitano disappears, taking with him a worthless old horse named Easter which the father was keeping only out of kindness. Horse and man ride away into the western mountains, and there Gitano presumably kills Easter and himself with a sword handed down as an heirloom of his family. Thus "The

Great Mountains" allegorizes the passing of the old Spanish order in California. "The Promise" takes up again the theme of Jody's desire to own a horse. This time the father promises him a colt to be born of the mare Nellie; Jody is to take the responsibility for the colt from the time of its conception, and thus the whole cycle of life will be made clear to him. When the colt is finally born there are difficulties, and the mare must be destroyed to save it. Jody has his colt, but he has learned that only through passion, cruelty, pain, and blood can new life come to birth. "The Leader of the People," the final section of *The Red Pony,* completes Jody's "education." A visitor comes to the ranch: his mother's father, an old plains scout who brought a wagon train to California in pioneer times. Scorned by the father as garrulous and foolish, the grandfather seems to Jody wonderful and heroic, a semi-mythical figure out of a past age. He tells of buffalo hunts and Indian attacks, and Jody can respond only with a description of his mouse hunts in the woodpile. The old man wryly comments on the irony of the comparison: "Have the people of this generation come down to hunting mice?" The visit ends sadly when the grandfather overhears an insulting remark the father makes about him. The old plainsman realizes he is superfluous, that his time has past. "There's a line of old men along the shore hating the ocean because it stopped them." With the disappearance of the frontier a new race of farmers has arisen, and there is no place for pioneers. This realization completes the coming to maturity of Jody, who has observed the life cycle in men and animals on the ranch and now perceives its operation in generations of human society. *The Red Pony* is one of Steinbeck's most successful works artistically; its style is faultless throughout, the mood is maintained without sentimentality, and the underlying motif is developed simply and unobtrusively. The novelette also lacks the profanity and coarseness which offends some readers in works like *The Grapes of Wrath,* and the relations of the boy with his mother and father and with his friend Billy Buck are related with great tact and insight.

The Grapes of Wrath (novel, 1939) is the story of itinerant farmers—the "Oakies" of the Depression period—who are driven from the Oklahoma dust-bowl to seek a new prosperity. The Joad family are lured to California by leaflets promising easy and well-paying jobs; they load themselves and their possessions into a decrepit automobile and strike out for the west. The family, headed by Tom Joad, includes the lusty and indecent Grampa, the suffering and religious Granma, the hard-working and tenacious Ma, the children Noah and Connie, and Connie's wife Rose of Sharon. At the end of their hectic trip, during which Granma dies and is buried without formality, their arrival in the San Joaquin Valley is a bitter disappointment. Jobs are ill-paying and hard to get, and the Oakies who crowd into the valley by the thousands are worse off than they were in the dust bowl. Violence, passion, and labor strife break out; Tom Joad is involved in a murder and after a while becomes a fanatic labor agitator. The most famous scene of the novel is the final one in which Rose of Sharon, her newborn baby dead, nourishes a dying man with her own milk; it is this scene which moralistic critics have found most objectionable.

Although the subject matter and dialogue of this novel are occasionally shocking, the total effect on most readers is moving and sympathetic. *The Grapes of Wrath,* which won Steinbeck a Pulitzer Prize in 1940, is generally considered his most important work; it is certainly his most controversial. Much of the sensation it caused was due to its subject matter, but apart from its lurid content it is still a remarkable book. In some respects it is Steinbeck's most naturalistic novel; its style is objective, it is highly detailed, and it shrinks from no banal or loathsome detail. It has, however, an underlying symbolic current which distinguishes it from American naturalism of the type of Dreiser; here it resembles Norris and Sinclair, although it is superior to anything these two authors have done. The implied political attitude is similar to that in *In Dubious Battle;* the conclusion is that only through organization can the itinerant fruit-tramps and other workers better their condition. If the attitude is generally left-wing, however, the book is not communistic; actually it stands closer to the social liberalism of the New Deal. The political aspects, however, are not here the main point of the novel as they were in *In Dubious Battle;* the interest is centered on the characterizations of the Oakies, the epic quality of the incidents, and the underlying symbolic motifs which break to the surface in such scenes as Rose of Sharon's feeding of the old man.

Cannery Row (novel, 1944) returns to the locale of *Tortilla Flat* but portrays different characters, this time chiefly Anglo-Saxon. As in the earlier book, however, the construction is episodic, consisting of little more than a set of interconnected short stories. The chief characters are the carefree and alcoholic Mack; his friends Hazel, Eddie the bartender, Hughie, and Jones; and the biologist Doc, who operates a small marine laboratory. Mack and his friends move into a house owned by Lee Chong, a Chinese storekeeper, and engage in a series of Rabelaisian adventures similar to those in *Tortilla Flat*. The climax of the novel is a surprise party which the denizens of Cannery Row throw for Doc, their friend and benefactor. This novel has the advantage over Tortilla Flat that it has at least one well-rounded and convincing character: Doc, unassuming and at home with the bums and harlots of Cannery Row, yet a sensitive person who enjoys poetry, fine wine, and Gregorian chants. The same locale and characters appear again in a sequel, *Sweet Thursday* (1954). Neither of these books should be considered among Steinbeck's major works, yet they are charmingly successful examples of their own genre of literature.

East of Eden (novel, 1953) is Steinbeck's first major novel since *The Grapes of Wrath* and evidently represents an attempt to create a work of important literary and mythical significance. The theme is the conflict between good and evil as symbolized in the Biblical story of Cain and Abel, here recast in the setting of the Salinas Valley. Actually the novel relates two recurrences of the Cain-Abel situation in successive generations. Adam Trask (Abel) is the favorite son of his father, a Connecticut farmer; because of this he incurs the jealousy of his brother Charles (Cain). Charles, who basically loves his brother in spite of his contempt and jealousy for him, fights him, but the matter ends inconclusively. Then, when Adam marries and has twin sons, the myth is reenacted on a ranch in the Salinas Valley. Caleb (Cain) worships his father and is jealous of Aaron, who without caring or deserving it wins Adam's preference. Finally, in his rage, he finds a way to get even with his brother. Aaron venerates the memory of his mother, whom he imagines dead. The truth about her is that she had been a prostitute before she met Adam, and after the birth of her sons has returned to her old profession. Finding that she is still alive and now madam of a Salinas house, Caleb vindictively takes Aaron to see her. Shattered, Aaron flees and in irrational despair joins the army. When word comes that he has been killed

Adam has a stroke; Cal feels the full weight of his own guilt. The old
Chinese servant Lee serves as a philosophical commentator on this
drama; he exhorts Adam to forgive Cal. But Adam leaves with his son
only a single enigmatic word: *Timshel*. This Hebrew allusion is interpreted by Lee and others to mean "Thou *mayest* rule over sin;" abandoning his son to evil, he nevertheless leaves him the possibility of
redemption through his personal effort if he wishes to accept good.
Thus *East of Eden* treats mankind's most basic enigma: the presence
of evil in the universe, and the cause of man's curse in the eyes of
God. Steinbeck's interpretation is in the end an optimistic one; mankind is abandoned by God in its struggle with evil, yet God, through
Adam the father of humanity, holds out hope of rehabilitation
through the gift of free will.

ERSKINE CALDWELL (born 1903)

Although Caldwell is a prolific writer who produced almost thirty
volumes between 1930 and 1950, his reputation continues to rest on
two novels: *Tobacco Road* (1932) and *God's Little Acre* (1933).
To these may be added a group of stories which come roughly from
the same period and are in the same style. Yet, although he is known
to the general public chiefly as the author of *Tobacco Road,* there is
some justification for viewing him as a writer whose main talent lies
in the genre of the short story. There is, in fact, a kind of episodic
quality even in his novels, a quality which suggests that they were
formed in his mind as story situations which he later welded together
into a novel. As for his stories, they fall into two general groups: the
comedies, many of them laid in Maine or in other parts of America
out of the South, and the naturalistic Georgia stories in the manner
of *Tobacco Road*. The comedies demonstrate his versatility as well as
his literary sophistication; they dispel the myth that he is a primitive
and somewhat naive Southern naturalist who "writes about what he
knows" and owes his success mainly to the shocking content of his
material. Actually he is far less primitive than, for example, Faulkner;
he is an educated person and a man of the world, a competent professional author who can write in many styles and on many subjects.
If he wrote his most successful fiction about the Georgia back-country
where he grew up, it is because he saw the literary possibilities of the
material and used it skillfully and effectively.

Nevertheless, from the standpoint of literary history Caldwell is mainly important as a Southern writer, and in his treatment of Southern materials he is a typical modern regionalist. He is concerned chiefly with the manners of the back-country Georgia farmer both black and white, and he describes these people and their land always in the implied contrast to the city. In other words his task is to reveal the country to the city reader; he writes for urban audiences with urban tastes and sensibilities, and the shock many readers feel from his writing is derived from the sharp contrast to their own urban environment. Ellen Glasgow and Willa Cather attempt to show us the universal and human in the lives of country dwellers; Erskine Caldwell shows us the grotesque, the strange, and the exotic. If naturalism means the presentation of the most brutal facts of human existence with utter candor, then Caldwell the Southern regionalist is a naturalist par excellence. The characters of his Georgia stories—sharecroppers, white trash, back-country pig farmers—demonstrate few human attributes; they resemble animals grotesquely clad in human form. In books such as *Tobacco Road* Caldwell has committed most of the literary crimes wrongly attributed to Faulkner. He presents pornography for its own sake, he is fond of shocking his audiences into attention, and he creates human beings devoid of any sense of decency. There is no doubt, however, that he is sincere in his desire to present the less savory aspects of Southern rural life as he sees them, and to produce eventual amelioration through the tactic of exposé.

The technique of Caldwell's sharecropper idylls is simple. He assembles a group of laconic and degenerate rustics, attributes to them a set of flesh-creeping and depressing antics, and relates the whole in the flattest manner possible without comment or emotion. This bald manner has won him a reputation as a cool and objective social observer; actually his insouciance is a studied literary attitude. "Atrocities related laconically"—this formula has won him fame, money, and even a measure of praise by critics. Caldwell has achieved a reputation as the leading, and most typical, journalist of Southern degradation.

LIFE: Erskine Caldwell was born in Coweta County, Georgia, in 1903, the son of a Presbyterian minister who traveled frequently as he was transferred from church to church throughout the South. His schooling was sporadic, and it was from his mother that he received most of his early learning. Later he attended a succession of colleges: Erskine College in South Carolina, the University of Virgina, the University of Pennsylvania, and another session at Virginia. He began writing as early as 1928; his first published works were two novelettes, *The Bastard* and *Poor Fool,* in 1929 and 1930 respectively. His first real success came with *Tobacco Road* (1932), which not only rose to the best-seller lists as a novel but went on in a dramatized version by Jack Kirkland to achieve one of the longest runs in the history of the American theatre. In 1933 his story "Country Full of Swedes" appeared in the *Yale Review* and won the *Yale Review* Fiction Award for the following year. Mr. Caldwell has been married three times: the first time to Helen Lannigan in 1925, a marriage which produced two sons and a daughter; to the photographer Margaret Bourke-White in 1939; and in 1942 to June Johnson, by whom he has another son. A 1941 trip to Russia with Margaret Bourke-White resulted in a number of books on the U.S.S.R., including the non-fiction *All-Out on the Road to Smolensk* (1942) and the novel *All Night Long* (1942).

CHIEF WORKS: *Tobacco Road* (novel, later drama, 1932) describes the life, times, and eventual decline of the Georgia share-cropper Jeeter Lester and his family. The plot actually consists of a set of episodes; the novel is really a set of integrated short stories. An in-law, Lov Benson, married to the twelve-year-old Pearl Lester, visits Jeeter and is clumsily robbed while Jeeter's daughter Ellie May serves as decoy. Jeeter's sister, the widow-preacher Bessie Rice, entices his son Dude to marry her by displaying a new automobile, which Dude later wrecks, killing his grandmother. Jeeter's only effort to farm his land consists of an attempt to borrow money for improvements; when this is not successful no one really cares when a fire burns up both house and Lester family.

God's Little Acre (novel, 1933) is a similar story laid in the hill country of Georgia. A mountaineer, Ty Ty Walden, wastes his life digging for gold on his land. His family is every bit as grotesque as Jeeter Lester's. It includes the promiscuous daughter Darling Jill and her sister Rosamund, whose husband Will betrays her with Griselda

Walden and later dies in a labor riot. These family calamities grieve Ty Ty only briefly; he is more interested in his prospecting. The characterizations in this novel are slightly more subtle and three-dimensional than they are in *Tobacco Road.*

STORIES: Most of Caldwell's stories are included in *Jackpot* (1940); a shorter collection is *Stories By Erskine Caldwell,* New York (1944). "Country Full of Swedes" (1933), originally published in the *Yale Review,* is typical of his light and gusty comedies, most of them written during his stay in Maine (1926-31). The story is related by a hired hand on the Maine farm of Jim Frost, who warns of the carnage and destruction likely when the Swedes, driven out of the sawmill towns by hard times, descend on their countryside. Stan, the narrator, is skeptical, but when the Swedes arrive their antics convince him. A small boy begins the destruction by climbing a tree after a cat; his father chops the tree down, and presently the Frost farm is virtually wrecked. But when Stan proposes revenge, Frost in terror pleads, "Good God . . . don't go making them mad." Henry Seidel Canby describes this story as "nothing but a symbol of the disturbing rush of vitality over the unvital, like a comber over a sterile beach."

"My Old Man's Baling Machine" is an eccentric-relative story that might well have been written by Saroyan. The hero's father is tricked by a traveling salesman into buying a paper-baling machine which he hopes will make him rich; he then proceeds to stuff every piece of paper into it that he can lay his hands on, including his wife's love-letters. Caldwell has written several other stories about this family, including "The Night My Old Man Came Home" and "Handsome Brown and the Goats."

"Saturday Afternoon" (1935) belongs to a markedly different group of stories: brutal tales of Negro-white relationships in the cotton country of Georgia. It is a lynching story, but an unusual one in construction; it relates the incident solely from the point of view of the town loafers, who feel no particular emotion at all toward the victim, a harmless "good" Negro named Will Maxie, but who partticipate in the killing out of sheer boredom of life in the Georgia village. The central character is the fat and sleepy butcher Tom Denny, whose friends wake him up from his afternoon nap so he won't miss the lynching. In spite of its apparent callousness, this story is one of the most effective anti-lynching pieces ever to be written by a Southern author.

"Kneel to the Rising Sun" (1935) is similar in mood. The cowed and stupid white sharecropper Lonnie is so subservient to his land-lord Arch Gunnard that he scarcely protests when his own father, out prowling for garbage in the middle of the night, is eaten by Gunnard's sleek pigs. A courageous Negro, Clem Henry, stands up to Gunnard and is consequently lynched by a mob; but Lonnie, feel-ing vaguely that something is wrong, lacks the character to oppose them. This story shows Caldwell at his most typical; his faults (sen-sationalism, grotesque exaggeration) as well as his merits (a power-ful plot, a total and dispassionate objectivity) are here seen in their purest form.

ROBERT PENN WARREN (born 1905)

Warren is a self-declared leader of the organized Southern agrarian movement, a group which set out to create a new Southern literature and to attack the conservatism and sentimentality of the "highcaste Brahmins of the Old South." He was the youngest member of the "Fugitive Group" of Nashville poets and critics, and he is the only member of that cénacle to achieve any prominence as a novelist. His success has been both a critical and a popular one; he has gained numerous awards including a Pulitzer Prize (1947), and Malcolm Cowley, one of his warmest advocates, has referred to him as "more richly endowed than any other American novelist born in the present century." He is also an important literary critic, the co-author with Cleaneth Brooks of *Understanding Poetry* and a leader of the New Criticism (see pp. 568-573). Finally, he is a poet. His poems, chiefly on Southern themes, are well fit to stand beside those of John Crowe Ransom and others of the Southern school, and are marked by a coolness and detachment lacking in the more impassioned Southern poets.

Sensitive and intellectual in temperament, Warren writes poetry of great subtlety and precision. This is perhaps not surprising consider-ing his background. What is surprising is that his fiction, while per-ceptive in the same way his poetry is, is nevertheless hard and natural-istic in the manner of Steinbeck, Hemingway, or Faulkner. While he does not totally resemble any one of these authors, he shares their laconic vernacular dialogue, their use of coarse or shocking detail, their apparent callous irony for literary effect. It is this hard quality of his style that saves his basically romantic plots from sentimentality. A lesser writer might have made a mawkish and sentimental historical novel out of the material of *World Enough and Time;* Warren treats it with the detached irony of modern naturalism, and the result is a first-rate novel.

As a regionalist Warren writes almost entirely about Kentucky, his home state. He has remarked, in the course of advising younger authors, that in Kentucky courthouses alone is buried enough material for a whole generation of writers. Yet he is more than a regionalist in the superficial sense of the word; he is concerned with more than mere local color or fictionalization of local history. On the surface his approach to Southern material might be described as sociological or political. Two of his three chief novels treat political themes, and even in *World Enough and Time* the contrast in ethics of various social classes is constantly implied. He also has "philosophical pretensions," although this is not to imply that his philosophy is unsound; it is simply that his philosophical comment often seems superimposed, superfluous, organically unconnected to his central plot. This difficulty is particularly apparent in *All the King's Men,* where the effort of the narrator Jack Burden to work out his personal philosophy often slows down the unfolding of the central plot. If his philosophical dissertations are not effective, however, his moral analyses are. The reader is made vividly aware of the moral implications of Willie Stark's career, and of the moral dilemma confronting Burden, through the unfolding of the action itself. The same is true of *Night Rider,* which is essentially a study in Percy Munn's personal moral problems and their final resolution through tragic expiation. In spite of the regionalistic preoccupations which dominate his work, Warren's novels are essentially studies in moral conflict laid in the richly suitable setting of the South.

An often cited flaw in Warren's fiction is his inability to limit his canvas. Like Faulkner and Wolfe, he is a writer of prolific imagination; he continually conceives scenes, characters, and situations which seem to run away with him and divert his attention from the central theme of his novel. The best example of this is the story of Judge Irwin in *All the King's Men,* which was intended as a "chapter in the longer story of the Boss" but which grows so large it almost dominates the novel. *Night Rider*, with its simpler structure and more limited cast, is superior in this respect; and *World Enough and Time*, in spite of its technical complexity, is Warren's most tightly organized novel.

As a poet Warren produces work of high quality but of rather limited originality. He resembles the other Fugitive Group and *Southern Review* poets in subject matter and even in form, but he is the most objective of the school; even his poems involving Negro-white conflicts are effective through their calm detachment rather than through their emotion. His poetry shows the effect of his highly developed critical faculty, yet his training as a critic has not inhibited his creativity. There is a quality in his verse that corresponds to the Faulkner-like naturalism of his fiction; he is closer to the earth than most other Southern poets. "Its strength no less than its fecundity," Untermeyer remarks of his poetry, "rises from Kentucky soil."

LIFE: Robert Penn Warren was born in Guthrie, Kentucky in 1905, in the section of Todd County which served as the setting for *Night Rider*. As a student at Vanderbilt University he became a member of the "Fugitive Group," a cénacle of young Southern writers who rallied around the bimonthly literary review *The Fugitive*. He later took a master's degree at the University of California and a B.Litt, as a Rhodes Scholar, at Oxford. He has spent most of his career as a university teacher, serving on the faculties of Southwestern College, Vanderbilt University, Louisiana State University, and the University of Minnesota. His first important published book was a biography, *John Brown: the Making of a Martyr*, in 1939. Mr. Warren was one of the founders of the *Southern Review* and served as editor of this important quarterly until its demise in 1942, when he became associated with the *Kenyon Review* as advisory editor. In 1947 *All the King's Men*, which had won the Southern Authors' Award in 1946, was awarded a Pulitzer Prize.

CHIEF NOVELS: *Night Rider* (1939) is based on an actual outbreak of violence between Kentucky farmers and tobacco companies in the early years of the twentieth century. The protagonist, Percy Munn, is a lawyer who has been educated out of the South and who returns to his home county to take the part of the farmers in the struggle. Moderate and reasonable by nature, disliking violence, Munn is a "good man" who is at first loath to become involved in the affair, but his innate idealism persuades him that his loyalty is due to the farmer class from which he sprang. He joins an Association formed by farmers and politicians to force the companies to raise their prices, and soon finds himself involve with unsavory companions: the brash and vulgar grower Bill Christian and the unctious and self-satisfied Senator Tolliver. The Association leaders also include Captain Todd, "a kindly, bearded man, a veteran of the Civil War," and the cynical but courageous Dr. MacDonald. Meanwhile Munn has voluntarily defended and procured an acquittal in a murder case for a local poor-white, Bunk Trevelyan, who thus becomes his admirer and defender. The Association goes about its work of persuading farmers to join together and refuse to sell their tobacco except at an agreed price, but the movement is a failure; selfish growers hold out and sell at the high prices caused by the shortage, and others betray their companions by selling secretly after they have signed with the Association. Senator Tolliver, selfish and opportunistic, abandons his friends and joins forces with the companies. Finally the hard core of the Association members band together in another organization, this time a secret one to send "night riders" out to destroy the tobacco of recalcitrant growers. Munn, drawn into this plot half against his will, soon finds himself deep in crime and violence. When Trevelyan, by this time a member of the night riders, betrays them, Munn is forced to murder him; other violence in which he is involved includes the burning of tobacco company warehouses. Finally he is a fugitive, accused of murder; he seeks out Senator Tolliver to kill him, but at the last moment, weary of violence, he relents. The novel ends as he is killed by a posse.

The point of the plot is that Munn, a man of integrity drawn into the struggle out of principle, is the one who is made to suffer from its consequences precisely because of his high character; except for MacDonald the others abandon him one by one, and in the end he is the scapegoat. An interwoven sub-plot describes his relations with his cold and hostile wife May and his affair with Sukie Christian, daughter of "Old Bill." Although the central interest of the novel lies in Munn's inner moral struggle, the descriptions of violence and death, related with magnificent detachment, contribute to the high quality of the work.

All the King's Men (1946) describes the career of Willie Stark, a Louisiana dictator and demagogue, as seen through the eyes of Jack Burden, a newspaperman who becomes one of his assistants. Stark's career is roughly based on that of Huey Long, although the parallel is confined to the public part of Long's career; the family relationships and the inner psychological tensions of Willie's organization are Warren's inventions. Willie Stark begins as a naive country lawyer who sincerely wants to better the lot of the "hicks" and "rednecks" from whose ranks he sprang; he is taken in hand by two people, Burden and the wisecracking "secretary" Sadie Burke, and with his natural talent for demagoguery he soon becomes a powerful figure. As the novel opens he is already governor, and Burden, a trained researcher, is engaged in digging up material on enemies Stark hopes to slander and blackmail. Meanwhile Stark's family life deteriorates; his wife Lucy, a country school-teacher, is repelled by his new coarseness and arrogance and leaves him, and his son Tom, spoiled and self-satisfied, is continually in trouble. The remaining important characters of the novel are Anne Stanton, daughter of an old Southern family, whom Burden loves but who eventually becomes Stark's mistress; Adam Stanton, her brother and Burden's friend, an eminent surgeon who accepts a position as director of a medical center Stark is building; and Judge Irwin, who has befriended Burden in his boyhood but is later betrayed by Burden because he has become Stark's enemy. The plot, becoming successively more involved, ends in a series of catastrophes: Irwin commits suicide and Burden learns that the man he has destroyed was actually his father; Tom, playing football while out of training through dissipation, breaks his neck and dies; and finally Adam, discovering his sister's relations with Stark, kills him and is in turn killed by Stark's bodyguard. As the novel ends Burden, disillusioned and cynical, nevertheless sets out with Anne to build a new life out of the wreckage of the old.

This novel is more than a mere fictionalized portrait of a dictator; it is an intricate network of moral conflicts and psychological relations in which each character exerts an influence on the others. The central character is Burden, cynical and detached yet retaining a basic decency. Stark himself is sometimes genuinely concerned for the people who worship him as an idol, sometimes callous and brutal. Adam Stanton, consecrated, idealistic, somewhat resembles the hero of Lewis' *Arrowsmith;* Anne, who serves merely as a focus for Burden's love and disillusionment, is less well motivated but still a convincing character. The minor characters—Sadie, the politician Tiny Duffy, the perverted chauffeur-gunman Sugar-Boy—are vivid and well-drawn. *All the King's Men,* winner of several literary awards including a Pulitzer Prize, is probably Warren's most important work.

World Enough and Time (1950) is a novel of passionate psychological and moral conflict in a historical Kentucky setting. Jeremiah Beaumont, a young lawyer in Kentucky in the eighteen-twenties, falls in love with Rachel Jordan, but she consents to marry him only on condition that he kill Colonel Cassius Fort, Beaumont's friend and spiritual father, who has earlier seduced her. He does so, but is afterwards tormented by agonies of conscience and philosophical doubt before he is finally executed for the murder. This novel is based on an actual incident, the so-called "Kentucky Tragedy" of 1824-25, in which Jeroboam O. Beauchamp was encouraged by his bride Ann Cook to murder Solomon P. Sharp. The case has served as the subject of several other literary works including Chivers' *Conrad and Eudora* (drama, 1834), Charlotte Barnes' *Octavia Bragaldi* (drama, 1837), Poe's *Politian* (drama, 1837), Hoffman's *Greyslaer* (novel and drama, 1840), and Simms' *Beauchampe* (novel, 1842).

POETRY: Warren's most important verse is contained in the volumes *XXXVI Poems* (1936), *Eleven Poems on the Same Theme* (1942), and *Selected Poems* (1944). Typical of his early work is the well-known "Pondy Woods" (1929), an account of a Negro lynching related in calm, reflective, but nevertheless moving verse. "Pro Sua Vita" and "Letter of a Mother," both from *XXXVI Poems,* are tributes to a mother-figure, the first on the occasion of her death, which suggests comments on the futility and irony of human birth, and the second expressing a vague womb-nostalgia, meditating over "The mother flesh that cannot summon back / The tired child it would again possess."

WILLIAM SAROYAN (born 1908)

William Saroyan began as an unknown and penniless writer in the Depression period, and his early books are his best: bitter, but poetically bitter, a naive and sentimental bitterness that is far from the harsh cynicism of a Dos Passos or a Farrell. He portrayed the lives of unfortunates, of human wrecks, of the meek and humble of the earth. He became a success doing this, and even made some money, but in achieving success he unfortunately left behind the people and the world his temperament best fitted him to write about. Like Wolfe, he is essentially an autobiographical writer, preoccupied with his own childhood and his own people. When he moved out of this milieu into the world of Broadway and Hollywood something essential in his work was no longer there. His best books are, and will remain, *The Daring Young Man on the Flying Trapeze, My Name Is Aram,* and the dramas written in the period around 1939: *My Heart's in the Highlands, The Time of Your Life,* and *Love's Old Sweet Song.* All these early works are concerned in one way or another with the lives of unsuccessful and humble people in the San Joaquin Valley of central California, especially the town of Fresno and its environs; they are sincere, spontaneous, youthful, and fresh. The later books are too often either sentimental *(The Human Comedy)* or insincere and studied, often with a view toward commercial success *(The Assyrians).*

The chief quality which strikes the reader in Saroyan's early works is their spontaneity, their naive but convincing warmth. Many stories have been written about young artists starving in garrets, but few have achieved the poignant and ironic understatement of the title story of *The Daring Young Man on the Flying Trapeze,* whose hero finds a penny in the street and thinks, "In the evening I shall polish it until it glows like a sun and I shall study the words." Yet, although parts of this story are masterfully written, Saroyan seems to have an almost pathological aversion to style. He has devoted a number of essays and prefaces to attacks on academic critics, on theories of literature, on rules of all kinds. He argues that a young writer should study not books but life, that he should write according to the "jump-into-the-river-and-start-to-swim-immediately" technique, that is, without any technique at all except the consciousness of what he wants to say. This attitude links him with the school of "automatic writers" of the twentieth century, especially with Gertrude Stein. His finished work does not greatly resemble Miss Stein's but it does often resemble Hemingway's. In "Seventy Thousand Assyrians" his hero goes to a barber college for a fifteen-cent haircut and thinks, "Outside, as Hemingway would say, haircuts are four bits." In spite of such satire, numerous Hemingway-like passages can be found in all his work up to approximately 1939; for all his condemnation of books and imitative writing, it is obvious that Saroyan is very well read in modern American literature and that the new techniques have had an obvious influence on his writing.

In spite of his Armenian background Saroyan is one of the most "American" of twentieth-century writers. His scenes are laid in the most American of locales—the bar-and-grill, the grocery store, the small-town neighborhood—and his style, especially his dialogue, is colloquial and unerringly faithful to the American idiom. In addition he has a tremendous, almost Whitman-like emotional attachment to America, a sentimental patriotism that becomes more prominent as his work progresses. The bitterness toward Depression America in *The Daring Young Man* (1934) is replaced in *The Human Comedy* (1943) by a sentimental affection for the homeland, an affection which is not at all contradicted by his continuing antagonism toward bourgeois materialism and other upper-middle-class aspects of American life. Saroyan's America is in a sense his private invention, yet it corresponds to an important element in the real America; and he has remained faithful to this image throughout his career. It is this element, the depiction of a sentimental, poetic, and anti-materialistic American undercurrent, that has made his work so popular abroad, especially in Europe; in France and Italy, for example, Saroyan is often considered one of the most important American authors of the century. Saroyan stands in the line of literary evolution represented by Thoreau, Whitman, and Mark Twain and continuing through Stein, Anderson, and other naturalists of the Twenties; it is a literary tradition hostile to form, concerned in its subject matter with the lives and tragedies of the humble, and spontaneous and highly subjective in style.

Out of this sentimental kinship with the humble and weak has come Saroyan's philosophy, or what passes for philosophy in his work: that there is a kind of success in failure, that the meek are blessed, and that the poor in spirit are compensated by a world of fantasy far more rewarding than the glittering and streamlined world of material success. To the "American Dream" with its promise of bourgeois luxury to be obtained through hard work, diligence, prudence, and thrift he opposes the "Cult of Failure," the sentimental admiration for the imprudent, the impulsive, and the poetic. Saroyan, at least in his early work, never portrays a character who is both successful and admirable; on the contrary he portrays many characters who are warm, lovable, and sympathetic precisely because they are impractical failures.

This attitude toward character is probably connected to Saroyan's Armenian background. As a member of a racial minority he felt himself, as a boy, to be an outsider in American culture, and this led him to a kinship with all the excluded, with the "proletariat" in its technical sense as "those who are in a society but not of it" (Toynbee). A list of the people Saroyan admires includes precisely all those elements tacitly excluded by the Chamber-of-Commerce patriot in talking about "the American way of life": the unemployed, barflies, Japanese, Assyrians, petty juvenile delinquents, prostitutes, vagabonds, itinerant Negroes, Greeks, drunken telegraphers, and miscellaneous job-drifters. Above all Saroyan admires his own people, the Armenians, persecuted for centuries, lacking a nation of their own, lacking even the acumen and diligence of the homeless Jews, lacking everything except the dignity of their history and their impractical and sentimental inner poetry. If Saroyan is a regionalist his region is not only a geographical area: it is also a people, the Armenians of California and all those who are kin to them through their inner goodness and their failure in the material world.

LIFE: Saroyan's early life is roughly that described in *My Name Is Aram,* which does not, however, fill in all the details. He was born in Fresno, California in 1908; his father, who died when he was two, had been a Presbyterian minister but later became a grape-rancher. After the death of the father the mother was obliged to send her children to an Alameda orphanage until William was seven, when the family was reunited in Fresno. Saroyan attended public schools, read avidly, and worked as a telegraph messenger. From the age of seventeen he was on his own, drifting from one odd job to another and finally settling down temporarily as manager of a Postal Telegraph branch in San Francisco. His first published stories appeared in 1934, and the same year he made the O'Brien volume of *The Best Short Stories* and published his own first volume: *The Daring Young Man* *on the Flying Trapeze.* The book was an immediate success; Saroyan paid off his debts, worked briefly in Hollywood, then returned to his writing. Since 1935 he has lived mainly in San Francisco and Fresno, with brief sojourns in New York City. *My Name Is Aram,* his second major book, consisted of pieces originally published in magazines, including *The Atlantic Monthly, The New Yorker,* and *Story.* From 1939 to 1941 he concerned himself chiefly with the drama; he directed or co-directed several of his own plays, including *My Heart's in the Highlands,* in New York, and turned down a Pulitzer Prize (1940) for *The Time of Your Life* because he felt a bourgeois society had no right to patronize "sincere" art. The Second World War affected him deeply, making him more socially conscious and intensifying his sentimental patriotism; out of this experience came *The Human Comedy,* a more idealistic work than anything he had previously published. Since the war his output has been prolific but has generally been considered inferior; the pieces of *The Assyrian and Other Stories* (1950), probably his best work after 1945, were written according to his own statement "in the hope of being sold to magazines for big money because a writer's got to live," a far cry from the bitter declaration of literary independence he expressed in *The Daring Young Man.*

CHIEF WORKS: *The Daring Young Man on the Flying Trapeze* (stories, 1934) contains Saroyan's most typical work and some of his best. The title story is the most important one in the volume; it is a simple impressionistic account of the death by starvation of an unpublished writer, related in a subjective but restrained style with faint overtones of irony. Paradoxically, although this story is the most "Saroyan-like" of anything Saroyan has written, it is also the most imitative of his works; the opening section particularly shows the mark of Joyce, Eliot, and the poignant silent comedies of Chaplin. Of the twenty-five other stories in the volume, typical examples deserve brief mention. "Seventy Thousand Assyrians" begins as a sketch of a barber in a San Francisco barber college and gradually turns into an essay on writing and a statement of literary creed. The style of the narrative sections often suggests the early Hemingway. "Love, Death, Sacrifice, and So Forth" is a satire on the typical Hollywood film, funnier yet more penetrating than most of its kind. "1, 2, 3, 4, 5, 6, 7, 8" is another starving-young-man story, also involving an attack on the mass-production society similar to that in Chaplin's *Modern Times;* and "And Man" is a sketch of the struggle between the sensitive boy and an insensitive society, personified in a school principal who straps the boy for taking walks in the country on school days. This last story treats themes later to be taken up in *My Name Is Aram* in a lighter and more whimsical style.

My Name Is Aram (stories, 1940) is virtually a novel; the stories are all about the same characters and contain a common thread of development. The book is frankly autobiographical; although Saroyan makes the conventional statement that the book is not about "any persons living or dead" he candidly adds, "neither is any person in this book a creation of fiction." The central figures are the members of the Garoghlanian family, Armenian farmers and vineyard workers in the San Joaquin Valley; the book is narrated in the first person by Aram Garoghlanian, a boy who has slightly more detachment and gravity than the puckish relatives who surround him and can thus view them with a certain objectivity. The best pieces of the book are the first story, "The Beautiful White Horse," involving the narrator's cousin Mourad who has a very flexible concept of what constitutes stealing and therefore sees nothing wrong with borrowing a neighbor's horse for six months to take early-morning rides; "The Journey to Hanford," about a "sad uncle" who has a constitutional apathy toward work; and "The Pomegranate Trees," about another uncle, Melik, who spends thousands of dollars trying to make the desert bloom into pomegranates and succeeds in producing only cactuses and sage brush. The conversation in the last-named piece between Aram and Melik over horned-toads is one of the most idiotic and yet most charming dialogues in modern literature. Most of the remaining stories are concerned with Aram's struggle against organized education ("One of Our Future Poets," "A Nice Old-Fashioned Romance") or with other anecdotes about eccentric uncles and cousins. *My Name Is Aram,* free from the bitterness of *The Daring Young Man* yet more sincere, straightforward, and unpretentious than Saroyan's later work, is probably his best book.

The Human Comedy (novel, 1943) is actually a set of sketches only slightly more unified than those of *My Name Is Aram;* as a novel it is episodic and lacks any single strong plot-line. Saroyan temporarily abandons his Armenians, although one or two appear as minor characters; the main characters are the Macauley family of Ithaca, California (actually Fresno), and a number of other residents of the town. Homer Macauley, the central figure, is a boy of high-school age who works, as Saroyan did, as a telegraph messenger; his friends in the telegraph office include the hard-boiled but basically kind manager Mr. Spangler and the alcoholic old telegrapher William Grogan, who dies at the end of a heart attack. The era is the period of the Second World War; Homer's brother Marcus is away in the army. The family also includes the four-year-old Ulysses and the sister Bess; the father has died some years before. Homer, as a telegraph messenger, has to deliver many messages telling mothers of the death of their soldier sons; he is depressed by this but at the same time matured through acquisition of a tragic view of life. The climax of the novel (and the shock which causes old Mr. Grogan's death) is the arrival of a telegram announcing that Marcus has been killed; Homer and his mother, both hardened to tragedy by the events of their lives, accept the news stoically and with resignation. Other notable scenes are the fascination of Ulysses with a friendly Negro who waves to him from a train (Chapter 1) and the interlude of the three lonely but madcap soldiers who treat two Ithaca girls to a movie (Chapters 17-20). This novel, which contains much good writing, is unfortunately marred by the excessive sentimentality with which Saroyan treats the war, soldiers, and patriotic matters generally. It is nevertheless his sole attempt at an integrated novel and one of his most important works. Parts of the story were made into a motion picture in 1944; Saroyan was originally offered a contract to collaborate on its production, but quarreled with the studio and quit before the picture was finished.

DRAMAS: Saroyan's most important dramas are contained in the volume *Three Plays* (1940); another book by the same title but dated 1941 contains three plays of lesser importance. The three dramas in the 1940 volume were all produced in New York by the Group Theatre, an outgrowth of the Theatre Guild, in 1939-40, and are similar in style and attitude. "My Heart's in the Highlands" (1939) is based on a 1936 Saroyan story and has also been published as a one-act play. In its longer form it is still intended to be played without intermission, but has assumed the scope of a three-act drama. Ben Alexander, an unsuccessful poet, lives in Fresno with his son Johnny; the two keep alive mainly by persuading Mr. Kosak, the local grocer, to give them food on credit. When Jasper MacGregor, an itinerant bugler, happens by they invite him to stay as a guest in the house, and his bugle-music is so beautiful that the neighbors crowd in to give them gifts of food. Mr. MacGregor, the romanticist whose "heart's in the Highlands," eventually proves to be a fugitive from an old folks' home, and is taken away by his keepers; meanwhile the owner of the house, who has not been paid for some time, rents it to somebody else, and father and son are thrown out into the world. The play ends as Johnny remarks, "I'm not mentioning any names, Pa, but something's wrong somewhere." The moral of the play is evidently that landlords should allow unsuccessful poets to live in their houses rent-free, in the same spirit in which Mr. Kosak has given them groceries. Whatever the dubious social implications of this theory, the play is a charming and poignant one, succeeding in spite of its lack of structure and its general obscurity. The *Three Plays* volume of 1940 includes an amusing set of criticisms of "My Heart's in the Highlands" taken from New York newspapers and magazines, showing the mixture of exasperation and bafflement with which critics greeted Saroyan's first important drama.

"The Time of Your Life" (1939), the second of the *Three Plays,* is a five-act drama, heavier and more involved than "My Heart's in the Highlands." The scene is a San Francisco bar, a "waterfront honky-tonk" presided over by the calm and philosophical bartender Nick. The other chief characters are the pure-hearted prostitute Kitty; the "loafer" Joe and his half-witted assistant and errand-boy Tom; Arab, an "Eastern philosopher and harmonica-player"; Krupp, a thoughtful waterfront cop who is ashamed of roughing up strikers; McCarthy, an intelligent and socially conscious longshoreman; Blick, a vulgar and obnoxious vice-squad detective; and Kit Carson, an old desert rat and Indian fighter. The plot is confused but basically consistent. The thick-headed Tom falls in love with Kitty and resolves to rescue her from her life of sin; Blick tries to make trouble for everyone in the bar and especially for Kitty, and is removed from the scene through an ingenious and undetectable murder by Kit Carson, whom everyone had previously taken for a garrulous and slightly crazy old idiot. The moral is that of most of Saroyan's work: that the little and confused people of the world, even in their vices, are more admirable than the big, the powerful, the organized, and the puritanical.

"Love's Old Sweet Song" (1940), the third drama of the volume, is a farcical love story set in Bakersfield, California in the back yard of "a beautiful unmarried small-town woman" named Ann Hamilton. The Greek boy Georgie Americanos, a telegraph messenger, serves as observer and commentator on the action. Through a joke Ann is sent a telegram announcing that Barnaby Gaul, a passer-by who barely met her when she was sixteen, is coming from Boston to ask for her hand in marriage; when an itinerant medicine man, Dr. Greatheart, happens by she takes him for her lover and he willingly accepts the part. Meanwhile the Yearling family, a large clan of migratory workers from Oklahoma, arrive and camp in Ann's back yard; Saroyan has a great deal of fun satirizing Steinbeck (in the person of Richard Oliver, an "unpublished novelist") and other writers who sentimentalize the plight of the "Oakies" while shrewdly using them for literary material. ("I don't know how I'm going to be able to write this and give it social significance," worries Oliver after the Yearling brothers give him a thorough thrashing.) Finally, after Dr. Greatheart, alias Barnaby Gaul, reveals that he is actually "Jim Doherty," Ann agrees to marry him, heedless of the fact that the Yearlings have burned down her house. An interlude in Act III of this three-act comedy depicts the lives of Georgie's father Stylianos and his grandfather Pericles, typical Saroyan eccentrics in the manner of *My Name Is Aram*.

The dramas of the 1941 *Three Plays* include "The Beautiful People," "Sweeney in the Trees," and "Across the Board on Tomorrow Morning," similar in style but inferior in quality to the three plays described above. *Razzle-Dazzle* (1942) collects a number of short plays, most of which are semi-dramatic sketches rather than genuine playable theatre dramas.

EUDORA WELTY (born 1909)

Eudora Welty began her literary career as a short-story writer, and proved herself so consummate an artist in this genre that many critics concluded that her talent was restricted to the limited scope of the story. Katherine Anne Porter, in the 1941 preface to *A Curtain of*

Green, remarked, "It is quite possible she can never write a novel, and there is no reason why we should." In *Delta Wedding* and again in *The Ponder Heart,* however, Miss Welty presently produced two exquisitely finished novels which not only showed a complete mastery of the form but demonstrated that her mature talent needed this wider scope to display its full power. She is a writer with few pretensions, and with no grandiose literary ambitions at all. Like Ellen Glasgow, she is a Southern writer, a kind of regionalist, and an intensely feminine writer who views human situations with a peculiarly feminine sensitivity; but there the resemblance ends. Miss Glasgow's stated purpose was to paint a complete panorama of Virginia life from Civil War times to the present; Eudora Welty has no other mission than to tell stories about the land and people she knows best. This land is the Mississippi Delta region, especially that part of it lying around Jackson, Mississippi, Miss Welty's home, and extending northward into the valley of the Yazoo River. To an outsider this region seems similar, even identical, to the Oxford district of Faulkner; yet it is typical of the South that Miss Welty's Delta inhabitants view northern Mississippi as a strange and distant land and its denizens virtually foreigners. The "low-born" Troy in *Delta Wedding,* from the hill country in northern Mississippi "up near the Tennessee line" (i.e., virtually Faulkner's region), is treated as an outlander by the self-satisfied and provincial Delta aristocrats of the Fairchild family.

With few exceptions, Miss Welty's best work is laid in this region and among its people, yet she is not a Southern regionalist in every sense. She does not treat the social and psychological implications of the Negro problem to any extent at all when compared with Faulkner; she has no plan for the regeneration of the South like Ellen Glasgow, and she is not particularly interested in the problem of the Southerner who emigrates into Northern culture (Wolfe, Glasgow). Moreover she has none of the sentimental traditionalism and patriotism of Ransom and the Fugitive poets. Whether she has captured the "real" South or not, she has created a fictional world of great charm, a world caught in the grip of an indolent and often ludicrous decadence, yet poetic, gallant, and above all vivid. We are emotionally moved by Faulkner, shocked into attention by Erskine Caldwell, and amused by Eudora Welty. Yet she is more than a humorist; in some respects her fiction gives us as good an insight into Southern society, even into the "problem of the South," as that of the other two authors. The comparison between the three is interesting in another respect: only Faulkner attempts to give us a complete cross-section of Southern society. Caldwell and Miss Welty are interested chiefly in the white population; they show the Negro only from the outside, and only in his relation to the white. But where Caldwell portrays chiefly the "crackers," the illiterate and landless tenant farmers of the back country and the small-town traders (Faulkner would call them Snopeses), Eudora Welty is concerned mainly with the faded aristocrats, Faulkner's Sartoris type. Even when she shows us vulgar townspeople (e.g., in "Petrified Man") she does so from the implied point of view of finer Southern ideals; and her eccentric and slightly mentally deficient country clans (*The Ponder Heart*) are nevertheless imbued with a proud and highly disciplined sense of family tradition. Her Fairchilds (*Delta Wedding*) are Faulkner's Compsons acting comedy instead of tragedy; both families share the same ingrown clan feeling and the same nostalgic consciousness of proud tradition amid the vestiges of decaying wealth.

But it is above all as a stylist that Miss Welty is superb. Her writing is careful, delicately whimsical even when she is relating farcical incidents, and unerring in diction and image. Her dialogues are as subtle and as colorful as those of any modern writer; on the one hand they are precise examples of Southern vernacular, and on the other hand they have a particular Eudora Welty flavor which is instantly recognizable and which no other Southern writer has achieved. Her narrative style is highly compressed; two or three ideas may be interwoven into a single sentence, and yet the result is not intricate or difficult in the way of James Joyce. Miss Welty began as a magazine writer, and even in her later works there is a great clarity and unpretentiousness about her style.

Robert Daniel distinguishes four styles or types of settings in Eudora Welty's work, as follows: (1) historical tales of the Natchez Trace ("First Love," "A Still Moment," and other stories in *The Wide Net*); (2) tales of the countryside, usually the Delta region of Mississippi, including her two novels and the best of her stories; (3) the middle-class town stories, e.g., "Asphodel" and "Petrified Man"; and (4) tales of the metropolis, including stories such as "Flowers

For Marjorie" and "Music From Spain," both from *The Golden Apples*. To these four categories must be added the stories of European setting contained in *The Bride of the Innisfallen*. For each of these settings Miss Welty has a different style and treatment; she is a conscious and versatile artist who writes skillfully to create a given effect, and her work shows a remarkable diversity. Yet it is in the tales of the Delta—the two novels and stories like "Why I Live at the P.O."—that Eudora Welty is at her finest, and it is through these stories that her position as an important writer is assured. ·

LIFE: Eudora Welty was born in Jackson, Mississippi in 1909. Her family was one of comfortable means; her father was president of an insurance company. She attended Mississippi State College for Women (1925-27) and earned a B.A. at the University of Wisconsin (1929). After further college work at Columbia University, she worked briefly in the advertising business but "as she had no real need of a job, she gave up the notion and settled down to writing." Her first story was published in 1936, when she was twenty-seven years old. Since then she has remained in Mississippi, with brief interruptions for travel. She is said to live a normal middle-class life in Jackson, and to take an active part in community and civic affairs; she describes herself as "underfoot locally."

Miss Welty first came into national prominence as a magazine-story writer; her early work appeared in *The Southern Review, New Directions, The Atlantic Monthly,* and *The New Yorker*. In 1942 and again in 1943 she received the O. Henry Memorial Prize for the short story. In 1944 she won an award from the American Academy of Arts and Letters "in recognition of her skill in the short story and her artistry in the subtle portrayal of character," and in 1955 she was awarded the quintennial Howells Medal for fiction. Her first novel, *Delta Wedding,* appeared in 1946 (*The Robber Bridegroom,* published in 1942, is more properly a novelette), and a second novel, *The Ponder Heart* appeared in its entirety in *The New Yorker* in December, 1953 and in book form in 1954.

NOVELS: *Delta Wedding* (1946) is a delicate and whimsical portrait of a family: the Fairchilds, of Fairchild, Mississippi, a fictional town on the Yazoo River near Delta City. The story, or rather the situation, since there is no cohesive plot, is seen chiefly through the eyes of a little girl, Laura McRaven, who comes to Fairchild for the marriage of her cousin Dabney Fairchild with the "low-born" northern Mississippian Troy Flavin, who works as an overseer on the Fairchild fields. The Fairchilds are a closely-knit clan who quarrel with each other but present an impenetrable wall to outsiders; those who marry into the family must either accepts its ways and lose their identity in it or be cast out. Their huge old house, full of sisters, aunts, cousins, and innumerable Negroes, is the center of a life of fascinatingly disorganized eccentricity; its fixtures include a demented but harmless aunt, an idiot child, a somewhat confused Negro witch-woman, and a number of precocious children. The chief events of the novel are the quarrel between an uncle, George Fairchild, and his wife Robbie, which begins when George ignores her safety to risk his life rescuing the feeble-minded Maureen, his niece, from a train (an act symbolic of the inward loyalty of the Fairchild clan); and the gradual acceptance of Troy by the clan, which admits him into its circle only on the assumption that Dabney will go on living in the family as before. None of this is related explicitly; it is conveyed chiefly through dialogue of a particular colorful and whimsical irony, and the story is revealed only gradually and obliquely. As the novel ends Troy and Dabney move into Shellmound, a spare Fairchild mansion which has remained vacant for years, and Robbie and George agree to occupy The Grove, another family house, so that their lives will remain within the Fairchild circle. Other characters are Battle, brother of George and head of the family; his Virginia-born wife Ellen, still an outsider after spending a generation in the family; the elder daughter Shelley; and Ellen's nine-year-old daughter India, a precocious child who is free from the smugness of most literary children of her type. A high moment in the novel is the account of the birth of Shelley, in which the bumbling Dr. Murdock anesthetizes himself with his gas machine and leaves Ellen to deliver her baby alone. This scene well demonstrates Miss Welty's skill in relating broadly farcical material in a subdued and faintly ironic style.

The Ponder Heart (1953) is similar in content but different in technique; it is presented in the form of a long monologue spoken by Edna Earle Ponder, one of the central characters. The Ponder clan resembles the Fairchild family, although it is neither as large nor as aristocratic. The key figure of the plot, Uncle Daniel Ponder, is an old gentleman so eccentric that on one occasion he is locked up in a mental institution; his apparent feeble-mindedness, however, is due mainly to his benevolent impulsiveness (the "Ponder heart") and to the fact that he lives in a private world of his own particular logic. The novel relates chiefly his marital adventures: how he was at one time captured by the designing Miss Teacake Magee and escaped only after a brief ordeal of matrimony, and how he is later tricked into marriage with the cheap and self-centered Bonnie Dee Peacock. Subsequently Bonnie Dee dies under ambiguous circumstances (the truth seems to be that Uncle Daniel playfully tickled her to death) and the Peacock clan, bent on revenge, has him charged with murder. The trial is the climax of the novel; it is an extended and skillfully related farce in which the vulgar Peacocks are contrasted with the tradition-proud and essentially upright Ponders. Uncle Daniel is acquitted, mainly because he gains the crowd's favor by passing out his entire fortune to them in greenbacks while the court is in session. The best of this short novel lies in the portraits of Daniel himself, of Bonnie Dee, and of Edna Earle, who is skillfully characterized as the one sensible member of the family through her own rambling style of telling the story.

SHORT STORIES: "Petrified Man," included in *A Curtain of Green* (1941), is typical of Miss Welty's comedies of lower-middle-class town life. The story is seen obliquely, related by Leota, a beauty-shop attendant, to her customer Mrs. Fletcher. The plot chiefly concerns Mrs. Pike, an incredibly vulgar friend of Leota's, who unmasks a side-show petrified man as a fugitive from justice who is wanted for raping "four women in California, all in the month of August." The real point of the story lies not in the plot but in the fascinatingly vulgar beauty-shop conversations, the preoccupation of the female characters with sex ("He's turning to stone. How'd you like to be married to a guy like that?"), and the general confused and earthy quality of Leota's narrative.

"Why I Live at the P.O." (also from *A Curtain of Green*) is a comedy of the Delta region foreshadowing the style of *The Ponder Heart*. Like the later short novel, it is a monologue related in a typical Welty-flavored Southern vernacular by its heroine. "Sister," who tells the story, is jealous of her sister Stella-Rondo, who has gone off to marry an itinerant photographer and now returns with a two-year-old girl, Shirley T., whom she declares is adopted. Sister, jealous, quarrels with her, and the whole family, including Uncle Rondo and the severe grandfather Papa-Daddy, takes Stella-Rondo's side. Finally Sister hauls away her possessions and moves into the post office, which belongs to her in virtue of the fact that Papa-Daddy has had her made postmistress through his political influence. Although Katherine Anne Porter refers to this story as "a terrifying case of dementia praecox," this is to take Miss Welty's comedy too seriously; the two sisters are no more feeble-minded than many other characters in Eudora Welty's work, and their "regression into childhood" is more whimsical than it is psychoneurotic.

"Death of a Travelling Salesman" (from *A Curtain of Green*) is slightly grimmer but still basically ironic. The hero, R. J. Bowman, a shoe salesman, is forced to take shelter for the night in the house of an eccentric couple—a haggard woman and her strong young husband Sonny—whose ménage is so strange and whose mannerisms so unnerving that he drops dead of heart failure just as he manages to escape from them. Miss Welty probably intended this story as a parody of the shocking backwoods stories of Erskine Caldwell and his school.

The Bride of the Innisfallen and Other Stories (collection, 1955) contains the better stories from Miss Welty's later period, some of them in European settings. The title story is an impressionistic account of a trip by train and ship from London to Ireland, seen chiefly from the point of view of a young American woman who is taking an "emotional vacation" from her husband. The interest of the story is contained in the characterizations of the passengers in the railroad compartment; since they are going to Cork, most of them are Irish, and their colorful friendliness and volubility are contrasted with the self-contained reticence of the English through whose country they are travelling. "Going to Naples," laid on an Italy-bound ship, is similar; it is obvious that Miss Welty is attracted to the romantic Irish and Italians for the same reason she loves her Delta Mississippians, that is for the contrast they offer to the "respectable" and slightly stuffy bourgeois temperament.

REALISTS AND NATURALISTS:
THE NEW GENERATION

In the period after the Second World War there emerged an important new group of young American writers, a school basically in the realistic-naturalistic tradition of the Twenties and stemming essentially from Hemingway, Dos Passos, Faulkner, Wolfe, and Anderson. John O'Hara, the oldest of this group, was born in 1905 and began publishing well before the war; the youngest, Norman Mailer, was born in 1923 and published his first book in 1948. In spite of this considerable spread in time, these writers are conveniently grouped together because they represent the second generation of twentieth-century realists, a group of authors who read the naturalists of the Twenties when they were young men and started in where Hemingway and his generation left off.

CHARACTERISTICS: (1) These younger writers resemble the earlier American naturalists first of all in attitude: they are skeptical, ironic, anti-puritanical, hard-minded, and basically materialistic, although they are not without traces of idealism. Four of the six authors treated here wrote war novels, and with one exception they are novels in the tradition of *All Quiet on the Western Front* and Dos Passos' *Three Soldiers:* cynical, anti-heroic, antagonistic toward the professional officer class and the military mind, basically pacifistic. Wouk's *The Caine Mutiny* is the exception, and its special qualities will be explained under the proper heading. When these writers treat domestic scenes they tend to do so in the manner of Sinclair Lewis and Scott Fitzgerald, satirizing the banality of middle-class life and antagonistic toward the hypocrisy that stems from American puritanism. Here again Wouk is the exception.

(2) In style the group writes in the idiom which is thought of as characteristically "American" in the twentieth century, and which derives from the naturalists of the Twenties: terse, vernacular, understated, and often hard-boiled. The tendency is toward pure narrative (especially dialogue) rather than discursive exposition; the authors are concerned to make us see "how it was" at first hand instead of telling us about the action in retrospect. The outstanding impression one receives from the post-1945 war novels is the studied detachment

of the author, the utter absence of emotional comment or sentimentalising. Here the line of development of the American war novel, from Crane through Hemingway to Jones, Mailer, and Shaw, is obvious.

(3) In construction the group owes something to war novels like *A Farewell to Arms* and to the Jazz Age novel of manners (e.g., Scott Fitzgerald) but more to Joyce, Faulkner, and Dos Passos; the typical construction of the post-1945 naturalistic novel is complex and ingenious, with flashbacks, shifting point-of-view devices, and experiments in chronological order. Perhaps the most influential single work in this respect is Dos Passos' *U.S.A.,* which was frankly imitated by Mailer in parts of *The Naked and the Dead* and which has also obviously left its mark on Shaw's *The Young Lions.* This kind of "pattern novel" technique, with its continual switching to different characters and its flashbacks into their past, is ideally suited to a war novel which presents a number of men of diverse backgrounds and then analyzes their contrasting reactions to the experience of war.

Of the six writers considered here, three (O'Hara, Shaw, and Salinger) are also consummate masters of the short story. In their story style the influence of their market—the commercial American magazine—is apparent. Salinger and Shaw wrote much of their short fiction for *The New Yorker,* and the well-known characteristics of this weekly (its brittle and sophisticated style, its fondness for stories of diffuse plot) became a part of their technique. O'Hara's magazine experience is more diversified; his stories rely more on plot and are more conventional in characterization. This peculiarly American genre, the magazine story, has reached a high stage of perfection in these three writers, as well as in others (Katherine Anne Porter, Eudora Welty) not considered in this group.

JOHN O'HARA (born 1905)

The relation of O'Hara to his environment is analogous to that of Thomas Wolfe. Born in a small Pennsylvania town, he moved on to a big-city culture and became a professional newspaperman and writer; yet as an author he remained fascinated with the places and the people of his boyhood, and he returns to this material consistently in his most important work. In a sense he is a kind of regionalist; his region is the south-central portion of Pennsylvania centering around Harrisburg and O'Hara's own home town of Pottsville (which he converts into the fictional town of Gibbsville). The population of this region is varied: Pennsylvania Dutch farmers, Polish coal miners, Italian shopkeepers and small tradesmen, Irish artisans, upper-middle-class townspeople mainly of Anglo-Saxon extraction, and a sprinkling of professionals (doctors, teachers) from out of the state. It is the last two groups with which O'Hara is chiefly concerned; that is to say he invariably writes from their point of view even though people from the first four groups appear as minor characters. O'Hara himself belonged to the last group; his father was a doctor who attended both the illiterate miners of the "patches" or small mining villages and the wealthy town gentry. In *The Doctor's Son* O'Hara portrays his own experience as a boy accompanying his father on his professional rounds, thus gaining invaluable knowledge of the people he was later to portray in his fiction.

O'Hara's Pennsylvania writing includes *The Doctor's Son,* the novels *Appointment in Samarra, A Rage to Live, The Farmer's Hotel,* and *Ten North Frederick,* and various stories published in other collections. With the exception of *The Farmer's Hotel,* a minor work, all the novels in this list have the same structure: they are fictional biographies of upper-middle-class Pennsylvanians involving a more or less complete social analysis of a small Pennsylvania city. O'Hara is never content to show us an individual; he must also show us the society which produced the individual. His novels contain much detailed data on the economy and industry of the region, and the changing social conditions which are causing some families to rise and others to decline. This sort of sociological documentation, however, serves only as background: his main interest remains centered on character. His typical hero (Julian English, Joseph B. Chapin) is a man born into a superior family in a small Pennsylvania town, educated at an Ivy League college, who returns to his home town and lives a "respectable" life as a leading citizen, concealing from the public the rottenness and unhappiness of his private life. In *A Rage to Live* the protagonist is a woman, but the pattern remains the same.

As an author who "takes the wraps off the social customs, the politics, the morals of a small American city," O'Hara at first sight resembles Sinclair Lewis. But there is an essential difference: Lewis is basically a satirist, and O'Hara, although not devoid of irony, approaches his subject much more seriously. Even though he attacks the hypocrisy and banality of middle-class life, it is obvious that he is impressed himself with the distinction of families like the Chapins with their Cadillacs, their Ivy-League educations, their social position, and the general aura of importance which surrounds them. Here O'Hara resembles Scott Fitzgerald more than he does Lewis. He is consciously a portrayer of "superior" people, even when he is attacking their standards. In spite of his political and social liberalism he can never view the miners, the immigrant shopkeepers, and the Negro servants of his region as anything but supernumeraries, background figures for his central drama; the bootlegger Al Grecco in *Appointment in Samarra* is one of his few convincing *déclassé* characters, and even he seems thin and stereotyped compared with similar characters in Hemingway or Dos Passos.

As a stylist O'Hara is facile but not highly precise. His writing is all first-draft; according to his own statement in an interview with Robert Van Gelder it goes to the printer just as it comes from his typewriter. Under these conditions its obvious finish is a tribute to his ear for dialogue and to his long experience as a newspaperman. Because of this technique, however, his construction is often awkward, his conversations, particularly intimate ones between husband and wife, gauche and unconvincing. He is not original in construction; *Butterfield 8,* the only one of his novels that shows any ingenuity in this respect, borrows its pattern from Dos Passos and Joyce. O'Hara's importance lies chiefly in his thorough knowledge of a certain region and a certain people, and his skill in recreating this private world in fictional form for the general reader.

LIFE: John O'Hara was born in Pottsville, Pennsylvania in 1905; his father was a physician, and O'Hara was one of seven children. Of Irish extraction, he was raised as a Catholic and educated at various schools including the Fordham Preparatory School and Niagara Preparatory School in Niagara, New York, from which he graduated in 1924. He had intended to go on to Yale, but the death of his father made further education impossible. Instead he went to work and held a number of odd jobs which provided him with valuable material for his later writing, ranging from guard in an amusement park to secretary to Heywood Broun. He gradually moved into newspaper work, serving as reporter on two Pennsylvania papers and going on to the

New York Mirror, the *Morning Telegraph,* and the *Herald Tribune.*
At one time he was also football editor of *Time.* In 1934 he turned
to screen-writing and worked in succession for four different motion-
picture companies. He was married in 1931 to Helen Ritchie Petit,
and again, after a divorce, to Belle Mulford Wylie in 1937. His first
novel, *Appointment in Samarra,* appeared in 1934. Meanwhile he was
turning out short stories at a prolific rate; a collection, *The Doctor's
Son and Other Stories,* appeared in 1935. His *Pal Joey* stories, which
appeared originally in *The New Yorker* as a set of sketches about
New York night life, were dramatized in 1941, winning success on
Broadway as a musical comedy, and were later made into a motion
picture. In 1955, after the death of his second wife, he was married
to Katharine Barnes Bryan. A long-time New York resident, O'Hara
has lived more recently in Princeton, New Jersey.

CHIEF WORKS: *Appointment in Samarra* (novel, 1934) describes
three climactic days in the life of Julian English, an automobile dealer
in Gibbsville, Pennsylvania. Julian, son of the Dr. Billy English who
appears frequently in O'Hara's fiction, is bitter and dissatisfied with
his life and tired of the monotony of his relations with his wife Caroline; basically an individualist, he is at the point of attempting to
break out of the pattern of conventional behavior that holds him fast
in the respectable society of the small town. As the novel opens he
does commit an act of rebellion, but it is a stupid and destructive
one: at a country-club party he throws a drink into the face of Harry
Reilly, who is not only his friend but also an influential member of
the community who has invested money in Julian's business. Julian's
collapse and destruction begin with this act. He begins drinking heavily, he insults the servants and antagonizes his wife, he flirts dangerously with the girl-friend of a local racketeer, and he gets into a low
argument in his club which ends in a general brawl. At one point he
considers simply driving out of Gibbsville and starting life anew
somewhere else, but he lacks the character to do this. Returning to
his home and finding it empty, he has a short drinking party in company with a young woman from a newspaper who has come to interview his wife; when he makes overtures to her he is repulsed. This
final failure disgusts him with his life and with himself, and he

commits suicide in his garage using the exhaust of his automobile to asphyxiate himself.

Other important characters in this novel include Julian's wife Caroline, oversexed and frustrated by Julian's indifference; Lute Fliegler, a contented automobile salesman who works for Julian; and Al Grecco, a cynical but competent bootlegger whose life becomes involved with Julian's at several points. There are also numerous passages filling in the economic and social background of Gibbsville. This short novel may be considered a kind of exercise for the more important treatment of similar themes in *A Rage to Live* and *Ten North Frederick*.

A Rage to Live (novel, 1949) is the fictional biography of Grace Tate, née Caldwell, daughter of the leading family in Fort Penn, Pennsylvania, an invented city roughly drawn after the capital town of Harrisburg. Grace's family is an old and proud one, and her parents raise her consciously in the tradition of aristocracy. To their surprise, however, she marries an "outsider," the New Yorker Sidney Tate, who is nevertheless considered acceptable because of his Yale background and his family's wealth. Grace and Sidney are at first happy living on a farm outside of Fort Penn, raising three children, and gradually assuming position as the most prominent family in the community. But Grace, first and foremost a Caldwell, continues to think of her husband as an outsider, and more and more her interests turn back to her own clan. In addition her character is dominated by a fierce "rage to live," a vitality so boundless that she cannot remain faithful to Sidney even though she loves him; she has a tempestuous affair with a local contractor, Roger Bannon, which soon becomes a matter for public gossip. Meanwhile the First World War comes; Sidney applies for a naval commission but is turned down for a physical defect. Shortly afterward he is stricken with infantile paralysis and dies, and a few days later Grace's small son Billy is carried off by the same disease. Struggling to reorganize her life, Grace rejects a chance to resume her affair with Bannon, but in spite of her inward struggles against her emotions she falls in love with Jack Hollister, a Fort Penn newspaperman. Although Hollister and Grace are innocent, Hollister's wife Amy senses their feelings toward each other, comes to an outdoor party where they are together, and fires several wild pistol shots at them without hitting anyone. This incident persuades Grace that her time of passions must come to an end, and that she must now resign herself to a graceful middle age. An epilogue describes her life a number of years later, in 1947; she has grown into a gracious if inwardly unhappy grandmother, living in New York and sustained by the obvious respect the young members of the Caldwell family show her. Another important character in *A Rage to Live* is Grace's brother Brock Caldwell, in his youth a playboy and a snob, who acquires character through gradual maturity and through marriage with a sophisticated Frenchwoman.

Ten North Frederick (novel, 1955) is O'Hara's most ambitious and most important work. Broader in scope than any of his previous novels, it includes a complete history of its locale and characters from Civil War times to the present. The central character is Joseph B. Chapin, the leading citizen of Gibbsville, a man whose life is dominated by a secret ambition to be President of the United States. The novel begins with Chapin's funeral and then goes back to recount the history of his life in a single long flashback. Born into the leading family in the town, Chapin never doubts his own superiority, just as he never doubts the superiority of Gibbsville and its society to all other places on earth, not excluding New York City. As a Yale student he has relations with Marie Harrison, sister of a friend; when she later dies from an abortion he feels a temporary remorse, but soon recovers from it. He marries Edith Stokes, who comes from a good Gibbsville family and is the proper and approved bride for him, and goes into a law partnership with Arthur McHenry, a boyhood friend who has also gone to Yale for his education. Chapin's law career is a success, and gradually political ambitions grow in him. In his forties he enters into negotiations with Mike Slattery, the local Republican boss, for the nomination for Lieutenant Governor. When Mike suggests that he make a large political contribution, "with no strings to it," he does so. But the Party leaders decide against his candidacy; they view him (perhaps rightly) as a snob with no appeal for the common voter. Chapin has thrown away a hundred thousand dollars on an ephemeral dream. But except for McHenry and perhaps Slattery, no one knows of his blasted ambition to be President; the world is unaware that his life has been a failure. Toward the end of his career he has a brief affair with Kate Drummond, his daughter's roommate; then he dies of a liver ailment aggravated by overdrinking.

Other important characters in *Ten North Frederick* are Chapin's wife Edith, who sees through him and is dissatisfied with her marriage but permits herself only one brief extramarital affair and then lives out her life maintaining her standards to the end; his daughter Ann, who falls in love with a musician named Charley Bongiorno and whose life is ruined when the family breaks up the affair; a son Joby (Joseph Jr.), whose character is broken by his strong-willed father and who ends up cynical and alcoholic; and Slattery, the politician, who views Chapin's stiff family pride somewhat ironically but nevertheless admires him and sympathizes with him as a man. As in *A Rage to Live,* there is much social documentation, including a complete analysis of the economic and commercial interrelationships of the town. The core of the novel, however, is the character of Chapin and his relations with his wife, his children, and Slattery.

O'Hara's remaining novels are less important. *Butterfield 8* (1935) is laid in uptown New York City and demonstrates the intricate pattern of relationships of the people who live within the telephone exchange indicated by the title. The central figure, Gloria Wandrous, is a fast girl of the flapper age who becomes involved in a descending circle of vice and is finally killed when she falls overboard from a steamer. *Hope of Heaven* (1938), set in Hollywood, describes the unhappy love affair of a scenario writer and a girl who works in a bookstore. *The Farmer's Hotel* (1951) is a short novel in which guests in a snowbound hotel become involved in a complicated intrigue of passion and tragedy.

STORIES: O'Hara's short stories are collected in *The Doctor's Son* (1935), *Files on Parade* (1939), *Pipe Night* (1945), and *Hellbox* (1947). The best known of his stories are contained in the first volume. Of these, "The Doctor's Son," the title story, is a long tale based on O'Hara's boyhood experiences following his father on his medical rounds. During a flu epidemic the narrator, James Malloy, visits the coal-mining "patch" of Collieryville with "Doctor" Myers, a young medical student, and falls in love with Edith Evans, daughter of a mine superintendent. But Edith's father dies in the epidemic, and James, who has seen Myers making love to Mrs. Evans, comes out of the experience matured and disillusioned; he never sees Edith again.

The best-known stories in *Files on Parade* are the "Pal Joey" letters, written by a semi-literate but expressive night-club entertainer on the road to a friend in New York City. The dialogue style is reminiscent of Damon Runyon. These stories and others about the same characters, most of them originally published in *The New Yorker,* were collected as *Pal Joey* in 1940 and converted by O'Hara and others into a musical comedy the same year. Stories from *The Doctor's Son* and *Files on Parade* are also contained in a letter collection, *The Great Short Stories of John O'Hara* (1956).

IRWIN SHAW (born 1913)

In spite of his occasional excursions into the drama and the novel, Irwin Shaw is first and foremost a short-story writer. Early in his career he mastered the art of a certain type of American magazine story: the mature, urban, and slightly ironic story constructed mainly out of conversations among witty and sophisticated city dwellers. Many of these stories were written for *The New Yorker,* and they show the style of brittle urbanity which that magazine has made famous. Thus his experience has made Shaw an expert stylist. His situations are often highly sentimental, but they are saved from mawkishness by the ironic objectivity of his treatment; emotion is always understated, and often the deep emotional reactions of the characters to their situations are conveyed only through implication.

Irwin Shaw's world is essentially a tragic one, even though Shaw himself is not a pessimist. He might perhaps best be termed a stoic; he is convinced of the basic hostility of the universe toward man, and he sees man himself as a selfish and egocentric creature essentially callous toward the sufferings of his fellows. Only occasionally is this grim picture relieved by some act of idealism, some unexpected attitude of unselfishness or tenderness. These isolated acts of decency illustrate Shaw's ethic: that even in a hostile universe, even in a callous and selfish society, the individual person occasionally shows impulses toward good. In *The Young Lions* the urban and detached playwright Michael Whitacre and the bitter young Jew Noah Ackerman, who have little in common on the social or intellectual plane, eventually find a basis for friendship in their common humanity, the core of decency and brotherhood they share beneath their complicated social exteriors. Shaw's attitude toward his own Jewish background is connected to this ethic of individualism. He obviously feels a certain emotional loyalty toward his race and its traditions (see the story "God on Friday Night") but nevertheless he refuses to consider himself primarily a Jew who stands in social opposition to a gentile majority. This attitude is magnificently illustrated in "Act of Faith," in which the Jewish soldier Seeger, at first troubled by a letter from his neurotically fearful Jewish father, eventually decides to sell his most precious possession to share the money on a Paris leave with his gentile friends.

Shaw is the type of author who is highly preoccupied with problems of literary technique, especially construction, and he often builds elaborate—if inconspicuous—symmetry and parallelism into his work. This tendency is most apparent in *The Young Lions,* where some critics have attacked his rather obvious ingenuity. It is not this rather pretentious complexity of construction, however, that marks Shaw as an important author; it is rather his unerring skill in dialogue and his mature urbanity in characterization, qualities which make him simultaneously one of the most cosmopolitan and the most American of modern writers.

LIFE: Irwin Shaw was born in 1913 in New York City and was educated in the Brooklyn public schools, later going on to Brooklyn College. As a college student he played football, wrote for the student newspaper, and wrote several plays produced by a local dramatic society. He was at one time expelled from the college for academic deficiencies (he failed calculus) but returned, after an interlude of odd jobs, to graduate in 1934. After his graduation he worked as a radio writer, producing serial scripts in a mass-production technique the demoralizing effects of which on a writer he has described in a story titled "Main Currents of American Thought." In 1936 he wrote his first work of literary importance, the play *Bury the Dead,* which was produced first by the experimental New Theatre League but soon attracted enough attention to be moved to a Broadway theatre for a successful run. On the strength of this success Shaw then went to Hollywood and wrote a number of screen plays, to which he attaches no importance whatsoever. In 1939 another play, *The Gentle People,* enjoyed a modest success and ran for four months on Broadway. Drafted in 1942 (he had requested 1-A classification although he could have been deferred), he served for the rest of the war in Africa, England, France, and Germany. Meanwhile he had achieved success as a short-story writer; his fiction was included in the O. Henry and O'Brien collections for the first time in 1940 and won numerous awards thereafter. One of his first war stories, "Walking Wounded," won the O. Henry Memorial Prize for 1944. After the war he turned again to playwriting, produced two failures, and then turned his hand to his first novel, *The Young Lions,* which appeared in 1948. It was generally considered a success, although some critics felt it did not fulfill the promise of his stories. *The Troubled Air,* another novel, appeared in 1951 and *Lucy Crown,* a third, in 1956.

CHIEF WORKS: *Bury the Dead* (drama, 1936) was written for the experimental New Theatre League, later ran successfully on Broadway, and has since been frequently produced by amateur and little theatre groups. Stylistically and structurally it resembles the drama of the German Expressionists, especially Toller and Wedekind; it is in the tradition of continental experimentalism also in its set, which is highly stylized, almost rudimentary. In dialogue, however, it is totally American, patterned after the World War literature of the type of *Three Soldiers* and *What Price Glory?* The plot is built around a sergeant and three soldiers who are detailed to bury six men killed somewhere in France in the First World War. The six dead men, however, refuse to be buried; they stand in their graves and demand an explanation of why they were "sold for twenty-five yards of bloody mud" while others live and make a profit from the war. A doctor is called to certify that they are actually dead, and a priest, a captain, and a trio of generals all try to persuade them to be buried. Finally the war department brings to France the women of the dead soldiers to persuade them to listen to reason. But one wife, the bitter and poverty-crushed Martha Webster, cries, "Tell 'em all to stand up!" As the play ends the corpses, walking over the inert form of a general, leave the stage like "men who have leisurely business that must be attended to in the not too pressing future"—i.e., to take their revenge on those who have instigated the war for their own profit. This drama is typical of the pacifism of the disillusioned Thirties, and its theme stands in sharp contrast to the attitude toward the

Second World War which Shaw was later to express in *The Young Lions.*

STORIES: The best of Shaw's stories are collected in *Sailor Off the Bremen* (1939), *Welcome to the City* (1942), and *Act of Faith and Other Stories* (1946); *Mixed Company* (1950) includes selected stories from all three earlier volumes. A few of the best known of these stories should be briefly described. "The Girls in their Summer Dresses" (from *Sailor Off the Bremen*) is typical of Shaw's light and urban *New Yorker* style. Michael, the hero, is happily married to Frances, whom he loves, but on the Sunday afternoon in which the story takes place a quarrel develops. It is spring, and Michael, a lover of beauty, cannot help admiring the splendid girls who pass on Fifth Avenue; but Frances, possessive and jealous, makes a scene about this, and at the end of the story it is obvious that the two are basically incompatible. "The Eighty-Yard Run" is the story of a football hero, Christian Darling, who makes a spectacular run one day in practice and then finds the rest of his life is an anti-climax. His wife Louise, who married him because he was a football hero, gradually surpasses him and becomes a magazine editor, while he is reduced to selling suits for a third-rate clothing manufacturer. Thus the story demonstrates the artificiality of "college hero" success and the way this kind of success destroys the character of a young man too immature to see it in perspective. "Act of Faith," from the volume of the same name, is a study of three soldiers in a camp in France, shortly after the end of the war, waiting to be transferred back to America. Norman Seeger, a Jew, receives a depressing letter from his father and learns that his brother Jacob has gone virtually insane through fear of anti-Semitic persecution. Meanwhile he is called upon to make a difficult decision. He and his two gentile friends Olson and Welch have a chance to go to Paris on leave, but have no money; the two ask Seeger to sell a German pistol which is his most prized possession, since he had to kill an SS major to get it (a symbol to Seeger of the Jew's triumph over Nazism). He also has a vague irrational feeling that he had better keep the pistol to defend himself against anti-Semites in America. But Seeger remembers that Olson and Welch have both risked their lives for him; when he asked them about their attitude toward the Jews he finds that they do not think of him as a Jew at all, but as a friend. Knowing now that he will be able to rely on Olson and Welch—and many others like them—when he returns to civilian life, he agrees to sell his pistol, remarking, "What could I use it for in America?" "God on Friday Night" (1939), originally published in *Story* magazine and frequently anthologized, is a portrait of a Jewish night-club entertainer, married to a blonde gentile girl, who comes home to his mother to ask her to pray for the son his wife is about to bear. The mother, who gave up her religion the day she married Sol's socialist father, nevertheless agrees to say the prayers. When the baby is born Sol and Violet, his wife, bring it to the mother, who lights candles for thanksgiving; and when her skeptical younger son Lawrence sneers sarcastically at this, she tells him, "Shut up, City College philosopher."

NOVEL: *The Young Lions* (1948), Shaw's most important full-length work, is a war novel following the fortunes of three soldiers, two Americans and one German, through the Second World War. Numerous other characters, all of them connected to these three, are also described in some detail. Michael Whitacre, a New York playwright, intellectual, a self-styled liberal, is rescued by the advent of the war from the vacuity and meaninglessness of his life and from an unhappy marriage. Although he could easily get a commission through influence, he joins the army as an enlisted man, serves for a time in a Civil Affairs unit, then requests combat duty and fights in the European campaign. Noah Ackerman, an unhappy young Jew, marries Hope Plowman, daughter of a rugged New Englander, and manages to overcome the old man's instinctive anti-Semitism. In the army, however, he does not have it so easy; he is constantly persecuted by ignorant and brutal draftees, and finally is forced to fight the ten biggest men in the company one by one. Emerging broken in body but not in spirit from this ordeal, he goes into combat in France and proves himself a capable and courageous soldier. Christian Diestl, the third main character, is a German soldier who enters Paris as a member of the victorious Nazi blitzkrieg, fights in North Africa under the hard and methodical Lieutenant Hardenburg, is wounded and returns to Europe, and finally retreats with the German army before the Allied invasion forces in 1944. The three meet in a symbolic and rather contrived climax in a Bavarian concentration camp just before the end of the war; Diestl kills Ackerman from ambush and is then stalked and killed by Michael, who by this time has developed from a vague and detached liberalism to a hard and angry resentment toward Nazism and everything it stands for.

This basic plot is reinforced with a complicated set of parallels and allegorical incidents. The novel opens with three chapters showing the activities of the three main characters on the same day: December 31, 1937. Diestl and Whitacre are often treated as "opposite numbers"—e.g., they are both refused commissions because of pre-war Communist associations, and they both have affairs with the same girl, Margaret Freemantle. In Chapter 4 Diestl is slightly wounded in the face in the capture of Paris, and on the same day, in Chapter 5, Whitacre is cut in the face when his neurotic wife throws a badminton racket at him. (For a more complete list of such parallels, see Aldridge, *After the Lost Generation,* pp. 151ff.) This novel has been acclaimed by some critics as the best work of fiction to be written about the Second World War; it is certainly one of the most ingenious and highly finished. Its detractors object to its "air of prefabrication and contrivance," its excessive ingenuity in construction, and the stereotyped quality of its characterizations: the ruthless Nazi, the muddled liberal, and the heroic and persecuted young Jew.

HERMAN WOUK (born 1915)

In the company of the other war novelists of World War II Wouk is an anomaly. He is conservative in temperament, religious in tendency, and has a great respect for stability, tradition, and established order. His most important work, *The Caine Mutiny,* avoids the clichés that have filled every war novel since *All Quiet on the Western Front* —the arrogant stupidity of officers, the superiority of the civilian soldier over the Prussianized professional, the monotonous obscenity. In fact *The Caine Mutiny* includes a specific satire on such novels in the description of *Multitudes, Multitudes,* the war novel which the pretentious and effete naval officer Tom Keefer is writing—a novel which is not without resemblance to *From Here to Eternity* and *The Naked and the Dead.* Wouk does not admire war, but he admits its necessity under special circumstances, such as the threat of fascism, and he accepts the fact that war involves a certain amount of stupidity, incompetence, and unfairness to individuals. But he is not anti-militaristic *per se;* he realizes that a military establishment, with its professional militarists, is necessary even in a democracy if democratic ideals are going to be maintained and made secure. He goes further: he believes that the military tradition, taken in itself, is a good and fine thing, and that a man cannot rise in a military organization unless he is a man of character. These "conservative" ideas are radical in the era of Dos Passos, Jones, Mailer, and Irwin Shaw.

In literary style too Wouk is a conservative. His approach to the novel is old-fashioned; he has scarcely been touched by the literary revolution led by Joyce, Faulkner, Dos Passos, and other twentieth-century experimentalists. The most remarkable quality of the style of *The Caine Mutiny* is its decorum. It is entirely devoid of the obscene language that fills most war novels (Wouk believes that "you don't use dirty language in somebody else's home," even when you enter the home as a writer of a novel) and it contains little shocking or violent incident. Only one man is killed aboard the *Caine* during its whole war service. Yet Wouk's novel loses none of its masculine hardness in observing this decorum; it is a thoroughly male book, devoid of prissiness or sentimentalizing.

Wouk's remaining work, although less important, follows this same pattern. He stands for all the domestic and traditional virtues: he believes in the American middle class, in the family, in the integrity of marriage, in patriotism, and in traditional religious values. None of this would be remarkable if Wouk were an ordinary American citizen; but as a writer, standing in the company of Sinclair Lewis, John Dos Passos, Ernest Hemingway, and his own post-1945 contemporaries, Wouk the conservative and traditionalist is virtually unique.

LIFE: Herman Wouk was born in 1915 in the Bronx and except for his naval service has lived most of his life in the New York area. His parents were Russian Jewish immigrants who came to America in 1905; his father at first supported the family by washing clothes and rose to become the president of a large and modern commercial laundry firm. His mother was the daughter of a rabbi, and the family was always Orthodox. According to Wouk, the two great influences on his ideas have been those of Rabbi Mendel Leib Levine, his grandfather, and the Columbia University philosopher Irwin Edman.

As a student at Columbia Wouk edited *The Columbia Jester,* a humor magazine, and wrote two varsity shows; he graduated with honors in 1934 with a major in comparative literature. After graduation he worked six years as a radio writer, at one time serving as script writer for the Fred Allen show. In June 1941 he left this position to work for the government as a dollar-a-year man writing and producing radio shows to popularize war bonds. When America entered the war he joined the Navy as a line officer, and served four years in the Pacific. His first ship, the U.S.S. *Zane,* a DMS (destroyer-minesweeper), won a unit commendation in the Solomons campaign. Wouk served in various positions including communications officer on this ship, and was then transferred to another DMS, the *Southard.* He rose to second in command (executive officer) of the *Southard* before it was finally wrecked in the Okinawa typhoon of October, 1945. All of this experience, as can be seen, found its way into *The Caine Mutiny.*

Meanwhile Wouk had begun writing fiction. His first novel, *Aurora Dawn,* was begun while he was still in the Navy and published in 1947; it was a Book-of-the-Month-Club selection and was favorably reviewed, and Wouk was launched as an author. *The Caine Mutiny,* in 1951, was his third novel. Its success was phenomenal. It sold over three million copies in various editions and was then dramatized, by Wouk and others, to become a Broadway hit; it was subsequently made into a motion picture which won an Academy Award. The book itself won a Pulitzer Prize and was selected by each of the four largest book clubs.

Wouk was married in 1945 to Betty Brown, a Phi Beta Kappa from U.S.C. whom he met while still in the service. His religious development is important in relation to his work. Converted to a "modern" skepticism at Columbia, he later returned to the traditional values of his Jewish heritage, and in the postwar period was active in a number of Jewish organizations. His gentile wife is a Jewish convert, and Wouk himself has taught literature at Yeshiva University in New York.

CHIEF WORKS: *The Caine Mutiny* (novel, 1951) is a war novel told chiefly from the point of view of the young naval officer Willie Keith, "because the event turned on his personality as the massive door of a vault turns on a small jewel bearing." A Princeton graduate and son of a wealthy doctor, Keith is uncertain what to do with his life; as the novel opens he is making his living as a night-club entertainer. He falls in love with a pretty young singer, May Wynn; but meanwhile the war breaks out, and Keith enters midshipman school at Columbia. When he gets his commission he is assigned to a decrepit converted destroyer, the U.S.S. *Caine.* Shortly after he joins the ship its captain, De Vriess, is detached and Commander Philip Queeg takes his place. Other important officers of the ship's company are Tom Keefer, a sophisticated intellectual who plans to write a novel about the war, and Steve Maryk, a San Francisco fisherman with a thorough knowledge of seamanship. It soon becomes apparent to officers and crew that Queeg is not only an unbearable martinet but apparently mentally unbalanced, especially under conditions of strain. He is over-meticulous about petty details and addicted to minor compulsions like the two ball bearings he continually plays with in his hand; he is afflicted with a mild paranoid tendency which convinces him that the ship has united in a conspiracy against him, and he tends to freeze up completely in moments of crisis to the point where he is incapable of giving orders or listening to reason. Keefer, who is well read in modern psychology, believes he is insane, and convinces Maryk of this; he tells him of Article 184 of Naval Regulations, which permits a junior officer to relieve his captain of command under "unusual and extraordinary circumstances" such as insanity. Maryk conscientiously begins to compile a notebook of Queeg's eccentricities in case such a crisis should ever arise. Meanwhile the *Caine* carries out its function as an escort ship and general errand-boy in the Pacific campaign. Queeg demonstrates his mental unbalance on many occasions. The most important of these is the "Yellowstain" incident during the Kwajalein invasion. Queeg, ordered to escort some landing boats into a beach under fire, instead deserts them, leaving a yellow dye-marker in the water to mark their point of departure; it is apparent that he did this either out of cowardice or out of temporary insanity.

The final crisis comes during a typhoon in the Philippine Sea in December, 1944. When the *Caine,* beaten by heavy seas, broaches to several times and almost founders, Queeg seems to lose command of himself and is unable to issue coherent orders. Maryk, by this time executive officer, countermands his confused orders and takes over the ship; the young Keith, who is officer of the deck, supports him. The ship is saved, and Queeg is transferred back to the United States for rest. But Maryk must undergo a court-martial; if he is found guilty of "conduct to the prejudice of good order or discipline," then Keith and Keefer will be faced with similar charges. Barney Greenwald, in peacetime a successful Jewish lawyer and now a Naval aviator, is assigned as defense counsel. His only chance lies in proving that Queeg was unbalanced, and his job is difficult; Queeg, now released from conditions of strain, is plausible and impressive, and three Navy psychiatrists declare him sane. But Greenwald, using every "smart lawyer" trick he knows of, succeeds in badgering Queeg until he breaks down in court and clearly demonstrates his paranoid personality; Maryk is acquitted. The *Caine* officers plan a party to congratulate Maryk and Keefer, whose war novel has been accepted by a publisher. Greenwald is invited, but comes only briefly to tell the group that they were wrong and Queeg was right. In a confused but eloquent drunken speech, he explains what the menace of fascism means to him as a Jew (his relatives have died in European concentration camps), and points out that while he and other civilians were hurriedly learning how to defend their country, it was only Queeg and those like him who were holding the line against the enemy. Militarism is therefore necessary and those who attempt to tear its ideals down (like Keefer with his anti-militaristic novel) are stupid and dangerous. He then throws a glass of (yellow) wine into Keefer's face and leaves.

Meanwhile the story of Keith's personal life has been woven into the novel. During a California leave in the middle of the war he meets May again and decides to marry her, but is later prevailed upon by his socially conscious mother that the marriage is beneath him and would interfere with his planned career as a scholar. At the end of the novel, however, he realizes that both loyalty and his continuing love call for him to marry her; he does so, even though her reputation has become somewhat tarnished by this time in the cynical world of night-club entertainment. Keith's character is shown developing throughout the novel; at the beginning he is a playboy and drifter without direction in life, and his war experience, along with his respect for his father, who dies during the novel, develops him into a strong and purposeful person of character.

Marjorie Morningstar (novel, 1955) is, like *The Caine Mutiny,* an anomaly among modern novels, in this case a tribute to female virtue and middle-class domesticity. Majorie Morgenstern, the heroine, is a Jewish girl in a Bronx family which rises socially and finally moves to fashionable Central Park West. Romantic as a young girl, she dreams of a stage career and has already picked out a name for herself: Marjorie Morningstar. At a summer resort she meets Noel Airman, a fascinating and sophisticated stage producer who spends most of the rest of the novel trying to seduce her—finally succeeding in a New York hotel. But Marjorie is basically virtuous, and she is not sure she is satisfied with the effete but superficial Noel. She is courted by three other men: the steady and unexciting Dr. Shapiro, Noel's assistant Wally Wronken, and Mike Eden, a "brilliant, devastating heel—a West Side version of a Scott Fitzgerald hero" *(Time)* whom she meets on a trip to Europe. But in the end she rejects all four and marries Milton Schwartz, a young Jewish lawyer, first telling him all the details of her relations with Noel and others. As the novel closes she has settled down to a comfortable middle-class existence in a New York suburb, in every sense an "average young matron." The most memorable parts of this novel are the scenes of Jewish home life in the nineteen-thirties, related by Wouk nostalgically but with great objectivity.

OTHER WORKS: *Aurora Dawn* (1947), Wouk's first novel, is a sophisticated satire on the radio advertising business in New York City. *The City Boy* (novel, 1948) is the story of eleven-year-old Herbie Bookbinder, who grows up in the Bronx and gradually comes to an acceptance of his own difference from his fellows (he is "brainy" and introspective) and an understanding of what he really is. It ends with his graduation into adolescence and his discovery of the adult world. *The Traitor* (drama, 1949) is an analysis of the problem of national security in the face of Communist conspiracy; its national-istic and conservative attitude antagonized many liberals at the time it appeared, before the Hiss trial and other spy revelations.

J. D. SALINGER (born 1919)

Salinger made an excellent reputation for himself as a writer of polished and subtle short stories before he published his first novel in 1951. *The Catcher in the Rye* confirmed and sustained this reputation and gained him a position as one of the more important American writers of the younger generation. The novel owed part of its popular success to its alleged shocking passages and to its selection by the Book-of-the-Month Club, but it is nevertheless a first-rate novel and one of the most convincing studies of adolescence ever to be written by an American.

Salinger is widely thought of, with justice, as a keen student of children. "All of my best friends are children," he himself has said. His extraordinary achievement in this area rests on two principles: first, he views children not from the adult point of view but from their own, from the inside, in a way few writers have succeeded in doing; and second, he concerns himself almost exclusively with extraordinary children. Many adult writers tend to make children seem younger than they actually are, to accentuate their babyish qualities, but Salinger does the opposite: he portrays children who are unusually mature for their age, who speak, or attempt to speak, like adults, and who wish to be accepted by adults on an adult basis. Models of this type are the little girl in "For Esme—With Love and Squalor" and Phoebe, the sister of the hero in *The Catcher in the Rye*. His adolescents speak in a curiously gauche dialect which belongs to their age, yet they too are seeking for acceptance in an adult world—in fact this is the whole plot of *The Catcher in the Rye*.

Stylistically Salinger is competent, painstaking, and precise, in the tradition of the *New Yorker* type of fiction which is his specialty. Like many other young American writers, he has an unerring ear for dialogue. His fiction is not strong on plot, and is sometimes virtually plotless; his stories are essentially character studies revealed through accurate, highly vernacular, and often clever dialogue. Yet for all his magazine-writer competence he is not stylized; there is a quality about his style that instantly identifies it as his own. Part of this is due to his characterizations, i.e., to the fact that he usually writes about the same kind of people who talk in the same way. In addition to this, however, his style is individual and original, bearing that unmistakable personal mark which is one of the characteristics of a quality writer.

LIFE: Jerome David Salinger was born in New York City in 1919; he was educated in New York schools and at a military school in Pennsylvania, which presumably provided him with the boarding-school background for *The Catcher in the Rye.* He attended three different colleges without taking a degree. His first published story appeared in *Story* magazine in 1940. He served in the Army from 1942 to 1946, participating in most of the European campaign and ending the war as a staff sergeant. His short stories have appeared in an assortment of American magazines ranging from *The New Yorker* to *The Saturday Evening Post.* In 1951 his first novel, *The Catcher in the Rye,* won critical acclaim and also caused a considerable sensation, mainly because one or two rather frank four-letter words offended some readers; its acceptance by the Book-of-the-Month Club assured its commercial success. In recent years Salinger has made his home in Westport, Connecticut.

CHIEF WORKS: *The Catcher in the Rye* (novel, 1951) is a sensitive psychological study of a prep-school boy, Holden Caulfield, whose parents live in New York. Holden in many ways exaggerates the normal tendencies of adolescence: he is hard-boiled and sophisticated in his own reveries but immature when confronted with a practical situation, he is basically good-hearted, even tender, but gruff and matter-of-fact on the outside, and he has a typical adolescent attitude toward sex; theoretically he is cynical and all-knowing, but in practice he is naive and chaste. His real difficulty, the reason he does not fit easily into the life of the Pennsylvania prep school, is that he is more sensitive and idealistic than the boys around him; this makes him bitter and unhappy, and to his teachers and others he seems a trouble-maker and a misfit. In the eighth chapter of the novel he runs away from the school and goes to New York, with only a vague notion in mind of what he is going to do; actually he is homesick, and half-afraid to approach his parents for fear of their disapproval. Arriving in the city, he registers at a hotel and is fleeced of his money by a prostitute and a cynical bellboy, who recognize him as a runaway and know he cannot complain to the police against them. After various other unsatisfactory experiments in New York high-life he secretly steals into his parents' apartment and visits his small sister Phoebe, for whom he feels a deep and protective affection, although he does not fully admit this to himself since it does not fit in with his outward pose of callousness. He also visits an old teacher, Mr. Antolini, the one adult in the world who understands and likes him; but the visit turns into tragedy through what is most probably a misunderstanding, and Holden flees under the impression Antolini has made homosexual advances to him. The next day he arranges to meet Phoebe at a museum, but she arrives with a suitcase, determined to run away with him because she instinctively understands he is unhappy. Touched by this, "so damn happy" and at the same time "damn near bawling," Holden decides to go home with her instead. In a brief epilogue (Chapter 26) he is in an institution recovering from an illness, probably a mental breakdown. Salinger's ending promises no happy future for Holden, and leaves him still struggling with the muddle of his adolescent temperament.

This novel, written in the first person, is a masterpiece of extended monologue; it is all related in Holden's own defiant, ungrammatical slangy, and cryptic way of talking, and yet manages to express great subtlety and insight. The relations between Holden and Phoebe are masterfully depicted; Holden never specifically analyzes his emotions toward his sister, yet the reader clearly sees his mixture of patronizing superiority and tender brotherly protectiveness. The dominant theme of *The Catcher in the Rye* is the helplessness of the adolescent—half child, half adult—in an adult society. Holden is too old for childish amusements, yet is punished cruelly when he tries to force his way into the adult world. He is punished as well for his finer qualities, his sensitivity; tenderness, fastidiousness, and insight are not virtues that are highly regarded by the normal inmates of prep-schools. The red hunting-hat which Holden wears through most of the novel is a symbol to him of defiant yet childish bravado in face of the conventions of the adult world.

STORIES: A representative selection of Salinger's stories is contained in *Nine Stories by J. D. Salinger* (1953). These stories, like most of Salinger's work, may be roughly classified in two groups: stories of upper-middle-class life in the New York region, and studies of small children. Of the first type, "Uncle Wiggily in Connecticut" is typical. Mary Jane and Eloise, who were college roommates together, meet in Eloise's house in Connecticut and proceed to get drunk while reminiscing about times past. In the course of the conversation it becomes apparent to the reader that both of them have made a failure of their lives, and that they have turned into selfish, superficial, and ignorant women. In a sense the story is an analysis of war marriages; both women married service men during the war, and both marriages failed to survive the monotony and banality of peacetime life. There is also a remarkable child named Ramona, who at first appears rather obnoxious but who wins the reader's sympathy when it becomes apparent that she is lonely and ashamed of her mother.

"For Esme—With Love and Squalor" is a story built around the typical Salinger child, grave, grown-up, and whimsically wise. In this case the central character is a little English girl who meets the narrator while he is a soldier stationed in Devonshire. Behind her serene sophistication Esme demonstrates all the British virtues: she is heroically matter-of-fact about the death of her father, who was "slain" in North Africa, and she is proper enough to write a quite adult letter to the narrator after he is transferred to Germany. This story, virtually plotless, is built around the tenderness which the soldier feels for the little girl and the contrast between the juvenile immaturity of his fellow soldiers and Esme's own precocious maturity.

JAMES JONES (born 1921)

As author of the most successful war novel of the period after 1945, Jones is *de facto* leader of what might be termed the Neo-Hemingway school of fiction among the younger generation of American writers. This is not to say that his style consistently imitates Hemingway's (although it sometimes does) or that he consciously took Hemingway as his model. He has admitted a debt to Thomas Wolfe, and actually *From Here to Eternity* outwardly resembles *Three Soldiers* and *What Price Glory* more than it does *A Farewell to Arms* or *For Whom the Bell Tolls*. Jones' novel nevertheless stands in the line of development in modern fiction that is commonly associated with Hemingway, and which owes a great deal to Hemingway as innovator and pathfinder. The qualities Jones shares with the older writer are those which the general public associates with the name of Hemingway: the understated and laconic dialogue, the violence presented without emotional comment, the stoic and hard-boiled view of character, the presentation of woman as a mere subjective object of masculine pleasure.

A comparison of *From Here to Eternity* with *A Farewell to Arms* or even *Across the River and into the Trees,* however, will demonstrate the differences between the two writers. Hemingway is concerned chiefly with personal and internal reactions; Jones, in spite of his subjectivity, views his characters mainly from the outside. Hemingway works on a small canvas; Jones attempts, at least, to be panoramic. Hemingway usually writes his entire novel from the point of view of a semi-autobiographical protagonist; Jones switches point of view frequently, so that each of his characters is seen in succession from the standpoint of the others. Finally, Hemingway generally uses coarse language and shocking incident in implied contrast to the higher human values in his story; Jones seems to show an adolescent fascination with vulgarity for its own sake. He does not even tacitly indicate disapproval of the premeditated murder which the hero of *From Here to Eternity* commits to revenge himself on a stockade guard. It is true that Prewitt himself is eventually destroyed through this act and that his victim is a brute and a sadist, yet Jones to the end apparently considers Prewitt merely an unfortunate victim of destiny who was ridden to the breaking point and who struck back in the way a man must if he is cornered. Hemingway's ethics are consistent, if unconventional; but Jones' ethics seem confused, poorly thought out, and in the end damaging to the integrity of his own hero.

It is not the ethical content of *From Here to Eternity,* however, which is its most important quality. Jones has a precise memory, a masterful eye for detail, and an acute ear for dialogue; his narrative style creates the illusion of reality—of "being there"—as well as the style of any contemporary writer. His characters instantly come to life as soon as they begin to speak; their language, monotonously and conventionally obscene, nevertheless has the interest which always attaches to unmistakable authenticity. His slang is convincing, never artificial or contrived, never "cute" or ingenious. In short, his skill in characterization is based mainly on dialogue. His best characters are those closest to his own personality; his women, for example, are two-dimensional and unconvincing. Most of all he fails in his presentation of officers; here his literary skill is hampered by his obvious subjective antagonism, his "enlisted man's complex" that makes it impossible for him to view officers with any objectivity. Thus his scenes in the Schofield officers' club are mere caricature, sometimes amusing but never convincing. Jones, a soldier, wrote about soldiers and even in a certain sense wrote for soldiers; this is the limitation of his method. Yet within these limits he has produced an important book, one of the most important American war novels to be written by a member of the post-1945 generation.

LIFE: James Jones was born in Robinson, Illinois in 1921 in a family that had been settled in the region for several generations; his father was a Northwestern graduate and a dentist. Although the family was a respectable one, its domestic life was not always serene; as Jones himself explains he grew up "in an atmosphere of hot emotions and boiling recriminations covered with a thin but resilient skin of gentility." The family suffered a severe blow from the Depression, and at an early age Jones was made aware of the ephemeral nature of social standing and financial security. When he graduated from high school jobs were hard to get, and on his father's suggestion he joined the Regular Army. Stationed at Hickam Field in Hawaii shortly before the Second World War, he became interested in writing through the discovery of Thomas Wolfe, whose family background he recognized as essentially similar to his own. His first novel was submitted to Scribner's in 1945 and rejected by the late Maxwell Perkins, who had earlier edited Wolfe; Perkins suggested, however, that Jones write another novel, and offered him an advance to support him while he did so. Additional financial backing was provided by Mr. and Mrs. Harry E. Handy of Robinson, who by this time were operating a sort of fiction school in this small Illinois town in which they maintained promising young writers and at the same time held them to a rigidly disciplined writing schedule. The result was *From Here to Eternity,* published in 1951 and an immediate success; it was a Book-of-the-Month Club Selection and won its author the National Book Award for fiction in 1952. In 1953 it was made into a successful motion picture. Critical opinion of the novel was also generally favorable, although some critics objected to its awkwardness in structure and its excessive crudeness in language. His financial position assured, Jones embarked upon another novel, this time centered on the life of a small

Illinois community; this was eventually published as *Some Came Running* (1957).

CHIEF WORK: *From Here to Eternity* (novel, 1951) begins as Robert E. Lee ("Prew") Prewitt, a soldier in Schofield Barracks in Hawaii, is transferred from a bugle corps to an infantry line company at his own request. The time is late 1940, approximately a year before the Japanese attack on the Hawaiian Islands. Prewitt, a tough uneducated boy from the coal-mining town of Harlan, Kentucky, has the character to make a good soldier, but he soon finds himself in trouble. A skilled boxer, he has previously blinded an opponent in an Army tournament and has made up his mind never to box again. Unfortunately the outfit into which he transfers is one in which favor and promotion go only to athletes. Captain Holmes, the company commander, is brow-beaten by his athletic-minded colonel to win victory for his company in the Post athletic competition at all costs, and he determines to force Prewitt to box or break him in the attempt. For months Prewitt undergoes the "treatment"—he is given dirty and unpleasant tasks to do, mistreated by non-coms, punished for minor infractions, and ostracized by other members of the company. He stands this as long as he can, but finally he is forced into a corner: Ike Galovitch, an illiterate and incompetent drillmaster, pulls a knife on him, and Prewitt knocks the non-commissioned officer down. For this he is sent to the post stockade, a virtual concentration camp where prisoners are tortured by sadistic guards and in some cases mutilated or murdered. Prewitt resolves to have revenge on S/Sgt. Judson ("Fatso"), and after he serves his term he waylays Fatso in a Honolulu alley, challenges him to a knife duel, and kills him. Prewitt, badly cut himself, goes A.W.O.L. and takes shelter in the house of Alma Schmidt, called Lorene, a prostitute with whom he fell in love before he went to the stockade. While he is convalescing the Japanese attack of December 7, 1941 takes place, and the war is on; after several days of restless brooding Prewitt, still ill, leaves the house to try to regain his outfit and is shot by a sentry who takes him for a deserter or a spy.

Around Prewitt's story are woven the stories of several other characters: Angelo Maggio, a likable Italian-American who dislikes authority, beats up two Military Police single-handed, and is eventually killed by sadistic guards in the stockade; Sergeant Milton Warden, a hard-boiled but competent professional soldier who has a dangerous affair with Captain Holmes' wife Karen; Colonel Delbert, a bull-headed and anti-democratic personification of the military mind; Isaac Bloom, a Jewish soldier who commits suicide when his long efforts to win the esteem of his fellow soldiers come to nothing; and Jack Malloy, a tough and unbreakable prisoner Prewitt meets in the stockade, a philosopher and natural leader of men who gives Prewitt the courage he needs to stand up under the inhuman punishment.

NORMAN MAILER (born 1923)

Harvard-trained and well read in modern literature, Mailer is a more consciously skillful writer than James Jones, and his work is free from the naive awkwardness that occasionally mars *From Here to Eternity.* Yet in another sense his literary background is an impediment; his style occasionally seems imitative and contrived, as though he were writing with the examples of Hemingway and Dos Passos consciously in mind. His political sophistication and his familiarity with the principles—and the jargon—of modern psychology are also apparent, but add little to the effectiveness of his fiction. He is at his best when he writes from direct personal experience, of incidents or conditions that moved him profoundly and which he is able to recreate for the reader. As a newspaper reviewer remarked of *The Naked and the Dead,* "For sustained terror and accurate translation of complete physical exhaustion, this has no parallel in American literature." Since the great experience of Mailer's life was evidently his war service, *The Naked and the Dead* is his best novel. The weakest parts of it, as might be expected, are those not written directly from experience: the psychology of General Cummings, the inner reflections of Lieutenant Hearn, and the flashbacks ("The Time Machine") in which he fills in the civilian backgrounds of the thirteen men who make up his platoon, many of them with past histories markedly different from his own. Likewise, in *Barbary Shore,* the parts we may presume to be autobiographical—the young writer who rents a room in Brooklyn to write a war novel—are good, and most of the presumably imaginary incidents are unconvincing. Mailer surmounted this difficulty to a certain extent in *The Deer Park,* where the screen writer Charley Eitel and even minor characters like the marijuana addict Paco and the producer Herman Teppis come alive in a convincing manner. Yet the trouble with *The Deer Park*—a vastly superior novel to *Barbary Shore*—is again connected to the derivative quality of the material. Whatever his experience of Hollywood might have been, Mailer is too obviously writing in the genre of the satire on Hollywood or Southern California customs—Huxley's *After Many a Summer Dies the Swan,* Waugh's *The Loved One,* or Schulberg's *What Makes Sammy Run?* Mailer has the merits that go with his faults; although he is often too conscious of his literary background, he is a competent and subtle literary craftsman, and his feeling for minute and vivid detail and his skill in structure make *The Naked and the Dead* one of the best of the post-1945 war novels.

LIFE: Norman Mailer was born in Long Branch, New Jersey in 1923 and grew up chiefly in Brooklyn, where he finished high school in 1939. He went on to Harvard with the idea of becoming an aeronautical engineer. During his freshman year, however, he became interested in writing, and was soon turning out stories at a prolific rate. In 1941 he won the *Story* magazine college writers' contest with a story entitled "The Greatest Thing in the World." He graduated from Harvard in 1943, and during a period of eight months while he was waiting to go into the Army wrote a novel called *A Transit to Narcissus,* a "romantic, morbid, twisted" study of life in a mental hospital, which was never published. The Army, according to Mailer's own statement, was an invaluable experience in his development as a writer. He served for about two years in the Philippines and in Japan in various jobs ranging from regimental intelligence clerk and aerial photograph expert to rifleman in a reconnaissance platoon, most of which experience found its way in one way or another into *The Naked and the Dead.* In 1944, while still in the service, he published "A Calculus at Heaven," a novelette about five American soldiers who are trapped by a Japanese platoon. Discharged in 1946, he immediately resolved to write a novel about the war. *The Naked and the Dead,* which further developed the idea he had expressed in embryonic form in "A Calculus at Heaven," appeared in 1948. This novel, one of the most successful books to come out of the war, was favorably greeted by critics and established Mailer as one of the leading

American writers of his generation. *Barbary Shore* (1951) was less successful; an excursion into a romantic and analytical style, it disappointed readers who expected another novel like *The Naked and the Dead.* Meanwhile Mailer traveled; he studied for a winter in Paris (1947-48), made visits to England, Spain, Switzerland, and Italy, and on his return wandered around America for some time while he worked on *Barbary Shore.* His third novel, *The Deer Park,* appeared in 1955 and was more favorably reviewed than any of his books since *The Naked and the Dead.* Mailer has been married once (1944) and later divorced; his political leanings are leftist but independent, and he describes himself as an "anti-Stalinist Marxist."

CHIEF WORKS: *The Naked and the Dead* (novel, 1948) is built around the structure of the typical war novel of World War I, e.g., Remarque's *All Quiet on the Western Front* or Barbusse's *Under Fire:* it follows a typical squad of men, of diverse backgrounds and character, into a combat situation and analyzes their individual reactions to the experience. Mailer's chief characters include a group he intends as a cross-section of American life: Julio Martinez, a Mexican boy from San Antonio; Sam Croft, product of an illiterate Texas cracker family who becomes a competent but callous professional soldier; Red Valsen, son of a Montana miner who "went on the bum" during the Depression and who joined the Army because "in the war you keep on moving"; Roy Gallagher, a South Boston Irish boy who had become involved in right-wing racist movements and was developing into a petty hoodlum before the war intervened to make him a soldier; Robert Hearn, a sensitive and over-mothered young lieutenant from a middle-class background, Harvard-educated, a half-hearted intellectual radical before he joined the Army to escape the boredom of his life; Woodrow Wilson, a Southern hillbilly who has passively drifted through life before the war; Edward Cummings, the division commander, West-Pointer and right-wing militarist from a conservative Midwestern family; Joey Goldstein, a Brooklyn Jew who is annoyed and tormented in petty ways by Croft and others because of his race; Willie Brown, in civilian life a salesman married to an unappetizing wife; "Polack" Czienwicz, a petty Chicago criminal; Roth, another Jew, more intelligent and analytical than most of the other enlisted men; and Steve Minetta, an Italian-American who is afraid he lacks the character to endure the discomfort and danger of combat. The action of the novel takes place on the imaginary Pacific island of Anopopei, which General Cummings' division captures from the Japanese after a long and muddled campaign. Hearn, who is Cummings' aide, rebels against the petty personal discipline which the general inflicts upon him and in punishment is put in charge of a reconnaissance platoon including most of the enlisted men among the characters listed above. This platoon is thereupon given an impossibly difficult task: to land on the far side of the island, march across the jungle, and conduct a reconnaissance of the Japanese forces to see whether an amphibious attack is feasible. Hearn takes command of the platoon but is resented by Croft, who shrewdly maneuvers the platoon into a position where Hearn is killed by the Japanese. Croft then takes over, tough and brutal, hated by the others but admired for his obvious competence as a soldier. Roth is killed in a fall from a mountain and Wilson is wounded by a sniper; four men are detailed to carry the wounded man back to the other side of the island. Two drop out, and finally Goldstein and a naive and religious Southerner named Ridges carry the backbreaking burden to the coast, following their orders out to the end even though Wilson dies on the way. When the survivors return to their base they find that their heroic struggle has been unnecessary; Japanese resistance has collapsed unexpectedly in a single day when General Cummings happened to be absent from the island, and the campaign is virtually over.

The attitudes in this novel are those implicit in most war novels by enlisted men: war is an obscene and meaningless sacrifice, most officers are incompetent and lacking in character, and the chief characteristic of combat is its senseless and ironic waste of effort. Another idea (expressed by General Cummings but perhaps shared by the author) is that a poor standard of living produces good soldiers, and vice versa. The pampered youths like Hearn fail to rise to the challenge of combat, while underprivileged boys like Croft and Martinez, the latter of whom distinguishes himself by a courageous single-handed reconnaissance behind enemy lines, find their true vocation in the army. Mailer's political radicalism is expressed through the arguments of Hearn in his conversations with Cummings; the general himself is intended as a caricature and psychological study of the military mind, with its ruthless disregard of human values and its right-wing and racist political principles.

The structure of *The Naked and the Dead* is intricate and carefully planned. Scenes involving the enlisted men in the reconnaissance platoon are alternated with conversations between Hearn and Cummings, in which the ideas latent in the situation are developed. As the novel proceeds to its climax an ironic contrast is apparent between the dogged and futile struggles of the platoon and the muddled strategy of the high command. Sprinkled throughout the narrative are two types of fictional vignettes imitated from Dos Passos' U.S.A.: "The Time Machine" presents brief flashbacks into the civilian lives of the various characters (Dos Passos' "Camera Eye"), and "Chorus," a slightly more original device, consists of small conversational interludes in dramatic form.

Barbary Shore (novel, 1951) is markedly different in style, decadent, analytical, and overrefined. The chief character and narrator, Mikey Lovett, is a young author who rents a room in a Brooklyn boarding-house to write a novel about the war. There he encounters four people whose lives become involved with his: the landlady Guinevere, a neurotic and unhappy nymphomaniac; McLeod, a former Communist and an amateur philosopher; Hollingsworth, a mysterious young man who seldom comes out of his room; and Lannie, a moody and impulsive young girl who has evidently just been released from a mental institution. These five people, along with Guinevere's three-year-old daughter, enter into a set of intricate and somewhat perverted relationships with each other. The mystery which Lovett at first does not understand is that McLeod is secretly Guinevere's husband; a second mystery, only gradually uncovered, is that McLeod, at one time a government employee, is suspected of having stolen "a little object" from his office in the interests of the Communist Party, and that Hollingsworth is an agent assigned to stalk him and produce a confession from him. McLeod, however, is suffering from a guilty conscience at having betrayed his political ideals; he agrees at one point to return the "little object" to its proper owners, but when Hollingsworth calls upon him to deliver, he refuses and Hollingsworth kills him. Lannie, by this time insane again, is presumably arrested for the murder. This novel is intended as an allegory of the anti-Communist witch-hunt as well as a general comment on the neuroticism of post-war America. The characters, each wrapped in his private egotism and pursuing his private lusts, are destroyed in the end through their lack of purpose or ideal, and only the heroic self-sacrifice of McLeod lends a positive note to the pessimistic ending. An interesting and original experiment, this novel is nevertheless less successful than *The Naked and the Dead,* and in his third major work Mailer returned to his earlier style.

The Deer Park (novel, 1955) is set in Desert d'Or, a mythical California desert resort somewhat resembling Palm Springs and populated with a grotesque and colorful set of Hollywood characters. The chief character and narrator is Sergius O'Shaugnessy, an Air Force veteran who has won a small fortune in a Tokyo poker game and comes to Desert d'Or to spend it. There he meets Charley Eitel, a Hollywood screen-writer who has been fired because he refused to identify former Communist associates when he was investigated by a Congressional committee. Sergius enters into an unsatisfactory romance with Lulu Meyers, an actress whose best days are over; and meanwhile Eitel, once married to Lulu, falls in love with Elena Esposito, mistress of a producer named Collie Munshin. The novel is devoted chiefly to the conversations of these people and their friends as they pursue their pleasureless and debauched amours and try to find some meaning in their cynical lives. The dialogues, vernacular, ironic, and sophisticated, are the best part of the book. Also memorable is the farcical scene (Chapter 20) in which the overbearing movie executive Herman Teppis tries to persuade Teddy Pope, a homosexual, to marry Lulu, not knowing she is already married to somebody else; the characterization of Teppis is a masterpiece of parody. As the novel ends Eitel agrees to cooperate with the Communist-hunters and regains his position in Hollywood; partly as an expiation of this he marries Elena, who has been injured in an automobile accident and is now penniless and helpless. Sergius goes off to New York to study and write, later opening a school for bull-fighters. *The Deer Park,* in spite of its cynicism and its chaotic plot, is an interesting and well-written novel; the characters of Eitel and Lulu are vivid, and the many minor characters are all well drawn. The title refers to the "Parc des Cerfs" in which Louis XV maintained a household of concubines, and a quotation from Mouffle D'Angerville implicitly identifies this depraved Deer Park, "that gorge of innocence and virtue in which were engulfed so many victims," with Hollywood, which depraves even the sincere Elena and the idealistic Eitel.

THE REACTION TO REALISM: PSYCHOLOGICAL AND ROMANTIC FICTION

One of the outstanding characteristics of the twentieth century is its cultural heterodoxy: it is an era in which a confusion of contradictory systems, attitudes, and philosophies exist side by side. It is difficult to form a neat judgment of a century which produced both Adolf Hitler and Albert Schweitzer, or to summarize the philosophy of an age in which John Dewey, Jean-Paul Sartre, and Jacques Maritain were all considered leading philosophers. This heterogeneous quality is found as well in twentieth-century literature. The dominant movement of the century is unmistakably realism, including its sub-movements of naturalism and regionalism. A small but important minority of writers, however, rejected this basic tendency and experimented instead with various forms of analytical, romantic, or psychological literature. Such writers tend to be highly individualistic and therefore difficult to classify under the traditional headings of literary history. In general, however, they may be said to fall into two groups:

Psychological Literature The term "psychological literature" is used in many different senses. In the France of the seventeenth century it referred to the analysis of moral sentiments and the conflict of ideas of right and wrong in the minds of tragic heroes, i.e., the kind of literature represented by Racine's *Phèdre* or Corneille's *Le Cid*. In the nineteenth century the term "psychological novel" was applied to novels of the type of Stendhal's, in which the hero's inner conflicts were analysed minutely for the reader. Later in the century the works of Poe, Baudelaire, and Dostoyevsky were termed "psychological" because they were preoccupied with unusual or abnormal states of mind. All these tendencies are revived in the psychological literature of the twentieth century. Writers like Thornton Wilder and Robinson Jeffers treat moral problems from the psychological point of view; Wilder and Katherine Anne Porter concern themselves with internal analysis of the motivations of their characters, and Jeffers and Sherwood Anderson (along with such Europeans as D. H. Lawrence.

Arthur Schnitzler, and Hugo von Hofmannsthal) concentrate their attention on the sexual or neurotic problems popularized by the Freudian and other schools of psychoanalysis. These authors differ widely in content and technique, but they are essentially alike in their purpose: to present human motivations from the inside, from the point of view of the mind concerned, rather than from the point of view of an external observer in the realistic tradition.

It is immediately apparent that many other writers, including some commonly considered realists or naturalists, come partly under this heading: the names of Henry James, Edith Wharton, William Faulkner, Eudora Welty, and J. D. Salinger come immediately to mind. There are indeed elements of psychological analysis in the work of all these writers, and in the end the question is only one of degree. Anderson is treated in this section and Faulkner in another merely because Anderson seems primarily concerned with abnormal mentality, whereas with Faulkner such themes are secondary to the prime purpose of his work.

Neo-Romanticism The history of twentieth-century European literature is marked by a curious revival of romanticism, which stands in direct opposition to the mainstream of realism in the period. The authors who participated in this romantic revival shared an interest in the exotic or unusual as opposed to the prosaic or ordinary, a certain flamboyance or preciosity of language, a liking for fantastic, heroic, or superhuman characters, and an inclination toward fantastic plot material. The movement included a number of European authors of first-rate importance: Maeterlinck, Loti, Cocteau, Saint-Exupéry, Rostand, Christopher Fry, Stefan George. In American literature the movement is not as important, although a number of authors already treated (Jack London, Elliot Paul, Thomas Wolfe, Willa Cather) demonstrate certain romantic qualities which serve to modify their basically realistic approach to literature. James Branch Cabell, however, is an anomaly: a complete and total romantic, an escapist, and a dealer in fantasy who perversely insisted on writing romantic novels in the age of Hemingway and Farrell and succeeded in making a best-seller out of at least one of them. *Jurgen* not only achieved a popular success but caused one of the great literary sensations of the post-1918 era. A writer like Cabell demonstrates the fallacy of thinking of literary history in terms of neat periods: neo-classicism, romanticism, realism. The Stendhals and Cabells of literary history show us that such terms represent types of literary personality rather than historical periods, and that an author who sincerely and capably writes in a style which is natural to him will achieve acceptance in any age.

SHERWOOD ANDERSON (1876-1941)

Anderson's most successful works are his stories and short pieces, especially the highly poetic and dramatic set of sketches of *Winesburg, Ohio*. Like Edgar Lee Masters, he seeks to avoid the artificial literary cénacles of the city and return to the more authentic life of rural America; like Masters also he sees the American small town as a suppressed volcano of frustrations, passions, and bitterness. Most of Anderson's characters are people a psychologist would term neurotic; many of them are amiable, a few dedicated or selfless, but none are entirely happy or complacent. Anderson belongs to the Lost Generation of Hemingway, Fitzgerald, and Dos Passos, and like these authors he is torn between affection and bitterness toward the land of his birth.

Anderson's attitudes are consistent throughout his work, although they appear only nebulously in his earlier books. He is suspicious and antagonistic in regard to middle-class virtue, and he is scornful of what is ordinarily called respectability in American life. He detests puritanism, and this has led him into an antagonism toward American religion. He is by no means irreligious; in fact there is a strong, almost mystical element of ethical religion in his work. His dislike of hypocrisy, however, causes him to view American Protestantism merely as the solace of frustrated clergymen, hysterical wives, and frigid spinsters. The characters in his stories we are meant to admire are the eccentrics: alcoholic artists, degenerate telegraph clerks, all the dregs and outcasts of respectable bourgeois society.

Anderson's style reflects an effort to capture the authentic colloquial atmosphere of American folklore. The language is simple and laconic, often resembling the dialogue of Hemingway. The stories are usually told in retrospect, as though seen through the veil of years; we hear about them as we would hear the half-forgotten scandal of a generation back. The stories in *Winesburg, Ohio* tend to follow a consistent pattern. First we are shown the protagonist, usually a neurotic or misfit, in the latter stages of his life and told the attitude of the town toward him. Then little by little the author reveals to us the factors which have made a human wreck out of this person who might have been happy and successful. The intolerance of a town has castigated and driven away a sensitive young teacher; misunderstanding has parted a young couple and warped the bride's life; sexual frustration has turned a useful citizen into a drunkard; or a family disgrace has preyed on the mind of a young boy until he grows up an eccentric. In the beginning of each story we feel a disgusted fascination toward these characters, but before we are done we understand them and sympathize with them. Thus Anderson demonstrates a basic proposition of modern psychology: that social misfits are not evil or reprehensible, that they are merely mental invalids warped by their contact with organized society and its rigid conventions.

LIFE: Sherwood Anderson was born in Camden, Ohio in 1876. His father, the prototype for the Windy McPherson of Anderson's first novel, was an easy-going drifter, full of tall tales and improbable anecdotes. Anderson had almost no formal education. As a young man he fought in the Spanish-American war, then returned to Elyria, Ohio, to work as manager of a paint factory and to write poetry in his spare time. One day, according to his own story, he simply stopped in the middle of a sentence he was dictating to a stenographer, threw everything up, and went off to Chicago to become a writer. The actual truth, however, seems to have been somewhat more prosaic; Anderson planned his literary career for some time before taking the decisive step. In Chicago his early writings were unsuccessful; the first book to be accepted by publishers was the novel *Windy McPherson's Son* in 1916. Several more novels were only moderately successful; Anderson's capsule irony was better adapted to the story. In *Winesburg, Ohio* he finally found his natural literary form; he burst in full flower upon an astounded postwar reading public, and was widely hailed as a writer of genius. *The Triumph of the Egg* (1921) was almost as successful, but most of Anderson's subsequent work is considered anticlimactic. An autobiographical book, *Tar: Middle West Childhood,* appeared in 1927.

Anderson was married four times and fathered altogether two sons and a daughter. In 1924 he settled in Marion, Virginia, where he served for many years as editor of two country newspapers—one Republican and the other Democratic. His death in 1941 was due to a trivial mishap; departing for a tour of Latin America, he swallowed a bit of toothpick at a farewell cocktail party, was removed from the ship ill at Colon, and died soon afterward of peritonitis.

CHIEF WORKS: *Winesburg, Ohio* (story cycle, 1919) is a set of connected stories or sketches dealing with the lives of the inhabitants of a fictional Ohio town. The central figure, and the author's alter ego, is the young George Willard, reporter on the *Winesburg Eagle*. George does not play an active part in the book until the last sketch; he serves merely as an observer and commentator. The best-known of the sketches are the following:

"Hands" tells the life story of Wing Biddlebaum, an eccentric and unhappy old man who feels a longing to befriend George but holds back through some gigantic and unnamed fear. As the story unfolds we learn the root of this fear. Biddlebaum was originally Adolph Myers, a sensitive young school teacher in Pennsylvania. His soul was extraordinarily concentrated in his hands; they were in constant movement, flitting about incessantly as he talked. Myers genuinely loved young people and was a fine and devoted teacher. But one day an idiot boy repeated his perverted dreams of his relations with Myers as a fact, and the town turned against him. Several boys told how he used to rumple their hair; Myers was driven out by the outraged citizens and barely escaped with his life. He has lived the rest of his years in constant fear of his sensitive hands, which he is afraid will reveal his repressed homosexual tendencies.

"Godliness" is a story in four parts, each of self-contained vignette. The central character is Jesse Bentley, an old farmer who rigorously dominates the lives of his wife, his daughter, and his grandson. Trained in his youth to be a minister, Jesse turns instead into a religious crank. He imagines that he, like the Biblical Jesse, is divinely chosen to rear a new race. His daughter Louise flees from him in terror and disgust and marries a town banker, John Hardy. Her son David, however, is induced to come back to the farm to live with old Jesse. The third quarter of the story is concerned with Louise's life, her persecution at the hands of other girls, and her desperate seduction of John, who she hopes will extricate her from an impossibly dull and narrow life. At last married to the respectable banker, she finds she has only changed one kind of monotony for another; she becomes a miserable, even a dangerous neurotic. The final quarter of the story comprises a sort of dénouement of all these conflicts. David Hardy, at fifteen, is taken by the old Jesse on a strange mission into the woods. The old man, having found a lamb born out of season, is driven by a senile obsession to sacrifice it to God in order that he may be chosen among men. He plans to daub David, his heir, with the blood; but David takes fright, strikes down Jesse with a slingshot, and runs away never to be seen again. The ironic parallels to the Biblical David and Jesse are obvious. "Godliness" is structurally a novel, condensed to occupy a mere fifty-five pages.

Poor White (novel, 1920) is a portrait of a midwestern farming town and its moral destruction by the encroachment of industrialism; the time is the end of the nineteenth century. The central character, a country boy named Hugh McVey, is inspired by wondrous tales of New England factories and cities by his foster parents, Henry and Sarah Shepherd. Later he settles in the small town of Bidwell, Ohio, and a grand dream is born in him: to transform Bidwell into a modern industrial city like those he has heard about from the Shepherds. He invents a crop-setting machine and manages to persuade Steve Hunter, a wealthy and educated local citizen, to sponsor a company to manufacture the invention. After several failures a successful machine is developed, and gradually Bidwell is industrialized. But the results are not quite as McVey had visualized. Factory workers, strangers with new and disturbing ways, invade the town, and many people, like Joe Wainsworth, the local harness-maker, lose their savings through unwise and hasty investments. To Wainsworth the factory becomes a symbol of everything hateful and menacing in the modern age; not only has he lost his savings through speculation, but his business collapses because people now prefer to buy machine-made harness. Brooding on this, he finally becomes unbalanced, murders Hunter, and attacks and almost kills McVey. This incident makes McVey begin to doubt the worth of the change he has wrought in the town. A secondary plot relates McVey's romance with Clara Butterworth, who returns to Bidwell after three years in the larger city of Columbus; the two are married at the height of McVey's success, and it is Clara who finally prevents Wainsworth from murdering her husband.

As the novel ends, McVey, disillusioned with the new world of the machine, finds consolation in his happiness with Clara and in plans for the future of the child which his wife is soon to bear. This novel, thematically similar to the tales of *Winesburg, Ohio,* thus ends on a more positive note, admitting the possibility of individual happiness even in a world of disillusionment and frustration.

The Triumph of the Egg (stories, 1921) is similar in general content to *Winesburg, Ohio* and may in a sense be considered a sequel to the earlier book; its tone, however, is lighter and more satirical, and the positive note is more often present. "The Egg," the best known of the stories, is an ironically bitter description of the narrator's father, who is driven by his ambitious school-teacher wife into one impractical enterprise after another in an effort to rise in the world. It ends with a simultaneously sad and hilarious scene in which the father, now proprietor of a restaurant, tries ineptly to amuse a customer by telling stories and doing tricks. The moral: be what you are. The father, who would have made an excellent farm hand, is a pitiful failure as a business-man.

Dark Laughter (novel, 1925) is a psychological study of the contrast between Negro and white temperament, combined with the usual Anderson themes of the sexual frustrations and inhibitions of the American middle class. Bruce Dudley, a young Chicago journalist, abandons wife and job to wander off across the country in a restless revolt against the conventionality and monotony of his life. Reaching New Orleans, he gets a job varnishing auto wheels in the Grey Wheel Company, and soon falls in love with Aline Grey, wife of the owner of the company. At the end of the novel the two elope, leaving Fred Grey, the husband, in a state of homicidal despair; he wants to kill either Dudley or himself, but lacks the courage to do either. Meanwhile Anderson has established the continual contrast between this frustrated and violent love-triangle of the whites and the easy-going hedonism of the New Orleans Negroes who observe them in silent amusement; as Grey returns to his house he hears the "dark laughter" of Negroes who mock the puritanical guilt-consciousness of his race.

Dark Laughter was Anderson's most popular novel, although it is considered inferior in quality to the stories of *Winesburg, Ohio* and *The Triumph of the Egg.* Anderson has admitted that the style of the novel—flowing, lyrical, and impressionistic—is indebted to Gertrude Stein.

JAMES BRANCH CABELL (born 1879)

Cabell today is usually treated more as a curious and eccentric literary phenomenon of the Twenties than as an important author in his own right. The tremendous vogue he enjoyed in the decade after the publication of *Jurgen* has died away, and now he is principally read by scholars, university students, and amateurs of literary curiosa. His popular decline is partly due to the triumph of the naturalists, an accidental literary and social process over which he had no control. Yet Cabell is a writer of great talent, perhaps even of genius, and it may be that another literary generation will come back to his work as the generation of the Thirties came back to Melville. Cabell is the kind of an author who is likely to prove durable, whatever temporary disfavor he may happen to fall into as public taste changes with the years. "The shifts of taste from age to age may now depress and now exalt the credit of the famous *Jurgen*," says Carl Van Doren, "but so have they done during the past five generations with *Tristram Shandy*, another masterpiece frequently baited by the sort of censor who dreads wit unless it picks its topics with caution. Both by its wit and by its beauty, *Jurgen* is entitled to survive."

Born into an old Virginia family in the generation after the Civil War, Cabell reached maturity at the moment the realistic movement in America was approaching its climax. When he began to write in the early years of the new century he tried to accommodate himself to this movement, and actually turned out a number of second-rate novels of mingled realism and romanticism. He soon realized, however, that he was no Dreiser or Crane; critics panned him unmercifully for factual errors in his settings, and he failed to achieve anything like a naturalistic verisimilitude. He then turned frankly to escapism and began to organize the great work of his career: the Poictesme series, purporting to be the chronicles of a mythical province lying between France and Spain. The climax of the series is the career of Manuel, a thirteenth-century Redeemer or religious prophet who comes to effect the salvation of the inhabitants of Poictesme and to provide them with their traditions and spirit.

The Poictesme books, especially *Jurgen,* are masterpieces of polished and slightly ironic escapism. More than any other American novelist Cabell expresses the escapist tendencies of the neo-romantic movement. The novels are infused with an irony suggestive of that of James Stephens, the Irish poet of elves and leprechauns, and there is also an element of Rabelais or Swift; the more exuberant passages in *Jurgen* caused it to be censored by the authorities in some states in 1919.

Although Cabell rejected the documentary accuracy of the naturalists, he actually organized his mythical province of Poictesme with great precision. Maps of the region have been drawn; its history is established from earliest times through the middle ages, and its chief heroes have all had their biographies written. Poictesme is one of the famous mythical lands of literature, Voltaire's El Dorado or Alice's land-down-the-rabbit-hole expanded into a vast and panoramic series of novels.

LIFE: James Branch Cabell was born in Richmond, Virginia in 1879; his family was an old and proud one, and Cabell always considered himself a Virginia gentleman first and a writer second. Educated at William and Mary College, he taught Greek and French there while still a student (1896-97). From 1898 to 1901 he worked as a journalist, serving on the *Richmond Times* and later on the *New York Herald*. Turning to free-lancing, he contributed a number of stories to leading magazines over a period of nine years (1902-10). He continued in his literary career therafter, except for a brief and surprising interlude in the West Virginia coal mines in 1911-13. His first novel, *The Eagle's Shadow,* a satirical romance of Southern society, appeared in 1901. The first of his Poictesme books was *The Soul of Melicent* in 1913 (revised as *Domnei* in 1920). *Jurgen* (1919) earned its author immediate fame, although its success was partly due to the scandal it aroused; a number of attempts were made to suppress it on the grounds of obscenity. When the tumult died Cabell continued in his quiet life as a Virginia gentleman and turned out approximately one book a year in the period from 1919 to 1947. Married in 1913, Cabell went on living for the rest of his life in Richmond, the town of his birthplace.

CHIEF WORKS: *Jurgen* (novel, 1919) is by far Cabell's best-known work. At the time of its publication it was suppressed for over eighteen months by the police through the instigation of the New York Society for the Suppression of Vice and similar organizations, and this of course helped it to achieve a great *succès de scandale*. Nevertheless the novel deserves to stand on its own merits as Cabell's masterpiece.

The greater part of the plot concerns the middle-aged pawnbroker Jurgen, who wanders off across the countryside in search of his wife Lisa, earlier abducted by Satan. Instead he finds the centaur Nessus, who directs him to the "Garden between Dawn and Sunrise." The rest of the novel is a fantastic picaresque. Jurgen meets Mother Sereda, the "Goddess who controls Wednesdays" and who bleaches the color out of everything in the world, descends like Aeneas into Hell, meets Queen Guinevere, encounters the magical Queen Sylvia Teriu, cavorts with the sensuous Anaïtis in the land of Cocaigne, marries Chloris, a dimpled Hamadryad, pursues, then flees from the cruel temptress Dolores, and visits the ghastly Florimel, who drowns unchristened children in a sea of blood. The influences of the *Odyssey* and of Rabelais' *Gargantua* and *Pantagruel* are apparent in this exuberant string of adventures. The chief qualities of the book's style are its whimsical irony and its delight in parodies, ranging from Rabelais to Greek mythology.

Other important volumes of the Poictesme series are (in order of their narrative sequence rather than date of publication) *Figures of Earth* (1921), *The Silver Stallion* (1926), *Domnei* (in revised version 1920), *The High Place* (1923), and *Something About Eve* (1927). A number of collections of short stories form part of the cycle, and the Poictesme material is also thematically connected to Cabell's romances of contemporary Virginia life, e.g., *The Rivet in Grandfather's Neck* (1915).

The Cream of the Jest (novel, 1917; revised 1920) is ostensibly a romance of contemporary life, although its dream-fantasy plot carries it far into the past in the spirit of *Jurgen*. Its hero, the author Felix Kennaston, bored by his humdrum modern life in general and his marriage in particular, comes into possession of a magic hieroglyphic talisman called the "sigil of Scoteia" which permits him to escape into a fantastic dream-world of the past. Here he finds himself in a previous incarnation in the mythical land of Storisende, where under the name of Horvendile he loved Ettarre, an "ageless, lovable, and loving woman of whom all the poets had been granted fitful broken glimpses." In other magical excursions he also visits the courts of Queen Elizabeth and Louis XIV of France and narrowly escapes being beheaded as an aristocrat during the French Revolution. Always beside him is the marvellous Ettare, whom he must not touch lest the dream be shattered. In his intermittent returns to modern life Kennaston becomes more and more estranged from his politely bored wife; after she dies he discovers the ironic truth that his magic talisman was actually nothing more than a broken top from her cold-cream jar. Kennaston is compelled at last to give up his youthful fantasies for the resigned and realistic complacency of middle age. Cabell has obviously drawn himself in the portrait of the romantic Kennaston, scholarly but inwardly rebellious, who escapes into the past through a talisman which is a symbol of imagination.

THORNTON WILDER (born 1887)

Wilder stands in marked contrast to his American contemporaries, especially the Hemingway-Dos Passos school of naturalism. He is consistently romantic (*The Cabala, The Bridge of San Luis Rey*) or fantastic (*Our Town, The Skin of Our Teeth*) in subject matter, and restrained, subtle, and highly polished in style; perhaps the best term to apply to his prose is classic. He is a highly intellectual writer in an age of proletarian or pseudo-proletarian naturalists, and an educated man in a time when even those American writers who have a liberal education (e.g., Steinbeck) strive assiduously to conceal the fact from their reading public. In fact, aside from his occasional use of American settings, there is little to mark Wilder as an American writer at all; in his literary and philosophical attitudes he is more properly a representative of the wider European tradition of letters. Here he resembles Henry James, his literary godfather and a writer he imitated in one of his most important novels, *The Cabala*.

Wilder has a warm regard for American life and expresses it in *Our Town* and *The Skin of Our Teeth,* but this does not lead him into chauvinism or naive provincialism. His real subject is humanity, and the long cultural tradition which has led it from the cave to the Europe and America of today. He is not interested in setting down a chronicle of his time (*cf.* Sinclair Lewis); to him all times and places are equally important. He has therefore been attacked by left-wing critics who believe that modern literature must be a document, that it must engage the pressing social problems of the day. Wilder believes that literature must press beyond these immediate exigencies to attain the essential and the universal. This attitude has caused him to be viewed in some quarters as an escapist and a sentimental romantic. The accusation, fair in the case of Cabell, is unfair when applied to Wilder.

Wilder's philosophy is a sort of broad and tolerant Christian humanism. He is little concerned with theology; he stands like Tolstoy for the brotherhood of man and for the spirit of tolerance and understanding. Christianity itself does not play a major part in his work, although it is commended by implication and contrast in *The Woman of Andros* and hovers like a shadow over *The Skin of Our Teeth*. In a 1928 preface Wilder declared his desire to present the highest and most basic religious principles of humanity without falling into "a repellent didacticism."

In actual practice his works are not primarily concerned with ideas. His characters are real flesh-and-blood creatures, and their main problems are moral and psychological ones; Wilder is interested chiefly in the internal life of his subjects. There is little documentation, even in his historical *Bridge of San Luis Rey* and *The Ides of March*. The latter work is precise as to historical fact, but nevertheless literary rather than scholarly; the documents involved are secondhand research materials, the very sort of data the Zola school sought to avoid.

Wilder differs from many of his American contemporaries as well in his careful attention to style. His models are Anatole France, James, Proust, Gide, and Mme. de Sévigné, each an acknowledged master of prose technique. He is a conscientious craftsman; he writes slowly and turns out a relatively small volume of work, but what he does produce is carefully polished. In fact some of his novels appear even too carefully wrought; in any case he does not err on the side of clumsiness. His strongest qualities are irony and subtlety. The first is seen at its best in the gravely satirical exposition of *The Cabala* and the adroit farce of *Heaven's My Destination,* and the second in the intricate emotional relationships of *The Bridge of San Luis Rey* and in the nuances of attitude and psychological reaction in *The Ides of March*. Finally, he is highly educated, especially in Western European history and literature, and he has no compunctions about incorporating his cultural background into his work. The nuances of social convention, of ecclesiastical procedure, and of aristocratic geneology in *The Cabala* are worthy of Proust, and *The Skin of Our Teeth* is virtually an allegorical Survey Course in European civilization. When Wilder's background and attitude are considered, the popular success of his work, especially *The Bridge of San Luis Rey* and *Our Town,* is even more remarkable than it seems at first sight.

LIFE: Thornton Wilder was born in Madison, Wisconsin in 1897. His father, a newspaper editor, was later appointed Consul-General in Hongkong and took the nine-year-old boy with him to China. Wilder was educated in China, at the University of California, at Oberlin, at Yale, at the American Academy in Rome, and finally at Princeton, where he took an M.A. in 1925. From 1921 to 1928 he worked as a teacher in a private school, but after 1928 he was able to live on the income from his writing; from 1930 to 1936, however, he served on the faculty of the University of Chicago on a part-time basis, teaching literature six months of the year and writing the other six months. His first novel, *The Cabala,* appeared in 1926, but he won wide recognition only with *The Bridge of San Luis Rey* in 1927. This novel won him a Pulitzer Prize, became a best-seller, and was made into a successful motion picture. He was awarded another Pulitzer Prize for *Our Town* (1928); this drama, along with *The Skin of Our Teeth* (1942) won him recognition as a leading American dramatist as well as an important novelist. His most recent novel, *The Ides of March* (1948), was received with less enthusiasm by the general public but won critical praise. Wilder, who has never married, has made his home in recent years in New Haven, Connecticut.

CHIEF WORKS: *The Cabala* (novel, 1926) is an intricate and subtle novel which may be read on at least three levels: as a Jamesian intrigue of social relationships in a European setting, as an analysis of decadent nobility in the manner of Proust, and as an allegory of Christianity, paganism, and modern civilization. The action takes place in Rome and is seen through the eyes of a young American student known only as "Samuele." Accompanied by his friend James Blair, a scholar and writer, he comes to visit the Italian capital and is soon introduced into the circle of "the Cabala," a mysterious social group which is said to wield wide power. The Cabala's members include Miss Grier, its ostensible organizer and leader; the Princess d'Espoli, a Frenchwoman whose obsession is the restoration of the Bourbon throne to France; Mlle. de Morfontaine, another French royalist whose dream is that France should again become a Catholic country; the Cardinal Vaina, a retired missionary to China and a universally respected churchman and scholar; and the Duchessa D'Aquilanera, member of the proud Colonna family and a "malignantly resourceful woman" famous for her sarcasms. Samuele agrees to try to rescue the Duchessa's son Marcantonio from the dissipations into which he has fallen; but the young American's puritanical inidgnation at Marcantonio's vices deranges the Italian boy, and he commits suicide. Samuele's other adventures with the Cabala are hardly more satisfactory. The Princess d'Espoli falls in love with Blair, who flees from her in chaste horror; meanwhile Samuele himself has secretly fallen in love with her. The Cardinal, a truly devout person but somewhat unconventional in doctrine, upsets the conventionally pious Mlle. de Morfontaine so greatly that she hysterically fires a pistol at him; he flees from Italy to return to China and dies aboard ship en route. At the end of the novel Samuele visits Miss Grier to demand an explanation from her of the curious mystery behind the Cabala, and she answers in a parable, refusing to say whether it is literally true or not: that the gods of ancient Greece did not die with the coming of Christianity, but still wander the earth, carefully concealing their identity from outsiders and consoling themselves with their own company. Thus the two parallel themes of the novel are: (1) the decadence or obsolescence of the anachronistic feudal nobility, with its ideals of Universal Catholicism and the divine right of kings, in the twentieth century; and (2) the "ghosts" of the past—including even the demons of paganism—which linger over the European soil. At the end the poet Virgil, appeared to Samuele in an apparition, tells him to "seek some city that is young"—i.e., to look to the future in some new and uncorrupted nation like America.

The Bridge of San Luis Rey (novel, 1927) is a pattern novel in which the lives of the various characters are linked together by a single catastrophic incident. The central theme is that of love; several types are portrayed and analysed. On a certain day of July, 1714 a precarious bridge across a gorge in Peru breaks, killing five persons who happen to be on it. These are the Marquesa de Montemayor; Pepita, her maid; Estaban, an Indian; Uncle Pio, coachman of a popular actress; and Jaimé, son of the actress La Périchole. Each of these persons loves another human being intensely and hopelessly; the types of love range from that of the Marquesa (drawn from the historical figure of Mme. de Sévigné) for her selfish daughter Clara to that of the primitive Esteban for his brother Manuel. The falling of the bridge occurs at the climax of each of these lives; it is, in fact, the only answer to the predicaments of the characters. The inhabitants of San Luis Rey attach no particular significance to the accident, but a scholarly monk, Brother Juniper, becomes interested in the incident and makes it his business to investigate the lives of the victims. His researches at last lead him to a profound respect for the omniscience and benevolence of the Providence which arranged so ingenious a solution to human problems.

This novel, which brought first fame to Wilder when it was published, is still his best-known work. Its chief literary affinities are with James and Proust, although the latter author probably had little direct influence on Wilder. The style of Mme. de Sévigné's letters is also frequently cited as an influence on the style of the novel.

The Woman of Andros (novel, 1930) is an idyll of classic Greece based partly on Terence's *Andria*. The scene is laid shortly before the birth of Christ on the Aegean island of Byrnos. A woman from the island of Andros, Chrysis, a hetaira or courtesan, has come to the island and totally bewitched all the young men, who banquet at her house and enjoy intellectual conversations in the Socratic manner. Pamphilus, son of Simos, is one of the youths attending these symposia. His father wishes to marry him to Philumena, a local maiden. Her father, Chremes, objects to young Pamphilus' relations with Chrysis and demands that he break them off. Pamphilus, however, refuses to give up his attachment to the fascinating woman, and it soon becomes evident that Chrysis herself is in love with him. The knot is drawn tighter when Pamphilus discovers that Chrysis has a younger sister, the virtuous Glycerium; he transfers his love to her and soon gets her with child. Chrysis, ill, is shaken by the news and soon dies; her household is sold, and Glycerium narrowly escapes being bound into slavery. Simos, pitying her, buys her from the slave-dealer, but she dies in childbirth. Pagan love and stoic virtue are mingled with pagan cruelty in this novel; the final lines tell how "the stars shone tranquilly down upon the land that was soon to be called Holy and that even then was preparing its precious burden." The nebulous reference to the advent of Christianity seems to condemn the decadent Greek culture by implied contrast.

Heaven's My Destination (novel, 1935) is an adroit and subtle satire on two facets of American life: the "mythology of salesmanship" (as in Miller's *Death of a Salesman*) and the tradition of fundamentalist evangelism (as in Lewis' *Elmer Gantry*). The hero, George Brush, is a devoted, idealistic, but priggish young man who makes his living as a textbook salesman but considers his work as an amateur evangelist more important. Essentially George's difficulty is that he is completely logical by nature and that he literally believes the Christianity of the Bible; he thus tries doggedly to live in the twentieth century according to the spirit of the Gospels, which involves him in a series of farcical mishaps. Typical of these is the story of his relations with Roberta Weyerhauser, a farmer's daughter who seduces him in a hayloft and whom he therefore conscientiously regards as his wife. He pursues her to Kansas City and insists on marrying her, even though he does not love her and she candidly hates him; when the marriage turns out to be a failure George is sincerely surprised and disillusioned. George also has a genius for getting locked up in small-town jails, usually because of his philosophy of non-violence (which he borrows from Gandhi) or because the local rustics misinterpret one of his frequent twenty-four-hour vows of silence and consider him either mad or criminal.

Wilder's attitude toward his hero has caused much controversy. The novel is obviously a satire, even a farcical one in spite of its restrained and mock-solemn style. Yet Wilder evidently sympathizes with George, who at worst is only a monomaniac and who may from another point of view be considered a sincere idealist who takes seriously the religion his fellow-men mouth hypocritically but lack the character to practice. George is in the end likeable, as maddening as his priggish earnestness may be to the other characters of the novel as well as the reader.

Our Town (drama, 1938) is a tribute to American life, a microcosm of life and death, love and marriage in a typical American village. The play is based structurally on the device of breaking down the "theatrical illusion" and letting the audience into the production of the piece which is also used in Pirandello's *Six Characters in Search of an Author*. There is a Stage Manager who serves as a sort of narrator or chorus; he introduces the characters and comments on the action. The plot centers around two neighboring families, those of Editor Webb and Dr. Gibbs. In the first act Dr. Gibbs comes in from a maternity case (the theme of birth), the Webbs cook breakfast (the sustenance of life) and the children go off to school. The young George Gibbs and Emily Webb play at puppy-love. In the second act, three years later, the couple are about to be married; their courtship and wedding is described (the cycle of life). In the third act, nine years later, Emily has died in childbirth; the cycle has completed itself. Emily's ghost appears; she abandons the living and joins the group of the dead, who advise her to forget her past existence and prepare for the future. This play thus attempts to demonstrate that even the humblest lives partake of the divine cycle of life, love, and death.

The Skin of Our Teeth (drama, 1942) is a fantastic *tour de force* resembling nothing else in Wilder's work. The hero is all humanity, personified in the figure of George Antrobus. He is Adam, Noah, in fact every great hero of humanity; he invents the wheel and the alphabet, lives through the Fall, the Flood, various wars, the Ice Age, and countless other catastrophes, and yet his life somehow struggles on. His wife Eva bears him two boys and a girl, but Cain, or Henry, the elder, murders his brother. A maid, Lily, serves as a sort of Liloth or personification of female sensuality. The first act takes place in the Ice Age, although the family is living in comfortable circumstances in Excelsior, New Jersey. It is so cold they are burning pianos in Hartford; gradually the wall of ice creeps southward. Refugees crowd into the home, including Homer, Moses, and the Muses. The second act takes place immediately before the deluge. The scene is Atlantic City; the convention of the Ancient and Honorable Order of Mammals, Subdivision Humans, is taking place, and George is to address the gathering. His theme is "Enjoy Yourselves." The Flood begins as the act closes; the family scrambles into a boat.

The third act returns to the suburban home. A war has just ended; Henry or Cain (personification of brute force) was the enemy. Lily, of course, was a camp-follower. The father, George, is now the creative

and inventive spirit in humanity, and continues with his inventions
of the wheel and the alphabet. The play ends as George, ever optimistic, prepares to fight for a better world with his weapons: books,
ideas, and human creativity.

The style of *The Skin of Our Teeth* is light and satirical, and the
profound meaning is only latent. The play is the most humorous of
Wilder's works; it might be viewed as a sort of parody of Joyce's
Finnegans Wake.

The Ides of March (novel, 1948) concerns the events leading up
to the assassination of Julius Caesar. The story is told entirely
through documents, proclamations, and letters of the participants.
The material is divided into four books as follows:

Book I mainly concerns Clodia Pulcher, patrician daughter of a
respected Roman family. Her mind has been disturbed by a variety
of experiences; she is violated by an uncle, and her beliefs are upset
by Caesar's skepticism. She is loved by the poet Catullus, but despises
him.

Book II depicts the arrival of Cleopatra in Rome and her relations
with Caesar; it describes her rôles both as a woman and as a queen.
Clodia discovers a plot whereby Marc Antony is to be discovered
embracing Cleopatra. Caesar happens along too soon, however, and
the plan is thwarted.

In Book III is related an incident which historically happened some
time before; Wilder concentrates the chronology for dramatic effect.
Clodia arranges for her wild young brother, Clodius, to be spirited
into the highly secret women's ritual of the Bona Dea. In the ensuing
scandal Pompeia, Caesar's wife, is accused of connivance, or even of
adultery with Clodius, and Caesar divorces her.

Book IV deals with the conspiracy to assassinate Caesar. Catullus
writes broadsides attacking him, and Brutus and Cassius plan the
actual murder. The novel closes with a description of the historical
assassination borrowed from Suetonius.

ROBINSON JEFFERS (born 1887)

Jeffers is the only major American writer of the twentieth century
to concern himself primarily with a form which has declined steadily
since the seventeenth century: the verse narrative. Yet there is nothing archaic or antiquarian about his technique; he writes in verse

not to imitate Milton or Dryden but because this medium seems natural to his personality and suited to the material he wishes to convey. His work is greatly influenced in content by Freudian psychoanalysis and by the modern interest in abnormal psychology in general. His longer poems, the best-known part of his work, are dark and heavy-laden, filled with scenes of death, violence, passion, pain, and incest. Jeffers himself is prone to attribute this element in his work to the influence of the classic tragedy—he has adapted Aeschylus and Euripides and written a modern version of the latter's *Medea,* and there is a consciously classic element in his own work. The real sources of his situations, however, are found in Freud and Jung; the dark and neurotic tone of his work resembles that of the Austrian poet Hugo von Hofmannsthal, another author influenced by the Viennese school of psychiatry. There are few normal characters in Jeffer's poems, and few dilemmas solved without recourse to bloodshed. Yet his principal interest is not in violence itself. His purpose is that of the practitioners of modern psychoanalysis—to uncover the secret springs of human motivation present in all of us but veiled out of propriety under ordinary circumstances. Jeffers does not argue that his characters are normal or even typical; he feels that the normal can best be understood through examination of the diseased. Moreover, as a poet he recognizes the dramatic value of exaggeration, violence, and monstrosity.

In spite of his superficial resemblance to Hofmannsthal, Jeffers does not share the basic pessimism of the Austrian poet. He believes positively in many things: the integrity of the individual, the healing and satisfying power of human love, the strength and honesty of the animal passions of all living creatures. Here, in his basic philosophy, he resembles D. H. Lawrence more than he does any other contemporary writer. He shares Lawrence's intense individualism, his antagonism toward conventional Anglo-Saxon puritanism, and his cult of natural action, his belief that only by following the inchoate instincts latent in his blood can the individual reach a consummation of his human possibilities. Thus his interest in sexual problems: since the sexual drive is that one which is most frequently inhibited by social conventions, it is the source of most neuroses and the root of the unhappiness of the civilized man. It is therefore natural that the neurotic preacher Barclay, of *The Women at Point Sur,* should begin his revolt against society with an inner religious awakening and end with an act of sexual iconoclasm which finally destroys him. Although the content of this verse narrative clearly indicates the parallel between Jeffers and Lawrence, it also suggests their basic difference: Jeffers, going a step beyond Lawrence, demonstrates the horrifying and destructive results of freeing a soul from social convention when it has no valid or practical controls to moderate its bestial impulses.

Jeffers' attitude toward politics is that of a thorough-going individualist. He is no Whitman or Sandburg, to affirm enthusiastically, "The people, yes"; he is suspicious of mankind in the mass, and on occasion even misanthropic. Where individuals can meet and exchange love as individuals, the relations of man to man can be clean and satisfying; but social groups, with their tendency to establish arbitrary conventions and taboos, are generally evil.

Jeffers is sometimes considered a kind of regionalist; most of his important work is set in the Monterey Peninsula region of California, especially around Carmel and Point Sur. Born in Pittsburgh, Jeffers came to California as a stranger and found in the Carmel region qualities that suited his personality and his artistic needs. He is fascinated with the wild and elemental quality of nature on the peninsula, with its wind-racked pines, its sea-fogs, and its violent changes of weather. In addition the population of the region includes non-Anglo-Saxon elements like Mexican farmers and Portuguese fishermen as well as various types of bohemians, aesthetes, recluses, and religionists. Jeffers with his personal tendencies might as well have written of Cape Cod or back-country Mississippi; his choice of the Carmel country was in a sense only a geographical accident out of which he has extracted copious literary material.

As a stylist Jeffers is striking, original, forceful, but hardly subtle; he is not primarily concerned with nuances of poetic effect or finer word values. His images are successful through their striking power rather than through precision or delicacy. His style is somewhat self-conscious; it is, however, free from irrelevancy and levity. Occasionally it is even painfully sincere. He is little interested in well-rounded characterizations, and for this reason his narratives are not really "verse novels" at all, but short modern epics. Jeffer's chief merit lies in his power to evoke striking, even shocking scenes and in his talent for making these scenes seem alive and interesting.

LIFE: John Robinson Jeffers was born in Pittsburgh in 1887, the son of a seminary professor and a remarkably talented mother. He was educated at a long series of colleges and universities including the University of Western Pennsylvania, Occidental College in Los Angeles, where he graduated at the age of eighteen, the University of Zürich, and the University of Southern California. He is widely travelled and competent in the major European languages. Married in 1913 to Una Kuster, he took up residence at Carmel, California, on the Monterey Peninsula. He later moved to Point Sur, near Carmel, where he was able to write under conditions of greater serenity; the major part of his creative career has been spent in the Carmel-Point Sur district.

Jeffers' first book of poems, *Flagons and Apples,* appeared in 1912. These early poems are unoriginal, however, and Jeffers did not definitely decide to become a poet until the publication of *Californians* in 1916. This book, at first published at the author's expense, was later reissued by the publisher and soon won Jeffers acceptance as an important new poet. His reputation continued to grow thereafter, especially during the Freudian boom of the Thirties.

CHIEF WORKS: "Tamar" (narrative poem, in *Tamar and Other Poems,* 1924), like all of Jeffers longer poems, is written in a sort of rhythmic free verse somewhat resembling Whitman. The theme is that of the Biblical curse of heredity: the sins of the fathers are visited on the children. A California rancher, David Cauldwell, is sexually intimate with his sister Helen. Years later his legitimate children, Lee and Tamar, begin to repeat the pattern. When Tamar is brought with child by her brother Lee she seeks to cover up by taking a lover, Will Andrews. Her dead aunt, Helen, however, speaks to her through the agency of another aunt, Stella, and persuades her to evil; under this influence she sets about to seduce her own father. Then, driven by a fanatic impulse to destruction, she collects father, brother, and lover in the house together and sets them upon each other. The poem ends as a half-witted relative, Jinny, sets fire to the house and burns up its inmates.

In spite of the Biblical antecedents of the thematic material of "Tamar," its moral point of view is classical, stemming essentially from Aeschylus. The catastrophe which ends the action comes out of the overweening and arrogant self-deification of the chief characters, the *hubris* of the Greek tragedy. The parallels to the *Oresteia* of Aeschylus, with its theme of passionate crime reenacted in suceeding generations, have been noted by critics.

"Roan Stallion" (narrative poem, from *Roan Stallion, Tamar, and Other Poems,* 1925) presents an even more striking theme, the lust of a woman for a horse, which she confuses with God because of the wild and elemental divinity of its animal strength. California, the sensitive and brooding quarter-Indian wife of the Monterey rancher Johnny, resents the drunken and clumsy attentions of her husband. The opening scene describes her courageous ride in a wagon into the town of Monterey through a storm to buy Christmas presents for her daughter Christine; during the wild ride her religious impulses, aroused by her knowledge that it is Christmas Eve, become confused in her mind with her awe before the "sexual" power of the storm and the raging river she crosses. Gradually she begins to associate this power with the magnificent red stallion her husband has recently brought home. Later, one night when her husband is absent, she rides alone on the mountain on the roan stallion, and begins to imagine a sexual rapport between her and the horse. When she returns she is menaced by her drunkenly amorous husband and flees to the roan stallion for protection. Johnny pursues her, the stallion attacks him, and California, instead of trying to aid him, takes the horse's side by killing a dog which is trying to defend its master. After Johnny has been trampled to death by the stallion she is moved by some reluctant human impulse to kill the horse, then she turns back to her daughter with the face of "a woman who has killed God."

California's blind instinctive worship of the stallion in this poem is intended as a kind of pantheistic allegory, an expression of a cult of the elemental and primitive as it is found in D. H. Lawrence, and with exactly Lawrence's symbolic union of the forces of sex and divinity. But Jeffers tacitly disapproves of the length to which California's sex-pantheism carries her, as magnificent as the conclusion of the poem may be. As in the *Medea* of Euripides, it is a *hubris* of sexual passion which brings California to her violent act of destruction.

The Women at Point Sur (verse narrative, 1927) centers around the Reverend Dr. Barclay, a Christian minister who loses his faith when his son is killed in the war; he abandons his city parish and comes to the Morhaus ranch on Point Sur to work out in his own mind a new religion based on freedom, love, and natural impulse. "There is nothing wicked in the world, no act is sin," he declares. But human nature, his own and that of his disciples, betrays him. Gradually he turns into a sort of prophet, adulated by his frustrated female followers. Confident of his own power and believing he is moved by a divine impulse, he first seduces an Indian servant-girl, Maruca, then violates his own daughter April. Other characters in the narrative include the Lesbian couple Natalia Morhaus and Faith Heriot, Natalia's husband Randal, and Barclay's wife Audis. After an intricate set of sexual involvements, all connected with Dr. Barclay's "mission," Natalia murders her infant, April takes her own life, and Dr. Barclay wanders off aimlessly in the hills to die of thirst and exhaustion, seeking for the peace "outside the stars, the other shore of me." His "religious" transformation has really been nothing but a neurotic nihilism which left him helpless before his animal impulses and has finally destroyed him and those around him.

"Cawdor" (narrative poem, from *Cawdor*, 1928) retells the Theseus-Hippolytus story from Greek mythology (cf. Euripides' *Hippolytus*). Cawdor, a middle-aged rancher, takes a young wife, Fera Martial, who falls in love with his son Hood. The young man rejects her overtures, and she, in a jealous rage, accuses him before Cawdor of forcing her. Cawdor, enraged, attacks and accidently kills his son. When he later learns that Hood was innocent he puts out his own eyes.

"Thurso's Landing" (narrative poem, from *Thurso's Landing*, 1932) concerns the decline of the family of Old Man Thurso, a rancher who fails at an impractical lime-kiln venture on the Monterey coast and kills himself some time before the action opens. He leaves his wife, his sons Reave and Mark, and Reave's wife Helen. Reave, a brooding angry character, resents his dead father's cowardly escape from life; Helen is bored, suffering from her mother-in-law's antagonism, and Mark is a disabled war veteran. The climactic action commences when Helen, desperate, runs off with another man. Shortly afterward Reave is crippled and made impotent by an accident. Mark, driven insane by an unspoken desire for Helen, hangs himself; and Helen murders Reave and poisons herself. The immediate emotional effect of this narrative is great, but the motivation of the characters is painfully weak.

"Give Your Heart to the Hawks" (verse narrative, from *Give Your Heart to the Hawks,* 1933) centers around a passionate and strong-willed woman, Fayne Fraser. As the poem opens her husband Lance surprises her in an embrace with his brother Michael and kills him. Fayne, willful and amoral, persuades Lance to conceal the crime and make it appear an accident, and he does so. But he lacks his wife's Medea-like strength of character, and is tormented by pangs of guilt; in his neurotic self-destructivity and masochism he seduces Michael's fiancée Mary Abbey, who shortly becomes pregnant. Mary commits suicide; and Lance, confessing everything to his puritanical father, succeeds only in driving the old man mad. As the poem ends Lance, fleeing with Fayne on horseback, loses his own mind, destroys the horse with an axe, and leaps from the cliff to his death. As for Fayne, she emerges with her strength of character unimpaired by these experiences; she turns courageously to the future which she will devote to the raising of Lance's unborn child. This powerful poem of Jeffers' later period presents a more complicated and ambiguous moral situation than most of his earlier verse narratives. Fayne is an impressive and striking woman, essentially creative rather than destructive; she is not "bad" in the ordinary sense, even in the sense in which the Medea of Euripides is bad, i.e., destructively and irrationally vindictive. Yet in the end she brings destruction on those around her, since her husband and the others lack her powerful will and self-confidence. In a world of ordinary men the heroic woman is out of place, and Fayne's strength of character brings only tragedy and ruin.

KATHERINE ANNE PORTER (born 1894)

In style as well as in attitude Katherine Anne Porter is frequently compared with her British contemporary Katherine Mansfield. With reservations, the parallel is a valid one. She shares Miss Mansfield's scrupulous and perspicacious attention to detail, her heightened, almost over-refined sensitivity to words, and her penetrating psychological insight, especially into the thought processes of children. The main difference between the two is that Miss Mansfield was a *déraciné,* an unhappy rebellious wanderer who rejected the environment of her childhood, and Miss Porter, in spite of her travels and residence in various parts of the world from Paris to Mexico, is and has remained a Southern writer. Her resemblances to Miss Mansfield, however, are more important than the differences. It is the acumen of her psychological analysis and the brilliant precision of her style, rather than her regionalistic subject matter, that have made her an important American author.

When the term "psychological" is applied to Miss Porter's work it should not be imagined that she is a doctrinaire Freudian, or that she is particularly influenced by any of the clinical schools of modern psychology. She is a psychological writer in the sense that Virginia Woolf and Proust were: in her insight into the hidden, sometimes unconscious thought processes that determine human behavior. Yet she achieves this without recourse to the over-ingenious stylistic tricks of a Joyce or a Virginia Woolf; her style is outwardly uncomplicated and conventional. It is so unpretentious, in fact, that the naive reader may view her work as less complicated than it actually is; it is the kind of prose that may be read on several levels according to the literary sophistication of the reader.

Born a Roman Catholic, Miss Porter has retained throughout her writing career a vivid sense of evil; she believes in evil as few other American writers of today do, and the struggle between good and evil (as in "Flowering Judas") is the basic conflict in her most characteristic stories. She is also extremely interested in racial types, racial characteristics, and racial conflicts, for example the contrast between the Anglo-Saxon, Slavic, and Indo-Mexican temperaments as they appear in "Hacienda." "Maria Concepción," one of her best-known stories, is virtually a study in the racial qualities of the Indian woman, although it also involves the broader universal qualities of elemental femininity. A similar theme is found in "Flowering Judas," where a struggle between Anglo-Saxon puritanism and Latin-Catholic emotionalism takes place within the mind of the heroine Laura.

Politically Miss Porter's bias is "to the left"—her own term. The combination of Catholic background (with its ever-lurking consciousness of sin) and socialist-humanitarian liberalism is well seen in the figure of Laura in "Flowering Judas," although as a matter of fact Laura is not an autobiographical character. If an autobiographical heroine is to be found in Miss Porter's work it is in the figure of Miranda, who appears as a little girl in "The Grave," recurs frequently in the stories from *The Leaning Tower,* and reappears in "Pale Horse, Pale Rider" as the heroine who like Miss Porter worked on a Denver newspaper during the First World War. The Miranda stories, in fact, if collected into chronological order, provide a sketchy but revealing fictionalized history of Miss Porter's own life.

Another parallel between Katherine Anne Porter and Katherine Mansfield is that neither writer's technique is suited to the novel as a literary form. Highly polished and succinct, Miss Porter conveys much in little space; the long stories like "Hacienda" and "That Tree" and the novelettes like those in the volume *Pale Horse, Pale Rider* might well have formed the material for novels in the hands of another writer. These "miniature novels" should be distinguished from the true short stories (e.g., "María Concepción" and "Rope") in which only a single facet of character is developed or a single incident related.

LIFE: Katherine Anne Porter was born in 1894 in Indian Creek, Texas in a family which traced its ancestry to Daniel Boone. Her family was Catholic, and she was educated in various convent schools in Texas and Louisiana. A sensitive child, she very early began to experiment with writing; her literary development was long and tedious, however, and she did not publish her first fiction until she was well into her twenties. Her first published story was "María Concepción" which she wrote in July, 1922. Thereafter she produced stories slowly but steadily; her first collection, *Flowering Judas and Other Stories,* did not appear until 1930. Miss Porter has travelled widely, and at one time served as a school teacher in Mexico. She has been married twice, in 1933 to Eugene Pressly, and American diplomatic official in Paris, and in 1938 to Albert Russel Erskine Jr., a professor at the University of Louisiana and business manager of the *Southern Review.* Divorced from Erskine in 1942, she has since lived for the most part in New York City, with occasional excursions to Hollywood as a screenwriter. Her most recent published volume is a collection of essays and short pieces, *The Days Before,* in 1952.

CHIEF WORKS: "María Concepción" (story, 1922) is a portrait of a young Indian woman in Mexico, illiterate, poverty-stricken, yet proud and wise in her native dignity. Her husband Juan works intermittently for an expedition of archeologists led by the American

Givens, but he is indolent and lacks character. Juan flirts with another girl, María Rosa, and when María Concepción discovers the intrigue he runs away with María Rosa to the sporadic war which can always be found going on in the region. María Concepción bides her time; when Juan returns she accepts him back, but goes secretly and kills María Rosa with a knife, saying, "For me everything is settled now." Opinion in the peon community condones the murder, and the authorities have no evidence to charge her with the crime; María Concepción goes home contentedly from the investigation with the baby of her rival, which as Juan's offspring she considers rightfully her own child. At the end, secure in the circle of her family, she feels a "strange, wakeful happiness."

The key quality in María Concepción's character is that she always acts instinctively, in accordance with her elemental impulses, and is therefore guiltless and serene in everything she does. Her reactions are basically savage (as opposed to civilized) and at the same time deeply feminine; e.g., it is feminine of her that her resentment is against her rival María Rosa rather than against Juan, toward whom she feels merely amorous and protective. Her "crime," as civilization would regard it, is the natural and instinctive act of a woman who feels her home menaced by the seductions of a rival.

"Rope" (story, 1928) is a satirical picture of a marriage between two quarrelsome, irrational, and confused bohemians, a penniless young couple who move into a remote country house to save money and then bicker continually over the small annoyances of their primitive life. In the end love conquers; the young people make up, and the cycle starts over again. This story presents in embryonic form a theme later to be developed more fully in "That Tree."

"Flowering Judas" (story, 1930) is often considered Miss Porter's most important work, a haunting and symbolically intricate narrative which superbly conveys the characters of its two principles. Laura, the heroine, is an American girl who teaches school in Xochimilco, near Mexico City. Because of her left-wing humanitarian principles she has become involved with Braggioni, "a leader of men, a skilled revolutionist" who is evidently the head of a large and complicated revolutionary organization. Braggioni is in love with her and makes clumsy overtures; but Laura, who has come to Mexico out of a romantic emotional attachment to the country, is nevertheless deeply

Anglo-Saxon: cool, reserved, always withholding a part of herself in her emotional relations with others. At the same time there is a latent attraction underlying her loathing for Braggioni, and this fills her with a vague consciousness of guilt. This guilt complex is increased by her political involvement: she has come to realize that Braggioni is basically cynical in spite of his outward sentimentality, that he constantly betrays comrades who are no longer useful to the movement, in fact that he is actually one of the fat and well-fed "bosses" against whom the pale and starving workers ought to be revolting. At the climax of the story she helps Eugenio, a young revolutionist who is in prison and despondent because Braggioni will not help him, to kill himself by smuggling drugs in to him. Later she has a disturbing allegorical dream in which the dead Eugenio appears to her and offers her the flowers of the Judas tree, saying, "This is my body and my blood." Laura's Catholic conscience has rebelled against the life of cynical compromise she is living, and all her suppressed guilt has risen in a dream to confront her.

It should be kept in mind that Braggioni is by no means the villain of this story. He is a "leader of men," a practical revolutionist who knows that life is basically disappointment and that all ideas are finally betrayed, and permits himself certain indulgences in the knowledge that his ends (his revolutionary ideals) justify his cynical means. He is partly correct in his assertion that he and Laura are basically alike except that he has more experience of life. "Some day," he says, "you will remember what I have told you, you will know that Braggioni was your friend." But Laura, cold, intellectual, and deeply religious, cannot compromise; for her the gulf between her ideals and her actual life is insupportable.

"That Tree" (story, 1934) is related by a young American living in Mexico. The hero, who has vague ambitions to be a poet, is at first quite happy loafing in the Mexican sunshine and living with an Indian girl who poses for some of his painter-friends. He is, however, more or less engaged to Miriam, a Minneapolis school-teacher, "a nicely brought-up Middle-Western girl, who took life seriously"; when she arrives in Mexico City to marry him his whole life is changed. Basically prim and priggish, Miriam is not impressed with his poetic aspirations and informs him flatly that he is an untidy loafer. He smolders under this taunting; they bicker, and finally Miriam goes back to America. Then comes the point of the story: the hero spends the years that follow doggedly trying to make something of himself to prove to Miriam "that he was not just merely a bum, fit for nothing but lying under a tree." He swallows his pride, sets aside his poetic ambitions, and becomes a successful journalist, although actually he has no interest in this profession and still (ostensibly) hates and depises everything that Miriam stands for. The fact is that the puritanical Anglo-Saxon element in his own character has given him a bad conscience and left him feeling vaguely that Miriam was right, that at the bottom he is nothing but a loafer. At the end of the story he invites her to come back, insisting to a friend in a drunken conversation that this time their relations are to be on another basis and that Miriam will "walk the chalk line"—a declaration that both he and the reader realize is nothing but a rationalization, since he instinctively feels the need of Miriam's discipline to counteract the indolent and ambitionless quality of his own character.

"Hacienda" (story, 1932) is set on a Mexican *pulque* plantation, where a Soviet motion picture company with an international staff comes to make a film. The heroine and narrator is a young female American writer who has been invited to watch the filming as a guest. The other important characters are Kennerly, an eccentric American business-manager; Uspensky, the Russian producer, and Andreyev, evidently his assistant; Don Genaro, the master of the estate; Doña Julia, his young wife; and Betancourt, a Mexican advisor to Uspensky. The long story consists mainly of conversations: sophisticated, international, often cynical. The central incident of the story, seen only obliquely through the comments of the characters, is the drama of a local Mexican boy, Justino, who accidently kills his sister with a pistol and is arrested for manslaughter, thereby delaying the shooting of the film. The incident is presented by Miss Porter with great subtlety; the evident sympathy which the narrator of the story feels for Justino is ironically contrasted with the callousness of the others toward his predicament. Justino can be released through payment of a rather large bribe, but Don Genaro's aristocratic pride is involved, and he refuses to let a mere country judge get the better of him; Justino stays in prison. At the end of the story it is apparent that only the "American" efficiency and aggressiveness of Kennerly holds together this motley and romantic assortment of Latins and Slavs so that the film somehow gets made in spite of all obstacles. The theme of "Hacienda" is that of the contrast of racial types: the impulsive but cynical Slavic mentality of the Russian producers, the American character of Kennerly, the decadent Spanish aristocracy of Don Genaro and his wife, and the simple and elemental instinct of the Indian plantation workers, personified in the boy Justino.

All the stories described above are included in the collection *Flowering Judas and Other Stories* (1935), and the first three were contained in an earlier volume by the same title published in 1930.

"The Downward Path to Wisdom" (story, in *The Leaning Tower and Other Stories,* 1944) is an intricate achievement in narrative technique, an adult domestic intrigue seen entirely from the point of view of a four-year-old boy. Stephen, the little boy, gradually becomes aware that his mother and father are living a life of mutual hatred, and that they are using him as a tool in their efforts to hurt each other. Sent away to visit his grandmother, Stephen meets a little girl, Frances, and makes friends with his Uncle David. But a misunderstanding arises over some balloons, and his mother and her brother David quarrel even more bitterly than mother and father had quarreled earlier. Stephen, sick at heart at his parting from Frances and now fully aware of the hate-filled lives of his elders, is taken back home with a new secret: that it is hatred that dominates the world. Thus the "downward path to wisdom" has brought him precociously to the pessimistic cynicism of an adult.

* * *

3. Drama in Transition

THE NINETEENTH CENTURY

For reasons which have not yet been satisfactorily explained, American drama was slower in reaching maturity than either fiction or poetry. A number of critics and literary historians have remarked that nineteenth-century American drama is marked not only by its relative lack of quality and integrity when compared with other types of American literature but by its lack of any national originality, any quality other than a superficial interest in "local color" and folklore that can be considered distinctively American. The century which produced Hawthorne, Poe, Whitman, Thoreau, and Mark Twain can boast of no dramatist of comparable quality. "It seems," says Barrett H. Clark, "in reading the hundreds of surviving plays of the nineteenth century, that the best of them were the work of more or less ingenious children who lived in a world that had done no thinking since 1620." This gulf between drama and serious literature continued well into the twentieth century, and was actually not bridged effectively until the period after the First World War. If a rough date can be assigned for the beginning of the modern American drama it is 1920, the year of O'Neill's *Beyond the Horizon* and the approximate era of the inception of the Theatre Guild. When it is remembered that *The Red Badge of Courage* was published in 1895 and Robinson's *Children of the Night* in 1897, it can be seen that the development of American drama lagged almost a generation behind the parallel processes in fiction and poetry.

The specific difficulties with nineteenth-century American drama were (a) that it had no higher purpose than merely to entertain, and thus too frequently degenerated into mere bathos or sentiment; (b) that when it had a serious purpose it too often tried to convey its message through sheer sentiment rather than through some more adept dramatic technique; and (c) that the theatre of the era was actor-centered rather than writer-centered, and that the play itself was therefore often considered merely a "vehicle" for the display of a

324

noted actor's histrionic talents. The first of these difficulties is well illustrated by the well-known genre of the American melodrama, with its helpless widows, inexorable landlords, and travelers lost in snow-storms, the type of old-fashioned play that is so often, and so justifi-ably, parodied in the twentieth century. The second is epitomized by *Uncle Tom's Cabin,* which in its dramatic version by George Aiken was one of the all-time successes of the American theatre; a noble and high-minded drama in concept, it nevertheless made its point through saccharine sentimentality and a prissy contrast between good and evil which a modern audience would find childish. The *Rip Van Winkle* of Boucicault and Jefferson (1865) demonstrates the third difficulty. One of a multitude of plays based on the tale of Washing-ton Irving, it was created specifically to serve as a vehicle for Joseph Jefferson, who played it for years and eventually became firmly asso-ciated with the rôle in the public mind. Although to judge by the success of the play his performances must have been good, at least by the standards of his audiences, the play today seems bad. Naturally the drama as an art form must always depend heavily on the contri-butions of actor, director, and producer, but after 1920 the emphasis was to shift markedly to the literary contribution of the playwright.

By modern standards, three names particularly stand out from the list of hundreds of nineteenth-century dramatists who were con-sidered successful in their own time. The first of these is DION BOUCICAULT (1820-90), Irish-born dramatist and actor, who won success in London before he came to America in 1853. A master of the melodrama and a writer who wrote as an actor and from the actor's standpoint, he was perhaps the most superficially successful playwright of the century. Those of his plays which seem to have the most lasting quality are *The Octoroon* (1859), a melodramatic picture of slavery based on a novel, *The Quadroon,* by Mayne Reid (1856) and roughly similar in its approach to the subject of *Uncle Tom's Cabin; The Colleen Bawn* (1860), one of a number of Irish folk-comedies with which Boucicault won the hearts of the American public; and the adaptation of *Rip Van Winkle* mentioned above, done in collaboration with the actor Joseph Jefferson. BRONSON HOWARD (1842-1908) is a more serious dramatist, one of the first American playwrights to experiment with genuine social criticism. His *Young Mrs. Winthrop* (1882) seriously treated the problem of divorce when the subject was still virtually unmentionable in polite society, and before the influence of European iconoclasts like Ibsen and Bourget had reached America. His Civil War play *Shenandoah* (1888), a great popular success, was less remarkable in quality and originality. Howard also frequently treated the America vs. Europe theme in the manner of Henry James; the most important plays in this genre are *The Banker's Daughter* (1878), *One of Our Girls* (1885), and *Aristocracy* (1892). Finally, JAMES A. HERNE (1839-1901) was one of the first American playwrights to strive for an indigenous and original national theatre, one which would include typical American qualities yet avoid the pitfalls of provincialism. His *Margaret Fleming* (1890) represents a sincere attempt to treat the problem of marital infidelity realistically. This play, although a relative dramatic success, was a commercial failure; but *Shore Acres* (1892), which was built around a faithfully realistic New England setting, won popular acclaim. *The Reverend Griffith Davenport* (1899) is a Civil War play far more mature and sophisticated than Howard's *Shenandoah;* in its ethical iconoclasm and its conflict between military and personal ethics it bears comparison with Bernard Shaw's *The Devil's Disciple*. Half melodramatic and half realistic, Herne is a transitional figure bridging the gap between his own century and the modern era of O'Neill, Sherwood, Odets, and Maxwell Anderson.

Another transitional figure who should receive mention is DAVID BELASCO (1859-1931), San Francisco-born playwright and producer, who refined and brought to perfection the school of photographic realism in the Broadway theatre. Belasco's late nineteenth-century productions were especially remarkable for their sets, which anticipated the settings of modern motion pictures in their painstakingly faithful authenticity. He is also said to have been the first theatrical producer to make effective use of the newly invented electric light for stage effects. His influence on later motion picture technique was considerable; in fact his best-known play, *The Return of Peter Grimm* (1911) was written in collaboration with Cecil B. DeMille, who later went on to Hollywood and won fame by adapting Belasco's super-realistic technique to the films. In the legitimate theatre, however, Belasco represented the high-water mark of a style which was soon to decline; when the more important playwrights of the post-1918 period appeared they generally conceded super-realism to the cinema and turned their talents in another direction. Other important dramas of Belasco, some of them written with collaborators, are *The Girl I Left Behind Me* (1893), *Madame Butterfly* (1900), and *The Girl of the Golden West* (1905). The last two of these plays are more familiar in their operatic adaptations by Puccini; in fact it is possible that future literary history will view Belasco chiefly as a supplier of plots for Puccini libretti. His important contribution to the history of American stage production, however, should not be underestimated.

EUROPEAN INFLUENCES

Meanwhile the European theatre was experimenting with far more original techniques, and when the time came its influence on the American drama was to be an important one. Two separate periods of experimentalism may be distinguished in the European drama of the late nineteenth century. The first of these is the realistic-naturalistic revolt, led by the social dramas of Ibsen around 1880 and followed by the dramas of the French naturalistic school. The second is the symbolic-expressionist tendency which began to assume importance about a generation later (*ca.* 1900) and reached its peak in the work of the pre-war German expressionists Wedekind, Kaiser, and Toller.

Undoubtedly the greatest single influence which the nineteenth century contributed to the modern drama is that of HENRIK IBSEN (1828-1906). A Norwegian of middle-class background, Ibsen is not a model naturalist in the later tradition of the Zola-Dreiser school, but his importance as a predecessor of later German, British, and American naturalists is great. In Germany and France his work exerted its main effect on the naturalistic school in the eighteen-eighties; in England and America the influence was delayed to the period immediately before the First World War. In this era his dramas excited tremendous social and literary controversy, and a certain familiarity with the basic principles of Ibsenism was part of the conversational stock of every cultured person. Today, after the triumph of feminism and the passing away of the social milieu in which he wrote, many of his dramas seem to have lost their point, and he is viewed chiefly as a master of dramatic psychology. Yet his attacks on Philistinism and hypocrisy are just as significant today as they were when they were written, and such recent plays as Arthur Miller's *All My Sons* (1947) consciously imitate the dramatic techniques which Ibsen brought to perfection over three-quarters of a century before.

Ibsen's dramas may be roughly divided into three groups. The first includes the poetic dramas of the period up to his visit to Norway in 1874; *Brand* and *Peer Gynt* are the most important of these. The tone of these early dramas is romantic; the settings are fantastic or exotic, and the characterization tends to be symbolic or allegorical rather than naturalistic. The second group, the social dramas that begin with *The League of Youth* as early as 1869, are written in prose; their settings are contemporary, and they treat naturalistic heroes involved in modern social or political conflicts. The third group of plays, symbolic or allegorical dramas with a mystical overtone, includes *Rosmersholm* (1886), *Little Eyolf* (1894), and *When We Dead Awaken* (1900). It is, however, the second group of plays that is most important in its influence on the American drama. In them Ibsen shifts his viewpoint continually and often takes contradictory sides of the same social question; *Hedda Gabbler* is in a sense a retort to *A Doll's House*. Yet he retains throughout his work one consistent aim: to present the truth unreservedly and fearlessly, in spite of the social denunciation this may call down upon him. Furthermore Ibsen's dramas are totally earnest; in spite of their high dramatic interest they never seek merely to entertain. Each of them treats a problem which Ibsen considers a basic and pressing one. Some of the problems are social, others personal, but in neither case are they trivial. Thus Ibsen lays the foundation for the "thesis play" or "problem play," the drama which treats a social or socio-domestic problem through dramatic conflict. Naturally to treat Ibsen merely as a social dramatist is an oversimplification; yet it is this element in his work which has been most influential in foreign countries, America among the others.

The first of these "social dramas" is *Pillars of Society* (1877), an attack on bourgeois ethics in which he bares the vicious hypocrisy which underlies middle-class "respectability." *A Doll's House* (1879), perhaps his most sensational play in its time, is a study of middle-class marriage and an eloquent plea for the emancipation of women; and *Ghosts* (1881) is likewise a study of the catastrophic consequences of marriage not based on true affection and respect. *An Enemy of the People* (1882), written in a burst of indignation which swept over Ibsen following the public attacks on *Ghosts,* is an exposé of the middle-class "vested interests" who turn savagely on the exponent of truth who menaces their property; it also contains a bitter denunciation of the stupidity and mob-instinct of the mass man. Finally, *Hedda Gabbler* (1890) shows the other side of the question earlier argued in *A Doll's House;* through its presentation of the destruction of a neurotic and frustrated "emancipated woman" it demonstrates the perils that lie in too hasty social change.

Other important European pathfinders in the naturalistic drama are GERHART HAUPTMANN (German, 1862-1946), whose *Before Dawn* (1889) is a powerful and brutal study in environmental determinism; MAXIM GORKY (Russian, 1868-1936), who created in *The Lower Depths* (1902) a drama which bridges the gap between naturalism and expressionism; and AUGUST STRINDBERG (Swedish, 1849-1912), also a transitional figure in the history of world drama, whose *The Father* (1887), *Comrades* (1888), and especially *Miss Julia* (1888) are considered classics of the naturalistic theatre. The various dramatic adaptations of Zola's novels (e.g., *Thérèse Raquin, L'Assommoir*) should also be mentioned, along with the naturalistic dramas of HENRI BECQUE (1837-99), the "Flaubert of the Theatre," whose *Les Corbeaux* (*The Ravens,* 1882) is said to have inaugurated the modern era in the French drama.

Zola and Becque were associated with a theatre group which was an important factor in the development of the French drama: the Théâtre Libre, founded in 1887 by André Antoine, an employee of the Paris gas company who became one of the leading theatrical entrepreneurs of France. In Berlin a similar theatre, the Freie Buehne, was founded by Otto Brahm in 1889. These two groups, the first two important experimental theatres in Europe, established an important example for the many American theatre groups such as the Theatre Guild which were to spring up after 1918.

Around the turn of the century there occurred a reaction against realism and naturalism in the European theatre which took several forms, the most important of which are the movements known as symbolism and expressionism. The first of these is often associated with the name of MAURICE MAETERLINCK (Belgian, 1862-

1949), who popularized and converted to dramatic form the literary principles of the French Symbolist poets. Maeterlinck's dramas are marked by a sense of the mystery of life, the irrational and inexplicable pattern of destiny, the transitory and fragile nature of human happiness, and the shadowy two-dimensional quality of his characters. The best known of his symbolist dramas are *Pelleas and Melisande* (1893), a fantasy in the setting of a medieval forest, and *The Blue Bird* (1908), a fairy tale which caused an enormous popular fad when it was played in the United States during the Twenties.

The founder of European expressionism was AUGUST STRINDBERG (Swedish, 1849-1912). In his *The Dance of Death* (1901) and continuing with *The Dream Play* (1902), Strindberg launched into a radical new style, the purpose of which was to imitate the disconnected but seemingly logical form of the dream. The background of his dramas ostensibly remained that of reality, but characterization, dialogue, and mood took on a portentous and nightmarish quality of fantasy. The two plays cited, along with *The Spook Sonata* (1907), are marked by a brooding pessimism, a Mephistophelian quality which struck a sympathetic note among the audiences of the fin-de-siècle; the tendency is apparent in such later dramas as O'Neill's *The Great God Brown* (1926).

Other important members of the European expressionist school were three Germans, FRANK WEDEKIND (1864-1918), GEORG KAISER (1878-1945), and ERNST TOLLER (1893-1939). The last of these is not particularly important as an influence on American drama, since his best-known play, *Masse Mensch,* appeared only in 1920 after the American experimental drama was well under way. The other two, however, were an important influence on such American dramatists as O'Neill and Rice. Their chief dramas include Wedekind's *The Awakening of Spring* (1891), which bitterly attacks the evils of puritanical repression of adolescent sexuality, and Kaiser's *From Morn To Midnight* (1916) and *Gas* (1917-20), the latter a grotesque and fantastic trilogy involving modern industrialism and the crushing of human dignity by the machine. Kaiser's dramatic technique is particularly important for its deemphasis of individuality and its tendency to treat humanity in the mass; even characters who do possess a certain individuality are given labels such as "Father," "Bank Clerk," or "Billionaire" rather than specific names. The dominant quality of all expressionism, however, is its weird, fantastic, or unreal atmosphere; the action seems to take place in a nightmare, everything is distorted or oversimplified, and the elements of conflict are presented in their bare or symbolic essence. The technique is well demonstrated in such American dramas of the Twenties as Rice's *Adding Machine* and O'Neill's *The Great God Brown.*

THE AMERICAN THEATRE
IN THE TWENTIETH CENTURY

The development of the American drama in the first half of the twentieth century can be roughly divided into three periods. The first of these, the era from 1900 to 1920, was a time of confused ferment and tentative experiment, a transitional period between the two centuries. American drama in these twenty years was preoccupied with two problems: the assimilation of the European influences described above, and the struggle to bring forth an indigenous and characteristically American drama. It was an era in which European plays were widely produced in America by amateur and university groups as well as by professional theatres; Ibsen, Hauptmann, Strindberg, Wedekind, and others of their kind became familiar to at least the more cultivated American audience. Meanwhile dramatists like Clyde Fitch experimented tentatively with the new technique of realism, producing plays which, in spite of their lingering Victorian and melodramatic qualities, were unmistakably precursors of the radically experimental dramas which were to come. At Harvard a relatively obscure college professor, George Pierce Baker, organized a class in playwriting which was to become one of the major forces in the formation of the new drama. His famous English 47 course (the "47 Workshop"), which he taught at Harvard from 1905 to 1925, helped to train such important American writers as Eugene O'Neill, S. N. Behrman, Sidney Howard, Philip Barry, John Dos Passos, and Thomas Wolfe. In addition to its importance as an influence on these writers, Baker's college course was also an interesting social phenomenon; it demonstrated that the American drama, scorned by serious critics in the nineteenth century, had by 1905 risen to the point where it was deemed worthy of study at such universities as Harvard and Yale.

The second period, 1920-30, may be justifiably termed America's dramatic Renaissance. It was an era of intense experimentation and originality, an era in which the pre-war process of ferment found its climax and fulfillment. There is a certain crudeness, a kind of rudimentary exaggeration, in the first works of any new literary movement, and the drama of this period, whatever its quality, cannot be described as refined or subtle. The old forms were being shattered; the decade was dominated by a spirit of iconoclasm. It was the era in which O'Neill came to the forefront as the leading American dramatist, and in which Rice, Sherwood, Howard, and Barry were trying each in his own way to create a new and native American drama. The experiments ranged from the raw naturalism of Anderson and Stallings' *What Price Glory?* to the radical expressionism of O'Neill's *The Great God Brown* and *Lazarus Laughed*. The era also marked the triumph of the Little Theatre movement, which had begun before the war in imitation of European experimental theatres, especially the Berlin Freie Buehne and the Moscow Art Theatre of Stanislavsky. In every major city of the nation amateurs and semi-professionals, along with a few professional actors, organized small theatres with the intention of producing experimental drama for a small, perceptive, and select audience. The influence of these relatively small theatres, however, cannot be measured by their box-office statistics. They were the means by which the new drama was gradually made attractive to a wider public; as they gained social acceptance and began to become a popular and "smart" means of entertainment, so did the new techniques of naturalism, symbolism, and expressionism gain acceptance among the general theatre audience. Among the more important of these Little Theatres were the Provincetown Players, which produced O'Neill's first play in 1916; the Toy Theatre in Boston; the Little Theatre in Chicago; and the Washington Square Players in Greenwich Village. Out of this last group developed an even more important theatrical organization, partly experimental and partly commercial in spirit: the Theatre Guild, which produced many European dramas in translation in the years following its founding in 1919 and in addition had the honor of bringing to the public such American plays as Rice's *Adding Machine* and O'Neill's *Strange Interlude*. The Theatre Guild gradually evolved into a commercial theatre group; by 1943 it reached the point of producing the popular musical comedy hit *Oklahoma!* Yet its importance as a focus of the experimental theatre movement in the Twenties and early Thirties cannot be overestimated.

The third period, which began around 1930 and continued through the Forties and Fifties, was an era of assimilation and refinement, a period in which the radical new techniques of the Twenties were popularized and perfected by a new generation of dramatists. There is scarcely anything new in the drama of this period which cannot be traced to the Twenties; yet some of the post-1945 dramas, for example Miller's *Death of a Salesman* and Williams' *A Streetcar Named Desire,* far surpass the more awkward experiments of the earlier era in their subtlety and maturity. Naturally many of the old generation of the Twenties continued to produce; O'Neill wrote his masterpiece *Mourning Becomes Electra* in 1931 and writers like Maxwell Anderson produced their most mature work after 1930. But by 1940 the interest had shifted to the new generation, and the period after 1945 was to see almost as many new dramatists come to the fore as the period after the First World War. It is interesting to note that by this time the process of European influence had reversed itself: plays like *Death of a Salesman,* when they were produced in Europe in the Fifties, created almost the sensation of the German expressionist dramas which were played in America in the Twenties. American drama, like the rest of American literature, had come into its own, and could now compete on equal terms in the arena of the world theatre.

CLYDE FITCH (1865-1909)

An enormously successful playwright in his own lifetime, Fitch is today considered important mainly for his historical contribution to the American drama. It is sometimes argued that his plays are too topical—too narrowly concerned with the immediate problems of his own time—to withstand the passing of years. This, however, is obviously not true of dramas like *The Girl With the Green Eyes;* female jealousy and marital infidelity are as effective drama today as they were in the days of Euripides' *Medea.* A sounder reason for the decline of Fitch's reputation is that his technique, considered advanced for its day, now seems naive and primitive after the great era of dramatic experimentation in the Twenties. It is now apparent that

Fitch was less a realist than a precursor of realism; he occupies a position in the theatre roughly analogous to that of his contemporary W. D. Howells in fiction. There are other parallels between Fitch and Howells: both were interested in moral and marital problems in upper-class American society circles, both treated sexual matters with Victorian caution even when dealing with such daring questions as that of divorce, and both served to introduce into American literature certain technical innovations from Continental sources. Fitch and Howells are transitional figures, men who considered themselves pathfinders of realism but actually only bridged the gap from Victorian literature to the true realism of the Twenties.

The structure of Fitch's most important social dramas (e.g., *The Climbers, Her Own Way*) usually combines a social theme with a highly melodramatic plot, customarily involving courtship or marriage. *Her Own Way* is typical; the attack on Wall Street speculation is presented through a plot of the utmost sentimentality, with the hero arriving unexpectedly in the last scene, clad in a soldier's uniform, to rescue the heroine and save the family from disgrace. Yet the characterizations in such plays rise far above the level of the ordinary nineteenth-century melodrama; Fitch's psychological insight might well have made him an O'Neill or an Arthur Miller had he been born in a later generation. As a moralist he is conventional, stoutly defending female virtue, masculine honesty, and the sacrament of marriage and attacking frivolity and irregular habits. He was often considered daring in his day; his *Sappho* (1900), based on the novel of Daudet, was fiercely attacked by critics as immoral. Today he seems conservative, both in technique and in content, yet he performed a valuable function as a pathfinder for the American theatre. He showed the way for the important generation of social critics and satirists who were to follow him; without Fitch the task of Howard, Kingsley, and Behrman would have been immeasurably more difficult.

LIFE: Clyde Fitch was born in Elmira, New York in 1909. Educated in a New Hampshire boarding school and at Amherst, he early showed an interest in the theatre, acting in student productions in college and attempting to upset the Amherst campus with his literary audacities. In 1888 he made the first of several trips to Europe; he was excited by the literary atmosphere of the Paris of the era, and made contact with the aesthetic movement which was then at its peak in London. Certain now that he wanted to make his career as a writer, he returned to New York and procured a recommendation from a friend, E. A. Dithmar, dramatic editor of the *Times,* to write a play for the famous actor Richard Mansfield. The play, *Beau Brummel,* was premiered in 1890 and was a splendid box-office success. Fitch wrote a number of other plays as vehicles for famous stage personalities, such as Julia Marlowe; most of these, however, are not typical of his best style, since they demanded a certain histrionic sentimentality to show off the talents of the actor. His better plays are marked by a close attention to documentation in the naturalistic tradition, a painstaking accumulation of facts that came to be known as "Fitchian detail." Yet it was Fitch's fate that the public always praised his plays for the wrong reasons. His greatest popular successes were *Barbara Frietchie* (1899), which owed its popularity mainly to the reputation of Julia Marlowe; *Captain Jinks of the Horse Marines* (1902), which presented Ethel Barrymore to the public in her first light comedy; and *The Stubbornness of Geraldine* (1902), which became a box-office hit mainly because one setting involved a pitching steamer which actually rocked through ingenious under-stage machinery. Fitch, however, stubbornly persisted in his efforts to bring true dramatic realism to the American stage, and *The Truth* (1906) won at least a grudging praise from critics. Fitch died on a trip to Europe in 1909, at Chalons-sur-Marne. His last play, *The City,* was produced a few months later in New York, and its success would have gratified him. His reputation, however, began to decline almost immediately after his death, and since the First World War his dramas have seldom been staged except by university and experimental theatres.

CHIEF WORKS: *The Climbers* (drama, 1901) is a melodramatic exposé of the wild financial speculation that lay under the surface of the elegant New York society of the turn of the century. When the husband of Mrs. Hunter, a supposedly wealthy society woman, dies it is discovered that he has been speculating foolishly and has left his family nothing but debts. His son-in-law Richard Sterling, husband of his daughter Blanche, has also been involved, and has secretly gambled away all his wife's fortune. A good-hearted aunt, Ruth

Hunter, comes to the rescue of the family and offers to let Sterling manage her funds; but Sterling, weak and characterless, speculates with this money too and soon loses it. Meanwhile Edward Warden, a family friend, seizes the moment to declare his love of many years for Blanche; and she, loathing her husband for his dishonesty, returns his love. But at the moment of crisis she realizes that duty binds her to her husband, whatever his character may be; she is not free to follow her own happiness. Sterling is overcome by shame; after a tumultuous inner struggle he takes his own life with an overdose of morphine. The chief interest in this play, in addition to the theme of the folly of speculation, lies in the inner moral conflicts of Blanche, Sterling, and Warden. Ruth Hunter, the aunt, speaks for the author when she persuades Blanche that the first duty of a married woman is to her husband whatever his faults. (Note the contrast to Ibsen; *cf. A Doll's House* and *Ghosts.*) The closing scene of Act I, in which a hypocritically grieving Mrs. Hunter, faced with months of formal mourning, cynically sells her new Paris clothes to a pair of friends at inflated prices, is one of the best-known passages in Fitch's work.

The Girl With the Green Eyes (drama, 1902) is a study in female jealousy and its destructive effect on normal human relations. John Austin, a candid and sincere young man, is genuinely in love with his wife Jinny; but she, dominated by an almost pathological jealousy, gives him little peace. The dramatic climax occurs when John unselfishly attempts to solve a domestic problem among Jinny's relatives. He learns that her brother Geoffrey, married to Ruth Chester, is actually a bigamist, having secretly married a housemaid some time before while under the influence of drink. When John, trying tactfully to work out some solution to this impasse, is obliged to have several discreet interviews with Ruth, his wife accuses him of infidelity. Unable to defend himself without revealing confidences, he leaves her. When the truth is finally revealed, Jinny, guilt-stricken, attempts to take her own life. When John learns of this he returns and their marriage is resumed, but on a new basis—this time free from jealousy and suspicion. This play, with its heroine dominated by a single personality quality, resembles an Elizabethan "comedy of manners" in its psychological over-simplification. From another point of view it is a precursor of the twentieth-century "psychiatric" drama, which presents the types and complexes of modern psychology in dramatic form.

Her Own Way (drama, 1903) is similar in theme to *The Climbers,* although its dramatic development is more successful. The story of financial speculation is neatly interlocked with a love-intrigue in which the heroine is confronted with the "moral dilemma" so popular in the fin-de-siècle theatre. Georgiana Carley has two suitors: Sam Coast, a wealthy self-made man with mining interests in the West, and Lieutenant Richard Coleman, a gallant young army officer whom Georgiana secretly loves. After an awkward and ambiguous declaration of love, Coleman goes off to fight the Philippine insurrectionists, and Coast is free to argue his suit. Meanwhile Georgiana's brother Steven has succumbed to the fever of speculation; not only has he gambled away all his family's money, but he has brought himself to the brink of personal disgrace. The wealthy Coast offers to extricate him from the situation, but only if Georgiana agrees to marry him. In this black moment Coleman is reported killed in the Philippines. After a number of weeks of suspense, however, he turns up alive to claim Georgiana and rescue the family with his own money. This highly theatrical love-plot is wholly nineteenth-century in its contrived suspense and melodramatic ending. The modern aspects of the play are the psychological study of the fever of speculation, the portraits of Georgiana's stepmother Mrs. Carley and her daughter Louise, both shallow society women who abandon Steven in his moment of crisis, and the character of Coast, a complex and convincingly sincere antagonist rather than a mere conniving villain in the nineteenth-century melodrama style.

The Truth (drama, 1906) belongs essentially to the same genre as *The Girl With the Green Eyes,* although the plot intrigue is more complicated. Becky Warder, a rather shallow young society woman, is conducting a flirtation with Fred Lindon, a friend of her husband. Lindon's wife Eve discovers the affair and sets detectives on the pair until she has acquired a complete dossier of their clandestine meetings. She presents Becky's husband Tom Warder with this evidence, and he questions Becky about the affair. She might extricate herself easily by telling the truth, but like Jinny (*The Girl With the Green Eyes*) she is dominated by a single personality flaw: in her case she is a pathological liar who embroiders on the truth even when she has no reason to do so. Warder's faith in her is destroyed through her obvious falsehoods, and he leaves her. She goes off broken-hearted to visit her father, who is living in rather irregular circumstances with a creature of bohemian habits named Mrs. Genevieve Crespigny. Roland, her father, also an inveterate liar, tricks Warder to come to her by sending a telegram informing him that Becky is gravely ill. But when Warder arrives Becky, resolving never to lie again, refuses to take part in the subterfuge. Since the trick was transparent any-how, and since Mrs. Crespigny has secretly told all to Warder in a private interview, this decision is the only thing that can save her. Warder takes her back, telling her, "We don't love people because they are perfect;" their marriage is restablished on the firm basis of the truth. Like *The Girl With the Green Eyes,* this play is a study in psychopathology, but with moral implications; its wholly human and personal conflict distinguishes it from Fitch's social dramas of the type of *The Climbers.* The last act of *The Truth* was declared by William Lyon Phelps to be the best dramatic scene that Fitch ever wrote.

The City (drama, 1909) is an experimental work more important as a forerunner of the naturalistic-expressionistic dramas of the Twen-ties (e.g., *The Adding Machine*) than as a literary work in its own right. The theme is the corrupting influence of the modern city on the individual; as in the *Massendrama* of the German expressionists, the city itself becomes the antagonist in the dramatic conflict. The play, however, owes more to the school of French naturalism and to the contemporary journalistic "muckraking" tradition than it does to German expressionism.

EUGENE O'NEILL (1888-1953)

O'Neill, usually considered the most important American play-wright of the twentieth century, wrote in many different styles during his long career. In the period before 1920 he used a sort of romantic naturalism similar to that of the contemporary Irish playwrights (e.g., Synge and O'Casey). Most of the plays of this period are sea stories; they include *Thirst* and the plays published in the volume *The Moon of the Caribbees* in 1919. *Anna Christie,* a full-length play dated 1922, also belongs roughly to this genre. These plays are fresh and sincere but not strikingly original; they show a certain awkwardness in style, and succeed mainly through the mood of intensity they manage to create rather than through psychological or stylistic subtlety.

In 1920 O'Neill's first major production, *Beyond the Horizon,* was staged in New York City. This play, along with *Diff'rent* (1920), was psychological in approach and relatively conventional in technique; both dramas demonstrated the contrast between basic human types and the evils which result from betraying one's nature.

In *The Emperor Jones* (1920) and *The Hairy Ape* (1922) O'Neill took a new tack. These plays, as well as *The Great God Brown* (1926), *Lazarus Laughed* (1927), and *Dynamo* (1929), greatly resemble the expressionism of the contemporary German school (Kaiser, Toller). They derive, however, from Strindberg more than from the Germans. *The Hairy Ape* is the best of the group; it caused a tremendous impact upon its first presentation, and the influence continued throughout the Twenties. Not only was it the first successful expressionistic play to be written by an American, but it was probably the most original American play ever written up to that time. In these expressionistic dramas O'Neill showed little interest in the radicalism of the European naturalists or in the German expressionistic technique of treating groups and social classes as dramatic individuals (*Massendrama*). His chief concerns were the personification of natural or atavistic forces (*The Hairy Ape* and *The Emperor Jones*), the changeable and ephemeral nature of human personality (*The Great God Brown*), and the establishing of fantastic theatrical moods (*Lazarus Laughed*).

O'Neill's interest in psychology, at the time a growing fad in intellectual circles, increased constantly during the Twenties. In addition to the early plays, *Desire Under the Elms* (1925) was strongly influenced by psychiatric concepts. The experimental *Strange Interlude* (1928) continued the tendency; the existence of subconscious attitudes was shown through spoken internal monologues sandwiched between the ordinary dialogue. In *Mourning Becomes Electra* (1931) this tendency reached its climax. The work might be described as a classic Greek trilogy recast in Freudian terms and presented with the theatrical devices and style of twentieth-century expressionism. For the fate of the Greek drama O'Neill substituted the subconscious desires, the frustrations, and the "complexes" which modern psychiatry has shown to underlie our external actions.

Finally, in a group of three plays written in the years before his death, *The Iceman Cometh, A Moon for the Misbegotten,* and *Long Day's Journey into Night,* O'Neill turned to a sort of decadent naturalism somewhat resembling Gorky or Chekhov. His interest in abnormal psychiatry is still evident in these plays, but the morbid pessimism latent in his earlier work now emerges to dominate the mood entirely. In technique the plays are straightforward and relatively conventional compared to his earlier experimental dramas; their dominant literary quality is the highly emotional dialogue, unconvincingly flamboyant and poetic in the case of the New York waterfront bums of *The Iceman Cometh* but more believable with the Irish acting family in *Long Day's Journey into Night.*

The many plays of this long and varied career, representing a variety of styles, techniques, and philosophies, nevertheless reflect one consistent aim: to present reality, the essential reality as O'Neill saw it, as honestly as he could and as totally as possible within the limitations of the stage technique. Early in the Twenties O'Neill stated that his aim was to "never be influenced by any consideration but one—'Is it the truth as I know it—or better still, feel it?' " His "feeling" of the truth changed considerably during his lifetime, and with it his dramatic style changed. But he constantly retained his unmistakably urgent quality of sincerity, the quality which set him sharply apart from most of his contemporaries and eventually won him a Nobel Prize and the mantle of greatness. O'Neill's consecrated quest for Truth was painstaking and tireless enough to overcome his natural shortcomings—his gaucheness of style, his philosophical naïveté—and carry him to his final destined position as America's greatest playwright.

LIFE: O'Neill was born into a theatrical family, and both profited and suffered from this fact. His parents, James O'Neill and the former Ella Quinlan, were professional actors; O'Neill himself was born in New York at a time (1888) when his parents were still active in the theatre. The life was an irregular one, a life in many ways unsuitable for a young child; in *Long Day's Journey into Night* O'Neill tacitly indicts his parents for the sentimental but heedless upbringing they gave their children. Both parents were Catholic, and O'Neill received his lower education at parochial boarding-schools. He spent a year at Princeton (1906-07) but was suspended; he left and went to work. In 1909 he married Kathleen Jenkins; a son was born, but the relationship ended in 1912. In 1910 he spent a year in the merchant marine as a common seaman; this experience gave him the material for a number of subsequent sea and waterfront plays. After a brief spell of tuberculosis he began to write plays; in 1914 he enrolled at Harvard to complete his broken education. His Harvard period was stimulating and rewarding; he was admitted to Professor Baker's famous Drama 47 class and became the most productive member and chief luminary of the group. In 1916 he became associated with the Provincetown Players, a group of actors and writers who ran a summer theatre in a Massachusetts resort. There O'Neill produced his first play, *Bound East for Cardiff.* The following year the Province-town group moved to New York City, where ten plays of O'Neill were performed between 1917 and 1920. His first major professional production, *Beyond the Horizon,* was presented at the Morosco Theatre in 1920 and won its author a Pulitzer Prize. For several years he was associated with the newly-formed Theatre Guild, which presented several of his plays. In 1936 his generally successful career was climaxed by the awarding of a Nobel Prize for Literature.

O'Neill was married three times, the last time to the actress Carlotta Monterey. In the later years of his life he suffered from Parkinson's disease, an ailment which caused a crippling tremor and made it almost impossible for him to hold a pen. He died of pneumonia in 1953.

CHIEF DRAMAS: *Beyond the Horizon* (1920) was O'Neill's first important full-length work. The two protagonists, Robert and Andrew Mayo, brothers on a New England farm, are markedly different in character. Andrew, strong, prosaic, and efficient, is a born farmer; his father confidently trains him to take over the farm after he is gone. Robert, sensitive and idealistic, detests the rude life of the farm; his long spells of illness and a year at college have set his imagination to working. He dreams continually of a romantic existence "beyond the horizon" he can see from the farmhouse window. In order to improve his health it is decided that an uncle, Captain Dick Scott, will take him on a voyage to distant parts of the world. Rob is excited by the prospect of traveling to the Orient and the South Seas; he looks forward to the imminent fulfillment of his romantic reveries. But on the night before his departure he and Ruth Atkins, fiancée of his brother Andrew, accidentally discover their love for each other. Swept away by his emotions, he gives up the sea voyage and promises to spend his life taking care of Ruth and her infirm mother. Andrew, bitter, impulsively goes to sea in Rob's place.

But through the "accident" of Rob's romantic infatuation for Ruth each of the main characters of the drama has been forced to betray his own nature. Rob, dreamy and inefficient, is a poor farmer, and under his management the farm rapidly degenerates. After his father dies the family becomes virtually bankrupt, and Rob's frustration makes him twisted and morbid. Andrew sees little adventure in the hard life at sea; what would have seemed romantic to Rob is only drudgery to him. Ruth, hard-working and loyal but insensitive, would have made an ideal wife for Andrew; tied to the idealistic Rob, she soon becomes dejected and slipshod. Rob and Ruth, however, find a certain consolation in their daughter Mary, who resembles Rob in personality.

When Andrew returns after three years his love for Ruth has faded, and he feels his place is not on the farm. He goes off to Argentina and becomes wealthy through trading and speculation. The paralyzed Mrs. Atkins, shrewish and petulant, makes life miserable for both Rob and Ruth. The disasters follow one after the other; their baby dies, and Rob's lungs become diseased. Still an idealistic dreamer, Rob looks ever forward to a better life "beyond the horizon," but his dream has become virtually a pathological delusion. In the final act Andrew returns from South America and finds a specialist to treat Rob; he confesses that through gambling in grain (i.e., betraying his true nature as a man of the soil) he has lost most of his fortune. The specialist gives Rob little chance to survive, but before he dies he tells Andrew and Ruth they must marry after he is gone. Then he drags himself out onto the road where, lying on the edge of a ditch, he can see the sun setting over the horizon he has never crossed.

The message of *Beyond the Horizon* is that each of us must follow out his own nature to its fulfillment; not to do so is to bring misery to one's self and to others. The main dramatic interest lies in the character of Rob: soft-minded, impractical, and indecisive, he nevertheless has a truly poetic sensitivity which might have brought him fame and happiness had he lived according to his nature.

The Emperor Jones (tragedy, 1920) centers around the character of Brutus Jones, an ex-Pullman porter who has become absolute dictator of a small Caribbean island. He rules ruthlessly and becomes constantly more obsessed with his own power. As the play opens the natives, driven to recklessness by his arrogance, rebel and take to the jungle; their voodoo war-drums boom with increasing tempo throughout the play. Jones, suddenly terrified, seeks to escape on foot from his castle. But the entire island seems to conspire to bring him to destruction: bushes seem to become animate, forms appear in the shadows, and the circle of drums closes in. Little by little Jones loses the rationality of the civilized man; he feels himself helplessly slipping back toward his primitive beginnings. At last losing his head, he runs wildly in a circle and wastes his ammunition firing at wraiths; at the end of the play even the silver bullet he has saved for himself has been fired. *The Emperor Jones* demonstrates the narrow line which separates the rational and civilized from the primitive and superstitious, even in civilized man.

Anna Christie (drama, 1921) opens as Chris Christopherson, a former sailor and now skipper of a New York coal barge, is awaiting a reunion with his daughter Anna, whom he has not seen since she was a child. Since the death of the mother the girl has lived with relatives on a Minnesota farm and later, as Chris thinks, as a nurse in St. Paul. When Anna appears on the scene it develops that, through poverty and boredom, she has fallen into a life of sin. She has been no ordinary prostitute, however; amid all her transgressions she has maintained an inward purity. Upon meeting, father and daughter are awkward, yet tender toward each other; both are anxious to conceal their unsavory pasts. Chris resolves to give up the low life he has been leading in taverns and saloons and devote his time to taking care of his daughter. The two take up housekeeping on the barge, and for a time both seem to find a new purpose in life. Then Mat Burke, a shipwrecked sailor, comes aboard the barge. With his lively Irish spirit he begins flattering Anna, and soon the two are in love. When Chris learns of this he is enraged; he hates the sea to which he has sacrificed his life and will have nothing to do with sailors. Now

the "old davil sea" is threatening to steal his daughter from him and
make her life miserable as that of his own wife—Anna's mother—
was.

Anna, however, still retains her sense of honor in spite of the
degradation she has been through. She feels her life has made her
unworthy to marry Burke, and in spite of her love she confesses
her past to him. Burke is enraged, charging he has been tricked; but
Chris now demands that he marry her. In the last act both men, their
ideals shattered by Anna's confession, decide to go back to sea again;
unknown to each other, they both sign on the same ship. But Anna,
purified in Burke's love, swears her old life is behind her and that
she will always be true to him. They decide to be married, and Chris
blesses the union. Chris and Burke, having signed articles, must still
go to sea; the "old davil" in its sinister way has caught them anyhow.
But Anna has been morally regenerated, and the three are friends;
the play ends on an optimistic note. The chief interest in this drama
lies in the psychological contrast between the three principals and in
Anna's moral crisis and eventual regeneration.

The Hairy Ape (drama, 1922) opens as Yank, a powerful and
illiterate stoker on an ocean liner, is boasting and ranting to his ship-
mates in the forecastle. Yank, all muscle and little mind, is a personification of brute energy, of the vigorous animal element in human
nature. Although his mates complain of their back-breaking and ill-
paid work in the stokehold, Yank exults in it and sets a dizzy pace
for the others. He knows that "he makes it go;" not only the ship,
but the whole civilized world is driven by energy supplied by him and
his fellows. He scorns religion, home, bourgeois standards, everything
but his satisfaction in his brute labor.

In the second act, however, a doubt is planted in his mind through
an encounter with a passenger on the ship, Miss Mildred Douglas.
Mildred, whose capitalist father owns the ship along with most of
the steel business of the world, is bored with her sheltered and artificial existence; she has tried to find escape in social work, but this
has proved synthetic and unrewarding. Aboard the ship she feels a
desire to see how "the other half"—the stokers in the fireroom—live.
Through her father's prestige she persuades an officer to take her
below. Yank, in the midst of one of his exultant and profane tirades,
is startled to see her appear suddenly before him. For her part

Mildred is terrified by the glimpse of real life she has seen; it is too powerful for her. She gasps in horror and cries to be taken away. This encounter has a profound effect on Yank. He tries to recapture his former exultation in his strength, but he cannot forget that another human being has seen him as a horrible and disgusting beast. Ashore in New York, he sets out to determine just what his place in the universe is. He is obsessed with a desire to find some class, some group, to which he can "belong." Snubbed by Fifth Avenue church-goers, he then rejects in turn the insidious Marxist temptations of his communist shipmate Long; he can feel no class hatred for the rich whose existence seems to him to lie in another universe. He tries to join the I.W.W., but is thrownout as a suspected provocateur when he proposes to blow up the capitalistic world with dynamite; again he does not "belong." In the final scene he visits the zoo and liberates a gorilla, which he hopes will accept him as a companion since humanity has rejected him. But the gorilla crushes him and runs away; Yank, dying, creeps into the empty cage, symbolically accepting the status of a caged and frustrated animal which he has actually been from the beginning.

Specifically a personification of brute energy, Yank is in a broader sense of symbol of mankind itself. Inexorably tied to his animal origin, man still aspires toward a higher existence; his basic search is for a realm to which he can "belong." Yank, failing to find this home in the higher regions, attempts to descend into the animal world. The unthinking brutes, however, destroy him as an interloper. Man is forever condemned to live an existence midway between the animal and the divine.

Desire Under the Elms (tragedy, 1924) is a violent drama of conflicting passions, partly Freudian and partly classic Greek in mood. The plot superficially resembles the Theseus-Hippolytus-Phaedra story as it is found in the dramas of Euripides and Racine; O'Neill transfers the basic situation to a New England farm in the period around 1850. Ephraim Cabot, a mean and avaricious New England farmer, takes a third wife, the young Abbie Putnam. His two elder sons, Simeon and Peter, despair of ever inheriting the farm and depart for California, selling their interest in the inheritance to their half-brother Eben, son of old Ephraim's gentle second wife. The young Abbie proves to be as avaricious and conniving as the family she has joined; she deliberately seduces Eben in an effort to produce an heir who will inherit the farm for her so that Ephraim's other sons will not get it. After the child is born Ephraim signs over the inheritance rights to it, and Eben, angered, confesses the child's illegitimacy to his father. Meanwhile Abbie has inadvertently and helplessly fallen in love with Eben; she is at the mercy of her passion. When Eben declares that he wishes the child were dead, she strangles it as a proof of her devotion. Eben goes for the police. But he is now emotionally involved with Abbie himself, and realizes he cannot live without her; he admits complicity in the crime and is arrested with her.

This drama, originally produced by the Provincetown Playhouse in Greenwich Village, was later moved to a Broadway theatre and went on to become a perennial road-show success. From a literary point of view *Desire Under the Elms* is interesting as a predecessor to the more important *Mourning Becomes Electra:* both plays use the same technique of transferring classic myth-situations into a modern quasi-Freudian setting.

The Great God Brown (drama, 1926) is a remarkable experiment in the problem of multiple personality, another subject which O'Neill derived from modern psychology. The two chief characters are William A. Brown, symbolizing the soulless and materialistic modern man, and his friend Dion Anthony (suggesting "Dionysus" plus "Saint Anthony"), a creative and pagan artist-type, unhappy and out of place in modern civilization. The dramatic development of the play depends heavily on the device of masks, which O'Neill uses to symbolize the outward and superficial aspects of personality and which the characters frequently remove or change. Dion and Brown are partners in a building enterprise, and Dion is naturally the creative half of the partnership. Dion's wife Margaret (who represents conventional married love) imagines that she loves him, but actually loves only his mask, which he wears to protect his sensitive inner nature from intrusion. Dion finds his insipidly virtuous wife unsatisfying, and consoles himself with Cybel, a prostitute (an "earth-mother" figure or symbol of elemental physical love). When Dion, drained of his creative imagination by Brown, weakens and dies, Brown takes possession of his mask and passes himself off as Margaret's husband. For a while he manages to fill both identities, but after a while he is accused (as Dion) of his own murder; he flees and is shot down by a police volley. Before he dies he is told by Cybel that "there is only love;" after he is dead she tells the audience "Always spring comes again bearing life." This simple and rather vague paganistic hedonism, however, does not express the real importance of *The Great God Brown* as a play; it is its radical expressionistic technique and its original approach to characterization that mark the drama as an important landmark in the American theatre.

Lazarus Laughed (drama, 1927) is similar in mood and theme but is even more radical in technique. Lazarus, the Biblical figure who was raised by Christ from the dead, returns to his people affirming the message he has learned through his unique experience: "There is only laughter! Fear is no more! Death is dead!" Eventually taken to Rome, Lazarus is killed along with his wife Miriam, assuring his followers to the end that "There is no death." In the final scene even his murderer, the mad emperor Caligula, is convinced of his message, and is grief-stricken at the thought, "I killed him and I proved there is death!" This remarkable play, written in a form of free verse, was produced by the Pasadena Playhouse in 1928 and has since been performed only occasionally by amateur and experimental groups; its extremely expressionistic form and its iconoclastic theme make it impractical for commercial production.

Strange Interlude (drama, 1928) is an ambitious work, consisting of nine acts and taking over four hours to play. In addition it uses experimental techniques never before attempted on the modern stage. Nina Leeds, the central character, is a personification of the female productive instinct ("God the Mother"), and the conflicts of the play arise out of the characters' efforts to find outlets for their erotic and reproductive impulses.

The nine acts, each consisting of a single scene, extend over a wide period in time. In the first act Nina, daughter of a puritanical professor, has become morbid over the death of her fiancé Gordon Shaw in the First World War. Gordon was a superb athlete and universally admired, yet Nina's father, secretly jealous, had prevented their marriage until after Gordon had gone overseas. Now Nina feels cheated of her natural satisfaction of reproduction. Also present is Charlie Marsden, a family friend and novelist who is secretly in love with Nina; she treats him with a playful condescension, calling him "good old Charlie." At the end of the act Nina, obsessed with the memory of her dead lover, departs to become a nurse in a hospital for invalid soldiers.

In Act II Professor Leeds has died, and Marsden, still secretly lustful toward Nina, awaits her return. But she enters with Sam Evans, a college friend of Gordon, a weak and immature youth who worships the memory of his more virile dead classmate. Sam, thinking of Marsden as Nina's "guardian" now that her father is dead, asks for her hand in marriage. Next enters Ned Darrell, doctor in the hospital where Nina works; he is a cool and competent scientist who prides himself on his objective attitude. He hints that Nina has been promiscuous with the wounded soldiers in the hospital out of a subconscious desire to atone for Gordon, and suggests a remedy in a marriage with Evans. Marsden agrees to help arrange the marriage.

In Act III Sam Evans and Nina are married and visiting Sam's mother; Nina is exultant to learn she is pregnant. But Mrs. Evans warns her that insanity is congenital in the Evans family; the baby must never be allowed to come to life. In Act IV Nina, still obsessed with a desire for a child, begs Darrell to provide her with one. This he agrees to do as a "prescription" which he, as her doctor, orders for her.

In Act V Nina's child by Darrell has been born and named Gordon in honor of the dead hero. But the afternoons of love with Darrell have had their effect: the two have become infatuated with each other in spite of Darrell's pose of scientific objectivity. Darrell, aghast at the results of his "experiment," sails for Europe. In Act VI Nina is happy with her baby, but Marsden, jealous, upsets her by reporting Darrell's philandering in Europe. Evans, proud of "his" child, is working hard and is on his way to success. Later in the act Ned Darrell returns from Europe and Nina sees he is still in love with her; she exults over her possession of three men, her husband Sam, the "father" Charlie, and the lover Ned.

Act VII takes place nearly eleven years later. Gordon quarrels bitterly with Darrell, whom he subconsciously realizes to be his mother's lover. Marsden, devoted to his own aged mother, is unhappy and ineffectual. Act VIII, ten years later, shows Gordon as a college senior. The rest of the characters, along with Gordon's fiancée Madeline Arnold, have gathered on the yacht to watch him row in a regatta.

All now realize that Gordon is a sort of reincarnation of the dead Gordon Shaw; thus Nina and Sam root for him to win but Darrell and Marsden, who have always resented the ghost of Shaw which has hung over Nina's life, hope young Gordon's boat will lose. Gordon wins, but Sam becomes so excited that he suffers a heart attack. In Act IX Sam has died. Nina is bitter that Madeline is taking her son from her. But before the act ends the characters arrive at something like contentment. Darrell, reconciled with his illegitimate son Gordon, agrees with Nina not to reveal the secret of the boy's birth; and Nina, her passions now dead, turns to a comfortable marriage with her old suitor Marsden. She concludes that the middle years of life, the years of passion, frustration, and bitterness, are only a "strange interlude" between the happiness of childhood and the serenity of old age.

The chief technical device of *Strange Interlude* is the "interior monologue" or spoken psychological aside, by which O'Neill attempts to reveal the inner thoughts of his characters. In the printed version of the play these "asides" are indented and set in smaller type than the outward dialogue. Unlike the asides of Shakespearean drama, O'Neill's are intended as totally unspoken, in some cases subconscious, expressions; they are interspersed with ordinary dialogue to indicate the contrast, often ironic, between spoken and unspoken thoughts.

The central figure of the play is undoubtedly Nina. Happy in her youth, she spends the middle years of her life as a tormented instrument of the reproductive instinct that lives within her; she is simultaneously virgin, priestess, mother, prostitute, and wife. More powerful than the men around her, she demands the love of all of them simultaneously. Yet this power brings her little happiness; it is only when her passions die with age that she finds contentment in marriage with the placid and "sexless" Charlie. The effectiveness of the play lies in its technical originality and in the powerful characterization of Nina; the main defect is O'Neill's tendency toward sentimental and mawkish inner dialogue.

Mourning Becomes Electra (tragic trilogy, 1931) is usually considered O'Neill's most important work. The story is based on the Agamemnon myth as found in Aeschylus' *Oresteia* trilogy, but the classic situation is bodily transferred to a modern setting and details of the plot are altered to conform to the new environment. The clan of the Atrides are reincarnated in the Mannons, the leading family in a small American town at the close of the Civil War.

In Part I of the trilogy Christine Mannon (representing Clytemnestra) awaits the homecoming of her husband Ezra (Agamemnon) from the war; during his absence she engaged in an illicit affair with a relative, the sea-captain Adam Brant (Aegisthus). Her daughter Lavinia (Electra), fervently loyal to her father, writes to him and to her brother Orin (Orestes) hinting to them of Christine's infidelity. When she warns her mother that Ezra is soon to return and that she must break with Adam, Christine resolves to murder Ezra and flee with her lover. On the night of Ezra's return Lavinia discovers the poison, and when Ezra dies she guesses the truth and secretly vows revenge.

In Part II Orin comes home from his father's funeral. Gentle and sensitive by nature, he has always been close to his mother; now he becomes fiercely jealous of her relations with Adam. His mother tries to distract him by suggesting a marriage with a neighbor, Hazel Niles. But Orin, his jealousy prodded by Lavinia, is not to be deterred; he traces Christine and Adam to a rendezvous on the latter's ship and kills Adam with a revolver. Stricken with grief, horror, and shame, Christine commits suicide as atonement for her guilt.

In Part III Lavinia and Orin depart on a long sea voyage which they hope will help them forget the horrible incidents of the past. But the family tendencies toward suspicion, jealousy, and incest persist; Lavinia, growing into her maturity, comes to resemble her mother, and Orin develops an almost pathological jealousy toward her. He threatens to reveal the details of Adam's death if Lavinia marries Peter Niles, her fiancé. Then he gradually begins to comprehend that his affection for his sister is not a normal one; horrified at his guilt, he takes his own life. Eventually the family curse overtakes Lavinia too; she frightens her fiancé away through the impetuous and perverted violence of her passion. Then, gradually growing more morbid and withdrawn, she shuts herself up in the deserted mansion to live out the rest of her days in solitude.

This drama represents an ambitious attempt to recast the Greek tragedy into the terms of modern psychology, i.e., to convey the modern psychological equivalent of the Greek concept of fate. For the destiny of Greek tragedy is substituted the determinism of blood and heredity. Lavinia, the central character, comes to destruction basically through the bad blood bequeathed her by her father, but this hereditary taint operates through the medium of psychological obsessions and fixations which make her unfit for normal life.

Long Day's Journey into Night (drama, published 1956) is a long-awaited posthumous play written by O'Neill in 1940 and withheld from the public for many years because of the delicate nature of its subject matter—the bitter domestic conflicts of O'Neill's own family. The chief characters are James Tyrone, an aging Irish-American actor; his wife Mary; James Jr. ("Jamie"), their elder son, and Edmund (based on the character of the author himself), the younger brother. The action adheres close to the classic unities, taking place on a single day in 1912 and confining itself entirely to the living room of the Tyrones' summer home. The play opens with the family conducting what is evidently a typical good-humored Irish family quarrel, but as the action proceeds the real truth is revealed: that the family is built on rottenness and deceit, and is rapidly degenerating. Mary, who as a girl was religiously inclined and dreamed of becoming a nun, regrets the irregular life of her marriage with Tyrone and longs for a decent and conventional home; through her bitterness she has gradually become a morphine addict. Jamie is a drunkard and libertine who out of sheer cynicism has encouraged his younger brother to follow in his footsteps, and Edmund, a would-be writer, is seriously ill from a combination of consumption and over-drinking. Tyrone, the father, is gradually revealed to be a histrionic and self-dramatizing windbag dominated by a single obsession: to acquire property and assure the security of his old age. His avarice has actually ruined the lives of all the others; when Edmund was born he economized on a cheap doctor for his wife, and it was this doctor who started her on the drug habit. Likewise his reluctance to spend money on doctors for Edmund has led his son into a serious illness. Yet this wreck of a family, each member continually deceiving and undermining the others, is held together by a fierce irrational affection which is stronger than their hatred; in their clearer and saner moments they realize their love for each other and regret their hasty and cruel outbursts. As the play ends, Mary, who had temporarily been considered cured, relapses hopelessly into a narcotic insanity again, unable to comprehend that her son is probably dying of tuberculosis.

Long Day's Journey was evidently conceived by O'Neill as part of an involved cycle of plays which in their entirety were to comprise a sort of dramatic autobiography. Two other plays fit into this cycle of material: *The Iceman Cometh* (1946) and *A Moon for the Misbegotten* (1952). The first of these, set in a sordid New York bar and peopled with characters reminiscent of the philosophical bums of Gorky's *The Lower Depths,* achieved a modest success on Broadway; the other is a study of the final disintegration of James Tyrone, Jr., or Jamie.

ELMER RICE (born 1892)

Rice is a prolific playwright who has written in an impressive variety of styles, ranging from radical experimentalism to the conventional form of the murder mystery. He owes his position as a major dramatist, however, chiefly to two plays written during the Twenties: *The Adding Machine* (1923), one of the first expressionistic dramas to be successfully produced on the American stage, and *Street Scene* (1929), a naturalistic-sociological study of the slums which brought him his greatest popular success. Rice is basically an idealist, an author with a deep social consciousness who has, as Clark puts it, "for thirty years exemplified the American playwright's concern with contemporary life and social problems." Yet he is at the same time a competent professional writer, capable of turning out an ingenious mystery play (*On Trial, Cock Robin*) or an amusing fantastic comedy *(Dream Girl, See Naples and Die)* almost on demand.

Throughout his career Rice was preoccupied with questions of theatrical technique, particularly of construction. He abandoned realism to experiment with the disconnected symbolism of the German expressionists in *The Adding Machine* and *The Subway;* in *Street Scene* he utilized the complex patchwork construction of such novels as Dos Passos' *Manhattan Transfer,* in which a large number of characters living in the same district are presented and the interrelationships of their lives gradually revealed. *On Trial,* his first successful play, was also one of the first modern dramas to be built around the flashback technique, a device which later became the stock-in-trade of the crime play. Neither a skilled stylist nor a profound thinker, Rice is at his best in solving intricate problems of plot, construction, and dramatic presentation.

LIFE: Elmer Rice (pseud. of Elmer Reizenstein) was born in New York City in 1892. After attending high school he went to work as a law clerk, meanwhile studying law in night school. He received his LL.B. from New York Law School in 1912, but never practiced. By this time determined to become a playwright, he wrote his first play and was surprised when it was immediately accepted; *On Trial* was produced in 1914 and launched him on a successful career as a writer. His subsequent efforts during the next ten years were less successful, however; between 1914 and 1923 he had only three plays produced, one of these (*The Iron Cross*) by a small experimental group. The other two plays from this period, *For the Defence* (1919) and *Wake Up, Jonathan!* (1921), were commercial ventures and unremarkable in literary quality. In 1923, however, the Theatre Guild produced *The Adding Machine,* which created a considerable sensation and won Rice a place as one of America's leading young playwrights. *Street Scene* (1929) was his greatest popular success; it won a Pulitzer Prize and was made into an outstanding motion picture.

Rice's career has been marked by a definite and consistent liberalism in politics. In 1936 he served briefly as a regional director of the Federal Theatre Project, but resigned in protest against alleged political censorship of the group's productions. Several of his plays from the Thirties are virtually political pamphlets: *We the People* (1933) is an angry and complex indictment of capitalistic society along socialist-Marxist lines, and *Judgment Day* (1934) is a warning, one of the first to appear in American literature, against the menace of fascism. In 1951 he risked his reputation and career to come to the defense of certain actors whose alleged left-wing associations were causing them to lose jobs in radio and television, arguing that he had always opposed political censorship of the arts in totalitarian countries like the Soviet Union and would continue to oppose it when it occurred in the United States.

Rice has been married twice, the first time to Hazel Levy (1915) and second, after a divorce, to the actress Betty Field (1942). After living most of his life in New York City, Rice has spent the recent years with his family on a Connecticut farm.

CHIEF WORKS: *The Adding Machine* (drama, 1923) is a ruthlessly satirical portrait of Mr. Zero, a white-collar nonentity hopelessly submerged in the mass of humanity in a large modern city. Employed for twenty-five years in a dull and futureless job as an accountant, Zero is bored with his henpecking wife and their banal friends (who have numbers, from one to six, instead of names) but lacks the character to break out of his monotony. He flirts briefly with a prostitute who lives in the same building, but when his wife discovers this he surrenders to her will and betrays the girl to the police; she is sent to prison for six months. He also considers an affair with Daisy Diana Dorothea Devore, a rather unattractive fellow-worker in his office, but lacks the initiative to do anything about this either. Dreaming idly of the day the Boss will reward him by elevating him to a high position in the office, he is rudely awakened when the Boss instead fires him to make way for a mechanical adding machine. In a temporary fit of insanity Zero murders the Boss and is executed for the crime. Coming to himself in the Elysian Fields, he finds there Daisy, who has committed suicide in order to be with him, and meets a new friend, Shrdlu, a proofreader who has murdered his mother and now yearns for punishment in a conventional hell—a punishment which to his disappointment is not forthcoming. Zero, in a conversation with Daisy, learns that she has loved him for many years and regrets the opportunities he has passed up in life. Then, in Scene Seven, in an interview with Charles, a kind of heavenly bureaucrat, Zero learns that there is no permanent repose even in death and that he is soon to be reincarnated as a super-nonentity in a new super-society. He learns, in fact, that he is the archetypical slave-soul, who has been reborn all through history as slave, serf, and employee. When he understands this horrible truth Zero at first refuses to be born again, but Charles easily turns his head by convincing him that a voluptuous girl named Hope awaits him in the life (i.e., an illusory hope keeps the nonentities and slaves of the world content with their lot). The third scene of the six which form this play is an amusing satire on lower-middle-class social life, a conversation between Zero and his friends in which every cliché and banality of the bourgeoisie is parroted in singsong fashion. *The Adding Machine* owes much to the school of continental expressionism; plays which it particularly resembles are Kaiser's *From Morn to Midnight,* written in 1916 and produced in America by the Theatre Guild the year before Rice wrote his play, and Capek's *R.U.R.*

Street Scene (drama, 1929) is a panorama of the daily life in a single block in the New York slums. The characters are carefully chosen to represent various ingredients of the New York population. The chief of these are Abraham Kaplan, a pessimistic and philosophical old Jewish Marxist; his son Samuel, a bitter and somewhat weak-charactered young intellectual; his daughter Shirley; Rose Maurrant, an Irish girl in love with Sam; her mother Anna, and her father Frank; and Filippo Fiorentino, a happy-go-lucky Italian immigrant, and his German wife Greta. The action depicts a typical day in the lives of these people and their neighbors, from an evening in June until the afternoon of the following day. The incidents of the day form a complex pattern; the central incident is the murder of Mrs. Maurrant and her lover Steve Sankey by Maurrant, who surprises the pair in the tryst. This tragedy momentarily shocks the neighborhood, but life soon resumes its normal pace. Rose tells Sam that she can never marry him now, since her mother's death and her father's arrest have left her with sole responsibility for her brother Willie, who is fast turning into a young hoodlum. Meanwhile life goes on; a Mrs. Buchanan who lives in the same building gives birth to a baby, and a new family moves into the rooms vacated by the Maurrants.

Street Scene is more than a mere exposé of slum conditions like Kingsley's *Dead End;* it penetrates further into the individual psychologies of its characters, and it attempts a symbolic contrast between the various social and racial types found in a large American city. It concludes honestly and objectively and offers no panacea for the slum problem; old Kaplan's dogmatic Marxism and Fiorentino's blithe hedonism are presented as facets of their characters rather than as solutions of the misery and viciousness of the slum. *Street Scene,* which ran for over six hundred performances on Broadway, was adapted in 1947 as an opera with music by Kurt Weill and lyrics by Langston Hughes.

SIDNEY HOWARD (1891-1939)

Sidney Howard is the direct literary descendant of Clyde Fitch, a dramatist who builds his conflict out of the psychological contrast between social types. Lacking a strong strain of originality, he formed his style out of a variety of influences: the contemporary French drama, the innovations of the pre-1920 American realists (especially Fitch), and the technical advice he received from George Pierce Baker in the famous "47 Workshop" at Harvard. It is symptomatic of his lack of originality that many of his best-known plays were adaptations from the French (e.g., *The Late Christopher Bean*) or from novels (e.g., *Dodsworth*); but it speaks for his skill as a dramatist that the majority of his plays achieved both popular and critical success on the New York stage.

In spite of his interest in the French drama, Howard is a thoroughly American playwright. He usually (but not always) transferred his European adaptations into an American setting, and he shows a skillful mastery of contemporary American idiom and manners. Yet the quality of American culture which particularly fascinates him is its diversity, specifically its racial minorities. His best-known plays are based on the manners of such minorities (*They Knew What They Wanted*) or regional cultures like that of small-town New England (*The Late Christopher Bean*). In spite of his thorough-going American quality Howard does not beat the drum for the "American Way of Life" in the conventional sense, neither is he a patriot as this term is ordinarily understood. He attacked the great American sacred cow of Motherhood in *The Silver Cord,* and in *The Ghost of Yankee Doodle,* his last play to be produced on Broadway during his lifetime, he dramatized a liberal's struggle against a fanatically intolerant nationalism. Yet he is basically conservative in temperament, accepting the sounder standards of his culture and avoiding the complete rejection of middle-class Americanism of such individualistic liberals as Saroyan and Steinbeck. Howard is above all a competent playwright and a careful student of American manners, the dramatic equivalent of such a novelist as J. P. Marquand. His contribution to the American theatre was not a spectacular one, but he was a skilled craftsman, and he left the theatre more sophisticated and more mature than he found it.

LIFE: Sidney Howard was born in 1891 in Oakland, California, the son of a steamship executive and a mother who was a trained musician. The contrast in his parents is significant; much of his work is concerned with the contrast between the "practical mind" and the artistic temperament. His father, however, was an avid enthusiast for culture, and the young Sidney's education was impressive; he was taken to Italy at twelve and had visited Europe twice by the time he was seventeen. Graduating from the University of California in 1915, he went on to Harvard to study playwriting under Professor George Pierce Baker. During the First World War he served in an ambulance outfit on the Western Front and in the Balkans, and was later commissioned as an aviator. After the war he worked briefly for a series of magazines including *The New Republic* and the old *Life* before he turned definitely to a dramatic career. His first play, a poetic melodrama of the Italian Renaissance entitled *Swords,* was produced in New York in 1921. A wide success, however, came to him only with *They Knew What They Wanted,* which was produced by the Theatre Guild in 1924 and won Howard a Pulitzer Prize the following year. The rest of his career was generally successful. He worked intermittently in Hollywood on screen adaptations, some of them from his own plays (*The Silver Cord, Christopher Bean*), and in addition adapted several novels for the stage. A marriage with the actress Clare Eames in 1921 ended in divorce in 1930; Howard's *Half Gods* is a drama of married life influenced by his own bitter experience with marriage. His death in 1939 on his Massachusetts farm was due to a tractor accident; the tragedy occurred at the height of his creativity, and it was known that he was working on at least two new plays at the time of his death.

CHIEF WORKS: *They Knew What They Wanted* (drama, 1924) is a somewhat sentimental melodrama of the marriage of an aging Italian wine-grower to a waitress. Tony Patucci, immigrant owner of a grape-farm in the Napa Valley of California, notices the young waitress Amy in a San Francisco restaurant and later courts her by mail, sending her instead of his own picture a photograph of his handsome young hired man Joe, a migrant worker and former I.W.W. agitator. Amy accepts; when she arrives she is indignant at the deception, but decides to marry Tony anyhow. The wedding takes place even though Tony, excited over her arrival, breaks both legs in an accident while going to meet her at the station. On her wedding night she is seduced by Joe, although both Amy and Joe immediately regret this betrayal of their friend Tony. When she later becomes pregnant she and Joe, fearing Tony's wrath, decide to run away together, although by this time they do not love each other. But when Tony hears of the baby he conquers his rage and begs her to stand by him, offering to accept the child as his own. At the end of the play each character has gotten what he wanted: Joe a temporary haven from the world and a temporary love for Amy, Amy a home of her own and a husband to provide her with security, and Tony a young wife and a child to bear his name. Morality and romantic love are less important than happiness, which comes from the satisfaction of basic biological needs. Other important characters are the priest Father McKee and the young Doctor, who conduct a long argument (religion vs. science) which extends through the play but comes to no conclusion. The main interest of the play, however, lies in the character of Tony: exuberant, spontaneous, and essentially pagan, a magnificent Latin hedonist exiled in a land of reserved Anglo-Saxons.

The Silver Cord (drama, 1926) is a bitter portrait of a pathologically possessive mother. The widowed Mrs. Phelps, smothering her two sons under a neurotically protective love, resolves to keep them forever little boys and to prevent them from marrying and thus escaping from her. The elder, David, goes off to Heidelberg to study architecture; there, free from his mother's influence, he marries Christina, a brilliant young research biologist. When the couple return to visit Mrs. Phelps they find that the younger son, Robert (Robin) has just become engaged to the charming young Hester. Mrs. Phelps immediately plots to frustrate Christina's career in a New York laboratory by keeping David at home, and sets Robert against Hester so effectively that the characterless younger brother breaks off the engagement while Hester is still a guest under the roof. Hester flees hysterically and is almost drowned in a hole in a frozen pond, while Mrs. Phelps calls from the house to warn her sons, who have gone to Hester's rescue, against catching cold in the winter air. This incident brings to a head the struggle between Mrs. Phelps and the two younger women, and Christina and David quarrel bitterly. David, forced to choose between mother and wife, chooses Christina, and the young couple go off together with the bitter and broken-hearted Hester. Robert, the weaker, stays behind, regressed completely into childhood and able to reply only, "Yes, Mother," to Mrs. Phelps' neurotic effusions of maternal love.

The Late Christopher Bean (comedy, 1932) is an adaptation based on René Fauchois' *Prenez Garde à la Peinture*. The young painter Christopher Bean has died poor and unknown in a small Massachusetts town, leaving most of his paintings in the house of the local Dr. Haggett. Ten years later, as the play opens, Bean is "discovered" by art critics, and a collection of his letters describing the missing paintings is published in *The Atlantic Monthly*. Immediately a succession of New Yorkers descend on the crusty but somewhat naive Dr. Haggett: an unscrupulous art dealer, Tallant, an expert forger and art speculator, and Maxwell Davenport, a respected art critic. The Doctor, who desperately needs money to send his two daughters to Florida so his wife can find husbands for them, is first tricked out of two of Bean's paintings by Tallant and then discovers that the rest have apparently been burned up as junk. Then a complication is revealed: Bean, it seems, was in love with Haggett's cook-and-maid, a stubborn young woman named Abby, and had painted a portrait of her which is now acclaimed as a masterpiece. The Haggett family tries desperately to trick Abby out of the painting, which is worth many thousands of dollars, but she clings to it out of a tenacious sentimentalism. Then seventeen more Bean canvases are unearthed. For a time the Haggett family joyously imagines itself to be rich, but then comes disillusionment: Abby reveals that she was secretly married to Bean, and thus the paintings are her property. A sub-plot describes the romance of Dr. Haggett's daughter Susan with a local paperhanger named Warren Creamer, who was trained by Bean as a painter and now shows signs of talent himself. The central interest of this comedy lies in the local color of the New England setting and in the eccentric Yankee characters of the Haggett family and their maid, thrown sharply into contrast by the arrival of the trio of effete New Yorkers.

Alien Corn (drama, 1933) is a play built thematically around two contrasts: American culture vs. Viennese culture, and the artist personality vs. the "Babbitt." The Viennese musician Ottokar Brandt and his pianist daughter Elsa come to the small Conway College for Women in the Middle West where Elsa has procured a job as a teacher. The society of the small town and the college faculty is dull and plebeian, however, and Brandt and his daughter long to return to Vienna. Elsa is torn between her sense of duty, which urges her to retain her teaching job to provide for her crippled father, and her artistic ambition, which makes her long to return to Vienna to study for a concert career. Meanwhile she falls in love with Harry Conway, the wealthy president and patron of the college; and Julian Varda-man, a young English instructor, falls in love with her. The climax of the drama comes when a joint concert is arranged for Elsa and Muriel Conway, wife of Harry Conway and an incompetent amateur soprano. The idea of the concert is to raise money to send Elsa back to Europe, but the young girl is revolted by Mrs. Conway's vulgarity and lack of talent, and refuses to go through with the plan. When she promotes and stages a recital of her own, Mrs Conway has her fired. Julian, who has burned his bridges behind him out of love for Elsa, commits suicide when he realizes she loves Conway; but Elsa rejects Conway's offer of marriage and security. At the end of the play, when a policeman asks her for her home address, she replies, "Vienna." She has chosen freedom instead of security, and art instead of a "normal" family life.

This drama is dominated by the character, not of Elsa, but of her irascible and temperamental father, intended by Howard as an epitome of the European artistic personality. The characterization is rather overdrawn, however, and the picture of American college life is some-what naive and stereotyped. The play owed much of the success of its Broadway run to Katharine Cornell, who played Elsa competently and convincingly and managed to overcome the characterization faults which are inherent in the drama.

PHILIP BARRY (1896-1949)

Most critics tend to view Barry as a sort of an American Noel Coward; typical terms applied to him are "dramatist of the best people" (Mersand) and "a writer of suave entertaining comedies about the well-bred, the well-to-do, the sophisticated" (Barrett Clark). This well describes the style of his light comedies, from *The Animal Kingdom* to *The Philadelphia Story* and *Paris Bound*. Another group of his dramas, however, are markedly different: the experimental plays including *White Wings, Hotel Universe, Tomorrow and To-morrow,* and *Here Come the Clowns*. These four plays differ widely in subject matter and profundity, but they share a common technique, which is at the bottom anti-realistic: they are symbolic, allegorical, and stylized, perhaps influenced by Continental expressionism but in any case directly opposed to the tradition of naturalism. In these plays Barry resembles Maeterlinck, Pirandello, and O'Neill more than he does Noel Coward or Sidney Howard. Although Barry's light comedies won him box-office success, it is undoubtedly this second group f plays upon which his permanent reputation must rest.

Barry is a Catholic of Irish extraction, and there is a definite eligious tendency running through his work. *Paris Bound* is an attack on divorce, and *John* and *Tomorrow and Tomorrow* adapt Biblical themes; the majority of his plays conclude on a note of moral conservatism. Occasionally, the morality is unconventional; in *The Animal Kingdom* the hero abandons his legal wife to return to his mistress, who he feels is his true mate in the biological and emotional sense. Barry is by no means an "official" Catholic dramatist as, for example, Mauriac and Chesterton are Catholic novelists; his point of view is individualistic and often iconoclastic. His main contribution to the development of the American theatre lies, not in his ideas, but in his revolt against realism, his original and highly effective use of whimsy, symbol, and fantasy for stage effect.

LIFE: Philip Barry was born in Rochester, New York in 1896 of Irish-American parents; his father was an immigrant who had come to America at the age of ten. Barry used his Irish-Catholic background in several plays, especially in *The Joyous Season* (1933) which describes a second-generation Irish family in Boston. Educated at Yale, he embarked first upon a diplomatic career, serving as a clerk in the Department of State in Washington and then as an attaché in the American Embassy in London. He found this boring, however, and in 1919 he enrolled at Harvard to study playwriting in George Pierce Baker's "47 Workshop." He spent two years under Baker, writing a number of plays and learning every aspect of theatre work from acting to scene-shifting. His first commercial production was *You and I* (1922), a comedy which won the Harvard Prize and ran for over six months on Broadway. The series of light comedies which followed it were generally successful, although *White Wings,* his first really original play, ran only three weeks in 1927. *Paris Bound,* produced the same year, was another box-office success, and established Barry in the public mind as the leading American writer of sophisticated comedy. The 1930 Theatre Guild production of *Hotel Universe* won him critical praise as well, and thenceforth he was considered among the more important American dramatists. His last box-office success was *The Philadelphia Story* in 1939; his subsequent plays were "something less than smash hits." Married in 1922 to Ellen Semple, he lived during much of his career in Florida; both he and his wife were Roman Catholics. Barry died of a heart attack in his New York apartment in December, 1949.

CHIEF WORKS: *White Wings* (drama, 1926) is a light fantasy that might have been written by G. K. Chesterton or the Irish poet James Stephens. The four acts of the play cover the years between 1895 and 1915; the theme is the passing of the horse and the triumph of the automobile. The subject, however, serves only as an excuse for an amusing parody of the usual sociological drama. Archie Inch, the hero, is the last of a long line of proud "White Wings" or city street-cleaners whose profession depends on the existence of the horse. He is in love with Mary Todd, but cannot marry her because her father is the inventor of the automobile, the arch-enemy of his clan. Mary, who really loves Archie, flirts sporadically with Kit Canari, a friend of Archie who gets in on the ground floor of automobilism and becomes a garage owner. Meanwhile the Inch family, including Archie's father and the dignified old Major Inch, his grandfather, steadily decline through their stubborn adherence to the obsolete tradition of the horse. When Archie's mother dies she makes him promis never to abandon his profession as a White Wing as long as a singl horse remains in the city. By 1915 there is only one horse left: Jo eph, a whimsical cab-horse owned by the philosophical cabby Herbert. Mary shoots Joseph with a revolver, and Major Inch dies quietly at the same instant; the age of horses is over. Archie and Mary are uni ed at last, and Archie's father, doggedly retaining his city job, is forced to become a garbage collector. It is interesting that this somewhat farcical comedy utilizes every trick of the vaudeville stage, from the horse with a pair of actors inside to the bird which falls out of the sky when a gun is accidentally discharged. Yet the final effect is a mixture of the comic and the poignant; through Barry's skill the audience is made to believe genuinely in the characters even while laughing at them.

Paris Bound (drama, 1927) argues that a passing infidelity is insufficient reason for a divorce which violates the sacrament of marriage and separates a basically happy couple. When Jim and Mary Hutton marry they are told by Jim's father of the tragedy of his own life: his wife had discovered him in a trivial affair with another woman and divorced him in spite of his love for her. He warns the young couple against allowing their happiness to be destroyed by such an incident. Five years later Mary discovers that Jim has been intimate with Noel Farley, an old sweetheart who loved him before his marriage, during a business trip to France. She decides to get a divorce, and when Jim leaves on another trip to Europe she herself enters out of defiance into an affair with the young composer Richard Parrish. But when Jim returns he does not question her about her relations with Parrish; she regrets her infidelity as well as her jealousy and resolves to say nothing to him about his affair with Noel. Thus the play concludes that "any two people who marry for love . . . and live before the world as man and wife create between them something they can never get away from."

Hotel Universe (drama, 1930) is an interesting experimental play which begins as a comedy of manners and gradually develops into an allegory involving the personality theories of Freudianism. Ann Field, an American woman who lives with her aged father Stephen in a villa in Southern France, is visited by a set of weekend guests, each of whom has made a failure of his life and reached a point of complete disillusionment and cynicism. Pat Farley, an actor and amateur wit whom Ann has long loved, is neurotically obsessed with the death of a young English girl who killed herself when he abandoned her; he has virtually decided to commit suicide. Lily Malone, an actress, is in the grip of an Electra complex—a morbid fixation on her dead actor-father. Tom Ames, born a Catholic, deeply although unconsciously feels the loss of his faith and wanders over the world aimlessly with his wife Hope, who wants instead to stay home with her children. Norman Rose, a Jewish banker, is held in the grip of his own successful career and unable to follow his real inclination to go off by himself and live a life of quiet contemplation; he has put off marrying Alice Kendall, another of the guests, whom he loves, because he subconsciously fears marrying a gentile. Then the mysterious Stephen, who has heretofore concealed himself, appears among them and transfers them to a semi-hypnotic state in which he becomes for each of them the key figure in his life: for Tom his boyhood confessor, for Lily her father, and so forth. Under the influence of this quasi-religious, quasi-Freudian father-figure each of the guests finds his way out of his neurotic impasse. Pat Farley courageously renounces suicide and returns to Ann, his old love; Lily finds sublimation of her father-fixation in a plan to play Cordelia in *King Lear;* Tom's Catholic guilt complex is brought to the surface and he recaptures something like his old faith; and Norman resolves to give up his burdensome career, marry Alice, and go off to Andorra with her. Meanwhile none of them have noticed that Stephen, his mission accomplished, has quietly died. The central figure of this involved allegory is Stephen himself, ostensibly a physicist by actually a symbolic manifestation of the divine, perhaps God himself—in the Freudian sense the ultimate Father-Figure.

The Animal Kingdom (drama, 1932), although a lighter play than *Hotel Universe,* is probably the most important of Barry's sophisticated dramas of manners. It develops a theme treated earlier in *Paris Bound,* but in a sense comes to the opposite conclusion. The talented and sophisticated young Tom Collier lives a happy if somewhat irregular life running a publishing house which prints high-quality books without making a large profit; his relations with his mistress, the designer Daisy Sage, are amiable and satisfying. Then he falls in love with Cecilia Henry, a girl who seems outwardly tolerant and urban but is actually highly conventional. When he marries Cecilia he soon finds himself confronted with a choice between his old bohemian life and the kind of existence which Cecilia represents: middle-class, successful, and stodgy. For a while he tries to adjust himself to marriage, renouncing Daisy and abandoning his old friends. But he finally realizes that Cecilia's "love" is actually selfish and materialistic; all she is really interested in is security for herself and her family. By alternatingly dispensing and cutting off her affection, she soon makes Tom a virtual slave, forcing him to compromise his publishing standards for commercial success and remaking his house, his habits, and even his personality. In the last act he rebels; tricking Cecilia into thinking she has defeated him again with her sexual wiles, he leaves her waiting upstairs while he sneaks out with Red Regan, his prizefighter-turned-butler, to go back to his "real" wife,

Daisy, who understands him and accepts and loves him for what he is. This play, however, is more than a mere attack on middle-class marriage. Its basic message is that the female security-instinct—the desire to have a husband for a "provider" and protector—must not be confused with genuine love. Tom's relationship with Daisy, monogamous, lasting, and essentially pure, is a more real marriage than his legal and economic responsibility to Cecilia.

SIDNEY KINGSLEY (born 1906)

Kingsley is a deliberate and conscientious craftsman who works slowly, produces a relatively small quantity of work, and polishes each play to perfection before he is done with it. His creative method is essentially that of the European naturalists, as much as he sometimes differs from them in content. He bases his writing on painstaking research; he customarily spends from two to five years gathering material before he writes a play. In preparing for the writing of *Men in White* he spent many months in New York hospitals, sometimes actually attending surgical operations disguised as an intern in order to obtain authentic basic data for his play. Likewise, before he wrote *Detective Story* (1949) he spent two years visiting police stations and detective squad rooms in New York City. In these plays and others like them his research method resembles that of a sociologist; the plays are virtually documentaries, based on first-hand data and organized into artistic form. In *The Patriots* (1942), on the other hand, his research method is that of the historian, based chiefly on books and documents. In either case he invariably accumulates a copious mass of data before he begins the actual writing of a play.

Although plays like *Dead End* and *Ten Million Ghosts* are in a sense exposés of modern "capitalistic corruption" and other evils of civilization, Kingsley is not exactly a political radical. He is, in fact, virtually without politics when compared with dramatists like Odets, Anderson, and Rice; his work shows a general humanitarian tendency and he shares with the Marxists the theory of environmental determinism, but he is reluctant to offer a near solution for society's ills in the form of any political program or philosophy. He is not a polemicist; he is first of all a professional playwright, concerned primarily with questions of dramaturgy and stagecraft. He operates on the principle that dramatic effectiveness can be obtained only through authenticity, and that authenticity is achieved through painstaking research. This formula has won him a position as one of America's leading dramatists of the post-1918 generation, and in addition has brought him financial success achieved by few other legitimate dramatists of the era.

LIFE: Sidney Kingsley (pseud. of Sidney Kieschner) was born in New York in 1906 and educated in New York City schools. While still a student at Townsend Hall, a secondary school, he began writing one-act plays; upon graduation he won a scholarship to Cornell, where he continued with his playwriting and gained valuable experience acting in student productions. In 1928 his *Wonder-Dark Epilogue* won a prize as the best one-act play of the year by an undergraduate writer. After college he worked briefly as an actor in a New York theatrical troupe, then spent several years as a scenario writer for Columbia Pictures. In 1933 the Group Theatre produced his *Men In White* (originally titled *Crisis*), and overnight Kingsley had won a reputation as a significant playwright. The play won a Pulitzer Prize in 1934 and was produced in London the same year; it was subsequently staged in many other European capitals, and was frequently revived in later years by small theatre groups. Sold to Metro-Goldwyn-Mayer, it was made into a successful motion picture. *Dead End* (1935) was an even greater critical and financial success; the New York stage production was acclaimed a sensation (partly due to its *succès de scandale*) and the expression "Dead End Kids" became a part of American slang. The script was again sold to Hollywood, and again a successful motion picture resulted. Nothing in Kingsley's later work matched the success of these two plays. *Ten Million Ghosts,* a pacifist drama in a semi-expressionistic technique, closed after eleven performances in 1936, and subsequent plays barely managed to break even. The play Kingsley intended as his third major work was *The Patriots,* a complicated historical drama based on the life of Thomas Jefferson which finally appeared in 1943. The play was acclaimed by reviewers and won the New York Drama Critics Circle Award for 1943, but lacked the dramatic interest to win box-office success; it was essentially a historical pageant rather than a conventional drama of conflict. Meanwhile Kingsley was serving in the army; after his discharge he wrote motion picture scenarios for a few years while gathering material for another play. This was *Detective Story,* which appeared in 1949 and was again successful both as a stage play and a motion picture. In 1951 Kingsley completed *Darkness at Noon,* an adaptation based on the Arthur Koestler novel; the play won another Critics Circle Award and was generally favorably reviewed. In 1954 appeared *Lunatics and Lovers,* a farcical comedy which demonstrated Kingsley's supple versatility as a stylist. Kingsley and his wife, the actress Madge Evans, have lived in recent years on a New Jersey farm.

CHIEF WORKS: *Men In White* (drama, 1933) presents a detailed picture of the daily routine of a modern hospital as well as a study of ethical conflict in the mind of a young doctor. George Ferguson, a young interne training in surgery under the noted specialist Hochberg in a New York hospital, is in love with the wealthy Laura Hudson and plans to marry her soon and take her with him to Vienna, where he plans to continue his studies. At present, however, he has little time for her because of the demands of his hospital position. Laura, jealous and annoyed, quarrels with him, and George has a brief affair with Barbara Dennin, a nurse. Laura and George soon make up their differences, but meanwhile Barbara finds she is pregnant. She seeks escape from her situation through an abortion, which results in a dangerous infection. When she is brought by coincidence to George's hospital for treatment the young doctor is faced with a moral dilemma: should he stand by Barbara and admit his guilt for her condition, or should he sacrifice Barbara to his future with Laura? But the matter is decided for him: Laura, learning of the affair, breaks off the engagement. He resolves to marry Barbara, even though he does not love her. But Barbara's illness is fatal, and George now believes his passing folly has lost him both women. Then, however, the wise surgeon Hochberg talks to Laura and convinces her that George's affair with Barbara was only an ephemeral passion; he explains also that George's devotion to his work, the original cause of the misunderstanding between the two young people, is a splendid and admirable thing and in no way incompatible with his love for her. The young couple are reconciled; George, now wiser and more steadfast in his ideals, goes off alone to Vienna, promising to marry Laura on his return.

Dead End (drama, 1935) is a bitter Depression play somewhat resembling Elmer Rice's *Street Scene* (1929) but more convincingly authentic in its use of slang and big-city local color. The setting symbolically contrasts the elegant apartments of the New York wealthy with the slum tenements in the dead-end streets behind them; the street in front of the apartment houses is temporarily closed for paving, and thus its tenants are forced to come and go via the rear entrance, the unsavory Dead End. The central character is Gimpty, a young cripple who grew up in the slums and struggled to win an education as an architect but is at present unemployed. He is in love with Kay, a prostitute who is the mistress of Jack Hilton, a wealthy tenant of the apartment. Other important characters are the "Dead End kids"—five young slum hoodlums named Tommy, Dippy, T.B., Angel, and Spit, all of them incurably warped by their environment. The climactic event of the drama is the visit to the street of Baby-Face Martin, a gangster who grew up in the neighborhood. After an inner moral conflict Gimpty decides to betray Martin to the police for the reward in order to be able to marry Kay and save her from her sordid life; when he does so, however, she convinces him that "This isn't the miracle we were looking for"—that the money would last them only a year or so, and then they would be at the mercy of the slums again. Kay goes off with Hilton, who has promised to marry her, on a yachting trip. Meanwhile a secondary plot has followed the fortunes of the Dead End kid Tommy and his sister Drina, who is in love with Gimpty. When Tommy, in a brawl, slightly wounds Mr. Griswald, a pompous tenant of the apartment building, Griswald threatens to prosecute and have him sent to a reform school. Drina unsuccessfully tries to convince Griswald that the reform school is only a school for crime, but he is adamant. Finally she appeals to Gimpty, and he agrees to use his reward money to hire a lawyer to defend Tommy. The play ends as Gimpty and Drina go off arm in arm, leaving the street to the obscene and raucous horseplay of the Dead End kids.

The chief importance of *Dead End* lies in its daringly frank picture of slum conditions and in the coarse and slangy dialogue of the Dead End kids themselves. The Gimpty-Kay story is somewhat melodramatic, and Gimpty himself is less believable than the more typical slum inhabitants. The symbolic contrast between slum and expensive apartment is ingenious, extending not only to the set and characters but into the plot itself; the apartment tenants, especially Mr. Griswald and his son Philip, attempt to ignore the corruption under their feet but are finally dragged down and soiled by it in spite of their hypocritical fastidiousness. The theme of environmental determinism is free from any political or partisan message; Kingsley offers no solution to the "problem of juvenile delinquency" other than the abolition of slums and the awakening of human tolerance in "respectable" people like Mr. Griswald.

MAXWELL ANDERSON (born 1888)

At first glance Maxwell Anderson is an anomaly in twentieth-century literature: a romanticist whose chief contribution to the theatre has been in the virtually obsolete form of the verse drama. There is, however, a thoroughly modern quality to Anderson's work, even when he is treating Elizabethan subjects in an archaic dramatic form; he invariably converts his characters into modern personalities with modern psychologies, and his political liberalism and cutting irony mark him as a typical American writer of his generation. Like Faulkner, Jeffers, and O'Neill, he was dissatisfied with the limited possibilities of prose realism, and he sought to break away from realistic conventions through some more subtle literary form. Instinctively romantic in temperament, he turned naturally to the lyrical verse drama which had grown steadily out of favor since the seventeenth century.

In practice Anderson's plays fall into three distinct groups. The first, the realistic prose dramas, begin with *What Price Glory* in 1924 and continue through *Truckline Café* in 1945 and his dramatization of William March's *The Bad Seed* in 1954. The second group, the historical dramas in verse form, includes *Elizabeth the Queen, Mary of Scotland, Joan of Lorraine,* and *Anne of the Thousand Days.* The best-known of these plays are concerned with the English sixteenth century, especially the reigns of Henry VIII and Elizabeth, and their style is a combination of the modern and the Shakespearian; even their form and structure follow the pattern of the Elizabethan drama. The third group comprises plays with a modern setting but in verse form, and includes *Winterset,* perhaps his most important play, and a number of minor dramas such as *High Tor* and the war play *Eve*

of St. Mark. The plays of the first group are written in the style of
modern naturalism, with realistic dialogue often spiced with slang
and contemporary allusions. The second and third groups are more
similar than might be expected; Anderson makes a deliberate effort
to modernize his historical characters, and conversely he imparts a
"classic" quality to the speech of the characters in his modern verse
dramas. Like the Elizabethan dramatists, he often writes the speeches
of his heroes and the more exalted portions of his action in a kind
of blank or free verse, and the comic, satirical, or vulgar portions of
his play in prose. The technique is seen at its most typical in *High Tor*
and *Knickerbocker Holiday*. Other plays like *Winterset,* which has
no comic relief and which substitutes a bitter irony for satire, are
written almost entirely in verse. His realism (and Anderson is in one
sense a realist) lies almost entirely in the area of content and attitude.
He is not the kind of romanticist represented by Robinson Jeffers,
living in isolation in a remote part of the world and detached as much
as possible from contemporary events; he is in intimate contact with
current events; he is in intimate contact with current events and his
interests are deeply involved in contemporary life. Two of his plays
(*Gods of the Lightning* and *Winterset*) are concerned with that great
cause célèbre of his generation, the Sacco-Vanzetti case, and even
so fantastic a comedy as *Knickerbocker Holiday* was intended as a
satire on the New Deal. For Anderson verse is a living form which
may, and ought to, be used for subjects of pressing interest for a
modern audience. The success of *Winterset* showed that his judgment
was not entirely wrong.

LIFE: Maxwell Anderson was born in Atlantic, Pennsylvania in
1888, the son of a Baptist minister. Educated in various parts of the
middle west as his father was transferred from one church to another,
he received his B.A. from the University of North Dakota in 1911.
He went on to take a Master's degree at Stanford (1914) and to
work at a variety of teaching and newspaper jobs. During the First
World War he maintained a rigidly pacifistic stand, which got him
into considerable difficulty before the war was over; he was dismissed
from a teaching position at Whittier College and fired from an editorial job on the *San Francisco Bulletin,* but refused to compromise
his ideals even in the face of hostile public opinion. This attitude,

undoubtedly connected to his Christian background, is part of a wider religious enthusiasm which Anderson has maintained throughout his career in spite of his political liberalism; he once referred to the theatre as "a religious institution devoted entirely to the exaltation of the spirit of man."

In 1918 Anderson went east to New York, where he worked intermittently for various publications including the *Evening Globe* and the *New Republic* until 1928. Meanwhile he had begun writing dramas; his first play, a verse drama in a contemporary setting entitled *White Desert,* appeared in 1923. His first success came with *What Price Glory?,* which he wrote in collaboration with Laurence Stallings in 1924. The play, which starred William Boyd and Louis Wolheim in rôles which became permanently associated with their names, was an instant success; the characters of Sergeant Quirt and Captain Flagg became a part of American folklore, and the story was later made into a successful motion picture. In 1930 appeared *Elizabeth the Queen,* the first of his verse dramas to achieve box-office success; he followed it with *Mary of Scotland* (1933) and *Winterset* (1935), which won him acclaim as a leading American playwright. During the Thirties he joined with Elmer Rice, Robert Sherwood, and others to organize the Playwrights' Group, a cooperative venture formed to produce plays written by its members. Anderson has won numerous awards and prizes during his career, including a Pulitzer Prize (1933) and two Drama Critics' Awards (1936 and 1937). He has been married twice, the second time (1933) to Gertrude Maynard. For many years a New York City resident, Anderson has more recently lived on a farm in Rockland County, N.Y.

CHIEF WORKS: *What Price Glory?* (drama, with Laurence Stallings, 1924) is the first American drama in the new realistic school of war literature represented by such novels as *All Quiet on the Western Front* and Dos Passos' *Three Soldiers.* The action is built around a long-standing feud between Sergeant Quirt and Captain Flagg, hard-bitten members of a U.S. Marine company in France during the First World War. When Flagg goes off to Paris for a week he leaves the company in charge of Quirt, who seizes the opportunity to appropriate Flagg's French girl Charmaine to himself. When Flagg returns he finds that Charmaine's father Cognac Pete has brought charges of seduction against Quirt and demands five hundred francs compensation plus marriage of his daughter to the sergeant. Flagg threatens to force Quirt into the marriage, but the war intervenes; the company is suddenly sent into action. Combat-weary, they are promised a month's leave if they can capture a German officer needed for intelligence purposes. Before they do, however, Quirt is wounded and sent back to the rear, where he escapes from a hospital and happily begins consorting with Charmaine again. When the German prisoner *is* captured Flagg returns to the rear area with the rest of the company and discovers Quirt's trick. They quarrel, then decide to gamble for the girl. Flagg wins, but at that moment new orders arrive sending the company back to the front in spite of the promised leave. Flagg, cursing, cedes Charmaine to the still invalided Quirt. But as the play ends Quirt, whose final loyalty is to the Corps and who is determined not to be outdone by Flagg, abandons the girl to follow his outfit back into the fighting.

In spite of its ostensible realism *What Price Glory?* is in many respects a romantic play. Its interest centers around the colorful characters of Flagg and Quirt and their perpetual friendly enmity; the constant quarreling between the two cannot disguise the fact that they respect each other and are really—perhaps unconsciously—close friends. The play differs from pacifistic war novels such as *All Quiet on the Western Front* in that it does not show war as totally brutal and meaningless, and indeed imbues it with a certain romantic aura of adventure. As Gassner remarks, "It is, indeed, far from certain that the authors were not themselves captivated by what they set out to deprecate." Most of the war color in the play was provided by Stallings, who served as a captain in the Marines during the war and lost a leg in combat at Château-Thierry; Anderson's contribution was mainly in dialogue and dramatic structure. It was the salty, realistic, and unerringly accurate dialogue which chiefly accounted for the stage success of this play.

Saturday's Children (drama, 1927) is typical of Anderson's prose comedies of manners. The theme is marriage, or rather the ironic contrast between the ecstasy of young love and the banality of the marriage which is its inevitable result. Florrie and Willie Sands, a young married couple, enjoy a typical American marital bliss of the lower-middle-class variety, that is to say they are constantly plagued by bills and quarrel petulantly in the intervals of their love-making. They accept their lot and make the best of it, however, and Florrie even undertakes to help trap a husband for her younger sister Bobby. Through Florrie's adroit strategy Bobby manages to trick Rims O'Neil, a likable but rather confused young man, into proposing to her. They marry, and immediately find themselves in the thick of the problems which have previously harassed Florrie and Willie: bills, dirty dishes, in-laws, petty deceits, quarrels, and banality. "What we wanted was a love affair," Bobby complains, "and what we got was a house and bills and general hell." Refusing to accept this, she leaves Rims, moves into a boarding house, and gets her old job back. When Rims comes to the boarding house to implore her to return, she refuses. Later that night, however, after the landlady has banished visitors from the house, Rims climbs stealthily in through the window, and she accepts him—as a lover and not as a husband. This wry but amusing study of middle-class marriage succeeds chiefly through its dialogue, which is cleverly and accurately vernacular.

Elizabeth the Queen (verse drama, 1930) is the best known of Anderson's historical dramas. The action is laid in the latter years of Elizabeth's reign (1599-1601) and the plot concerns the rebellion led by the Earl of Essex. The aging queen, suppressing her natural affection for Essex, tricks him into dissolving his army and then imprisons him in the Tower. She offers him pardon in return for renunciation of his ambitions, but he refuses, unwilling to be content with second place in the kingdom and preferring death to ignominy. This play, written in traditional English blank verse, represents an attempt to achieve a stylistic compromise: Anderson sought to revive the splendor and high poetry of the Elizabethan drama and at the same time remain natural and idiomatic enough to be acceptable by modern audiences. *Mary of Scotland* (1933) and *The Masque of Kings* (1937) are similar in style and treatment.

Both Your Houses (drama, 1933) is a satirical attack on political chicanery, one of the first serious criticisms of corruption in the Federal government in American literature. Alan McClean, an idealistic young congressman, is appointed to an Appropriations Committee because other members consider him too naive and inexperienced to cause any trouble. But McClean soon discovers that almost all the members of the Committee represent corrupt vested interests, and that an appropriations bill originally intended for a Nevada dam has actually been laden with graft through the old tradition of log-rolling. When he tries to expose the corruption he finds that the evidence will prove damaging to Simeon Gray, another congressman whose daughter Marjorie is Alan's sweetheart. He persists in his efforts, however, and opposes the bill to the end even though the others succeed in getting it passed. As the play ends he resolves to begin a vigorous personal campaign to expose the log-rolling and corruption which are the traditional means of getting legislation passed in the Congress.

Winterset (verse drama, 1935) is usually considered Anderson's most important play. Set in a New York tenement district near the river, it deals with people and places much like those in Rice's *Street Scene* or Kingsley's *Dead End,* but does so in an entirely different technique; its mood, tragic and highly poetic, is the antithesis of naturalism. Thirteen years before the action begins an Italian workman and anarchist named Romagna has been unjustly executed for a murder committed during an attempted payroll robbery. The murder was actually committed by Trock Estrella, who has just been released from prison as the play opens. Garth, a young musician and son of the Jewish scholar Esdras, was a witness to the crime; and the killer Trock, who is ill and has only six months to live, suspects him of wanting to give evidence to the police. He threatens Garth, who protests that he has no intention of talking and that his interests are the same as Trock's, since he is technically guilty of murder too. Then Mio, the young son of the executed Romagna, arrives on the scene, wandering about the world seeking evidence which will cleanse the name of his innocent father. He falls in love with Miriamne, Garth's sister, before he realizes her relation to his natural enemy Garth, and is then faced with a cruel moral dilemma: to restore his father's reputation he must destroy the brother of the girl he loves. Meanwhile, through a coincidence, Judge Gaunt, who had sent Romagna to the electric chair, appears, distraught and half insane with remorse and obsessed with the idea of justifying himself before the world; Esdras temporarily takes him into his home to protect him. The crisis of the play occurs when Trock has Shadow, an obnoxious gunman, shot and thrown into the river; Shadow, not yet dead, appears wounded and bent on revenge in the Esdras tenement, and

Trock is forced to kill him again for good, this time in the presence of Esdras, Garth, Mio, and Miriamne. When the police arrive Mio, knowing Trock as the criminal who should have died instead of his father, denounces him for the murder of Shadow. But Garth and the others, fearing Trock's vengeance, fail to back Mio up, and the police depart with the demented Judge Gaunt leaving Trock untouched. Mio, now knowing he faces certain death at the hands of Trock, goes off to meet his fate; when he is killed Miriamne also exposes herself to fire and is struck down by a bullet from the gangsters' machine gun. As the play ends Esdras tells the dead Mio that the glory of man is "not to cringe, never to yield, but standing, take defeat implacable and defiant." The implied reproach to the sensitive but cowardly musician Garth is obvious. *Winterset,* in structure a tragedy in the Elizabethan manner, is highly refined and artificial in style, rich in metaphor and in the ironic turns of language which Elizabethans called "conceits." Its diction is archaic and imaginative, making little attempt to imitate the modern vernacular.

High Tor (verse drama, 1936) is a fantasy or allegory contrasting traditional American individualism and self-reliance with the aggressive business-philosophy of the twentieth century. Van Dorn, a fiercely independent young man who lives alone on High Tor, a peak overlooking the Hudson River in upstate New York, quarrels with his fiancée Judith, who wants to live a normal domestic life and tries to persuade him to sell his mountain to entrepreneurs who wish to mine its valuable trap-rock. Two pompous business-men, Biggs and Skimmerhorn, arrive on the mountain to deal with him, hoping to trick or coerce him into surrendering the valuable rights, but become involved in a farcical imbroglio involving a set of Dutch ghosts left over from a seventeenth-century ship and a gang of incompetent bank-robbers, Dope, Elkus, and Buddy. A satchel full of money stolen by the bank-robbers comes eventually into the hands of Biggs and Skimmerhorn, who are then trapped in the scoop of a steamshovel and arrested by the police for the crime. Meanwhile Van has romanced with the attractive Lise, one of the phantoms from the Dutch ship, who serves as a symbol of his desire for a pure love uncontaminated by banality and materialism. After the two unscrupulous business-men are arrested, however, Lise goes off in her ship leaving Van to Judith, who now repents of her mean decision and agrees to accept Van on his own terms. Van finally agrees to sell the mountain for a large sum to Skimmerhorn's father, a business-man of a blunter and more honest sort, and go west with Judith to seek an unspoiled new region where he can retain his individualism. John, an Indian who is about to die and who makes Van promise to bury him on the mountain, provides philosophical comments through the play, concluding at the end, "Nothing is made by men but makes, in the end, good ruins." Thus modern American "progress" and materialistic aggressiveness are repudiated completely. Unlike *Winterset, High Tor* is not written completely in verse; comic scenes and speeches of characters like Biggs and Skimmerhorn are in vernacular prose similar to that of Anderson's realistic dramas.

ROBERT SHERWOOD (1896-1955)

Sherwood is an acknowledged master of the technique of the high comedy, but he writes high comedy of a very special kind, resembling the philosophical comedy of Bernard Shaw more than the Noel Coward "comedy of manners." His *Road to Rome,* in fact, is essentially the same kind of play as Shaw's *Caesar and Cleopatra,* a comedy of ideas in which historical figures are converted into modern characters with modern psychologies. Although Sherwood is by no means as partisan and dogmatic a thinker as Shaw, there is a consistent thread of idea running through his work: he is a pacifist and humanitarian (although his pacifism at one period turned into militant anti-fascism) and he is an advocate of natural human behavior as opposed to social convention. These two concepts are epitomized in *Idiot's Delight;* the polyglot Europeans and Americans who meet in the remote Italian hotel are friendly and tolerant as long as they follow their natural instincts, but when they are infected with the mass hysteria of nationalism they turn into stereotypes of war-mongering patriots. In *The Petrified Forest* and *Reunion in Vienna* natural action is contrasted with artificial (social or conventional) action; Sherwood believes that a genuine individual impulse which comes from within, even if it is what society condemns as immoral, is wiser than conduct determined solely by external morals, laws, or conventions. Amytis in *The Road to Rome* is the model Sherwood heroine in this respect: she is unmoved by the hysteria of Roman chauvinism which infects her husband Fabius, she gives herself to Hannibal when

it seems natural and proper for her to do so, yet in the end she violates the stereotyped conventions of romanticism by going back to her
husband rather than becoming Hannibal's concubine. When the play
is over it is apparent that she has acted rightly in each case, and that
Rome, her husband's career, and her own destiny have been served
by her feminine intuition.

Sherwood spent a number of years of his life in Europe, and he
always retained an admiration for European civilization and a respect
for the European cultural tradition. Almost half his plays are either
laid in a European setting or based on European characters; in his
best-known American play, *The Petrified Forest,* the heroine is half
French and the chief male character a former American expatriate
who constantly contrasts European and American culture to the det-
riment of the latter. Yet this apparent rejection of "the American
way of life" is merely the normal iconoclasm of a writer who grew
to maturity during the Twenties. Sherwood's later work—especially
his *Abe Lincoln in Illinois* and *Roosevelt and Hopkins*—shows him
to be a writer who is deeply concerned with American problems and
conscious of his American heritage, which he views from the standpoint of a sincere humanitarian and liberal.

LIFE: Robert Emmet Sherwood was born in New Rochelle, New
York in 1896. He evidently inherited his artistic inclinations from his
parents; his father was an investment broker with an enthusiastic
interest in the theatre and his mother a talented painter and illustrator. The family was well-to-do, and Sherwood had an excellent education, first at Milton Academy and then at Harvard. In 1917, however, he left college in his junior year to enlist in the Canadian Black
Guards; he saw the worst of the combat on the Western Front, was
wounded at Amiens, and spent many months in hospitals. From this
experience came his lifetime detestation of war, which found its way
in one way or another into most of his plays.

Sherwood had begun writing plays while still an undergraduate at
Harvard, and had also written for student publications including
Lampoon, for which he wrote a particularly ingenious parody of
Vanity Fair. When he was mustered out of the service in 1919 he was
invited to join the *Vanity Fair* staff, and served on the magazine as
dramatic critic until the next year, when he resigned in protest against

the firing of Dorothy Parker, whose criticisms were considered too caustic by the publishers. During the following years he wrote for a number of periodicals including the old *Life* and *Scribner's*. Meanwhile, he had retained his interest in playwriting, and 1927 saw the production of his first play, *The Road to Rome*. The production was a success, and thenceforth he was able to make his living as a playwright, achieving both critical and popular success; he received three Pulitzer Prizes between 1936 and 1941, and served from 1937 to 1941 as president of the Dramatists' Guild.

A lifetime liberal, Sherwood took an active part in politics under the New Deal administration of Franklin Roosevelt, especially after 1940; during the war he served as chief of the overseas branch of the Office of War Information, and is credited with writing many of Roosevelt's best speeches. A close friend of Harry Hopkins, he inherited his voluminous papers after his death; out of this mass of material he compiled an important historical study of the New Deal, *Roosevelt and Hopkins: An Intimate History* (1948). This work, over a thousand pages long, not only became a best-seller but won Sherwood a reputation as a first-rate researcher and historian.

Sherwood was married twice, to Mary Brandon in 1922 and to Mrs. Madeline Connelly, former wife of the author Marc Connelly, in 1934. Toward the end of his carreer he wrote extensively for television and motion pictures; one of his movie scenarios, *The Best Years of Our Lives,* won an Academy Award. He died of a heart attack in New York in November, 1955. "In the American theatre," wrote Maxwell Anderson in a funeral sermon prepared for reading by the actor Alfred Lunt, "the death of Sherwood has an effect comparable to the removal of a major planet from the solar system."

CHIEF WORKS: *The Road to Rome* (drama, 1927) is a philosophical comedy laid in Rome in the period of the Second Punic War (*ca.* 216 B.C.). Fabius, newly elected Dictator of Rome, is a typical political windbag and chauvinist who boasts emptily of the victory the Romans will win over the invading Carthaginian forces led by Hannibal. His half-Greek wife Amytis, however, has no interest whatsoever in politics and can see little sense in a useless war which will kill thousands of men and bring no gain to either side. She is intrigued, however, by descriptions of the ruthless Hannibal, who sounds to her much more attractive than her prosaic husband. When news comes that the Roman legions have been defeated in the disastrous battle of Cannae and that Hannibal's forces will shortly sack Rome, she flees, ostensibly to go to take shelter with her mother on the seacoast. Actually, however, she steals secretly with two trusted slaves into the camp of Hannibal, curious to see what he is like and perhaps hoping for an escape from her humdrum and conventional existence. Hannibal at first orders her put to death, then is intrigued by her beauty and obvious intelligence; she willingly surrenders herself to him. The next day Fabius, with his chief general Scipio, comes to the Carthaginian camp to treat for terms. But Hannibal has already been convinced by Amytis of the senselessness of destroying the city and slaughtering all its inhabitants; his unthinking soldier's nationalism has been shattered completely by her woman's common sense. He withdraws his army from the city and goes instead to raise the siege of Capua, inviting Amytis to come with him and share his life. But she refuses, telling him that he must not spare Rome to win her but because "every sacrifice made in the name of war is wasted." She goes back to rejoin her husband Fabius, who announces bombastically that the Carthaginians have retreated because "Hannibal, with all his elephants all his men, could not subdue the high moral purpose of Rome."

In spite of its setting *The Road to Rome* is no historical drama. it makes to attempt to achieve an authentic Roman atmosphere, and uses the historical background only as a convenient frame for a philosophical comedy. Much of the Roman setting, in fact, is actually a satire on the modern American state (e.g., the clichés repeated by Fabius, a parody of the speech of a modern politician), and the Greek attitude which Amytis upholds bears a certain analogy to modern European culture, especially the French. The psychology of the chief characters is thoroughly twentieth-century, and even minor characters like the Carthaginian soldiers are treated as satires on their modern equivalents.

Reunion in Vienna (drama, 1931) is a study of social transition, the passing of the old Hapsburg order in Austria and the coming of a new and modern generation to replace it. The story is laid in Vienna in 1930 on the hundredth anniversary of the birth of the late Emperor Franz Joseph I. The handful of aristocrats left in Vienna plan a party for the occasion at a fashionable hotel, and invite Frau Elena Krug, famous before the war as mistress of the Crown Prince Rudolf Maximillian and now wife of the eminent psychiatrist Anton Krug. Elena at first refuses, but when she learns that her old lover Rudolf, exiled for years, is actually going to enter Austria illegally to attend the dinner, she comes to the hotel. Rudolf proposes a renewal of their love, but she refuses, telling him that an era has passed and that now she is another woman, the wife of Dr. Krug. Rudolf is unable to understand her attitude; he pursues her to her home, where he meets Anton and cynically reveals his desire to him. Anton leaves the matter up to Elena; meanwhile he leaves the couple alone in the house while he goes off to consult with the political authorities about plans for the safe re-exiling of Rudolf, who will probably be shot if he is captured by the police. Rudolf is so impressed with this courtesy, and with the implied trust Anton has shown in Elena, that he willingly agrees to leave the country and renounce his rights over his old mistress. He has comprehended what his fanatic followers and hangers-on have not: that the day of the Hapsburgs is gone and can never come back, and that the future belongs to Dr. Krug and his kind. Sherwood wrote this realistic "romantic comedy" especially for Alfred Lunt and Lynn Fontanne, who played Rudolf and Elena respectively in the original production.

The Petrified Forest (drama, 1934) is a study of decadent Western civilization, a culture in which the intellectuals who have been dominant for so long are finally at the point of extermination through self-induced sterility. The play is evidently influenced by Eliot's poem *The Waste Land,* which is referred to twice in the course of the action. The setting is the interior of a gas station and lunch stand on the Arizona desert. The proprietor, Jason Maple, is a pompous self-appointed patriot who conceals his lack of character under an American Legion uniform. The remaining important characters are his daughter Gabrielle (Gabby), whose French mother has despaired of life on the bleak desert and gone back to Europe; his father Gramp, an old pioneer who is disgusted with twentieth-century culture; Boze Hertzlinger, a former star athlete and now employee of the café; Alan Squier, a "lost generation" American expatriate who has lived for several years on the French Riviera, married to a wealthy woman, but has now come back to hitchhike his way through America in search of some meaning in life; and Mr. and Mrs. Chisholm, a pair of middle-class travelers from Ohio. The plot centers around the capture of the café by Duke Mantee, a killer and fugitive from the law, and his gang; this crisis brings out the latent qualities of each of the characters and brings their lives to the climactic point. Alan, who has fallen in love with Gabby, willingly allows himself to be shot by Mantee in order that the young girl may use his insurance money to escape from her dull life and go to France to study art. Mrs. Chisholm who is also bored with her life, offers to "crawl into the hay" with Mantee, but a gun battle intervenes to prevent this; meanwhile, however, she has seen through her husband's insipid conventionality. Jason is unmasked as an incompetent coward, and Duke Mantee, the anti-social criminal, is typified by Alan before he dies as "the last great apostle of rugged individualism" in the Petrified Forest of outmoded ideas. The final message of the play is a plea for a life of wider experience than the usual existence dominated by convention and banality; even Duke seems more admirable than the blustering "patriot" Jason, who does only what society expects of him and parrots second-hand ideas in place of a philosophy. It should be noted that Alan is not the "hero" of the play in the ordinary sense; he is intended as a personification of the decadent generation of the Twenties, which can only talk instead of act and which confines its intellectual leadership to presiding over the degeneration of culture.

Idiot's Delight (drama, 1936) is set in a remote Italian hotel on the Austrian border on the eve of a hypothetical war. In this microcosm are assembled a set of symbolically contrasting characters: Dr. Waldensee, a German scientist consecrated to the study of the cause of cancer; Quillery, a French socialist and pacifist; Mr. and Mrs. Cherry, English newlyweds preoccupied with their own personal happiness; Harry Van, an American nightclub entertainer, with his troupe of six showgirls; Achille Weber, a French munitions manufacturer; and Weber's mistress Irene, a self-styled White Russian refugee. Other characters important in the plot are Pittaluga, the proprietor of the hotel; the Austrian waiter Dumptsy; and Captain Locicero, an Italian officer in command of the nearby airfield. In the first act the characters are friendly and tolerant toward each other and indifferent to the clouds of a major European war which are gathering on the horizon; Quillery is a professional pacifist, Dr. Waldensee holds science and humanity above his loyalty to Germany, and the others are mainly concerned with their individual search for happiness. Then war breaks out suddenly and news comes that Italian planes from the airfield have bombed Paris; immediately all the main characters are caught up in the hatreds of the war. Quillery speaks out violently against the bombing of Paris and is shot by the Italians; Dr. Waldensee decides to go back to Germany to contribute his knowledge to germ warfare, and the others plan to return home to join their respective armies. It is not Weber, the "warmonger" and target of Quillery's pacifistic diatribes, who is responsible for the war but humanity itself, normally peaceable but irrational and fanatic as soon as the war fever is whipped up. As the play ends Irene denounces Weber and he abandons her; she joins forces with Harry, who recognizes her as a girl he met long ago in Omaha, and they begin "Onward Christian Soldiers" as the first French bombs crash down on the hotel. This play, written in 1936, is a remarkably accurate prediction of the outbreak of the Second World War. It is also interesting that Sherwood was able to predict the change of heart of many liberals who turned from pacifism to militant anti-fascism between 1932 and 1939, and ironic that he himself was to undergo this same change of opinion; by 1940 he was an impassioned anti-Nazi and anti-communist who attacked the Russian invasion of Finland in *There Shall Be No Night* and supervised anti-fascist propaganda as a high official of the O.W.I.

Abe Lincoln in Illinois (drama, 1938) is a historical play in twelve scenes following the career of Lincoln from his period as a New Salem storekeeper to the time of his departure for Washington as President-Elect. Sherwood treats Lincoln as a personification of the American ideal of humanitarianism plus personal ambition and self-realization, and attempts in the play to show the development of the idea in Lincoln himself. The play was awarded a Pulitzer Prize in 1939.

CLIFFORD ODETS (born 1906)

The talent of Clifford Odets burst dramatically onto the American theatrical scene in the middle of the Depression era. In a single year, 1935, he wrote four plays and won a reputation as the outstanding member of the new left-wing school of young American dramatists.

Odets today is still remembered chiefly for these 1935 plays, especially *Waiting for Lefty* and *Awake and Sing*. His subsequent work,
while less important in the development of American drama, has
nevertheless shown him as a playwright of a great deal of versatility.
Paradise Lost (1935) and *Rocket to the Moon* (1938), along with
Night Music (1940), are satires of middle-class American domesticity, usually involving a love plot but virtually devoid of political comment; *Golden Boy* (1937) is a penetrating study of the American cult
of success, symbolized through the figure of an Italian boy who cannot decide whether he wants to be a prizefighting champion or a
violinist. The most important of Odets' post-1945 plays is *Country
Girl* (1950), in which the central conflict is again personal and
domestic rather than social. Taken as a whole, Odets' work reveals
him as a dramatist whose talent lies mainly in the portrayal of the
inner conflicts and struggles of the big-city American middle class—a
class which in the Thirties shaded off imperceptibly into the tenement
proletariat of the Bronx.

Odets was a professional actor for several years before he wrote
his first play, and he has an intimate technical knowledge of the
theatre. With the possible exception of *Waiting for Lefty,* which
borrows some of the technical innovations of European expressionism, his plays are not experimental or radical in technique; they are
sound and competent in construction and written always with an eye
to the practical limitations of dramatic production. As is often the
case with dramatists with an extensive theatrical background, Odets'
plays do not read as well as they play; they sometimes seem gauche or
oversimplified in book form and come to life only when put upon the
living stage. This is particularly true of *Waiting for Lefty,* which is a
sort of a visual pageant rather than a purely "verbal" drama and must
be seen in production to be properly appreciated.

Odets' most striking talent, however, and the quality which chiefly
accounted for the success of his early plays, is his skill in dialogue.
He has an unerring ear for the speech of the big-city masses—brash,
colorful, cynical, enriched by the influences of a half-dozen immigrant
languages and seasoned with a poetic bitterness born from the poverty
and hopelessness of life in the metropolitan tenements. His command
of this idiom, the language of his own people, makes the parallel
efforts of Kingsley (*Dead End*) and Rice (*Street Scene*) seem ama-

teurish by contrast. He is naturally at his best in the Jewish dialect—
Golden Boy with its Italian hero is less successful in dialogue than
Awake and Sing. This idiom is strongly influenced by the underlying
Yiddish substratum of its speakers, even using Yiddish syntax
("Please, I'm making a story? I fell in the chair like dead."). In
Odets' drama the dialect seems colorfully foreign and at the same
time deeply and characteristically American; above all it has the
unmistakable ring of authenticity. The same criticism may be made
of his characterizations—they are best when they are closest to his
own background, and weakest in characters (like the doctors in Episode V of *Waiting for Lefty*) who are farther from his own experience.
Likewise *The Country Girl* is the best of his later plays because he is
writing about what he knows—the backstage lives of actors in the
big-city theatre. Odets' permanent place in the American theatre is
assured, not by his efforts at left-wing propaganda, but by his skill in
dramatic composition and his mastery of the idiom of an important
segment of American culture.

LIFE: Clifford Odets was born in Philadelphia in 1906; both his
parents were Jewish Lithuanian immigrants. He was raised in New
York and Philadelphia and attended schools in both cities. At fifteen,
however, he left high school to work as a radio writer and announcer;
at nineteen he was earning a living by reading dramatic poems over
the radio. By 1928 he had established his career as an actor, working
in stock companies and obtaining an occasional minor part in Theatre
Guild productions. In 1930, along with Harold Clurman and Herbert
Biberman, he helped to organize the Group Theatre, which was conceived as a sort of junior Theatre Guild to produce plays by younger
dramatists and which began under the protection of the older organization. At this time Odets' ambitions were still confused; he dreamed
vaguely of becoming a concert pianist and also experimented tentatively with writing novels. He worked as an actor in Group Theatre
productions for three years before he wrote his first play. This was
Awake and Sing, which he wrote to express the "strangulations of
family life" as he had known them in his own youth. The Group
rehearsed the second act of the play but decided not to produce it;
meanwhile they went on to stage Kingsley's *Men in White.* The fol
lowing year (1934) Odets wrote *Waiting for Lefty* in three days for

a one-act play contest sponsored by the New Theatre League. Staged by the League, the short play created an enormous sensation and made Odets a celebrity overnight. The Group Theatre now reconsidered his work; it produced *Waiting for Lefty* on Broadway in early 1935 and commissioned another short play, *Till the Day I Die,* to complete the bill. In February the Group also produced *Awake and Sing,* which achieved a considerable box-office success. Odets, his reputation made, went to Hollywood, where he stayed for three years, contributing to the scripts for such important films as *The General Died at Dawn.* In 1937 he was married to the motion-picture actress Luise Rainer; the union was a stormy one, and the two were divorced in 1940. Odets subsequently spent several periods in Hollywood, where he worked both as screenwriter and as director. Meanwhile his political attitudes had changed with the changing atmosphere of the times. His early plays adhered closely to the Communist Party line; *Waiting for Lefty* is probably one of the most violently partisan proletarian dramas ever to be produced on the Broadway stage. Even as late as 1939, writing a preface to his first six plays, he remarked, "We are living in a time when new art works should shoot bullets." But by 1942 he was content to describe himself as "some kind of a socialist" and had disavowed formal Party connections. In 1952, at the height of the Congressional anti-Red "purges," he testified before the House Committee on Un-American Activities that he had been a Party member briefly in 1934 but had resigned when pressure was put upon him to write party-line propaganda. Odets was married for the second time in 1943 to the actress Bette Grayson, she died in 1954. Since the war he has divided his residence between New York and California.

CHIEF WORKS: *Waiting for Lefty* (one-act drama, 1934) consists of six "Episodes" plus a number of incidental scenes, all played on a bare stage without benefit of scenery. The sequence of action is outwardly disconnected and the general mood is fantastic, suggesting the Continental expressionistic drama of Kaiser and Wedekind and the similar American experiments of O'Neill and Rice. The action is concerned with a strike of New York taxicab drivers during the Depression, and approximately half the scenes take place in a drivers' meeting in which the theatre audience is addressed over the footlights as though it were the membership of the meeting. Retorts, heckling, and comments are frequently heard from this audience, thus effectively breaking down the conventional barrier between stage and theatre-goer. The play opens as Harry Fatt, a corrupt union leader who actually serves the capitalistic bosses, tries to persuade the drivers not to go out on strike. Flashback scenes then show typical incidents in the lives of the strikers. The driver Joe is exhorted by his wife Edna to strike to provide food for his starving children, and the young Sid tells his fiancée Florence he cannot marry her until the drivers' wages are increased. Meanwhile the drivers await the arrival of Lefty Costello (symbol of aid from the international workers' movement), the one leader they trust and respect. When news comes that Lefty has been found dead, murdered by the bosses' police, the workers turn into a howling mob which chants, "Strike, strike, strike!" as the curtain comes down. In addition to its interest as an extreme example of proletarian drama, *Waiting for Lefty* is important as one of the first American plays to utilize the bare-stage technique and the break-ing down of the audience barrier which were later used in such important dramas as Thornton Wilder's *Our Town* (1938).

Awake and Sing! (drama, 1935) was written before *Waiting for Lefty* but produced slightly later. All the action takes place in the Bronx tenement flat of the Bergers, an impoverished Jewish family including three generations. Jacob, the grandfather, is a philosophical and studious old Jew who has been unable all his life to convert his idealism into action. Bessie, his daughter and the real head of the family, is aggressive and hard-working but unhappy, obsessed with a desire for bourgeois prosperity and respectability; her husband Myron is a "born follower" who lacks the character to seize what he wants out of life. Their son Ralph, an impractical thinker and dreamer, resembles his grandfather in character. Their daughter Hen-nie, a stenographer, is an individualist who "travels alone" and feels loyalty to no one, even to her own family; she is made for love and motherhood, but so far has been unable to find a husband. Also frequently present in the flat are Uncle Morty, a self-made man and successful clothing merchant who patronizes the Bergers but does little to aid them, and Moe Axelrod, a bitter and cynical sensualist who lost a leg in the war and is now out only for himself; he loves Hennie, but she despises him. The crisis of the action arises when Hennie announces she is pregnant by an unknown lover. The hard

Bessie, taking the situation in hand, forces her into a marriage with Sam Feinschreiber, a recently arrived immigrant whom Hennie does not love. Meanwhile Bessie works to break up Ralph's romance with his fiancée Blanche, whom she dislikes because she is a moneyless orphan. The two idealists in the household, Ralph and the old Jacob, seem helpless before the cynical ruthlessness of the others. Then Jacob, who owns a three-thousand-dollar life insurance policy made out to Ralph, takes the dog up on the roof for an airing and leaps to his death, presumably in order to give Ralph a new start in life. The family immediately begins squabbling over the money, but Ralph, disgusted, willingly hands it over to Bessie. By this time Blanche has abandoned him; he resolves to go out into the world alone and struggle for his living, exulting in the new strength that his freedom has given him. Hennie, bored by her monotonous life with Sam, elopes with Moe to go on "a big boat headed south," and the dissolution of the family is complete. The title of this drama comes from an Old Testament passage quoted by Jacob before he dies: "Awake and sing, ye that dwell in the dust, and the earth shall cast out the dead." Thus the play demonstrates the viciousness of a certain kind of family, which sacrifices everything, even happiness, to material success and ruthlessly suppresses the individual needs and longings of children. The wise grandfather Jacob, with his combination of Old-Testament humanitarianism and Marxist criticism of bourgeois capitalism, serves as a spokesman for the ideas Odets himself held during the period.

S. N. BEHRMAN (born 1893)

Since the success of *No Time for Comedy* in 1939 and the relative decline of Philip Barry, Behrman has assumed a position as the leading American writer of high comedy. The difference between high comedy and comedy of manners is a subtle one, but it may be perceived by comparing *End of Summer* or *No Time for Comedy* with Noel Coward's *Private Lives,* or any of the more sophisticated comedies of Kaufman and Hart. Both types achieve their humor through character contrast and verbal wit, but Behrman's comedy is based in the end on significant social, moral, or personal problems, problems which might equally well serve as subjects for tragedy or serious melodrama. Behrman is not a "social dramatist," nor is he a profound philosopher; but the superficial and attractive surface of his comedy invariably conceals a serious comment on life which is the more effective for being presented in witty and engaging form. A typical example is *No Time for Comedy,* which at first glance appears to be a mere "triangle story" about a man who cannot decide which of two women he loves. Underneath, however, are fundamental problems: the duty of an artist to strive for the amelioration of his society versus his duty to his own artistic principles, the rôle of feminine inspiration in the life of an artist, and—most basic of all— the attitude of an individual toward corrupt social forces over which he has no control.

It is often remarked that Behrman sprang almost full-blown into maturity as an artist; he had no discernible formative period, and *The Second Man,* his first major drama, is as mature in idea and technique as his most recent work. Although his work is generally consistent both in attitude and in style, he does show a considerable versatility. In addition to his own comedies he has adapted three European dramas for the American stage, the most important of which is Werfel's *Jacobowsky and the Colonel* (1944), a play which Behrman might well have written himself. In 1954 he adapted Marcel Pagnol's trilogy *Fanny* as a Broadway musical, and he has also published two major non-fiction works: a biography of the New York art dealer Joseph Duveen, and a set of autobiographical reminiscences about his early family life in Worcester, Massachusetts. Both originally written for *The New Yorker,* they were later published in book form as *Duveen* and *The Worcester Account* respectively.

Behrman is neither a political polemicist or a dramatist of idea, yet there is a consistent thread of attitude running through his work. Like most important American writers of his generation, he is a liberal and humanitarian and thus an anti-fascist; he deals frequently in his drama with the radical movement of the Depression era (e.g., in *End of Summer*), but he treats it with great objectivity. His obvious sympathy for the cause of the masses never leads him into the partisan radicalism of Odets or Maxwell Anderson. Moreover, he differs from these two playwrights and their kind in his suspicion of conventional heroism; the iconoclasts, the rebels, and the prophets in his dramas are often revealed at the end as hopelessly incompetent. When the young lover Austin, in *The Second Man,* attempts in a high moral passion to shoot Storey, who he believes has seduced his fiancée, he only makes a fool of himself, for two reasons: he is a poor pistol shot, and he is wrong about the seduction. In the end it is the sophisticated, blasé, and compromising Storey who is right. Likewise in *No Time for Comedy* the dramatic romanticism of Amanda is contrasted with the level-headed realism of Linda, who realizes that, heroic gestures aside, it is more important to know how to live than to know how to die. In Behrman's view heroism and high comedy are mutually incompatible; as soon as the merciless light of satire is turned onto heroism it is exposed as nothing but dangerous and irrational bluster.

LIFE: Samuel Nathaniel Behrman was born in Worcester, Massachusetts in 1893 in a simple middle-class Jewish family he has skillfully described in *The Worcester Account*. An avid reader in his youth, he began to write at an early age; he wrote a one-act play while still in high school, sold it to a vaudeville circuit, and then got a job acting in it himself. After attending Clark College in Worcester he went on to Harvard, where he studied playwriting alongside Sidney Howard in Baker's "47 Workshop" (1916). Unable to find a job after he left Harvard, he took an M.A. at Columbia, studying under Brander Mathews and John Erskine. Meanwhile he had written his first important play, *The Second Man*. It was basically ahead of its time, and the theatre was in a period of doldrum; Behrman worked for eleven years before he succeeded in getting it produced. During these intervening years he worked on two dramatic collaborations, with J. Kenyon Nicholson and Owen Davis, and served intermittently as a book reviewer and theatrical press-agent. *The Second Man* was finally produced by the Theatre Guild in 1927. The production was a success, and Behrman was established as a Broadway playwright. He continued to turn out approximately one comedy every two years until the period of the Second World War. He also visited Hollywood several times to work on screen plays (*Queen Christina, A Tale of Two Cities*) and adapted a number of foreign works for the American theatre including Somerset Maugham's story *Jane,* Giraudoux's drama *Amphitryon 38,* and Werfel's *Jacobowsky and the Colonel*. Most of these works, along with his own plays, were box-office hits as well as critical successes. Married in 1936 to Elza Heifetz, sister of the violinist Jascha Heifetz, Behrman has lived a quiet and retired life in comparison with most other New York dramatists; he has frequently contributed short stories and articles to popular magazines and has revealed a secret ambition to write a novel. In 1954 his adaptation of Marcel Pagnol's *Fanny* was the hit of the Broadway season.

CHIEF WORKS: *The Second Man* (drama, produced 1927) is built around a romantic intrigue involving two couples who shift relationships in the manner of Noel Coward's *Quadrille*. The chief characters are Clark Storey, a writer of slick commercial magazine stories; Monica Grey, a vivacious young girl of twenty; Austin Lowe, a dedicated young scientific researcher; and Mrs. Kendall Frame, a wealthy dilettante. The plot depends on the fact that Kendall and Austin have money, while Storey and Monica do not, and that Kendall and Storey are practical while Monica and Austin are romantic. As the play opens both Kendall and Monica are in love with Storey, although Kendall is annoyed at him because of his careless and independent ways and because she believes he is interested in her only for her money. The latter charge is true: Storey, who is normally sexed but incapable of love, knows through his common sense that he and the wealthy Kendall would be happy together but that a marriage with Monica would be stifled by poverty. Austin, fumbling and incompetent in personal life, is unable to win Monica; and she, meanwhile, is open and shameless in confessing her love for Storey. Storey tries to throw the young pair together by leaving them alone in his apartment and ordering a dinner for them, but they quarrel, and for a time Austin develops an interest in Kendall. Monica makes overtures to Storey but is rejected; in a last desperate effort she accuses him, in the presence of the other two, of being "the father of her unborn child." Storey, defeated, agrees to marry her, and the angry Kendall plans to leave for Europe for an indefinite stay. But the next morning Austin appears in the apartment, distraught, and tries to kill Storey with a pistol. Missing, he is overcome with humiliation and despair, and goes to another room to sleep off his fatigue. When Monica arrives at the apartment and learns of Austin's rash and "heroic" act she believes in his love for the first time, and falls in love with the new man he has become. The lovers depart, and the cynical and sophisticated Storey appears to be beaten at last. But he quickly calls up Kendall on the phone and comes to an understanding with her; worldly and free from sentimentalism, the two realize that they can best find happiness with each other. The dramatic interest in *The Second Man* lies in the contrast between the attitudes of the two pairs of lovers: Storey and Kendall, wiser than the younger couple, realize that money is as important as love in making marriage succeed. The title refers to a remark Storey makes about himself, explaining why he is incapable of sentiment or sincerity: "There's someone else inside me—a second man—a cynical, odious person, who keeps watching me, who keeps listening to what I say, grinning and so-phisticated, horrid . . ." Yet it is this "second man" who is the wiser of the two parts of Storey's personality, sensing that a romantic marriage with Monica would be doomed to disillusionment and failure.

End of Summer (drama, 1936) is a somewhat more serious play than *The Second Man,* involving a contrast in social classes in addition to its theme of personal conflict. Paula Frothingham, a wealthy young heiress, is in love with Will Dexter, a college student of radical tendencies who plans on editing a left-wing magazine after he graduates. He quickly makes friends with Mrs. Wyler, Paula's grandmother and a member of the vigorous Victorian generation which rose from poverty to make the millions on which the Frothingham family now lives in luxury. Mrs. Wyler dies during the time covered by the play, leaving her money to Paula, and the young couple plan to use the inheritance to found Will's magazine. Leonie, Paula's mother, represents the middle generation, lacking Mrs. Wyler's vigor but also lacking the idealism and social consciousness which mark Paula and her contemporaries. Frivolous and impractical, Leonie is nevertheless a charming representative of the late Victorian millionaire class, which achieved an unmatched elegance and sophistication in its time but is already being destroyed by social change. Leonie, a natural flirt, has an extremely complicated romantic life; still married to Paula's father Sam Frothingham, she plans an affair with the Russian refugee Count Mirsky and then falls in love with Dr. Kenneth Rice, a psychiatrist whom she engages to treat Count Mirsky's neurosis. Meanwhile the younger generation is struggling against the older; Will's college chum Dennis McCarthy, a brash and sarcastic young intellectual, taunts Kenneth about his alleged medical omniscience, and Will finds Paula's father inalterably opposed to her marriage with a "radical." The drama begins to resolve itself when it becomes apparent that Kenneth, the suave opportunist of psychiatry, is cynically plotting to win Leonie for her money. When Paula discovers that Kenneth is actually attracted to her instead of her mother, she tricks him into confessing his "love" in front of Leonie, and thus succeeds in having him banished from the house. Will and Paula, denied Mrs. Wyler's money by Sam, who is the executor of her estate, nevertheless (presumably) marry and strike out to make a living through their own efforts; and Leonie, in a final romantic gesture, promises to back Dennis in publishing the radical magazine. Thus the "end of summer" has seen the complete collapse of the Frothingham clan and their way of life: Mrs. Wyler is dead, Paula has willingly descended into the working class with Will, and even Leonie has joined forces with the proletariat by supporting Dennis, who jokingly tells her, "Come the revolution—you'll have a friend in high places." *End of Summer* is thus an allegorical study of the shifting American social classes in the period from the nineteenth century through the Depression era.

No Time for Comedy (drama, 1939) is usually considered Behrman's most important work. Built basically around the conventional love-intrigue which also forms the plot of *The Second Man,* it is in another sense an extremely personal and subjective work in which Behrman attempts to work out his own attitude toward the violent political events of the late Thirties. The central figure, Gaylord ("Gay") Esterbrook, is a successful writer of comedies much like those of Behrman's early work; he is married to Linda Esterbrook, an actress who has played in most of his dramas, skeptical by temperament and ironic in her attitude toward her husband's talent. Gay, fallen into a creative impasse, imagines he has found new stimulation in Amanda Smith, a wealthy society woman who seeks to "develop his latent powers" and inspire him to greater and more profound works. Linda, who discovers this platonic but dangerous relationship through Philo Smith, Amanda's husband, resolves to fight for Gay, and thus the basic conflict of the drama is established. Amanda represents the positive inspiration which a woman can provide for a creative artist, seeking always to encourage him to greater and more significant work; with her assistance Gay plans a pretentious and falsely profound drama entitled *Dilemma* which is to explore the mysteries of immortality. Linda, who actually loves Gay more than Amanda does, nevertheless realizes his limitations and tries to prevent him from "living beyond his intellectual means;" she knows he is an excellent writer of entertaining comedy, but fears he would produce only pompous claptrap if he tried to be profound. Thus she is a "negative" influence on his talent, but a healthy one, an influence which will encourage his true talents and save him from his own weaknesses. A social issue is also involved: under Amanda's influence Gay convinces himself that the grim political events of the time (fascism, the war in China, the Spanish Civil War) demand a more serious attitude toward art, in short that the Thirties are "no time for comedy." The conflict is debated by Gay and Linda in a long dialogue in Act III; Gay is undecided whether to go off with Amanda to fight in the Spanish War or stay with Linda to write more comedies to make the time seem a little less gloomy. As the curtain falls he is on the telephone, still agonizingly undecided; but the presumption is that he will stay with Linda. If he does he will write a play called *No Time for Comedy,* that is, precisely the play in which he is now acting. The attitude of Linda—and of Behrman—toward the question of evils like fascism is expressed in a speech in Act I: "I gather the besieged Spaniards love the American films . . . Why grudge them a little fun in their last moments? . . . We can only laugh at our plight. That's what distinguishes us from the animals . . ."

LILLIAN HELLMAN (born 1905)

If Lillian Hellman had written only *The Little Foxes* and *Another Part of the Forest,* she might well be classified as a regionalist; she was born in New Orleans and has a genuine insight into Southern manners and culture, and these two plays treat social movements and processes discussed by other Southern writers from Ellen Glasgow to William Faulkner. She is also, however, the author of *The Children's Hour,* a drama built on abnormal psychology and set in an Eastern girls' school; *Days to Come,* a play involving American labor-management conflicts; *The Watch on the Rhine,* one of the best anti-Nazi plays of the war period; and *The Searching Wind,* laid partly in a European setting and concerned with diplomacy and international intrigue. Here conventional classification breaks down. Miss Hellman is sometimes treated as a "social dramatist," and there is some justification for this label too; almost every one of her plays makes apparent the social attitudes, tendencies, and processes which lie behind personal destinies. At the same time her plays are not "sociological" dramas in any sense; her characters are genuine individuals, not social symbols, and her interest remains centered on the individual conflict of personality which arises out of the contrasting natures of her characters. Thus in *Watch on the Rhine* Teck and Kurt come into conflict not so much because one is a Nazi sympathizer and the other an anti-fascist as because one is depraved and unscrupulous and the other a man of character. The central interest is always on persons rather than on social ideas. If it can be said that in a sense all modern realistic drama derives from Ibsen, Miss Hellman follows in the tradition of *Hedda Gabbler* rather than *A Doll's House* or *An Enemy of the People.*

In spite of her sex Miss Hellman is anything but a feminist; in fact it would be difficult, through mere reading of her plays, to identify the author as a woman. Here she differs from Ellen Glasgow, or from female playwrights like Clare Booth (who incidentally resembles Miss Hellman in both subject matter and political attitude). Not only is her interest equally disturbed between male and female characters, but she often shows a remarkable knowledge of the male side of life and insight into the masculine mentality. With the possible exception of Tennessee Williams, few male dramatists of her generation have demonstrated such a convincing understanding of the psychology of the opposite sex. This is perhaps best demonstrated in *Watch on the Rhine,* which is almost wholly a masculine story in which the female characters play only peripheral parts.

Politically Miss Hellman is a liberal, an anti-Nazi and anti-fascist who "believes more in the rights of the working man than in any other rights" and who has undergone Congressional scrutiny for her alleged left-wing associations. In spite of this bias her plays are never didactic. Even *The Searching Wind,* her most sweeping indictment of fascism and appeasement, is tolerant and objective; the diplomat Alexander Hazen, who argues for appeasement, is more misguided than sinister and is at the bottom motivated by humanitarian principles.

Stylistically Miss Hellman's drama is noteworthy for its sophistication and polish, for its adroitly vernacular dialogue, for its unerring accuracy in transcribing the manners of diverse cultures from the small Southern town to the diplomatic circles of pre-war Rome. In spite of its obvious intelligence her drama is invariably facile and easily comprehensible to the ordinary audience, a quality which has enabled her to achieve an impressive box-office success with at least three plays and at the same time to win the praise of serious dramatic critics.

LIFE: Lillian Hellman was born in New Orleans in 1905; her family background was Jewish. The family moved to New York when Miss Hellman was five, but returned to New Orleans intermittently; she attended schools in both cities. She studied at New York University for three years but left without a degree; she later studied for a semester at Columbia. After leaving N.Y.U. she went to work in the publishing business and simultaneously began writing short stories, only a few of which were published. She first became interested in playwriting through a job as a reader for a dramatic publisher. Her first play, *Dear Queen,* written in collaboration with Louis Kronenberger in 1931, was unproduced. In 1934, however, she wrote *The Children's Hour,* which created an enormous sensation in its Broadway production; it ran for 691 performances—virtually a record for a "problem play"—and was widely thought to have missed winning a Pulitzer Prize only because of its alleged indecency. After her next play, *Days to Come* (1936), a strike story typical of the Depression era, she visited the Soviet Union (1936-37) and spent some time in Hollywood as a screenwriter; she subsequently returned to Hollywood frequently on writing assignments and collaborated on motion-picture versions of *The Children's Hour* and *Watch on the Rhine.* This second play, which appeared on Broadway in 1941, won her the annual Critics' Circle Award and also achieved a considerable box-office success. In 1945 she visited the Soviet Union for the second time. In the following years she was active in several organizations described as "left-wing," and in 1952 she was called to testify before the House Committeee on Un-American Activities. She denied she was a Communist at the time, but refused to discuss her previous political experience. In a subsequent letter to the Committee she stated that for ethical reasons she was obliged to refuse to testify about the political activities of her friends and associates or persons

she had known in the various organizations to which she had belonged; the Committee did not pursue the matter. Miss Hellman has
been married once, to Arthur Kober, and was divorced in 1932.
During recent years she has lived on a farm near New York.

CHIEF WORKS: *The Children's Hour* (drama, 1934) is set in a
girls' boarding school operated by two young unmarried women,
Karen Wright and Martha Dobie, who first met in college and who
have labored and saved for several years to get the school on its feet.
Also teaching in the school is Mrs. Lily Mortar, Martha's aunt, a
former actress and a woman of somewhat dramatic temperament.
A problem arises when a pupil, Mary Tilford, who has always been
somewhat unstable, develops a fit of hysteria when punished for a
minor offense. The young Doctor Joseph Cardin, Karen's fiancé,
examines Mary and announces that her supposed "heart attack" is
only shamming. That night Mary escapes from the school and goes
home to her grandmother, Mrs. Amelia Tilford, and for revenge reveals to her an involved web of gossip, partly taken from remarks
made by Mrs. Mortar and partly pure fabrication, suggesting that
Karen and Martha have been sexually intimate. Mrs. Tilford believes
the story, since she imagines Mary to be an innocent child who could
only be telling the truth; actually Mary has heard hints of female
homosexuality from several other sources, including an illicit reading
of Gautier's novel *Mademoiselle de Maupin*. Shocked, Mrs. Tilford
spreads the news, and the school is ruined. When another pupil,
Rosalie Wells, comes temporarily to stay in the Tilford home, Mary,
through knowledge of a minor theft Rosalie has committed, black-
mails her to back up her story. Thus complete disaster falls on Karen
and Martha; their libel suit against Mrs. Tilford loses in court, and
Karen's fiancé Cardin, confused and now half-suspecting the rumors
are true, abandons her. Then Martha confesses to Karen her secret
guilt: that she actually had felt an unnatural affection for her, although
the impulse has never taken an overt form. Rejected by the shocked
Karen, Martha commits suicide. Shortly afterward Mrs. Tilford arrives to beg forgiveness of the pair; she has discovered Mary's du-
plicity and now knows they were innocent. Karen, her life ruined,
agrees to accept Mrs. Tilford's sincere contrition and her financial aid
in starting over again in a new life.

As a psychological portrait of an abnormal child *The Children's Hour* bears comparison with Henry James' "The Turn of the Screw" and with the less important *The Bad Seed* by William March, later dramatized by Maxwell Anderson. Miss Hellman borrowed the idea for *The Children's Hour* from the Scottish crime writer William Roughead's book *Bad Companions* (1930), which contained a chapter entitled "Closed Doors, or The Great Drumsheugh Case" relating an 1809 Edinburgh scandal caused by a child who claimed two headmistresses at her school had "an inordinate affection" for each other.

The Little Foxes (drama, 1939) portrays the decline of the Southern aristocracy and the rise of an aggressive new social class in a small Alabama town. The central characters are the Hubbard family —the hard, cynical, avaricious Ben; his weak-charactered brother Oscar, and his ambitious sister Regina. Oscar is married to the former Birdie Bagtry, daughter of the genuine ante-bellum aristocratic family of the town; Regina's husband is Horace Giddens, an honest and philosophically inclined banker who as the play opens is away in Baltimore under treatment for a heart ailment. Ben, the natural leader of the family, has found a scheme to make them all rich, involving a partnership with the Chicago financier William Marshall in a plan to build a cotton mill in the town. Ben and Oscar each put up $75,000 and demand an equal contribution from Regina; she cynically tricks her ailing husband Horace to come home in order to get the money out of him. When Horace refuses, Ben encourages Oscar's weak-willed son Leo, who works in Horace's bank, to steal $80,000 worth of bonds from Horace's safe-deposit box. In return for this favor Regina is to marry her daughter Alexandra to the dissolute young Leo. Horace, however, sees through this plot and detects the theft. The bitterness of this family quarrel is too much for his heart, however, and he dies, as Regina, calmly looking on, refuses to bring him the medicine he needs. Regina, however, has been brought to her senses by these violent events and now sees her family in its true nature for the first time. Through her knowledge of the theft she forces Ben and Oscar to give her the dominant share of the partnership; then she turns to seek a true understanding with her daughter Alexandra for the first time.

The chief character contrast in this play is that between the Hubbards and Birdie, who represents the true Southern aristocratic tradition which has gone into decline since the disaster of the Civil War. Horace, along with the faithful Negroes Addie and Cal, is on Birdie's side, deploring the selfish and pushing ambition of Ben and Oscar, believing, as Addie says, that "There are people who eat the earth and eat all the people on it," and that it is not even right for others to "stand and watch them do it."

Watch on the Rhine (drama, 1941) is set in an average American middle-class home, that of the widowed Fanny Farrelly, who has living with her a son, David, and a pair of house guests, the Roumanian refugee Count Teck de Brancovis and his American-born wife Marthe. As the play opens Fanny welcomes to the house her daughter Sara, who is returning to America after a long residence abroad with her husband Kurt Müller, a clandestine German fighter against Nazism, and her children Joshua, Bodo, and Babette. Although Fanny and David cannot understand the fanatic political consecration of Kurt, which has caused much physical suffering and hardship to himself and his family, they greet him warmly and attempt to make him and his family feel at home. The conflict, however, is provided by Teck. A weak-charactered failure in his own career, he is jealous of Kurt and also sees in him a chance to make a small fortune. He pilfers Kurt's luggage for evidence which he takes to the German Embassy, and as a result several of Kurt's companions are arrested in Europe. Soon Kurt finds himself at the complete mercy of Teck, who demands a ten-thousand-dollar bribe before he will keep quiet in order that Kurt may return secretly to Germany to aid his imprisoned friends. Kurt at first promises to comply, but he knows that cooperation with the unprincipled Teck is useless. Only violence can resolve the situation; he strikes Teck down and drags him offstage to murder him. The Farrellys, who are of course indignant at Teck's perfidy, are nevertheless shocked at first by this act, but finally realize that evil based on violence (e.g., Nazism) can be fought only on its own terms. They assist Kurt to escape in Fanny's car, although they realize that the eventual revelation of the murder will cause trouble for them with the police. A sub-plot is concerned with the personal relations of Teck and Marthe, who married him because she was dazzled by his title but was soon disillusioned. She turns instead to David, who has previously flirted superficially with her but now accepts her sincerely in a gesture symbolic of his new-born sympathy for the liberal struggle against fascism in Europe.

The Searching Wind (drama, 1944) is a structurally intricate play exploring the reasons for the democratic appeasement of fascism in the Thirties and the human factors which went to make up this social attitude. The plot utilizes the flashback technique; the first and last scenes take place in Washington in 1944 and the intervening scenes fill in the lives of the characters from 1922 to 1938. The chief characters are Alexander Hazen, an American diplomat; the talented Catherine (Cassie) Bowman, his fiancée in 1922; her best friend Emily Taney, whom he eventually marries; and Sam, the son of Alex and Emily, a soldier during the Second World War. As the action proceeds it becomes apparent that Alex's wife is one of compromise and rationalizing, in spite of his basic good nature and idealism; the pattern extends from his betrayal of Cassie and marrying of Emily to his career as a diplomat, in which he contributes importantly to the American policy of appeasement which reached its climax at the time of the Munich Conference in 1938. In the last scene Sam reveals that his leg, which has been damaged by a war wound, will have to be amputated; the family realize that Alex's political attitudes of years before have finally caused this tragedy in their own circle. As the play ends Cassie remarks, "I don't want to see another generation of people like us who didn't know what they were doing or why they did it . . . We were frivolous people." Moses Taney, Emily's father, also provides philosophical comment on the action. This play, written at the height of the Second World War, is remarkable for its objectivity and detachment toward the political issues involved; Alex is portrayed as a sincere idealist who is far from a villain, merely, as Cassie remarks, a man who "didn't know what he was doing."

Another Part of the Forest (drama, 1946) is a "sequel in reverse" to *The Little Foxes;* it portrays the earlier history of the Hubbard family in the period around 1880. At this time the family is headed by the hard and ambitious Marcus Hubbard, who made a fortune through illegal commerce during the Civil War and is now replacing the aristocratic Bagtry clan as the chief force in the region. His family, however, provides little assistance to his ambitions; his wife Lavinia is weak-minded and preoccupied with religion, his son Oscar is a half-witted roué, and his elder son and heir Benjamin is a rebellious and ambitious enemy who opposes him at every turn. His daughter Regina is conducting a secret affair with John Bagtry, scion of the aristocratic family, and Oscar has fallen into a vulgar concubinage with a prostitute named Laurette Sincee. Meanwhile Marcus, encouraged by Ben, plans to gain control of the Bagtry plantation through secretly lending money to the daughter of the family, the childish and light-headed Birdie Bagtry. He leaves the affair in the hands of Ben, who tries to trick him by pretending that the loan is for ten thousand dollars but keeping five thousand for himself. When Marcus discovers the deception a fierce struggle breaks out between father and son. Then Ben discovers, through the maundering of his mentally incompetent mother, the secret disgrace of his father's life: that he had not only operated as a smuggler during the War but that he had once led Union troops through a swamp to slaughter twenty-seven Confederate boys in a hidden training camp. Armed with this knowledge, Ben forces his father to sign over to him all his wealth and surrender control of the family; in his ambition and ruthlessness he has proved himself Marcus' equal. Ruling his family with an iron hand, he marries Regina to Horace Giddens, a young clerk who lives in Mobile and is thus far away enough not to have heard the scandal of her affair with John. He also (as we learn in *The Little Foxes*) forces Oscar to marry Birdie in order to get control of the Bagtry wealth. Miss Hellman evidently considered *The Little Foxes* and *Another Part of the Forest* as part of a trilogy; in a 1952 interview she announced she was contemplating a third play to complete the series.

ARTHUR MILLER (born 1915)

Along with Tennessee Williams, Arthur Miller represents the culmination of the process of evolution in the American theatre which began in the era of Clyde Fitch and extended over a half-century of development and experimentation. Thus Miller's work is not highly original in technique; it represents an organic synthesis, an endproduct in which the diverse elements which went to make up the final result are not always apparent on the surface. Basically Miller is a realist, and his technique might be described as naturalism; he concerns himself (unlike Tennessee Williams) with the typical and outwardly normal in American life, and his style is straightforward and vernacular. He deliberately creates characters who are ordinary instead of extraordinary. Where Williams' Serafina (*The Rose Tattoo*) is an exotic personality who interests Americans through her contrast to their own background, Miller's typical heroes Joe Keller (*All My Sons*) and Willy Loman (*Death of a Salesman*) are normal American business-men and husbands; their tragedy provokes sympathy precisely because it is the tragedy of average American life.

Yet Miller's realism is not as simple as that of Clyde Fitch or Dreiser, or even of Odets. It is a more complex form of art, a technique that uses in one form or another most of the devices developed by the experimentalists of the Twenties: the free verse of Maxwell Anderson, the fluidity in space and time of the Expressionists, the breaking-down of the audience barrier of Brecht, Wilder, and others, and the inner psychological analysis of O'Neill's *Strange Interlude*. *A View From the Bridge* well demonstrates this heterogeneous quality of Miller's work; basically realistic, it nevertheless contains free-verse passages, a narrator who speaks directly to the audience (*cf. Our Town*), fantastic and unrealistic shifts in chronology, and an underlying web of psychological pathology which suggests O'Neill's *Mourning Becomes Electra*. But since Miller's "experimental" devices are ones which have been stylized and perfected by a generation of use in the theatre, they are conventional enough to be easily grasped by the average audience; Miller in no sense appeals primarily to an avant-garde public. Thus his drama demonstrates the process of filtering-down through which the radical experiments of avant-garde literature eventually reach and influence popular art.

Miller's favorite material, and the setting of the majority of his important plays, is the bourgeois family. *All My Sons* and *Death of a Salesman* are built chiefly around father-son relationships, and *A View From the Bridge* around the tension between a father and stepdaughter (incidentally his niece). Although it cannot be said that any of these families are strictly speaking "normal" ones, they are at least "typical;" any playwright is usually obliged to exaggerate the normal for dramatic conflict. Willy Loman is not an "average" American salesman; he is the symbolic archetype of the American salesman. Another theme found almost invariably in Miller's work, connected to his interest in the family, is the American Dream of material success—the cult of the dollar. It is this neurotic avarice, this frenzied effort to "provide for the family" and "rise in the world," which destroys both Joe Keller and Willy Loman in spite of their basic decency. And intermingled with these two themes is often found a third: the warped and distorted passions which result from the suppression of the sex drive in puritanical society. This last element is seen most obviously in *A View From the Bridge*, Miller's least realistic play, which not only shows the destructive effect of repressed love but presents latent homosexuality and incest, the latter two portrayed in a manner which is no less subtle for being made comprehensible to the average audience. In spite of his apparent simplicity Miller is a complex artist, one who has carefully integrated his experimental techniques into a personal and original form of realism.

LIFE: Arthur Miller was born in New York in 1915; his father, an Austrian immigrant, was a well-to-do manufacturer by the time the son was born. Schooled in Manhattan, he went on after a period of odd jobs to the University of Michigan, which accepted him in spite of his poor scholastic record partly because of his talent for creative writing. He wrote his first play at Michigan; it won several prizes, and he was encouraged to continue. He turned out approximately two plays a year during the time he was an undergraduate, several of which brought him awards and money prizes. After graduating from Michigan (1938) he returned to New York and did radio writing for a living, meanwhile continuing to write plays. In 1947 *All My Sons* brought him acclaim from critics and a certain amount of popular success. Miller came into his own with *Death of a Salesman* (1949); the drama won a Pulitzer Prize and a Critics' Circle Award (both 1949), enjoyed a phenomenal run on Broadway, and later toured the country with considerable success. In *The Crucible* (1953) Miller departed radically from his previous realism; the play, an allegory built around the New England witch trials of the seventeenth century, drew an ironic parallel to the anti-Red "witch hunts" of the Fifties. Meanwhile Miller was in trouble with Congressional investigators; in 1957 he was convicted in a Federal court of a contempt charge arising out of his refusal to reveal the names of associates in alleged left-wing activities of earlier years. He has been married twice, the first time to Mary Slattery (two children) and the second time, after a divorce, to the motion-picture actress Marilyn Monroe.

CHIEF WORKS: *All My Sons* (drama, 1947) is a study of the effect of the Second World War in a typical American family. Joe Keller, the central character, is a sixty-year-old manufacturer and small businessman; his son Larry, a flyer, was reported missing during the war, and Joe's wife Kate has ever since nourished an obsessive and neurotic belief that her son will some day be found alive. Another son, Chris, brooding and idealistic, fought in the war in the infantry and now works in his father's plant. As the play opens Ann Deever, formerly Larry's fiancée, comes to visit the Kellers, and the secret shame of the family is revealed: during the war Joe had been in partnership with Ann's father in a concern which had shipped defective cylinder heads to the Army Air Corps, causing the deaths of several young men; both had been arrested, but Joe had been exonerated while Deever was sent to prison for a long term. Now Chris, who has long loved Ann, plans to marry her, but his mother is opposed; clinging to her belief that Larry is still alive, she tells Chris that marrying Ann would be an act of betrayal to his brother. Then George Deever, Ann's brother, arrives; he has just visited his father in prison and has become convinced that Joe is also guilty of the crime. He angrily accuses Joe and attempts to take Ann away with him. But the mother Kate, his old friend, succeeds in placating him. As the action proceeds, however, a doubt begins to grow in the mind of the idealistic Chris about his father's innocence. By persistent questioning he finally elicits the truth: that Joe had known about the defective parts and had approved their shipment, later denying his part in the fraud when he was accused. Joe tries to defend his action by arguing that many others did the same thing during the war, that in fact all war procurement was based on the profit system and was basically selfish, and that he committed the fraud solely to win financial security for his family and his sons. Yet it was Joe who symbolically killed his own son Larry; Ann produces a letter to prove that Larry, in disgust over news of his father's fraud, virtually committed suicide in his own plane. Joe finally realizes that the American boys who fought in the war were "all his sons," and that he was as responsible to them as to his own family; he now knows himself to be a murderer. Tormented with guilt, he commits suicide; the mother, before neurotic but now the strongest member of the family, tells Chris, "Don't take it on yourself. Forget now. Live." Thus *All My Sons* demonstrates the basic ethical weakness of the American business morality, which justifies all through success and often ignores human values; Joe, setting out to succeed in the typical American way, has murdered his own son and brought destruction on himself and his family.

Death of a Salesman (drama, 1949) treats a similar theme: the conflict between business ethics and the emotional relationships of a family. The central character, Willy Loman, is a travelling salesman with a home in Brooklyn who covers a New England territory by automobile; the action concentrates on the last two days of his life, although events many years back are filled in through flashbacks. A successful salesman in his youth, Willy has gradually become tired and ineffectual; in spite of the encouragement of his loyal wife Linda, he knows his life has been a failure. His two sons Biff and Happy are a disappointment; Happy is apparently bogged down for life in a dull and monotonous job, and Biff has turned into a drifter and petty criminal. As the flashbacks are presented they gradually reveal the root of this tragedy: Willy's dogged faith in the magic of salesmanship, his conviction that personality, a glad hand, "contacts," a quick smile, and good clothes will bring you everything you want in life. Biff, a champion athelete in high school, was his favorite of the two boys, and he had ruined his character through pumping him full of this philosophy. "I never got anywhere," says Biff, "because you blew me so full of hot air I could never stand taking orders from anybody!" The climax of the action is a flashback scene in a Boston hotel room, where Biff surprises his father in a clandestine meeting with another woman. Shaken and disillusioned, he drifts gradually into a life as a loafer and ne'er-do-well. Other flashbacks present Willy's older brother Ben, an adventurer and self-made man who travelled in all parts of the world and made a fortune several times over. To Willy his brother is a symbol of the success that can come through enterprise and courage. The contrast between Willy and Ben points up an incidental theme of the play: that Willy has been born a generation too late, that in a pioneer age he might have made a fortune as an enterprising frontier merchant. This theme is suggested by Willy's constantly expressed longing for the outdoors, his nostalgia for his old car with an open windshield, and his pathetic efforts to raise vegetables in the dank Brooklyn soil. Another theme is implicit in the contrast between Biff and his school admirer and hanger-on Bernard, a timid and bookish failure as a boy when Biff is at the height of his triumph as an athlete. When Willy meets Bernard years later he finds that the "bookworm," through hard work and application, is now a successful lawyer, living exactly the life that Willy planned for his own sons. As the play ends, Willy, who has finally lost his job, commits suicide, leaving his twenty-thousand-dollar insurance policy to give his sons a start toward a new and better life. In addition to the chronologically intricate flashbacks, the chief technical devices of *Death of a Salesman* are the continual reappearance of Ben, actually only a revery or hallucination in Willy's mind, and the trick of revealing Willy's inner thoughts through his mumbling to himself. Each of the flashbacks, in fact, is set off by a thought which occurs in Willy's mind and suggests to him some incident or person in the past. This last device, commonly used in motion pictures, is adapted by Miller for the stage through use of an ingenious stage setting in which quick time-changes can be made through lighting different parts of the set.

A View From the Bridge (drama, 1955) is actually a short full-length play in structure, although it is little longer than the average one-act drama. Its hero, Eddie Carbone, is a longshoreman of Italian descent who works on the New York docks. He and his wife Beatrice have raised a niece, Catherine, now seventeen years old, as their own daughter. Still loyal to their relatives in Italy, Eddie and Beatrice agree to take into their flat a pair of illegal Italian immigrants ("submarines" in waterfront slang), Marco and Rodolpho, who plan to work on the docks to get money to send to their families in Italy. Marco, the elder, is married and has a tubercular wife, but his younger brother Rodolpho, blond and handsome, is unmarried. Catherine and Rodolpho immediately fall in love, but Eddie angrily opposes the match. He finds a variety of reasons to justify his attitude: he points out that Rodolpho is penniless and that Catherine is too young to be married, and he detects in the young Italian signs of a latent homosexual tendency—which is merely implied in the dialogue and never stated directly. The real reason, however, is that Eddie himself is secretly in love with his niece, and cannot bear to think of letting her go. He first realizes this latent feeling one day when he comes home drunk and finds Rodolpho and Catherine making love; in an angry scene he seizes and kisses her, then fights inconclusively with Rodolpho. Half-crazed with his mixed emotions and ready to do anything to prevent the marriage, he violates the code of his people by betraying Marco and Rodolpho to the Immigration authorities. The two are arrested, but Marco suspects Eddie of the betrayal. When the two are released on bail they come to get Catherine to take her to be married; a fight breaks out and Eddie is killed by a blow from Marco. The ending is tragic in the best classical sense: Eddie is destroyed through his tragic flaw, his ignorance of his own passions, and through his sin of betraying Marco and Rodolpho to the police. The action of *A View From the Bridge* is introduced and commented upon by Alfieri, a character who serves both as a lawyer who advises Eddie in his problem and a narrator who speaks directly to the audience. Another unusual technical device in the play is the use of poetry, a kind of free verse in which Alfieri comments on the action in the manner and style of a classic chorus. In its original Broadway production (1955) *A View From the Bridge* was presented on a double bill with another short play by Miller, *A Memory of Two Mondays,* a rather disconnected but effective study of the emotional relationships of employees in a New York automobile parts warehouse.

TENNESSEE WILLIAMS (born 1914)

Considered from the standpoints of both critical and popular success, Williams is undoubtedly the most important new dramatist to emerge onto the American theatrical scene in the period after the Second World War. A highly original playwright who has a knack for creating vivid and striking characters, he is not easy to classify by conventional literary standards. He is a regionalist whose interest in the South is incidental to his central concern: human character, personal emotions, the crisis of personality. He is a naturalist who has created some of the most sordid settings and the most debased characters in the modern drama, yet he has a fairy-tale touch that imparts an air of fantasy to his most realistic plays. "Everyone should know nowadays the unimportance of the photographic in art," he wrote in the preface to *The Glass Menagerie:* "that truth, life, or reality is an organic thing which the poetic imagination can represent or suggest, in essence, only through transformation, through changing into other forms than those which were merely present in appearance." This is a clear-cut rejection of traditional realism in the theatre. On the other hand, while his interest in exotic settings and strange and perverted personalities might be considered romantic qualities, his objectivity, his total detachment from his characters and their struggles, sets him apart from romantic dramatists like William Saroyan or Maxwell Anderson. Like Arthur Miller, he utilizes many of the experimental devices of the expressionists and other avant-garde dramatists of the Twenties, but he integrates them into a style which is wholly personal and individual. Like most first-rate authors, Williams belongs to no clear-cut school.

The dominant theme of Williams' work is one which constantly recurs in twentieth-century literature: rejection of the American middle-class Protestant culture and its standards, especially its puritanism and its hypocritical standards of respectability. Like Saroyan and Steinbeck, Williams turns for dramatic material to the exotic and foreign elements in the American population: the Italians and Creole whites of Louisiana, and the decayed aristocrats of a declining Southern culture. Behind the action of most of his plays a social process can be seen in operation: the Southern plantation class, vigorous and highly cultivated in the ante-bellum period, declines with the economic decline of the South, becomes corrupt and characterless, and is finally absorbed into the energetic commercial class (often of foreign extraction) which is gradually assuming control of the economy. In *The Glass Menagerie* the dominant class is still the aristocracy, decadent as it is; a mother, lost in escapist reveries of her aristocratic youth, perverts and destroys the happiness of her middle-class children. In *Twenty-Seven Wagons Full of Cotton* a virile Sicilian cotton-gin operator symbolically defeats a characterless plantation-owner and seduces his childish and mentally incompetent bride; in *A Streetcar Named Desire* and *Cat on a Hot Tin Roof* members of the former landowning class are seen in various stages of decline. *The Rose Tattoo,* with its verile, hot-blooded, and hedonistic Sicilians, frankly champions physical love in its most violent and unsophisticated form;

the two middle-class housewives who appear briefly in the play provide
an ironic contrast between Latin vigor and prurient middle-class
puritanism.

But mere social change by itself is unrewarding as a source of
dramatic conflict. For his immediate plot material Williams makes
use of a subject of more immediate interest: the sexual passions,
especially in their exaggerated or frustrated form. Sexual maladjust-
ment plays a part in almost all of his major dramas, and the most
important of the plays (*A Streetcar Named Desire, The Rose Tattoo*)
implicitly contrast uninhibited sexual behavior, which Williams admires, with the perversions, neuroses, and hysteria which arise from
frustration of this basic human need. This is not to say that Williams
is a "psychological dramatist"; his work is free from the vocabulary
and dogma of modern psychiatry, and he owes almost nothing to
Freudianism and its related schools of psychopathology. In this respect he resembles D. H. Lawrence more than he does Robinson
Jeffers or Eugene O'Neill; it is when his characters follow their "blood
instinct" (e.g., the Stanley and Stella of *A Streetcar Named Desire*)
that they are happy and satisfied, whatever their social position, and
it is when this instinct is denied or misdirected (as in the Blanche of
the same play) that neurosis and unhappiness result. And, like
Lawrence, Williams has no interest in the sensational aspects of sex,
no desire to shock merely for the sake of shocking, or in order to
attract attention. He is so suspicious of this kind of sensationalism,
in fact, that he deliberately cut a number of profane speeches out of
Cat on a Hot Tin Roof when he heard that rumors were spreading in
the theatrical world that he had written a shocking play. Here he
stands in sharp contrast to such writers as Henry Miller, who, whatever his basic intent, seems to take an impish pleasure in shocking the
complacent and conventional through words banned in polite usage.
Williams chooses his language, as he does his material and his characters, because it seems fitted to the poetic concept he has of the play.

LIFE: Tennessee Williams was born Thomas Lanier Williams in the
small town of Columbus, Mississippi in 1914. Although in later years
he made much of the alleged conflict of "Puritan and Cavalier" strains
in his blood, his family came from white Protestant stock on both
sides; his grandfather was an Episcopalian minister, his father a travel-

ling salesman, and his mother of Quaker stock. Until Williams was twelve the family lived in the grandfather's rectory, then the father was transferred north to St. Louis. The twelve-year-old boy felt lonely and unwanted in the stodgily respectable middle-western city, and the experience undoubtedly contributed to the aversion toward lower-middle-class respectability which is apparent throughout his work. He began to write at an early age, publishing some poetry under his real name when he was still in his boyhood. Meanwhile he completed his schooling in St. Louis and went on to college in the middle of the Depression; unable to continue because of the financial situation of the family, he dropped out after two years. There followed a long period of monotonous work as clerk in a shoe factory, while he continued with his writing in his free time. Under the combined strain of job and writing his health failed, and he went to live with his grandparents in Memphis. Gradually his writing, mostly stories at this time, began to sell, and he became self-sufficient enough to reenter college. He graduated from the University of Iowa in 1938, went on with his writing, and worked at a succession of odd jobs. In 1940 he was granted a Rockefeller fellowship which enabled him to write *Battle of Angels,* his first mature play; staged by the Theatre Guild, the play was opened for trial in Boston, but was abandoned during the trial run. Classified 4-F by the draft, Williams went back to his writing and his odd jobs. Then a Hollywood screenwriting contract provided him with enough money to write *The Glass Menagerie;* it was produced on Broadway in 1945, achieved a box-office success, and won the Critics' Circle Award for that season. In 1947 *A Streetcar Named Desire* brought him even greater success, and his reputation as a leading playwright was established. Between 1945 and 1955 he won two Critics' Circle Awards and two Pulitzer Prizes, the latter for *A Streetcar Named Desire* and *Cat on a Hot Tin Roof.* Several of his plays during the period were made into successful motion pictures. In spite of his frequent residence in New York and California, Williams prefers to live in New Orleans, in the Creole quarter he used as the setting for *A Streetcar Named Desire.* Politically independent, he claims to be merely a "Humanitarian." He was unmarried in 1955.

CHIEF WORKS: *The Glass Menagerie* (drama, 1945) is a "memory play" involving the technique of broken chronology in which the

recollections of a narrator present on the stage introduce and comment upon incidents taken from his earlier life. This narrator is Tom
Wingfield, a somewhat bitter young man who spent years working
in a St. Louis warehouse before he finally became a merchant marine
sailor. The other important characters in the seven scenes are his
mother Amanda Wingfield, an impoverished widow who nostalgically
recalls the youth in which she was a vivacious Southern belle with
many suitors, and a daughter Laura, crippled, moody, and unattractive to men. Like her mother, Laura lives in a world of illusion; she
finds her escape in the "menagerie" of glass animals which she cher-
ishes in the sordid St. Louis flat. Each of Laura's pitiful attempts to
face reality have come to nothing; her mother has sent her to business
college, but the atmosphere of the school made her physically ill, and
Amanda discovers that she has not been attending her classes for several weeks. Tom, who is an avid reader and dreams of becoming a
poet, is forced to work at a monotonous job in a shoe warehouse to
support the family; he grows rebellious when he sees no way out of
the impasse and turns to petty dissipation. A constant bicker goes on
between him and Amanda over his way of life. Finally Amanda
persuades him to invite one of his fellow-employees from the warehouse to dinner; when Amanda learns that Laura is to have a "suitor"
she is filled with a nervous elation, and makes a pitiful attempt to tidy
up the flat. Jim O'Connor, the guest, is "a nice, ordinary young man"
who gets along well with Laura; by coincidence it happens that he is
a secret beau for whom Laura had a clandestine admiration in high
school. As her desperate need for a lover becomes apparent, however,
Jim grows apprehensive; finally he confesses to her that he is engaged to another girl and will soon be married. After Jim leaves,
Amanda bitterly upbraids Tom for bringing an engaged man as a
suitor for Laura. Tom, his disgust at the sordid family situation rising
to the point of rebellion, storms out of the flat—ostensibly to go to
the movies, but actually to go off to sea. As the play ends Tom, now
a detached narrator of his own life drama, confesses to the audience
the feeling of remorse toward his sister which has pursued him ever
since he abandoned her to her lonely spinsterhood.

In addition to the unrealistic device of the actor-narrator, *The
Glass Menagerie* utilizes another surrealistic or expressionistic trick:
a screen on which are projected magic-lantern slides bearing images

or titles which comment ironically on the action. This device, intended to "give accent to certain values in each scene," was omitted in the Broadway production.

A Streetcar Named Desire (drama, 1947) is set in the Creole quarter of New Orleans "on a street which is named Elysian Fields" and which is reached by taking a streetcar named Desire and transferring to one named Cemeteries—i.e., an analogue of life itself. Stella Du-Bois, daughter of an old but now impoverished Southern family, has come to New Orleans and married Stanley Kowalski, an artisan of Polish extraction, strong, virile, a heavy drinker and a great poker player. As the play opens Stella's sister Blanche, who has remained home in the family mansion in Laurel, Mississippi, comes to "visit" —actually she is coming to live with them, since everyone else in the family has died and Blanche, through incompetence and debauchery, has lost the family mansion to creditors. Although Blanche has pretensions to elegance and pretends to feel a fastidious repugnance for the surroundings in which Stella and Stan live, it soon becomes apparent that she is not only a neurotic but an alcoholic and a shameless nymphomaniac. She at first attempts to vamp Stan, but he, content with his satisfying relations with Stella, ignores her. Then she takes up with Harold Mitchell ("Mitch"), an unmarried friend of Stan, somewhat younger than she (Blanche is apparently in her late thirties and anxious over the approach of middle age). At first this affair goes well, and Mitch's interest in Blanche seems to be based on genuine love. Once when they are alone Blanche confesses to Mitch the secret tragedy of her life, which has left her guilt-ridden and lonely ever since: married at sixteen, she accidently discovered that her young husband was a homosexual, and drove him to suicide through her recriminations. Mitch accepts her in spite of this, and a marriage, the solution to Blanche's problems, seems in the offing. But meanwhile she has made an enemy of Stan through her haughty air of superiority, her hypocritically fastidious ways, and her secret drinking. When Stan learns the truth about her past—that she was virtually banished from Laurel after she had taken up a life of debauchery— he tells the full story to Mitch, who breaks off relations with her. To complete his revenge Stan roughly attacks her one night when Stella has gone to the hospital to have a baby. Her "fiancé" gone and her pose of superiority toward Stan shattered, Blanche relapses into a psychotic world of self-delusion, consoling herself with an imaginary friend, the wealthy Shep Huntleigh, who is shortly to invite her on a yachting cruise of the Caribbean. Stella has no choice but to send her to a mental hospital; a doctor and a matron call for her, she struggles frantically against the female matron, but is led away quietly by the male doctor.

Two themes are interwoven in *A Streetcar Named Desire:* (1) the decline of the landowning Southern aristocracy, symbolized by Blanche and Stella, and its defeat at the hands of the modern commercial-industrial class, personified in Stan; and (2) the contrast between hysterical female sex-frustration (Blanche) and normal and healthy physical relations (Stella and Stan). As a human being Blanche is pitiable, especially when we understand the past history which has made her what she is; but as a visitor in the house of Stan and Stella she stands for evil, and she brings evil to everyone she touches. Particularly obnoxious is her ingrown and perverted delicacy, which contrasts strongly with Stan's hard-drinking, profane, vulgar, but basically healthy attitude toward life.

The Rose Tattoo (drama, 1950) centers around the character of Serafina delle Rose, a Sicilian dressmaker who lives with her daughter Rosa in a small Gulf Coast village. Happily married to Rosario, a virile Italian truck-driver who has a rose (evidently a symbol of physical love throughout the play) tattooed on his chest, she is expecting another child as the play opens. When she is visited by Estelle Hohengarten, a harlot, she agrees to make a rose-colored shirt for Estelle's sweetheart without realizing that Estelle is actually intimate with her Rosario. Then news comes that Rosario, smuggling narcotics in his truck under a load of bananas, has been killed in a fight with the police. Serafina, morbidly brooding on her grief, locks herself in her house and for months refuses to dress or to attend to her business. Cherishing her dead husband's ashes in an urn, she regresses constantly farther into her melancholia. When Flora and Bessie, two priggish middle-class ladies, call for a blouse they have ordered, Serafina is rude to them, and for revenge Flora repeats to her the common gossip about the unfaithfulness of her husband; Serafina, stunned, becomes even more sullen and brooding. Her daughter Rosa, seventeen and just graduated from high school, picks this moment to introduce to her mother her boy-friend, a sailor named Jack Hunter. Serafina, skeptical over the faith of men, forces Jack to swear before an image of the Virgin that he will "respect the innocence of the daughter, Rosa, of Rosario delle Rose."

In Act II a complication is introduced: by accident a young truck driver, Alvaro Mangiacavallo, calls at the house, and Serafina in spite of herself is struck with his resemblance to her dead husband. When Alvaro clumsily makes advances to her she rejects him, then gives him permission to return that night. Act III begins with a farcial courting scene in which Alvaro, hot-blooded but inept, is constantly repulsed by the inwardly confused Serafina. When Alvaro learns that her resistance is caused by loyalty to her dead husband, he proves through a telephone call that Rosario had actually been unfaithful to her; in a torment which fast becomes a passion, Serafina then gives her love to him. The next morning Alvaro arises stupified with a terrible hangover and confusedly makes advances to the sleeping Rosa, who has meanwhile returned from a date. A terrible three-cornered argument results; but in the end Serafina blesses Rosa's marriage with Jack and forgives the clumsy Alvaro for his mistake. Life has triumphed over the cult of death in the Delle Rose household: Serafina's long dead love has been reborn in the person of the handsome young Alvaro. The success of *The Rose Tattoo* is the triumph of the characterization of its heroine. Alternating between an animal-like brooding and a fiery and hot-blooded passion, Serafina is simultaneously a vivdly original human being and a symbol of healthy and unashamed womanhood, uninhibited by Anglo-Saxon puritanism and the middle-class bugbear of respectability.

Cat on a Hot Tin Roof (drama, 1955) is set on a Mississippi plantation owned by "Big Daddy" Pollitt, an energetic planter who rose from a "red-neck" overseer to become a multimillionaire. As the play opens Big Daddy is dying of cancer, a fact known to everyone in his family but his wife Big Mama. His children, who have gone to college and become "respectable" and successful, now gather around to fight over the spoils. An elder son Gooper and his wife Mae have brought their five children to the plantation to win Big Daddy's sympathy, but the howling and ill-mannered brats only set his nerves on edge. His younger son Brick, an alcoholic, takes little part in the controversy; but Brick's wife Margaret, the "cat on a hot tin roof," nervous and sexually frustrated, determines to fight vigorously for her husband's rights. The climactic scene occurs when Big Daddy, who has been assured that his illness is curable and that he will soon be well, has a conversation with Brick in which he begins to probe into his son's reasons for drinking. This reason Brick has scarcely admitted even to himself: it is a secret fear that his affection for a college friend, Skipper, was an unnatural one. Margaret, angry over Brick's failure to make love to her, has accused him of this, and now under his father's grilling he realizes it is true. In his desperate effort to get back at Big Daddy he tells him the truth that he is incurably ill of cancer. In a mixture of despair and hot-tempered anger at the lies that have been told him, Big Daddy shuts himself up in his room. Then, in a family conference, the truth about Big Daddy is told to Big Mama, and Gooper attempts to wheedle her into giving him control of the property. Margaret, seeing her cause failing, tries to rally Brick to help her, but he is apathetic. Finally, in a last desperate effort to win Big Daddy's sympathy, she sends word to him that she is going to bear Brick's baby. As the play ends she has determined to make this lie a reality, and in her dogged strength of character she finds the means to force Brick into serving as the father for her child. The ending is inconclusive, but the implication is that the flighty but courageous Margaret has won her battle against the hostility of her relatives and the apathy of her husband.

For the Broadway production of *Cat on a Hot Tin Roof* (1955) Williams was induced to write a new third act which differed considerably from the original printed version, chiefly as the result of suggestions from the director Elia Kazan. The chief difference between the two versions is that the Broadway ending is more specific and leaves less to be conjectured, also that a definite change is shown in the character and attitude of Brick. Some ambiguity was also felt about the characterization of the heroine in the original version. As Williams later wrote, Kazan "felt that the character of Margaret, while he understood that I sympathized with her and liked her myself, should be, if possible, more clearly sympathetic to the audience." This sentence is an important clue to the character of Margaret; she is by no means a dangerously hysterical neurotic like the Blanche of

A Streetcar Named Desire, merely a healthy and normally sexed young woman who has been turned into a "cat on a hot tin roof" by her husband's inattention. In the Broadway version of the play this point is made clear by Big Daddy's acceptance of Margaret in the final scene. Both versions of the third act are available for comparison in *Theatre Arts* XLI:6 (June, 1957), pp. 33ff.

* * *

4. Tradition and Revolt in Poetry

THE HERITAGE OF THE NINETEENTH CENTURY

Like the rest of American literature, American poetry in the nineteenth century tended to be strongly derivative from its European heritage. While American poets sometimes treated indigenous themes, they usually did so in the manner of transplanted English poets, using the verse forms, the imagery, the literary conventions, even the philosophical content of the European tradition. A typical example is William Cullen Bryant, a poet who wrote consciously as an American, using what he thought were American materials, but nevertheless produced what was essentially a Wordsworthian poetry in the British romantic tradition. Even his ideas—the joyousness of kinship with nature, his political liberalism, his nebulous Deism and Unitarianism—he shared with the English romantics, and the influence of Wordsworth on his diction is obvious. The same judgment might be made of Longfellow, Whittier, Holmes, Lowell, even Sidney Lanier; there was little in their verse which would have surprised the average English reader, nothing which marked their technique as indigenously and unmistakably American.

To this generalization there are three major exceptions, each of them important in its influence on twentieth-century poetry.

EDGAR ALLAN POE (1809-49), in some respects a conventional romantic, was in other respects a remarkably advanced poet in technique as well as in content. Perhaps his most important legacy to modern poetry is his fascination with the emotive values of individual words, his tireless effort to find exactly the word which would produce the desired psychological or emotional reaction in the reader. In his essay "The Philosophy of Composition" he purported to reveal the process by which he had composed his famous poem "The Raven," describing the infinite pains he had taken to select the word "nevermore" to establish the mood of the poem, and then to build around it a structure of calculated emotional effect. Twentieth-century poets, applying to Poe's basic concept the more detailed theories of modern psychology and semantics, developed the technique to a high degree; it is perhaps seen best in the poetry of the Imagist school (Pound, Amy Lowell, H.D.) and in the poets influenced by them. Likewise Poe's conviction that only a short lyric can sustain a high poetic level, his preoccupation with intricate metrical and rhyme patterns, and his "Gothic" or deliberately grotesque subject matter all had their due impact on the revolution in American poetry which took place around 1914.

An even more important influence was that of WALT WHITMAN (1819-92). Abandoning conventional verse forms entirely, Whitman wrote "free verse" a half-century before the term was coined and before it was recognized as an essentially new technique in poetry. Not only did his *Leaves of Grass* (1855) abandon traditional prosody and metrics, but it lacked any apparent organization or structure. Its content might roughly be described as naturalistic; it was drawn from a broad knowledge of life rather than from an academic erudition or from a genteel "observation of nature" in the manner of the New England nature-poets. Whitman knew intimately, and celebrated in his poems, all kinds of Americans from farmers to big-city prostitutes; he observed a multitude of trades and professions, travelled widely, and mingled with ordinary people rather than with poets and scholars. He was scornful of Victorian decorum; his poems contained words, incidents, and ideas that shocked many of his contemporaries. He wrote with utter frankness, both about himself and about the more unsavory details of the world about him. Finally, his poems contained a strain of grandiose egotism, an elemental vitality, a "barbaric yawp" which reflected the energetic self-confidence of a new nation. His two Lincoln poems "When Lilacs Last in the Dooryard Bloom'd" and "O Captain! My Captain!" influenced a dozen important twentieth-century poems on Lincoln, from Markham's "Lincoln, the Man of the People" to Sandburg's "The Long Shadow of Lincoln." His influence in technique is even more important: one only has to glance at the appearance on the page of Sandburg's *Chicago Poems* or Cummings' *Sonnets Actualities* to realize the tremendous impact of Whitman on the poets of our own age.

Finally, EMILY DICKINSON (1830-86), most of whose poems were not published until after her death, exerted an important influence on at least a minority of twentieth-century poets. In some re-

spects a romantic, she treated conventional subjects (nature, unre-
quited love, death) but always in an ingeniously original manner.
Her poetry is highly condensed, like that of Poe; she often achieves
her most brilliant and subtle effects with a mere half-dozen lines.
Even more important for its mark on twentieth-century poetry is her
elliptical method, her half-playful cryptic quality which always implies more than it says and conveys its meaning as much through
suggestion as through denotational content. Although many of her
poems are concerned with highly dramatic material, she understates
emotion; there is a faint current of irony in her style which reappears
in the twentieth century in such poets as Frost (who has admitted
his debt to Miss Dickinson), Cummings, Amy Lowell, Sara Teasdale,
Edna Millay, and Edgar Lee Masters. Her metrics and rhyme also
anticipate modern poetry; her slightly diffuse "slant rhymes" (*pearl/
alcohol, Heaven/given*), her lines lengthened or shortened for calculated effect, continually found imitators in the experimental poetry
of the post-1914 era.

BRITISH INFLUENCES

In addition to the obvious tradition bequeathed to American literature
by the English romantics and Victorians (Wordsworth, Coleridge,
Byron, Shelley, Keats, Tennyson, Browning, Arnold), two late nineteenth-century British poets are particularly important for their influence on twentieth-century verse.

GERARD MANLEY HOPKINS (1844-88), a Jesuit priest whose
poetry was almost unknown during his lifetime and whose work was
not published until 1918, deeply impressed the postwar generation
of poets who were deliberately searching for new techniques. His
curious metrical system, which he called "sprung rhythm," suggested
the most radical experiments of the twentieth century, and his vividly
condensed imagery was as advanced as that of the formal Imagist
school of Ezra Pound and Amy Lowell. In addition to these two
technical innovations, he sought to rid his verse of particles, relative
pronouns, suffixes, and other non-imagistic elements of language;
each word was to contribute to the total "inscape" (his term for a
single unified imagistic effect). His verse cannot be properly appre-

ciated unless it is read aloud; his metrical innovations and his imagistic nouns and verbs were intended entirely for auditory impact. Poetry, according to Hopkins, was to communicate chiefly the experience of nature, and the flow of language was to match the original sensation through its rhythm and general organization. Hopkins' difficult and often obscure verse is still unknown to the general public, but his impact on a half-dozen leading English and American poets alone would mark him as an important literary figure.

Even more important is the influence of WILLIAM BUTLER YEATS (1865-1939), Irish-born poet and dramatist whose long career spanned the period from the Victorian era to the post-1918 experimentalism. Yeats' work mirrored each of the periods through which he passed: as a member of the Symbolist movement (1890-1900) he wrote under the influence of Pater, Ruskin, and the French Symbolists; then, joining the Abbey Theatre group in Dublin around 1900, he turned to an active interest in the drama, in content revolutionary and in style more or less naturalistic with poetic overtones. In the Twenties he returned to poetry, producing a subjective, sensual, and emotionally charged verse marked by a pessimism similar to that of Housman or Hardy. Yeats was a valuable friend and advisor to a whole generation of younger poets: T. S. Eliot and Ezra Pound associated with him personally, and a number of other American poets underwent his influence either through Eliot and Pound or through independent reading of his work. The exuberant spontaneity of "The Lake Island of Innisfree," the precise and evocative symbolism of "The Wild Swans at Coole" and "Leda and the Swan," the metaphysical and contemplative allegory of "Sailing to Byzantium," each of these moods found its echo in some aspect of later American poetry.

CONTINENTAL INFLUENCES

The influence of the French Symbolist movement on Yeats and his group has already been noted above. Paradoxically, this Continental movement itself owed something to American literature. The spiritual godfather of Symbolism in France was CHARLES BAUDELAIRE (1821-67), who evidently provided the name for the school through his use of the word *symboles* in his poem "Correspondances" and who anticipated both its revolutionary poetic techniques and its grotesque and often morbid subject-matter by more than a generation. Baudelaire himself was profoundly influenced by an early reading of Poe, in whose verses and tales he found confirmation of the theories that lay in embryonic form in his mind. Taking the cue from Poe's meticulous attention to the sensual and psychological associations of words, Baudelaire built his poetic method on a "correspondence" or association of the five senses; a visual image might suggest an audible sensation, for example, or a perfume (as in "Hymne à la Beauté") might suggest abstract beauty.

The theory was advanced and refined by ARTHUR RIMBAUD (1854-91), who in his famous sonnet "Voyelles" attributed definite colors of the spectrum to the various vowel sounds: "A black, B White, I red, U Green, O blue . . ." Typical of his method in application is "Bateau Ivre," a long poem in which a pilotless boat drifting down a river toward the sea symbolized the poet's soul seeking escape from the conventions of society. In addition to Rimbaud, the French Symbolist school also included STÉPHANE MALLARMÉ, its acknowledged leader or *chef de cénacle,* whose work was pervaded by a deep, if somewhat contrived, pessimism and melancholy; PAUL VERLAINE, whose work showed the influence of Poe as well as anticipating Freudianism through its probing into unconscious associations; HENRI DE REGNIER, who made extensive use of Greek pastoral and pagan themes; and PAUL VALERY, a member of the second generation of Symbolists who died only in 1945, and whose *La Jeune Parque,* published in 1917, anticipated the theological-Symbolist style of Eliot's later poems (e.g., *Ash Wednesday*).

Other important European influences on contemporary American poetry are that of DANTE, especially apparent in Eliot and Pound; medieval French and Italian poetry, especially that of the troubadours, which found an echo in the work of many moderns from Pound to John Crowe Ransom; and the twentieth-century French movements or SURREALISM and DADA, which in their total abandonment of rational content, their esoteric and often incongruous symbols, and their fascination with dream-states and the unconscious mind provided poetic ideas for certain American experimentalists, especially Wallace Stevens and E. E. Cummings.

GENERAL CHARACTERISTICS OF CONTEMPORARY AMERICAN POETRY

American poetry in the twentieth century shares with the poetry of other nations two tendencies which at first glance seem mutually contradictory. The first of these is "verse naturalism," the tendency to avoid artificiality and return to a natural vernacular idiom; and the second is technical experimentation, the plunge into various forms of esoteric symbolism, experimental reconstruction of language, and novel systems of prosody. The combination of these two elements is well seen in such a poem as Eliot's *The Waste Land,* a difficult work involving an intricate hierarchical structure of symbols and obscure allusions to mythology, anthropology, and classic literature, but also containing passages of faithfully transcribed vernacular ("He's been in the army four years, he wants a good time, / And if you don't give it him, there's others will, I said . . .").

The naturalistic and vernacular quality in modern poetry causes no difficulty to the average reader; "verse naturalists" like Robinson and Frost who write almost exclusively in this idiom often achieve a wide popularity. It is the "experimental" quality of modern poetry that baffles and enrages the ordinary public, and has in a period of a half-century almost completely alienated the more advanced poets from the great mass of the population. Comparatively speaking, the public which enjoys the poetry of T. S. Eliot, Ezra Pound, or Wallace Stevens is an infinitely smaller percentage of the total population than the public which read the poems of Tennyson or Poe. Poetry has never, except in rare instances, been the preoccupation of the great masses of people, but never before the twentieth century has poetry been written for such a small and clannish group of readers. The reasons for this cabalistic regression are two: first, that the possibilities of conventional forms of poetry had been exhausted—that after Tennyson, Browning, Arnold, and the poets of their age everything that could be said in traditional verse had already been said—and second, that a new and more complicated society was deemed to deserve new poetic techniques capable of portraying or reflecting its complexity. The style of the nineteenth century, poets felt, was hopelessly inadequate as a means of expressing poetically the age of the airplane and the radio. The poet, confronted by this intricate and often ominous technology, was forced into a search for a poetic language as technical as the age which produced it. In the words of T. S. Eliot: "Our civilization comprehends great variety and complexity, and this variety and complexity, playing upon a refined sensibility, must produce various and complex results. The poet must become more and more comprehensive, more allusive, more indirect, in order to force, to dislocate if necessary, language into his meaning." The phenomenon was only a part of the increasing specialization which was felt in every aspect of life in the twentieth century; the scientist, the mathematician, the theologian, the psychologist, the poet, the technician in every field followed the line of his own highly intricate technique until he became virtually cut off from the rest of the population. Thus modern poetry often seems to the layman hopelessly obscure; the average citizen, after a single glance at Pound's *Cantos* or Eliot's *Four Quartets,* turns in despair back to his newspaper. Like modern music and modern painting, modern poetry demands a higher effort from the reader who wishes to appreciate fully its more complex modes of expression.

HISTORY: THE LITTLE MAGAZINES AND
OTHER RALLYING-POINTS

Because of the technical complexity described above, the more advanced forms of modern poetry soon lost contact with the lay population, and the poet found himself isolated in his own culture. The result was a tendency for poets to band together with their own kind, to form coteries, schools, groups, and movements. Never before had so many new labels been coined for literary cénacles: impressionism, expressionism, Symbolism, surrealism, Dada, Vorticism, futurism, modernism. Undoubtedly the most important of these groups for its influence on the development of American poetry was the Imagist movement, founded in England around 1909-15 by Ezra Pound and Amy Lowell and later transferred to American soil by Miss Lowell. The group, in addition to publishing widely in magazines, produced four important anthologies: *Des imagistes,* edited by Ezra Pound and published in Europe in 1914, and three successive volumes of *Some Imagist Poets,* published in America under the guidance of Amy

Lowell in 1915 and the two following years. The mark of Imagism can be seen in many later poets, from Eliot to Eberhart and Shapiro; in addition the movement served as a medium of exchange of ideas, a kind of club from which young poets could derive mutual inspiration and advice.

A similar function was performed by the countless small magazines which sprang up after 1912 to serve as rallying-points for the new poetry. The most famous and most important of these "little magazines" was *Poetry: A Magazine of Verse,* founded by Harriet Monroe in Chicago in 1912. Receptive to experimental forms but rigidly demanding in its literary standards, *Poetry* performed a tremendously important function in encouraging new forms in American poetry. The magazine, which never championed any single movement or school, was at least partly responsible for bringing to public attention the work of T. S. Eliot, Robert Frost, Carl Sandburg, Amy Lowell, H. D., Ezra Pound, Vachel Lindsay, and Hart Crane. *The Little Review,* also a Chicago magazine, was founded in 1914 by Margaret C. Anderson; it differed from *Poetry* chiefly in that it divided its attention equally among verse, fiction, and criticism. Most of the poets listed above also appeared in *The Little Review,* which also published W. C. Williams, W. B. Yeats, Wallace Stevens, and Carl Sandburg. *The Little Review* performed another great service to modern literature when it serialized James Joyce's *Ulysses* (1918-20), an action which caused one issue to be confiscated by postal authorities for alleged obscenity. *The Little Review* moved frequently during the Twenties, to San Francisco and New York and finally to Paris; it ceased publication—symbolically—in 1929 at the end of the era it had helped to create.

Other important little magazines, most of them founded during the Twenties, are *Fugitive,* which served as a focus for the Nashville "Fugitive Group," *Transition, The Seven Arts, Dial, Hound and Horn,* edited by university students and particularly receptive to younger poets, and *The Sewanee Review,* more academic in character and chiefly concerned with Southern literature. In the Thirties and the post-1945 era a new generation of literary magazines sprang into existence: *The Kenyon Review, The Hudson Review, The Partisan Review,* which until 1939 served as an unofficial organ of Stalinist criticism, *New World Writing,* a semiannual anthology, and *New*

Directions, an annual anthology edited by James Laughlin and sponsored by the publishing house of the same name. These publications, along with dozens of others, most of them non-profit or financed through philanthropy, provided an important means of expression without which many younger poets might have remained unpublished and eventually turned to other pursuits.

Finally, the function of colleges and universities in encouraging the new movement in poetry should be mentioned. Not only did many colleges set up workshops and seminars to give valuable training to young poets, but college teaching especially after 1945 became an important source of income for poets and other writers. The alienation from the general public discussed above resulted in severe financial hardship for the average poet; there is scarcely a quality poet in the twentieth century who was able to make a living through his writing alone. A variety of sources of secondary income were found: Frost for a time was a working farmer, and T. S. Eliot for years held an editing position in a publishing house. But it was the university which, in America, provided the largest amount of financial support for poets whose writing was not remunerative in itself. Many poets, from the "Fugitives" who gathered at Vanderbilt University in Nashville in 1922-25 to the later generation of Richard Eberhart and Delmore Schwartz, held teaching positions in English or other subjects; while others, like Frost, were simply engaged as "poets in residence" to lecture occasionally while continuing to work at their poetry. Summer writers' conferences also provided incidental income for poets, as well as encouraging talents among would-be writers. It is safe to say that without the assistance of the American university the new movement in poetry would have been seriously handicapped and might never have assumed the importance and magnitude in the cultural life of the nation it had attained by 1955.

EDWIN MARKHAM (1852-1940)

Few modern poets have enjoyed so great a popularity in their lifetime as Edwin Markham. He made his name famous with a single poem, and he remained a famous man until his death at the age of eighty-eight. During his career he was frequently addressed as "the dean of American poetry" and "the poet laureate of labor;" Joyce Kilmer hailed him as the greatest living poet, and H. L. Mencken referred to "The Man With the Hoe" as "the greatest poem ever written in America." Today he is usually regarded by critics as more important as a predecessor than as an important poet in his own right. His position in American letters is often compared with that of William Dean Howells, roughly his contemporary. Just as Howells anticipated twentieth-century realism in content and purpose without achieving its experimentalism in style and construction, so Markham foreshadowed the themes and social attitudes of twentieth-century poetry but remained conservatively Victorian in technique. His "The Man With the Hoe" and "The Toiler" are comparable in content to such social-protest poems as MacLeish's "Burying Ground By the Ties;" his "Lincoln, the Man of the People" anticipates Sandburg, and his "Judas Against the World" suggests such quasi-archaic modern ballads as Eliot's "Journey of the Magi" and Pound's "Ballad of the Goodly Fere." In style, however, Markham resembles the poets he himself admired, all of them pre-Victorian: Bryant, Byron, Wordsworth, Tennyson, sometimes Whitman or Poe.

At his worst Markham tends to lapse into doggerel, and there is scarcely one of his poems that does not have in it lines of a singsong banality (e.g., in "The Man With the Hoe," ". . . How will you ever straighten up this shape . . . ?"). He was not a consistently talented poet, and he seemed to lack a competent organ of self-criticism; a more sensitive talent would have noticed and deleted these clichés and doggerel passages. Yet even in his weaker poems there are occasional passages of great beauty and originality; in these rare moments he seems to attain the height of a Poe or a Shelley. The opening lines of "The Man With the Hoe" are typical of his best "Wordsworth style;" the often cited image of the ravens pecking out the brain of the hanged murderer in "The Ballad of the Gallows-Bird" might have come from the pen of Poe or Baudelaire.

Although Markham was no mere newspaper rhymer, he was a "popular poet" in every sense. Many of his important poems, including "The Man With the Hoe," first appeared in newspapers, and others were published in popular magazines such as *The Ladies Home Journal, Century,* and *Scribner's.* He was free from technical sophistication; he felt no urge to find a newer or a better poetic way to express his sentiments. It is interesting to compare his "On the Suisun Hills" with Dylan Thomas' "Fern Hill" and Ransom's "First Travels of

Max;" all three treat recollections of an idyllic boyhood close to nature, but Markham's poem is trite in style, even in imagery, compared with the intense and allusive twentieth-century techniques of Thomas and Ransom.

Thus Markham's final importance must rest upon his content. He is not the first American poet to treat "democratic" themes or to hail the age of the common man—Whitman had done this before him, and the theme is latent in Emerson and Whittier. He was, however, the first important American poet to use poetry as a vehicle for proletarian purposes, to express a frank and deliberately class-conscious revolutionary sentiment. "The Man With the Hoe," prophesying a time when ". . . this dumb terror shall rise to judge the world / After the silence of the centuries," is revolutionary poetry, at least in embryonic form; the theme is found throughout Markham's work, and marks him as an important predecessor of MacLeish, Sandburg Langston Hughes, Clifford Odets, and Maxwell Anderson.

LIFE: Edwin Charles Markham was born in 1852 in Oregon City, Oregon, the son of pioneer parents; his father had led an immigrant train from Illinois into the Oregon Territory. When Markham was five his father died and the family moved to the Suisun Valley in central California. For ten years the young Markham lived the life of a farm boy amid the scenes he has discribed in "On the Suisun Hills." Meanwhile he had encountered literature; through the inspiration of a teacher in a little country school he made his acquaintance with the standard poets and first conceived his ambition to become, some day, a poet himself. When he was fifteen the family moved again, this time to the Santa Clara Valley south of San Francisco. Here Markham attended the State Normal School to prepare himself as a teacher, later going on to Christian College in San Jose. From that time until his first successful poems brought him financial independence he made his living as an educator, serving in various positions from teacher in a small Sierra mining town to principal of the Observation School of the University of California in Oakland.

Markham began to write poetry while he was still a student, although with little success. In 1886 occurred one of the most important inspirations of his life: in the March issue of *Scribner's* for that year he saw a black-and-white reproduction of Millet's painting *The*

Man With the Hoe, and was fascinated. "It held my soul, as one is held by some object of menace and terror," he wrote later. He immediately jotted down the rough draft of a poem, which eventually served as the opening passage of his poem in its completed form. It was not until twelve years later that he finished the work; then, viewing the original Millet canvas on exhibit in the house of the San Francisco society leader Mrs. William Crocker, he worked three days over his earlier version and produced the work as it is known today. "The Man With the Hoe" appeared in the *San Francisco Examiner* in 1899 and created an immediate sensation. The poem was widely reprinted throughout the world, and editorials hailed it as the predecessor of a new literary age. A number of sequels followed, all of them inspired by famous works of art—"The Toiler," "The Sower," "The Angelus"—and Markham's poems became the standard declamation pieces for a generation of school children. Meanwhile his first published volume, *The Man With the Hoe and Other Poems,* had appeared in 1899. In 1900 he wrote "Lincoln, the Man of the People," which lent its title to his second volume published in 1901. It is indicative of Markham's widespread popularity that when the Lincoln Memorial in Washington, D.C., was dedicated in 1922 this poem was chosen out of more than two hundred and fifty others by a committee of laymen headed by Chief Justice William Howard Taft as the dedicatory piece to be read at the ceremony. Markham continued to write prolifically throughout his long career, but few of his later poems achieved the success of the poems written before 1914. Married in 1897 to Anna Catherine Murphy, he moved east to New York with his first success in 1901 and later established a permanent residence on Staten Island. His wife died in 1938. During the latter years of his life Markham, a dignified and striking figure (Louis Untermeyer described him as "looking like a blurred composite photography of four Hebrew prophets and all the New England poets"), was widely honored and eulogized; a Carnegie Hall meeting on the occasion of his eightieth birthday was attended by many famous members of the literary world. His health failed rapidly during the Thirties; in 1937, after an attack of encephalitis, he was declared legally incompetent, and in 1940 he died in his Staten Island home of pneumonia.

IMPORTANT POEMS: "The Man With the Hoe," Markham's best-known poem, was inspired by the painting of the French pastoral landscapist Jean François Millet (1814-75). Beginning with an impressionistic description of the painting's subject, the poem goes on to pose a long rhetorical question (11. 5-26) inquiring the reason for the misery and hardship which have fallen upon man, this "Thing the Lord God made and gave / To have dominion over sea and land." The development of the poem then leads into a prophecy of social revolution, again phrased in question form, predicting an age when "this dumb terror shall rise to judge the world." The mood of this warning, however, is less political than religious, suggesting a moral or theological righting of wrongs rather than an outright social upheaval. In a note in the original volume edition Markham explained that he saw Millet's subject as "a plundered peasant, typifying the millions left over as the debris from the thousand wars of the masters and from their long industrial oppressions, extending over the ages." Like many of Markham's longer works, the poem is written in unrhymed pentameters (English blank verse).

"The Toiler: the Hoe-Man of the Ages," inspired by Rodin's statue *The Thinker,* is similar. The ending, however, is stronger and more effective than that of the earlier poem, rising to a climactic picture of the cheated toiler who is given as his reward "a crust to taste" and finally commenting bitterly, "How patient he has been with God!" In the same genre are "The Sower" and "The Angelus," both suggested by paintings of Millet. The first of these is particularly notable for its "social irony;" the poet, contrasting the sower of the grain with the rich who eat its bread, remarks, "Yea, this vicarious toiler at the plow / Gives that fine pallor to my lady's brow." These rhymed couplets, also found in "The Angelus," are in the tradition of the English heroic couplets of the age of Dryden and Pope.

"The Ballad of the Gallows-Bird," written in 1896 and first published by Mencken in *The American Mercury,* was considered by Markham himself to be his best poem. A long, fantastic, and grotesque ballad in rhymed quatrains, it suggests the influence of both Poe and Coleridge, especially the latter's "The Ancient Mariner." The ballad is narrated by a murderer, who first describes how he believed himself saved from the gallows through an accident, fled away to wander through strange regions, and at last realized he was

dead and condemned to hell. The best part of the poem is the moving
and effective climax in which the damned soul, wandering aimlessly
across a nightmare landscape in search of his bereaved wife, encounters a gallows and there sees his own body "A-swing in the spectral
light."

"Lincoln, the Man of the People," first written for a Lincoln
Birthday Dinner in New York in 1900, was later selected for reading
at the dedication of the Lincoln Memorial in 1922. Like the similar
poetic tributes of Whitman and Sandburg, the poem stresses Lincoln's
humble origin ("the tried clay of the common road") in contrast
with his heroic destiny ("A man to match the mountains and the
sea"). The lines beginning, "The color of the ground was in him,
the red earth" (11. 16ff) are particularly notable for their vernacular
simplicity and dignity, anticipating the similar techniques of Sandburg and Masters. The reference to "Captain" in the closing passage
is an obvious echo of Whitman's "O Captain! My Captain!", probably
the best-known poetic lament for the death of Lincoln.

"Judas Against the World" is another ballad, written to correct
"a serious mistake that the whole world has made concerning Judas."
Markham argues that, since Judas committed suicide as soon as he
discovered that Jesus yielded to arrest, he did not intend to betray
the Saviour; rather "he expected so powerful a person as Jesus to
resist arrest and go gloriously free." Narrated by Judas himself, the
poem presents a powerful if somewhat stilted and melodramatic picture of the last hours of Jesus. It is also interesting as a possible
influence on Ezra Pound's "The Ballad of the Goodly Fere," which
also presents a novel interpretation of the Crucifixion story in ballad
form.

EDWIN ARLINGTON ROBINSON (1869-1935)

Like Markham, Robinson is a poet who has long been popular
among lay readers—the "non-literary" public—but the tremendous
scope of his work and the power of his mastery over words marks
him as the greater poet of the two. In spite of its consistent tone his
work shows a great versatility. Among the general public he is known
chiefly for the short epigrammatic characterizations like "Miniver
Cheevy" and "Richard Cory" and for the romantic verse novel
Tristram, which brought him wide fame and financial success. Critics,

however, especially in academic circles, consider his most important contribution to lie in certain sonnets and shorter lyrics (e.g., "Many Are Called"), in a handful of medium-length philosophical poems, the best-known of which is "The Man Against the Sky," and in *Merlin* and *Lancelot,* the two Arthurian narratives which are regarded as more penetrating and less sentimental than *Tristram.* But verse narrative and philosophical poetry have gone out of style, and will perhaps remain so; Robinson's fame in the future is likely to rest upon "Miniver Cheevy" and poems like it, bitter, original, modern in their salty irony, and easily appreciable by the public which buys and reads popular anthologies of poetry.

In both his short epigrams and his longer verse narratives Robinson shows a consistent interest in character; most of his better-known poems succeed in creating vivid and original personalities which stick in the reader's mind. His technique of characterization, influenced by his early interest in the theatre, is that of a dramatist rather than a novelist; he conveys character through dialogue (many of his longer poems consist almost entirely of conversation) rather than through internal analysis. In this respect his characterization technique resembles that of Eliot ("The Love Song of J. Alfred Prufrock," "Portrait of a Lady") rather than that of Robinson Jeffers, who is marked as a true "verse novelist" through his technique of objective and detached psychological analysis. Yet even Robinson is objective in another sense; his characterizations are usually studies of his yellowmen rather than himself. His best-known characters are eccentrics, noble failures, monomaniacs, amateur philosophers, and stoically bitter old men. In a sense Robinson is treating his own problem in creating such figures, since he too was an "outcast," a misunderstood and unhappy refugee from normal life, who often doubted his own genius and lived on the whole an unhappy existence. But when he put pen to paper he transferred this personal attitude into figures who were not himself, who were outside his consciousness, who in fact were often based on eccentric persons Robinson had met in real life; two acquaintances he is known to have used as models for his poetry were Alf.ed Louis, an eccentric Jewish philosopher who is thought to have suggested the fictional Captain Craig, and Joseph Lewis French, a colorful vagabond who followed and pestered Robinson during most of the latter part of his life.

Such characterizations, half-failures whose genius is insufficient to bring them fame but only enough to fill them with a deep and bitter sense of superiority, often illustrate Robinson's basic philosophical attitude: a despairing metaphysical pessimism like that of Thomas Hardy combined with a classical stoic acceptance. Robinson's life was bitterly unhappy; if ever there lived a man who had reason to believe "the fates were against him," it was he. Yet, like his own character Cliff Klingenhagen, he drank his wormwood like a philosopher, even taking a certain sardonic satisfaction in the depth of his misfortune and finding the strength to endure in his own hardy New England character. Another typical creation of Robinson is Mr. Flood, who ironically "drinks to the bird" of passing time and talks to himself when there is no one else to talk to. Robinson is not without resemblance to the British poet W. E. Henley, who in the midst of misfortunes "black as the pit from pole to pole" still thanked "whatever Gods may be" for the strength of soul to withstand them.

Robinson's attitude toward religion also approximates that of Henley. He is essentially an agnostic, continually stressing the unknowability of divine things and yet clinging to a dogged abstract belief in some Power or Meaning in the universe beyond the comprehension of human intelligence. At the bottom, however, he is neither a philosopher nor a theologian; he is a poet whose beliefs even in the realm of religion are expressed instinctively in concrete images. One of the most prevalent of these symbols, one which pervades virtually his whole work, is the antithesis between light and dark, which reflects both his own basic pessimism and the influence of the Christian culture in which he wrote. "Dark" to Robinson is the misery and meaninglessness of mundane life, full of evil and pain for even the happiest of mortals; darkness also occasionally symbolizes the nothingness we fear lurks beyond death. "Light" is the vision of all that is not material, of the ideal whatever it may be. To Robinson's Lancelot the Dark is his sin, the seduction of Guinevere and the betrayal of his king, and the Light is the life of religious devotion into which he longs to escape. In "Credo," where perhaps the image is most clearly expressed, the poet first complains of being lost in the darkness (life), then speaks of the "black and awful chaos of the night" (oblivion); yet at the end he "feels" the coming of a Light which may be thought of in terms of a quasi-Christian salvation.

Some critics argue that Robinson's philosophy of "immediate pessimism plus ultimate optimism" is a result of his New England heritage, with its firmly imbedded Calvinistic doctrine modified by the later mysticism of the Emersonian transcendentalists. Whatever its sources, the concept is one which may be found in almost all of Robinson's poems which touch upon ultimate questions.

Robinson's language is that of a sparse and laconic down-easter; he mistrusts rhetoric and verbosity, and has an apt command of the curt and colorful Yankee idiom of the Maine coast. His dialectisms are naturally more effective in poems in a modern setting, and some critics, for example Ivor Winters, have poked fun at the New England expressions he puts into the mouths of a Merlin or a Rembrandt. Other critics view the laconic quality of his verse as a symptom of an inward Puritanical repression; Robinson preserves a rigidly Victorian decorum in his love scenes, and refused to read Daudet's *Sapho* for years because he had heard it was pornographic. Whatever the reason, Robinson is not a poet who is likely to fall into maudlin rhetoric or Swinburnian romanticism; at his best his tone is that of a quiet and drily bitter New England cynic.

Robinson began in his college days as an admirer of classic literature and a translator of Virgil and Horace. Rejecting the romanticism of William Vaughn Moody and his group, at that time dominant on the Harvard campus, he turned to a vernacular style which he apparently derived from personal sources, although he was familiar with Wordsworth. He was practically unaffected by the contemporary naturalistic movement in fiction. His content owes much to Baudelaire and the French Symbolists as well as to Thomas Hardy's verse; this last influence is the only one in his work which may be termed in any sense "naturalistic." Robinson views life as a drama in which each man consciously or unconsciously selects a rôle in which to appear before his fellows. Sometimes this mask is torn away, as in the case of Richard Cory; in other cases the deception fails to succeed, as with Miniver Cheevy. But whenever the illusion is stripped away and the reality underneath is laid bare, we find life to be bleak, hostile, and friendless. The happiest characters in Robinson's poetry are those, like Cliff Klingenhagen and Eben Flood, who continue to maintain the illusions and fantasies which bring contentment even when they inwardly realize them to be false.

LIFE: Edwin Arlington Robinson was born in 1869 in Head Tide, Maine; shortly after his birth the family moved to the town of Gardiner, Maine, where he grew up and which he converted to the "Tilbury Town" of his poems. His family was an old and respected one; he was descended on his mother's side from a colonial governor of Massachusetts and from a sister of the poetess Ann Bradstreet. The immediate family, however, tended toward the eccentric; his brother Dean, a doctor, was a lifetime alcoholic and narcotics addict, and his father was an amateur spiritualist who experimented with levitation when he was on his deathbed. As a child Robinson suffered from ear infections, which he believed had been originally caused by a blow from a schoolteacher; he was operated on several times for mastoiditis, and eventually suffered a partial loss of hearing. Delicate and introverted, he studied the classics avidly as a high-school student. He later persuaded his family to send him to Harvard, although the family finances permitted only a two-year stay at college. At Harvard, however, he got his start as a poet; he published in student magazines and made contacts which were later to prove useful. From 1896 to 1902 he lived in New York City, working at odd jobs and writing in his spare time. His first poems were published at his own expense in 1896; a more important collection, *The Children of the Night,* appeared in 1897. His first wide success came with *Captain Craig* in 1902. This poem found a powerful supporter in Theodore Roosevelt, then President of the United States, who championed Robinson warmly. From 1905 to 1910 he held a minor government position in New York city granted him through the President's intervention.

Meanwhile his popular success continued to grow, reaching a peak with *Tristram* in 1927. In the period after the World War he received many honors and awards including three Pulitzer Prizes (for *Collected Poems,* 1922, *The Man Who Died Twice,* 1925, and *Tristram,* 1928). Today, however, his best work is considered that written before the war. Robinson during his later years spent his summers at the Mac-Dowell Colony in Peterborough, New Hampshire, a literary cénacle of which he was the chief luminary. He never married, and on the whole his life seems to have been an unhappy one; he did not seem to derive any particular pleasure from anything other than the writing of his poetry. He died of cancer in New York in 1935.

CHIEF WORKS: THE LONG POEMS. "Ben Jonson Entertains a Man From Stratford" is a dramatic monologue somewhat in the style of Browning; it is spoken by Jonson to an unnamed countryman who has come to London and inquires news of his fellow-townsman Shakespeare. Two characterizations are involved, as in Browning's "My Last Duchess;" Jonson characterizes himself through his speech, and he characterizes Shakespeare through anecdotes and through his personal interpretation of the great poet's character. Jonson (actually, of course, Robinson) sees Shakespeare as a self-consciously ambitious man who bitterly resented the favors society had granted to lesser persons; he is unhappy in London, "where he sees too many lords." His ambition is to be "Duke of Warwick," as Jonson drily remarks; he hopes for a title and wealth to show his Stratford compatriots how far he has risen in the world. This is the source and meaning of his greatest works, even including the sonnets into which he has poured the best of his genius. A characteristic of Jonson's style which Robinson imitates in the poem is his flowery and slightly pedantic Latinity, e.g., "a deal of circumambient hocus-pocus" and "a patent and intrinsical equavalence."

"The Man Against the Sky," which lent its title to a volume published in 1916, is an important example of Robinson's metaphysical pessimism. The solitary man who crosses a hilltop into the sunset in the opening lines is emblematic of man in general approaching death. After this image is established the poet then conjectures as to several attitudes that man may take toward the experience of death: he may overcome it through stoic fortitude, he may deny its existence through a conventional religious faith, he may greet it with an indifference born of disillusionment with the world, or he may be a mechanistic materialist who sees himself as "a living reason out of molecules" and death as a mere incident of physics and chemistry, and thus accepts the scientific necessity of his own oblivion. Then, after a few lines dwelling on the universality and inevitability of death, the poet demands an answer to a large question: why, if death is inevitable and oblivion follows, should man bother to do anything, even perpetuate his own species ("launching other lives to voyage again / A little farther into time and pain")? The only answer is that "if we know anything" there is a Word, a divine perfection, which sometimes appears to us "in incommunicable gleams / Too permanent for dreams." Although we cannot know the exact nature of this Divinity or even guess at its purpose, these premonitions of its existence are the only solace available to us in our journey "beyond our sunset fires." The poem ends, however, on a fundamentally pessimistic note; Robinson evidently found the premonition of Divinity which he describes little comfort in his own pessimistic stoicism.

"Captain Craig" is a long narrative poem which lent its title to the volume published in 1902. The narrator, evidently the poet himself, describes and characterizes his old acquaintance Captain Craig, a New England eccentric, amateur philosopher, vagabond, and indigent, relating many conversations and quoting documents such as Captain Craig's letters and last testament. Gradually Captain Craig emerges as an Emersonian philosopher whose outward sarcasm conceals a detailed if somewhat crotchety erudition and even a transcendental faith: in his will he refers to himself as "Sage-errant, favored of the Mysteries." His ethic is one of altruism, contrasting sharply with the materialistic selfishness of late-nineteenth-century civilization. Robinson's dim agnostic expectations of immortality are also expressed; the Captain tells his young friends, "I can do no more / Than hope for all of you that you may find / Your promise of the sun." Yet Captain Craig must not be confused with Robinson himself; he is a fictional creation who is at once ridiculous, wise, and pitiable, and the poem is a character study rather than a personal philosophical essay.

Merlin (narrative poem, 1917) is a character study of the magician-figure of the Arthurian legends treated from a modern point of view. The chief historical sources are the *Morte d'Arthur* of Sir Thomas Malory (*ca.* 1470) and the metrical "Merlin and Vivien" from Tennyson's *Idylls of the King* (1859). Where both Malory and Tennyson portray Merlin as a mysterious and senile necromancer, however, Robinson shows him as a forceful and intelligent man at the height of his powers, capable of passionate love and in every way equal in character to Arthur and the other Knights of the Round Table. There are two distinct stories involved in the poem: the love of Merlin for the Breton beauty Vivian, and the disintegration and collapse of Arthur's kingdom through the Lancelot Guinevere tragedy. The two stories are only loosely connected, and this lack of unity is felt by some critics to be a flaw in the poem. Where Tennyson's theme is

"Sense at war with Soul" (i.e., the universal conflict between fleshly sin and spiritual idealism), Robinson's poem has at least two themes. The first is the operation of fate: like Cassandra, Merlin is a seer who perceives the tragedy toward which the kingdom is moving but is powerless to avert it. The second theme is that of Merlin's personal moral problem; his love for Vivian, which represents a carnal temptation, prevents his coming to Arthur's aid until it is too late. Since, however, the fall of the kingdom is fated anyhow, the force of the second theme seems logically weakened; Robinson has difficulty establishing any harm actually caused by Merlin's "sin." The action of the poem is briefly as follows: Merlin, encountering the fascinating Vivian at her castle of Broceliande in Brittany, is so attracted to her that he withdraws from the world into the castle for ten years, thus founding the legend that he descended into a "living grave" for that period of time and miraculously emerged alive. The knight Dagonet arrives at Broceliande and exhorts Merlin to come to Arthur's aid; he goes, but finds the situation hopeless and returns to Vivian. Back in Broceliande, he broods over his duty to his monarch and over the foolishness which has led Arthur into his present situation; his illegitimate son Modred has raised a rebellion and killed several knights, and Lancelot has carried off Guinevere, killing Gawaine's brothers Gareth and Gaheris. Merlin blames all this on sin, especially the sin of Arthur; but Vivian, sensual, feminine, and amoral, cannot understand and is contemptuous of this "puritanism." Finally Merlin returns to Camelot out of an abstract sense of duty, but he knows the end is destined and that he can do nothing. Thus the central conflict of *Merlin* is the struggle in Merlin's mind between his love for Vivian, whom he finally loses because of his brooding over the fate of the kingdom, and his duty to Arthur, who in turn is faced with a similar conflict himself.

Lancelot (narrative poem, 1920) is similar in style and treatment, and relates many of the same incidents from another point of view. The central figures here are Lancelot, the trusted knight of Arthur; Guinevere, the Queen; Gawaine, a courageous and upstanding knight and onetime friend of Lancelot; and the King himself. The action centers around the seduction of Guinevere by Lancelot, especially an incident in which Arthur pretends to go off on a hunting trip but returns unexpectedly to surprise the pair in a tryst. Surrounded in the castle, Lancelot fights his way to freedom with Guinevere but is forced to kill twelve knights in doing so, including Gareth and Gaheris, the favorite brothers of Gawaine. Withdrawing with Guinevere to the castle of Joyous Gard, Lancelot prepares for a war with Arthur; but meanwhile he begins to be assailed by doubts of conscience. Thus the conflict of the poem is introduced: Lancelot vacillates between the "Dark," his present life of sin, and the "Light," the life of the spirit, specifically a withdrawal into a life of religious contemplation. The conflict is well expressed by Lancelot himself in a soliloquy which concludes Section VII of the poem. Lancelot exhorts Guinevere to return to Arthur, but she refuses, proposing instead that they should flee together to France. Finally he takes her back to Camelot, but in spite of his contrition is formally banished by Arthur. In Section VIII Arthur attacks Lancelot at Joyous Gard, but meanwhile he has other difficulties; the base Modred, his bastard son by the sister of Lot's wife, has seized the opportunity to raise a rebellion. When Gawaine, who is mortally wounded, exhorts Lancelot to return to the defense of Arthur, Lancelot at last does so, but it is too late; he arrives with his army to find the last battle over and Arthur and Modred both dead. He then seeks Guinevere, who has retired to a convent, and begs her to accept him now that Arthur is dead. She, however, has thought out the moral issues which Lancelot himself discussed with her at Joyous Gard, and has decided to devote herself to a religious life. She convinces Lancelot, and they part. He rides away, desolate and conscious only of nothingness, but feeling somehow that he is moving toward divinity: "Always in the darkness he rode on, / Alone; and in the darkness came the Light." The theme of the poem, however, is not specifically a religious one; it is rather the basic human conflict between the physical and the spiritual, and the destruction which may result from the struggle of these forces in a human soul. *Lancelot* is considered by many critics to be one of Robinson's most important poems; Ivor Winters calls it "one of the few deeply impressive narrative poems written in English in more than two hundred years."

Tristram (narrative poem, 1927) draws from the same source materials as *Merlin* or *Lancelot,* and in addition is based to a certain extent on the medieval Tristan-Isolt romances of Gottfried von Strassbourg and Thomas. The core of the story is the love of Tristram for

two women: Isolt of Brittany, daughter of King Howel, called Isolt
of the White Hands; and Isolt of Ireland, wife of King Mark, also
known as Isolt the Fair. According to the story, the Cornish knight
Tristram first fell in love with the Irish princess Isolt when he visited
her land to ask her hand for his monarch, King Mark. Later, after
the marriage of Mark and Isolt, the two renew their love. (Robinson,
in his process of modernization, discards the love-potion which motivated this love in the medieval versions as well as in the opera of
Wagner). They meet for a prolonged tryst at Joyous Gard, the castle
of Lancelot, but Mark learns of Isolt's hiding place and kidnaps her,
removing her in a ship. Tristram later returns to Cornwall in search
of Isolt; they meet, with the permission of Mark, but Tristram's
treacherous cousin Andred surprises them and murders both. This
ending is radically different from that of the standard legend, in which
Tristram dies in Brittany after a battle. Robinson's poem goes on
after Tristram's death to describe how his body was taken to Brittany
in a ship, ending with a passage in which King Howel attempts to
comfort his broken-hearted daughter. *Tristram* is the most romantic,
or most sentimental, of Robinson's three Arthurian poems; it was
widely popular at the time of its original publication, and made him
financially independent after years of poverty.

SHORTER POEMS: "Eros Turannos" is a succinct portrait of a
marriage, told from the wife's point of view. Fearing her husband
and regretting the rash choice that committed her life into his hands,
she nevertheless lacks the courage to violate the mores of a Victorian
society by rebelling against him. She can only endure—a favorite
theme of Robinson. At the end her life seems to her like a "stairway
to the sea / Where down the blind are driven." The Greek title signifies "the tyrant love."

"Richard Cory" is one of Robinson's best-known poems, although
its surprise ending, superficial and contrived, marks it as a lesser
work. Cory, the cynosure of the community, nevertheless takes his
own life; we can never judge a man's happiness from the outside.

"Cliff Klingenhagen" is a sardonic portrait of a misfit in life who
has learned to savor and enjoy his own failure, perhaps an ironic
portrait of Robinson as he conceived himself. The poem is ambiguous;

Cliff Klingenhagen is described sarcastically, especially in the last lines, yet he shows an admirable stoicism in the courage with which he quaffs the bitter portion of wormwood.

"Credo" is a sonnet which states in fourteen lines the basic theme of "The Man Against the Sky" (see above). The poet, lost in skepticism, living in a modern materialistic world where "there is no star / In all the shrouded heavens anywhere," nevertheless senses "the coming glory of the Light;" even when faith crumbles under the impact of rational skepticism the poet feels an irrational premonition of some Divinity in the universe.

"How Annandale Went Out," another sonnet, is one of Robinson's bitterest and most cutting short poems. The theme, euthanasia, is a shocking one for the period around the turn of the century. The man Annandale dies, and the narrator, who is both a physician and the dying man's friend, shortens his anguish by mercifully ending his life; the "slight kind of an engine" is evidently a hypodermic needle. Structurally the poem, a miniature dramatic monologue in sonnet form, is a masterpiece of technique.

"Miniver Cheevy" is one of several thumb-nail portraits of small-town characters contained in *The Town Down the River* (1910). The technique resembles that of Masters' *Spoon River Anthology;* the "Tilbury Town" of the setting is Robinson's fictionalization of his Gardiner, Maine. As for Miniver Cheevy, he is a hopeless romantic misfit who lives only in the past and sees everything in our time as gall and wormwood; this effectively prevents him from making anything of himself.

"Many Are Called," which some critics consider Robinson's finest sonnet and one of the best modern sonnets in English, is a study of the vocation of the poet. The theme is also found in sonnets of Keats and Shelley; Robinson differs from these English romantics in his subtle irony, which enables him to view the profession of poetry somewhat more objectively. Of all the poets who exhort the Lord Apollo "in ecstasy, in anguish, and in vain" (a good example of satirical anti-climax), "even the loudest are outside"—i.e., mere bombast and purple language will not make a poet. The gift of talent falls on poets only infrequently and inexplicably; it is a kind of divine grace, which cannot be prayed for and which comes only "by will of him on whom no man may gaze." Thus Robinson combines his own ironic mistrust of his talent with a steadfast belief in the basic divinity of the spark of poetry in mankind.

ROBERT FROST (born 1875)

Frost is generally thought of as the chief modern representative of the New England tradition of poetry. It is more accurate, however, to say that he expresses the native New England character more than he does the genteel and somewhat bookish literary tradition of Long-fellow, Whittier, and Holmes. In his person as well as in his poetry he is a typical Yankee: laconic, matter-of-fact, conservative, yet possessed of a tremendous energy and power to work. In personality he exactly resembles the Yankee farmer of his own "Brown's Descent," who falls clean out of his steep farm on a winter morning and has to walk back by the road, "a matter of several miles," but retains his composure so thoroughly that he does not even let his lantern go out during his willy-nilly descent. Likewise most (although not all) of Frost's poems are laid in New England and treat typical New England characters, most of them farmers and other rural dwellers. Yet there is nothing narrow or parochial about Frost's regionalism; it never takes the political turn of the regionalism of so many Southern writers, nor does it prevent him, as Amy Lowell's love of New England did, from appreciating other regions. Frost in practice has spent most of his life in large cities or college towns; he lived for over three years in England, and a number of poems, including the famous "Once By the Pacific," are based on his recollections of California. Frost is a regionalist not because he is a violent partisan of one region's way of life over another's, but because New England provided him with a rich fund of material which suited his personality and his poetic method.

A sturdy individualist, Frost has remained almost untouched by contemporary fads and styles in poetry. In spite of his wide reading, in fact, he can be said to have undergone almost no literary influences. There is nothing of the "experimental" in his technique, no influence of Pound, Eliot, or the modern avant-garde school of poetry. One reason for this is that Frost formed his literary attitudes before the avant-garde movement was well under way; another is that he has an instinctive distrust of literary exhibitionism, of poets who contrive to be deliberately obscure in order to be thought original. Thus his language is drawn almost entirely from the vernacular. He avoids the sometimes brutal slang of Sandburg; his accent is that of a soft-spoken New England farmer who views life with a sort of wry optimism. He has a fine feeling, not only for the fertility of the earth and the friendly relationship between man and soil, but for the taciturn type of New England farmer that he himself, born in the west, eventually became. There is little artificial or poetic diction in Frost, and no poetic pretension at all. The effortless air of his verse is deceptive; actually its beauty and simplicity are the result of a careful and sensitive attention to detail. Like Wordsworth, he strives to achieve a natural and idiomatic language in his poetry. He is, however, in the words of one critic, "far less bloodless" than the somewhat pedestrian Wordsworth. It would be difficult to imagine the English poet writing the wry "The Egg and the Machine" in which Frost expresses an anarchistic urge to throw turtle eggs at a locomotive. Behind Frost's laconic prose-like quality is an inner emotion, an enthusiasm, sometimes even an anger—which he rigidly controls in the same manner as the farmer Brown who fell down the hill with his lantern. At the same time he is not a naturalist in the style of Zola, or even of Steinbeck; he has no desire to unearth the unsavory, the merely brutal, to shock his readers' sensibilities. "There are two types of realists," he has said. "The one who offers a good deal of dirt with his potato to show that it is a real one; and the one who is satisfied with the potato brushed clean. I'm inclined to be the second kind . . . To me, the thing that art does for life is to clean it, to strip it to form."

Underneath the simple vernacular of Frost's poetry, however, lies a deceptive depth of metaphor. He is by no means a "metaphysical" or "philosophical" poet, yet there is meaning in each of his poems, and it is almost never a trivial meaning. In the preface to his 1939 *Collected Poems* he wrote, "A poem begins in delight and ends in wisdom." In reading his poetry one is constantly aware of the ultimate realities: life, death, food, work, hatred and friendship, sex and the rhythm of nature. Many of his poems are about animals, but Frost does not sentimentalize them in the manner of the romantics; he is concerned chiefly, almost wholly, with humanity, and animal life is interesting to him only as it provides some kind of analogy to human problems. He is a believer in life, earthly and mundane life with no

supernatural trappings; there is a definite strain of hedonism, of sensuous appreciation of the experience of being alive, in his poetry. Yet
he has no morbid abhorrence of death; in such poems as "After
Apple-Picking" and "A Leaf-Treader" he expresses an unheroic and
acquiescent acceptance of the inevitable end of all living things. Often
in his poetry the death-wish is contrasted with the life-instinct (e.g.,
"Stopping By Woods on a Snowy Evening") or spirit with matter,
the infinite with the mundane and immediate (e.g., "Birches"). Like
most poets, Frost is constantly aware of conflicts or contrasts in the
world about him; in his case the dichotomy often takes the form of
the practical (the mundane, the material) versus the spiritual or
intangible. The idea is, of course, most obviously expressed in
"Birches," where the poet concludes that one must occasionally climb
toward heaven but must always return to earth, and that it is "good
both going and coming back." Another strain which runs throughout
his poetry is that of individualism; his desire to stand alone, to make
his own decisions, leads him into what is virtually a philosophical
anarchism. The best expression of this is found in "West-Running
Brook," where the perverse current of water is used as an analogue
of the individualist's desire to "swim against the stream"; the theme
is found in some form, latent or specific, throughout most of his work.

It is in style and structure that Frost is most revolutionary, although
even here his experiments are cautious compared with those of the
"modernist" poets of the Twenties. He almost never writes in a traditional form (sonnet, rhymed couplet); he often uses rhyme, but
usually in an erratic and inconsistent manner, always subordinating
it to the thought. When, as in "Brown's Descent," he writes in a conventional form like the ballad meter, he often does so for comic or
ironic effect. (Another example is found in the couplets of the mock-
heroic "The Egg and the Machine"). Most of his lyrics are short; even
such medium-length pieces as "West-Running Brook" and "From
Plane to Plane" are much briefer than the similar poems of Robinson
or Markham. Here too Frost is the laconic New Englander; he expresses himself as eloquently on the consequences of passion in the
nine lines of "Fire and Ice" as Robinson does in the many pages of
Tristram. As simple as his poetry is, Frost never stoops to explain; he
leaves the reader with a brief succinct statement which he may under-

stand or misunderstand as he pleases, or interpret according to the wisdom of his own experience.

LIFE: Robert Frost was born in San Francisco in 1875 (although the date is disputed, and Frost himself has stated it as 1874), and lived in California for the first ten years of his life. His father, however, was a New Englander who sympathized with the Southern cause during the Civil War (he christened his son Robert Lee) and emigrated to California to make his living in journalism and politics. The father died when Frost was ten, and the mother moved with her son back to Lawrence, Massachusetts, where she earned her living as a schoolteacher. After high school Frost enrolled at Dartmouth, but gave college up after a semester. For several years he worked as bobbin boy in a Lawrence mill and at several other nondescript jobs. He married in 1895; two years later he entered Harvard, where he managed to stick out two years of work in English. In spite of his aversion to college, however, he was a good student who made better than average marks in Greek and classical studies. After Harvard, which he left without a degree, he taught school in New England for three years and worked intermittently at a variety of odd jobs; in 1900 he moved his family to a farm near Derry, Vermont, where for eleven years he struggled to wrest a living from the rocky and obdurate soil. Meanwhile he had begun to write poetry, although with little success. In 1912, however, he decided definitely to commit himself to a literary career; he left with his family, which now included four daughters, to live in England. For three years he remained abroad, living in the suburban town of Beaconsfield and in a small cottage in Gloucestershire. In 1913 his first volume, *A Boy's Will,* was accepted by a British publisher. His second book, *North of Boston* (1914), also appeared first in England; it was the first of his works to demonstrate the real stature of his talent, and when he returned to the United States in 1915 he found himself already a celebrated literary figure. In the following years he continued to produce poetry slowly but steadily, publishing about fifteen volumes of verse plus two collections (*Collected Poems,* 1939, and *Complete Poems,* 1949) between 1913 and 1955. Meanwhile he lived intermittently on various farms in New Hampshire and Vermont and held a variety of teaching jobs in institutions ranging from the Breadloaf School of Middlebury College (which he helped to found in 1920) to Amherst, where he held the title of "Poet in Residence." His poetry has won many awards, including four Pulitzer Prizes (1924, 1931, 1937, and 1942) and the Poetry Society of America medal (1941). Frost's wife, born Eleanor Miriam White, died in 1938; three of his four daughters grew to maturity. In recent years he has lived in Cambridge, Massachusetts and spent his summers on a Vermont farm. In 1950 he received a remarkable honor: the United States Senate passed a unanimous resolution honoring him on his seventy-fifth birthday. Thus Frost, who published his first volume only at the age of forty-eight, had arrived at his seventies in the almost undisputed position of dean of American poetry.

IMPORTANT POEMS: "Mending Wall" was the leading poem in *North of Boston* (1914). Frost describes how he and his farmer-neighbor each spring used to walk along their common wall to replace the stones that had fallen during the winter, arguing amiably as they did so; the poet claimed the fence was unnecessary where friendship existed ("My apple trees will never get across / And eat the cones under his pines . . .") and the neighbor doggedly insisting that "Good fences make good neighbors." The meaning of this poem is a rather diffuse one, lying essentially in the contrast between the iconoclastic hater of walls and boundaries (the poet) and the conservative lover of tradition who clings doggedly to his old ways (the neighor). More specific interpretations—each of which is true in its own way—are (1) that the poet represents the liberal and international attitude and the neighbor an old-fashioned and conservative nationalism, mistrusting neighbors and preferring to build a wall around himself and his possessions; and (2) that the tradition-bound neighbor, described as "like an old-stone savage armed," represents primitive man, still carrying in his mind an aboriginal mistrust of his fellow, and the poet, more civilized, stands for a friendly and cooperative brotherhood of humanity.

"The Death of the Hired Man," also from *North of Boston,* consists of a dialogue between Warren, a farmer, and his wife Mary. Silas, their old hired man, has returned, sick and decrepit, after a long absence. He habitually stays with them during the hard winters but is lured away by good wages around haying time. They feel a genuine sympathy for him but do not know quite what to do; they know they ought to send him to his wealthy brother in the city, but are afraid this will hurt Silas' pride. As the poem proceeds it develops into a subtle analysis of typical male and female attitudes toward justice and mercy. Warren is outwardly antagonistic toward Silas, whom he regards as an unreliable worker and an economic liability. Mary, whose emotions are closer to the surface, begs him to forgive Silas and give him shelter this one last time. His home is here, she argues, since (a famous Frost line) "home is the place where, when you have to go there, they have to take you in." As they talk Silas is dying in the next room. When Warren goes in to him and discovers him dead, his monosyllabic report shows that he feels as tenderly toward Silas as Mary does; he has merely concealed his feeling beneath his rough masculine exterior. This poem is often cited as one of the finest genre pieces in American poetry.

"After Apple Picking" begins realistically, with a description of the poet's fatigue after picking apples, but soon begins building in allegorical meaning. The "strangeness of sight" which the poet felt after looking through the sheet of ice skimmed from the drinking trough is the premonition of old age, or of death itself; the ice indicates that autumn, the traditional poetic symbol for the end of life, is drawing near. Then, in a "dream," the poet utilizes the apples as a symbol of his own achievements of a lifetime, perhaps more specifically his poetry. He now sees more clearly the imperfections in what he has done (". . . every fleck of russet showing clear") and realizes how thoroughly the habit of work is ingrained in him ("My instep arch . . . keeps the pressure of a ladder-round"). The rewards for a lifetime of work—perhaps critical praises for his poetry—now pour in freely upon him, but he is overtired from the work itself and cannot savor them. Then the reason for his fatigue: his own demanding standards, which led him to reject any creation of inferior quality (". . . all / That struck the earth, / No matter if not bruised . . . Went surely to the cider-apple head / As of no worth"). At the end, through a half-serious reference to the woodchuck's sleep, he conjectures as to the nature of death—a sleep which he fears will still be troubled by feelings of regret for not having achieved the perfection he had struggled toward. The use of rhyme in this poem is interesting; beginning with a quatrain rhymed *abba* (although erratic in the length of its lines), the poem continues to rhyme occasionally, lending an odd dream-like quality to the development of the theme as it progresses down the lines. This use of erratic line-length and occasional rhyme, which Amy Lowell might have called polyphonic, occurs frequently in Frost's medium-length poems.

"Birches" (from *Mountain Interval,* 1916) is similar in technique, combining a realistic genre picture with a latent level of more profound meaning. The poet opens with a description of a game enjoyed by New England country lads: they climb young birches to the very top, taking care not to lean to either side, then swing outward, bending the birch down in a long arc and eventually descending to the ground. Then, following the stanza-break (line 40) the poem considers the philosophical implication: that when the petty details of life (cobwebs, twigs) grow too annoying, it is refreshing to "climb toward heaven" (i.e., to seek exaltation in the spiritual) provided one can always come back to earth (the solidly satisfying routine of daily life). Thus the poet rejects both the pure life of the spirit, the ascetic existence as practiced by saint and recluse, and the unrelieved and sordid monotony which is the destiny of those who are aware of nothing but material existence. The alternation between the two worlds is "good both going and coming back"; the spirit renews our energy for the material world, and the world provides us with elemental satisfactions (food, sleep, love) which eventually through satiety revive our longing for the spiritual. This poem contains one of Frost's most specific statements of his own metaphysics and ethics—his "religion," if the term can be used for so undogmatic a set of concepts.

"Brown's Descent, or, The Willy-Nilly Slide" tells an anecdote from the life of a taciturn farmer who lived on a steep hill. One frosty morning he slid all the way to the bottom and had to walk back by the road, a matter of several miles. The poem may be viewed as a half-satirical, half-serious answer to an ancient philosophical problem: how does the wise man act in the face of adversity and torment? Frost's answer suggests a calm and matter-of-fact New England tenacity: one should hang onto the lantern (i.e., retain composure amid reverses), see to the practical necessities ("Ile's / Bout out!") and then seek a solution, not by attacking adversity head-on (trying to climb back up the icy hill) but by finding a roundabout way of surmounting the problem, even if patience is required (going home by the road, "a matter of several miles").

"Fire and Ice" is a short poetic epigram conjecturing as to the nature of the end of the world. Fire and ice (symbolizing "hot" passion and "cold" hatred respectively) are suggested as the means of destruction; the poet has had experience of both. The implied corollary is that the wise man balances his life between these destructive extremes, loving and hating when the impulse comes but abandoning himself to neither. Note that the poem, while by no means formal, utilizes only three rhymes in its nine lines and follows a generally consistent iambic meter.

"West-Running Brook," which lent its title to the volume published in 1928, is an expression of Frost's social attitude, or rather his steadfast and sometimes eccentric individualism. Presented in the form of a dialogue between a pair of lovers, the poem describes a New England brook which perversely runs west when all normal brooks run east to the Atlantic. Yet even in this perverse brook itself are rebellious elements; the "white wave" introduced in line 20 struggles upstream, "not gaining but not losing," and suggests to the lovers (as to Frost) an analogy of their own defiance of society and convention ("It is from this in nature we are from. / It is most us").

"Once By the Pacific," which Frost playfully cited as having been conceived "as of about 1880"—when he was six—is a descriptive piece suggested by a memory of a Pacific storm, which battered the cliffs so cruelly that the poet felt an apprehension over the solidity and permanence of the continent. The implied theme is that even in the middle of our rocky-steady rational assurance in the permanence of our selves and our existences, we are occasionally troubled by a vague fear of the unknown, of elemental nature, of the wild and uncontrolled forces which in the end dominate the universe. Civilization is only a thin veneer; the reference to "God's last *Put out the light*" stresses the impermanence of man's works as well as mankind's very existence.

"The Bear," like many of Frost's poems, begins with a nature-picture: the wild bear of the woods embracing the choke-cherry. The bear, which unknown to itself is confined to a limited area of woods set aside by men, feels free; but men, who know too well the limitations of their existence, feel confined even in the universe. Man is forever confined between the macrocosm and the microcosm (symbolized by the telescope and the microscope), limits "in conjunction giving quite a spread," but nevertheless rankling to the restless and exploring human mind. Or (in Frost's second metaphor) man is confined between the traditional philosophical extremes, "At one extreme agreeing with one Greek / At the other agreeing with another Greek" —perhaps the contrast between Plato (spirit) and Democritus or Epicurus (matter), or between the universal philosophical poles of idealism and materialism. Although this seems to most men an adequate space in which to exist, the poet finds the limits annoying; he would prefer to be the wild bear, ranging wherever his fancy suggests and never suspecting the existence of boundaries he cannot cross.

"The Egg and the Machine" is an attack, playfully written in traditional English heroic couplets, on the machine age of the twentieth century. The poet personifies the locomotive through a kind of emotional animism and focusses on it all his annoyance with the arrogant and ubiquitous machines of our time. When the protagonist's eye falls upon a turtle egg (symbol of the unique and magic perfection of nature, a perfect shape in which life is mysteriously contained), he feels now "armed for war," and threatens to fling the egg into the headlight of the next locomotive that passes. This gesture, of course, will not stop the locomotive, but it is a supreme answer to the machine: the egg, produced by the lowly turtle, is nevertheless a more wonderful object than all the locomotives and other gadgets which ingenious men have devised.

"Stopping By Woods on a Snowy Evening" is Frost's best-known short lyric. The poet, halting his sleigh in the midst of the snowy woods, finds the gloom inviting, but remembers he has "miles to go before I sleep"—practical duties call him from the deep, almost religious beauty of the frozen woods. The thought is usually interpreted as a death-wish, which the poet overcomes as he reflects on the practical life which lies ahead of him.

"A Leaf-Treader" similarly deals with the conflict between the death-wish and the life-instinct. The poet, "autumn-tired," i.e., sensing the approach of the autumn of his life, is saddened by the falling leaves, which suggest overwhelmingly that everything is drawing toward an end. Yet he is cheered by remembering that "it was no reason I had to go because they had to go," and he ends with an exhortation to himself to "keep on top of another year of snow." Thus the human will dominates the ever-present latent wish to retire from the struggle into an easeful oblivion.

"Two Tramps in Mud-Time" begins with an anecdote of two tramps, itinerant lumber-workers, who proposed to the poet to relieve him of his wood-chopping chore for pay. The poem then develops into a consideration of the relation between "love and need"—play and work, or avocation and vocation. "My object in life," the poet explains, "is to unite / My avocation and my vocation." He has done this in his wood-chopping, which is both a pleasure and a necessity. The implied suggestion is that this should also be the goal of a poet, or of anyone who has a job to do—"Only where love and need are one, / Is the deed ever really done . . ." Thus Frost rejects the common American tradition that one works at an unpleasant job from Monday to Friday and spends only a brief weekend of "recreation"—the things one really wants to do.

CARL SANDBURG (born 1878)

Sandburg's literary reputation has undergone many vicissitudes during his long career. When his *Chicago Poems* first appeared in 1916 they caused a tumult of controversy. He was accused of "gutter naturalism," of coarseness and brutality; his verse was called mawkish, awkward, and distorted, and he was widely condemned for failing to distinguish between prose and poetry, for having included large sections of documentary material in his verse. But gradually he attracted a small but devoted band of followers, mostly other poets; "Chicago" won the Levinson Prize as early as 1914, and soon other literary prizes and awards were accorded him. *Cornhuskers* (1918) and *Smoke and Steel* (1920) enhanced his reputation, and meanwhile the literary temper of the nation changed overnight as the new era of the Twenties opened. Sandburg came into his own; alongside the work of Dos Passos, Hemingway, and Pound his poetry seemed almost genteel, and its proletarian vigor, flavored with a faint intellectual irony, appealed to the taste of the Jazz Age. By 1928 Sandburg was being invited to Harvard as Phi Beta Kappa poet; his triumph was complete. The same year he published *Good Morning, America,* which was to be virtually his last significant collection of lyrics. Since 1929 he has directed most of his energy to other projects: his vast Lincoln scholarship, his work as a folklorist and song-collector, a long historical novel, an autobiography. Meanwhile his early poems have come to be less highly regarded; a generation of younger poets have refined and improved upon the techniques he made popular in the Twenties, and today the verses of *Chicago Poems* often seem mawkish and immature. To a public which has read James T. Farrell the awe of Sandburg at Chicago's sin ("They tell me you are wicked and I believe them, for I have seen your painted women under the gas lamps luring the farm boys . . .") seems slightly naive. Yet Sandburg was a great pathfinder in American poetry, an important link between the free-verse naturalism of Whitman and the big-city modernist poetry of the generation of the Thirties. He has been rightly called "the laureate of industrial America" and "the American national poet." He has more right to the second title than, for example, a poet like Frost, who writes rural and individualistic verse in a society that is growing constantly more urban and collectivized, or any of the poets of the experimental movement (Eliot, Pound) whose technical complexity places them beyond the comprehension of the general public. In any account of twentieth-century poetry Sandburg must loom large, if only for his importance as a breaker of old forms and the first significant poetic spokesman of the machine age.

Stylistically as well as in content Sandburg derives from Whitman, although he substitutes for Whitman's dynamic optimism a more cautious and slightly cynical skepticism of the twentieth century. In vocabulary and idiom he is a vernacularist; he utilizes slang, trade jargon, colloquialisms, and popular metaphors with a masterful ease, and with a finished dramatic effect no poet before him had achieved. His work is dominated by energy, the force and enthusiasm of a new nation. He has nothing in common with the genteel European tradition; he lacks the classical background of Robinson and he rejects the cynical scorn for American culture of such expatriates as Pound and Eliot. He glories in America's exuberance, in its strength and youthful vitality. Politically liberal, he speaks out bitterly against war, against industrial exploitation, and even against materialism itself (*cf.* "Limited"). In spite of his stylistic cynicism and irony he is essentially a romantic; he views everything as larger, more wonderful, and more powerful than it is in reality. Much of his force derives from his trick of describing his visions of power in short, blunt words, in the diction of the streets and the smoking-rooms. Sandburg is an indigenous American poet in several respects: in his romantic enthusiasm, in his diction and poetic method, and even in the fresh naïveté with which he attacks the most difficult problems of poetry and life.

LIFE: Carl August Sandburg was born of Swedish parents in Galesburg, Illinois in 1878. He had few advantages in youth; he earned his own living from the age of thirteen, working at a variety of odd jobs from milkman to farm hand. After serving in the Spanish-American War he enrolled at Lombard College in Galesburg; he attended this school for four years but never received a degree. He was, however, awarded an honorary Litt.D. in later years when his poetry had made him famous. At Lombard he attracted the attention of Professor Philip Green Wright, who detected a definite talent for poetry in the young war veteran; Professor Green not only encouraged his writing but financed the publication of his first book of poems. *In Reckless Ecstasy* appeared in 1904; the thin volume of verses, most of them derivative and immature, attracted no immediate attention. Sandburg, continuing to write, meanwhile supported himself with a newspaper job in Milwaukee, where he also met and married Lillian Steichen, sister of the famous photographer Edward Steichen. From 1910 to 1912 he served as secretary to the mayor of Milwaukee, which if nothing else gave him a practical background in American politics. In 1914 the newly created magazine *Poetry* began publishing and championing his verse; "Chicago," which appeared in *Poetry* that year, won him the Levinson Prize and brought him his first success. *Chicago Poems* (1916) created the sensation we have noted above. Four more important volumes of poetry appeared between 1918 and 1928, by which time Sandburg had arrived at a position as a leading American poet. Thereafter his poetry output decreased; after 1925 he turned his attention increasingly to his voluminous biography of Lincoln (*Abraham Lincoln: the Prairie Years,* 1926, and *Abraham Lincoln: the War Years,* 1939) and to his collection of native American folk songs (*The American Songbag,* 1927). *The People, Yes,* which appeared in 1936, was a hybrid work, consisting partly of original poetry and partly of folklore and native locutions he had gathered in his personal researches. During the Second World War he wrote a series of newspaper columns and made radio broadcasts for the Office of War Information. A lifetime midwesterner, he moved in his sixties to a farm near Flat Rock, North Carolina, in the Smokies, where he has lived since.

CHIEF WORKS: The poems of Sandburg's early period (1904-28) may be roughly divided into two groups. The first of these are the vigorous, often emotional lyrics of urban and proletarian life in the manner of Whitman's *Leaves of Grass,* written in a kind of prose-poetry alternating with short incisive rhythmic assertions; the second are the small carefully-polished word-pictures resembling the work of Amy Lowell and the other Imagists. Of the poems of the first type, "Chicago" is by far the best known. The strong short lines of the opening ("Hog Butcher for the World"), the key words all capitalized in the manner of a newspaper headline, soon give way to a Whitmanesque rhapsody ("They tell me you are wicked . . .") utilizing a Biblical parallelism and a flowing effect obtained by long strings of adjectives connected by "and." The theme is an exultant tribute to Chicago's strength and vitality; the poet admits the crime and misery which exist in the city, but celebrates the youthful energy that makes it seem a "tall bold slugger."

In a similar genre are "Grass," a bitterly ironic statement on war; "Cool Tombs," which reminds the reader that all greatness, all love, all life, ends "in the dust . . . in the cool tombs"; "Limited," which satirized the American pride in material gadgets, symbolized in the train which like everything else will eventually become "scrap and rust"; "Jazz Fantasia," an interesting attempt to apply the Whitmanesque style to a description of negro jazz, utilizing slang and onomatopoeia ("husha-husha-hush . . ."); and "Flash Crimson," an ironic "prayer" in which the poet, momentarily sensing the "flash of crimson" which is the divine vision of spirit in the universe, willingly accepts the ugliness, the pain, and the hardship which are man's lot on earth.

Of the imagistic word-pictures, the most famous is "Fog," a short lyric consisting of a single metaphor and suggesting the minute perfection of Japanese poetry. "Nocturne in a Deserted Brickyard" is similar, again centering around a single image, in this case the attribution of a liquid or flowing quality to the moonlight.

The People, Yes (1936) is an epic tribute to American democracy, comprised partly of original poetry and partly of a hodgepodge of idioms, folk expressions, slang terms, popular metaphors, yarns, and tall tales. The dominant theme is that "the people will live on;" in spite of their ignorance and blundering, in spite of their irrational mistakes and their blind passions the people carry with them a strength and endurance which will maintain them through all hardships. "This old anvil laughs at many broken hammers." The mingling of poetry and document in this book recalls the technique of Dos Passos' *U.S.A.* trilogy, which also includes popular materials such as songs and newspaper headlines to set the mood of an era.

The American Songbag (anthology, 1927) is a comprehensive collection of folk songs gathered over a period of many years. About a hundred of the songs had never before been published; Sandburg extracted them directly from farm hands, hoboes, railway men, and hill people.

"The Long Shadow of Lincoln" was presented by Sandburg as a Phi Beta Kappa poem at William and Mary College in 1944. Beginning with a line from an 1862 Lincoln speech, "We must disenthrall ourselves," the poem takes this admonition as the essence of the man: a calm, "sad," "cool," and "kind" composure before the problems which face humanity. The refrain of "dust alive" (also "dream-dust") characterizes not only the dead Lincoln but all mankind, formed of dust yet eternal through its possession of spirit and intelligence. This long poem with its restrained and carefully controlled emotion is considered the most important poetic work of Sandburg's later years.

EZRA POUND (born 1885)

Except for the notoriety of his 1946 indictment for treason and the public debate over the Bollingen Prize affair, Pound has remained throughout his career virtually unknown to the general public. Yet he has exerted a tremendous influence on the whole movement of modernist verse; Eliot has referred to him as "the most important living poet of the English language." Pound invented the term Imagism and founded the school that bore the name; he played a large part in forming the styles of Eliot, Hart Crane, MacLeish, and the generation that followed them, and he vigorously championed the work of Eliot, Joyce, Tagore, and other writers when they were relatively unknown.

His own poetry is a subject of great controversy; Allen Tate called the *Cantos* "one of the three great works of poetry of our time," but Edward Fitzgerald along with many others found Pound's work hung about with "a dismal mist of unresolved confusion." Of three qualities of his poetry, however, there can be no controversy; its tremendous erudition, its striking originality, and its technical and intellectual brilliance.

It is Pound's erudition that most discourages the average reader who first approaches his poetry. He is, among his other accomplishments, a competent comparative literature scholar familiar with literary history from its earliest beginnings to the present time, conversant with the prosody of Anglo-Saxon, Provençal, medieval Italian, and Chinese poetry, and adept at most of the ordinary modern languages. Moreover he has no desire to hide these accomplishments; in fact he wears them like so many badges. The *Cantos* are an intricate network of allusions to, and quotations from, hundreds of obscure and esoteric literary works ranging from Latin poetry to the *Analects* of Confucius. "Thus it is clear," comments a critic, "that we cannot *know* everything about *The Cantos* until we have read not only everything Pound has written, but everything he has read as well." Not many readers are willing to subject themselves to such a discipline.

Among the many literary and philosophical influences which found their way into Pound's work may be cited a few of primary importance: (1) Homer, whose epics Pound knew intimately in the original language, and whose *Odyssey* provides one of the main thematic threads for the *Cantos;* (2) the medieval Italian poets, especially Dante, whose *Divine Comedy* also influenced the structure of the *Cantos,* and Cavalcanti, whose sonnets and ballades Pound translated in 1912; (3) classic Chinese poetry, a volume of which Pound edited and translated under the title *Cathay* in 1915; (4) Browning, who suggested to him the basic form for his *Personae,* and whose hero Sordello reappears frequently in Pound's work; (5) the American Orientalist Ernest Fenollosa (1853-1908), whose essay *The Chinese Written Character as a Medium for Poetry,* edited by Pound in 1936 but read by him much earlier, provided him with basic aesthetic concepts which he incorporated into his poetry; (6) the German anthropologist Leo Frobenius (died 1938), who furnished Sir James Fraser with much of the anthropological data for *The Golden Bough* and whose theory of mythology Pound used in his own work; and (7) Thomas Jefferson, whose economic views greatly influenced Pound's attitude toward modern capitalism.

Stylistically Pound is dynamically brilliant, if not always coherent. He writes from tremendous conviction, a conviction ironical and sophisticated rather than naive. Unfortunately this power of enthusiasm all too readily degenerates into invective; Pound is probably the most irascible of modern poets. Not only does he despise the reading public, but he is belligerent toward critics, scornful of all authors who make money as well as the majority of his fellow poets; it is a rare craftsman who can win a word of praise from Pound. His early poetry more or less resembled the work of the other Imagists (Amy Lowell, H. D., John Gould Fletcher). Around 1915 he became intrigued with Oriental poetry of various kinds; the verse of Li Po and Japanese forms such as the *hokku* undoubtedly had an influence on his subsequent work as well as on the Imagist movement as a whole. The later poems, especially the *Cantos,* lack the enamel-like simplicity of his Imagist period; after 1918 he variously referred to his own style as "Vorticism" or "the ideogrammic method" (a term suggesting the influence of Chinese poetry). In this period Pound resembles the Eliot of *The Waste Land,* although if there is a connection it is probably Pound who influenced Eliot.

Pound's ideas are emphatic but sometimes seem confused. In his early period he was much concerned with the theme of personal freedom, which he found in a variety of writers from Jefferson to Henry James and which he offered as the basic of his own ethic; yet by 1941 he had allied himself with Italian fascism so completely that he was making anti-American broadcasts on the Rome radio and serving as an adviser for the Italian government in its progaganda war against America. The link between these apparently incompatible extremes lies in Pound's concept of the term "usury." The Latin word *usura* and the term "usurious society" occur frequently in his later work, and the concept is woven deeply into the *Cantos;* it is simultaneously Pound's politics, his economics, his personal ethics, and even his criterion for the criticism of art. Briefly, Pound convinced himself that usury (i.e., capitalism, banks, the lending of money for interest, the whole money economy) was the basic evil in organized society and the first symptom of the degeneration and collapse of all

civilizations throughout history. Athenian society before approximately 450 B.C. was tribal and aesthetic rather than usurious; thus
the poetic achievements of Aeschylus and Sophocles. With the inception of a money economy Athens entered a decadent period, which
was reflected in its epigonistic literature and its baroque art. Another
example, one of Pound's favorites, is that of medieval Italy. The
poetic triumph of Dante and Cavalcanti and the superb art and architecture of the Quattrocento occurred in an age when usury was a
mortal sin; with the advent of modern commerce and capitalism
around 1500 Italian society degenerated, and so did its art. It was
because of this hatred of *usura* that Pound vented his spleen on modern capitalism, voiced paranoid warnings of "international Jewry,"
viewed Churchill and Roosevelt as sinister villains, and found a hero
in Mussolini, whose syndicalist economics seemed to him to be a
return to the usury-free middle ages. Such ideas, however, were subjective and emotional rather than rational in Pound. "As a political
thinker," comments Untermeyer, "Pound was not only ineffectual but
absurd; as a person he was intermittently unbalanced." As a poet,
it might be added, he is believed by many critics including Allen Tate
and T. S. Eliot to be one of the greatest creative talents of the century.

LIFE: Ezra Pound was born in Hailey, Idaho in 1885; he half-
satirically refers to himself in *Mauberley* as "born / In a half savage
country, out of date; / Bent resolutely on wringing lilies from the
acorn." His parents, however, soon moved to Pennsylvania; Pound
entered the University of Pennsylvania at fifteen, and had commenced
a private study of comparative literature by the time he was sixteen.
Traditional college courses annoyed him, however, and he changed
to the status of special student to avoid the requirements of a fixed
curriculum; he later took a bachelor's degree at Hamilton College.
In 1905 he returned to the University of Pennsylvania and was
granted an M.A. the following year; meanwhile he served briefly as
an instructor on the Pennsylvania staff. After a brief excursion to
Europe he returned to what he thought was a career as a college
teacher, but the experiment lasted only four months; he was dismissed
from the staff of Wabash College for a long list of reasons, "all accusations," he later asserted, "having been ultimately refuted save that
of being 'the Latin Quarter type.' " Returning to Europe in 1907, he

spent some time in Italy; his first volume of poems, *A lume spento,* was printed in Venice in 1908. The following year he established himself in London, where he remained until 1920. He met W. B. Yeats and soon gained acceptance into the Yeatsian circle; before long, however, he had acquired a coterie of his own. *Personae,* a second volume of verse published in London in 1909, was favorably greeted by critics; thenceforth his reputation, at least in avant-garde circles, increased constantly.

In 1914 Pound collected and published an anthology of poet: y under the title *Des imagistes,* a book which played an important part in launching the Imagist movement both in England and in America. When the group was taken over by Amy Lowell, however, he gradually drifted away from it; the poems of *Lustra* (1916) anticipate his later and more mature style. Shortly after this Pound began to apply the term "Vorticism" to his poetry; the label, which he shared with Wyndam Lewis, was intended to signify a highly "centered" or unified poetic effect, as in Imagism, but swirling, like a vortex, with a dynamic energy in contrast to the static quality of Imagist poetry. Meanwhile Pound had produced a number of important translations and adaptations, including lyrics of the thirteenth-century Italian poet Guido Cavalcanti (1912) and a set of adaptations of Chinese poetry (*Cathay,* 1915). In 1920 appeared the first major work of his new period: *Hugh Selwyn Mauberley,* a somewhat esoteric and highly allusive cycle of poems (actually a single poem divided into sections) which influenced such later works as Eliot's *The Waste Land* and *Gerontion* and Hart Crane's *The Bridge.* The same year he moved to Paris, where he remained until 1924, an intimate of the Left-Bank expatriate circle which included Hemingway and James Joyce. It was through Pound's influence that Joyce's *Portrait of the Artist* was accepted by the Egoist Press, and Pound also played a large part in bringing the work of Eliot to the attention of publishers and editors. In 1924 he moved again, this time to Rapallo, on the Italian Riviera, where he remained more or less permanently for the next two decades. The first of his *Cantos* appeared in 1925 as *Cantos I-XV;* he continued to publish sections of this major work through 1955. Meanwhile his economic and political views led him to sympathize increasingly with the fascist regime in Italy; as early as 1935 he had published *Jefferson and/or Mussolini,* and by 1941 he was openly broadcasting anti-American propaganda on the Italian radio. In 1942 he was indicted for treason *in absentia* in the American courts, and in April of 1945 he surrendered himself to advance units of the conquering American army. Imprisoned in a stockade near Pisa, he sketched out amid great hardships and discomfort the poems of the *Pisan Cantos,* which were published in 1948. After his return to America for trial he was examined by a committee of psychiatrists and found insane; the indictment was therefore set aside, and he was committed to St. Elizabeth's Hospital in Washington, D.C., as an incurable psychotic. The next year a violent controversy broke out over his work; in February of 1949 he was announced as winner of the newly-established Bollingen Award, sponsored by the Library of Congress. The award committee, which included T. S. Eliot, W. H. Auden, Allen Tate, Robert Penn Warren, and Katherine Anne Porter, defended their choice of a poet who had been indicted as a traitor and was presently confined in an insane asylum by stating, "To permit other considerations than that of poetic achievement to sway the decision would destroy the significance of the award . . ." The award was attacked by the poet Robert Hillyer in a celebrated *Saturday Review* article, and the controversy continued for several months. The prize was eventually granted as announced, although as a result of the dispute the sponsorship for the Bollingen Award was transferred from the Library of Congress to Yale University. Pound's most recent volume of *Cantos,* entitled *Rock-Drill,* appeared in 1955.

CHIEF WORKS: The most important poems of Pound's early period are contained in *Personae* (1909) and *Exultations* (1909); poems from both volumes are reprinted in the 1926 edition of *Personae.* The word *personae* signifies "masks," here used in the sense of personalities which the poet assumes in order to create a dramatic monologue or characterization. Not all the poems of the 1926 volume, however, come under this heading; some are simple Imagist impressions in the style of H. D. or Amy Lowell. Of the true *personae* in the volume, the best known is "Sestina: Altaforte," a dramatic monologue spoken by the medieval Bertrand de Born, put in Hell by Dante "for that he was a stirrer up of strife." (See *Inferno,* Canto XXVIII.) In contradiction to Dante, Pound portrays Bertrand, a thirteenth-century troubadour and knight, as a lusty and energetic warrior who cries that "The man who fears war . . . is fit only to rot in womanish peace." The form of the poem loosely imitates troubadour verse-forms like the ballade which Bertrand is known to have written.

"A Girl," an often-anthologized favorite from Pound's early period, is an Imagistic impression of a young girl and at the same time a subtly symbolic network of metaphors: on the immediate level the girl is compared with a tree, yet the underlying sub-metaphor treats the tree as the girl's lover, permeating her very essence through his intense sympathy.

Even briefer is "In a Station of the Metro," in form an English-language version of the two-line Japanese *hokku,* which, after the suggestive word "apparition," concludes with a single metaphor comparing the faces in the crowd to "petals on a wet, black bough."

Hugh Selwyn Mauberley (1920) is the first major long poem of Pound's work as well as the first poem to demonstrate his mature technique and attitude. The Mauberley of the title is an imaginary poet of the pre-1914 era, invented by Pound partly as a tongue-in-cheek analysis of himself in his early period and partly as a satire on the poetic temper of the fin-de-siècle. Mauberley, however, does not appear until the latter part of the poem, the first half of which is devoted to various poetic excursions in Pound's own voice. The work in its entirety consists of eighteen separate poems which form an integrated whole, although their connection is not immediately apparent upon first reading. The first of these sections, "E. P. Ode Pour L'Election de Son Sepulchre," is a parody of Ronsard's famous self-written epitaph; Pound, writing as though he were a superior, pompous, and slightly hostile critic of his own work, describes himself as "out of key with his own time" and concludes wryly in the last stanza that he passed from men's memory in the thirtieth year of his age, i.e., 1915, approximately the end of his Imagist period. The second section is also well known; it characterizes the age in which the poem was written, especially English literary circles of the pre-war era, which demanded a "mould in plaster" (stylized nineteenth-century verse) rather than the "alabaster" of true classic poetry. Section III continues the theme, revealing the age as dominated by "A tawdry cheapness." Other interesting sections are the seventh, titled "Siena mi fe'; disfecemi Maremma" (a quotation from Dante), which characterizes Pound's friend Victor Gustave Plarr under the pseudonym Monsieur Verog and thereby sums up the literary temper of the Nineties; "Mr. Nixon," the ninth section, a satire on the modern successful novelist of the type of Arnold Bennett; and "Mauberley," the opening section of the second part, in which the title-figure of the poem is characterized as a minor artist of limited creativity but retaining a pride and self-respect which he derives from a long literary tradition. This theme is continued through the remaining four sections of the work.

The *Cantos* (1925-55) are the major work of Pound's career, a gigantic unfinished poetry cycle which in its final form is to contain one hundred cantos or chapters. The various sections of the work which have so far appeared are *Cantos I-XVI* (1925), *XVII-XXVII* (1928), *A Draft of XXX Cantos* (1930), *Eleven Cantos: XXXI to XLI* (1934), *The Fifth Decad of Cantos* (1937), *Cantos LII-LXXI* (1940), *The Pisan Cantos* (1948), and *Rock-Drill* (1955). Although the *Cantos* are confused and seemingly disconnected upon first reading, critics have discerned in them a highly involved formal structure, comparable in some ways to the plan of the *Divine Comedy*. The two dominant themes are said to be (1) the idea of the Descent into Hell, derived from Vergil and Dante, and (2) the motif of metamorphosis, the divine transformation of one thing into another, as found in Ovid and as treated by modern mythologists such as Ranke and Fraser. The theme of the *Odyssey,* an extended sea-voyage replete with adventures many of which are erotic in nature, also recurs periodically. At least two cantos of the voluminous work should receive individual mention. Canto I, one of the best-known as well as the most straightforward and explicit sections yet published, is actually a loose translation or paraphrase of Book XI of the *Odyssey* via the Renaissance Latin version of Andreus Divus, who is mentioned in the final lines of the canto. The passage in which the ghost of the sailor Elpenor describes the manner of his death ("Ill fate and abundant wine" through ". . . that I swung mid fellows") has been cited as a splendid example of Pound's elliptical style, which skips over trivial details to achieve a classic Greek simplicity. Canto XLV, often anthologized, is a kind of ode or dissertation on *usura,* including Pound's theory of the relation between the usurious society and the decline of the arts. The style, in sharp contrast to the discursive quality of most of the *Cantos,* is Biblical, containing extensive parallelism and utilizing a consciously archaic English to establish a dignified and prophetic mood. Much history, transcribed almost literally but in Pound's highly individual and condensed style, is included; Cantos LII through LXI list in detail the succession of Chinese dynasties and their accomplishments, and Cantos LXII through LXXI include a fairly complete history of nineteenth-century America. Also interesting is Canto LXXIV of the *Pisan Cantos,* which includes an ironic picture of Pound's imprisonment by the U. S. Army in Pisa: ". . . and they digged a ditch round about me / lest the damp gnaw thru my bones."

It is likely that future criticism will view the *Cantos* as more important for their influence on other poets than as works of intrinsic quality in their own right. Among the poems in which a definite influence of the *Cantos* has been noted are Eliot's *The Waste Land,* Hart Crane's *The Bridge,* and MacLeish's *Conquistador.*

AMY LOWELL (1874-1925)

If there is any single book which can be said to have announced the opening of a new era in American poetry in the twentieth century, it is Amy Lowell's *Sword Blades and Poppy Seed,* published in 1914 only a year after her fruitful encounter with Ezra Pound in England. Pound was an expatriate who published mainly in Europe, and Eliot's *Prufrock,* also first published in England, was not to appear until 1917; Miss Lowell's volume was the first book to come to the attention of the American public which bore vividly and unmistakably the mark of the new poetic style. This book, along with her later work, still seems modern today; alongside it the poetry of Robinson and Markham seems hopelessly Victorian, and even the early work of Masters and Frost slightly old-fashioned.

Miss Lowell was the co-founder (with Pound) and chief American representative of the poetic movement known as Imagism, which loomed large in poetry of the Twenties and still continues to exert a certain influence. The basic tenets of the movement she derived from Pound and other *imagistes* she encountered on a 1913 trip to Europe. Upon her return she utilized these principles to found a group centering around herself and held together by her vigorous and forceful personality. From the group proceeded several anthologies of verse, all titled *Some Imagist Poets* (1915-17) and edited chiefly by Miss

Lowell; she was also an active contributor to *Poetry* magazine, which after 1914 served as an informal rallying-place for American Imagists. Imagism as Amy Lowell conceived it meant the abandonment of the trite and worn-out poetic conventions of the nineteenth century and a return to the language of ordinary speech; the restriction of the length of a poem to a few dozen lines, i.e., its confinement to a single impression or emotion; and, most important, an emphasis on sharp and clearly-cut images of sight, sound, smell, and touch. Imagist poetry strives for a sort of "enameled" quality, a brightly-hued but simple series of impressions which contribute to a single final effect. It avoids the intellectual and abstract, and emphasizes the concrete; it abandons maudlin sentimentality, and it favors direct images to allusions or references. Because of her hostility to sentimentality Miss Lowell is sometimes accused of a lack of emotion, a deficiency of human feeling; Untermeyer remarks of her verse that "motion too often takes the place of emotion," and the *Oxford Companion to American Literature* notes that "it has been criticized as dealing too exclusively with sensual images, particularly visual ones, and as neglecting emotional values." That this is an unfair accusation can easily be seen in her best-known poem, "Patterns." This poem, typical of Miss Lowell's style in general, explores the very depths of human emotion, portraying an emotional experience so severe that it virtually shatters the personality of the heroine, but it does so without sentimentality. Miss Lowell's poetry shows us emotion controlled by discipline, by a deliberate act of will proceeding from strength of character.

Unlike Ransom, MacLeish, or the later Eliot, Amy Lowell is a "pure poet" who is concerned almost entirely with the craft of poetry, with the poetic medium as a means of artistic communication; she has no message to convey, no world-view to promulgate. Her task is to absorb experiences from the world around her and then communicate them to the reader through carefully chosen and polished language. Thus a second accusation is sometimes made against her: that her poetry "lacks content," that it is deficient in idea, in short that it is trivial and superficial. It is so in the same sense as Shakespeare's sonnets, the lyrics of Sappho, or the shorter verses of Poe, all of which are "pure poetry" rather than didactic or intellectual verse.

It was Amy Lowell who popularized the term *vers libre* (free verse), thus provoking the endless jokes of the Twenties about "the thousand little magazines that died to make verse free" and jests of a similar nature. She illustrated the technique of free verse in her own poetry to some extent, especially in the period 1914-16; but a term which more exactly describes her technique, a term she herself invented for an essay on John Gould Fletcher, is "polyphonic prose." " 'Polyphonic' means 'many-voiced,' " she explained in the essay, "and the form is so-called because it makes use of the 'voices' of poetry, namely: meter, *vers libre,* assonance, alliteration, rhyme and return." In practice polyphonic prose represented a rebellion against conventional poetic forms, especially against the classical notion that a poem must choose one form, meter, or rhyme pattern and then stick to it. Miss Lowell's polyphonic technique adapted the language to the subject; thus a variety of forms might be used within a single poem as the mood or content of the poem changed.

In content Amy Lowell is simply "imagistic," i.e., she interests herself in any aspect or facet of life that seems colorful or vivid. Flowers and other emblems of nature (birds, trees) play a large part in her verse, although not in the conventional sentimentalized manner of the romantics; nature is merely utilized subjectively as a source of strong sensory impressions to be savored by poet and reader. If there is one dominant idea which runs through her work, it is that of the conflict between natural action and convention—the "patterns" which provide the title for her best-known poem. Born into a rigidly conventional New England background, she was nevertheless a highly individualistic person; she felt herself, and continually expressed in her poetry, the inward struggle between individual desire and the thousand restrictions, models, patterns, and customs which society imposes upon its members. Her personal attitude toward the problem is well summed up in "The Sisters," in which she views three famous poetesses from the standpoint of convention vs. liberty and finds herself less inhibited than Mrs. Browning and Emily Dickinson but still unable to abandon herself to the frank hedonism of a Sappho.

LIFE: Amy Lowell was born in Brookline, Massachusetts in 1874, and except for occasional travel remained in this small New England town all her life. Her family was a prominent one in New England cultural and political life; a brother, Abbott Lawrence Lowell, was president of Harvard, and another, Percival Lowell, a famous astronomer. Educated in private schools and through travel abroad, she had every advantage in her youth that a highly cultivated society could offer. A glandular imbalance caused her to become abnormally stout, and she never married. In her twenties she interested herself chiefly in politics, a radical area of activity for a woman in the nineteenth century; she was a rigid Republican with pronounced rightwing views on the "place of the working class" and remained so until her death. Around 1902 she first began to develop an interest in poetry; she began studying the subject and writing experimentally, but did not publish her first book until she was thirty-six. Meanwhile her parents had both died, and she assumed charge of the family estate, Sevenels, in Brookline, where she lived for the rest of her life. *A Dome of Many-Colored Glass,* her first volume of verse, appeared in 1912. On a 1913 trip to England she met Ezra Pound, eleven years younger than she was but already an established young modernist poet. The meeting was an important one; Miss Lowell returned to America an avowed Imagist, and soon assumed command of the American wing of the movement, which grew to include Richard Aldington, Hilda Doolittle, F. S. Flint, John Gould Fletcher, and others. In 1915 and in each of the two following years the group issued an anthology titled *Some Imagist Poets,* edited by Miss Lowell. Her own poems continued; *Sword Blades and Poppy Seeds* had appeared in 1914, and *Men, Women, and Ghosts* followed in 1916. Miss Lowell, now the acknowledged leader of a cénacle, had become a colorful figure, an immense and impressive woman who smoked black cigars, wore men's hats, and swore fierce men's oaths. Yet there was nothing essentially masculine about her; her mind was totally that of a woman, and her *outré* mannerisms were merely a shell which concealed a deep feminine sensitivity. A lifetime admirer of Keats, she devoted her last years to a critical biography of the romantic poet which has been accepted as one of the basic volumes of Keatsian criticism. Seldom in good health in later years because of her bulk, she died of a cerebral hemorrhage in 1925. Three separate volumes of poetry, including some of her best work, were published after her death: *What's O'Clock,* awarded a Pulitzer Prize in 1925, *East Wind* in 1926, and *Ballads For Sale* in 1927.

CHIEF WORKS: "Patterns" is the best-known poem of *Men, Women, and Ghosts* (1916) and an often-anthologized favorite among Amy Lowell's works. It is cast in the form of a monologue, but not a "conversational" one like the dramatic monologues of Browning or Robinson's "Ben Jonson Entertains a Man From Stratford;" the monologue is rather interior, a kind of soliloquy suggesting the stream-of-consciousness technique of fiction. The narrator, an English lady of some earlier day (the period is established only by the costume), walks down her garden paths dreaming of her lover, a soldier fighting in France. But the lover has been killed in "a pattern called war;" she cries bitterly that she will never know his embrace. A number of different types of "patterns" are portrayed in the poem. On the immediate material level the lady's dress, the formal garden in which she walks, and even the lady herself are patterns (with her fan, powdered hair, and fine dress she is a "picture" of a lady rather than a person). Yet these patterns are only symbols of the real patterns that confine her—the social codes which demand of her a formalized standard of behavior. The conflict of the poem is one between these conventions and her inward desires: ". . . my passion / Wars against the stiff brocade." She longs to divest herself of the brocaded gown— i.e., to rebel against restricting conventions—and enjoy her love passionately and unashamedly. But she cannot, for two reasons: as a lady in a formal age she must adhere to propriety, and besides her lover is dead—he too has conformed to the "pattern" expected of him as a soldier. The lady continues to behave as is expected of her by society; she does not break down when the news of her lover's death is brought her, but does the "proper" thing in inviting the messenger to take some refreshment. Inwardly, however, a despairing revulsion has taken place, and she cries to herself, "Christ! what are patterns for?" In addition to its dramatic form the chief structural device is its use of refrain (which Miss Lowell referred to as "return"), especially the repetition of the motif "stiff, brocaded gown . . . squills and daffodils."

"Evelyn Ray," from *What's O'Clock* (1925), is a short ballad combined with a vivid impressionistic word-picture of the setting, evidently a New England farmhouse. Two men have quarreled over the girl Evelyn Ray; they duel, and both are killed. Then, after an abrupt transition (11. 75-76), the poet turns to a personal contemplation of the story which continues through the remaining fifty lines of the poem. Analyzing the situation of the lovers in Christian terms, she wonders what Evelyn Ray will do in Eternity with two lovers, both of whom died for her; the likelihood is that she will be called to answer for the deaths of the two young men, perhaps because of her fickleness or her indecision. The poet concludes, "Better be nothing, Evelyn Ray;" it is better that one's body should pass to nothingness, furnishing nourishment for the buttercups, than that we should have to answer in another life for all our mistakes on earth. After generalizing thus over the flaws in the Christian theology the poem ends on an even more general note, averring that a creed is always "the shell of a lie" and that it is better for Evelyn Ray and her lovers to have lived in a physical world and to return at last to physical substance. This poem is thus one of the few of Amy Lowell's in which she expresses a specific philosophical attitude toward ultimate questions; the dominant tone, however, is artistic and personal rather than theological.

"Lilacs," also from *What's O'Clock,* is a nostalgic portrait of Miss Lowell's New England, which to her is typified by the many-colored fragrant blossoms of the lilac, which blooms in May. The poem consists almost entirely of a set of disconnected images of New England scenes, tied together by the refrain, "Lilacs, / False blue . . ." etc. Technically it is interesting as an example in its most characteristic form of Miss Lowell's polyphonic prose, with its occasional prose passages interspersed with free verse and refrain. "Lilacs" is said to have been Miss Lowell's favorite among her own poems.

"The Sisters," also from *What's O'Clock,* is a conversational and somewhat whimsical portrait of three great female poets: Sappho, Mrs. Browning, and Emily Dickinson. Miss Lowell discusses herself as the fourth of the "sisters," although in the end she feels little kinship with the others. Sappho's abandoned hedonism is impossible for a New England spinster—"This tossing off of garments / Which cloud the soul is none too easy doing / With us today." Mrs. Browning, on the other hand, is too conventional, hopelessly hedged about with Victorian propriety; Miss Lowell regretfully concludes that she would never have dared to call her by her domestic nickname "Ba." As for Emily Dickinson, she is both too Victorian and too exacting—i.e., she is a prim and precise poetess who is satisfied with nothing less than the perfect turn of language in every phrase. Miss Lowell, who has not the subtlety for this sort of thing, would nevertheless "somersault all day / If, by so doing, I might stay with her." In the end it is Emily Dickinson's old-maid prudishness which would have alienated her from Miss Lowell; she "chated her despair with games of patience"—i.e., her chaste resignation after her unhappy romance—and "fooled herself by winning" or by coming eventually to enjoy her colorless spinsterhood. Miss Lowell concludes by blaming everything on Queen Victoria, or perhaps Martin Luther—in short the stultifying restrictions which modern puritanical society imposes on women, even women of genius.

H. D. (born 1886)

Hilda Doolittle, who signed her verses "H. D.," was one of the first American poets to enlist under the banner of Imagism, and went on to become one of the most important of the group. Unlike most of the others, she remained loyal to the movement throughout her long career; in fact she has been called "the only true Imagist." Ezra Pound, the founder of the movement, alleged that Amy Lowell, in spite of her vigorous promotion efforts, was not an Imagist at all; in fact he sardonically referred to her personal brand of the technique as "Amygism." Meanwhile he himself, in *Mauberley* (1920) and later in the *Cantos,* had moved away from a pure Imagist style. H. D., who continued to champion the technique through the Thirties, ended as virtually *de facto* leader of the movement.

Like most Imagism, the verse of H. D. superficially resembles Oriental poetry, especially the highly polished miniature Japanese forms such as the *hokku.* Her real historical roots, however, lie in the tradition of classic and decadent Greek lyrics, especially the poetry of Sappho and that of the decadent *Greek Anthology.* Her allusions to classical culture emphasize the sensual and erotic; the dominant symbols are the Cyprian Aphrodite (the love-goddess in her most sensual aspect), traditional courtesans such as Lais, satyrs and other Dionysians, and the Dionysus-Apollo antithesis (flesh versus mind). The Cyprian city of Paphos, celebrated in antiquity as a sort of classic Gomorrah and the site of a famous temple to Aphrodite, often recurs in her verses. This cult of classic hedonism is of course merely H. D.'s personal form of reaction against Victorian puritanism; it is a theme found in Pound and the early Eliot as well as in many other poets of her generation. In H. D., however, the theme is used so consistently that it becomes a sort of personal mythology, which after much reading of her poetry assumes a highly distinctive and original quality of its own. This private symbolism must be mastered before her work as a whole can be appreciated.

It is not this, however, for which H. D.'s poetry is generally praised; it is instead the minute perfection, the perfect polish, the inevitability of image, which mark her short impressionistic lyrics. She has a gift for fresh and unusual metaphor, invariably graphic; the heat is referred to as a thick substance, almost like soil, which must be "plowed" by the wind, or sea waves are described as pine trees, resembling "pools of fir." There is no narrative in her verse, little characterization, and almost no philosophy; it is "pure poetry" in its purest form, devoted solely to perfection of metaphor, to the recreation in the reader's mind of a single perfectly polished image.

LIFE: Hilda Doolittle (later Aldington) was born in 1886 in Bethlehem, Pennsylvania, where her father was a professor of mathematics and astronomy at Lehigh University. When she was nine years old her father was appointed Director of the Flower Astronomical Observatory of the University of Pennsylvania; thus her formative years were spent in Philadelphia. After a private secondary school she went on to Bryn Mawr, but was forced to leave after two years because of poor health. She had begun writing while still in college; she translated Latin lyrics for publication and, after leaving Bryn Mawr, wrote children's stories for a Presbyterian paper published in Philadelphia. In 1911 she took a step which proved a turning point in her life: a trip to Europe, during which she became interested in the new movements in poetry and met Ezra Pound in London. Quickly converted to Imagism, she began writing under Pound's influence and sponsorship; her work appeared in his anthology *Des imagistes* in 1914 and later in the Amy Lowell Imagist volumes in 1915-17. Pound also recommended her work to Harriet Monroe, editor of the newly-founded *Poetry,* and the magazine not only published her poems but awarded her its Guarantors Prize in 1915. Meanwhile Miss Doolittle had married Richard Aldington, a British member of the Imagist cénacle, and established herself more or less permanently in England. Her first volume, *Sea Garden,* appeared in England in 1916. She continued to produce poetry slowly but steadily, meanwhile working in collaboration with her husband at translations of Greek lyrics; during Aldington's war service in the British army she substituted as editor of his magazine *The Egoist. Hymen,* her second volume of poetry, appeared simultaneously in England and America in 1921; next followed *Heliodora and Other Poems* (1924) and *Collected Poems* (1925). Meanwhile she had separated from Aldington; in 1920 she visited America and settled temporarily in California, but soon returned to Europe. After 1921 she lived in London and in a small town in Switzerland on the shore of Lake Geneva. She traveled frequently, especially to Greece. In 1938 she was awarded the Levinson Prize by *Poetry* magazine; although she has tended to remain in the second rank of contemporary poets, critical comment on her later work has been generally favorable. Her most important recent volumes are *The Walls Do Not Fall* (1944), *Tribute to the Angels* (1945), and *The Flowering of the Rod* (1946), which together form a trilogy in unrhymed verse centering around the experience of the Second World War.

TYPICAL POEMS: H. D.'s verse is generally consistent in style as well as in theme, and examination of a limited number of poems will demonstrate the tendencies of her work. "Pear Tree," one of her best-known visual images, is a short poem of sixteen lines, some of them only three syllables long, characterizing the impression of the pear tree through reiteration of the adjective "silver" and through suggestions of its lifting, arm-like quality: "higher than my arms reach / you have mounted. / O silver . . ."

"Heat," another short poem often anthologized, is unusual in that it attempts to communicate non-visual images: in this case temperature, humidity, and the tactile sensation of heated air. The dominant metaphorical device is the comparison of the heat to a solid substance which must be "cut apart" by the wind, through which fruit cannot drop, and which may be "plowed" like heavy soil.

"Lais," typical of H. D.'s many poems inspired by Sappho and the *Greek Anthology,* is a portrait of the legendary Grecian courtesan in middle age, lifting her mirror and finding no longer the face of "dark flame and white" of her youth. In addition to its vivid images the poem depends for its effect mainly on refrain: each of the last four stanzas begins with the word "Lais," and the antithesis *white/dark* recurs rhythmically.

"Holy Satyr" is in the same genre, marked stylistically by its extremely short lines in the Hellenistic Greek manner. The satyr, half-man, half-goat, a quasi-divine follower of Dionysus, is the subject of a poem of adoration which is partly hymn and partly love-song. Except for the reference to "leaf-circlets" (the classic laurel wreath of acclaim) the symbolism is chiefly erotic.

"The Islands" is a curiously rhythmic love-song which begins with an evocation of the chief islands of the Greek archipelago, especially those whose names suggest vague allusions to eroticism. Section II of the seven sections introduces the real theme: "What are the islands to me / if you are lost—." Love of land brings peace, but "Beauty sets apart"—love is the antithesis of peace, thus the poetess cannot savor the charm of the islands while love is unsatisfied. The reiterated refrains of the poem as well as the imagistic and non-consecutive content suggest words to be set to music; the diction as well seems chosen to convey a euphonious, quasi-musical effect.

"Heliodora" is the title poem of a volume published in 1924. In form it is a narrative dialogue, virtually unique in H. D.'s work; by another writer the same material might have been treated as a short story. The poetess, lingering (evidently in a café) with a lover, conducts a playful game of metaphors, but the young man (younger than she) has the greater talent with words. Inspired by her competition and by the wine, he seizes upon the metaphor of "a lily that laughs" for a smiling girl's kiss; with this beginning he goes on to compose a poem, actually included within H. D.'s poem, praising a young girl in the archaic style of the Greek lyric. A little drunk ("the wine-bowl crashed to the floor . . ."), he leaves, and the poetess thinks to herself that "there will never be a poet / in all the centuries after this" who will be so original and adept at metaphor. This romantic but slightly ironic poem suggests Ernest Dowson or Oscar Wilde as viewed through the slightly skeptical eyes of a Katherine Mansfield; the poetess admires the talent of her friend, yet there is a suggestion of feminine pride, of slight annoyance when he bests her in the game of metaphors.

JOHN GOULD FLETCHER (1886-1950)

Along with Pound, Amy Lowell, and H. D., John Gould Fletcher was one of the original members of the Imagist movement founded in England shortly before the First World War. He was not, however, a lifetime Imagist; the early poems of *Fire and Wine* and its four companion volumes published before 1915 were radically exhibition-istic and lacked the restraint of the Imagist technique (he later referred to them as "my literary wild oats"), and the work of his late period (after 1935) is conventional, even conservative, often taking the form of long odes or elegies on traditional set subjects. His most important poems fall into two groups: (1) the Imagist poems published in the Amy Lowell anthologies (*Some Imagist Poets,* 1915-16-17) and in his two volumes *Irradiations—Sand and Spray* (1915) and *Goblins and Pagodas* (1916); and (2) the long poems, influenced by Imagism but more contemplative and philosophical in nature, the best of which are found in *XXIV Elegies* (1935). Although this last volume includes poems written over a period of twenty years, it represents a tendency in his work which had previously remained latent at least as far as publication went; the appearance of *XXIV Elegies* introduced a new style which was to dominate the remainder of his work.

The most striking quality of Fletchers' early verse is its powerful graphic imagery; he not only sees what the less sensitive fail to see, but he perceives unusual relationship, juxta positions, and contrasts in nature which are not apparent to the ordinary eye. In "Irradiations" clouds, wind, and trees are compared one after the other to animals, the first two to horses and the last to elephants, in a masterful net-work of metaphors. In his later poems the images are more conventional and he shows an unfortunate tendency toward abstraction, which the original Imagists sought above all to avoid; yet these longer poems succeed through their very size in achieving a momentum and impressiveness impossible to obtain in a shorter lyric. After 1935 his poetry tends to resemble Sandburg, or even MacLeish. Moreover, in this later period he begins to show a kinship with these poets in content; his longer poems often contain liberal or radical political ideas, and he expresses a definite antagonism toward the blind materialism of machine-age society. In this genre, however, he is a poet of secondary importance; his main fame rests on his contribution to the Imagist anthologies and to his other poems of the 1914-16 period.

LIFE: John Gould Fletcher was born in Little Rock, Arkansas in 1886 of well-to-do parents who instilled in him a love for the classics and foreign languages. He was educated at Andover and at Harvard (1903-07); he found himself a social misfit in college, but meanwhile read widely and began to "scribble verses," as he later described it. In 1906 his father's death left him financially independent; the following year he left Harvard without a degree, although he was within four months of graduation. For about a year he wandered aimlessly about America, visiting Colorado and New Mexico; in 1908 he left for Europe. The following year he settled in London, where he remained, with numerous visits to the Continent, until 1914. Meanwhile, in the single year of 1913, he published the five volumes of his "wild oats" poetry: *The Dominant City, Fire and Wine, Fool's Gold, The Book of Nature,* and *Visions of the Evening.* His encounter with Pound and Imagism did not occur until after the last of these books had appeared; the influence of the movement was first apparent in Fletcher's contributions to *Some Imagist Poets* (1915-16-17) and in his *Irradiations—Sand and Spray* (1915). In 1914 he had returned to America, where he became a close friend of Amy Lowell; in 1916 he returned to England, married Florence Emily Arbuthnot, and remained until 1933. With the breakdown of his marriage and a turning in his literary career he came back again to America; he married for the second time, to Charlie May Simon, in 1936. Thereafter he lived mainly in Arkansas, traveling widely in America and Mexico. In 1939 his *Selected Poems* won him a Pulitzer Prize. During the late Thirties his interest began to turn to prose; he wrote a history of Arkansas for a Little Rock newspaper in 1936, and also experimented without music success in novel-writing. His autobiography *Life Is My Song* appeared in 1937. His death in 1950 was by drowning, apparently through suicide; his wife subsequently explained his final illness and death as caused by despair over "the Machine Age and its machine wars."

TYPICAL POEMS: "Irradiations" (from *Irradiations—Sand and Spray,* 1915) is an integrated cycle of poems consisting of a set of impressionistic studies from nature. The first four sections, which contain impressions of rain, wind, and fog in a large city, are the best known. Section V animizes the houses of the city as "careless drowsy giants" and the remaining sections are concerned more and more with the poet's subjective emotions. "Sand and Spray," from the same book, is similar; the impressions are those of a stormy day on a beach, and the five sections are labelled with musical terms ("Allegro furioso," etc.) to suggest the movements of an orchestral suite. "Sand and Spray" is more typical of pure Imagism than "Irradiations," which is faithful to the technique only in its first four sections. In addition the shorter lines and briefer images of "Sand and Spray" make it resemble more the pure Imagism of Amy Lowell and H. D.

XXIV Elegies (1935) is the most important work of Fletcher's later period. The twenty-four poems of the volume treat subjects of great diversity from Tintern Abbey (subject of the well-known poem by Wordsworth) and the city of London to skyscrapers and Thomas A. Edison. The "Elegy on London" is a word-picture of the British capital suggested by the similar poems of Juvenal (*Rome*) and Samuel Johnson (*London*) but emphasizing the grotesque and grimy power of a modern industrial city. The poem is dominated by the subtle theme of bells, a motif which is constantly reinforced and rises to a climax in Section IV; it is then seen to be an echo of the poet's nostalgia for the city, which he associates with his own creative aspirations: "Still deep within my heart . . . Deep clang of bells, the cry that bids life stay . . ."

The "Elegy on an Empty Skyscraper" is similar in style but more modern in concept, suggesting the poetic treatment of big-city themes by Sandburg and Hart Crane. Fletcher again utilizes animism; the half-built skyscraper is personified as a giant, standing with heavy feet sunken in the "molten pavements," who speaks to the poet of the emptiness of material creation, the "Vain flight of shadow where the chasms cry."

The "Elegy on the Russian Revolution" is an interesting experiment in a modern epic style. Evidently influenced by the heroic tradition in Russian poetry (Pushkin, Lermontov), the poem first sketches a grandiose panorama of Russia and then personifies the Revolution as a great red dawn, coming out of the East like a foaming red horse whose "hoof withers the grass."

"Elegy on the Last Judgment" is, in spite of its title, more politi-

cal than theological; the Judgment to come is evidently a social revolution or war in which the inequities of capitalist society will be wiped
out in a final violent cataclysm. The elegy ends, however, on a more
metaphysical note, suggesting the passing of the seasons and the
recurrence of life (Section III), through which "Earth in its long
death-agony turns from flame / To sparks and ash that kindles flame
again." This poem, like most of the others in *XXIV Elegies,* technically resembles Sandburg, Benét, and Hart Crane more than it does
the Imagist poetry of Fletcher's earlier period.

ELINOR WYLIE (1885-1928)

An intensely individual poet who never associated herself with any
literary school or movement, Elinor Wylie nevertheless most resembles the Imagists in style; her shorter lyrics have the same polished,
"enameled" quality, and she sometimes even surpasses them in precision and vividness of image (*cf.* "Velvet Shoes"). But she differs
from the Imagists in one important quality, and it is one which dominates her work: her subjectivity. She writes from a frankly personal
point of view; all her poems are in one way or another about herself,
and when she writes satire she can generally be found to be poking
fun at some pompous or excessively serious quality in her own character. Here her work parallels that of Edna Millay; indeed her poetry
may be considered a kind of hybrid between that of Miss Millay and
H. D., with a slight admixture of Shelley and the English metaphysical
poets.

It is difficult to find a poem of Mrs. Wylie's that is entirely serious,
or one that is entirely trivial. Even in her gravest and most pretentious
work there is a faint suggestion of self-mockery; and her light verse,
which often approaches the comic, has always a subtle thought-
provoking quality about it. Although her poetry is not intellectually
difficult, it reveals her as an extremely erudite person, one whose
poetic background is enriched from sources as disparate as the Hellenic Greek lyrics (Callimachus, Theocritus) and the English meta-
physicians (Donne, Blake). Another important influence is that of
Shelley; not only did Mrs. Wylie borrow his poetic mood, especially
that of his sonnets, for her later poems, but she considered herself a
kind of spiritual kindred to the English poet, and consciously modeled her life upon his. Like Shelley and the other British romantics,

she is anti-materialistic, resenting the necessities of mundane existence and the banal and degrading weaknesses of the flesh; yet she treats this theme too with a faint touch of irony (e.g., "The Eagle and the Mole"). In prosody Mrs. Wylie is highly rhythmic; she does not share the tendency toward free verse common to most poets of her generation, and her metrical patterns often approach the musical (according to her husband William Rose Benét, she actually intended some of her lyrics to be sung). A poetess of great diversity, Mrs. Wylie is simultaneously a traditionalist who echoes the themes of Sappho and Donne and an intensely modern, "advanced" woman whose mood and imagery reveal her kinship with Edna Millay and the other poetesses of her generation.

LIFE: Mrs. Elinor Wylie was born Elinor Hoyt in Somerville, New Jersey in 1885. Both her parents were Pennsylvanians, and when she was two years old the family moved to a Philadelphia suburb. Educated in private schools, she visited Europe with a grandfather and sister at eighteen. Shortly after her debut, disappointed over an unhappy romance, she impetuously married Philip Hichborn; a son was born of the marriage, but the union was never a satisfactory one. Three years later (1910) she eloped with Horace Wylie, also married and fifteen years her senior. The couple moved to England; in 1912 Hichborn took his own life, although his domestic troubles were not the primary cause of his suicide. Wylie and Mrs. Hichborn were later married, and she used the name Wylie to sign her poems for the rest of her career. Her first volume, a small and rather immature collection entitled *Incidental Numbers,* was privately printed in England in 1912. In 1915 she and Wylie returned to America; although by this time they were properly married, they found social circles in Washington and Philadelphia closed to them, and they eventually established themselves (1919) in New York. A number of Mrs. Wylie's poems appeared in magazines during the next few years, and in 1921 she published her first important collection: *Nets to Catch the Wind.* Two years later she and Wylie were divorced, and in 1923 she was married for the third time to William Rose Benét, himself a well-known poet. During the rest of her career Mrs. Wylie (as she continued to call herself professionally) visited England frequently, spending a long sojourn there in 1927. Meanwhile her writing continued; in the eight years from 1921 to 1928 she produced four volumes of poetry and four of prose. At the time of her death from a heart attack in New York in 1928 she was completing her revisions to her final book of poems, *Angels and Earthly Creatures.*

TYPICAL POEMS: "The Eagle and the Mole" (from *Nets to Catch the Wind,* 1921) is a wry moral allegory somewhat in the genre of the English metaphysical poets. The poem advises those delicate souls who abhor the crudity of fleshly existence either to rise above it in heroic loneliness (symbolized by the eagle), or, if courage for such heroism is lacking, to burrow beneath it, living the gloomy and bitter life of a recluse (symbolized by the mole). The mole, depicting as holding intercourse with the "roots" of things, with "rivers at their source," nevertheless seems rather foolish among his "disembodied bones"; a typical Elinor Wylie irony pervades the advice.

"Velvet Shoes," also from *Nets to Catch the Wind,* is in Mrs. Wylie's quasi-Imagist style, consisting entirely of images of snow, smoothness, and silence; Untermeyer calls it "perhaps the whitest poem ever written."

From the same volume, "Sanctuary" is a wry twelve-line allegory resembling the style of Emily Dickinson. Longing for a firm thick-walled house of bricks (security, emotional self-sufficiency), the poetess realizes only too late that this means suffocation (or spiritual death).

"Peregrine" (from *Black Armour,* 1923) is typical of several ballad-like poems in Mrs. Wylie's work; metrically its form is that of the rondo. The miniature characterization describes, with slight irony, a legendary vagabond who is perhaps intended to stand for the modern wanderer-male of the Lost Generation (Hemingway, Fitzgerald).

Another often-anthologized ballad is "Peter and John," from *Trivial Breath,* 1928. The apostles Peter and John recount dreams in which each hung upon the gallows; John in his dream saw himself as the Christ, but Peter (who denied Christ thrice before the cock crew) reveals in the last lines that he in his dream was Judas Iscariot. This emotionally restrained but highly charged poem depends for its effect chiefly on its striking images ("In the falling sun / He burned like a flame") and on its evocative and repetitive rhythm, typical not only of the classic English ballad tradition but of such modern ballads as those of Housman, Edna Millay, and Auden.

SARA TEASDALE (1884-1933)

Sara Teasdale's short, highly polished, and nostalgic lyrics are the poetic reflection of her own unhappy life. She modeled her early verse on that of Christina Rossetti, with whom she had much in common; both women, deeply feminine, nevertheless resented and rebelled against their subservient rôle in a man's world, and both express in their poetry a sensitive, ironic, and slightly bitter attitude toward love. To Sara Teasdale it seemed there were only two choices open to a woman who sought love: a purely negative "feminine" passivity, which she rejected ("But how can I give silence / My whole life long?"), and a lonely but independent solitude, which she eventually chose (see "The Solitary"). At her weakest she is sentimental; at her best she is succinct, accurate, and evocative.

In prosody Sara Teasdale is conservative, following her model Christina Rossetti. Her favorite form is the quatrain, which she perversely continued to use in the middle of the free-verse craze of the Twenties. In her first poems she often used blank verse; her later work is more often rhymed. Her quatrains in the form *abxb* often resemble those of Emily Dickinson, although Miss Teasdale is even more conservative in rhyme than the nineteenth-century poetess, following conventional rules where Emily Dickinson often experimented with oblique or "slant" rhymes. Miss Teasdale's epigrammatic cleverness is sometimes slightly too contrived; since good poetry is meant to be reread, a poem which depends for its effect on a surprise or clever twist in the last line often loses its initial charm with the passing of time. The best of her poems follow the more subtle pattern of "The Long Hill," probably her best-known verse, which ends with a slight wry turning of thought: "the rest of the way will be only going down." Almost bare of imagery and metaphor, her verse is highly condensed, stark, achieving a mood of disillusion without cynicism and nostalgia without sentimentalism; she is the master of the poetic epigram of regret.

LIFE: Sara Teasdale was born in St. Louis in 1884 of parents who were already middle-aged at the time of her birth; her effort to adjust

herself to a difficult family situation contributed to the neuroticism
which followed her throughout her life. Educated at home and at a
private school, she was a precocious child; she very early encountered
the poetry of Christina Rossetti which made a deep impression on her
and formed in her a resolution to become a poetess herself. Her first
poems were published when she was still in her girlhood; in 1907
appeared her first volume, *Sonnets to Duse,* an immature and tentative collection not typical of her best work. *Helen of Troy and Other
Poems* (1911) marked the beginning of her mature poetic career;
the promise was sustained in *Rivers to the Sea* (1915), *Love Songs*
(1917), and *Flame and Shadow* (1920). Meanwhile her personal life
had led her into complications and unhappiness. An intermittent ha-
bitué of Chicago poetic circles, she met there Vachel Lindsay, who
courted her for a number of years without success; in one of the intervals of her indecision she impulsively married Ernest R. Filsinger, a
St. Louis business man. In 1925 Lindsay himself was married; Miss
Teasdale divorced Filsinger in 1929, and in 1931 Lindsay died by
suicide. For the rest of her life Miss Teasdale lived in New York
City, torn, as one writer puts it, between "the desire to be loved and
the greater desire to be alone." Her later poetry (*Dark of the Moon,*
1926, and *Strange Victory,* 1933) is disillusioned and calm, often
concerned with the theme of the passing of time and the approach of
old age. She died in 1933 from an overdose of sleeping pills which
caused her to drown in her bath.

TYPICAL POEMS: "Night Song at Amalfi," built of three parallel
quatrains, is a protest against the passive rôle in love to which women
are committed by tradition. Longing to respond passionately to the
demands of her love, the poetess, inquiring of heaven and sea
(perhaps spirit and flesh), is told to reply only with silence.

"The Long Hill," almost identical in form, is an allegory of middle
age—the "crest" of which Miss Teasdale was despairingly aware in
the later years of her life. One does not notice the summit of life
because "brambles"—the cares of daily existence—are distracting.
Youth is left imperceptibly behind, and once one becomes aware of
having reached middle age there is no turning back, since the rest of
the way is downward.

"The Solitary," also formed of three quatrains, offers an intimate glimpse into Miss Teasdale's personality during her later years. Looking back without regret at the anxious and unhappy dependence upon others which dominated her youth, she feels herself now "self-complete as a flower or a stone."

"Effigy of a Nun," a poem of medium length, is evidently inspired by a medieval statue of a nun seen in a European museum. Contemplating the expression of the nun, the poetess comprehends that she understood all the ways and pleasures of the world and yet rejected them, finding contentment in the splendor of her own triumph over the flesh ("She must have told herself that love was great, / But that the lacking it might be as great a thing . . ."). The parallel to Miss Teasdale's own life is obvious; she too voluntarily chose solitude, then "learned too well in her long loneliness / How empty wisdom is, even to the wise."

"Appraisal," an irregularly-rhyming poem of seventeen lines which departs from Miss Teasdale's usual quatrain form, is a mature and sophisticated portrait of a lover who is seen by the poetess in all his faults: his indecision, his "cautiousness like garments/Frayed and thin, with many a stain—". Yet even though she views her beloved with the pitiless clarity of intelligence, she accepts him willingly for his merits: his proud will, his gentleness, his sense of humor. This poem is one of many brief love-poems in Miss Teasdale's work, a selection of which is found in *Love Songs* (1917).

T. S. ELIOT (born 1888)

Beginning around 1909 as an avant-garde poet whose esoteric work was read only by a small circle of cognoscenti, Eliot has through the years acquired popular prestige until a 1954 *Life* article could describe him as "the world's most distinguished living poet." His acceptance parallels the gradual acceptance of modern poetry by the public, at least that lettered and educated portion of the public which reads something more than its daily newspaper. Meanwhile Eliot as a poet has not remained static. His poetry, beginning with *Prufrock and Other Observations* (1917) and continuing through the dramas of the post-1945 era, shows a definite progression in content as well as in technique. Four periods may be roughly distinguished in this long poetic career. Eliot's first published poems (1909-17), while not lacking in originality, were strongly derivative; they were influ-

enced in technique by Imagism, by the dramatic monologues of
Browning, by Elizabethan drama, and by the work of the French
impressionist poet Jules Laforgue (1860-87). Several of the poems
of this period (e.g., "Dans le restaurant") were actually written in
French; the two most important of them, "The Love Song of J. Alfred
Prufrock" and "Portrait of a Lady," are monologues or miniature
dramas partaking of the rhythm of Elizabethan verse. With *The
Waste Land* (1922) a new period begins; Eliot, still influenced by
Pound in technique, now began to develop a more personal religious
and ethical system, marked by an increasing interest in the English
metaphysical poets (Donne *et al.*) and Oriental religions (Buddhism,
Vedanta) and a fascination with anthropological mythology inspired
by reading of Sir James Frazer's *The Golden Bough* and Jessie L.
Weston's *From Ritual to Romance*. The trend from dramatic to philosophical poetry continues in the third period (1930-40), which is
dominated by the serious and theological *Ash Wednesday;* and it finds
its climax in the fourth period, beginning with *Four Quartets* in 1943
and continuing through the two dramas *The Cocktail Party* and *The
Confidential Clerk*. The difficult *Quartets,* abstruse and lacking strong
imagery, are dominated by the religious principles Eliot had first publicly professed in 1927; the same ideas are also latent in the two
plays. By 1950 Eliot had arrived at a philosophical position comparable to that of his contemporaries Huxley and Waugh: rejection of
Western materialism combined with an eclectic spiritualism including
elements of Oriental and Occidental religions. Eliot himself, in an
unpublished lecture, has distinguished three periods of "metaphysical poetry" in world literature which have produced work of
superlative quality: the Medieval (school of Dante and Cavalcanti);
the Renaissance (school of Donne); and the Modern (school of
Baudelaire and Laforgue). To these might be added the Contemporary: the school of Eliot and the younger poets who have taken him
as their model.

Although Eliot has passed through several periods or stages in his
long poetic career, his style and content follow a consistent pattern
of development throughout his work. The elements in his poetry
which rose to predominance during his later years are detectable in
embryonic form even in his earliest work, and nothing he acquired
along the line of his literary evolution was ever totally abandoned.

Thus, examining his poetic work as a whole, a number of dominant characteristics or tendencies may be described:

(1) Eliot has a strong feeling for the PAST, especially for the literary and religious traditions of the past. It is probably this attitude which has led him to abandon the relatively new American culture for the more traditional society of Britain. In his poetry the tendency takes the form of an interest in myths and ancient religions, as well as a preoccupation with obscure and difficult literary allusions. To Eliot the past is not something dead which is studied in books, but a memory vigorously manifested in present events; in his view mythology transcends time. He is fond of introducing figures from ancient Greece, such as Tiresias, into modern settings, or of drawing parallels between contemporary and archetypical situations. His interest in the work of Jung and Frazer (see below) is connected to this tendency.

(2) Eliot is fascinated with SYMBOLS, especially the mental symbols the psychiatrist and anthropologist Carl Jung calls archetypes. Archetypes or primordial images are symbolic concepts common to all mankind which relate to problems of man's natural or social environment; they are frequently concerned with fertility fetishes or with man's erotic nature. Much of Eliot's poetry presupposes a knowledge of these theories, and is therefore fully meaningful only after reading Jung, Frazer, and other authors.

(3) A political conservative, Eliot is anti-democratic on intellectual grounds; i.e., he feels little kinship with the unlettered masses and believes the important forces of society to lie in the educated, the talented, and the aristocratic. His apotheosis of heroism in *Coriolan* has led his critics to accuse him of a sort of proto-fascism, but this is unfair. A more judicious statement is Eliot's own in the 1928 introduction to *For Lancelot Andrewes,* where he describes himself as "an Anglo-Catholic in religion, a classicist in literature, and a royalist in politics."

(4) Eliot, especially in his earlier poems (before 1930), often portrays inadequate characters who feel a sense of their own impotence and the banality of their lives, who seek to rebel in an heroic fashion against their situations, but who generally fail through half-measures. This recurring theme is sometimes called the PRUFROCK motif, after the character in "The Love Song of J. Alfred Prufrock," but it occurs frequently elsewhere. Eliot finds this personality symptomatic

of the plight of modern man in the broader sense; in *The Waste Land* the concept is depersonalized and pervades the entire poem.

(5) In his poetic technique Eliot takes his departure from the Imagists and from Ezra Pound, although from this starting point he evolved constantly toward a more personal and more original style. His use of free verse, his snatches of conversation, and the generally disjointed appearance of his verse resemble Imagism, while his copious allusions, his juxtaposition of ancient and modern, and the fact that he writes consciously for a small group of erudite readers show his kindship to Pound. Eliot specifically acknowledged his admiration of, and debt to, Pound in the dedication of *The Waste Land*. A *Times Literary Supplement* review well summarized the character of his earlier poetry when it described it as having "two marks of 'modernist' work, the liveliness that comes from topicality and the difficulty that comes from intellectual abstruseness."

LIFE: Thomas Stearns Eliot was born in St. Louis, Missouri in 1888. His ancestry was distinguished; his family included President Charles W. Eliot of Harvard as well as a number of earlier writers, educators, and divines. He took his undergraduate degree at Harvard, where he was exposed to Santayana and Irving Babbitt; he then went to Paris to study at the Sorbonne (1910-11). Returning, he resumed his studies at Harvard, but made another trip to Europe immediately after the outbreak of the war. In 1915 he married an Englishwoman, Miss Vivienne Haigh-Wood, and took up his residence in London. He returned to America periodically, sometimes for considerable visits, but his loyalties leaned more and more to Britain during the early Twenties. From 1915 to 1922 he earned his living as a teacher, free-lance writer, and editor; in 1922 *The Waste Land* won the Dial Award and brought him both fame and a certain amount of economic security. The same year he founded a review, *The Criterion,* which he continued to publish for seventeen years. Neither his poetry nor his editorial ventures, however, brought him total economic independence, and he retained during most of his career a part-time position as literary editor for a British publisher.

In 1927 Eliot became a British subject, and the following year, in the introduction to *For Lancelot Andrewes,* he made the statement of literary, religious, and political conservatism quoted above. Since then he has become increasingly concerned with religion in his poetry and drama, and has in fact become one of the major metaphysical poets of the century. At the same time his style has diverged from that of the Imagists, becoming constantly more abstract as his content becomes more metaphysical. This tendency reached its climax in *Four Quartets* (1943); a concise statement of his final politico-religious position is contained in the essay *The Idea of a Christian Society* (1940). In recent years Eliot's interest has turned increasingly to the drama; he wrote four major plays between 1935 and 1953, and at least two of them (*Murder in the Cathedral* and *The Cocktail Party*) were successful in theatre productions. In 1948 Eliot was awarded the Nobel Prize for Literature "for his work as a trail-blazing pioneer of modern poetry;" the same year he visited America to reside briefly at the Institute for Advanced Study at Princeton. He returned to America in 1950 for another visit, this time lecturing at Harvard and at the University of Chicago.

CHIEF WORKS: "The Love Song of J. Alfred Prufrock" (1915) is the major poem of Eliot's first collection, *Prufrock and Other Observations* (1917). The style is free verse broken by occasional rhymes, the medium of most of Eliot's early poems. The epigraph from Dante, translated, readers, "If I thought my answer were to one who could ever return to the world, this flame should shake no more; but since none ever did return alive from this abyss [Inferno], if what I hear be true, without fear of infamy I answer you." In a parallel manner Prufrock, the "I" of the poem, speaks his thoughts within the abyss of his own soul; he lacks the courage to rebel, and his love song is one he never voices aloud.

Prufrock (his name suggests a dull and slightly pretentious respectability) is an ineffectual gentleman, no longer young, who is growing weary of the artificial London society in which he monotonously passes his days. He yearns for a more vital and adventurous existence, but lacks the courage to embark upon it. Since he is living in a puritanical Anglo-Saxon society, his rebellious thoughts turn first to erotic adventure. The first section (11. 1-12) is an invitation to an unknown and perhaps as yet unchosen partner to embark upon such an adventure: an expedition into the less savory quarters of the city is implied. The refrain (11. 13-14, 35-36) ironically typifies the shallow aestheticism of tea-party society, the life Prufrock wishes to escape. Lines 15-34 extend the image of urban squalor, suggesting a clandestine adventure, and end with a temporizing compromise. Afraid of ridicule, from line 36 onward Prufrock seems to grow increasingly uncertain; he asks, "Do I dare disturb the universe?" In 1. 82 and again in 11. 110ff he confesses his own inadequacy, admitting that he is after all no prophet or tragic hero. In the closing lines (119-130) his abortive revolt against convention is symbolized in several sea-images; the mermaids who sing "each to each" are uninhibited creatures luxuriating in their natural setting and producing exquisite unpremeditated song. Prufrock overhears the beckoning song of the mermaids, but realizes this invitation to adventure is not meant for him. The final three lines reveal the reason: although escape into the nirvana of sensualism, both physical and intellectual, is temporarily successful, "human voices wake us, and we drown"—mundane affairs press in upon us and we are recalled to conventional life. This closing passage, like the previous descriptions of fog and slums, is typical of the Imagist technique and if taken out of context might well be treated as a short Imagist poem complete in itself.

Prufrock is a type of character that Eliot knew well from first-hand acquaintance: the cultured, sensitive, but bored gentleman of Cambridge or London society, the literary man or professor, whose sense of decorum and fear of ridicule prevent him from seizing life and savoring it in a more virile manner. In the wider context the poem describes the human conflict between sensual desires and longings and the restrictions of civilization. Each human being longs for a nirvana where social censure will be forgotten in a passionate enjoyment of the senses; but most people, like Prufrock, are deterred by fear of ridicule and feelings of inadequacy.

"Portrait of a Lady" (poem, 1917) is laid in a similar setting. The speaker is a young man; his companion is a lady, somewhat older who wishes to hold him although she realizes their affair cannot hope to be permanent. For his part the young man is torn between sympathy and a longing for freedom. Perhaps a little too refined and sensitive, the lady leads a highly artificial life among her flowers, her Chopin recitals, and her "few friends." In the penultimate stanza (11. 102-108) the lady, in spite of her sophisticated manner, scarcely conceals her anguish at the parting; yet the young man realizes this last separation is to be a permanent one.

The poem symbolically covers a cycle of time from winter to winter. Section I takes place in December; in Section II it is April and the lilacs are in bloom. In the final section October completes the circle and accentuates the young man's restlessness, nostalgia, and boredom. The last stanza in Section II (11. 71-83) is the chief expression of the young man's attitude toward the lady, an attitude dominated by sympathy but lacking real passion. Like "Prufrock," this poem is a character study intended to communicate the mood of a certain social environment.

"Sweeney Among the Nightingales" (poem, 1918) is one of several Eliot poems involving the character of Sweeney, an "ape-necked" symbol of unthinking modern materialism. The epigraph from Aeschylus ("Alas, I have been smitten deep with a mortal blow") suggests the tragedy of Agamemnon's death and establishes the motif of archetypical murder and lust. Sweeney is observed in a bawdyhouse; all the persons present are vulgar and sensual, concerned only with their immediate physical desires. They are unaware of the wider and more sublime existence around them, mentioned in sections 2, 3, 9, and 10. Sweeney himself "guards the horned gate"—i.e., blocks the messages from the dead (traditions of the past) which might help him and his companions to escape from their plight. The rhythms of nature (the stars, etc.), the ecstatic experience of religion (the nearby convent), and the ever-present tragedy of Agamemnon are close at hand, even in our modern life; but Sweeney and his kind are insensible toward them. Eliot here pleads for a renewed contact with tradition and with the spiritual forces of human experience, the means by which mankind can rise again to sublimity.

A variant interpretation of the poem compares Agamemnon's death with a sordid and evil plot prepared against Sweeney by Rachel, the lady in the Spanish cape, and "someone indistinct" with whom the host converses. In either case the basic contrast is that between tradition and sublimity on one hand and contemporary banality on the other.

In "Burbank with a Baedeker: Bleistein with a Cigar" (poem, 1919) the same theme is repeated in the setting of Venice. Eliot views the city, the traditional home of the arts and of aristocratic luxury, as today vulgarized by the commercialism which was present from the inception of the city and which has finally conquered it. Burbank with his guidebook denotes intellectual curiosity, love of culture, and respect for tradition; he arrives to find Venice (symbolized by Princess Volupine, whose name suggests both the Latin root for "fox" and the word "voluptuous") in a state of decadent decline. Burbank "falls" for the Princess, but she is more receptive to the attentions of Bleistein, the vulgar embodiment of avarice, and Sir Frederick Klein, representative of a new commercial order. Bleistein's blatant commercialism is that of the mongrel cosmopolite who strikes crudely toward his goal, whereas Sir Frederick, perhaps British, assumes a veneer of culture and is accordingly more effective.

The imagery of the poem continually contrasts the glory of Renaissance Venice with the rats and slime of the modern city. In a wider context Venice stands for Western culture as a whole. From the creative magnificence of the middle ages and Renaissance it has degenerated into a sordid commercialism; fortune turns from the Burbanks of the world to the opportunistic Bleisteins.

"Gerontion" (poem, 1920) begins with an epigraph from *Measure for Measure* (III:1) suggesting that neither youth nor age has any importance, since life is essentially illusion. The title signifies "a little old man." Again the contrast is that between human life in a framework of tradition and spiritual kinship with the past and a bestial existence governed solely by the needs of the moment. The old man is a prisoner in contemporary society, a world obsessed with gain, ignorantly atheistic, and rotten from within. One of its chief qualities is instability, symbolized by the "rented house" in which the old man lives. Heroism is dead; the old man admits that he did not fight at Thermopylae (the "hot gates") or at any of the other battles of the ancient world against barbarism. He is "waiting for rain" (the refreshing and lifegiving spiritual vitality that comes like rain from above) but instead is continually tormented by winds, symbol of modern restlessness and uncertainty. Beginning with line 17 Christianity is introduced in contrast to contemporary avarice and vulgarity. In 11. 54ff, beginning "I that was near your heart," Gerontion refers to the estrangement of modern man from the religion which sustained him up to the time of the Renaissance. The penultimate section (11.

60ff) concludes that commercialism (the spider symbolizes the intricacy of modern finance) is likely to triumph permanently. Modern man, alienated from the spiritual forces which previously nourished him, is condemned to live in the "rotting house" of his cosmopolitan and rootless society.

The Waste Land (poem, 1922) is the most important work of Eliot's earlier period. The theme is again the banality and barrenness of the contemporary world contrasted with the richness of traditional spiritual and mythological forces. There are two chief sources for the structure and symbolism of the poem: Jessie L. Weston's *From Ritual to Romance* and Sir James Frazer's *The Golden Bough*. Some knowledge of both these books is essential to an appreciation of the poem. Miss Weston's book is a psychological and anthropological study of the Holy Grail legend. The story of the Grail appears in slightly different forms in many cultures, but it always concerns a dry, sterile, and cursed land (the "waste land") ruled over by a Fisher King whose sexual impotence is connected with the plight of his realm. The wanderer or knight who arrives to voice the ritual demand for the Holy Grail is the talisman through which king and land are restored to virility. Frazer's work begins in an attempt to explain another widespread racial myth: the priest of the sacred wood who is killed each year by a candidate who thereby becomes the new king and priest. According to Frazer and Miss Weston, both myths can be traced to primitive fertility rites; and students of comparative mythology believe that the element of sacrifice common to both has eventually found its way into Christianity as the ritual of the Eucharist. Miss Weston explains that secrets of these mystery religions were transmitted into Western Europe in pre-medieval times by Syrian and Phoenician merchants, and eventually emerged in the middle ages as the legend of the Grail.

In writing *The Waste Land* Eliot also utilized Carl Jung's theory of primordial images or archetypes (see above).

With these materials Eliot constructs a poem of which the dominant theme is the contrast between human universals and modern materialism and banality. The epigraph is from the *Satyricon* of Petronius: "With my own eyes I saw the Sibyl suspended in a jar at Cumae, and when her followers said to her, Sibyl, what do you want? she replied, I want to die." Thus two motifs of the poem are suggested: universal mythology and the death-wish deriving from boredom.

The poem itself is divided into five sections. The first, "The Burial of the Dead," introduces the motif of the recurrence of life out of death and corruption, but depicts April as "the cruellest month," since it destroys the serene oblivion of winter (death) in order to create new life. A snatch of banal conversation is interposed; the thematic contrast between sublimity and banality is established. The concept of "rootlessness" or lack of stabilizing tradition is suggested in the conversation and in the subsequent soliloquy (11, 19-30). An exhilarating snatch of Wagner's *Tristan und Isolde* is quoted (31-35), but is followed by a bleaker line from the same opera: "Empty and bare the sea" (1. 42). In line 44 appears Madame Sosostris, a vulgarized clairvoyant who is the only descendant of the wise necromancers (or Sibyls) of the ancient world. She tells fortunes through the Tarot pack of cards, each of which bears a symbolic image. The Phoenician sailor is to reappear in the poem, and the man with three staves is identified by Eliot in a note as the Fisher King himself. The section ends with an allusion to the superstition of planting corpses with crops to insure fertility; the "Dog" connects the incident with the Egyptian Osiris myth, which also concerns the resurrection of life.

In Section II, "A Game of Chess," the motif is the absence of mythical meaning in contemporary marriage. Philomel, in an ancient myth violated by a king and transformed into a nightingale, can now produce only discordant sounds for the modern ear (11. 99-110). Irony is achieved through reference to the sublime passions of Cleopatra and Dido. Snatches of neurotic modern conversation are introduced (11. 120ff) and at line 139 begins a vulgar cockney dialogue concerned with abortion and other unsavory aspects of modern conjugal relations. The refrain "HURRY UP PLEASE IT'S TIME" is the call of the English pub-keeper at closing time. The idiotic farewells of the patrons then fade into the poignant song of Ophelia from *Hamlet* (11. 169ff). Again sublimity is present, but the vulgar generation is too distracted to notice it.

The title of Section III, "The Fire Sermon," recalls a famous Buddhistic discourse on lust and fornication. Opening with a pastiche of Spenser's wedding song, the section soon contrasts this idyllic picture with the squalor of modern love ("Sweeney to Mrs. Porter in the spring"), heralded by motor horns and associated with the horror of rats. Mr. Eugenides (line 209) recalls the Syrian merchants who, according to Miss Weston, brought the mysteries to Europe; now they bring only sordid merchandise. Toward line 227 the narrator becomes Tiresias, the blind seer of Greek mythology who was the wisest of humans because he had been both woman and man; thus he embodies the sexual tension which is the motif of the section. Tiresias, present in modern London, views the sordid tryst of a typist and a clerk in a tenement bedroom. Modern love, promiscuous and perfunctory, has lost its mystery and has become no more significant than the playing of a phonograph record. The section ends with the song of the three Thames Daughters (inspired by the Rhine Maidens of *Die Götterdämmerung*), who relate the manner of their dishonoring, and with a final echo of the Buddhistic sermon.

The short fourth section, "Death by Water," parallels the drowning of the Phoenician sailor of "The Burial of the Dead" with the previously established archetype of death and subsequent resurrection.

The final section, "What the Thunder Said," begins on a note of hopelessness: "he who was living" (Adonis, Osiris, Christ, symbol of the incarnation of Divinity) is now dead, and contemporary man is dying spiritually. The rock (spiritual sterility) is contrasted to water, universal symbol of the beginning of life. The "falling towers" of the cities of the Near East and Europe are mentioned (11. 373-376); the civilization which began in Greece and the Holy Land is toppling. The cock-crow (line 391), heard as Christ was seized by the soldiers, recalls the story of the Passion; rain (symbol of recurring life) shortly results. But this image is abandoned, and the poem turns to the Hindu myth of the thunder from the Upanishads. The protagonist has now become the Fisher King himself; he wonders what action he can take against the ruin of his land. Three quotations follow. The first is from Dante: "Then sprang he back into the fire that refines them." The sinner Arnaut Daniel, viewed by Dante in Purgatory, gladly accepts his suffering since he knows it will bring redemption. The second is from the anonymous *Vigil of Venus:* "When shall I become as the swallow?" Eliot's note connects this with Procne, in the Greek myth changed to a swallow to escape her suffering. The third, "The Prince of Acquitaine at the fallen tower," is from a sonnet of Gerard de Nerval; it refers to the poet whose life is ruined but who proposes to

begin anew. The childish jingle of London Bridge stresses the theme
of decay and collapse. The poem then ends with a Sanscrit benedic-
tion; the word *shantih* is equivalent to "the Peace that passes all understanding." But this consolatory note is almost ironic in the context
of the previous pessimistic passage. Thus the poem's theme is that
the mythical death and rebirth of Osiris, Adonis, or Christ, the ritual
which has nourished mankind for centuries, is not longer possible,
since our age has lost its contact with the past and has become spiritually sterile. *The Waste Land* is not, as is sometimes thought, a mere
portrait of the generation of the Twenties; it is an analysis of the
predicament of modern man in his relation to the universal spiritual
forces of nature.

"The Hollow Men" (poem, 1925) is similar in tone and content
but much less extensive in treatment. The epigraph is from Conrad's
The Heart of Darkness, which depicts the contrast between the
artificiality of civilization and the elemental but savage power of
primitive superstition. The Hollow Men are the citizens of modern
Western culture, synthetically stuffed with opinions, ideas, and faiths
they cannot feel. The senselessness of the modern man's daily routine
is indicated in the childish nursery rhyme which begins Section V.
The fourth stanza of this section ("Between the desire . . .") suggests
the impotence of the Prufrock-Gerontion type of figure who is reduced to inaction through the "Shadow" of thought. The chief feature of modern culture is its banality and pettiness; the world ends
"not with a bang but a whimper."

Ash Wednesday (poem, 1930) is a poetic contemplation expressing the religious ideas which Eliot had worked out in 1927-28. The
major theme is the neo-Platonic love of Dante, Cavalcanti, and other
medieval Italian poets; the Lady who dominates the poem is a symbol
of perfection or beauty through which man may be drawn to God.
There are many echoes of the Bible and of Church litanies.

Four Quartets (poetry, 1943) is a volume consisting of four sym-
metrical meditations on philosophical and religious subjects. The
images of the poems are intended to communicate the subjective experience of religious faith. Each quartet is named for a geographical
location and identified with one of the four humors of medieval medicine. "Burnt Norton" takes its name from a manor-house in Gloucestershire; its element is fire. "East Coker" is a small village in Somer-

setshire; the element of the poem is earth. The "Dry Salvages" are rocks off the New England coast; the element is water. "Little Gidding" is the site of a religious community of the seventeenth century; the dominant element is air. The quartets follow a quasi-musical structure, and each poem is identified with an aspect of Christian religious experience.

DRAMAS: *Murder in the Cathedral* (1935) is the most important of Eliot's early plays. In form a verse tragedy, it takes for its subject the historical incident of the murder of the Archbishop Thomas à Becket by followers of Henry II in Canterbury cathedral in 1170 A.D. The form is rigidly classical, and a chorus is included in the manner of the Greek tragedy. There is little action except for the murder itself; the play consists largely of a set of philosophical dialogues in which Thomas converses with his murderers and with others. The central scene is the debate with four Tempters who symbolize the inner conflict in Thomas' mind: his youthful love of pleasure, his later ambition for power, the threat of the feudal barons, and his own egotistical desire for martyrdom. Rejecting all four temptations, Thomas goes on to deliver a masterful sermon in which he defines his own attitude toward the tragedy which is approaching him: "The martyr no longer desires anything for himself, not even the glory of martyrdom." When the king's knights arrive later to murder him he offers no resistance. After the deed the knights present a foolish and unconsciously ironic defense of their crime, and the drama ends as Thomas' priests thank God "who has given us another Saint in Canterbury."

The Cocktail Party (drama, 1949), laid in a modern setting and written in an informal and vernacular free-verse style, has proved the most successful of Eliot's plays in the theatre. As the action opens four of the chief characters have become involved in a banal sexual impasse: Edward Chamberlayne, a successful solicitor, is having a clandestine affair with Celia Coplestone; his wife Lavinia is in love with Peter Quilpe, and Peter himself is courting Celia. Edward and Lavinia plan a cocktail party, but on the day it is to take place Lavinia leaves her husband, and he is forced to entertain the guests himself and make lame excuses for her absence. The most important guests at the party are Julia Shuttlethwaite, outwardly a silly woman dominated by her affected mannerisms, and an "Unidentified Guest" to whom Edward impulsively reveals his domestic troubles. The "Un-identified Guest" is actually Sir Henry Harcourt-Reilly, a kind of psychiatrist who is as much a spiritual practitioner as a medical one. The action gradually reveals that he has been called in on the case by Julia, who underneath her giddy silliness is actually a wise and intuitive woman. Dr. Reilly persuades Edward and Lavinia that they must break out of the shells of egotism which have isolated them from each other; realizing the seriousness of the situation, they do so, and their marriage continues on a new and firmer basis. As for Celia, who suffers from the sense of isolation from her fellow beings as well as from a "consciousness of sin," Reilly recognizes in her a true Saintly personality; he sends her to a sanatorium, and then advises her to follow her own destiny as her heart guides her. She becomes a member of a religious order, goes off as a nurse to a remote tropical island, and there is martyred by the natives in a particularly horrible manner. Peter, also following his destiny, becomes a screenwriter, thus finding contentment at his own level of ability; Reilly tells him, "You understand your *métier,* Mr. Quilpe—which is the most that any of us can ask for."

Underneath this comedy-of-manners plot, which might have been written by a Sidney Howard or a Philip Barry, is a metaphysical undercurrent which is wholly Eliot's. Reilly, Julia, and her playboy friend Alex are beneath their superficial appearances deeply religious persons; the toast (actually an incantation) which they recite at the end of Act II clearly shows them to be members of some kind of spiritual cult—or perhaps they are Divinities masquerading under human form. Although Reilly at first appears to dominate the plot, it is Julia who is the real power behind him; she is evidently a kind of priestess or an earth-mother figure who knows all and who controls the latent instincts and impulses of her friends. Unlike *Murder in the Cathedral,* however, the play does not arrive at a neat theological conclusion; its philosophical meaning is latent and suggested rather than specific.

Other Eliot dramas are *The Family Reunion* (1939), similar to *The Cocktail Party* and set in an English country house, and *The Confidential Clerk* (1953), a poetic allegory of man's search for a father and a belonging-place.

HART CRANE (1899-1932)

A tempestuous but indecisive person in his private life, Hart Crane possessed a great poetic talent which he never succeeded fully in expressing in his work. He died young, leaving his ambitious project *The Bridge* as the chief monument of his talent; his reputation, which was never widespread, has remained confined to a small circle of critics, students, and fellow poets. Yet his admirers, many of them among the foremost literary critics of his generation, saw in him an authentic poetic genius; Gorham Munson believed that even at the age of thirteen Crane was "writing at a level that Amy Lowell never rose from," and his biographer Brom Weber called him "unquestionably the major poetic talent of twentieth-century America."

Most critics of Crane's poetry agree that its chief difficulties arose out of his intellectual shortcomings. Not only was his education inadequate for the kind of poetry he was trying to write, but he never forced himself into the mental discipline of thinking out his beliefs, and as a result he was never quite sure what he was writing about. Allen Tate, who knew him personally, said of him, "Crane was the archetype of the modern American poet whose fundamental mistake lay in thinking that an irrational surrender of the intellect to the will would be the basis of a new mentality."

Conscious of his lack of formal education, Crane was an avid reader, and many literary influences found their way into his work. Paradoxically, he came to poetry via the modern poets (Sandburg, Lindsay, Fletcher, Eliot) and only later steeped himself in the Elizabethan and other classic literatures which had helped to form these poets themselves. He felt himself attracted to Poe and especially to Rimbaud through a kinship of personality; although he dramatized the parallel, there is indeed a resemblance in the tragic, debauched, and unhappy lives of the three poets. Finally, the influence of the madcap and irrational French movement of Dada provided Crane with an excuse to follow his own chaotic inclinations and to abandon the form and coherence of modern poetry. In a famous letter which he wrote to *Poetry* magazine in 1926 in a controversy with its editor Harriet Monroe over certain metaphors in "At Melville's Tomb," Crane succinctly stated his credo: "I may very possibly be more interested in the so-called illogical impingements of the connotations of words

on the consciousness (and their combinations and interplay in metaphor on this basis) than I am interested in the preservation of their
logically rigid significations at the cost of limiting my subject matter
and perceptions involved in the poem." Miss Monroe's reply, which
objected to his "crowded and tortured lines," struck to the real difficulty of his method: that in spite of his attempted surrender of the
intellectual and abandonment of logic there is a forced and cerebral
ingenuity about Crane's poetry that distinguishes it from the true
irrationality of Dada or the "automatic writing" of Gertrude Stein.

Although Crane's work acquired originality and technical complexity all through his career, his content remained fairly consistent. The
dominant experience of his life was the revolt against his father, his
middle-class background, and the crass and sordid commercialism
he associated with both; his poetry is marked by an insistent, almost
obsessive antagonism toward puritanism and middle-class convention.
He turned in his rebellion to a vigorous hedonism and an escape into
exoticism; many critics consider his best poems those written in Cuba
and the West Indies. Yet Crane never managed to free himself entirely
from the world of factories and middle-class convention. His attitude
toward science, technology, and industry is an ambiguous one; he
thought of himself as an elemental creature of nature, profoundly
anti-civilized, yet in spite of his professed abhorrence for "the machine" he is fascinated with it as a symbol and makes frequent use
of it in his poetry. His major work, *The Bridge,* is nothing less than
a Whitmanesque paean dedicated to American civilization in general
and the Brooklyn Bridge in particular. Crane is a poet who succeeds
through his native literary genius, his highly original and sensitive
power of words, rather than through the inconsistent and often muddled content of his work.

LIFE: Hart Crane was born in Garrettsville, Ohio in 1899; his
father, at first a small-town merchant, later became a successful and
wealthy candy manufacturer after the family moved to Dayton and
then to Cleveland. His mother, an ardent Christian Scientist, had little
in common with the father, and Crane's parents were separated while
he was still a child. To this "curse of sundered parentage" he attributed much of the confusion and unhappiness of his later life. Crane
showed evidences of poetic talent very early in life; he wrote finished

verse at the age of thirteen, and at sixteen, in spite of the disapproval of his father, he went away to New York to make a career as a writer. For the rest of his life he vacillated between his poetic calling and the necessity of earning a living; he worked intermittently and grudgingly in his father's business, wrote advertising copy, held various jobs as munitions worker and laborer during the First World War, and at one time even served as manager of a tea-room. Two personal vices, alcohol and homosexuality, constantly interfered with his creative efforts; he became gradually more embittered and maladjusted throughout his life in spite of the efforts of his friends to help him to a normal and happy adjustment to his own nature. In New York he became an intimate of vanguard literary circles, a friend of Waldo Frank, Vachel Lindsay, Sherwood Anderson, Malcolm Cowley, and others, and a contributor to *The Little Review, Poetry,* and *The Seven Arts.* Out of tremendous personal struggles he wrote the tentative poems of his early period: "Porphyro in Akron," "Black Tambourine," "Faustus and Helen," and the more important "At Melville's Tomb." His first volume, *White Buildings,* appeared in 1926. Meanwhile Crane was still dogged by poverty and living mainly through the generosity of friends; then, in early 1926, he received a sum of money from the philanthropic banker Otto Kahn which enabled him to work in relative comfort on the poem he planned as the central work of his career: *The Bridge.* He worked at this long poem for several years, living part of the time on a family plantation on the Isle of Pines in Cuba; after appearing in fragments in various magazines it was published in complete form in 1930, and won Crane the Levinson Prize of *Poetry* magazine for that year. In 1931 Crane went to Mexico on a Guggenheim grant to write a long poem based on the Cortez-Montezuma story. His personal problems, however, had not yet been solved; he was still struggling with his homosexual nature, he had begun to fear that his poetic talent was running out, and he had become a confirmed alcoholic. The prospect of facing reality again in America was too much for him; he committed suicide by dropping overboard from the ship which was carrying him back to New York in April, 1932.

CHIEF WORKS: "At Melville's Tomb" is the best-known poem from Crane's early volume *White Buildings* (1926). The visit to the sea-

side tomb is used as a starting-point for a series of images connected
with the sea, especially with wrecks and drownings at sea. In the first
stanza, in an unusual and often-cited image, the "dice" (ground fragments) of drowned men's bones "bequeath an embassy" (i.e., are
thrown up on the beach as an embassy or message of their fate),
having "numbers" or mere quantity, but no individual identity. The
second stanza is dominated by the image of the calyx, which suggests
simultaneously a cornucopia or horn of plenty, the vortex made in
the water by a sinking vessel (throwing up a "scattered chapter" of
wreckage), and the involuted shape of a shell. The third stanza develops the idea that "frosted" (or imperfectly seeing) eyes may "lift
altars" through rising toward heaven; even an unspoken urge to
divinity in a sense creates Gods that did not exist before. The fourth
and final stanza returns to the thought of the drowned mariner and
novelist, who will never navigate (either on earthly seas or in the
realm of the mind) again; the "fabulous shadow" of Melville now
belongs to the sea, the eternal resting-place of mysteries. Such a
logical paraphrase, however, does not indicate the true nature and
merit of the poem, which succeeds through its vivid and unusual
images rather than through anything it "says" on the rational level.

   The Bridge (poem, 1930), Crane's masterwork, is a long poem
consisting of a set of more or less related sections, all of them tied
together by a common theme: the myth of America, its growth, its
nature, and its gigantic stature and vitality. The dominant image is
that of Brooklyn Bridge, which was to Crane both the embodiment
of triumphant American materialism and a "bridge" from the material world into a higher, perhaps spiritual, realm. The introduction
or proem describes the bridge itself in a highly intricate set of images
in which the themes of whiteness, of energy, and of flame recur. The
sections which follow are named, and take their themes from various
aspects of American life and history. Section I, "Ave Maria," centers
around the "legend" of Columbus; in monologue form the great dis-
coverer relates the emotions of his return to Spain, especially his
conviction of a divine purpose behind his voyage. Section II, "Powhatan's Daughter," is made up of a number of shorter poems: in
"Harbor Dawn" the poet awakens from his vision of Columbus in a
room near New York harbor, in "Van Winkle" he goes on his way
to work preoccupied with legends from American history, in "The

River" he reverts to a chaotic series of autobiographical memories suggesting the technique of Pound's *Cantos* and ranging from hoboes seen in his Ohio childhood to cross-country train trips, "The Dance" returns to the world of the Indian for a Dionysian whirl of music and sacrifice, and "Indiana" describes the unspoken goal toward which the section has been moving, union with Pocahontas, daughter of the Indian chief Powhatan, symbol of the maternal fertility of the American earth.

The short Section III, labelled "Cutty Sark," is a piece of impressionistic poetry again suggesting the narrative sections of Pound's *Cantos* or the more experimental parts of Dos Passos' *U.S.A.;* snatches of conversation from waterfront bars are interspersed with visions of underseas creatures and the sunken paradise of Plato (*Critias, Timaeus*) and the ancients (the Atlantis myth). Section IV, "Cape Hatteras," begins with a poetized geological history of the eastern seaboard, rising gradually to a consideration of the American destiny suggested by the memory of Walt Whitman, who is first quoted ("Recorders ages hence . . .") and then rhetorically addressed. The section continues to describe America's technical triumphs, e.g., the airplane ("Seeing himself an atom in a shroud— / Man hears himself as an engine in a cloud!"), then warns of the absolute ruthlessness of scientific invention and the danger involved in allowing it to control our lives (the stanza beginning "The nasal whine" and ending ". . . of blind ecstasy!"). At the end of the section the poet again affirms his kinship with Whitman and his loyalty to the kind of America portrayed in Whitman's poetry. Section V, "Three Songs," includes three short poems of an erotic or Dionysian tendency, still reinforcing the theme of American energy and fecundity; Section VI, "Quaker Hill," apparently written as an afterthought, is an ironic treatment of the "Promised Land" myth in America. Section VII, "The Tunnel," is more important; on the surface it is an account of a trip by subway from Manhattan to Brooklyn via the East River tunnel. The images and allusions of the section combine to convey a total description of urban experience, from the banal conversations overheard on the subway to the consciousness of complete helplessness which man feels in the "mechanical jungle." The concluding Section VIII, "Atlantis," returns to the underwater-kingdom myth of Plato; Crane intended the section as "a mystic consummation toward which all other sections of the poem converge." To this end most of the themes, images, and references of the preceding sections are reiterated at least briefly; the dominant image is that of Cathay, which Crane uses as a symbol of "an attitude of spirit, rather than material conquest . . .", in other words the unmaterialistic and even spiritual enthusiasm for America which dominates Whitman's *Leaves of Grass*. The importance of *The Bridge* is considered to lie less in such chaotic philosophizing, however, than in the many brief and intense imagistic passages which give life to the poem. The most often cited are the images of the seagull and the elevator ("Till elevators drop us from our day . . .") in the proem and the vivid pictures of city life in "The Tunnel," the most popular and most often anthologized section of the work.

EDGAR LEE MASTERS (1869-1950)

Although he wrote voluminously during his long literary career, Masters' fame rests on a single book: *Spoon River Anthology*. Its publication in 1914 was an important event in American literary history, anticipating the work of Sherwood Anderson, Robinson Jeffers, and other writers of the psychological school in the post-war era and paving the way for Lewis' bitter satire of middle-class manners in *Main Street* and *Babbitt*. In style there is little that is remarkable about Masters' book; the pioneers of the new poetic technique, Amy Lowell, the *Poetry* magazine group, and Ezra Pound, had already laid down the lines modernist poetry was to follow before 1914. The originality of *Spoon River Anthology* lay in its content. It ruthlessly exposed the hypocrisy and frustration of American village life, laying bare the perverted puritanism, the pompous respectability, the hidden sexual transgressions, perversions, and tragedies that previous writers had glossed over or simply ignored. Masters did for the village what Stephen Crane, in *Maggie: A Girl of the Streets,* did for the big city; he blasted away the puritanical conventions which had previously inhibited authors who sought to treat certain aspects of American life and thus paved the way for the utter frankness of the fiction of the Twenties.

Masters' remaining work falls far below *Spoon River Anthology* in importance, and most critics believe in quality as well. His many volumes of poetry can be classified roughly in two groups: sequels to, or imitations of, *Spoon River Anthology,* of which *The New Spoon River* (1924) is the best known; and subjective or descriptive lyrics, written from a personal point of view—e.g., the poems of *Songs and Sonnets* (1910) and *Songs and Satires* (1916). In this section style Masters occasionally achieves a poem of striking quality e.g., ("Week-End by the Sea"); his later attempts to recreate the atmosphere of *Spoon River Anthology* are usually disappointing.

Masters' attitudes and ideas in *Spoon River Anthology* are lucid, forceful and consistent. He is opposed to virtually everything the middle class stands for: external respectability, the adulation of the dollar and material success, the legalistic concept of justice, and the dogma of sexual chastity. Masters is invariably on the side of the type which later became termed the "introvert": the withdrawn, the unhappy, the poor in spirit, the frustrated and misunderstood artist-type, the plain girl, the solitary and simple-minded farmer. In a sense he stands for the traditional American pioneer values and attacks the artificial and urbanized culture of the twentieth century; one of the few completely sympathetic characterizations in *Spoon River Anthology* is that of Lucinda Matlock, the woman of vigorous pioneer stock who tells her effete descendants that "life is too strong for them." But Masters' talent is basically a negative and satirical one, and the majority of his characterizations are bitterly ironic.

Stylistically *Spoon River Anthology* is straightforward and lucid, owing something to Whitman in the unhampered flow of its free verse. Occasionally, as in "Petit, the Poet" and the prologue "The Hill," he rises to a rhythmic lyricism, but more commonly the style of the book is conversational, succinct, imitating the laconic understatement of the gravestone epitaph. *Spoon River Anthology* has been called a novel in free verse; its style is indeed closer to that of fiction than it is to most of the poetry of the twentieth century.

LIFE: Most of the important events in Edgar Lee Masters' life found their expression in one way or another in *Spoon River Anthology*. He was born in 1869 in Garnett, Kansas of pioneer stock, but his family moved to Lewiston, Illinois (the presumed model for Spoon River) when he was still a child. He attended Knox College in Galesburg, Illinois, then went home to read for the bar in his father's law office. After practicing briefly in Lewiston, he moved to Chicago

(1892), where he continued to practice law intermittently until 1920. Meanwhile he had begun writing poetry; his first volumes, beginning with *A Book of Verses* (1898), were traditional in style and meter, influenced by the *Rubaiyat* of Fitzgerald, by Browning, and by Swinburne. In 1912 an accidental event convinced him to abandon his law career and at the same time contributed to the ironic cynicism of his later work: his partner defaulted, and Masters found himself in legal difficulties and ostracized through the machinations of his political enemies. He turned to full-time writing, inspired and advised by his friend William Marion Reedy, the editor of *Reedy's Mirror*. Reedy lent him *The Greek Anthology;* the volume of classic poems provided him with the title and the basic idea for *Spoon River Anthology,* sections of which began to appear in Reedy's magazine in May, 1914. The work was published in volume form the same year, creating an enormous sensation; it was widely attacked by moralists and puritans, but the publicity only added to its popularity. Masters' succeeding volumes returned to his earlier poetry style; in 1924 he attempted a sequel in *New Spoon River,* but he had lost the sure touch of the earlier book. He produced approximately twenty-five volumes of poetry between 1904 and 1942; his complete works include over fifty volumes.

Masters was married twice, the first time to Helen Jenkins in 1898 and the second time, after a divorce, to Ellen F. Coyne in 1926. With his second wife he lived during his later years in the Hotel Chelsea in New York. In 1944 he was hospitalized, suffering from pneumonia and malnutrition; various literary societies including the Author's League came to his aid and provided financial assistance to pay his medical bills. He spent his last days in a convalescent home in Philadelphia, where he died in 1950.

CHIEF WORK: *Spoon River Anthology* (1914) consists of a set of short poetic characterizations in the form of epitaphs from an Illinois village graveyard. Each of the personalities of the book is allowed to describe himself, but it is not true, as sometimes stated, that each "tells the truth about himself." In many cases the characters are consciously hypocritical, and in other instances they simply do not know the truth about themselves; the reader learns the truth only through putting together facts from various epitaphs. A typical example is seen in the characterizations of Else Wertman and Hamilton Greene. The German serving-girl Else confesses in her epitaph that she was the mother of Hamilton, who was charitably raised by her employers as their own child. Since Greene, her master, was father of the child, the secret was kept from everyone, even from the boy Hamilton. He grew up to become a famous statesman; in his epitaph, with unconscious irony, he attributes his success to the "will, judgment, logic" he inherited from his father and the "vivacity, fancy, language" of his mother.

Of the more than two hundred and fifty other characterizations (the number varies in different editions) a few of the best known should be noted. "A. D. Blood" is typical of several epitaphs of pompous and hypocritical dignitaries. Blood, who in his lifetime had been a professional puritan and scourge of saloons and sin, is subjected after death to an ironic indignity: a "worthless" pair of lovers nightly conduct their amours using his gravestone as a pillow.

"Anne Rutledge" is a brief but effective portrait of the Illinois girl who was loved by the young Lincoln but died of a fever before they could be married; according to legend (recorded, for example, in Carl Sandburg's Lincoln biography) the future president was deeply marked by the experience, becoming thenceforth "a changed man keeping to himself the gray mystery of that change." Thus the dramatic Whitmanesque conclusion of Anne Rutledge's self-portrait: "Bloom forever, O Republic, / From the dust of my bosom!"

"Lucinda Matlock" is a portrait of a hard and vigorous pioneer woman who found satisfaction, even glory, in the hard frontier life which broke lesser souls. Her epitaph is one of the few exultant statements in the book. After bearing twelve children and living to ninety-six, she tells her "degenerate," discontented, and brooding twentieth-century descendants, "Life is too strong for you— / It takes life to love Life."

"Petit, The Poet" is in a sense Masters' whimsical self-portrait. The unsuccessful village rhymer, turning out romantic conventional verse in old-fashioned forms ("Triolets, villanelles, rondels, rondeaus . . ."), resembles Masters himself in the period before 1914, when he turned to the cutting satire of Spoon River Anthology. The tragedy of Petit's life is that he realizes only after he is dead and buried that superb poetic material had lain all about him in the village.

Instead he wrote "little iambics, / While Homer and Whitman roared in the pines!"

VACHEL LINDSAY (1879-1931)

The poetry of Vachel Lindsay has two great qualities which rescue it from mere jingling rhyme: a tremendous vitality and enthusiasm, and a solidly rooted basis in American folklore. Its most striking quality is of course its rhythm; poems like "The Congo" and "General William Booth Enters Into Heaven" were deliberately written to be chanted, and Lindsay himself toured about the country chanting them. Their published versions even include stage directions to guide the reciter in public presentation, and at least one of them ("General William Booth") is intended to be sung to the tune of a traditional hymn. This emphasis on rhythm arose out of Lindsay's determination to restore poetry to the realm of the popular arts, to make it a genuine source of enjoyment for the illiterate; he himself coined the term "The Higher Vaudeville" for his concept of poetry. There is nothing academic or subtle about Lindsay's verse; he is the absolute antithesis of Ezra Pound or T. S. Eliot. Because of his strong rhythms and his use of popular materials he is sometimes treated with contempt by serious critics, who apply to him the epithet that Emerson applied to Poe: "the jingle man." Yet at least a half-dozen of his poems seem destined for a permanent place in American literature, if only for their originality and vitality. "His gospel is no less original for being preached through a saxophone," remarks Untermeyer.

Actually Lindsay's "verse to be chanted to a bass drum" represents only one of his several styles. Such poems as "Kansas," "Factory Windows Are Always Broken," and "The Raft" are objective and descriptive pieces based on the life of the middle west, its vistas and its people; their tone is subdued, at least compared to his more popular work, and the imagery and treatment are conventional. His tributes to heroes of American history (Lincoln, Nancy Hanks, Johnny Appleseed, John P. Altgeld) are restrained, calm, almost reverent in their eulogy in spite of their Whitmanesque lyricism. Yet another style is found in poems like "The Chinese Nightingale" and "The Voyage": sentimental, fantastic in metaphor, resembling Imagism in mood and evidently influenced both by this movement and by Chinese poetry. In spite of this versatility Lindsay won popular success only in one genre: the boisterous and highly rhythmic songs of the type of "The Congo." This narrow public view of his work undoubtedly contributed to the discouragement and bitterness which marked the later years of his career.

In spite of his diversity of styles Lindsay is remarkably consistent in content. His great subject is America: its history, its legends, its contemporary life. Even "The Chinese Nightingale," his most exotic poem, is built around the figure of the Chinese-American laundryman, a familiar figure in American culture. Unlike most of his contemporaries, Lindsay is almost totally uncritical in his enthusiastic acceptance of his nation. His patriotism is as irrational and emotional as it is infectious, and his view of history is that of a schoolboy; he accepts everything—legends, myths, folklore, and fact—and incorporates it indiscriminately into his poetry. History to him is made up of personalities, each of them invested with a mythical aura of heroism: John L. Sullivan, Woodrow Wilson, Daniel Boone, Johnny Appleseed, Andrew Jackson, William Jennings Bryan. His factual knowledge of the lives of these heroes seldom goes beyond what might be found in a grade-school primer; his view of them is drawn from folk mythology rather than from historical scholarship. Lindsay thus has a valuable gift which modern poets, with the possible exception of Sandburg, have lost: an authentic emotional kinship with the mind of the masses. "The country has produced no one more distinctively American than Vachel Lindsay," states Wells in *The American Way of Poetry*.

LIFE: Vachel Lindsay was born in Springfield, Illinois in 1879; his nostalgic attitude toward this city, the state capital and a town heavy with Lincoln tradition, undoubtedly contributed to his interest in popular history. His education was extensive but erratic; he attended Hiram College for three years (1897-1900), then, deciding to become an artist, went to Chicago to study at the Art Institute (1900-03), later going on to the New York School of Art (1904). Finding himself unable to sell his drawings, he set out in 1905 on a vagabond trip around the country, supporting himself partly through the sale of a thin volume of poetry called *Rhymes To Be Traded For Bread*. Soon he found poetry and lecturing more remunerative than art; for the next five years he travelled around the country like an itinerant revivalist, preaching "The Gospel of Beauty," as he himself called it, reciting his own poems, and selling copies of his work. He gradually formulated his concept of "communal art," the basic idea of which was to remove the arts from the custody of the intellectuals and academicians and return it to the people, to make it into a "Higher Vaudeville" which would once again, as in the days of Homer, provide a real source of entertainment for the unlettered masses. When winter made tramping in the open impractical he lectured for the Anti-Saloon League or for the Y.M.C.A. In 1913 he published his first major volume, *General William Booth Enters Into Heaven. The Congo and Other Poems* followed in 1914. The title poems of these two volumes remained his most popular works; in later years he complained that whenever he attempted to speak seriously to an audience about poetry or art they demanded that he "cease his trifling" and give them "The Congo" or "General William Booth Enters Into Heaven." His *Collected Poems,* a volume of great diversity but of uneven quality, appeared in 1923. In 1925 he married Elizabeth Conner, whom he had met on a lecture tour in California; two children were born of the marriage. For the next six years the Lindsays divided their residence between Spokane, Washington and Springfield, Illinois. Lindsay's later years were in general unhappy ones. None of his work after 1914 achieved the success of his first two books; in addition his health deteriorated, and his impatience with the interminable lecturing and reciting of his "bass-drum poems" to audiences unsettled his nerves and made him dejected and bitter. Fearing poverty and evidently sensing a deterioration of his poetic talent, he took his own life on December 5, 1931.

IMPORTANT POEMS: "General William Booth Enters Into Heaven," title poem of the volume published in 1913, is a poetic tribute to the founder of the Salvation Army (1829-1912) intended to be sung to the tune of the revivalist hymn "The Blood of the Lamb." Booth is followed into Heaven by the motley assortment of sinners he has saved, from "Bull-necked convicts" to "drug fiends pale;" the procession is accompanied by Salvation Army workers who are described in Lindsay's typical boisterous alliteration and onomatopoeia ("Big-voiced lasses made their banjos bang"). The meter is an interesting one which Lindsay uses frequently in this type of poem: a four-beat line, accentuated in this case by the actual beating of a drum, in which any number of off-beats may intervene. Although the meter is theoretically similar to that of Anglo-Saxon verse as well as to the "sprung rhythm" of Gerard Manley Hopkins, Lindsay uses it in a highly original manner which suggests a half-savage, almost primeval emotionality. Similar rhythms are found in "The Congo" and "Simon Legree."

"The Congo," title poem of the volume published in 1914, purports to be "a study of the Negro race" but is actually only a poetic interpretation of a set of popular American stereotypes about the Negro. The poem is divided into three sections, which treat three aspects of the Negro character. The first, "Their basic savagery," offers a vision of a Negro revel in primitive Africa, showing the Congo Negroes as a savage and warlike people who steal the cattle of upland tribes, kill whites and Arabs, and steal pygmies for slaves. The refrain, "Mumbo-Jumbo will hoo-doo you," with its suggestion of witchcraft which lingers as a racial memory in the mind of the Negro, dominates the section. Section II, "Their irrepressible high spirits," transfers the scene to a celebration of American Negroes, but the hoodoo refrain is still present. Section III, "The hope of their religion," depicts a sermon by "a good old Negro in the slums of the town;" Christianity has replaced paganism and driven witchcraft under the surface ("Never again will he hoo-doo you"). Yet at the end the vulture (symbol of the repressed but ever-lurking primitivism of the Negro mind) repeats the hoodoo refrain. In addition to this refrain, the poem is tied together by another couplet, evidently occurring in the mind of the poet who perceives the vision of the poem: "Then I saw the Congo, creeping through the black, / Cutting through the jungle with a golden track." The effect of this poem has unfortunately been marred by the passing of time and the evolution of social progress; written before the First World War, it presents a stereotyped and anthropologically naive interpretation of the Negro which later generations have in general rejected.

"A Negro Sermon:—Simon Legree" (1914) is similar in style to the poems discussed above. The figure of Legree is based more on the dramatic version of *Uncle Tom's Cabin* by George Aiken than it is on the original novel by Harriet Beecher Stowe. The striking originality of the poem lies in its evangelistic sermon form, enlivened with the refrain (evidently shouted by the congregation) of "And he went down to the Devil."

"John Brown," another poem of the same period, is also intended for antiphonal recitation, with the interrogative refrain, "What did you see in Palestine?" This poem is also interesting for its combination of folklore and Biblical elements; Brown, the legendary-historical martyr of Abolition, is seen from the illiterate Negro point of view as a prophet in the Biblical tradition who takes his place in Palestine alongside Father Noah and other figures from the Old Testament.

"Abraham Lincoln Walks at Midnight" (1914) is a simple and poetically conventional portrait of Lincoln, written during the First World War. Lindsay imagines the ghost of Lincoln, returning to his Illinois home, tormented and saddened by the dreadful slaughter of the twentieth-century war.

"The Chinese Nightingale," title poem of the volume published in 1917, is a modern American equivalent of Coleridge's "Kubla Khan," a visionary fantasy drawn from the world of the poet's revery rather than from life. It opens, however, on a realistic note; the poet, visiting his friend the Chinese laundryman Chang, inquires the reason he stays awake so late at night, and Chang responds with a confession of the exotic reveries in which he indulges through the aid of a joss-stick and a charmed nightingale. Part of the poem is spoken by the nightingale itself and other sections by a "Chinese lady of high degree" evoked in the course of the vision. The theme is the age-old heritage of culture and beauty which Chang, as humble as he is in America, possesses as a member of the Chinese race; the imagery of the middle part of the poem is suggested by that of classic Chinese poetry. The refrain, sung by the nightingale, is "Spring came on forever;" to the aged Chinese living in his world of fantasy the passing of time has ceased to exist. Some of the highest poetry is found in the last stanza; here Lindsay achieves one of the few coherent and persuasive philosophical comments in his work. The poem concludes, "Man is a torch, then ashes soon;" yet love, which sets man aflame into a "torch," is an ultimate reality, inspiring the song of the nightingale and making Spring "come on forever."

"The Ghosts of the Buffaloes" (from *The Chinese Nightingale and Other Poems*) in some respects marks a return to Lindsay's earlier chanting style; the technique, however, is more subtle and the poem as a whole more thoughtful and controlled. In a midnight vision the poet, in his home in the middle west, sees a herd of stampeding buffalo pursued by Indians galloping off to the west. The vision of buffalo and Indians, symbolizing the westward migration and final extinction of the Indian race, is contrasted with the "caroling" of crickets, a recurrent melody which suggests the security and complacency of modern American life. On another level the theme of the poem is that of dreaming; since "Life is the west-going dream-storm's breath" (e.g., transitory and unreal), reality, by a logical paradox, lies only in dream itself. Thus the vision of the Indians in the early stanzas of the poem can serve to inspire and invigorate a creative mind, like that of the poet's, even in the commonplace twentieth century. Although never as popular as his "bass-drum poems," this poem is considered by critics to be among Lindsay's finest; one writer attributes to it "a subtle beauty of melody that he never surpassed."

STEPHEN VINCENT BENÉT (1898-1943)

A competent folklorist as well as a first-rate poet, Benét writes in a consciously native and vernacular American idiom. More than any other poet of his time he has made effective use of the fascinating body of American folklore—tall tales, legends, folk songs—which had existed from Colonial times but which scholars first began collecting and compiling around the turn of the century. But Benét, unlike Whitman and his followers (Sandburg, Hart Crane), approaches American life from a thoroughly literary point of view; he is not the kind of poet who goes out among the people, pencil in hand, and accurately transcribes the turns of their language to put it in his verse. The two forms in which Benét was most successful, the epic (*John Brown's Body*) and the folk-ballad, are literary types of a venerable tradition in Indo-European culture, found in the literature of virtually every nation from Homer's Greece to medieval France and Germany. Like Vergil, Benét felt the lack of a ballad-epic tradition in his own country; and like Vergil he set out to create one in conscious imitation of the naive and authentic ballad tradition of more primitive cultures. The basic concept can be attacked on aesthetic grounds; when a highly civilized culture attempts to produce primitive literature, the result is generally thin and synthetic. Although Benét did not perhaps succeed as well as Vergil, he came as close to creating the American Epic as any other poet from Longfellow through Hart Crane.

Benét's first poems, published when he was only seventeen, were dramatic monologues evidently influenced by Browning and Robinson, and he retained throughout his career an interest in dramatic poetry, in characterization, and in narrative. An accomplished novelist and short-story writer, he writes fiction like a poet and poetry like a novelist; his talent is simultaneously narrative and lyric, and he can seldom divest himself of either quality. His chief failing is probably his lack of originality; not only are his subjects usually drawn from other sources (historical, traditional), but his techniques too are derivative; there is no single stylistic quality which can be identified as uniquely his own. The influence of Whitman is obvious, as is that of MacLeish; Untermeyer cites the presence in *John Brown's Body* of "the long cadences of Sandburg" and "the jingling beat of Lindsay." In *Burning City,* a collection of poems published in 1936, Benét is slightly more original than in his earlier work; in spite of their indebtedness to MacLeish these poems often achieve a vivid and striking union of the laconic vernacular of the folk-ballad and the stream-of-consciousness style of the modern psychological novel. Benét's early death (he died at forty-four) cut short a development which might have led into a more subtle and highly original poetic technique.

LIFE: Stephen Vincent Benét was born in Bethlehem, Pennsylvania in 1898, son of an army colonel with literary and poetic tastes; he was well read from his earliest youth, and his writing, in spite of his superficial primitivism, reveals his wide reading and considerable erudition. He was raised in various army posts where his father was assigned; a large part of his boyhood was spent in Benicia, California, on San Francisco Bay. His education was thorough; he received a B.A. from Yale in 1919 and an M.A. from the same university in 1920, then went on to France to do graduate work at the Sorbonne. Meanwhile he had already begun publishing poetry; his first book of poems, *Five Men and Pompey,* appeared as early as 1915. From 1920 to 1926 he supported himself chiefly through his novels, most of them historical romances; in 1923 his narrative poem *King David,* highly influenced by Vachel Lindsay, won the poetry prize offered by *The Nation.* In 1926 he was offered a Guggenheim Fellowship which enabled him to go to Paris to work on *John Brown's Body;* this book-length epic poem, which appeared in 1928, made him famous overnight and was awarded a Pulitzer Prize the following year. Additional success came with the folk-tale "The Devil and Daniel Webster" (1937), which was later dramatized and converted into an opera with music by Douglas Moore. With the outbreak of the Second World War he wrote a number of propaganda pieces to aid in the war effort, including a short history, *America,* for distribution abroad by the Office of War Information. He died of a heart attack in his home in New York City in March, 1943. An unfinished poem left after his death was later published as *Western Star* (1943), and was awarded a Pulitzer Prize in 1944.

IMPORTANT POEMS: "The Ballad of William Sycamore" (from *Tiger Joy,* 1925) is one of several imitations of traditional ballads in this early collection. Written in quatrains in an uneven trochaic meter, the poem consists of a first-person autobiography of its hero, born under "a tall green fir," who married "a girl like a Salem clipper" and raised many sons only to lose the eldest at the Alamo and the youngest at Custer's last stand. The final stanza, addressing the modern audience, advises them derisively to "Go play with the towns you have built of blocks;" urban civilization seems childish and artificial to William Sycamore, the archetype of the pioneer. This poem departs from the traditional ballad form chiefly in its point of view; true ballads are seldom first-person, and almost never cover a character's entire career from birth to death. The spirit and tempo of the ballad, however, are faithfully imitated. "The Mountain Whippoorwill," from the same collection, is also well known among Benét's ballads.

John Brown's Body (narrative poem, 1929) is a book-length historical narrative of the Civil War which consciously imitates the form and atmosphere of the classic epic. The individual passages, however, are based on the folk-ballad style rather than imitated from the epic in the manner of Longfellow's *Hiawatha* and *Evangeline.* Opening with a prelude, "The Slaver," which depicts the moral doubts of a young mate on a slaving vessel as it carries its human cargo toward America, the poem goes on to relate the chief incidents

of the Civil War through 1865 and the assassination of Lincoln.
Dominating the entire narrative is the legendary tradition of John
Brown, the abolitionist who was executed for an abortive raid on the
Federal arsenal at Harpers Ferry in 1859. Into the historical back-
ground are interwoven a number of fictional characters, each typi-
fying a social group or an aspect of the American population: Jack
Ellyat, an idealistic Connecticut law student; Clay Wingate, an aristocratic Southern cavalryman, and his fiancée, the "Southern belle"
Sally Dupré; Luke Breckinridge, an illiterate and ignorant mountaineer who fights for the South without even understanding who
the Yankees are; Spade, a runaway Negro; Jake Diefer, a stolid
Pennsylvania farmer who hires Spade as his hand after the war; and
Melora, a mountain girl whom Ellyat loves before he is captured
and sent to a Southern prison. The meter of the poem is diverse,
ranging from Whitmanesque free verse (the peroration to John Brown
at the end of Book One) to rhythmic imitations of Negro spirituals
(the song "Sherman's Buzzin' Along to de Sea" in Book Eight). The
poem ends with an ode to the equalitarian and industrial civilization
which won over the aristocratic and agrarian society of the South.
The best parts of *John Brown's Body* are usually considered to be the
fictional episodes; the historical incidents, especially the battles, suffer
from a certain depersonalized quality. Henry W. Wells argues that
the work "labors under a number of embarrassments as a poem,
being one-third history, one-third novel, and one-third poetry." This
lack of unity prevents it from being a true epic; it is instead a historical verse novel in a rich diversity of styles, the poetic equivalent
of Dos Passos' *U.S.A.* plus Tolstoy's *War and Peace*.

"Nightmare Number Three" is the best known of the somewhat
grotesque poems on modern subjects contained in *Burning City*
(1936). The subject is one frequently encountered in contemporary
literature: the revolt of the machines against their human masters
(*cf.* Capek's *R.U.R.*). Benét's medium-length poem is set in the middle of New York City, where the concrete mixers, automobiles, bus-
ses, even the elevators suddenly unite in rebellion against humanity.
The effect of the poem is achieved through its combination of shocking subject-matter with the laconic and vernacular American idiom:
"But the horses might help. We might make a deal with the horses."
The underlying theme is of course the danger inherent in a machine

civilization in which mechanisms gradually assume more importance than human beings.

TALE: "The Devil and Daniel Webster" (1937, as opera libretto 1939) is by far the best known of Benét's shorter narrative pieces; it is often anthologized and frequently produced in its dramatic form. Jabez Stone, a luckless and crusty New England farmer, sells his soul to the Devil in exchange for a promise of ten years' prosperity. When the debt comes due Stone, terrified, appeals to Daniel Webster, the greatest lawyer and orator in American history, to defend him. A "trial" takes place before a kind of kangaroo court; the jurors, chosen by the Devil, consist of twelve of America's most notorious traitors. Webster, appealing to this set of scoundrels as men rather than as Americans, succeeds in winning them over through his unmatched eloquence, and Stone is acquitted. In addition to its dramatic and operatic versions this tale has been made into a successful motion picture under the title *All That Money Can Buy*.

Benét's older brother, WILLIAM ROSE BENÉT (1886-1950), was also a well-known poet, winner of the 1942 Pulitzer Prize for *The Dust Which Is God,* husband of the poetess Elinor Wylie and important as a reviewer and critic, especially for *The Saturday Review of Literature*. His most important work as an anthologist was the editing, with Norman Holmes Pearson, of the *Oxford Anthology of American Literature.*

CONRAD AIKEN (born 1889)

In his youth strongly influenced by Eliot, his classmate at Harvard, and by the Imagism of John Gould Fletcher, Conrad Aiken in his later career gradually developed a strong and original poetic style of his own. Essentially he is a conservative in techinque; he shows little interest in experimental poetic devices and is conventional in rhyme and meter. His first three volumes, *Earth Triumphant and Other Tales in Verse* (1914), *Turns and Movies* (1916), and *The Jig of Forslin* (1916), are primarily devoted to narrative verse, the weakest of them strongly influenced by Masefield, Fletcher, and Masters and the best of them imitations of the early T. S. Eliot. The influence of Eliot continues in his next three books, *Nocturne of Remembered Spring* (1917), *The Charnel Rose* (1918), and *The House of Dust*

(1920); paradoxically the last of these, "a poem of the soul of a city," is said to have itself influenced *The Waste Land*. Aiken first began to emerge into his mature poetic style with *Punch: The Immortal Liar* in 1921; thenceforth his poetry is chiefly lyrical, although a narrative or monologue is sometimes also involved.

In this later poetry, his most important work, Aiken is musical rather than imagistic; his fascination with echolalia and the auditory qualities of language recalls the poetry of Poe and Lanier. (Aiken is said to have memorized a pocket volume of Poe at the age of thirteen.) According to his own statement of his purpose, he seeks to divest verse of its intellectual content, its allusive quality, even its metaphor, in order to move toward "absolute" poetry, "a poetry in which the intention is not so much to arouse an emotion . . . as to employ such emotion with the same cool detachment with which a composer employs notes or chords." This musical quality is well seen in "Morning Song From Senlin," Aiken's best-known lyric, as well as in the shorter poems from *Punch: The Immortal Liar* and from *Priapus and the Pool* (1922).

In addition to his reputation as a poet, Aiken is also important as a novelist and short-story writer. His fiction is strongly marked by two influences: medicine, especially surgery, and interest derived from his physician father, and modern psychology, especially the Freudian concept of the subconscious and the Jung-Ranke theories of archetypes and atavisms. He is perhaps at his best in his stories, where he achieves a remarkable mood, an atmosphere of almost metaphysical unreality, in the short space of a few pages. A prolific writer, Aiken produced over two dozen books of verse and ten volumes of fiction between 1914 and 1952. He has been accused of writing too copiously, and there is indeed much that is second-rate in his work; his most important achievements are the poems of the 1921-29 period and a handful of stories like "Mr. Arcularis" and "Silent Snow, Secret Snow." It is likely also that his remarkable autobiography, *Ushant* (1952), will be more highly regarded with the passing of time.

LIFE: Conrad Aiken was born in Savannah, Georgia in 1889, the eldest of three sons. Although his well-to-do family provided him with many advantages, his boyhood was hardly a normal one; his father, a brilliant but somewhat eccentric doctor, forced him to attend an eye operation at the age of nine, and two years later the family was shattered when the father took his mother's life and then his own. Conrad went to live with an aunt in New Bedford, Massachusetts; he attended Middlesex School and went on to Harvard. Always an avid reader, he began writing poetry while still in college. In 1911 he took a year off to travel to Europe, returning to graduate a year later. Married in 1912 to Jessie McDonald, he returned to Europe with his wife for a year's honeymoon; on his return he established himself in Cambridge, where a small independent income made it possible for him to devote himself entirely to his writing. Around 1915 he became a close friend of John Gould Fletcher, whom he took as his poetic mentor during the period. He continued to produce both verse and fiction voluminously during the Twenties and Thirties; his *Selected Poems* won him a Pulitzer Prize in 1929. During the Thirties he spent much time in England, where with his second wife, the former Mary Hoover, he operated an informal summer school in writing and painting. In 1950-51 he held the Library of Congress Chair of Poetry, and in 1953 his *Collected Poems* won the National Book Award as the most distinguished volume of poetry published that year. In recent years Aiken and his wife have lived in Brewster, Massachusetts and in a New York City apartment.

TYPICAL POEMS: "Miracles," a medium-length poem in intermittently rhyming quatrains, is typical of Aiken's early period. After an opening description of twilight conveyed through accurate imagistic devices, the theme of Mary's sorrow for Christ is introduced, dominated by the unseen presence of angels round the Virgin as she carried her Son from the cross. The final stanza pleads that we today, "persuaded by searching music," may also feel about us presences, "clear things" which may be perceived through an intimate surrender to nature and a heightened sensitivity to the spiritual.

"Morning Song From Senlin" is part of a longer poem contained in *The Charnel Rose* (1918). The song, sung by the hedonistic but spiritually sensitive wanderer-figure Senlin, depends for its poetic effect chiefly on its rhythm, its strong musical quality, and the evocative cadence of its words. Senlin, prosaically dressing before his mirror, transcends his banal situation through his consciousness of divinity ("Should I not pause in the light to remember God?") and through awareness of his own insignificance in the astronomical cosmos, conveyed through mention of his own "small" and "white" face and through several images of the turning of the earth: "a swiftly tilting planet" . . . "The earth revolves" . . . "There are suns beneath my floor . . ." The final quatrain, with its reference to vines, dewdrops, and bird-songs, returns the poem to the mundane and practical world, which Senlin nevertheless finds beautiful through his inward awareness of the spiritual and cosmic. The song is often cited as Aiken's best-known lyric.

"The Puppet Dreams," from *Punch: The Immortal Liar* (1921) typifies the more purely lyrical quality of Aiken's later work. The short disconnected songs which make up the poem are dominated by the theme of escape in exoticism; Sheba is introduced as a personification of Oriental sensualism, and the mention of the rise and fall of stars introduces a transcendental note that is seldom lacking in Aiken. Evidences of the influence of Imagism are still apparent in this later work: e.g., "The peach-trees lean upon a wall / Of gold and ivory."

"And in the Hanging Gardens" is one of a number of narrative poems which Aiken wrote in his early and middle periods. Some of these are influenced by Markham and Eliot; this one resembles Keats. The dominant image is that of rain, falling into the hanging gardens around a palace, evidently in the Orient or Near East. A princess is reading a letter; as the poem proceeds we learn that it tells of the death of her lover in the "northern desert." Meanwhile the foolish king (evidently her father) intoxicates himself with wine, throws his goblet out the window, and then descends the stair to find it again, stopping to taste "One drop of wine wherewith wild rain has mixed." Neither are aware of the knave of diamonds, who steals in the dark to attack the grieving princess, unprotected by her weak-minded and drunken father. This poem, suggests Keats' "The Eve of St. Agnes," is marked by its intensity and vividness of image: the moon "inflaming the lilac heads," the "sandy wind" that withers the grass.

"One Star Fell and Another" is a didactic anecdote typical of Aiken's later work. The poet, walking with a friend, perceives two falling stars almost in an instant, and thinks "How prodigal that sky is of its stars!" The two friends conclude that we humans too must be prodigal with our "words and worlds," with our love, our thought.

ourselves. The theme is thus the *carpe diem* of romantic poetry: let us live fully, giving all we have to life, lest by holding back, by abstention, we miss something of what life has to offer in return.

FICTION: At least two of Aiken's best-known stories should be briefly mentioned. "Silent Snow, Secret Snow" is a fantasy of a child's dream-world, a sensitive study of the transition from childish daydreaming to neurosis. The small boy Paul Hasleman abandons himself to reveries of falling snow (he evidently lives in the South, and thus to him snow is wholly a thing of the imagination) and derives a secret pleasure from fancying the sound of the approaching footsteps of the postman in the silent whiteness. Withdrawing into his dream, he gradually loses contact with his teacher, his parents, even the doctor who is called in to treat him. When his impatient father grows angry, Paul regresses completely into the dream-world, aware of nothing but the insistence of the falling snow. The postman in this story is evidently a personification of death, and the snow fantasy itself a death-wish.

"Mr. Arcularis" treats a similar theme through an adult protagonist. The hero, recovering (as he imagines) from a major operation, leaves the hospital to go on a sea-voyage. But the voyage is a fantastic one which takes place in a dream: Harry, the chauffeur who takes him to the ship, is actually Charon, the classic boatman of the Styx, and each of the other characters or references is significant in the death-symbolism. The mention of the Harvard bar suggests Tennyson's "Crossing the Bar," an allegory of death; Miss Dean, suggested to his mind by memory of a hospital attendant, is an angel, and the coffin which Mr. Arcularis imagines in the ship's hold is his own. While he is dreaming Mr. Arcularis is still on the operating table in the hospital; the throbbing of the ship's engines which pervades the story is the sound of his own heartbeat, and the sensation of cold which he feels is the declining vitality of his own dying body. As the story ends he dies, in his fantasy shooting off in a "long magnificent, delirious swoop of dizziness" toward the North Star. The moving and Poe-like metaphysical quality of this story is relieved by its humor (Mr. Arcularis' stale jokes) and by its irony: the game of chess which the comic parson (symbol of Calvinistic religion) insists on playing in the very face of death is theology, an abstract science holding little interest for either Mr. Arcularis (the soul at the point of death) or Clarice Dean (an angel, therefore divinity itself).

WILLIAM CARLOS WILLIAMS (born 1883)

Beginning before the First World War in frank imitation of Ezra Pound and the Imagists, W. C. Williams gradually evolved into a highly original and effective variety of free verse. Many of his subjects are taken from nature, and most of his images are visual ones, but he is by no means an ordinary "nature poet." His verse is never effusive or emotional; its main quality is a severe, almost naked starkness. Williams is basically romantic, but his scientific training and his masculine reserve lend him a control and hardness that preserve him from sentimentality. He is occasionally ironic, but never facetious; his whole work, even in his earliest Imagist period, is consistently mature in attitude and technique. Anti-sentimental and anti-Victorian, Williams is one of the most "masculine" of modern poets.

In style and diction particularly Williams rejects the sentimental literary heritage of the Victorians; he strives constantly to achieve the "brusque nervous tension, the vigor and rhetoric" of vernacular American speech. Although he avoids slang, his language is thoroughly idiomatic; he seldom uses a word which is beyond the vocabulary of the ordinary reader, and the rhythm, the intonation of his language is that of common speech. He has been accused of metrical inconsistency; actually his metric is that of idiomatic conversation. A careful study of his typography and punctuation will show that they too are intended to reproduce the rhythm, the pauses and emphases, of ordinary speech; in spite of the visual quality of his images he has a keen ear for linguistic nuances.

In content Williams tends toward "pure poetry"; he seldom moralizes or indulges in philosophical sermonizing, and if he has any religious principles they are not prominent in his poetry. Politically he is liberal, with a tendency to the left; criticism of bourgeois capitalism is sometimes found in his fiction (e.g., the story "Jean Beicke") but almost never in his poetry. The same thing is true of his medical background; he uses his scientific training and his experience as a doctor frequently in his fiction, but it seldom appears in his poetry except in an occasional term or phrase borrowed from medicine. As a writer of fiction—he has published four novels and a number of first-rate short stories—Williams is conventional in style but cuttingly ironic, sometimes even apparently callous, in attitude; his medical stories contain some of the most powerful descriptions of disease and suffering in modern fiction. In his fiction as in his poetry, however, Williams is objective rather than indifferent; he shows the sympathetic detachment of a man who has combined the writing of literature with a full-time career as a practicing physician.

LIFE: William Carlos Williams was born in 1883 in Rutherford, New Jersey, a small town where he remained to live and practice medicine all his life. His ancestry was polyglot: his father's family was English, and from his Puerto Rican mother he inherited a mixture of Basque, Dutch, Spanish, and Jewish blood. His religious background was likewise diverse; his mother, born a Catholic, and his Episcopalian father both later turned to Unitarianism. Williams, the eldest child of the family, attended a private school in Switzerland and went on to the University of Pennsylvania, where he received a medical degree in 1906; he thereupon returned to Europe to do graduate work in pediatrics at the University of Leipzig. Upon his return to America he married (1912) and settled down to medical practice in Rutherford. Meanwhile he had turned to writing poetry as an avocation; his first book, a tentative and rather imitative volume entitled *Poems,* appeared in 1909. *The Tempers* (1916) demonstrated a more mature command of style, although it was strongly influenced by Pound and the American Imagists. Gradually poetry assumed a place in his life at least equal in importance to his medical career. He found no handicap in conducting two careers simultaneously; "One feeds the other, in a manner of speaking," he has explained. In 1926 he won the coveted Dial Award for "services to American literature"; from that time on he produced poetry at a steady but modest rate and continued to retain his reputation as a major American poet. Among the many other awards and distinctions which came to him during his career were a National Book Award (1950) and a Bollingen Prize, which he shared with Archibald MacLeish in 1952. In the same year he was appointed Consultant in Poetry to the Library of Congress, but because of political opposition to his alleged left-wing principles he never actually served in the office. From 1942 to 1951 he devoted himself chiefly to a long narrative poem entitled *Paterson,* based on the history and social background of the New Jersey industrial city, which he intended as a kind of epic of the American racial and cultural heritage. His autobiography appeared in 1951.

TYPICAL POEMS: "Metric Figure" (1917) is a characteristic example of Williams' vivid and succinct studies of nature subjects. The short poem consists entirely of a description of the rising sun shining through poplars; the final effect depends on the striking metaphors (the leaves as "little yellow fish") and on the climax of the last three lines, in which the gleam of the sunrise "Outshines the noise / Of leaves clashing in the wind." This confusion of the impressions of sight and sound suggests the influence of Pound, who in turn derived the device from the French Symbolists.

"Tract" (1917) is an exercise in extended irony, consisting of a set of instructions for a funeral addressed to a set of conventionally pompous townspeople. The effect of the poem is achieved through contrast between the conventional gestures of grief (the polished black verse, etc.) and the manifestations of genuine feeling (the weathered farm wagon "with gilt wheels," a brave and sad little touch which the poet feels is appropriate to the personality of the deceased).

"Poem" (the short lyric beginning "By the road to the contagious hospital," from *Spring and All,* 1923) is a poem of only twenty-seven lines which echoes some of the imagery as well as the concepts of Eliot's *Waste Land.* Beginning with a description of a bleak winter scene on a road through muddy fields, the poem turns (stanza five) to the tentative awakening of spring and the "naked,/cold, uncertain" leaves of grass which are the first evidence of the return of life to the world. At first unconscious, the spring plants gradually acquire awareness as they come to life: "rooted, they/grip down and begin to awaken." Thus the poem depicts the cyclical rebirth of life, which is here, through the allusion to the "awakening" and awareness of plants, connected to intelligence and thus to humanity. An adroit touch is the transition from winter images to images of spring, achieved in a mere seven words in the fifth stanza; the two lines of the stanza are connected organically to the preceding passage by the word "lifeless," which echoes "leafless" in the fourth stanza. The simple and understated ending is typical of Williams' pared-down style.

"The Red Wheelbarrow" (1923) is one of the shortest serious poems ever published by an American poet. The structure is rigidly formal; the poem consists of four miniature stanzas of four words each. Three images are involved: the wheelbarrow, described simply as "red," the qualifying adjectival phrase "glazed with rain," which relieves the excessive severity of the second stanza, and the contrasting white chickens of the final stanza. This poem suggests the cameo-like technique of the Japanese *hokku,* which influenced Pound and the other Imagists.

"The Yachts" (1935) is a medium-length descriptive piece inspired by a yacht race, one of the best-known poems of Williams' later period. The construction involves a paradox or shift in attitude; the yachts are first described as fragile compared to the boundless power of the sea (stanzas 1 and 2), then, toward the end, as triumphing over the sea's fruitless efforts to crush them. Meanwhile the sea, which has been personified in the first stanza, becomes virtually humanized before the poem ends; in stanza 9 it consists of "bodies" which reach out frantic arms to halt the yachts. The frenzied images of the angry sea continue up to the last stanza, and the poem ends with the calm triumph of human craftsmanship over nature: ". . . the skillful yachts pass over." From a technical point of view the poem is interesting as an exercise in sustained personification; aesthetically its chief merit lies in its powerful imagery ("Mothlike in mists, scintillant in the minute/brilliance of cloudless days . . .").

WALLACE STEVENS (1879-1955)

Wallace Stevens is an extraordinary literary phenomenon, a successful insurance executive who became simultaneously one of America's most important modern poets. Even more remarkable, there is nothing of the Babbitt or the business-man mentality about his poetry; in fact criticism of it is more often directed toward its alleged obscurity, the highly specialized intricacy of its aesthetic. Stevens is a highly modern, even esoteric type of poet whose work, never popular with the general public, is appreciated chiefly by a small band of scholars, critics, and fellow poets. In these circles he is as highly regarded as any other poet of the century. "*Sunday Morning,*" writes Ivor Winters, a critic who is by no means always favorable to Stevens, "is probably the greatest American poem of the twentieth century and is certainly one of the greatest contemplative poems in English . . ."

A Harvard graduate and a wide reader, Stevens writes from a consciously aristocratic and educated point of view; his poetry is solidly erudite as well as thoroughly mature and sophisticated. The chief influences in his work are the aesthetic theories of Plato and Coleridge (both of which, however, he rejects in certain particulars) and the poetic techniques of the French Symbolists. Like Mallarmé, Verlaine, and the other members of the Symbolist school, Stevens is fond of brilliant visual effects, strong impressionistic images, and evocative but logically diffuse lines. One particular device he borrowed from the Symbolists is the intricate interchanging of sensual impressions, intermingling sight and sound, odor and texture. Following along the lines suggested by Rimbaud's famous sonnet "Voyelles" and by the critical theories of Mallarmé, he attributes definite and fixed values to various colors; for instance the color blue to Stevens invariably connotes poetry, the romantic, the life of the sensibilities, especially the world of the imagination (e.g., in "The Man With the Blue Guitar"). On this theoretical basis Stevens builds a poetry that is simultaneously vivid, erudite, and technically competent. In content it is often epicurean or hedonistic. "The world of *Harmonium* is rich, almost effete," says O'Connor in a remark which might be applied as well to the rest of Stevens' work. "It is a world of comfortable living, *objets d'art,* voyages in the Caribbean, French phrases, sophisticated knowledge and wit."

Moreover, this world is all there is for Stevens; although he has a considerable interest in metaphysics he rejects all Platonic or Christian concepts of immortality. The spirit exists for Stevens, but only as a substance that infuses matter in its mundane state. He has a tendency, in fact, to equate spirit with imagination, a term which has great importance in his aesthetic system. It is imagination (whether of a poet or of an ordinary concept-forming individual) which lends order to the confused diversity of the universe which would otherwise be mere chaos. And Stevens believes above all in order, in an orderly universe and in an orderly approach to the imaginative realm of poetry. Order is, in fact, his *summum bonum,* serving for him in the way the concept of virtue serves for the ordinary Christian. Yet this idea of order is not a political one; he is not, for instance, a religio-political conservative in the way that T. S. Eliot is. To Stevens order is the pattern, the sense, which the human imagination imposes upon experience. The higher the civilization the more sensitive and complex the imagination, and therefore the more refined the order which the imagination evokes. Stevens' concept is most clearly expressed in a poem which is otherwise not very important, "The Idea of Order at Key West" (1935), but it is implied throughout his work.

Another remarkable thing about Stevens' poetic career is that he turned seriously to writing only in his maturity and published his first volume, *Harmonium,* at the age of forty-three; thus he sprang full-blown onto the literary scene without the usual period of tentative and immature searching for an individual style. His poetry, written over the long period of time from *ca.* 1913 to the time of his death in 1955, is remarkably homogeneous in quality; the main development in it is that his later work (after 1936) tends to be more technically intricate and difficult.

LIFE: Wallace Stevens was born in Reading, Pennsylvania in 1879; his ancestry was Dutch. He attended Harvard (1897-1900) and went on to the New York Law School; he was admitted to the bar in 1904. After practicing law for a short time in New York City he transferred to the insurance business; in 1916 he joined the legal department of the Hartford Accident and Indemnity Co., and in 1934 he became a vice-president of the firm. He thus lived for the major part of his career in Hartford, Connecticut, where the home office of the company was located. Meanwhile he had entered upon a second, almost secret career as a poet. He had published verse while still a Harvard undergraduate, and during his period of law practice in New York he had associated with the modernist cénacle including W. C. Williams, Marianne Moore, and Alfred Kreymborg. Between 1914 and 1923 he published about one hundred poems in magazines, from *Poetry* and *The Little Review* to *The New Republic.* In 1914 and again the following year his work won prizes from *Poetry.* His first volume, *Harmonium,* was published by Knopf in 1923 chiefly through the influence of Carl Van Vechten; the book was not a commercial success, selling fewer than a hundred copies, although it received high praise from some critics. In his early period Stevens also wrote several verse dramas; his *Three Travellers Watch a Sunrise* was produced in 1920 by the Provincetown Players with Edna Millay in the leading rôle. In 1920 *Poetry* awarded him the coveted Levinson Prize, and in 1922 *The Dial* presented him as a distinguished contributor. His volumes continued to appear at a steady rate: *Ideas of Order* in 1935, *Owl's Clover* in 1936, *The Man With the Blue Guitar and Other Poems* in 1937. Meanwhile Stevens continued to live in relative obscurity, shunning literary publicity and conscientiously performing his duties as an insurance executive. Many honors came to him in his later years: election to the National Academy of Arts and Letters in 1946, a Bollingen Prize in 1950, a National Book Award in 1950 and another in 1955, and a Pulitzer Prize (for his *Collected Poems*) in 1955. He died in Hartford in August, 1955.

IMPORTANT POEMS: "Anecdote of the Jar" (1916) is on the surface a simple allegory of a jar placed on a hill in Tennessee and somehow transforming the wilderness. Critics, however, have widely disagreed as to its interpretation. Stanley P. Chase wrote, ". . . the little poem is meant to suggest nothing more than the superiority . . . of the simplest bit of handicraft over any extent of unregulated nature," and O'Connor speaks of the jar "imposing its order" on the wilderness. But Ivor Winters argues that, although the jar does dominate the wilderness, "it does not give order to the wilderness—it is vulgar and sterile, and it transforms the wilderness into the semblance of a deserted picnic ground." This latter interpretation has come to be the accepted one; it is not until the jar is placed in the middle of it that the wilderness becomes "slovenly." Man's works blight the naturalness of the countryside and make it shabby and synthetic; the poem is an objective picture of the slovenly borderline between civilization and wilderness.

"Peter Quince at the Clavier" (1923) is a soliloquy built around the idea that human emotions are equivalent to music and that music itself is "feeling then, not sound." The Biblical legend of Susanna and the elders is used as a skeleton; each emotion of Susanna and her watchers is interpreted in musical terms. Though these emotions die away with the passing of man (Stanza IV), abstract beauty lives on in successive individuals; Susanna's memory stirs music (emotions) in moderns like a "clear viol."

"Sunday Morning" (1923) is Stevens' best-known poem, and has been called one of the most important American poems of the century. It consists of eight stanzas of exactly fifteen lines each. In Stanza I we are introduced to the protagonist, a lady arising on a Sunday morning and taking her breakfast on a terrace. The Sunlight intensifies the pungence of the orange she is eating and the bright green wings of her cockatoo. These images do not seem quite real to the lady, however, since she is meditating on the meaning of death. Stanza II introduces the theme of the poem: what divinity does the lady possess, and what is the meaning of this divinity in the light of the obvious reality of death? The poet answers provisionally that delights of the senses are more valuable than any ephemeral hope of life after death.

But in V the lady refuses to accept this hedonistic solution; the human desire for immortality is too strong even in the midst of sensual pleasure. But, the poet answers, death is necessary in order to set life into relief; our appreciation of life is heightened by the everpresent consciousness of death. In VII a new religion is predicated; the poet describes a ritual in praise of the generative principle of life. Men will find comfort and strength in their "heavenly fellowship of men that perish." In the final stanza the immortality of Jesus is rejected, and by implication the hope of human resurrection is also abandoned. Man is inescapably destined to live on the earth, a whirling ball in "an old chaos of the sun." Yet nature, life, and the generative principle are all about us; in the final lines the doctrine of hedonism and life-worship is reiterated.

In "Le Monocle de Mon Oncle" (poem, 1923) the style is more intricate and Stevens' hedonism tempered by a more thoughtful examination of the meaning of life. The images of the poem constantly contrast sensual experience, (the red bird, the apple, the skull, the pool of pink, and the lilacs) with thought and contemplation (the Chinese philosophers, the poet himself as a "rose rabbi"). The poem, however, does not treat of human nature in the wider sense as much as it does the nature of the poetic personality. Stanzas VI-X trace the evolution of the poetic temperament through youth and maturity to old age. In the final stanza (XII) the poet confesses to some difficulty in comprehending love; he now sees nuances where all seemed simple in his youth. The reference to "fluttering things" in the last line also suggests an interest in the realm of idea and spirit as opposed to the world of the flesh. Thus this poem comprises a statement of Stevens' more mature poetic and philosophic principles which may be contrasted with the ideas of his earlier work.

"The Emperor of Ice Cream" is reputedly one of Stevens' most obscure poems. The dominant theme is that of death, symbolized through a funeral which is evidently that of a poverty-stricken old lady; the obsequies are prepared by "the roller of big cigars," a personification of strong and lusty vitality, who is ordered in what is perhaps Stevens' most famous single line, to whip "In kitchen cups concupiscent curds," i.e., apparently to prepare funeral libations which are aphrodisiac in nature. For life must struggle with death; even as the funeral guests bring "flowers in last month's newspapers" we are reminded that "The only emperor is the emperor of ice-cream," i.e., that the only reality or truth, the ruling force in our lives, is necessarily the pleasure of the senses. Thus it is implied that man, believing in and serving "the emperor of ice-cream," gives to the enjoyment of the senses a validity, even a transcendental significance, which Christians previously gave to the idea of immortality through their faith in it.

ARCHIBALD MACLEISH (born 1892)

In marked contrast to the popular "ivory tower" concept of the poet, MacLeish is a highly social being, intimately in contact with his environment and sensitive to the atmosphere of ideas—intellectual, political, and economic—in the world around him. His long career has led him through a number of literary periods, each of which was conditioned by the changing social environment. In his early period, when he first began to write seriously as a poet (1923-30), he was considerably influenced in technique by Ezra Pound, T. S. Eliot, and the technical innovators of the age. His work of this period is introverted and subjective, concerned with aesthetic and personal problems; in style it is imagistic, highly polished and subtle, but lacking in strongly original content. With the end of the art-for-art's-sake epoch of the Twenties, MacLeish abandoned his pure aestheticism and became increasingly conscious of his social and cultural heritage as an American; the poems of this period (1930-33), e.g., *Frescoes for Mr. Rockefeller's Center,* are broad in scope, thoughtful, often dominated by a strong consciousness of the American historical tradition. His tendency toward political engagement increased during the New Deal era; in his third period (approx. 1933-48) he is frankly collectivist, left-wing, internationalist, and anti-fascist. Much of his work in this period wavers between literature and propaganda; and during most of the period he held public office under the Roosevelt administration. Finally, in 1949, with his acceptance of a teaching position at Harvard, he shifted his interests once more to pure poetry and to a philosophical rather than political attitude toward the world around him. His most recent poems (e.g., *Songs For Eve,* 1954) are personal in theme and refined, subtle, and lyrical in technique.

Yet it is probably the work of the second and third periods (1930-48) which will insure MacLeish a permanent place in American literature. It is here that he is most original, most strikingly American and vernacular. Many critics object to the political bias of his work in this period, arguing that poetry must not be confused with propaganda. MacLeish's attitude, however, was a sincere one; he was personally convinced that poetry must be made to serve higher ends than the mere communication of subjective impressions. More than any other writer he helped to convince the American intellectual public of the need of opposing fascism with organized force. Even more important, he succeeded in this period in coming to grips with two problems which most poets prefer to ignore: the antagonism between the political order and the artist class in modern society, and the increasing power of the mass media (radio, newspapers, motion pictures) over the public mind. His answer to the first problem was political engagement; until the artist himself takes an active part in the political life of his society he will continue to be misunderstood and persecuted. (MacLeish himself, seeking confirmation in a political office, was once subjected to the ordeal of being grilled publicly by a congressman about the "meaning" of his poetry.) As for the second problem, his answer was similar: the artist, whether poet, composer, or painter, must contribute actively to the mass media and must develop new and more subtle artistic techniques to rescue them from banality. If poets object to the kind of motion pictures turned out by hack writers, they must write motion pictures themselves. Thus, in addition to working frequently as a screen-writer, MacLeish experimented with the ballet (*Union Pacific*), the drama (*Panic*), the radio play (*The Fall of the City*), and the documentary news-magazine (*Land of the Free*). Yet none of these undertakings has destroyed his integrity as a poet. He has achieved distinction in both realms, as poet and as propagandist; at one extreme his "You, Andrew Marvell" has been called the finest American short poem of the century, and at the other *The Fall of the City* seems assured of permanent fame as one of the great radio plays of our time.

LIFE: Archibald MacLeish was born in Glencoe, Illinois in 1892. His family was well-to-do, and he was educated at Hotchkiss School and at Yale (B.A. 1915). Married while still a student, he nevertheless served in the First World War as a volunteer member of an ambulance unit and later as a Field Artillery officer; his brother, an aviator, was killed in Belgium. After the war he entered the Harvard Law School, which awarded him an LL.B. in 1919. After teaching for a year at Harvard he practiced law for three years in Boston. Meanwhile he had begun writing poetry. His first book of poems was published in 1917, and in 1923 he took the decisive step in his life by abandoning his law career and going with his wife and two children to France to write. The family stayed in Europe until 1928; from 1924 onward MacLeish published approximately one volume of poetry a year through the period of the Thirties. Returning to America, he settled on a Connecticut farm; in 1932 a trip to Mexico provided the inspiration for the long narrative poem *Conquistador,* which won a Pulitzer Prize for that year. For a brief period during the Thirties he served on the staff of *Fortune* magazine; meanwhile his political activities on behalf of the Roosevelt administration increased. In 1939, in recognition of this active political attitude and of his poetic attainments, he was appointed Librarian of Congress; the appointment was strongly opposed in some circles, but MacLeish proved to be a capable and popular public administrator. In 1940 he published a highly controversial essay of political belief under the title *The Irresponsibles,* particularly attacking the generation of writers of the Twenties whose sentimental pacifism, as he considered it, had helped to turn public opinion away from an active participation in European affairs. During the Second World War he held another important public office: Director of the Office of Facts and Figures, the agency which later developed into the U. S. Information Service. In the period immediately after the war he was active in United Nations affairs, serving as chairman of the American delegation to the first UNESCO conference in Paris in 1946. In 1949 he accepted a teaching position at Harvard, the Boylston Chair of Rhetoric and Oratory, one of the most venerable professorships offered by an American university. His poetry output continued; in 1952 his *Collected Poems* were simultaneously awarded a Pulitzer Prize, the Bollingen Prize, and the National Book Award as the best volume of poetry published that year.

IMPORTANT POEMS: "Ars Poetica" (1926) is a short free-verse statement of MacLeish's youthful poetic principles. At this time MacLeish's attitude stands squarely for art-for-art's-sake and against political commitment. The key line in the poem is the final one: "A poem should not mean but be." Poetry has no other significance than its own existence, its own illumination of statement, and its own beauty.

"Immortal Autumn" (1930) presents a novel thought on the autumn season. It is eminently the "human season," the poem argues, because in nature retreats and becomes invisible; the birds and the leaves disappear, leaving man alone on his planet. The final line calls for love and understanding between men in a world where humanity is bereft of nature.

"You, Andrew Marvell" (1930) is the best-known of MacLeish's early lyrics. The title alludes to Andrew Marvell's "To His Coy Mistress," which contains the couple, "But at my back I always hear / Time's winged chariot hurring near." The chariot of Marvell's poem suggests death, and in MacLeish's poem the gradual encroachment of the shadow of night over the globe of the earth achieves a similar impression. The shadow of dusk is seen falling, first over Babylon and the Near East, then through the classic lands to the Atlantic; at last it reaches the poet, lying "face downward in the sun" somewhere in America. The path of the dusk-line from east to west parallels the march of civilization, which began in the Euphrates valley, passed to Greece and Rome, thence to Europe, and came finally to America. In technique the poem is interesting for its sustained grammatic suspense; it consists of a single long sentence of parallel clauses connected by "and."

"Memorial Rain" (1930) is a tribute to the war dead in a form suggested by the classic English elegy. The reflections of the poet alternate with the conventionally patriotic remarks (". . . these happy, happy dead") of a diplomat making a memorial speech; thus the mood of the poem is one of irony mixed with sorrow. The setting, an American military cemetery in Belgium, reminds the poet of "one" (evidently MacLeish's aviator brother) who lies under foreign earth remembering his Illinois home and troubled by the constant and monotonous wind (symbol of unrest). The ambassador's speech is at last interrupted by the coming of rain, which drives away his audience; and with the moisture "seeping / Between cracked boards" (symbol of the cycle of life, of the merging of the body with earth) peace comes again to the dead soldier. In addition to its content the poem is interesting from a technical point of view; its concrete, even blunt images (e.g., the rain seeping in to the corpse) are relieved by the subtle originality of diction (the "thin grating" of ants, the "spurts of water that ravel in the dry sand") and by its use of half-rhymes and other prosodic innovations (*thin/continues, lake/like,* the slight variations in the "o" vowels in lines 3-4). This poem, which owes something to Ezra Pound, nevertheless marks the transition in MacLeish's work to the more mature and politically conscious style of the Thirties.

"Burying Ground By the Ties" (1933) is the best-known piece from *Frescoes for Mr. Rockefeller's City.* The speakers are the thousands of foreign-born workmen who helped to build the Union Pacific line through the Rockies, and by extension all of America's foreign-born proletariat. Deprived of status as "true" Americans, they are nevertheless the foundation of the wealth which the rich enjoy. Yet their only satisfaction lies in knowing that they "laid the steel to the stone stock of these mountains." This is one of the first of MacLeish's poems to show a definitive political attitude.

The Fall of the City ("verse play for radio," 1937) was the first radio script to be written by an established poet. The plot, laid in a mythical city, is an allegory of fascism. The play opens as an announcer, viewing the crowd milling about in the central plaza of the city, relates the situation: a woman recently dead has come back to life and is about to speak to the people. As the crowd listens she tells them in oracular accents that the city of masterless men is to take a master, and there will be "blood after." Confusion sweeps over the crowd; then a messenger arrives to warn of a conqueror who has taken all countries "east over sea-cross." Faced with the menace, the people are terrified. An orator speaks to them, exhorting them to pacifism; only with "freedom" (i.e., passiveness), he tells them, can freedom be preserved. His motto is "weakness conquers." After the orator (personification of the pacifists and isolationists of the nineteen-thirties), another messenger arrives to report that the conqueror has now landed and is marching on the city. The people become frantic with fear and begin to accuse their leaders of treason. Then the priests (symbols of organized religion) speak to them; they argue that salvation will be found only if the population turns back to its traditional gods. Next comes a general, a personification of the spirit of preparedness; he calls the politicians and priests "foolish old men" and warns that freedom can be preserved only if men unite to fight against it. But the people do not listen; they are hypnotized by the imminent arrival of the conqueror. When he appears, clad in armor, they fall on their faces before him; in their supine attitude they do not notice that when the conqueror opens his visor his armor is empty. The shell of armor might easily be toppled, but the people cannot see this; they have fallen down before a nonentity because they are afraid of the responsibility of their freedom. Fascism does not conquer free and courageous men; it triumphs only over the morally weak who are tired of "the long labor of liberty" and too cowardly to fight against their enemies.

E. E. CUMMINGS (born 1894)

Opinion is about equally divided as to whether Cummings is a poet of genius or merely a facetious exhibitionist. In either case he is one of the most highly individual literary figures of his generation, as strikingly original in technique as he is eccentric and irrepressible in personality. Above all he is the enemy of complacent middle-class respectability: "the godless are the dull and the dull are the damned," he stated in a 1941 poem. His spontaneous individualism has led him as well to revolt against traditional poetic technique; not only does he abandon conventional structure and content, but he rejects even the usual techniques of conveying information and emotion through the printed word. His experiments in typography have become his trademark; the mere appearance of his poetry on the page instantly identifies its author. Comparable idiosyncracies are present in his syntax, punctuation, and diction.

Cummings is primarily concerned with the auditory impact of language; his verse is meant to strike the ear and not the eye. This is instantly apparent when Cummings is heard reading his own poetry on phonograph records; the curious innovations in typography which give his verse such an odd appearance on the page are then seen merely as aids to oral reading, as guides to timing, accentuation, syllable stresses, and even to pitch. He breaks lines to indicate stress; he sometimes capitalizes key words for the same reason, and he uses punctuation to indicate the rises and climaxes in tone. In his more radical poems he avoids capitalization for any purpose, even spelling his name "e. e. cummings." These eccentricities have been widely imitated, but it requires a poet of Cummings' skill to make them vivid and meaningful.

In content Cummings is (a) a total individualist, virtually a philosophical anarchist, and (b) a kind of Dionysian hedonist. These two attitudes serve as his politics and ethics respectively, although they are hardly systematic enough to be considered under these terms. His aversion to social groups, to right wings and left wings, to organizations, clubs, parties, institutions, and committees of all kinds approaches the pathological; Cummings is the individualist *par excellence*. In spite of their alleged respect for "rugged individualism," Americans are a nation of joiners, a highly gregarious people; thus Cummings, the absolute individualist, often finds himself at odds with "the American Way of Life." His personality is essentially satirical; he lacks that quality so necessary in the Good Citizen, an awe in the presence of venerable institutions. Basically a serious person, he refuses to be caught in the attitude of seeming to take anything seriously, even his own poetry; he is one of the few modern poets of the modernist school who has enough sense of humor to combine poetry with genuine comedy. Horace Gregory has compared his bawdy humor to that of the Italian Commedia dell'arte; a comparison with Rabelais is also apt.

As for his ethics of hedonism: Cummings is enthusiastically on the side of love, poetry, springtime, freedom, and sensual pleasure. The Dionysian quality in his poetry ("o sweet spontaneous earth") is connected to his antagonism toward puritanism and Anglo-Saxon propriety; much of his more serious poetry is concerned with tributes to the earth as a source of life, to female beauty as a symbol of the life force, and to vitality and sensory beauty in every form. Erotic themes play a large part in his work; more than any other American poet of his time he has revived the romantic love-poem, the lyrical tribute to the beauty of the beloved, which has tended to grow out of style since the eighteenth century when it was the chief subject of lyric poetry.

Cummings is a controversial figure, and opinions of his importance differ widely. Theodor Spencer has termed him "the most truly delightful lyric poet in America," and Lloyd Frankenburg in 1950 called him "one of the major lyric poets of our time." On the other hand Allen Tate has complained that "he replaces the old poetic conventions with equally limited conventions of his own," and Untermeyer concludes, "Robbed of typographical oddities, reduced to essential statements, most of [his] verse is not so spectacular as it first appears." In the future, as the startling quality of Cummings' typographical experiments wears off, he will probably be admired chiefly for his content as one of the important romantic lyricists of his generation.

LIFE: Edward Estlin Cummings was born in Cambridge, Massachusetts in 1894. His father was a well-known Congregationalist minister. Cummings attended Harvard, where he received a B.A. in 1915 and an M.A. in 1916; immediately thereafter he embarked for France, where he served as a volunteer ambulance driver. His radical and pacifist remarks, however, soon brought him under the suspicion of the French authorities, and he found himself confined for several months in an internment center for "subversive aliens." He related these experiences in a saucy and highly original novel, *The Enormous Room* (1922). After serving out the rest of the war in the American army, he returned to New York and set himself up as a poet. Two years of this brought little success; he returned to Paris, where he remained until 1924 studying painting. Meanwhile he continued to write poetry; when he returned to America he found that his novel

and his first collection of verse had earned him a considerable reputation. In 1925 he won the *Dial* prize for poetry; he continued to
produce verse at a prolific rate until 1930, when he returned for
several years to Paris.

Married in 1928 to Ann Barton, Cummings was later divorced;
since 1933 he has lived chiefly in New York. His interest in painting
continued; he has exhibited several times with the Society of Independent Artists in Paris and has held several one-man shows in
America including two (1944 and 1949) at the American-British
Art Centre. In 1952 he was invited to give the annual series of
Norton Lectures at Harvard University; his rather eccentric and
highly informal talks were later published as *i: six nonlectures*
(1953). In 1955 Cummings received a special citation from the
National Book Awards committee for his definitive volume *Poems,
1923-1954.*

TYPICAL POEMS: "La Guerre" (from *Tulips and Chimneys,* 1923)
consists of two antiphonal sections which contrast the evil of war
with the changelessness of the "sweet spontaneous earth." The love-
death conflict in the second section, which finally results in the rebirth of spring, suggests the Greek Persephone-Pluto myth; a semi-
religious paganism is often implied in Cummings' "Dionysian" lyrics.

"Chanson Innocent," from the same collection, is similar. Beginning as a kind of child's song accompanied by the whistling "far and
wee" of the balloon-man, it builds rhythmically to a climax in which
the balloon-man (now "goat-footed" and thus recognized as a satyr
or follower of Dionysus, a symbol of joyous Bacchic abandon) ends
the poem with a final exultant note of his pipe. The two compound
adjectives "puddle-wonderful" and "mud-luscious," which strikingly
convey the child's delight in spring, are often-cited examples of Cummings' verbal experiments.

"Portrait VIII" (the poem beginning "Buffalo Bill's / defunct,"
also from *Tulips and Chimneys,* is a whimsical but sincere tribute to
the legend of the famous American cowboy. The running together of
"break onetwothreefourfive pigeons justlikethat" is a typical instance
of Cummings' effort to convey reading directions through typography.

"The Cambridge ladies who live in furnished souls" (also from
Tulips and Chimneys) is a satirical "sonnet" characterizing the re-

spectable ladies of Cambridge, Massachusetts, priggish, religious, superficially cultivated, gossip-mongering, who are too narrow and prim to be aware of the tremendous vitality of the world all about them; thus they do not notice that the moon "rattles like a fragment of angry candy."

"Poem, Or Beauty Hurts Mr. Vinal" (from *is 5*, 1926) is one of Cummings' best-known satires, a devastating portrait of the business-minded middle-class American citizen. The poem consists mainly of parodies of advertising slogans interspersed with bombastic Fourth-of-July oratory; the passage in the middle beginning "i do however protest" turns to a personal attack by the poet on the stereotyped banality of advertising, motion pictures, and other mass media. The poem ends with a ribald but masterful description of obsession with patent medicines and the cult of personal fastidiousness in America.

"Next to of course god" (Poem III of Section Two of *is 5*) is similar but shorter, consisting entirely of a parody of a banal patriotic oration. The speaker, after spouting unconvincingly about the "heroic happy dead" who "rushed to the slaughter," then pauses to drink "rapidly a glass of water;" the sudden and incongruous return to the prosaic turns his pretentious speech into a comic mockery.

"Since feeling is first" (Poem VII, Section Four, in *is 5*) is one of the best known of Cummings' love-lyrics. The traditional *carpe diem* theme is treated in half-serious, half-whimsical modern terms; the poet, insisting to his mistress that his intelligence is unimportant beside her beauty ("your eyelids' flutter"), implores her to love him, since life is short and death ("no parenthesis") is long. Relatively conventional in form, this short poem is one of Cummings' most successful treatments of the theme of love, avoiding exhibitionistic eccentricity on one hand and sentimentality on the other.

"Space being (don't forget to remember) Curved" (Poem VII in *ViVa*, 1931) is a boisterous pastiche of the clichés of modern science and its inevitable result, the arrogant self-glorification of the human race; "god being Dead," man has become the Lord of Creation. His supremacy is illustrated through an incongruous and mocking example: at the least crooking of his trigger finger, "earth's most terrific / quadruped" (the elephant) "swoons into billiard Balls!" Cummings, the total individualist, rejects even modern scientific humanism as a philosophical dogma. This theme, that of man's arrogance in assuming his superiority over the rest of the universe, is one frequently found in Cummings' later work; see also "pity this busy monster, manunkind" (1944).

JOHN CROWE RANSOM (born 1888)

It is one of the tenets of the New Criticism that the literary critic must be a creative artist in his own right. Ransom, one of the founders of the movement, fulfils the condition; he is equally important as a critic and as a practicing poet. During his period of teaching at Vanderbilt University he was one of several Nashville poets who founded *The Fugitive*, a literary review which served as the rallying-point of the so-called "Fugitive Group" and helped to set off a considerable literary revival in the South. He is a Southerner by instinct and by choice; his poetry combines the experimental techniques of the newest literary schools with the aristocratic traditions of the ante-bellum South. He is by no means an easy poet; although his verse is never deliberately esoteric, he writes consciously for a small group of specialists who appreciate his technical subtlety. The outstanding feature of his style is his ability to combine serious content with wit or irony. He seldom descends to outright humor or burlesque, but his most profound ideas appear hidden behind a faintly satirical veil. This lightness is cruder in his early poems, where it might well be termed wit; in the poems after 1924 it more commonly takes the form of a delicate semi-whimsical seasoning.

Ransom's metrics are conservative for the twentieth century, but he is more daring in his rhyme and diction. He readily uses slant rhymes in the manner of Emily Dickinson (*"ready-study"*); he resembles Dickinson too in his use of whimsical personifications of nature as in "Lady Lost." His poems often achieve their finest effects through a carefully calculated harshness; he refines dissonance and assonance to the point of preciosity. The weakest of his poems are those in which scholarly erudition predominates; the best are the delicate studies in whimsy and pathos of the type of "Bells for John Whiteside's Daughter." Latent in all of Ransom's verse is the concept of aristocracy; he deeply deplores the decline of the ante-bellum South with its Cavalier tradition and its deeply inbred sense of chivalry, and he takes for his enemies the new and brash commercial class which is attempting to force industry and urbanism onto the

South. Many of his poems implicitly contrast agrarianism with urbanism, or chivalry with commercialism (e.g., "Captain Carpenter"). Yet Ransom is aware of the decadence of Southern aristocracy; death and corruption are among his favorite themes, and even his symbols of aristocracy have a certain senile air about them. Ransom is a curious poetic mixture; he looks toward the past in subject matter and attitude, yet is a vigorous pathfinder in technique.

LIFE: John Crowe Ransom was born in Pulaski, Tennessee in 1888, the son of a Protestant minister. Educated at Vanderbilt University (B.A. 1909), he went on to Oxford as a Rhodes Scholar and earned a second bachelor's degree in *Litterae Humaniores* in 1913. Returning to America, he joined the faculty of Vanderbilt; except for a brief interruption to serve as an artillery officer in the First World War, he remained in the English department at that school until 1937. He soon became the central figure in the "Fugitive Group" which also included Allen Tate and Robert Penn Warren, and in addition began publishing poetry; his first volume, *Poems About God,* appeared in 1919. This book, somewhat tentative in style, is generally considered inferior to *Chills and Fever* (1924), which contains some of his best-known poems. In 1931-32 he visited England on a Guggenheim Fellowship, lecturing at the College of the South West of England at Exeter. In 1937 he left Vanderbilt for Kenyon College in Ohio, where he founded the *Kenyon Review;* by 1945 he was the acknowledged leader of the "Kenyon Critics" and one of the chief spokesmen of the New Criticism. The Summer 1948 issue of *The Sewanee Review* contained a series of articles on Ransom's significance as a poet and critic by various friends and students, including tributes from both Tate and Warren. In 1951 he received the Bollingen Prize in Poetry as well as the Russell Loines award in literature from the American Institute of Arts and Letters, both awards made chiefly on the basis of his *Selected Poems* (1945).

IMPORTANT POEMS: "Bells for John Whiteside's Daughter" (1924) is a half-whimsical, half-pathetic threnody for a small girl. Fallen into a "brown study" (death), the little girl amazes all who remember her liveliness when she was alive. The central section of the poem (11. 8-16) is devoted to a recollection of the child driving geese to the pond; this image is left in the reader's mind as he again is reminded (11. 13-16) of the little girl's death, which "vexes" so much those who loved her.

"Here Lies a Lady" (1924) again presents the theme of death. The lady passed through six fevers and six chills before she died; in the former her fingers flew over imaginary "old scraps of laces," perhaps memories of her life, and in the latter she turned "cold as a thin stalk" in a foreshadowing of death. The lady, however, is to take consolation in the love and respect of those she leaves behind: her husband, child, and relatives. She thus dies "in great honor." The vaguely implied theme of this poem is decadence; Ransom's interest in the decline of the South is the underlying note. Yet the allegory is not stated specifically; it appears only when one recalls the poet's background and interest.

"First Travels of Max" (1924) describes an expedition into the woods made by a small boy, Max Van Vrooman. Max's family is old, aristocratic, and very respectable; yet when he is forbidden to enter "Fool's Forest" his contrary nature make him immediately want to disobey this order. In the woods he encounters a variety of wild beasts, and at last interviews a Red Witch who threatens him with ill luck and damnation. He escapes even from her, boasting bravely that he will return when he is grown to cut off her head. Max goes back to his well-kept home. Yet we know he will again venture into the woods (symbol of evil or debauchery) in the manner of every Southern aristocrat who grows bored with his respectable manor life. Thus "First Travels of Max" is a delicate study in the connection between aristocracy and decadence.

"Antique Harvesters" (1924) opens in the contemplative vein of a classic pastoral, but soon reveals itself as a study of the decline of the Southern agrarian way of life. The harvesters, as they gather the grain from the land, are conscious of standing on ground drenched in the blood of heroes (of the Confederacy); the hunters who appear in pursuit of a ghostly fox suggest the aristocratic manor life of the ante-bellum South. In Stanza V the South is personified as a "Lady" who soon reappears as a "Proud Lady;" to the suggestion that he abandon the South for more prosperous regions, the harvester replies with scorn that he will always remain the Lady's defender and champion. It is true the South is in a state of decline (VIII, 1), yet if you imagine that she is about to die, remember that the earth itself lives but on the mercy of God and may be approaching its end at any moment (VIII, 5-6).

"Piazza Piece" (1924) is a light but melancholy dialogue between an aging gentleman and a young woman. Their remarks can scarcely be termed conversation, since neither hears the other; the gentleman is desperately aware of his age and his ineffectiveness as a swain, and the lady is thinking only of her unknown "truelove" who is to come. The poem combines the neo-Platonic concept of love with the resigned pessimism of a decadent age.

"Captain Carpenter" (ballad, 1924) is a meaningful burlesque of the traditional English ballad form. Captain Carpenter, a model ballad hero, has the misfortune to be born into the modern age; thus he finds himself, to his chagrin, defeated by all the rogues, witches, and devils he sets out to conquer. Mutilated and humbled, the Captain (symbol of aristocratic chivalry and courage) is not yet subdued; he continues to fight until a final "rogue in scarlet and gray" (symbol of modern callousness and efficiency) cuts out his heart. The poet concludes with a curse on all those avaricious and heartless rascals who wound and murder true chivalry in the world. The implicit contrast in the poem is that between Southern tradition and modern commercialism.

For Ransom as a literary critic see also "The New Criticism," pp. 571ff.

MARIANNE MOORE (born 1887)

Like Pound and Hart Crane, Marianne Moore is a poet's poet, read and appreciated chiefly by specialists; T. S. Eliot believes that "her poems form part of the small body of durable poetry written in our time." But unlike Pound and Crane she is not a "difficult" poet; her work is limited in popularity not because it is obscure but because it is highly specialized in content and attitude. She is not "socially conscious" in the political sense; she is not an embattled humanitarian, and she is not usually concerned with profound philosophical or religious problems. In her own words, her purpose is to create "imaginary gardens with real toads in them;" i.e., to describe an impressionistic world of the imagination, but to do so in images so concrete and vivid that they spring to life in the reader's mind. Her attitude is objective; she does not permit herself surface displays of emotion, and her poetry is almost devoid of any passionate warmth toward her fellow man. In a sense she is a nature poet; she has a fondness for small living things struggling valiantly to hold their own against a hostile universe. In all living things, even in vegetable organisms, she sees the operation of a wonderous life force; in one poem she marvels, "What sap / went through that little thread / to make the cherry red!"

Stylistically her poetry is chiefly remarkable for its vivid and highly original images: an elephant is described as "black earth preceded by a tendril." Structurally her work is fragmentary, virtually anarchistic; one critic objects that hers is "an outlook that has to break things into small pieces to see them," and another applies the term "mosaic" to her disconnected and apparently irrelevant series of images. Miss Moore's own term for this quality in her work is "elasticity," which she opposes to "logic;" in other words her sequence of ideas is intuitive rather than logically consecutive. The influence of the Imagist movement is apparent; the idea also has something in common with the method of Gertrude Stein in such books as *Tender Buttons,* where an irrational and wholly feminine intuition guides the selection of words with a rich associative content.

LIFE: Marianne Moore was born in St. Louis, Missouri in 1887. Her grandfather was a Presbyterian minister and her brother a clergyman and Navy chaplain; in her private life Miss Moore has remained a serious and rigidly moral church-goer. Educated at Bryn Mawr (B.A. 1909), she went on to study stenography at the Carlisle Commercial College in Pennsylvania and then to teach for four years at the Carlisle Indian School. She had begun writing while still a student; in 1915 *The Egoist,* a British review devoted chiefly to Imagist verse, published her first poem to appear in a major magazine. From 1918 she lived in New York City, first in a Greenwich Village apartment and later in a Brooklyn flat, which she and her chaplain brother first rented because it was conveniently near to the Navy Yard where he was stationed. Miss Moore remained in this apartment for the rest of her career, living frugally and working steadily at her poetry. In 1921, after a number of her poems had appeared in magazines, her friends including Hilda Doolittle published at their own expense a small volume of her work entitled simply *Poems. Observations* followed in 1924; between 1921 and 1951 she published seven volumes of verse, including a volume of *Selected Poems* (1935) with an introduction by T. S. Eliot and a *Collected Poems* (1951). From 1921 to 1925 she worked as a librarian in a Brooklyn branch library; in 1926 she became editor of the important literary review *Dial,* a position she held until the magazine ceased publication in 1929. Many awards and recognitions came to her during her long career; among them were the Dial Award in 1924, the Levinson Prize of *Poetry* magazine in 1932, the Hartsock Memorial Prize in 1935, the Bollingen Prize (for her *Collected Poems*) in 1951, and a Pulitzer Prize in 1952. For nine years (1944-53) she labored at her painstaking translation of *The Fables of La Fontaine,* which finally appeared in 1954. A wide reader, Miss Moore interests herself in virtually every aspect of learning, from classic languages to zoology and botany; she is said to be an avid lecture-goer and a keen observer of the objects and persons around her. *Predilections,* her first volume of prose essays, appeared in 1955.

TYPICAL POEMS: "To a Steam Roller" (1924) is typical of the whimsical and slightly rococo style of her early work. The steam roller, which crushes down the "sparkling chips of rock" (perhaps equivalent to individual objects of beauty) and then walks back and forth on them, suggests a comparison with humans who must categorize everything according to a dogmatic system. Toward the end of the poem the stupid and ponderous machine is incongruously compared to a butterfly, an image suggesting a contrast between the steam-roller mentality of the dogmatist with the poet's own whimsical and intuitive changeability.

"Poetry" (1935) expresses Miss Moore's chief statement of her poetic philosophy and of her intent as a poet. She begins by confessing that she dislikes poetry: "there are things that are important beyond all this fiddle." Upon first approach poetry seems to everyone, even to a poet, a trivial exercise much less important than the more physical and concrete occupations in life. But if one reads it "with a perfect contempt," i.e., without expecting anything, much value may be found in it. The middle sections of the poem (stanzas 2-5) discuss the obscurity of some modern poetry, the importance of other forms of language like "business documents and school books," and the stupidity of the "immovable critic," who is depicted in the guise of an ill-tempered and flea-bitten horse. The final stanza presents the key phrase: poetry must present "imaginary gardens with real toads in them." The real lover of poetry likes it first of all because he likes its "raw material," i.e., the physical sensations of life; he then demands that its technique be "genuine," i.e., unaffected, free from deliberate obscurity, and motivated by true emotion on the part of the poet.

"In Distrust of Merits" (1944) is one of Miss Moore's rare statements on contemporary social issues, a thoughtful consideration of the implications of the Second World War. Beginning pessimistically in the mood of disillusioned pacifism which has inspired so many war poems, the poem gradually evolves into an analysis of the millions of personal hatreds which go to make up the national war psychology. If war is to have any point (stanza 5) we must promise never again to hate "black, white, red, yellow, Jew, / Gentile, untouchable;" the only possible meaning in war is that "hearts must feel and not be numb." The final stanza, rising to a magnificent climax, turns to a searching analysis of the poet's own emotions toward the war: has she too felt hatred toward the official enemies? "There never was a war that was / not inward;" this is the conclusion of the poem. Wars arise, not from conflicts of international interests, but from the sum of the hatreds of individuals; until hatred is replaced by love in the heart of each human being wars will continue. This idea is one which Miss Moore expressed frequently in the period after 1941; in her reply to a 1955 biographical questionnaire she stated, "I feel that the unselfish behavior of individual to individual is the basis for world peace."

EDNA ST. VINCENT MILLAY (1892-1950)

Much of Edna Millay's popular fame rests upon two factors: the sensation of her remarkable "Renascence," written at the age of nineteen, and the personal legend which sprang up about her and made her into a living symbol of the Greenwich Village bohemian life of the Twenties. This is not to disparage her skill as a poet: "Renascence" is a superb poem, and some of the sonnets of her later period deserve a permanent place in American literature. Her success was a lucky coincidence of talent and time; her particular literary gift exactly fitted the temper of the era in which she first began to publish.

Her work, especially in her earlier poems, is suffused with a spirit of rebellion, an iconoclasm which questions all traditional values and finds most of them wanting; yet she is not basically a skeptic. The best term to apply to her attitude is perhaps "romantic," but she is so only in the ironic and half-mocking style of a Byron or a Stendhal. She has been called, in fact, "the feminine Byron of the early 1920's;" the main difference is that Miss Millay's longer poems often show an earnestness and philosophical thoughtfulness that the great British romantic seldom achieved. Her shorter lyrics are mainly concerned with the theme of love, generally in a bitter-sweet, half-ironic mood of regret. In her sonnets this theme is on the surface somewhat posed and literary, but it is based on a deep personal sense of melancholy, even of dread; as Miss Millay grew older she became increasingly concerned with the thought of death and of the usefulness of all human endeavor. Her political disillusionment contributed to her attitude: her liberal idealism, which grew to maturity during the Twenties, was shattered by the Sacco-Vanzetti case and the Depression, and she was never able to recover her intellectual equilibrium, to come to terms with the harsh realities of the world as it was. Basically a romantic personality, she was superbly at home in the Twenties; she found herself out of place in the bleak and disturbing world of Hitler, the Depression, and the atomic bomb.

Stylistically Miss Millay is conventional compared with most of her contemporaries. "Renascence," her best-known poem, is written in old-fashioned iambic tetrameter, and many of her most successful poems are impeccably correct sonnets. Some of her longer works (e.g., *Conversation at Midnight*) are written in a kind of blank verse in reverse, in lines which rhyme but lack any meter but that of ordinary conversation; a number of her lesser-known poems approach the technique of free verse. But she is no innovator, either in content or in style; nothing she wrote would have seemed completely strange to the readers of Byron or Shelley. Edna Millay's work demonstrates that even in the twentieth century it is not necessary to indulge in startling technical innovations to write poetry that will give high pleasure and emotion to readers.

LIFE: Edna St. Vincent Millay was born in Rockland, Maine in 1892; she was educated at Barnard and at Vassar, where she received a B.A. in 1917. She had begun writing in her childhood; her first poems appeared in the pages of the juvenile magazine *St. Nicholas.* In 1912 "Renascence," written when she was only nineteen, was published in an anthology of younger poets entitled *The Lyric Year,* and won her instant fame; the poem was compared to Bryant's *Thanatopsis* and its author hailed as a new Emily Dickinson, Christina Rossetti, Elizabeth Barrett, or Sappho. Upon graduation from Vassar she went to New York, where she became a part of the Greenwich Village literary cénacle and a member of the Provincetown Players. In addition to acting frequently in productions of this experimental group she herself wrote three verse dramas during the Twenties; in 1927 she wrote the libretto for Deems Taylor's *The King's Henchman,* called "the first American grand opera." Her first volume of poetry, *Renascence,* appeared in 1917; most of the shorter lyrics in the book were similar in mood to the title poem. She continued to publish frequently, producing about one book of poetry every two years. In 1923 she was married to Eugen Boissevain, a Dutch importer who gave up his business to serve as business manager for her poetic career. Moving with her husband to a farm in the Berkshires in upstate New York, she continued to write under her maiden name; in addition she occasionally wrote humorous verse and light prose under pseudonyms, most of it under the name "Nancy Boyd." Her sudden death on the Berkshire farm in 1950 was due to a heart attack. *Mine the Harvest,* a posthumous volume including poems written between 1939 and 1950, was generally praised by critics when it appeared in 1954.

IMPORTANT POEMS: "Renascence" (1912) is a contemplative poem in simple tetrameter couplets on the subject of the individual's relation to infinity. Unlike most poems of the type, which attempt to convey a single point or opinion, "Renascence" contains several shifts in attitude, showing the evolution of the poet's thought in its progress from one idea to another. In the last stanza the poet, lying on a solitary mountaintop, longs to "touch infinity" (i.e., to have all wisdom, to learn the secrets of the universe) and is startled into a scream by discovering how easy this is—that infinity is at the fingertips of anyone who will reach out for it. But the third stanza reveals a disturbing and terrifying discovery; now omniscient, the poet is burdened with the weight of all human sin and suffering ("For my omniscience I paid toll / In infinite remorse of soul."). Having in a sense become God, she now bears all God's griefs and responsibilities. A death-wish follows at the end of the stanza; and in stanzas 4, 5, and 6 the wish is granted. The poet, lying underground, feels the kindly pattering of the rain over her grave, and her longing for the simple physical pleasures of existence is renewed. This marks the second turning of the poem; having longed for, and received, infinity, she is now awakened to a new realization of the joy of mortal existence. This wish too is granted (stanza 7), and in stanza 9 she savors to its fullest the mere physical sense of being alive ("Like one gone mad I hugged the ground . . ."). The poem concludes (stanza 10) that, although human beings must necessarily live in an imperfect physical world, the infinite is within the grasp of all: "The soul can split the sky in two, / And let the face of God shine through." The poem is not, however, basically "spiritual" or religious in the Christian sense as is sometimes argued; it expresses no concept of a future existence, and its religious aspect lies merely in its concept of an infinity, or a consciousness of significance, of grandeur, of meaning in the universe lying all about us in our mundane existence.

"What Lips My Lips Have Kissed" (from *The Harp-Weaver and Other Poems,* 1924) is typical of Miss Millay's love-sonnets in a melancholy and poignant vein. The poet, reflecting on the many forgotten lovers of her years of passion, compares herself (lines 9-11) to a lonely winter tree from which the birds "have vanished one by one," an image probably drawn from Shakespeare's famous Sonnet LXXIII ("That time of year thou mayst in me behold"). The last two lines, however, in their understated simplicity, rescue the poem from this rather affected literary metaphor and end it on a superbly moving note.

"Euclid Alone Has Looked on Beauty Bare," also from *The Harp-Weaver,* deals with a rather abstract theme: the perfect beauty of mathematics as compared to the imperfect beauty of all material objects. The abstract quality, however, is relieved by the sharply vivid imagery of light in the sestet, as well as the reference to the "massive sandal" of the goddess of beauty "set on stone" in the final line. In a broader sense this sonnet is concerned, not only with the beauty of mathematics alone, but with the superiority of abstract forms of beauty over the concrete forms, an idea found in the neo-Platonic philosophy of aesthetics.

"Oh, Sleep Forever in the Latmian Cave" (from *Fatal Interview,* 1939) is another sonnet of Miss Millay frequently anthologized. The classic Endymion-Selene myth is viewed from a rather ironic modern standpoint; the moon-goddess, bewitching the young mortal through her beauty, nevertheless comes out second best in the amorous encounter, since Endymion can at least escape from his love through the climactic oblivion of death, while she "wanders mad, being all unfit / For mortal love, that might not die of it." The implied theme, however, is not a trival one: that our human mortality, which we dread as a loathsome sentence, nevertheless serves to intensify our experience, to heighten our pleasure in love through the ever-present consciousness of the oblivion which follows death.

KENNETH FEARING (born 1902)

The poetry of Kenneth Fearing has two striking characteristics: in form it is erratic, highly original, often "documentary," imitating the format of the police report or the newspaper story; and in content it is violently and caustically anti-bourgeois, attacking American middle-class smugness and complacency with a merciles satire. Fearing resembles E. E. Cummings in many respects; he uses unusual typography and punctuation devices, he flavors his poetry with the impish irreverence of his own personality, and he shares Cummings' antagonism toward the middle-class business world. The main difference between the two is that Fearing is the more facile and obvious poet; he lacks Cummings' subtlety of image and aesthetic sensitivity, and he does not go as far as Cummings in experimental form and construction. What he gains is a kind of documentary immediacy achieved through his use (usually satirical) of the materials of mass media; it is essentially the technique of Dos Passos' *U.S.A.* applied to poetry. Many of his poems are dialogues in slang or big-city vernacular; others take the form of theatre programs, dying statements of condemned criminals, miniature portraits in the manner of *Spoon River Anthology,* parodies of popular songs, or mock funeral dirges. Much of his effect is attained through ironic contrast in the form of incongruous juxtaposition; the banal but desperate statement of the condemned criminal in "Jack Knuckles Falters" is interspersed with headlines about the marriages of Rumanian princes and earthquakes in Peru. When he is serious (as in "Pantomime" or "Breakfast With Hilda") he is generally dull. He is at his best when his mock-seriousness is unexpectedly shattered by his derisory satire—as in the transfiguration of the deceased business-man in "Portrait (2)," whose soul, "roving . . . amiably through space in a Plymouth 6" at last finds peace "soothed by Walter Lippmann and sustained by Haig & Haig." Fearing is superlatively the poet of the city streets, slangy, skeptical, full of the color and contrast of big-city life; his command of vernacular and the offhand sarcasm of his manner mark him as one of the most thoroughly and typically American poets of his generation.

Fearing has also won considerable success as a novelist. His fiction, however, is not considered by critics to be of the literary quality of his verse; as a commercial writer who has supported himself by ghost-writing and hack-writing throughout his poetic career, he evidently writes his novels principally to earn money.

LIFE: Kenneth Fearing was born in Oak Park, Illinois in 1902. The son of an attorney, he was educated in Oak Park schools and at the University of Wisconsin (1921-24). After holding a number of odd jobs ranging from salesman to mill-hand in Chicago, he went to New York and began to earn his living as a free-lance writer. Much of his writing has been purely commercial, and most of it has appeared under pseudonyms; he wrote at least one book in collaboration with two other writers under the common pen-name "Donald F. Bedford." Meanwhile he had begun to write verse in his spare time; his poems began to appear in magazines in the late Twenties, and in 1929 he published his first poetry volume, *Angel Arms.* Since then he has published frequently in *Poetry, The New Yorker,* and other magazines, and in addition has produced five more volumes of verse, including a *Collected Poems* in 1940. Fearing lives in New York City and has been married twice, the second time to the painter Nan Lurie. In spite of the uneven quality of his work his handful of first-rate poems have won him a position as a leading American poet; Horace Gregory has praised him for having "converted the bromides of tabloid journalism . . . into a brilliant art," and Henry W. Wells finds the "significant roughness" of his verse "peculiarly American."

IMPORTANT POEMS: "Jack Knuckles Falters" (from *Angel Arms,* 1929) consists entirely of a banal death-statement made by a condemned criminal before his execution; the statement is interlarded with mocking newspaper headlines which emphasize the stereotyped falseness of the statement. This poem is one of several among Fearing's work which portray the stupidity and banality of the criminal mind; "St. Agnes' Eve," also from *Angel Arms,* is another.

"Dirge" (from *Poems, 1930-1935*) is an often-anthologized favorite and probably Fearing's most important single poem. The mock funeral chant laments the total pointlessness of the life of its insipid hero, a small office worker who hoped to become an "executive type" but was destined only for a nameless obscurity among the millions of his kind in a big city. The fifth stanza ("and wow he died . . .") embarks on a chanted parody of the comic strip with its surfeit of humorous but catastrophic disasters; the seventh stanza ("Very much missed . . .") points up the obscurity of the hero by sarcastically implying that he will be missed only as a statistical unit, a newspaper subscriber and a subway rider. Returning to the comic-strip vocabulary, the poem ends in an ingeniously ironic imitation of the sound of funeral bells, which clang over the dead hero like the "wham" and "bop" of the funny-paper disasters.

"Portrait (2)" (from *Dead Reckoning,* 1938) is similar; its hero, however, is a slightly different social type: a smug and outwardly successful executive from the post-Depression era. The theme of the poem is that everything about its hero is artificial, machine-made, and spurious, from his false teeth to his mind, which has been reconstructed by a partnership of psychoanalysts. Only his soul is his own —yet even the soul, in the final lines of the poem, is sarcastically revealed to be a production of mass production, soothed by the euphemistic pronouncements of a radio commentator and sustained by the Scotch which is the official beverage of the executive class. Fearing treated this theme several times; another good example is "Obituary" (from *Poems, 1930-1935*), which portrays a similar hero whose only "true-blue pal" was the ambulance attendant who carried his body away.

SOME YOUNGER POETS

In addition to the poets discussed above, who in most cases had published the major body of their work before 1945, the work of a number of younger poets should be briefly mentioned. Born roughly around the time of the First World War, these poets constitute a second generation which underwent its literary formation under the influence of Eliot, Pound, Auden, and the other modernists of the Twenties. The group began publishing in the late Thirties, in some cases (e.g., Jarrell and Shapiro) not until the time of the Second World War. Since they belong, so to speak, to the "second wave" of modern poets, their work is necessarily derivative; it utilizes the devices, styles, forms, even the attitudes of the older generation which revolutionized modern poetry during the Twenties. Yet their work, at least their better work, is not merely imitative; the web of influences in which they operate has become so intricate and diffuse that the influence of a single poet is seldom detectable in their work. In addition they share an experience which the older generation lacked: they grew to maturity in the atmosphere of European fascism, world tension, and the social upheaval of the Depression and New Deal, and most of them were young enough to participate directly in the Second World War. The war particularly left its mark on their work, not only in content but in attitude, in a pessimism, a certain mature cynicism which is evident in their common outlook.

RICHARD EBERHART (born 1904), somewhat older than the others, began publishing poetry as early as 1930. A Master of Arts from Cambridge, he has held a position as a college teacher during most of his career, although his history includes a year as tutor to the King of Siam (1930) and service during the Second World War as a naval officer. His poetry is often concerned with nature-subjects or with the simple objects of daily existence; his first volume, *A Bravery of Earth,* came out of his experiences on a freighter trip around the world. A typical Eberhart poem is "The Fury of Aerial Bombardment," a consideration of the religious implications of war ending with a simple and moving reference to the young men, now dead, who "distinguished the belt feed lever from the belt holding pawl" in the Naval gunnery school where the poet was an instructor.

KENNETH PATCHEN (born 1911), raised in the Ohio steel-mill country, briefly attended the University of Wisconsin and afterwards held a variety of odd jobs while he began to write his first poems. Awarded a Guggenheim Fellowship in 1936, he produced his first volume, *Before the Brave,* the same year. A radical modernist, Patchen is influenced by European surrealism in technique; his work has a genuine and striking originality, but its weakness is its total subjectivity and its disregard for the accepted values of language. Several of his books, including *The Journal of Albion Moonlight* (1941), *Memoirs of a Shy Pornographer* (1945), and *Sleepers Awake* (1946), are written in a heterogeneous style which combines poetry and prose with exercises in verbal experimentation resembling those in Joyce's *Finnegans Wake.* His best-known single poem is probably "Do the Dead Know What Time It Is?", a narrative vignette in a tavern in which the hero's conversation with a harlot is constantly interrupted by the harangue of a maudlin and philosophical old drunk.

DELMORE SCHWARTZ, born in Brooklyn in 1913 of Jewish extraction, was educated at Wisconsin, N.Y.U., and Harvard and has taught college English during most of his career; from 1940 to 1947 he held a position on the Harvard faculty. From 1943 to 1946 he served as editor of *The Partisan Review,* and he has since held several other important editorial positions. His first volume of poetry, *In Dreams Begin Responsibilities,* appeared in 1938. His work is rich in concrete imagery but built on a basis of thoughtful philosophical content; it often involves a metaphysical theme, e.g., the relation between spirit and flesh. A typical example is "In the Naked Bed, In Plato's Cave," in which the poet, lying in his bed in a room on a busy street, imagines for an instant that he is in the cave of shadows which Plato invented as an allegory of the relation between the Material and the Ideal (*Republic,* Book VII). "The Heavy Bear," another of Schwartz's best-known poems, symbolizes the poet's corporeal body as a heavy and somewhat stupid bear which he (the "real" he, his ego or spirit) must carry with him through the world. A gross and appetitive creature, the bear constantly drags his owner down to a lower level of existence, but he realizes he can never divest himself of its burdensome flesh; human beings are inexorably condemned to "the scrimmage of appetite."

KARL SHAPIRO, born in 1913 in Baltimore, was deeply marked as a poet and thinker by his experience as a soldier in the Second

World War; his first two major books, *Person, Place, and Thing* (1942) and *V-Letter and Other Poems* (1944) appeared while he was still serving in the South Pacific. *V-Letter* won a Pulitzer Prize in 1945; Shapiro has since published several more volumes of verse and criticism. In 1947 he was appointed Consultant in Poetry to the Library of Congress; from 1948 he has held teaching positions in various universities, and beginning in 1950 he served as editor of *Poetry* magazine. As a poet Shapiro is original in form and content without being eccentric; Eliot and Auden are often cited as influences on his style. Although his work is thoughtful, it is neither pessimistic nor cynical; Babette Deutsch wrote in a review of his *Poems, 1940-1953,* "His interest in his immediate surroundings, together with his verbal facility, set him apart from those of his fellows who stand in the street damning a disjointed world . . ." A typical poem is "The Leg," in which a soldier who has lost a leg in combat at first feels as though part of his soul has been amputated with it, that he must "pray for the part that is missing," then comes to understand the body itself as "a sign / To love the force that grows us," i.e., divinity, or the life force in the universe. As the poem ends the soldier realizes that this knowledge, "the substance of our understanding," is a kind of immortality that transcends the flesh.

RANDALL JARRELL (born 1914) is another poet who was strongly influenced by his experience in the war, during which he served as an instructor in the Air Corps. A Master of Arts from Vanderbilt, he has served on the faculties of various American colleges including Kenyon College (1937-39) and Princeton (1951-52). His poetry is highly condensed, compact, and unerringly precise; a battle alarm on an aircraft carrier is described as a "jew's harp's sawing seesaw song" which "plucks at the starlight where the planes are folded." A student of psychology in college, he often utilizes the concepts and symbolism of the Freudian and other schools of modern psychology; at the same time he is one of the few poets of his generation to treat the theme of love with seriousness and dignity (e.g., in "Burning the Letters"). A typical poem is "Pilots, Man Your Planes," a vivid and objective description of air combat in the South Pacific. Another well-known Jarrell poem is "The Death of the Ball Turret Gunner," a short monologue of only five lines, spoken by the dead aircraft gunner, in which the round ball turret serves as a symbol of the womb to which the gunner subconsciously longs to return. The deliberately brutal last line of the poem provides a shocking return from the dream-world of the gunner's subconscious to the physical horror of modern war.

PETER VIERECK (born 1916), holder of a Ph.D. in history from Harvard, is a well-known essayist as well as a poet. As a political writer he is one of the leading spokesmen of the "New Conservatism," which he defines as "a revolt against revolt," anti-Fascist and anti-Communist. He published four volumes of essays and three volumes of verse, in addition to single poems in magazines, between 1941 and 1955; his first volume of poems, *Terror and Decorum,* won a Pulitzer Prize in 1948. Stylistically Viereck is ingenious, vernacular, with a weakness for trick effects and eccentricities; one critic has objected to his "combined will to preach and to be pert." During the Second World War he served as a sergeant in the African and Italian campaigns, and like Jarrell and Shapiro has written some of his most important poems out of his war experience. Although he is a pacifist in principle, he differs sharply from most of his contemporaries in his romantic attitude toward the adventure of war. In *"Vale* From Carthage" he commemorates the death of a soldier friend in a philosophical mood recalling the *Frater ave atque vale* of Catullus; and in "Kilroy," a vernacular and sentimental lyric built around a bit of G.I. folklore, he compares the peripatetic American soldier of 1944 to the wanderers and heroes of all history from Ulysses to Columbus. The concluding lines suggest that the young men who missed this great experience of their generation will regret it throughout their lives: *"And in the suburbs Can't sat down and cried."*

ROBERT LOWELL, born in 1917 in Boston, was educated at Harvard and at Kenyon College, where he studied under John Crowe Ransom. His war experience was somewhat confused; he first (1943) tried to enlist in the Armed Forces but was rejected, and when he was later drafted he refused to serve because of his moral objection to the bombing of civilians. As a result he served five months in prison as a conscientious objector. A Catholic, Lowell is a thoughtful poet in content and a conservative in technique. His philosophical attitude is sometimes compared to that of Gerard Manley Hopkins, but he shows a puritan strain, stemming perhaps from his New England background, which is lacking in the nineteenth-century Jesuit poet. Lowell's dominant theme is a search for faith in a modern world of materialism and skepticism; his contemporary Peter Viereck has termed him "the best qualified to restore to our literature its sense of the tragic and lofty." A typical poem is "The Holy Innocents," a short contemplative lyric in which the poet sees from his automobile (symbol of modern material civilization) a pair of oxen "blunder hugely up St. Peter's hill." The oxen, the "Holy innocents" of the title, are then developed as a symbol of human innocence, of the childlike faith which the world of the automobile has lost. In the last line the poet sadly remarks the absence of the spirit of Jesus from modern life: "Lamb of the shepherds, Child, how still you lie." In 1947 Lowell was awarded a Pulitzer Prize for his second volume of poetry, *Lord Weary's Castle*.

* * *

5. Recent American Criticism

GENERAL TENDENCIES

One of the phenomena of twentieth-century literature, in America as well as in Europe, is that criticism has come into its own as a separate and autonomous creative genre, proceeding out of the fields of fiction, drama, and poetry, but in a sense partaking of a life of its own. The twentieth-century critic is concerned, not only to explain and criticize the work of primary authors, but to argue and defend a literary aesthetic which may lie as much in the realm of philosophy or sociology as it does in literature. This tendency is especially obvious in the field of poetry criticism. Poetry has often become in our time a form of literature created by experts and for experts. Such literature demands expert criticism, and criticism which is under little obligation to make itself comprehensible to the general public; and this type of criticism has been produced in abundance in the first half of the twentieth century.

Another salient feature of twentieth-century literature is its diversity: numerous distinct schools and movements evolve side by side in the same era and compete for the attention of the same readers. This tendency has found its due reflection in criticism. Whereas during the romantic and realistic periods of the nineteenth century a single school of literary criticism could be said to predominate at any one time, in the twentieth century the field of literary criticism becomes a battleground on which myriad and mutually incompatible schools of criticism engage in struggle. The most striking characteristic of twentieth-century critics is their tendency to group themselves into schools; and it is easiest to comprehend and appreciate the whole field of criticism if these schools are first defined and analyzed.

IMPRESSIONISTIC CRITICISM

This term, a broad and generic one, may be said to include the work of all those critics who bring to the analysis of literature no single method, dogma, or prinicple, but who judge each literary work by the immediate personal impression it produces on the critic. The term therefore does not define a school, but merely serves to describe all those critics whose attitude is primarily eclectic and subjective. The connection with the school of impressionism in creative literature (fiction and poetry) is slight; an impressionistic critic is likely to admire Eliot as much as he does Proust. The impressionistic critics thus significantly represent an attitude characteristic of the twentieth century: they are relativists who strive for a detached and supple appreciation of excellence in literature no matter what form or technique it may assume. The impressionistic critic wishes to convey to his readers his own personal appreciation of a work or an author, and by this means eventually to widen popular interest in literature; he is a detached observer who interests himself in the literary parade not out of a compulsion to classify and categorize literary work but through a desire to appreciate the best literature of our time and then communicate this appreciation to his readers. Thus most impressionistic critics (Mencken is an exception) are mainly concerned with analyzing what they find admirable rather than what they find bad.

American impressionistic criticism, which began to assume importance around the turn of the century, owed much to European models. The term impressionism itself was borrowed from the French, and American impressionists shared a definite internationalism in attitude. Not only did they stand opposed to the various schools of "nationalistic" criticism which called for an independent and totally native American literature, but they borrowed much of their theory from the school of impressionistic criticism which was already well established in Europe by the turn of the century. Two British critics were particularly important in influencing their American contemporaries. GEORGE SAINTSBURY (1845-1933) was an indefatigable scholar as well as an enthusiastic and forceful stylist; in such work as *A History of Criticism* (1904) and *A History of the French Novel* (1919) he not only served to stimulate an interest in foreign literature among his fellow Englishmen but brought to English prose a highly personal vivacity which it had seldom seen since the age of Swift and Addison. SIR EDMUND GOSSE (1849-1928), a comparative literature scholar, was equally international in attitude; he was influential in introducing the English-speaking public to modern Russian and Scandinavian literature, and he was one of the first English critics to take notice of such important French writers as André Gide and Maurice Barrès. On the continent the leading impressionistic critic during the first decade of the century was JULES LEMAÎTRE (1853-1914), a French university professor and Academician whose familiarity with the aesthetic theories of his time made him the least dogmatic and the most appreciative of critics. His seven volumes published under the general title *Les Contemporains* (1885-89), along with his *Impressions de Théâtre* (1888-98), comprise a complete and valuable literary chronicle of their time. Another important French impressionistic critic of the era was RÉMY DE GOURMONT (1858-1915), who spent most of his career as a *Mercure de France* reviewer. He is often treated as the official critic of the Symbolist school; himself a poet and a novelist, he early recognized the importance of the Symbolist poets and was instrumental in gaining them a wider popular acceptance. His most important criticism is contained in *Promenades littéraires* (1904-23).

BENEDETTO CROCE (1866-1952), philosopher and critic and perhaps the greatest Italian literary figure of the twentieth century, may be classed with the impressionistic critics through his eclectic attitude and his ability to appreciate literary personalities markedly different from his own. A deep-rooted idealist, he sees the universe, including all human experience, as essentially spirit. Yet his predilection for spirit over matter does not lead him into romanticism; in fact an antagonism toward excessive emotionalism in literature is one of his few biases. His most important works of criticism and aesthetics are *Brevario di Estetica* (1913), *La Letteratura Della Nuova Italia* (1914-15), and *Ariosto, Shakespeare, e Corneille* (1920).

The author who is chiefly responsible for bringing the spirit of European impressionism into American letters is JAMES GIBBONS HUNEKER (1860-1921). Talented in many fields, Huneker studied music in Paris and returned to New York to take up a career as a music critic and journalist. During the first twenty years of his career he wrote chiefly on music and the arts; when he finally turned to literature he did so as a critic firmly grounded in comparative aesthetics. Although his attitude as a literary critic was tolerant and eclectic, he was especially attracted to the European decadents and iconoclasts of the late nineteenth and early twentieth centuries: Nietzsche, Ibsen, Shaw,

Huysmans, Rimbaud, Villiers de l'Isle-Adam, and Strindberg. As a stylist Huneker is fresh and spontaneous; he makes up in interest what he lacks in concision and force. His main importance in the history of American literature is that he helped to turn public interest toward the extremely influential field of fin-de-siècle European literature, which had previously been neglected in the enthusiasm for America's own literary awakening. Without Huneker such important influences as that of Laforgue on T. S. Eliot might never have occurred, or might at least have taken a different form. Huneker's most important critical works are *Melomaniacs* (1902), *Overtones* (1904), *Iconoclasts: A Book of Supermen* (1909), and *Promenades of an Impressionist* (1910). Huneker's curious novel *Painted Veils* (1920) is probably his best-known work.

H. L. MENCKEN (1880-1956), considerably influenced by Huneker at the beginning of his career, is generally considered an impressionistic critic, although his irascible individualism and dogmatism separate him sharply from most of the European members of the movement. Mencken's attitudes resemble Huneker's in some respects; he shares his interest in European culture, especially music, and he served as a warm defender and champion of the older critic. His style and attitude, however, differ markedly from Huneker's: Mencken is a fiery polemicist, at his best in cutting satire directed against the idols of American bourgeois culture. He participated actively in all the controversies that rocked American society during the Twenties (prohibition, evolution, censorship of literature, etc.); he applied his energies not only to literary criticism but to social, economic, and political affairs. A conservative in regard to social questions (e.g., the Negro problem in the South), he is violently radical on moral questions; his particular anathema is reserved for Victorian morality. As a literary critic he consistently attacks such schools as the New Humanism for their insistence on a moral element in literature. He is scornful of academic scholarship, although he produced an important work of scholarship himself in *The American Language*. Perhaps most important, Mencken performed an invaluable service to American letters through his lifelong defense of literary freedom and his attacks on censorship. He was particularly assiduous in defending works of the naturalistic school, not because he sympathized with its aims and techniques, but because it was this group that found itself most under attack by would-be censors. Thus, in the fervor of his hatred of the Philistines, Mencken came warmly to the defense of Dreiser's *The "Genius,"* although he considered the novel itself only mediocre.

Mencken wrote most of his literary criticism for two magazines: *The Smart Set* in the period 1908-23 and *The American Mercury* thereafter. His most important book-length works of criticism are the six volumes of *Prejudices* (1919-27). Other critical works include *George Bernard Shaw, His Plays* (1905) and *A Book of Prefaces* (1917). In his later career Mencken turned to the field of linguistics and philology, and produced the important study *The American Language* (1936-47 with supplements).

GEORGE JEAN NATHAN (1882-1958), an avowed disciple of Huneker, served with Mencken as editor of *The Smart Set* (1914-23) before the two went on to found *The American Mercury* (1924). From 1930 Nathan was editor-in-chief of *The American Mercury,* and as such established himself as one of the important literary authorities of the era. In the tradition of Huneker, he adopted an attitude of extreme sophistication and detachment; he lent the brash and chaotic era of the Twenties an almost Epicurean quality of aristocracy. He resembles Huneker also in his lack of interest in ideology; he once stated, "The great problems of the world—social, political, economic, and theological—do not concern me in the slightest." Instead he interested himself in "the surface of life"—the delightful complexity and fascination of the more immediate aspects of existence. Nathan's criticism is largely associated with the theatre; he was probably the best-known serious dramatic critic in American letters from 1920 to 1940. As a play reviewer he championed the early plays of O'Neill and other experimental dramatists of the Twenties; he violently attacked the vulgar elements in the American theatre, and continuously demanded and encouraged an American drama which would take its place in the world theatre of Aeschylus, Shakespeare, and Racine. His best-known collections of reviews and shorter pieces are *Mr. George Jean Nathan Presents* (1917), *Art of the Night* (1928), and *The Morning After the First Night* (1938); his theoretical views are best found in *The Critic and the Drama* (1922) and *The New American Credo* (1927). Nathan also edited the important annual *Theatre Book of the Year* beginning in 1943.

EDMUND WILSON (born 1895), Princeton-trained, went on to

a career as a literary journalist and by 1938 had established himself as an important critic. Most of his early literary criticism was written for magazines, including *The New Republic,* on which he served as associate editor; in the period after the Second World War he became a steady contributor to *The New Yorker.* Wilson's style is informal, conversational, and highly personal; he is disparaged by some academic critics because of his alleged superficiality. Yet he has a genuine erudition and a sound judgment; his deceptively relaxed style conceals a profound literary acumen. His most important literary criticism is contained in *Axel's Castle* (1931), *The Triple Thinkers* (1938), *The Wound and the Bow* (1941), *The Boys in the Back Room* (1941), and two volumes of reviews published as *Classics and Commercials* (1950) and *The Shores of Light* (1952). Like Mencken, Wilson differs from conventional impressionists in holding strong social views; but unlike Mencken he is a thorough-going and consistent liberal. For a time during the Thirties he was sympathetic to Communism; he visited the Soviet Union for five months in 1935 and wrote a favorable account of his journey after his return. He later became disillusioned with the Soviet experiment, chiefly because of Russian censorship and "liquidation" of writers and artists, but he remained a collectivist with pronounced left-wing views. In 1940 he published *To the Finland Station,* a masterful philosophical and historical study of the evolution of the Marxist doctrine up to its culmination in the arrival of Lenin in St. Petersburg in 1917. During the Second World War Wilson began to turn to an interest in psychoanalysis; his analytical essays on Dickens, Kipling, and Henry James are masterful contributions to the genre of psychoanalytical criticism. Wilson is also the author of a work of fiction, *Memoirs of Hecate County,* which enjoyed a considerable *succès de scandale* at the time of its publication in 1946.

THE NEW HUMANISM

One of the most important critical movements of the twentieth century, the New Humanism as a literary school is confined almost entirely to America; yet in its basic premises it opposes the spirit of twentieth-century American culture. Essentially the New Humanism represents a return to classicism; or rather, since America cannot be said to have had a classical period, a movement to instill into American letters the principles of ancient and Continental classicism. Thus the movement is vehemently opposed to romanticism, especially to its cult of individualism, its reliance upon emotion as the final arbiter of conduct and criticism, and its admiration of originality and eccentricity in literature. The New Humanists also attack naturalism, the dominant literary movement in America during the Twenties, for its flagrant violations of decorum, its lack of form and symmetry, and its doctrine of determinism. As a credo of scholars and aesthetes the New Humanism above all demands that literature be based on discipline: moral discipline in content and formal discipline in technique. Along with their mistrust of determinism the New Humanists often express a suspicion of science as a whole; they associate modern science and liberalism with the moral and literary chaos which they feel have come to dominate our age. Psychoanalysis and other psychological doctrines are condemned for a double reason: their dogma is based on fallacious scientific pretensions, and their method places strong emphasis on the emotional and romantic elements in the human mind. Although the New Humanism, based on classicism, is not basically religious in its attitude, most New Humanists argue that religion, as one of the chief elements of discipline in modern society, must underlie social institutions and perform an essential part in literature. Thus the movement has a strong conservative element which develops, not only out of its hostility to liberalism, but out of its insistence on discipline in every realm of social and aesthetic activity. The New Humanists likewise oppose the democratic and Marxist doctrine of "literature for the masses"; literature, as they see it, should be written for the fit few on the level to which the worthy should be aided to attain. The attitude of the New Humanists toward contemporary American culture is somewhat paradoxical. On the one hand More and Babbitt continually called for a genuine and original American literature which would take its place with the great classic literatures of other ages (the Hellenic fifth century, the Elizabethan, the French seventeenth century); yet on the other hand they failed to recognize this literary awakening in the thoroughly American work of Hemingway, Steinbeck, and the other naturalists of the post-war period.

The New Humanists enjoyed their greatest prestige in the period before 1914; by 1920 the tide of opinion had begun to turn away from them. In 1930 opposition to the movement was focused through publication of an anthology, *The Critique of Humanism,* which included attacks by Hartley Grattan, Malcolm Cowley, and others. Among the charges laid to the New Humanists by their critics is that none of them were creative artists; primarily philosophers and moralists, they had no first-hand knowledge of the creative process or the artistic personality.

PAUL ELMER MORE (1864-1937) is along with Irving Babbitt the founder and chief exponent of the New Humanism in America. After a period of teaching at Harvard and Bryn Mawr, he retired in 1897 to take up a monastic existence at Shelburne, New Hampshire, where he wrote the first of his *Shelburne Essays* (1901-14). In these important studies he challenges the chief idols of American culture: humanitarianism, liberalism, and, in literature, naturalism. He holds Jean-Jacques Rousseau responsible for beginning the trend toward emotionalism which has become the curse of our age; he is also concerned with attacking the scientific doctrine of evolution, particularly in the person of its champion Huxley. Religion plays an important part in More's work as it does in his life. He retired to Shelburne mainly out of a desire to find religious meaning in human experience; he eventually achieved this through a merging of neo-Platonism with a diffuse and aesthetic form of Christianity. As a critic More writes expertly, but hardly in a fresh or forceful style; he has the manner of a scholar rather than a polemicist. His criticism is remarkable for its range of subject matter, its extensive erudition, its depth of insight, and its stylistic precision; his style is neoclassic in the best sense of the word. In addition to the *Shelburne Essays* in eleven series his most important critical works are *Platonism* (1917), *The Demon of the Absolute* (1928), and *On Being Human* (1936).

IRVING BABBITT (1865-1933) was associated with More as the co-founder of the New Humanism. His background and training lay chiefly in the field of Romance studies; he was trained at the Sorbonne and for a large part of his career taught French at Harvard. The twin pillars of his critical philosophy are Christianity and classicism. In his first important work, *Literature and the American College* (1908), he condemned the tendencies of modern literature, especially naturalism and decadence, and called for a return to the traditional disciplines of classicism. His most important work is The New Laokoön (1910), an impassioned attack on romanticism and naturalism, the latter of which

Babbitt considers merely romanticism turned upside down. *The Masters of Modern French Criticism* (1912) surveys the history of French literature in the nineteenth century in an effort to find the cause of the decay of classic principles and the triumph of determinism and naturalism. *Rousseau and Romanticism* (1919) combines a detailed analysis of the origin of romanticism with a manifesto calling for the replacement of emotionalism in literature by the higher standards of discipline and idealism. Relativism, both in philosophy and in literature, is also condemned; Babbitt argues for absolute and permanent principles of literature, ethics, and social organization. In addition to Rousseau the authors whom Babbitt condemns most severely are Keats, Shelley, Blake, Hugo, Baudelaire, and Swinburne.

STUART P. SHERMAN (1881-1926) came under the influence of Babbitt while he was a graduate student at Harvard (*ca.* 1904); during the immediate post-war period he was one of the chief exponents of the New Humanism, although by the end of his career he had evolved to a more liberal point of view. Strongly influenced by Matthew Arnold, he was a thorough-going moralist, a "judicial" critic as opposed to an impressionist; he attacked the naturalism of Dreiser, Moore, Wells, and Synge in *On Contemporary Literature* (1917) and engaged in a lifelong polemic with Mencken and other libertarian critics over the alleged immorality of modern fiction. Conservative and intensely patriotic, Sherman vigorously defended the American Puritan tradition during the era of its greatest unpopularity around 1920. For many years professor at the University of Illinois, Sherman went to New York in 1924 to serve as book review editor of the *New York Herald Tribune*. In the last two years of his life his attitude mellowed considerably; he praised naturalists like Sherwood Anderson, even H. G. Wells, whom he had previously attacked in *On Contemporary Literature,* and went so far as to laud his old enemy H. L. Mencken "as an educator if not as a critic." His early death in 1926 was due to a boating accident.

NORMAN FOERSTER (born 1887) is another important spokesman of the New Humanism. A lifetime college professor, he served on the faculty of the University of North Carolina (1914-30) and later became director of the School of Letters of the University of Iowa (1930-44). Socially conservative, Foerster is a strong champion of "liberal" education, i.e., an education based on the classics, on the traditional disciplines of literature and scholarship, and on the cultural heritage of Western civilization. As a literary critic he is tolerant and genteel, at least compared to the vigorously partisan Sherman. Not a highly original thinker, he confined himself to expounding and disseminating the ideas of More and Babbitt in his *Nature in American Literature* (1923), *American Criticism* (1928), and *The American Scholar* (1929). In addition to his personal writing he performed an important function as an editor; his *A Reinterpretation of American Literature* (1928) is an important compilation of essays summing up the position of the New Humanists.

PSYCHOLOGICAL AND PSYCHOANALYTICAL CRITICISM

The new concepts of Freud, Jung, Adler, Brill, and others exerted a considerable influence on twentieth-century literature. This influence was perhaps most important in the novel and drama, but the new psychological concepts also produced their corresponding school of literary criticism. The critics of this movement differ greatly from each other, not only because they based their critical apparatus on different psychological schools, but because psychology and psychoanalysis by their very nature encourage diverse interpretations. It can be said, however, that critics of the psychological school share certain basic concepts:

(1) Following Freud, the psychological critics hold that art and literature are born in the human subconscious as a product of the id, and after taking form there acquire their outward structure and texture in the conscious mind of the artist. The artist is essentially a neurotic personality; his repressions and frustrations have caused his libido to be diverted into the artificial outlet of artistic creativity. According to some critics, the quality and quantity of his creativity is proportional to the degree of his frustration; the greatest artists are the greatest neurotics. The artist differs from the ordinary neurotic, however, in that his heightened sensitivity makes it possible for him to translate his frustration into highly complex works of art; artistic creativity is the most socially valuable form of neurosis. Artistic activity not only

relieves the neurotic tension of the artist, but for the critic provides an interesting and revealing insight into the inner thought processes of the creator.

(2) Proceeding as it does from the subconscious, art is most successful when it seeks to portray the subconscious processes of the mind. This does not mean that the author must consciously express psychological theory; in fact, according to psychological critics, even pre-Freudian authors such as Sophocles and Tolstoy used psychoanalytic theory without understanding its full significance. This in no way vitiates the validity of their presentation of such concepts. Many psychological critics hold that a great work of literature manifests its greatness precisely and solely through its power to reveal the subconscious life of its characters and its author; the absence of such content argues against the quality of a heretofore admired work of literature.

(3) According to psychological critics, literature at its best demonstrates the universal mythology and symbology which modern psychoanalysis claims to have discovered. Such subconscious manifestations as the Oedipus complex (Freud), archetypes such as that of the death and resurrection of the hero (Jung), and personality factors like the introvert-extravert contrast (Adler) are demonstrated, not only in modern authors familiar with psychological theory, but in classic authors who are thought to have used such concepts subconsciously. Psychological critics are particularly concerned with identification of symbols in literature, and again these symbols may be considered to be of conscious or of subconscious origin.

(4) In America and England especially psychological criticism is greatly concerned with attacking puritanism and sexual repression as they are found in our society. The fulfillment of the individual personality can be achieved only if the individual's complete physical, mental, and spiritual development is allowed him, and this is often impossible in the restrictive atmosphere of a puritanical society. Therefore literature ought to portray the morbidity and frustration which arise through repression of natural instincts, and conversely should depict the perfection of personal fulfillment possible under conditions of freedom. Literature which holds up for admiration asceticism, self-denial, abnegation of physical pleasure, or obsessive consciousness of

sin is undesirable, since its final effect will only be to cause additional frustration and unhappiness.

Some typical critics of the psychological school in America are:

FLOYD DELL (born 1887) was one of the first American critics to attempt the application of Freudian doctrine to literature. His influence on American letters, however, was mainly an informal one; he wrote no full-length work in defense of psychological literature. As an editor of the *Masses* (1914-17) and the *Liberator* (1918-24) he criticized literature from a basically Marxian point of view and only occasionally brought psychoanalytic theory to bear. He underwent psychoanalysis himself in 1917-18, and thenceforth turned increasingly to the Freudian point of view; he was instrumental in bringing Freudianism to the attention of Sherwood Anderson, who later utilized it extensively in his writing. As a speaker, reviewer, and conversationalist Dell was able to convert numbers of New York authors and artists to the Freudian doctrines, at least temporarily. His own writing was chiefly in the genre of the novel; his most important critical work, involving social as well as literary criticism, is *Love in the Machine Age* (1930). His autobiography, *Homecoming* (1933), provides an interesting picture of the fad of Freudianism in the Greenwich Village literary set of the Twenties, although Dell also describes his later disillusionment with certain aspects of Freudian doctrine.

WALDO FRANK (born 1889), American novelist and essayist, founded and edited the influential *Seven Arts* in New York (1916-17); he performed an important function in this and other publications in presenting European and Latin American culture to America. Conversely, several of his works are explanations of American culture for foreign readers. Throughout his work Frank is concerned with depicting America as a nation dominated by puritanism and oppressed with an intellectual sterility in which its artists and authors work only with the greatest difficulty. He makes extensive use of the Adlerian terms "introversion" and "extraversion" in describing the position of the artist in America; American materialism is a "vast and juiceless California fruit," a synthetically extraverted product, and the artist as an introvert is ruthlessly suppressed by this dominant element in our society. Frank offers "organic wholeness," the "origin and end of all our creative being," as the goal of artistic activity; the puritanical censor, by denying the individual his natural emotional and physical outlets, deliberately frustrates this process of self-realization.

Although Frank recognizes the importance of Freud and Jung in forming modern thought and uses their concepts widely in his own work, he is by no means a slavish disciple of either psychologist. He criticizes Freud for his excessive stress on man's reason and for his consequent neglect of the mystery and spirituality hidden in the subconscious. He finds Jung more receptive to his element of the mystic in the subconscious, but criticizes him for his insistence on the absolute universality of his archetypes and for his relatively narrow culture as compared to Freud. Frank is also critical of popular manifestations of Freudianism: the fad of psychoanalysis among the intellectuals, the bandying of half-understood psychoanalytical terms in conversation, and the tendency to explain failure and wrong-doing through facile recourse to psychological theory.

JOSEPH WOOD KRUTCH (born 1893), American critic and essayist, was a loyal Freudian from the time of the First World War up to 1932, when he partially repudiated psychoanalysis in *Experience and Art*. His best-known work of psychological criticism is *Edgar Allan Poe: A Study in Genius* (1926), which converts the career of Poe into a "Freudian melodrama" and treats the poet's life as a case-history of complexes and frustrations. *The Modern Temper* (1929) and *Five Masters* (1930) are also influenced by psychological doctrines.

Other sometime exponents of the psychoanalytical theory of literature are VAN WYCK BROOKS (born 1886), whose *The Ordeal of Mark Twain* (1920) was one of the pioneer studies in psychological criticism; and EDMUND WILSON (see above, p. 557), who followed in Brooks' footsteps to write penetrating psychological studies of Dickens, Kipling, and Henry James and continued to utilize Freudian concepts in modified form throughout his career.

NATURALISTIC, SOCIOLOGICAL, AND
MARXIST CRITICISM

The naturalistic movement in literature, which may be viewed as a scientific-materialistic reaction to the idealism and romanticism of the nineteenth century, is reflected in literary criticism by the various schools which may be roughly grouped together under the title of socio-logical or proletarian criticism. On the continent the godfather of this literary philosophy is HIPPOLYTE TAINE (1828-93), a rigid deter-minist who provided the theoretical basis for the naturalistic literature of Zola, Daudet, and the Goncourts. In American literature socio-logical criticism tends to treat and interpret literature already written rather than provide a foundation for future literatures; it is thus critical in the real sense of the word rather than philosophical as is much of the work of Taine.

Modern sociological and materialistic critics, while differing widely, tend to share at least two fundamental concepts:

(1) They present literature as a reflection of history, especially of the historical development of economics, technology, and class rela-tions. Literary movements and periods (romanticism, realism, neo-classicism) are treated as reflections of wider social phenomena; the romanticism of Poe and Lanier is a manifestation of the aristocratic ideals of the ante-bellum South just as the realistic reaction which fol-lowed it is an outgrowth of the Civil War and the triumph of Northern industrialism. Such socio-economic phenomena as the rise of the proletariat and the conflict between agrarianism and industrialism find a significant reflection in literature, and literary works are held to be valid and meaningful only when they reflect such processes.

(2) Their concept of characterization in literature is that the indi-vidual human is a being motivated mainly by his environment rather than by his internal will; his destinies are determined by the economic, social, industrial, and political processes going on about him. This is simply the philosophical concept of determinism applied to literary criticism; the sociological critic views the individual as the virtual pawn of his environment.

Proletarian and Marxist criticism, a school which proceeded out of the main body of naturalistic-sciological criticism and subsequently acquired special qualities through its contact with the political move-ments of socialism and communism, adds to these concepts the following:

(1) History is to be viewed chiefly in terms of the class struggle, and social progress is achieved only through class warfare and revolu-tion. Human social activity in the past has been motivated mainly by the efforts of various classes—the bourgeois during the Renaissance

and the proletariat in the nineteenth century—to unseat the dominant class immediately above. The individual is important only in relation to his social class; in literature he is to be shown as a mere unit or symbol of his class. The class war being the only means whereby social progress is to be accomplished, the heroic individual is the one who works to intensify the class war, and his natural antagonist is the character who seeks to delay or alleviate class tensions. The Marxist critics demonstrate such processes, not only in works written under the direct influence of Marxism, but in the work of classic authors (Crevecoeur. Melville, Whitman) who have, it is argued, used class concepts without realizing it.

(2) Since the class war is inevitable and progress is to be achieved only through revolutionary upheaval, literature is to be judged chiefly in the light of its effectiveness in inspiring class consciousness and in preparing the proletariat for revolution. (This is, of course, not the case in countries where a Marxist revolution has already taken place; in such circumstances the duty of a Marxist author is to support the social reforms undertaken by the regime.) Conversely, the Marxist critic attacks literature which tends to inhibit class consciousness and revolutionary activity; this includes sympathetic portrayal of Christian renunciation, aesthetic escapism, or bourgeois or capitalistic standards.

V. F. CALVERTON (1900-40), critic and editor, is an example of an American sociological critic who experimented in Marxism but remained aloof from the formal Communist movement. After attending Johns Hopkins University he founded and edited *The Modern Quarterly,* later *The Modern Monthly,* a publication devoted to radical social and literary criticism. He visited the Soviet Union in 1927 but returned disillusioned; turning completely from political Communism, he remained an independent radical for the rest of his career. His first important book-length work was *The Newer Spirit* (1925), in which he attempted to establish the basis for a purely sociological theory of literature. The dominant theme of the book is that class concepts shape and determine the literary consciousness. In *Sex Expression in Literature* (1926) he developed the thesis that literary treatments of sexual problems are determined chiefly by economic forces. His most important critical work is *The Liberation of American Literature* (1932), in which he attempts to interpret the history of American literature in terms of the Marxian concept of class struggle. He also refutes the "pollyannistic fallacy" that proletarian literature need be optimistic and idealistic in content, and maintains that tragedy must, under any form of society, be the highest expression of the artistic impulse.

VERNON PARRINGTON (1871-1929), literary historian and sociologist, shares Calverton's socio-economic interpretation of literature but is less influenced by Marxism in his view of social processes. Beginning with an expository study of Sinclair Lewis (1927), he then turned to the major work of his career: the three-volume *Main Currents in American Thought: an Interpretation of American Literature from the Beginnings to 1920* (1927-30). This vast work treats the history of American literature from a socio-economic point of view; writers are considered, not for their aesthetic qualities, but for their importance as manifestations of social, political, and economic processes. Parrington is particularly concerned with the far-reaching influence New England puritanism has exerted on American thought, an influence which he feels to be deeply stultifying. Although the general tone of the work is radical, Parrington is by no means hostile to democratic processes; *Main Currents* is based less on Marxism than on a peculiarly American form of agrarian radicalism, and a firm faith in the democratic ideal is constantly implied.

MICHAEL GOLD (born 1891) is a typical orthodox Marxist critic; he was associated during most of his career with the organized Communist movement. Beginning as a copy-reader on the *New York Call*, he next served as assistant editor of the old *Masses*, then as editor of the radical *Liberator* (1920-22). In 1933 he helped to found the *New Masses*, a publication which served as a center of Communist social and artistic criticism during the Thirties. He also contributed frequently to the *Daily Worker* and other Communist newspapers. Gold, a novelist and short-story writer by preference, has not produced a definitive full-length work of literary criticism; his most important statements are to be found in his *New Masses* articles and in his contribution to *Proletarian Literature in the United States* (1935), an anthology which he helped to edit. Most of his criticism is negative; he is a skilled satirist and polemicist, but is less convincing when praising authors with whose ideas he agrees.

GRANVILLE HICKS (born 1901), another left-wing critic and editor, approached radicalism from the direction of religion; he began his writing career as a liberal Christian but turned to an active Marxism during the Depression. He served for a time as editor of the *New Masses,* but resigned both this position and his membership in the Communist Party at the time of the 1939 Soviet-German pact. He has since maintained an independent radical position. His chief critical work, dating from his orthodox Marxist period, is *The Great Tradition* (1933), a study of American literature since the Civil War treating literary history as a manifestation of Marxian socio-economic theory.

Other contemporary critics associated at one time or another with the Marxist movement are WILLIAM PHILLIPS and PHILIP RAHV, for many years editors of the influential *Partisan Review,* which also repudiated the Party line around the time of the Soviet-German pact; WALDO FRANK, earlier treated (see p. 563) as a psychological critic; JAMES T. FARRELL, naturalistic novelist whose *A Note on Literary Criticism* (1936) calls for a socially conscious propaganda; and EDMUND WILSON (see above, p. 557), strongly influenced by Vico, Taine, and Marx, who analyzed the social function of literature in *The Triple Thinkers* (1938) and offered a Materialistic-Marxist approach to the study of political history in *To The Finland Station* (1940).

THE NEW CRITICISM

The term "the New Criticism" is applied to an important literary and critical movement which began to take form during the Twenties and emerged into prominence in the period after the Second World War. The basic concepts of the school, however, had been argued as early as the turn of the century; it appears that the term "the New Criticism" itself was first used in a 1910 address by Joel E. Spingarn at Columbia University. Spingarn, a professor of comparative literature, argued that since art is expression and criticism the study of that expression, the New Critic ought to confine himself to an examination of two question: (1) What did the artist intend to do? (2) How well did he do it? This anti-judicial manifesto, published at the very height of the prestige of the New Humanism, marked the turning of the tide toward the aesthetic and technical attitudes which were to dominate American criticism increasingly in the Thirties and Forties.

Although the New Criticism was developed chiefly in the universities by university professors, it began partly as a reaction against academic

pedanticism, at least against antiquated and pedantic historical scholarship of the kind that piles up documentary data on Shakespeare's life
and times but fails to grasp the essential aesthetic merit of Shakespeare's work. The movement was also influenced by the development
of modern semantics, an area of philosophical and linguistic study
which began to assume importance in the Twenties. In a sense the
New Criticism merely applies the principles of semantics to the field of
literature, although certain concepts not found in semantics were
adopted by the movement after its formation.

The New Criticism is chiefly an American movement, although such
British poets as Auden, Spender, Thomas, and Edith Sitwell share with
it certain concepts of poetic theory. The chief tenets of the New
Criticism may be listed as follows:

(1) The New Critics are hostile to traditional literary criticism and
to academic methods of literary history; they feel that university scholarship in the past has concerned itself too narrowly with analysis of
the period in which literature is created, the social milieu in which it
developed, and the movement or school into which it may be grouped.
Thus criticism has tended in the past to fall into a mere pigeonholing of
literature, a process not essentially different from the classifying techniques of botany or geology. The New Criticism prefers to take each
literary work by itself and consider it as a work of art without regard
to its origin; it is after all the work and not the period which primarily
interests the reader. Likewise, the New Criticism revolts against biographical studies which attempt to explain a literary work through
examination of the personality, life, and attitudes of its author. This,
according to the New Critics, tends to degenerate quickly into pure
biography, which has little connection with the enjoyment of literature.
In short, the New Criticism sets aside all consideration of the origin of
a literary work to focus attention strictly upon the work itself.

(2) The New Critics argue that previous literary criticism—e.g.,
the New Humanism and the various schools of sociological criticism—
have been excessively preoccupied with the moral element in literature.
Their concern with philosophical, ethical, or intellectual content has
blinded them to the fact that literature is primarily language intended
to produce enjoyment and that it is not message or moral that makes
good literature; a good poem may be built around a bad idea, and a

bad poem around a good idea. Dante's erroneous medieval notions of cosmology in no way vitiate the merit of the *Divine Comedy*.

(3) The New Criticism therefore turns from consideration of the moral or philosophical content of a work to analysis of its technique; the New Critics are chiefly, almost exclusively, concerned with problems of style, language, structure, meter, and metaphor. Many of them are poets in their own right; they view poetry as a craft which must be learned for itself rather than as a mere vehicle for philosophical ideas. A typical passage of the New Criticism conducts a detailed analysis of a poem, line by line, weighing the purpose and effectiveness of each device in turn. The New Critics are also much concerned with levels of meaning in poetry; they are adroit at demonstrating multiple symbolism, allegorical significance, or subtle psychological associations. Because of their almost exclusively technical approach to literature the New Critics concern themselves chiefly with poetry; their interest in fiction and drama is slight.

(4) According to the principles of the New Criticism, the craft of literary criticism itself is an art comparable with the arts of poetry or painting. Criticism has two purposes: to inform and enlighten the reader about literary works, and to provide enjoyment through the style and texture of the critical material itself. Literary criticism is thus treated as one of the chief branches of literature rather than as a subsidiary field deriving from the others.

SEMANTIC AND PHILOSOPHICAL BACKGROUND: I. A. RICHARDS. Among the language experts who provided the philosophical basis for the New Criticism the British semanticist I. A. Richards (born 1893) is most important. Richards collaborated with C. K. Ogden on *The Meaning of Meaning* (1923), an exercise in the psychological interpretation of language involving the nature of the symbol and its relation to the thing symbolized. One of the main concepts of this influential book was the distinction between denotation and connotation, i.e., the rational significance of a word as opposed to its emotional or associational impact on the mind. Richards went on to write, in his own name, *The Principles of Literary Criticism* (1926), *Coleridge on Imagination* (1934), and *A Philosophy of Rhetoric* (1936). The first of these is the most important in its influence on the New Criticism; its main thesis is the idea that symbolic statements (e.g., poetic images) evoke attitudes rather than convey information.

Another key concept in Richards' semantics is the distinction between "scientific statement" and "pseudo-statement." A scientific statement, concerned with the transmission of hard physical data, conveys a meaning the truth of which can be verified by means known to man. The pseudo-statement, of which a poem is an example, scorns logic except as a subordinate to emotion and employs words as sensory stimuli and emotive symbols without regard for their denotative meaning. Both types of statements are valid, and both convey valuable information; the difference is simply in the technique of communication. The parallel between such theories and the highly connotative modern poetry technique of T. S. Eliot or Ezra Pound is obvious.

WILLIAM EMPSON (born 1906) is an important student and disciple of Richards; he provided Richards' rather abstract principles with more specific application to the field of practical criticism. His most important work is *Seven Types of Ambiguity* (1929), in which he argues that poetry by its very nature invites two or more different readings of its meaning. He then proceeds to demonstrate seven varieties of his multiple-meaning phenomenon, involving various degrees of specificity in the technique by which the poet conveys his mental state to the reader.

T. S. ELIOT (born 1888), while not a formal member of the New Criticism, made certain contributions to its literature and has often associated himself with the group. In "Tradition and the Individual Talent" (1917) Eliot argued that in the process of composition the poet deliberately submerges his own personality; the merit of the finished product is in large measure the degree of its objectivity. This idea is connected with the New Critics' rejection of biographical interpretation of poetry and their insistence upon detailed examination of the work itself. Eliot differs from the orthodox New Critics, however, in his conviction that literature must have a strong metaphysical or ethical content; *For Lancelot Andrewes* (1928) contains the famous statement in which Eliot terms himself "an Anglo-Catholic in religion, a classicist in literature, and a royalist in politics." Other important Eliot works of criticism are *The Sacred Wood* (1921), *Dante* (1929), *Selected Essays* (1932), *The Use of Poetry and the Use of Criticism* (1933), and *Notes Toward a Definition of Culture* (1949). For Eliot as a poet and critic see also pp. 479-492.

JOHN CROWE RANSOM (born 1888) has in recent years been

accepted as the leader of the New Criticism in America. As a Rhodes Scholar (1910-13) Ransom came into contact with the new linguistic and literary movements in Britain. From 1914 he taught literature at Vanderbilt University and participated in the influential "Fugitive Group" of poets and critics in Nashville. In 1930 he published *God Without Thunder,* one of the basic texts of the New Criticism; *The World's Body* (1938) and *The New Criticism* (1941) followed. From 1937 Ransom taught at Kenyon College in Ohio, where he edited *The Kenyon Review,* a publication which became a focus of the New Criticism in the post-war period. Ransom's version of the New Criticism is a difficult and highly specialized one, largely concerned with structural organization and "texture" in poetry, and with the relation between these two factors. He is especially assiduous in attacking literary moralization and philosophizing; he has vigorously criticized Ivor Winters for the latter's insistence on some sort of moral content in literature.

For Ransom as a poet see also pp. 534-537

ALLEN TATE (born 1899), also a former member of the "Fugitive Group" of Nashville writers, has been closely associated with Ransom on the *Kenyon Review.* In addition to his many essays in this publication and in the *Southern Review* and *Sewanee Review,* Tate's most important works are *Reactionary Essays on Poetry and Ideas* (1936), *Reason in Madness* (1941), and *On the Limits of Poetry* (1948). Tate is particularly concerned with analyzing other schools of criticism; he has capably attacked the Marxist critics and the New Humanists, in both cases on the basis of their didacticism, and the impressionistic critics like Huneker and Mencken for their lack of consistent critical apparatus. Tate carries technical virtuosity in criticism to a high point; he is one of the most expert stylists of the movement.

An important concept in Tate's criticism is that of "tension." He believes that a poem is not a static object but an equilibrium of dynamic forces, which cannot be understood unless the basic tensions of its construction are understood. Like Eliot and Ransom, Tate is temperamentally a conservative with a strong respect for tradition; always hostile to Marxist-socialist materialism, in 1950 he announced his conversion to the Catholic religion.

YVOR WINTERS (born 1900) has been intermittently associated with the New Criticism, although he has disputed heatedly with

Ransom. Winters devotes much effort to attacking romanticism in its various forms; he views the deterministic doctrines of naturalism with equal mistrust. He parts company with Ransom chiefly on the question of the relation of morality to poetry; although Winters is opposed to outright didacticism in literature, he believes a literary work ought to contain some ennobling or thought-provoking concept which will raise it above the level of mere verbal experiment. Winters is one of the most painstaking of the New Critics in analyzing poetic structure and texture; he applies to the poem under discussion all the patience of a jeweler disassembling a fine watch. His most important works are *Primitivism and Decadence* (1937), *Maule's Curse* (1938), *The Anatomy of Nonsense* (1943), and *In Defense of Reason* (1947), the last of which comprises parts of the first three books plus certain added material.

Other important exponents of the New Criticism are KENNETH BURKE (born 1897), who analyzes the nature of symbolic action in *The Philosophy of Literary Form* (1941); R. P. BLACKMUR (born 1904), a poet-critic whose *The Double Agent* (1935) is remarkable for its patient analysis of the textual quality of poetry and the relation of texture to structure; and CLEANTH BROOKS (born 1906), a Yale professor who collaborated with Robert Penn Warren on *Understanding Poetry* (1938) and himself wrote two important critical works: *Modern Poetry and the Tradition* (1939) and *The Well Wrought Urn* (1947).

* * *

Bibliography

This bibliography is compiled for the convenience of students of modern American literature who wish to make further study of the authors and literary movements treated. It does not pretend to be complete; in the case of some authors who published fifty or more separate items during their careers, a complete list of works would be both inconvenient and confusing. The bibliography therefore includes (a) the most significant or important works of each author, and (b) a selected list of critical or biographical materials for further reference.

Dates of publications of works in volume are in all cases those of the first edition. In the case of poems, short stories, or other works not originally published in volume form, the bibliography generally gives the date of first volume publication, since the magazines or reviews of original publication are not often available to the ordinary reader.

Especially significant or useful works are indicated with an asterisk (*).

AMERICAN LITERATURE: GENERAL

Van Wyck Brooks, *New England: Indian Summer,* N.Y. 1940, and *The Confident Years,* N.Y. 1952; James D. Hart, *The Oxford Companion to American Literature,* N.Y., 1956; Robert Van Gelder, *Writers and Writing,* N.Y., 1946; Harry R. Warfel, *American Novelists of Today,* N.Y., 1951; Edward Wagenknecht, *Cavalcade of the American Novel,* N.Y., 1952; Stanley J. Kunitz and Howard Harcraft, eds., *Twentieth Century Authors,* N.Y., 1942.

W. D. HOWELLS:

Venetian Life, 1866; *Italian Journeys,* 1867; *The Lady of the Aroostook,* 1879; *A Modern Instance,* 1881; *The Rise of Silas Lapham,* 1884; *Indian Summer,* 1885; *A Hazard of New Fortunes,* 1889; *Criticism and Fiction,* 1891; *The Quality of Mercy,* 1892; *A Traveller from Altruria,* 1894; *The Kentons,* 1902; *The Leatherwood God,* 1916.

ABOUT: O. W. Firkins, *William Dean Howells: A Study,* Harvard U. P., 1924; Herbert Edwards, *"Howells and the Controversy Over Realism in American Fiction,"* American Literature, November, 1931; James L. Woodress, Jr., *Howells and Italy,* Duke U.P., 1952.

HENRY JAMES:

Roderick Hudson, 1876; *The American,* 1877; **Daisy Miller,* 1879; **The Portrait of a Lady,* 1881; *Washington Square,* 1881; *Princess Casamassima,* 1886; *The Aspern Papers,* 1888; *Terminations,* 1895; *What Maisie Knew,* 1897; *The Spoils of Poynton,* 1897; *The Turn of the Screw,* 1898; *The Two Magics,* 1898; *The Wings of the Dove,* 1902; *The Ambassadors,* 1903; *The Golden Bowl,* 1904; *The Altar of the Dead,* 1909; *Letters,* 1920. SEE ALSO *The Great Short Novels of Henry James,* ed. Philip Rahv, N.Y. 1945.

ABOUT: Van Wyck Brooks, *The Pilgrimage of Henry James,* N.Y. 1925; Elizabeth L. Cary, *The Novels of Henry James,* N.Y. 1905; **J. W. Beach, *The Method of Henry James,* Yale U.P. 1918; **F. O. Matthiessen, *Henry James, the Major Phase,* Oxford U.P. 1944.

HAMLIN GARLAND:

Main-Travelled Roads, 1891; *Jason Edwards: An Average Man,* 1892; *A Spoil of Office,* 1892; *A Little Norsk,* 1892; *Crumbling Idols,* 1894; *Rose of Dutcher's Coolly,* 1895; *The Captain of the Gray-Horse Troop,* 1902; *Hesper,* 1903; *Cavanagh, Forest Ranger,* 1910; *Other Main-Travelled Roads,* 1910; **A Son of the Middle Border,* 1917; *A Daughter of the Middle Border,* 1921; *Trail-Makers of the Middle Border,* 1926; *Back-Trailers from the Middle Border,* 1928.

ABOUT: Edward Wagenknecht, *Cavalcade of the American Novel,* N.Y. 1952.

STEPHEN CRANE:

*Maggie, a Girl of the Streets, 1893; *The Black Riders and Other Lines* (poetry), 1895; **The Red Badge of Courage,* 1895; *The Little Regiment,* 1896; *The Open Boat and Other Tales of Adventure,* 1898; *The Monster and Other Stories,* 1899; *Whilomville Stories,* 1900; *Men, Women, and Boats,* 1921. SEE ALSO R. W. Stallman, ed., *Stephen Crane, an Omnibus,* N.Y. 1952.

ABOUT: Wilson Follett, *"The Second Twenty-Eight Years: A Note on Stephen Crane, 1871-1900," Bookman,* Jan. 1929; Thomas Beer, *Stephen Crane: A Study in American Letters,* N.Y. 1923 (reprinted in *Hanna, Crane, and the Mauve Decade,* N.Y. 1941); John Berryman, *Stephen Crane,* Methuen, 1951; R. W. Stallman, "Stephen Crane," in *Critiques and Essays on Modern Fiction,* ed. John Aldridge, N.Y. 1952.

FRANK NORRIS:

Yvernelle, a Tale of Feudal France (narrative poem), 1892; *McTeague,* 1899; *A Man's Woman,* 1900; **The Octopus,* 1901; *A Deal in Wheat,* 1903; *The Pit,* 1903; *The Responsibilities of the Novelist,* 1903; *The Third Circle,* 1909; *Vandover and the Brute,* 1914.

ABOUT: Franklin Walker, *Frank Norris, a Biography,* N.Y. 1932; *Ernest Marchand, *Frank Norris, a Study,* Stanford U.P. 1942.

JACK LONDON:

NOVELS: *Children of the Frost,* 1902; *The Call of the Wild,* 1903; *The Sea Wolf,* 1904; *White Fang,* 1905; *The Game,* 1905; *The Iron Heel,* 1907; *Martin Eden,* 1909; *Smoke Bellew,* 1912; *The Valley of the Moon,* 1913; *The Star Rover,* 1914.

AUTOBIOGRAPHY: *The Cruise of the Snark,* 1911; *John Barleycorn,* 1913.

ABOUT: Charmian London, *The Book of Jack London,* N.Y. 1921; Joan London, *Jack London and His Times,* N.Y. 1939; *Irving Stone, *Sailor on Horseback,* N.Y. 1938.

O. HENRY:

STORY COLLECTIONS: *Cabbages and Kings,* 1904; *The Four Million,* 1906; *Heart of the West,* 1907; *The Trimmed Lamp,* 1907; *The Gentle Grafter,* 1908; *The Voice of the City,* 1908; *Options,* 1909; *Roads of Destiny,* 1909; *Whirligigs,* 1910; *Strictly Business,* 1910; *Sixes and Sevens,* 1911; *Rolling Stones,* 1913; *Waifs and Strays,* 1917; *Postscripts,* 1923. SEE ALSO *The Complete Works of O. Henry* (one volume), N.Y. 1937.

ABOUT: *E. Hudson Long, *O. Henry, the Man and His Work,* U. Penn. Press, 1949.

EDITH WHARTON:

Novels: *The House of Mirth*, 1905; *Ethan Frome*, 1911; *The Reef*, 1912; *The Custom of the Country*, 1913; **The Age of Innocence*, 1920; *A Son at the Front*, 1923; *Old New York*, 1924.

Stories: *Xingu and Other Stories*, 1916.

Criticism: *The Writing of Fiction*, 1925.

About: Percy Lubbock, *Portrait of Edith Wharton*, N.Y. 1947; *Blake Nevius, *Edith Wharton, a Study of Her Fiction*, Univ. Calif. Press, 1953.

GERTRUDE ATHERTON:

*The Californians, 1898; *Before the Gringo Came*, 1894; *The Conqueror*, 1902; *Rezanov*, 1906; *Tower of Ivory*, 1910; *Julia France and Her Times*, 1912; *The Black Oxen*, 1923.

Non-fiction: *Adventures of a Novelist*, 1932; *Golden Gate Country*, 1945.

About: *Saturday Review of Literature*, May 28, 1932.

THEODORE DREISER:

Novels: *Sister Carrie*, 1900; *Jennie Gerhardt*, 1911; *The Financier*, 1912; *The Titan*, 1914; *The "Genius,"* 1915, **An American Tragedy*, 1925; *Chains*, 1927; *The Bulwark*, 1946; *The Stoic*, 1947.

About: Robert H. Elias, *Theodore Dreiser: the Apostle of Nature*, N.Y. 1948; *F. O. Matthiessen, *Theodore Dreiser*, N.Y. 1951.

BOOTH TARKINGTON:

The Gentleman from Indiana, 1899; *Monsieur Beaucaire*, 1900; *The Two Vanrevels*, 1902; *The Conquest of Canaan*, 1905; *The Flirt*, 1913; *Penrod*, 1914; *The Turmoil*, 1915; *Penrod and Sam*, 1916; **The Magnificent Ambersons*, 1918; *Alice Adams*, 1921; *The Midlander*, 1923; *Growth*, 1927; *The World Does Move* (autobiography), 1928; *The Heritage of Hatcher Ide*, 1941; *Kate Fennigate*, 1943; *The Image of Josephine*, 1945.

About: Robert Cortes Holliday, *Booth Tarkington*, N.Y. 1918; Edward Wagenknecht, *Cavalcade of the American Novel*, N.Y. 1952.

GERTRUDE STEIN:

*Three Lives, 1908; Tender Buttons, 1914; The Making of Americans, 1925; Matisse, Picasso, and Gertrude Stein, 1932, *The Autobiography of Alice B. Toklas, 1933; Four Saints in Three Acts, 1934; Everybody's Autobiography, 1937; Picasso, 1938; Paris France, 1940; Wars I Have Seen, 1945; Brewsie and Willie, 1946.

ABOUT: *Donald Sutherland, Gertude Stein: a Biography of Her Work, Yale U.P., 1951; *Elizabeth Sprigge, Gertrude Stein, Her Life and Work, N.Y. 1957.

UPTON SINCLAIR:

NOVELS: *The Jungle, 1906; The Metropolis, 1908; King Coal, 1917; Oil!, 1927; Boston, 1928; World's End, 1940; Between Two Worlds, 1941; Dragon's Teeth, 1942; Wide Is the Gate, 1943; Presidential Agent, 1944; Dragon Harvest, 1945; A World to Win, 1946; Presidential Mission, 1947; One Clear Call, 1948; O Shepherd Speak!, 1949.

ABOUT: Floyd Dell, Upton Sinclair: A Study in Social Protest, N.Y. 1927; *Malcolm Cowley, "Man of Good Will," New Republic, January 11, 1943.

SINCLAIR LEWIS:

NOVELS: Our Mr. Wrenn, 1914; Free Air, 1919; *Main Street, 1920; *Babbitt, 1922; Arrowsmith, 1925; Elmer Gantry, 1927; Ann Vickers, 1933; Work of Art, 1934; It Can't Happen Here, 1935; Gideon Planish, 1943; Cass Timberlane, 1945.

ABOUT: *Carl Van Doren, Sinclair Lewis: A Biographical Sketch, N.Y. 1932; Harrison Smith, Sinclair Lewis, N.Y., 1925 (outdated); Maxwell Geismar, The Last of the Provincials, N.Y. 1947.

ELLIOT PAUL:

Indelible, 1922; Impromptu, 1923; Imperturbe, 1924; Low Run Tide, 1929; Lava Rock, 1929; The Amazon, 1930; The Governor of Massachusetts, 1930; *The Life and Death of a Spanish Town, 1937; Concert Pitch, 1938; Hugger-Mugger in the Louvre, 1940; *The Last Time I Saw Paris, 1942; Linden on the Saugus Branch, 1947; A Ghost Town on the Yellowstone, 1948; My Old Kentucky Home, 1949.

ABOUT: Robert Van Gelder, Writers and Writing, N.Y. 1946.

HENRY MILLER:

*Tropic of Cancer, 1931; *Tropic of Capricorn, 1939; Black Spring, 1939; The Cosmological Eye, 1939; The Colossus of Maroussi, 1941; The Air-Conditioned Nightmare, 1945; Nights of Love and Laughter, 1955; A Devil in Paradise, 1956.

ABOUT: Nicholas Moore, Henry Miller, 1943; Bernard H. Porter, ed., The Happy Rock: A Book About Henry Miller, Berkeley, 1945; *Kenneth Rexroth, introduction to Nights of Love and Laughter, N.Y. 1955.

JOHN P. MARQUAND:

The Unspeakable Gentleman, 1922; Lord Timothy Dexter, 1925; Ming Yellow, 1934; No Hero, 1935; Thank You, Mr. Moto, 1936; The Late George Apley, 1937; Think Fast, Mr. Moto, 1937; Mr. Moto Is So Sorry, 1938; Wickford Point, 1939; *H. M. Pulham, Esq., 1941; So Little Time, 1943; Last Laugh, Mr. Moto, 1942; Repent in Haste, 1945; B. F.'s Daughter, 1946; Point of No Return, 1949; Melville Goodwin, U.S.A., 1951; Sincerely, Willis Wayde, 1955.

ABOUT: Edward Wagenknecht, Cavalcade of the American Novel, N.Y. 1952; Robert Van Gelder, Writers and Writing, N.Y. 1946.

JOHN DOS PASSOS:

Three Soldiers, 1921; Streets of Night, 1923; Manhattan Transfer, 1925; Orient Express, 1927; U.S.A. (The 42nd Parallel, 1930; Nineteen-Nineteen, 1932; The Big Money, 1936); District of Columbia (The Adventures of a Young Man, 1939; Number One, 1943; The Grand Design, 1949); Most Likely to Succeed, 1954.

ABOUT: Delmore Schwartz, "John Dos Passos and the Whole Truth," Southern Review, IV (1938), pp. 351ff.; James T. Farrell, "Dos Passos and the Critics," American Mercury, XLVII, 1939; Joseph Warren Beach, American Fiction, 1920-1940, N.Y. 1941.

F. SCOTT FITZGERALD:

STORY COLLECTIONS: Flappers and Philosophers, 1920; Tales of the Jazz Age, 1922; All the Sad Young Men, 1926; Taps at Reveille, 1935.

NOVELS: This Side of Paradise, 1920; The Beautiful and Damned, 1921; The Great Gatsby, 1925; Tender Is the Night, 1934; The Last Tycoon, 1941.

MISCELLANEOUS: *The Crack-Up,* 1945.
ABOUT: *Arthur Mizener, *The Far Side of Paradise,* N.Y. 1951,
Alfred Kazin, ed., *F. Scott Fitzgerald, the Man and His Work,* N.Y.
1951; Maxwell Geismar, *The Last of the Provincials,* N.Y. 1947.

ERNEST HEMINGWAY:

STORY COLLECTIONS: *Three Stories and Ten Poems,* 1923; *In Our
Time,* 1924; *Men Without Women,* 1927; *Winner Take Nothing,*
1933; *The Fifth Column and the First 49 Stories,* 1938.

NOVELS: *The Sun Also Rises,* 1926; *A Farewell to Arms,* 1929;
To Have and Have Not, 1937; *For Whom the Bell Tolls,* 1940; *Across
the River and Into the Trees,* 1950; *The Old Man and the Sea,* 1952.

NON-FICTION: *Death in the Afternoon,* 1932; *Green Hills of Africa,*
1935.

ABOUT: Louis Henry Cohn, *A Bibliography of the Works of Ernest
Hemingway,* N.Y. 1931; *Carlos Baker, *Hemingway: The Writer As
Artist,* Princeton U.P. 1952; *Philip Young, *Ernest Hemingway,* N.Y.
1952; John A. Atkins, *The Art of Ernest Hemingway,* N.Y. 1952;
Malcolm Cowley, *"Hemingway and the Hero,"* *New Republic,* CXI
(1944), pp. 755ff.

THOMAS WOLFE:

NOVELS: *Look Homeward, Angel,* 1929; *Of Time and the River,*
1935; *The Web and the Rock,* 1939; *You Can't Go Home Again,*
1940.

STORIES: *From Death to Morning,* 1935.

CRITICAL ESSAY: *"The Story of a Novel,"* in Maxwell Geismar, ed.,
The Portable Thomas Wolfe, N.Y. 1948.

ABOUT: *Herbert J. Muller, *Thomas Wolfe,* Norfolk, Conn., 1947;
Pamela H. Johnson, *Hungry Gulliver* (in England *Thomas Wolfe*),
N.Y. 1948; Bernard DeVoto, *"Genius Is Not Enough,"* *Saturday
Review of Literature,* April 25, 1936.

JAMES T. FARRELL:

NOVELS: *Studs Lonigan (Young Lonigan,* 1932; *The Young Manhood of Studs Lonigan,* 1934; *Judgment Day,* 1935); *Gas House
McGinty,* 1933; *A World I Never Made,* 1936; *No Star Is Lost,*
1938; *Father and Son,* 1940; *My Days of Anger,* 1943; *The Face of

Time, 1953; *Tommy Gallagher's Crusade*, 1939; *Ellen Rogers*, 1941; *Bernard Clare*, 1946; *The Road Between*, 1949; *This Man and This Woman*, 1951; *Yet Other Waters*, 1952.

CRITICISM: *A Note on Literary Criticism*, 1936; *The League of Frightened Philistines*, 1945; *Literature and Morality*, 1947.

ABOUT: W. M. Frohock, *The Novel of Violence in America*, Dallas, 1950; Joseph Warren Beach, *American Fiction, 1920-1940*, N.Y. 1941. For Danny O'Neill series see *Time*, November 23, 1953.

REGIONALISM AND RURAL NATURALISM: GENERAL

Louis D. Rubin, Jr., and Robert D. Jacobs, *Southern Renascence: The Literature of the Modern South*, Baltimore, 1953; Allen Tate, *et al.*, eds., *I'll Take My Stand*, N.Y. 1930.

ELLEN GLASGOW:

NOVELS: *The Descendant*, 1897, *Phases of an Inferior Planet*, 1898; *The Voice of the People*, 1900; *The Battle-Ground*, 1902; *The Romance of a Plain Man*, 1909; *The Miller of the Old Church*, 1911; *Virginia*, 1913; *Life and Gabriella*, 1916; *The Builders*, 1919; *One Man in His Time*, 1922; **Barren Ground*, 1925; *The Romantic Comedians*, 1926; *They Stooped to Folly*, 1929; *The Sheltered Life*, 1932; **Vein of Iron*, 1935; *In This Our Life*, 1941.

STORIES: *The Shadowy Third*, 1923.

AUTOBIOGRAPHY: *The Woman Within*, 1954.

CRITICISM: *A Certain Measure*, 1943.

ABOUT: *Maxwell Geismar, *Rebels and Ancestors*, N.Y. 1953; Josephine Jessup, *The Faith of Our Feminists*, N.Y. 1950; Frederick P. McDowell, "Ellen Glasgow and the Art of the Novel," *Philological Quarterly*, XXX (1951), pp. 328ff.

WILLA CATHER:

NOVELS: *Alexander's Bridge*, 1912; *O Pioneers!*, 1913; *The Song of the Lark*, 1915; **My Antonia*, 1915; *One of Ours*, 1922; *A Lost Lady*, 1923; *The Professor's House*, 1925; *My Mortal Enemy*, 1926; **Death Comes to the Archbishop*, 1927; *Shadows on the Rock*, 1931; *Lucy Gayheart*, 1935; *Sapphira and the Slave Girl*, 1940.

STORIES: *The Troll Garden*, 1905; *Youth and the Bright Medusa*, 1920.

CRITICISM: *Not Under Forty,* 1936.

ABOUT: René Rapin, *Willa Cather,* N.Y. 1930; Mildred R. Bennett, *The World of Willa Cather,* N.Y. 1951; *David Daiches, *Willa Cather,* Cornell, 1951.

OLE RÖLVAAG:

Giants in the Earth, 1927; *Peder Victorious,* 1929; *Pure Gold,* 1930; *Their Father's God,* 1931; *The Boat of Longing,* 1933.

ABOUT: *Theodore Jorgenson and N. O. Solum, *Ole Edvart Rölvaag: A Biography,* N.Y. 1939.

PEARL BUCK:

NOVELS: *East Wind: West Wind,* 1930; *The House of Earth (The Good Earth,* 1931; *Sons,* 1932; *A House Divided,* 1935); *The Mother,* 1934; *The Exile,* 1936; *Fighting Angel,* 1936; *This Proud Heart,* 1938; *The Patriot,* 1939; *Other Gods,* 1940; *Dragon Seed,* 1941; *The Promise,* 1943; *Portrait of a Marriage,* 1945; *Pavilion of Women,* 1946; *Kinfolk,* 1949; *God's Men,* 1951; *The Hidden Flower,* 1952; *Come My Beloved,* 1953.

STORIES: *The First Wife,* 1933; *Today and Forever,* 1941; *Far and Near,* 1948.

AUTOBIOGRAPHY: *My Several Worlds,* 1954.

ABOUT: Harry R. Warfel, *American Novelists of Today,* N.Y. 1951; *James Gray, *On Second Thought,* Univ. Minn. Press, 1946.

WILLIAM FAULKNER:

NOVELS: *Soldiers' Pay,* 1926; *Sartoris,* 1929; *The Sound and the Fury,* 1929; *As I Lay Dying,* 1930; *Sanctuary,* 1931; *Light in August,* 1932; *Pylon,* 1933; *Absalom, Absalom!,* 1936; *Intruder in the Dust,* 1948, *Requiem for a Nun,* 1950; *The Fable,* 1954.

STORIES: *These Thirteen,* 1931.

MISCELLANEOUS: Malcolm Cowley, ed., *The Portable Faulkner,* N.Y. 1946; *The Faulkner Reader,* N.Y. 1954.

ABOUT: Irving Howe, *William Faulkner, a critical Study,* N.Y. 1952; Frederick J. Hoffman and Olga W. Vickery, eds., *William Faulkner: Two Decades of Criticism,* Mich. State Coll. Press, 1951; *William Van O'Connor, *The Tangled Fire of William Faulkner,* Univ.

Minn. Press, 1954; Robert Coughlan, *"The Private World of William Faulkner," Life,* September 28-October 5, 1953.

JOHN STEINBECK:

The Pastures of Heaven, 1932; *Tortilla Flat,* 1935; *In Dubious Battle,* 1936; **Of Mice and Men,* 1937; *The Long Valley,* 1938; **The Grapes of Wrath,* 1939; *The Moon Is Down,* 1942; *Cannery Row,* 1945; *The Wayward Bus,* 1947; *The Pearl,* 1948; *East of Eden,* 1953; *Sweet Thursday,* 1954. SEE ALSO Pascal Covici, ed., *The Portable Steinbeck,* N.Y. 1943.

ABOUT: *Harry T. Moore, *The Novels of John Steinbeck,* Chicago, 1939; Lewis Gannett, *John Steinbeck, Personal and Bibliographical Notes,* N.Y. 1939; Edmund Wilson, *The Boys in the Back Room,* San Francisco, 1941.

ERSKINE CALDWELL:

STORIES: *American Earth,* 1931; *We Are the Living,* 1933; *Kneel to the Rising Sun,* 1935; *Southways,* 1938; **Jackpot,* 1940; *Georgia Boy,* 1943; *Stories by Erskine Caldwell,* 1944; *The Courting of Susie Brown,* 1952.

NOVELS: **Tobacco Road,* 1932; **God's Little Acre,* 1933; *Journeyman,* 1935; *Trouble in July,* 1940; *All Night Long,* 1942; *House in the Uplands,* 1946; *The Hand of God,* 1947; *This Very Earth,* 1948; *Episode in Palmetto,* 1950; *A Lamp for Nightfall,* 1952; *Love and Money,* 1954.

NON-FICTION: *You Have Seen Their Faces* (with M. Bourke-White), 1937; *All Out on the Road to Smolensk,* 1942; *Call It Experience,* 1951.

ABOUT: *Introduction by Henry Seidel Canby to *Stories by Erskine Caldwell,* N.Y. 1944; John D. Wade, *"Sweet Are the Uses of Degeneracy," Southern Review,* I (1936), pp. 449ff.; *Malcolm Cowley, *"The Two Erskine Caldwells," New Republic,* CXI (1941), pp. 599ff.

ROBERT PENN WARREN:

BIOGRAPHY: *John Brown: The Making of a Martyr,* 1929.
VERSE: *XXXVI Poems,* 1936; *Eleven Poems on the Same Theme,* 1942; *Selected Poems,* 1944.

NOVELS: *Night Rider*, 1939; *At Heaven's Gate*, 1943; *All the King's Men*, 1946; *World Enough and Time*, 1950; *Band of Angels*, 1955.
STORIES: *The Circus in the Attic*, 1949.
CRITICISM: *Understanding Poetry* (with Cleanth Brooks), 1939.
ABOUT: Harry R. Warfel, *American Novelists of Today*, N.Y. 1951; *Louis D. Rubin, Jr. and Robert D. Jacobs, eds., *Southern Renascence: The Literature of the Modern South*, Baltimore, 1953.

WILLIAM SAROYAN:

FICTION: *The Daring Young Man on the Flying Trapeze*, 1934; *Inhale and Exhale*, 1936; *Three Times Three*, 1936; *Little Children*, 1937; *A Native American*, 1938; *The Trouble with Tigers*, 1938; *Love, Here Is My Hat*, 1938; *Peace, It's Wonderful*, 1939; *My Name Is Aram*, 1940; *Fables*, 1941; *The Human Comedy*, 1943; *Dear Baby*, 1944; *The Adventures of Wesley Jackson*, 1946; *The Assyrian and Other Stories*, 1950.
DRAMA: *The Time of Your Life*, 1939; *My Heart's in the Highlands*, 1939; *Love's Old Sweet Song*, 1940; *The Beautiful People*, 1941; *Razzle-Dazzle*, 1942; *Don't Go Away Mad*, 1949.
AUTOBIOGRAPHY: *The Bicycle Rider in Beverly Hills*, 1950.
ABOUT: James Gray, *On Second Thought*, N.Y. 1946.

EUDORA WELTY:

STORIES: *A Curtain of Green*, 1941; *The Wide Net*, 1943; *Music from Spain*, 1948; *The Golden Apples*, 1949; *The Bride of the Innisfallen*, 1955.
NOVELETTE: *The Robber Bridegroom*, 1942.
NOVELS: *Delta Wedding*, 1946; *The Ponder Heart*, 1954.
ABOUT: Katherine Anne Porter, Introduction to *A Curtain of Green*, N.Y. 1941; Robert Daniel, *"The World of Eudora Welty,"* in Rubin & Jacobs, eds., *Southern Renaissance*, Baltimore, 1953.

JOHN O'HARA:

NOVELS: *Appointment in Samarra*, 1934; *Butterfield 8*, 1935; *Hope of Heaven*, 1938; *A Rage to Live*, 1949; *The Farmer's Hotel*, 1951; *Ten North Frederick*, 1955.
STORIES: *The Doctor's Son*, 1935; *Files on Parade*, 1939; *Pipe Night*, 1945; *Here's O'Hara*, 1946; *Hell Box*, 1947.

NON-FICTION: *Sweet and Sour*, 1954.
ABOUT: Robert Van Gelder, *Writers and Writing*, N.Y. 1946.

IRWIN SHAW:

DRAMA: *Bury the Dead*, 1936; *The Gentle People*, 1939.
STORIES: *Sailor Off the Bremen*, 1939; *Welcome to the City*, 1942; *Act of Faith and Other Stories*, 1946; *Mixed Company* (collection), 1950.
NOVELS: *The Young Lions*, 1948; *The Troubled Air*, 1951; *Lucy Crown*, 1956.
NON-FICTION: *Report on Israel*, 1950.
ABOUT: *John W. Aldridge, *After the Lost Generation*, N.Y. 1951.

HERMAN WOUK:

NOVELS: *Aurora Dawn*, 1947; *The City Boy*, 1948; *The Caine Mutiny*, 1951; *Marjorie Morningstar*, 1955.
DRAMA: *The Traitor*, 1949; *The Caine Mutiny Court-Martial*, 1954.
ABOUT: *"The Wouk Mutiny," Time*, 66:48-50 (September 5, 1955).

J. D. SALINGER:

The Catcher in the Rye, 1951; *Nine Stories*, 1953.
ABOUT: Arthur Heiserman and James E. Miller, Jr., *"J. D. Salinger: Some Crazy Cliff," Western Humanities Review*, X:2 (Spring, 1956), pp. 129ff.; Harrison Smith, *"Manhattan Ulysses, Junior," Saturday Review of Literature*, 34:12 (July 14, 1951).

JAMES JONES:

From Here to Eternity, 1951; *Some Came Running*, 1957.
ABOUT: A. B. C. Whipple, *"James Jones and His Angel," Life*, 30:143 (May 7, 1951).

NORMAN MAILER:

"A Calculus at Heaven" (in the anthology *Cross Section*), 1944; *The Naked and the Dead*, 1948; *Barbary Shore*, 1951; *The Deer Park*, 1955.
ABOUT: John W. Aldridge, *After the Lost Generation*, N.Y. 1951; Maxwell Geismar, *"Nightmare on Anopopei," Saturday Review of Literature*, 31:12 (May 8, 1948).

SHERWOOD ANDERSON:

NOVELS: *Windy McPherson's Son,* 1916; *Marching Men,* 1917; *Poor White,* 1920; *Many Marriages,* 1923; *Dark Laughter,* 1925.
STORIES: **Winesburg, Ohio,* 1919; *The Triumph of the Egg,* 1921.
AUTOBIOGRAPHY: *Tar: Middle West Childhood,* 1926; *Memoirs,* 1942.
ABOUT: Cleveland B. Chase, *Sherwood Anderson,* N.Y. 1927; *Lionel Trilling, "Sherwood Anderson," Kenyon Review,* Summer, 1941; Irving Howe, *Sherwood Anderson,* N.Y. 1951.

JAMES BRANCH CABELL:

The Eagle's Shadow, 1904; *Gallantry,* 1907; **The Cream of the Jest,* 1917; *Beyond Life,* 1919; **Jurgen,* 1919; *The Jewel Merchants,* 1921; *The Silver Stallion,* 1926; *Music from Behind the Moon,* 1926; *The White Robe,* 1928; *The Way of Ecben,* 1929.
ABOUT: Don C. Bregenzer and Samuel Loveman, eds., *A Round Table in Poictesme* (anthology of criticism), Cleveland, 1924; Carl Van Doren, *James Branch Cabell,* N.Y. 1932; H. L. Mencken, *James Branch Cabell,* N.Y. 1927.

THORNTON WILDER:

NOVELS: *The Cabala,* 1926; *The Bridge of San Luis Rey,* 1927; *The Woman of Andros,* 1930; *Heaven's My Destination,* 1935; *The Ides of March,* 1948.
DRAMA: *Our Town,* 1938; *The Skin of Our Teeth,* 1942.
ABOUT: Edmund Wilson, *Classics and Commercials,* N.Y. 1950, pp. 81ff.; W. T. Scott, *"Our Town and the Golden Veil," Virginia Quarterly,* January, 1953.

ROBINSON JEFFERS:

Flagons and Apples, 1912; *Californians,* 1916; *Roan Stallion, Tamar, and Other Poems,* 1928; *Dear Judas and Other Poems,* 1929; *Descent to the Dead,* 1931; *Thurso's Landing and Other Poems,* 1932; *Give Your Heart to the Hawks,* 1933; *Solstice,* 1935; *Such Counsels You Gave to Me,* 1937; *Be Angry at the Sun,* 1941.
ABOUT: Rudolf Gilbert, *Shine, Perishing Republic: Robinson Jeffers and the Tragic Sense in Modern Poetry,* Boston, 1936; Lawr-

ence Clark Powell, *Robinson Jeffers, the Man and His Work,* Pasadena, 1940.

KATHERINE ANNE PORTER:

Flowering Judas, 1930; *Hacienda,* 1934; *Noon Wine,* 1937; *Pale Horse, Pale Rider,* 1939; *No Safe Harbor,* 1941; *The Leaning Tower,* 1944; *The Days Before* (essays), 1952.

ABOUT: Charles Allen, *"Southwestern Chronicle: Katherine Anne Porter," Arizona Quarterly,* II:90-95 (Summer, 1946); Lodowick Hartley, *"Katherine Anne Porter," Sewanee Review,* XLVIII:206-216 (April, 1940); *Ray B. West, Jr., "Katherine Anne Porter and Historic Memory,"* in Rubin & Jacobs, eds., *Southern Renascence,* Baltimore, 1953.

MODERN AMERICAN DRAMA: GENERAL

*Barrett H. Clark and George Freedley, eds., *A History of Modern Drama,* N.Y. 1947; John Gassner, *Masters of the Drama,* N.Y. 1954; Joseph Wood Krutch, *The American Drama Since 1918,* N.Y. 1939; *Frank H. O'Hara, *Today in American Drama,* Univ. Chicago Press, 1939; *Eric Bentley, *The Playwright as Thinker,* N.Y. 1946; Burns Mantle, *Contemporary American Playwrights,* N.Y. 1938.

CLYDE FITCH:

Beau Brummel, 1890; *The Moth and the Flame,* 1898; *Barbara Frietchie,* 1899; *Sappho,* 1900; *The Climbers,* 1901; *Captain Jinks of the Horse Marines,* 1901; *The Stubbornness of Geraldine,* 1902; *The Girl with the Green Eyes,* 1902; *Her Own Way,* 1903; *Her Great Match,* 1905; *The Woman in the Case,* 1905; *The House of Mirth,* 1906; *The Truth,* 1907; *The City,* 1909.

ABOUT: John Mason Brown, *Upstage,* N.Y. 1930.

EUGENE O'NEILL:

DRAMA COLLECTIONS: *Thirst and Other One-Act Plays,* 1914; *Bound East for Cardiff,* 1916; *Moon of the Caribbees,* 1919.

FULL-LENGTH DRAMAS: *Beyond the Horizon,* 1920; *The Emperor Jones,* 1921; *The Hairy Ape,* 1922; *Anna Christie,* 1922; *All God's Chillun Got Wings,* 1924; *Desire Under the Elms,* 1925; *The Great God Brown,* 1926; *Marco Millions,* 1927; *Lazarus Laughed,* 1927;

Strange Interlude, 1928; *Dynamo*, 1929; *Mourning Becomes Electra*, 1931; *Ah, Wilderness!*, 1933; *The Iceman Cometh*, 1946; *A Moon for the Misbegotten*, 1952; *Long Day's Journey Into Night*, 1956.

ABOUT: *Barrett H. Clark, *Eugene O'Neill, the Man and His Plays*, N.Y. 1929-47; John Mason Brown, *"Eugene O'Neill: 1888-1953,"* *Saturday Review of Literature*, December 19, 1953; Edwin A. Engel, *The Haunted Heroes of Eugene O'Neill*, Harvard U.P., 1953.

ELMER RICE:

On Trial, 1914; *The Adding Machine*, 1923; *Wake Up, Jonathan!*, 1928; *Street Scene*, 1929; *Cock Robin* (with Philip Barry), 1929; *Close Harmony* (with Dorothy Parker), 1929; *See Naples and Die*, 1929; *The Left Bank*, 1931; *We, the People*, 1933; *Judgment Day*, 1934; *Two on an Island*, 1940; *Dream Girl*, 1945; *The Show Must Go On*, 1949.

COLLECTIONS: *Morningside Plays*, 1917; *Plays*, 1933; *Seven Plays*, 1950.

ABOUT: Burns Mantle, *Contemporary American Playwrights*, N.Y. 1938.

SIDNEY HOWARD:

Swords, 1921; *They Knew What They Wanted*, 1924; *Lucky Sam McCarver*, 1925; *McCobb's Daughter*, 1926; *The Silver Cord*, 1926; *The Late Christopher Bean*, 1932; *Alien Corn*, 1933; *Dodsworth*, 1934; *Yellow Jack*, 1934; *Paths of Glory*, 1935; *The Ghost of Yankee Doodle*, 1937.

ABOUT: Barrett H. Clark, *"The United States,"* in Clark and Freedley, eds., *A History of Modern Drama*, N.Y. 1947; Joseph Mersand, *The Play's the Thing*, N.Y. 1948.

PHILIP BARRY:

You and I, 1923; *White Wings*, 1926; *Paris Bound*, 1927; *Cock Robin*, 1928; *Hotel Universe*, 1930; *Tomorrow and Tomorrow*, 1931; *The Animal Kingdom*, 1932; *Bright Star*, 1935; *Spring Dance*, 1936; *Here Come the Clowns*, 1938; *The Philadelphia Story*, 1939; *Liberty Jones*, 1941; *Without Love*, 1942; *Second Threshold*, 1951.

NOVEL: *War in Heaven*, 1938.

BIBLIOGRAPHY 589

ABOUT: Joseph Wood Krutch, *The American Drama Since 1918*, N.Y. 1939; John Mason Brown, *Upstage*, N.Y. 1930.

SIDNEY KINGSLEY:

Men in White, 1933; *Dead End*, 1935; *Ten Million Ghosts*, 1936; *The World We Make*, 1939; *The Patriots*, 1942; *Detective Story*, 1949; *Darkness at Noon*, 1951; *Lunatics and Lovers*, 1955.
ABOUT: John Mason Brown, *Two on the Aisle*, N.Y. 1938.

MAXWELL ANDERSON:

VERSE DRAMAS: *Elizabeth the Queen*, 1930; *Night Over Taos*, 1932; *The Sea Wife*, 1932; *Mary of Scotland*, 1933; *Valley Forge*, 1934; *Winterset*, 1935; *High Tor*, 1937; *The Masque of Kings*, 1937; *Knickerbocker Holiday*, 1938; *Key Largo*, 1939; *Candle in the Wind*, 1941; *Eve of St. Mark*, 1942; *Joan of Lorraine*, 1946; *Anne of the Thousand Days*, 1948.
REALISTIC PROSE DRAMAS: *What Price Glory?*, 1924; *Saturday's Children*, 1927; *Both Your Houses*, 1933; *Storm Operation*, 1944; *Truckline Café*, 1945; *The Bad Seed*, 1954.
ABOUT: Joseph Wood Krutch, *The American Drama Since 1918*, N.Y. 1939.

ROBERT SHERWOOD:

DRAMA: *The Road to Rome*, 1927; *The Love Nest*, 1927; *The Queen's Husband*, 1928; *Waterloo Bridge*, 1930; *This Is New York*, 1930; *Reunion in Vienna*, 1931; *The Petrified Forest*, 1935; *Idiot's Delight*, 1936; *Tovarich*, 1936; *Abe Lincoln in Illinois*, 1938; *There Shall Be No Night*, 1940.
NOVEL: *The Virtuous Knight*, 1931.
HISTORY: *Roosevelt and Hopkins: An Intimate History*, 1938.
ABOUT: John Mason Brown, *Seeing Things*, N.Y. 1946.

CLIFFORD ODETS:

Waiting for Lefty, 1935; *Awake and Sing*, 1935; *Till the Day I Die*, 1935; *Paradise Lost*, 1935; *Golden Boy*, 1937; *Rocket to the Moon*, 1938; *Night Music*, 1940; *Clash by Night*, 1941; *The Big Knife*, 1948; *The Country Girl*, 1950; *The Flowering Peach*, 1954.

ABOUT: Burns Mantle, *Contemporary American Playwrights*, N.Y. 1938.

S. N. BEHRMAN:

ORIGINAL DRAMAS: *The Second Man*, 1927; *Meteor*, 1929; *Serena Blandish*, 1929; *Brief Moment*, 1929; *Biography*, 1932; *Rain from Heaven*, 1934; *End of Summer*, 1936; *Wine of Choice*, 1938; *No Time for Comedy*, 1939; *The Talley Method*, 1941.

ADAPTATIONS: *Amphitryon 38*, 1937; *The Pirate*, 1942; *Jacobowsky and the Colonel*, 1944; *Jane*, 1952; *Fanny*, 1954.

NON-FICTION: *Duveen*, 1952; *The Worcester Account*, 1954.

ABOUT: E. M. Gagey, *Revolution in American Drama*, Columbia U.P., 1947.

LILLIAN HELLMAN:

The Children's Hour, 1934; *Days to Come*, 1936; *The Little Foxes*, 1939; *Watch on the Rhine*, 1941; *The Searching Wind*, 1944; *Another Part of the Forest*, 1946; *The Autumn Garden*, 1951.

ABOUT: Burns Mantle, *Contemporary American Playwrights*, N.Y. 1938; Harry Gilroy, *"The Bigger the Lie,"* New York Times, December 14, 1952.

ARTHUR MILLER:

DRAMA: *All My Sons*, 1947; *Death of a Salesman*, 1949; *The Crucible*, 1953; *A View from the Bridge*, 1955.

NOVEL: *Focus*, 1945.

ABOUT: John Mason Brown, *Still Seeing Things*, N.Y. 1950; Brooks Atkinson, *Broadway Scrapbook*, N.Y. 1947.

TENNESSEE WILLIAMS:

Battle of Angels, 1945; *The Glass Menagerie*, 1945; *27 Wagons Full of Cotton*, 1946; *You Touched Me* (with Donald Windham), 1947; *A Streetcar Named Desire*, 1947; *Summer and Smoke*, 1948; *The Rose Tattoo*, 1950; *Camino Real*, 1953; *Cat on a Hot Tin Roof*, 1955.

NOVELETTE: *The Roman Spring of Mrs. Stone*, 1950.

STORIES: *One Arm*, 1950; *Hard Candy*, 1954.

ABOUT: Paul Moor, *"A Mississippian Named Tennessee,"* Harpers,

197:63ff. (July, 1948); Norris Houghton, *"Tomorrow Arrives Today,"* Theatre Arts, 30:83ff. (February, 1946).

MODERN AMERICAN POETRY: GENERAL

Henry W. Wells, *The American Way of Poetry,* Columbia U.P., 1943; Edward Davison, *Some Modern Poets,* N.Y. 1928; Rica Brenner, *Poets of Our Time,* N.Y. 1941; Margaret C. Anderson, *My Thirty Years' War,* N.Y. 1930; *Cleanth Brooks and R. P. Warren, *Understanding Poetry,* N.Y. 1938; Louis Untermeyer, ed., *Modern American Poetry,* Mid-Century Edition (anthology), N.Y. 1950.

EDWIN MARKHAM:

The Ballad of the Gallows Bird, 1896; *The Man with the Hoe and Other Poems,* 1899; *Lincoln and Other Poems,* 1901; *The Shoes of Happiness and Other Poems,* 1915; *Gates of Paradise and Other Poems,* 1920; *New Poems: Eighty Songs at Eighty,* 1932; *The Star of Araby,* 1937; *Collected Poems,* 1940. SEE ALSO *Poems of Edwin Markham,* selected and arranged by Charles L. Wallis, N.Y. 1950.

ABOUT: *Charles L. Wallis, preface to *Poems of Edwin Markham,* N.Y. 1950.

E. A. ROBINSON:

POETRY COLLECTIONS: *The Torrent and the Night Before,* 1896; *The Children of the Night,* 1897; *The Town Down the River,* 1910; *The Man Against the Sky,* 1916; *The Three Taverns,* 1920.

VERSE NOVELS: *Captain Craig,* 1902; *Merlin,* 1917; *Launcelot,* 1920; *Avon's Harvest,* 1921; *The Man Who Died Twice,* 1924; *Tristram,* 1927.

ABOUT: *Herman Hagedor, *Edwin Arlington Robinson, a Biography,* N.Y. 1938; *Ivor Winters, *Edwin Arlington Robinson,* Norfolk, Conn., 1946.

ROBERT FROST:

A Boy's Will, 1913; *North of Boston,* 1914; *Mountain Interval,* 1916; *New Hampshire,* 1923; *West-Running Brook,* 1928; *Collected Poems,* 1930; *A Further Range,* 1936; *Collected Poems,* 1939; *A Witness Tree,* 1942; *Steeple Bush,* 1947; *Complete Poems,* 1949; *The Road Not Taken,* 1951; *Hard Not to Be King,* 1951; *Aforesaid,* 1954.

ABOUT: Gorham B. Munson, *Robert Frost*, N.Y. 1927; *R. P. T. Coffin, *New Poetry of New England: Frost and Robinson*, Johns Hopkins Press, 1938; *Sidney Cox, *A Swinger of Birches*, N.Y. Univ. Press, 1957.

CARL SANDBURG:

POETRY: *Chicago Poems*, 1916; *Cornhuskers*, 1918; *Smoke and Steel*, 1920; *Slabs of the Sunburnt West*, 1923; *Good Morning, America*, 1928; *The People, Yes*, 1936.

BIOGRAPHY: *Abraham Lincoln: The Prairie Years*, 1926; *Abraham Lincoln: The War Years*, 1939.

NOVEL: *Remembrance Rock*, 1948.

COLLECTION: *The American Songbag*, 1927.

ABOUT: Karl W. Detzer, *Carl Sandburg*, N.Y. 1941; Henry W. Wells, *The American Way of Poetry*, Columbia U.P., 1943.

EZRA POUND:

A Lume Spento, 1908; *Personae*, 1909; *Exultations*, 1909; *Provença*, 1910; *Canzoni*, 1911; *Ripostes*, 1912; *Lustra and Other Poems*, 1917; *Hugh Selwyn Mauberley*, 1920; *Personae*, 1926 (includes poems from the earlier *Personae* and from *Exultations*); *The Cantos of Ezra Pound*, 1948 (also published in several sections under other titles, 1925-1955).

ABOUT: *Hugh Kenner, *The Poetry of Ezra Pound*, Norfolk, Conn., 1950; John J. Espey, *Ezra Pound's Mauberley, a Study in Composition*, Univ. Calif. Press, 1955; Peter Russell, ed., *An Examination of Ezra Pound* (collection of essays by various critics), Norfolk, Conn., 1950.

AMY LOWELL:

POETRY COLLECTIONS: *A Dome of Many-Colored Glass*, 1912; *Sword Blades and Poppy Seed*, 1914; *Men, Women, and Ghosts*, 1916; *Can Grande's Castle*, 1918; *Legends*, 1921; *A Critical Fable*, 1922; *What's O'Clock?*, 1925; *East Wind*, 1926; *Ballads for Sale*, 1927.

CRITICISM: *Six French Poets*, 1915; *Tendencies in American Poetry*, 1917; *John Keats*, 1925.

ABOUT: *S. Foster Damon, *Amy Lowell*, N.Y. 1935; Glenn Hughes, *Imagism and the Imagists*, Stanford U.P., 1931.

H. D.:

POETRY COLLECTIONS: *Sea Garden*, 1916; *Hymen*, 1921; *Heliodora and Other Poems*, 1924; *Collected Poems*, 1925; *Red Roses for Bronze*, 1932; *Collected Poems*, 1940; *The Walls Do Not Fall*, 1944; *Tribute to the Angels*, 1945; *The Flowering of the Rod*, 1946; *By Avon River* (includes essay), 1949.

PROSE: *Palimpsest*, 1926; *Hedylus*, 1928.

DRAMA: *Hippolytus Temporizes*, 1927.

ABOUT: Harold H. Watts, "*H. D. and the Age of Myth*," *Sewanee Review*, 56:287ff. (April, 1948).

JOHN GOULD FLETCHER:

The Dominant City, 1913; *Fire and Wine*, 1913; *Fool's Gold*, 1913; *The Book of Nature*, 1913; *Visions of the Evening*, 1913; **Irradiations —Sand and Spray*, 1915; *Goblins and Pagodas*, 1916; *The Tree of Life*, 1918; *Granite and Breakers*, 1921; *Parables*, 1925; *Branches of Adam*, 1926; *The Black Rock*, 1928; **XXIV Elegies*, 1935; *Selected Poems*, 1939; *South Star*, 1941; *Burning Mountain*, 1946.

AUTOBIOGRAPHY: *Life Is My Song*, 1937.

ABOUT: Harriet Monroe, *Poets and Their Art*, N.Y. 1926.

ELINOR WYLIE:

POETRY COLLECTIONS: *Incidental Numbers*, 1912; **Nets to Catch the Wind*, 1921; *Black Armour*, 1923; *Trivial Breath*, 1928; *Angels and Earthly Creatures*, 1929; *Collected Poems*, 1932.

PROSE: *Jennifer Lorn*, 1923; *The Venetian Glass Nephew*, 1925; *The Orphan Angel*, 1926; *Mr. Hodge and Mr. Hazard*, 1928; *Collected Prose*, 1933.

ABOUT: William Rose Benét, foreword to *Collected Poems of Elinor Wylie*, N.Y. 1923-38; **Nancy Hoyt, *Elinor Wylie: The Portrait of an Unknown Woman*, N.Y. 1935; Harriet Monroe, *Poets and Their Art*, N.Y. 1926.

SARA TEASDALE:

Sonnets to Duse, 1907; *Helen of Troy and Other Poems*, 1911; *Rivers to the Sea*, 1915; *Love Songs*, 1917; *Flame and Shadow*, 1920;

Dark of the Moon, 1926; *Strange Victory*, 1933; *Collected Poems*, 1937.

ABOUT: Louis Untermeyer, *From Another World*, N.Y. 1939.

T. S. ELIOT:

POETRY COLLECTIONS: *Prufrock and Other Observations*, 1917; *Poems*, 1919; *The Waste Land*, 1922; *Poems, 1909-1925*, 1925; *Ash Wednesday*, 1930; *Four Quartets*, 1943.

ESSAYS: *The Sacred Wood*, 1920; *For Lancelot Andrewes*, 1928.

DRAMA: *Murder in the Cathedral*, 1935; *Family Reunion*, 1939; *The Cocktail Party*, 1949; *The Confidential Clerk*, 1953.

ABOUT: *F. O. Matthiessen, *The Achievement of T. S. Eliot*, Oxford U.P., 1947; *Elizabeth Drew, *T. S. Eliot, the Design of His Poetry*, N.Y. 1949; *George Williamson, *A Reader's Guide to T. S. Eliot*, N.Y. 1957; B. Rajan, ed., *T. S. Eliot, a study of His Writings by Several Hands*, London, 1947.

HART CRANE:

White Buildings, 1926; *The Bridge*, 1930; *Collected Poems*, 1933.

ABOUT: *Philip Horton, *Hart Crane: The Life of an American Poet*, N.Y. 1937; *Brom Weber, *Hart Crane: A Biographical and Critical Study*, N.Y. 1948; Malcolm Cowley, *"A Preface to Hart Crane,"* *New Republic*, April 23, 1930.

EDGAR LEE MASTERS:

A Book of Verses, 1904; *Songs and Sonnets*, 1910; *Spoon River Anthology*, 1914; *Songs and Satires*, 1916; *The New Spoon River*, 1924; *Selected Poems*, 1925; *Poems of People*, 1936; *More People*, 1939; *Illinois Poems*, 1941.

DRAMA: *Maximilian*, 1902; *The Trifler*, 1908; *The Leaves of the Tree*, 1909.

AUTOBIOGRAPHY: *Across Spoon River*, 1937.

ABOUT: Robert Van Gelder, *Writers and Writing*, N.Y. 1946; Amy Lowell, *Tendencies in Modern American Poetry*, N.Y. 1917.

VACHEL LINDSAY:

The Tree of Laughing Bells, 1905; *Rhymes to Be Traded for Bread*, 1912; *General William Booth Enters Into Heaven and Other Poems*,

1913; *The Congo and Other Poems*, 1914; *The Chinese Nightingale and Other Poems*, 1917; *The Daniel Jazz*, 1920; *The Golden Whales of California*, 1920; *Collected Poems*, 1923; *Selected Poems*, 1931.

AUTOBIOGRAPHY: *Adventures While Preaching the Gospel of Beauty*, 1914.

ABOUT: *Edgar Lee Masters, *Vachel Lindsay*, N.Y. 1935; Henry W. Wells, *The American Way of Poetry*, N.Y. 1943.

STEPHEN VINCENT BENÉT:

POETRY: *Five Men and Pompey*, 1915; *Young Adventure*, 1918; *Heavens and Earth*, 1920; *King David*, 1923; *Tiger Joy*, 1925; *John Brown's Body*, 1928; *Burning City*, 1936; *Western Star*, 1943; *The Last Circle*, 1946.

FICTION: *Young People's Pride*, 1922; *Jean Huguenot*, 1923; *Spanish Bayonet*, 1926; *Thirteen O'Clock* (includes "The Devil and Daniel Webster"), 1937; *Tales Before Midnight*, 1939.

ABOUT: *Henry W. Wells, *The American Way of Poetry*, Columbia U.P., 1943; Robert Van Gelder, *Writers and Writing*, N.Y. 1946.

CONRAD AIKEN:

POETRY: *Earth Triumphant and Other Tales in Verse*, 1914; *Turns and Movies*, 1916; *The Jig of Forslin*, 1916; *Nocturne of Remembered Spring*, 1917; *The Charnel Rose*, 1918; *The House of Dust*, 1920; *Punch: The Immortal Liar*, 1921; *Priapus and the Pool*, 1922; *Selected Poems*, 1929; *John Deth and Other Poems*, 1930; *Time in the Rock*, 1936; *Collected Poems*, 1953.

STORIES: *Bring! Bring!*, 1925; *Costumes by Eros*, 1938; *Short Stories*, 1950.

NOVELS: *Blue Voyage*, 1927; *Great Circle*, 1933; *King Coffin*, 1935; *Conversation*, 1940.

AUTOBIOGRAPHY: *Ushant*, 1952.

ABOUT: Frederick J. Hoffman, *Freudianism and the Literary Mind*, Baton Rouge, 1945; Mark Schorer, *"For Aiken: Reparation,"* New Republic, 126:19 (March 31, 1952).

WILLIAM CARLOS WILLIAMS:

POETRY: *Poems*, 1909; *The Tempers*, 1913; *Al Que Quiere*, 1917; *Kora in Hell*, 1921; *Sour Grapes*, 1922; *Spring and All*, 1923; *Col-*

lected Poems, 1934; *The Complete Collected Poems,* 1938; *The Wedge,* 1944; *Paterson* (Books I-IV), 1946-51.

NOVELS: *A Voyage to Pagany,* 1928; *White Mule,* 1937; *In the Money,* 1940; *The Build-Up,* 1952.

ESSAYS: *In the American Grain,* 1925.

STORIES: *The Knife of the Times and Other Stories,* 1932; *Make Light of It,* 1950.

ABOUT: Lloyd Frankenberg, *Pleasure Dome,* N.Y. 1949; *Vivienne Koch, *William Carlos Williams,* Norfolk, Conn., 1950.

WALLACE STEVENS:

POETRY: *Harmonium,* 1923; *Ideas of Order,* 1935; *Owl's Clover,* 1936; *The Man with the Blue Guitar,* 1937; *Parts of a World,* 1942; *Esthétique Du Mal,* 1944; *A Primitive Like an Orb,* 1948.

ESSAY: *"The Noble Rider and the Sound of Words,"* in Allen Tate, ed., *The Language of Poetry,* Princeton U.P., 1942.

ABOUT: *William Van O'Connor, *The Shaping Spirit: A Study of Wallace Stevens,* Univ. Chicago Press, 1950; Ivor Winters, *The Anatomy of Nonsense,* Norfolk, Conn., 1943.

ARCHIBALD MacLEISH:

POETRY: *Tower of Ivory,* 1917; *The Happy Marriage,* 1924; *The Pot of Earth,* 1925; *Nobodaddy,* 1925; *Streets in the Moon,* 1926; *New Found Land,* 1930; *Public Speech,* 1936; *Actfive,* 1948; *Songs for Eve,* 1954; *Collected Poems,* 1952.

NARRATIVE POEMS: *The Hamlet of A. MacLeish,* 1928; *Conquistador,* 1932.

RADIO SCRIPTS: *The Fall of the City,* 1937; *Air Raid,* 1938.

ESSAYS: *A Time to Speak,* 1941; *The Irresponsibles,* 1940; *The American Cause,* 1941.

ABOUT: Edmund Wilson, *"Archibald MacLeish and the Word,"* in *Classics and Commercials,* N.Y. 1950.

E. E. CUMMINGS:

POETRY: *Tulips and Chimneys,* 1923; *&,* 1925; *XLI Poems,* 1925; *is 5,* 1926; *ViVa,* 1931; *no thanks,* 1935; *Collected Poems,* 1938; *50 Poems,* 1940; *One Times One,* 1944; *Kaipe,* 1950; *Poems, 1923-1954,* 1955.

PROSE: *The Enormous Room,* 1922; *Eimi,* 1933; *i: six nonlectures,* 1953.
ABOUT: M. L. Rosenthal, *"Mr. Joy and Mr. Gloom,"* New Republic, September 18, 1950; *Life,* November 24, 1952 (biogr. sketch); M. N. S. Whitely, *"Savagely a Maker," Poetry,* July, 1947.

JOHN CROWE RANSOM:

POETRY: *Poems About God,* 1919; *Chills and Fever,* 1924; *Grace After Meat,* 1924; *Two Gentlemen in Bonds,* 1926.
CRITICISM: *God Without Thunder,* 1930; *The World's Body,* 1938; *The New Criticism,* 1941.
ABOUT: Ivor Winters, *The Anatomy of Nonsense,* Norfolk, Conn., 1943.

MARIANNE MOORE:

POETRY: *Poems,* 1921; *Observations,* 1924; *Selected Poems,* 1935; *The Pangolin and Other Verse,* 1936; *What Are Years?,* 1941; *Nevertheless,* 1944; *Collected Poems,* 1951.
TRANSLATION: *The Fables of La Fontaine,* 1954.
ESSAYS: *Predilections,* 1955.
ABOUT: Lloyd Frankenberg, *Pleasure Dome,* N.Y. 1949; T. S. Eliot, *"Introduction to Marianne Moore,"* in *Selected Poems,* N.Y. 1935; Winthrop Sargeant, *"Humility, Concentration, and Gusto,"* New Yorker, February 16, 1957; Charles Tomlinson, *"Abundance, Not Too Much: The Poetry of Marianne Moore,"* Sewanee Review, LXV:4 (Autumn, 1957), pp. 677ff.

EDNA ST. VINCENT MILLAY:

POETRY: *Renascence,* 1917; *A Few Figs from Thistles,* 1920; *Second April,* 1921; *The Harp-Weaver and Other Poems,* 1924; *The Buck in the Snow and Other Poems,* 1928; *Fatal Interview,* 1931; *Wine from These Grapes,* 1934; *Conversation at Midnight,* 1937; *Huntsman, What Quarry?,* 1939; *Make Bright the Arrows,* 1940; *Collected Sonnets,* 1941; *Collected Lyrics,* 1943; *Mine the Harvest,* 1954.
DRAMA: *Two Slatterns and a King,* 1921; *The Lamp and the Bell,* 1921; *Aria Da Capo,* 1921; *The King's Henchman* (libretto), 1927.
ABOUT: *Elizabeth Atkins, *Edna St. Vincent Millay and Her Times,* Univ. Chicago Press, 1936; John Crowe Ransom, *"The Poet as*

Woman," in *The World's Body,* N.Y. 1938; Edmund Wilson, *The Shores of Light,* N.Y. 1952.

KENNETH FEARING:

POETRY: *Angel Arms,* 1929; *Poems,* 1935; *Dead Reckoning,* 1938; *Collected Poems,* 1940; *Afternoon of a Pawnbroker,* 1943; *Stranger at Coney Island,* 1949.

NOVELS: *The Hospital,* 1939; *Clark Gifford's Body,* 1942; *The Big Clock,* 1946; *The Loneliest Girl in the World,* 1951; *The Generous Heart,* 1954.

ABOUT: Kenneth Burke, *The Philosophy of Literary Form,* N.Y. 1941; John Peale Bishop, *Collected Essays,* N.Y. 1948.

SOME YOUNGER POETS:

Richard Eberhart: *A Bravery of Heaven,* 1930; *Reading the Spirit,* 1936; *Song and Idea,* 1940; *Poems New and Selected,* 1944; *Poems 1946-1953,* 1953. Kenneth Patchen: *Before the Brave,* 1936; *First Will & Testament,* 1939; *The Journal of Albion Moonlight,* 1941; *The Dark Kingdom,* 1942; *Memoirs of a Shy Pornographer,* 1945; *Sleepers Awake,* 1946; *Red Wine and Yellow Hair,* 1949. Delmore Schwartz: *In Dreams Begin Responsibilities,* 1938; *Genesis,* 1943; *Vaudeville for a Princess and Other Poems,* 1950. Karl Shapiro: *Person, Place, and Thing,* 1942; *V-Letter and Other Poems,* 1944; *Essay on Rime,* 1945; *Trial of a Poet and Other Poems,* 1947; *Poems, 1940-1953,* 1953. Randall Jarrell: *Blood for a Stranger,* 1942; *Little Friend, Little Friend,* 1945; *Losses,* 1948; *Selected Poems,* 1955. Peter Viereck: *Terror and Decorum,* 1948; *Strike Through the Mask,* 1950; *The First Morning,* 1952; *Shame and Glory of the Intellectuals* (prose), 1953.

Robert Lowell: *Land of Unlikeness,* 1944; *Lord Weary's Castle,* 1946; *The Mills of the Kafanaughs,* 1951.

MODERN AMERICAN CRITICISM: GENERAL

Charles J. Glicksberg, *American Literary Criticism, 1900-1950,* N.Y. 1952; Frederick J. Hoffman, *Freudianism and the Literary Mind,* Baton Rouge, 1945; Granville Hicks, *et al., eds. Proletarian Literature in the United States: An Anthology,* N.Y. 1935; C. Hartley Grattan, ed., *The Critique of Humanism: A Symposium,* N.Y. 1930; *J. P. Pritchard, *Criticism in America,* Univ. Oklahoma Press, 1956.

J. G. HUNEKER:

Melomaniacs, 1902; *Overtones,* 1904; *Iconoclasts: A Book of Dramatists,* 1905; *Visionaries,* 1905; *Egoists: A Book of Supermen,* 1909; *Promenades of an Impressionist,* 1910; *Painted Veils* (novel), 1920.

ABOUT: Benjamin Decasseres, *James Gibbons Huneker,* N.Y. 1925.

H. L. MENCKEN:

George Bernard Shaw: His Plays, 1905; *A Book of Prefaces,* 1917; *Prejudices,* 1919-27; *The American Language,* 1936-47.

ABOUT: Edgar Kemler, *The Irreverent Mr. Mencken,* Boston, 1950.

GEORGE JEAN NATHAN:

The Eternal Mystery, 1913; *Mr. George Jean Nathan Presents,* 1917; *The Popular Theatre,* 1918; **The Critic and the Drama,* 1922; *Materia Critica,* 1924; *The New American Credo,* 1927; *Art of the Night,* 1928; *The Intimate Notebooks of George Jean Nathan,* 1932; *The Morning After the First Night,* 1928; *Encyclopaedia of the Theatre,* 1940. With H. L. Mencken: *Europe After 8:15,* 1914; *The American Credo,* 1920.

EDMUND WILSON:

Axel's Castle, 1931; *Travels in Two Democracies,* 1936; *The Triple Thinkers,* 1938; *To the Finland Station,* 1940; *The Wound and the Bow,* 1941; *The Boys in the Back Room,* 1941; *Memoirs of Hecate County* (fiction), 1946; *Classics and Commercials,* 1950; *The Shores of Light,* 1952.

PAUL ELMER MORE:

Shelburne Essays, 1901-14; *Platonism,* 1917; *The Demon of the Absolute,* 1928; *On Being Human,* 1936.

ABOUT: Robert Shafer, *Paul Elmer More and American Criticism,* New Haven, 1935.

IRVING BABBITT:

Literature and the American College, 1908; *The New Laokoön,*

1910; *The Masters of Modern French Criticism,* 1912; *Rousseau and Romanticism,* 1919; *On Being Creative,* 1932.
ABOUT: F. Manchester and O. Shepard, *Irving Babbitt,* N.Y. 1941.

STUART P. SHERMAN:

Matthew Arnold: How to Know Him, 1917; *On Contemporary Literature,* 1917; *Americans,* 1922; *The Genius of America,* 1923; *Points of View,* 1924; *Critical Woodcuts,* 1926.
ABOUT: Jacob Zeitlin and Homer Woodbridge, *Life and Letters of Stuart P. Sherman,* N.Y. 1929.

NORMAN FOERSTER:

Nature in American Literature, 1923; *American Criticism,* 1928; *The American Scholar,* 1929.
EDITED: *A Reinterpretation of American Literature,* 1928.

FLOYD DELL:

Moon-Calf (novel), 1920; *Love in the Machine Age,* 1930; *Homecoming,* 1933.
ABOUT: Upton Sinclair, *American Outpost,* N.Y. 1932.

WALDO FRANK:

Our America, 1919; *The Re-Discovery of America,* 1929; *In the American Jungle,* 1937.
ABOUT: Gorham B. Munson, *Waldo Frank,* N.Y. 1923.

JOSEPH WOOD KRUTCH:

Edgar Allan Poe, 1926; *The Modern Temper,* 1929; *Five Masters,* 1930; *Experience and Art,* 1932.
ABOUT: Charles I. Glicksberg, *"Joseph Wood Krutch,"* Sewanee Review, January-March, 1936.

V. F. CALVERTON:

The Newer Spirit, 1925; *Sex Expression in Literature,* 1926; *The Liberation of American Literature,* 1932; *The New Ground of Criticism,* 1930; *The Awakening of American Literature,* 1939.
ABOUT: Charles I. Glicksberg, *"V. F. Calverton,"* Sewanee Review, July-September, 1938.

VERNON PARRINGTON:

Sinclair Lewis: Our Own Diogenes, 1927; *Main Currents in American Thought,* 1927-39.

ABOUT: See *New Republic,* February 15, 1939.

MICHAEL GOLD:

John Brown, 1923; *Proletarian Literature in the United States* (ed.), 1936; *Change World!,* 1937.

GRANVILLE HICKS:

Eight Ways of Looking at Christianity, 1926; *The Great Tradition,* 1933; *One of Us,* 1935; *John Reed,* 1936; *I Like America,* 1938.

ABOUT: Charles L. Glicksberg, *"Granville Hicks and Marxist Criticism,"* Sewanee Review, April, 1937.

I. A. RICHARDS:

The Meaning of Meaning (with C. K. Ogden), 1923; *The Principles of Literary Criticism,* 1926; *Coleridge on Imagination,* 1934; *A Philosophy of Rhetoric,* 1936.

ABOUT: J. C. Ransom, *The New Criticism,* Norfolk, Conn., 1941.

JOHN CROWE RANSOM:

God Without Thunder, 1930; *The World's Body,* 1938; *The New Criticism,* 1941.

ABOUT: Delmore Schwartz, *"Instructed of Much Morality,"* Sewanee Review, Summer, 1946.

ALLEN TATE:

Reactionary Essays on Poetry and Ideas, 1936; *Reason in Madness,* 1941; *On the Limits of Poetry,* 1948; *The Hovering Fly,* 1948.

ABOUT: Charles I. Glicksberg, *"Allen Tate and Mother Earth,"* Sewanee Review, July-September, 1937.

YVOR WINTERS:

Primitivism and Decadence, 1937; *Maule's Curse,* 1938; *The Anatomy of Nonsense,* 1943; *In Defense of Reason,* 1947.

ABOUT: William Barrett, *"Temptations of St. Yvor,"* Kenyon Review, Autumn, 1947.

* * *

Index

Date Due